TOUCHING
THE
MOON

TOUCHING THE MOON

THE STORY OF MY LIFE
WRITTEN FOR MY GRANDCHILDREN:
KATHI, LARA, MIKE, JOE, AND JIM

John Coutinho

American Literary Press, Inc.
Five Star Special Edition
Baltimore, Maryland

Touching the Moon

Copyright © 2003 Dr. John Coutinho, P.E.

Library of Congress
Cataloging-in-Publication Data
ISBN 1-56167-774-4

Library of Congress Card Catalog Number:
2002114937

Published by

American Literary Press, Inc.
Five Star Special Edition
8019 Belair Road, Suite 10
Baltimore, Maryland 21236

Manufactured in the United States of America

Many of the stories at the beginning of this book this book were initially prepared as class assignments in a course on "Creative Writing" conducted   by   Ms. Josephine Atwater of the Community College of Baltimore County, 1998-2000. Some of the illustrations were graciously provided by Mr Lawrence Feliu of the Northrop Grimman History Center, Bethpage, NY. Mr Alan Reese, Managing Editor of the publisher, was of great assistance in helping me cope with my onerous computer. My wife, Eleanor, patiently read the manuscript and corrected many typographical errors. My friends in Germany reviewed the sections that they were acquainted with.

Photo of Coutinho

Coutinho Coat of Arms

The Coutinho coat of arms is one of the 72 of the prominent families of the former Kingdom of Portugal that decorate the ceiling of the Great Hall of the National Palace at Sintra, where Napoleon first capitulated to Wellington, (Convention of Sintra, 1808). The five red five pointed stars on a gold background represent the five wounds of Christ.

The Coutinho coat of arms was granted in perpetuity in 1130 by the King of Portugal to Don Garcia, Lord of Leomil, for his services in cleansing Northern Portugal from the Moors, who were eventually all evicted to northern Europe and North Africa by 1492. Arms were used to identify families before the introduction of family surnames. Don Garcia's grandson assumed the family surname of Coutinho.

The expulsion of the Moors from Spain and Portugal assured that the area would be spared the continuing bitter, religious conflict that still plagues other parts of the world today, 2002 AD.

C O N T E N T S

INTRODUCTION

TOUCHING THE MOON

Expressions such as "Touching the Moon" in the past generally have referred to objectives that were supposedly unattainable. With the Apollo Program, the unattainable was reached, to the applause of the entire world watching on television. Most engineers just dream of being associated with such a program, but as luck would have it, I was at the right place at the right time and was trained and able to make a contribution to this historic project, and now to act as an eyewitness to some of the events that made it all possible.

My entire life has been spent reaching for difficult goals. I was born in Portugal and came at the age of four with my parents to Washington, D. C. I flunked first grade at the Trinity School in Georgetown because I could not speak English. My parents moved to another neighborhood with a Catholic school, St. Martin's, where the nuns where more supportive. Although there were 50 boys in class, the nuns encouraged me to the point that in the eighth grade I was at the head of the class, including in English.

My father was a professor at the School of Foreign Service at Georgetown University and felt that I should learn more about the world than was taught in American schools. He also believed in the "sink or swim" theory. I was dropped off in Germany for the rest of my education. At that time I could not speak a word of German, but when I returned to the United States with a degree in aeronautical engineering, I spoke German like a native.

Luck was really with me when I found my first job in February, 1939 at the Grumman Aerospace Corporation in Bethpage, N. Y. Mr. Grumman, a former US Navy pilot, was one of the few men in the industry at the time who was convinced that the aircraft carrier was going to be the main battle ship of the US Navy. A carrier based fighter aircraft is much more difficult to design than a land based aircraft with the same flight performance, since the latter do not have to carry the heavy provisions for carrier operation. I was taught that Grumman was in business to build the world's best carrier based fighter aircraft, and that if we did so, the Navy would have no choice but to buy our products and we would have no money worries.

I found this philosophy, this constant striving for the very best, quite appealing. While other companies spent much of their effort improving what they had, Grumman built one new aircraft after the other, always extending the state of the art, with larger, heavier, more powerful aircraft, with the highest possible performance. And I was always at the leading edge of development, reaching into uncharted regions.

Grumman started small in the space program in the late 1950's with the ECHO I, a big inactive, bright metal balloon on which we could bounce radio signals. On a clear night you could just see it, a small bright dot in the dark sky. Eleanor and I were enchanted beyond words looking up at the night sky in our back yard and realizing that we had changed the map of the sky!

One project followed another until we won the development contract for the Orbiting Astronomical Observatory (OAO), a large telescope with a 36 inch diameter mirror, designed to map the sky. At 3900 pounds, it was the largest and heaviest spacecraft ever built up to that time. The National Aeronautics and Space Administration (NASA) estimated that they required a year to do the proposed mapping job. After that time, the OAO was still fully functional, and NASA searched the world scientific community for jobs that could be done on the OAO. It was finally shut off after seven years of service. Scientists who ran their programs on the OAO concluded that it would have been a more useful spacecraft if it had been manned with an on-board intelligence.

Next came the Apollo Project to put men on the moon, and Grumman was ready.

THE GENERATION THAT PUT MEN ON THE MOON, IN PERSPECTIVE

By Charles Anderson
Retired Grumman Employee

We were before television, before penicillin, polio shots, antibiotics, and frisbees. Before frozen foods, nylon, Dacron, Xerox, Kinsey. We were before radar, fluorescent lights, neon signs, credit cards, and ball point pens. For us, time sharing meant togetherness, not computers; a chip was a piece of wood, hardware meant hardware, and software was not even a word. In our time, closets were for clothes, not for coming out of, and a book about two young women living together abroad could still be called "Our Hearts were Young and Gay." In those days, "Bunnies" were small rabbits and a rabbit was not a Volkswagen.

We were before Batman, the Grapes of Wrath, Rudolph the Red Nose Reindeer, and Snoopy. Before DDT and vitamin pills, Vodka and the White Wine craze, disposable diapers and the Jefferson nickel.

Before scotch tape, audio tape and video tape, the Grand Coulee Dam, M & M's. the automatic shift, the Lincoln Continental and the Jeep. When we were in school, pizzas, Cheerios, frozen orange juice, instant coffee and McDonald's were unknown. We thought fast food was what you ate during lent. We were before AM and FM radio, tape recorders, CD's and CD players, before electric typewriters, word processors and answering machines, dish and clothes washers, hair and clothes dryers, freezers, electric blankets, panty hose and drip dry clothes.

We were before men wore long hair and earrings, and woman wore tuxedos. We were married first and then lived together, how quaint!! We were before Alaska and Hawaii were states, before Israel and the United Nations. Transatlantic flight belonged to Charles Lindbergh and Amelia Earhart. In our time, cigarette smoking was fashionable, grass was mowed, coke was a drink, and pot was something used for cooking. In 1935, MADE IN JAPAN was junk and making out was something you did on an exam. "Out of Luck" meant what it said, today - "lucked out" means just the opposite.

In our day there were were five and ten cent stores where you could buy things for five and ten cents. A penny post card cost a penny and a newspaper was sold for two or three cents. A new car was available for under $700.-, gasoline was just eleven cents a gallon, but alas, our weekly salary was $ 25. We made do with what we had. We were the last generation that was so naive as to think it was necessary for a woman to have a husband to have a baby!!"

There is much, much more. It took fifty years between the invention of the airplane that opened up access to the entire world until people started to rely on air transportation. Fancy luxury long distance trains came and went. Today, SIX HUNDRED MILLION air passengers a year keep the US airlines busy. And never before in history has there ever been anything like our crime rate. We have been the most creative generation in history, for good and for bad! And to top it off, we put men on the moon and brought them back safely to Earth!!!

CHILDHOOD MEMORIES

MY BIG,   BEAUTIFUL, RED   BALL
(One of my earliest recollections)

My mother says that when I was very little I was born in Portugal. My mother says that Portugal is a beautiful country where she took part in the Festival of Roses in Sintra in the mountains where the King and Queen had their big summer houses. My mother rode with her friends in a great big wagon covered with roses and waved to all the people in the street.

My mother says that some bad people made the King go away. My father was the King's friend and he had to go away, too. He got a job at the Portuguese Embassy in America. After he found a place for me and my mother to live in America, we went there too. We had to go on a great big ship on the ocean.

My mother says the ocean was dangerous because of the war and the submarines, but I wasn't afraid. My mother says the ship would sail down the coast of Africa, then the shortest way across the ocean, and up the American coast. My mother says it was a very long trip and took many months, but I don't think so. I looked very hard for the coasts of Africa and America, but never saw any.

My mother says I would climb the rope ladders on the ship and frighten her, but I don't think so. My mother says that one day I fell and broke my collar bone and had to spend a long time in the ship's hospital, but I don't remember. My mother says she has trouble buying jackets for me because one shoulder is higher than the other because of my fall, but I don't think so; I just grew that way. My mother says I am super active, always getting into trouble, but I don't think so. I am a very nice and obedient child.

My mother says that I had my fourth birthday during the trip, but I don't remember. I always get a lot of clothes for my birthday and have to try on everything for everybody to see and I can't go out and play. Clothes are not presents. Clothes are something they have to give you anyway, like your dinner to make you grow up big and strong. Clothes take up a lot of room in Santa Claus's sack and there is not enough room left for all the toys us children have asked for.

One day while I was playing, I found a big, beautiful, red ball. It was so exciting!   My mother said I could never take the ball out on the deck, but could play all I wanted to in the big hall in front of the ship's dining room. It was such fun! My mother and her friends would throw the ball to me, and sometimes I would catch it, but most of the time I would have to run after it and throw it back to my mother.

One day I was playing alone in the big hall when I had to go see my mother. I carried the ball very carefully and stepped out on the deck. Somehow the ball slipped out of my arms and rolled down the sloping deck. I screamed as loud as I could: "MAMA, MAMA! HELP! MY BALL, MY BALL!" but the ball would not stop! The ball rolled over the side of the deck and fell far down into the water. I ran right to the Captain's office .and yelled at him: "STOP THE SHIP! SEND A MAN OUT TO PICK UP MY BALL!" The Captain said he couldn't do that, but I knew he could have if he had wanted to. I cried as loud as I could, stamped my feet, and jumped up and down, but all the Captain would say was that he was my friend, which he wasn't.

I ran back to the deck where I had lost my ball and could see a little red dot moving up and down with the waves far away. As I watched the dot became smaller and smaller, and finally I could not see it any more. My big beautiful, red ball was gone. I will never forget it.

UNDER THE SINK

As a child, I had two retreats that I used depending on where my mother was. If she was practicing her music, my retreat would be under the baby grand. If my mother was working in the kitchen, my retreat would be under the sink From this place I could also watch her in most of the dining room and hear her moving about in the living room. When I was not outside playing with my friends, these retreats were my hang-outs. There I felt safe and protected and could play with my toys as I pleased. Under the baby grand, I kept some of my big toys like my wind-up train and my set of cubic blocks. My ambition was to build a tower of blocks from the floor to the bottom of the baby grand. I would place one block carefully on top of another, and then another, but somehow the tower would always fall down before it reached the bottom of the baby grand. It was frustrating, but I would always try again.

In those days, the space under kitchen sinks was not blocked off with a cabinet front like it is today, and I had free access to this space. Here I kept some more of my smaller toys, such as my top, erector set, and my stereoscope.

My top had a stem sticking up out of its cover. When you pushed down on the stem, it would wind up the top. When the top was released, it would spin and play a song that always delighted me. My erector set consisted of a lot of small metal pieces that could be joined with small bolts to make little structures or vehicles. I liked to make four wheeled wagons. I would place my toy soldiers in the wagon and give them a ride. I remember that when I became older, and did not play with my erector set any more, my mother wanted to gather up all the little pieces and give the set to the Salvation Army. She could not find all the small missing pieces, so she gave the set away the way it was. For years now and then she would find a small piece here and there in little crevices all over the house.

My father would once in a while take a business trip and always bring me a toy. One time he brought me a stereoscope with three-dimensional pictures of the Zeppelin airship. The pictures showed the airship being built, and then its majestic flights over lofty mountain tops and vast oceans. I was so thrilled that I spent hours upon hours studying these pictures and dreaming about traveling in an airship. These dreams stayed locked in my heart until I got my job at Grumman and tried to get a pilot's license. My dreams were shattered by a lousy doctor who determined by test that my eyes did not have the depth perception required for a pilot's license.

After I grew up, I visited several houses similar to the one I lived in as a child and inspected the space under the sink. I was always amazed at how small the space was.

MY MOTHER'S BABY GRAND

I remember that when I was a child, I would go to sleep every night with my mother playing the piano. She wanted to be a professional musician. Her diploma from the Lisbon Conservatory of Music was carefully packed in her chest of drawers underneath the bed sheets, flat and safe. She was very concerned about maintaining her skills, so whenever she could, she practiced. She wanted to practice six hours a day, but I don't think she had time for that. If she did not think she had practiced enough during a day, which was practically every day, she would play into the night while I fell asleep.

When my parents died, I brought the baby grand home where it graced our living room for many years. My wife enjoyed playing, but I could not get my sons to become interested. They were already playing other instruments at school.

When we decided to move to a retirement community, we sold our house in Aberdeen and had to decide what to do with the baby grand which we all loved. One of our grand-daughters has fun playing the piano, so we decided to give it to her. At present she has no place to put it, so we sent it to her parents' house where it now decorates their living room. My daughter-in-law plays the piano and enjoys entertaining her friends with her music. She is delighted with the tone of the baby grand.

My mother's baby grand, that put me to sleep when I was a child, has now been a treasure in the family for four generations.

BOYHOOD PASTIMES

FREEDOM

I grew up in Washington in a different world from today. I had freedoms that my children never had. There were few cars around and they presented little danger to children. We had to forcibly restrict our childrens' radius of activity to protect them from the automobile traffic all around us. This was a big difference from my boyhood, when I was free to roam around the city of Washington as I pleased. I think I had these freedoms because my parents had them when they grew up. But there has been a sudden change in our lives. The automobile is now king of the road. The lives of suburban children today are regulated by the school bus schedule. They don't become free until they acquire their driver's license and access to a car.

EVARTS STREET

During my years in grade school, we lived on Evarts Street Northeast, off North Capitol Street and three blocks south of Michigan Avenue. If you looked south on North Capitol, you could see the Capitol at the end of the street. It was less than two miles away.

Evarts Street was a short one-block street between North Capitol and a cemetery fence. The street continued on the other side of the cemetery, but that was inaccessible to us. The houses on the north and south sides of the street were standard Washington row houses, with nice front yards.

It was a new development when we moved in. Almost all the men on the block were government employees, mostly Irish Catholic. There was no traffic on the street, and there was seldom a car. The houses were serviced from an alley in the back. The few people that had cars, treasured them and kept them in garages.

PLAYMATES

There were five boys my age on the block. We got along well and played together. We did not associate with girls, and we did not play with children two or more years younger than ourselves. We ignored boys who were two or more years older than we were. We had our own world and excluded everybody else.

This gang became my extended family. I was the only foreigner, but the other boys had never met a foreigner before. They had no preconceived notions, and I was fully accepted.

PLAYGROUNDS

We had three play grounds. The first one was Evarts Street. A full, clear block without traffic, augmented by sidewalks and front yards. It was a clean, expansive area.

Then there was the District drinking water filtration plant across North Capitol Street. Most of the plant was underground, and covered by a beautiful, grassy field, five city blocks long and a large city block wide, interspersed with ground-level man holes every thirty feet in both north south and east west directions. The man holes never bothered us at all.

Every block there was a row of filtration towers, some thirty feet in diameter and sixty feet high. We never went near them, there were always men working around. All around the outside of the plant there were large trees and ornamental plantings.

Our third playground was the thick woods along the north side of Michigan Avenue. That property was part of the vast parcel belonging to the Old Soldiers' Home where they took care of the surviving Civil War veterans.

Chalk

In 1920 when we moved into our new house on Evarts Street, the sidewalks were finished, but not the road pavement. In the rough ground of the road, we boys found large chunks of chalk, some two to three inches in diameter. None of us had ever seen chalk like this before. It was great fun for drawing pictures on the sidewalk and on the walls of houses that ran along the alleys. However, our chalk pictures were quickly washed away by the next rain. After a short time, they paved the road and that was the end of our chalk supply. It was great fun while it lasted.

Baseball

Evarts Street was a large, safe, clean playground and became our favorite baseball field. I owned a bat and glove, and everyone else provided a piece of equipment. In those days they didn't have soft balls, we played with standard hard balls.

We developed our own version of baseball suitable for five or less players, similar to what was later called stick ball. Every time there was a strike or a walk, everyone advanced one position, from from second to first base, to pitcher and catcher, until he got a chance at bat.

Evarts Street was also good for other games, such as hide and seek.

Racing and Touch Football

In the football season, we would go over to the filtration plant. It was the greatest place for running. We would race one another. I would win a lot of times, I was the fastest runner in the group. Running was a lot of fun.

Another game we played was touch football. This also required a lot of running. The filtration plant provided the wide open spaces for it.

"Butter Bread"

The vigorous games we played at the filtration plant were quite exhausting, and sometimes we decided that we needed refreshments. We would count our pennies, and if we had five, we would go to the store across the street and buy a loaf of "butter" bread, that is, white bread that has been coated with butter before baking, price five cents. We would bring it back to the shade of a nice tree, break it apart with our hands, and everybody got several chunks. I cannot imagine now why we thought it tasted so good.

Camping and Spitting

Sometimes we would go into the thick woods north of Michigan Avenue. Here we would make believe we were camping out and go hunting for imaginary deer and bears. In camp, to make life more interesting, we would play cards.

One important exercise we did here was to practice the manly art of spitting. In those days, barber shops, bars, hotels, and public places were all equipped with shiny brass spittoons, and woe the man who missed. Although public spitting is no longer in style, if you look for it, you can occasionally watch on television some baseball players in the pit indulging in some fancy spitting.

Our make believe campfire was also the scene of some important discussions, such as the one described under the heading of "Future Statesmen" below.

Rainy Days

The sun did not always shine. On rainy days when we could not play outside, each boy would take a book and we would all meet in the house of one of the boys and read our books. Then we would be so quite that you could hear a pin drop. At that time, I was reading the "Tom Swift" series of boy adventurer stories that I borrowed from the public library.

The host's mother would occasionally come in and serve us some sarsaparillas and cookies.

Parades

Whenever there was a big parade in Washington, and there were several every year, we would tramp down to Pennsylvania Avenue as a gang and squirm our way through the crowd to get a good place at the curb.

Sometimes we would get to see the President of the United States. All parades had some military units with a band and flags. When the American Flag went by, we always stood at attention with our right hands over our hearts. The men around us would always take their hats off.

Future Statesmen

Sometimes we would have a deep discussion at our "campfire" in the woods on what we were going to be when we grew up. Being so exposed to parades and other festive occasions involving the President, all the boys except me wanted to become President of the United States. There was always quite an argument until we decided who it should be. We usually did not like to give the job to anyone who had been selected at one of our previous conclaves.

The next most important job was Secretary of War. We went through the entire cabinet until everyone had a job. I was the only one who spoke a foreign language, so I became the Secretary of State. I had no competition and was quite content with my job. I never ran for President.

At that time, on New Year's Day, anybody could go to the White House, and after standing in line for an hour or so, shake hands with the President. We boys figured out that shaking hands with people all day long was one of the most important basic duties of the President. So the boy that we had selected for President would spend the rest of the day practicing hand-shaking with all the other boys, to strengthen his hand for his serious, future duties.

Patriotic   Holidays

The Fourth of July was a big holiday with fireworks at the Washington Monument. For this occasion we would go to watch with our families, not as a gang. We had sparklers, but no fireworks, they were strictly forbidden in Washington.

Another significant holiday was Decoration Day, May 30. The land west of Catholic University at that time was a large meadow full of wild flowers. We would all go there early in the morning of Decoration Day and in a few hours we would each have quite a few bouquets of fresh flowers, mostly daisies with some ferns. The cemetery entrance was on North Capitol Street, a few blocks south of

Evarts Street.

There was a steady stream of people entering the cemetery to decorate the graves. Everybody brought their own flowers, but some people always thought that they could use an extra bouquet. We stood there with our flowers on each side of the entrance, and usually within an hour or two, we sold all our flowers for 25 cents a bouquet. This was great big bucks for us.

Palm Sunday and Easter

Palm Sunday provided a reason for an excursion to the Franciscan Monastery. The big attraction was the large bin of palms, you could take as much as you pleased. We each took an armful. We came home and started to make little crosses and other trinkets out of the palms. We gave our family members, friends and neighbors as many as they would take, but at the end of the day we still had a pile of left over trinkets and palms. This was a big problem, since the palms were blessed, we could not throw them in the garbage. We finally took them the next day into the woods, built a fire and burned them. Our gang obeyed the rules.

Every Easter, all the boys, including me, got new suits and shoes. We were allowed to wear them to church and until after the noon meal.

Dinner Time

On normal weekdays, all boys were called home from our games at four thirty, were scrubbed and had their clothes changed, so they would look presentable when their fathers came home from work for dinner at about five o'clock. Life in Washington was quite formal in those days.

Boys Club

Several summers my mother sent me every weekday to the District's Boy's Club. The Club had a well equipped gym, a pool room, and a baseball field, but no swimming pool which I would have liked. I learned to play cards and pool quite well, but most of the time I spent on the baseball field. One day I was up at bat when the ball came at me just as I wanted it to. I swung at the ball with all my might and hit it squarely. The ball made a beautiful arc over the rear fence. I leisurely trotted around the bases for a home run. Never, in the rest of my life, have I hit a ball like that again.

Thunder Storms

I remember that there was a thunder storm every hot afternoon or early evening that cooled down the hot temperatures. I also remember the long stretches of hot muggy days when all of the energy would be drained out of you. I guess the truth lies somewhere in between my two memories.

When I was smaller and my parents went out, they got a babysitter, Miss Leshire, to stay with us. My sister, Helen, was five years younger than me. Miss Leshire was a kind, elderly person, who was terrified of thunder storms. When we had thunder and lightning, she would get out a statue of the Blessed Virgin and set it up on a table as far from the windows as possible. Then she would light a candle in front of it and sit there saying her rosary.

In contrast to Miss Leshire's behavior, my mother had no fear of storms. She would stand at the window and watch the lightning, it fascinated her. She explained to me that lightning had something to do with energy transfer. This was the only time that I can remember, that my mother explained something to me that I could not understand.

Crystal Sets

On my own, my specialty was building crystal sets and installing antennas. I had a little shop in the basement where I did my work. I could only get Washington stations on my sets, but I met boys who claimed that they had received Pittsburgh, then the strongest station in the U.S.

I had books on how to do all this. My mother helped me out financially. She helped me to get up on our roof where I installed an antenna as long as the house. Such antennas have to be properly grounded because they attract lightning. I would take a four foot long piece of copper pipe and hammer it about three feet into the ground. The antenna had to be attached to this pipe by a heavy copper wire. This wire was cut at a place where it was convenient to install a thin wire into the house to the crystal set.

At the cut, I installed a "lightning arrester." This little gadget consists of two one-half-inch wide copper plates. One edge of the plates is cut into sharp triangles, one sixteenth of an inch high. The two plates are mounted on a base so that their sharp points are opposing one another, about two hair widths apart. One plate is attached to the ground, the other one to the antenna and the crystal set.

The theory is that the grounded plate has greater attraction for a stroke of lightning than the thin wire to the crystal set, and the electricity jumps the small gap in the lightning arrester.

In a thunder storm, I would carefully watch the little gap between the two plates in the lightning arrester. A stroke of lightning was not necessary to demonstrate how the thing worked. Just the electrically charged wind blowing over the house was sufficient to load the antenna with a charge large enough to generate a current to the ground. As I watched, there would be a steady stream of sparks from the antenna plate to the ground. I was fascinated and happy that my crystal set and house were safe from lightning.

During a National Presidential Nominating Convention that was taking place at the time, my father asked me what I could hear on my crystal set. I set him up with my earphones listening to the final balloting. He sat there listening all afternoon, then went back after supper. It was a new experience for him. My mother, Helen, and I stayed in the kitchen giggling and laughing at his enthusiasm for my crystal set..

I provided several family friends with crystal sets and installed antennas for them. I became quite an expert on climbing up on roofs.

The demand for my expertise did not last long. Just as I was getting good at it, they came out with tube operated radios, and crystal sets became obsolete.

PARADISE LOST

Evarts Street, when I was growing up, was truly a wonderful place to live. Today, the place has turned into a Black neighborhood. The street is full of cars, there is no space to play ball. The filtration plant is fenced in and the grass grows tall and wild. Our beloved woods are gone, replaced by fancy new apartment houses.

The new suburban neighborhoods where we now raise our children simply don't have the atmosphere and flavor of Evarts Street. With advancing technology, something of human value during our growing years has been lost.

ELEMENTARY EDUCATION

ST. MARTIN'S SCHOOL

When I was six years old, my mother enrolled me in Trinity Catholic School in Georgetown. The nuns were not friendly, and when I tried to teach them Portuguese, they would not listen. At the end of the year, they would not promote me to second grade because they said my English was not good enough to handle the work.

During the summer, my father bought a new house on Evarts Street, just off North Capitol Street, from which he could walk to work at both Catholic and Georgetown Universities. My father was a great walker.

Our new house was in St. Martin's Parish which had a brand new grammar school, but only a basement church. The nuns were Sisters of Notre Dame and we became friends right away. They taught me English. Since I already knew my letters and numbers in Portuguese, they just taught me the English names to things I already knew. It wasn't hard. The nuns said I made remarkable progress.

The school was strictly segregated, I do not remember ever seeing any girls there. My sister was five years younger than me, but she was a girl who wanted my toys. We hardly ever spoke.

For a grown-up, the school was about a ten minute walk from our house, but usually it took me over half an hour because there were so many things to see on the way, like seeing what was playing at the near-by movie house.

Washington street cars in the center of the city have their third power rail underground. There is a small slot in the ground halfway between the two tracks, and a collector reaches down from the bottom of the street car through this slot to an underground rail. On North Capitol Street, just a few blocks north of the school, there is a switching station. There is big hole in the ground between the tracks where a man in the hole removes the underground collector from the bottom of the streetcar while the conductor raises the trolley to the overhead power line. On the way home from school, a group of us would always wait for a street car to come along, so we could watch the power delivery being switched from underground to overhead or vice versa. We would talk real nicely to the conductor and ask him for a ride home. Often the conductor would let us get on the car, but at other times he would say no. Then we'd wait for the next car, and if three conductors said no, we would give up and walk home, but we would get home quite late.

Washington is rather unique in that it has lots of trees along its residential streets. In the fall the streets would be full of leaves, but the people would sweep them into the gutters for the city to collect them. I found it to be great fun to walk in the gutters and kick the leaves. Often there would be water in the bottom of the gutter, and I would arrive home with my feet cold and soaked. My mother would put me to bed because I would be getting a cold.

My mother was frustrated trying to keep me out of the gutters, and my parents finally decided to send me for my third grade to Mt. Washington Academy, a boy's boarding school in Northwest Baltimore. The nuns there were all my friends. My parents came to see me every week, but I wasn't lonesome. While I was there, we had confirmation. My mother examined me carefully before we went to church, and said it was the first time she had seen me really clean behind the ears. Since that day, I have always cleaned myself behind the ears real well.

After my year at Mt. Washington, I came back to St. Martin's and didn't walk in the gutters any more. Every day started with a half hour of religion, the nuns taught us from the Baltimore Catechism. We were told to obey our parents. We learned about the ten commandments, the seven sacraments, the organization and history of the church, and how to relate to other people. In the higher grades, we discussed the parts of the mass and other services, and the nuns helped the boys who wanted to learn how to serve at mass. Girls were never discussed.

After religion, there was a daily spelling drill, which was taken very seriously. We also had a lot of English composition at which I became very good. In the last couple of years we diagramed sentences. I wondered what for, but have found that even today when faced with a tricky sentence, the best thing to do is to diagram it and try to make two out of one. I never could tell the difference between an adjective and an adverb, and what it means for one word to modify another, but I muddled through pretty well. In addition to desk work, we had daily mental arithmetic drill and oral reading. By the sixth grade I was becoming very good in my school work and the nuns told my parents that they would allow me to skip a grade to make up for my first grade fiasco. My mother wanted to go along, but my father would not hear of it. He felt I had to have more training in English. His pet exercise for me was to make me copy by hand several pages of some good English text. He was impossible to please.

We had at least a hour's home work every day, which I did as soon as I got home, while telling my mother what had happened at school. This way I had the rest of the evening free and could read, play with my friends, or build crystal sets and listen to the radio. Regardless of my father's fears, I felt pretty secure at the head of the class.

Looking back on all this, I think my most important subject was competitive mental arithmetic. At first I had to translate all numbers into Portuguese, do the arithmetic, and translate the answers back into English. The nuns were very patient and watched me carefully. These nuns were smart! Finally the day came when I did my mental arithmetic in English. The language you do your mental arithmetic in is your mother tongue. I now think the nuns knew this. After reaching this point, I became better in all my subjects.

St. Martin's had no gym or other athletic facilities. Across the street was a brand new public school with a beautiful large gym and a great swimming pool, but the kids over there were no smarter than we were at St. Martin's. We did have a Boy Scout Troop which I joined and we had great times on overnight trips sleeping in the woods.

WASHINGTON

Next to St. Martin's, the next most important place in Washington for me was the public library. The now boarded-up classical building was on the edge of the down town business section. I had to take a street car to get there, but once there, I loved roaming around the the town with the big stores and their beautiful window displays, everything was so fancy. Then there was the now long gone Earle Theater which let kids in before 6 pm for 15 cents. I often went with a friend, and we got a first run movie plus an hour's live show. It left me with a life-long interest in the theater.

Washington at that time was a beautiful city, everything so new and clean. Even as a small boy, I recognized that the city was planned with great imagination, I could wander around all over and never get lost. The north-south streets were numbered consecutively, and the east-west streets were laid out in alphabetical order.The people were wonderful; hard-working, friendly, and helpful. Where else would fussy parents like mine let their kid wander around, all over downtown, even after dark? At every street car stop in the morning there would be a pile of newspapers on top of a milk box, and an empty cigar box on top of the newspapers. People going to work would help themselves to a paper and drop the money in the cigar box. Nobody ever stole anything If a cop caught somebody driving while drunk, he would tell the driver to move over into the passenger's seat and he would get in the car and drive the drunk home. Once home, the cop would make sure that the drunk was adequately being taken care of before returning to his beat.

Every year Bishop Shahan, the Rector of Catholic University, and a few of his associates, would come to our house and have Christmas Dinner at noon, but the party would last deep into the night, long after I had been sent to bed. It was a gala affair, the men wore black ties and the ladies long dresses. My mother would play the piano. We attended several affairs of this type at friends' houses throughout the year.

Unfortunately, my beautiful Washington no longer exists. I have heard hotel door men tell out-of-town guests not to go out for a walk, it's too dangerous. Washington today is the murder capital of the world. St. Martin's is a poor, broke, black, inner-city parish. The church is kept locked, except during services. The newspapers at the street car stops are gone. A popular black man, M. Barry, was recently elected mayor, and immediately created 10000 new civil service jobs for blacks in the District Government. There are over 100 independent police jurisdictions in the Metropolitan Area. Local problems stagger the imagination. No one in public office has a full understanding of all that's wrong with the area. It's not just a matter of the right hand not knowing what the left is doing, it's any finger of the left hand not knowing what the other fingers of the same hand are doing. No coordinated action is possible. Today, Washington is the worst administered Metropolitan Area in the whole world, and it all happened in the name of progress!

MY FAMILY

JOAO ANTONIO COUTINHO

My paternal grandfather was born in Lisbon, Portugal, studied medicine, and joined the Portuguese Navy as a medical officer for a tour of duty. A photograph of him in his Navy uniform is on page 19. He looks just like my son Alan. We have records showing that he served as the medical officer in Goa (Portuguese India), Angola, and the Canary Islands.

After his Navy tour, he settled in Lisbon and conducted a medical practice, specializing in tropical diseases. He was very well off and was recognized as a member of the upper class in Lisbon. I am named after him and was expected to follow in his footsteps and study medicine.

LUIZA AMANDINA de SIQUEIRA

My paternal grandmother was a very aristocratic lady. She had four children, two boys and two girls, but one boy died as a small child.

My two aunts were well educated. One was a poet. I have a published play that she wrote.

My other aunt became infected with the flu bug that infected the world shortly after World War I and killed tens of millions of people. My grandfather had passed away by then. The doctor treating my aunt recommended that moving her to a tropical climate might save her life. My other aunt was married to a Portuguese government official, and he managed to get transferred to Goa, Portuguese India. So the family moved to Goa. My sick aunt lived a few more years, but eventually she died. However, the rest of the family stayed on in Goa. My father visited them once, and he was appalled at the slip-shod way the Portuguese government was running the place. My grandmother died there at the age of 92.

Sequeira, spelled with an "e," is a very common name in Portugal, Spain, and Latin America. Siqueira with an "i" is the name of a family prominent in Portuguese history. Their coat of arms consists of five golden sea shells arranged in a 2-1-2 pattern on a blue background. It is reproduced, like the Coutinho's coat of arms, on the ceiling of the National Palace in Sintra. A book entitled "O Paco de Cintra" by E. Casanova and F. Lino, published by Impressa National, Lisbon, 1903, contains a reproduction of the ceiling of the Great Hall of the National Palace. The ceiling is domed, so a reproduction on a flat surface would be highly distorted.   The ceiling is shown in

Lieutenant Joao Antonio Coutinho
Portuguese Navy

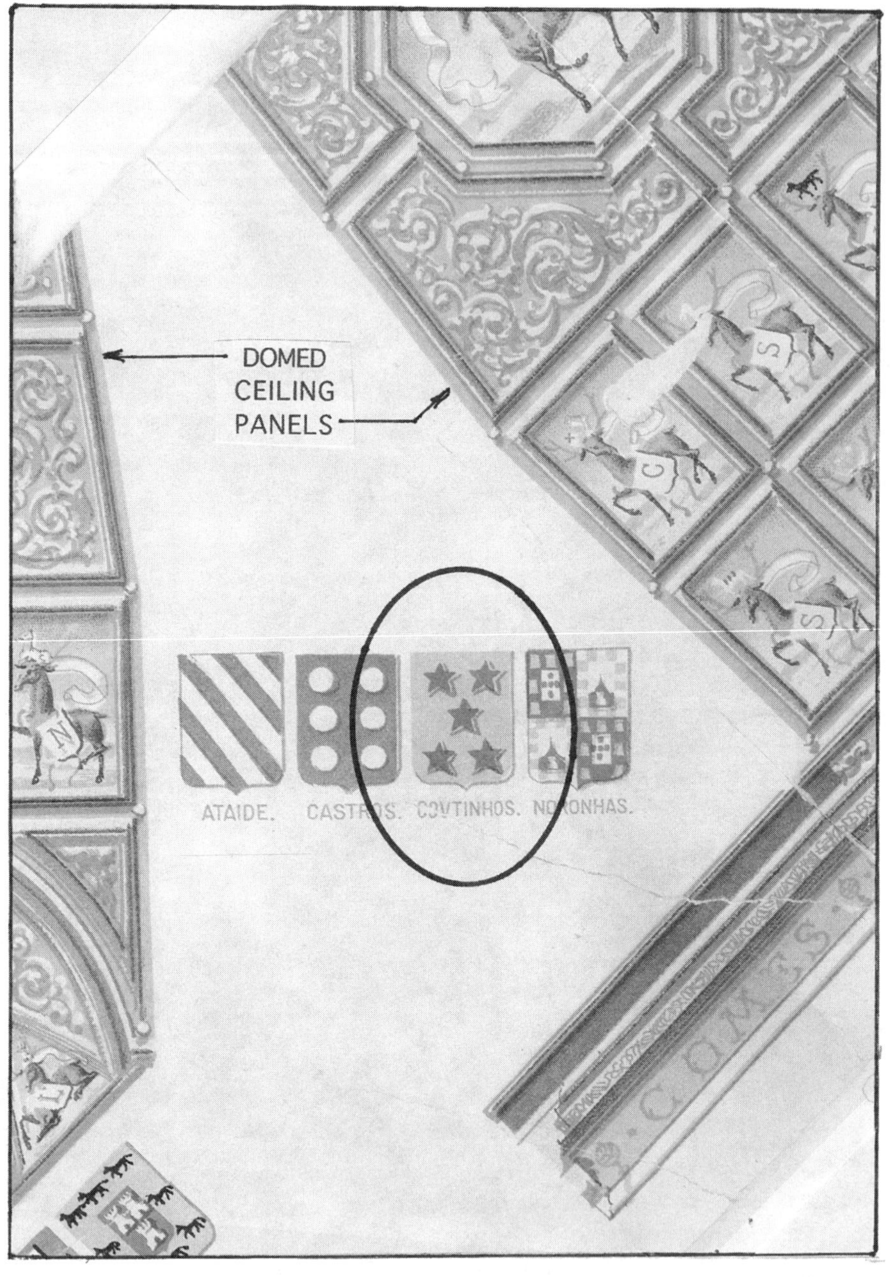

Coutinho's Coat of Arms
as it appears on the ceiling of theGreat Hall,
National Palace, Sintra

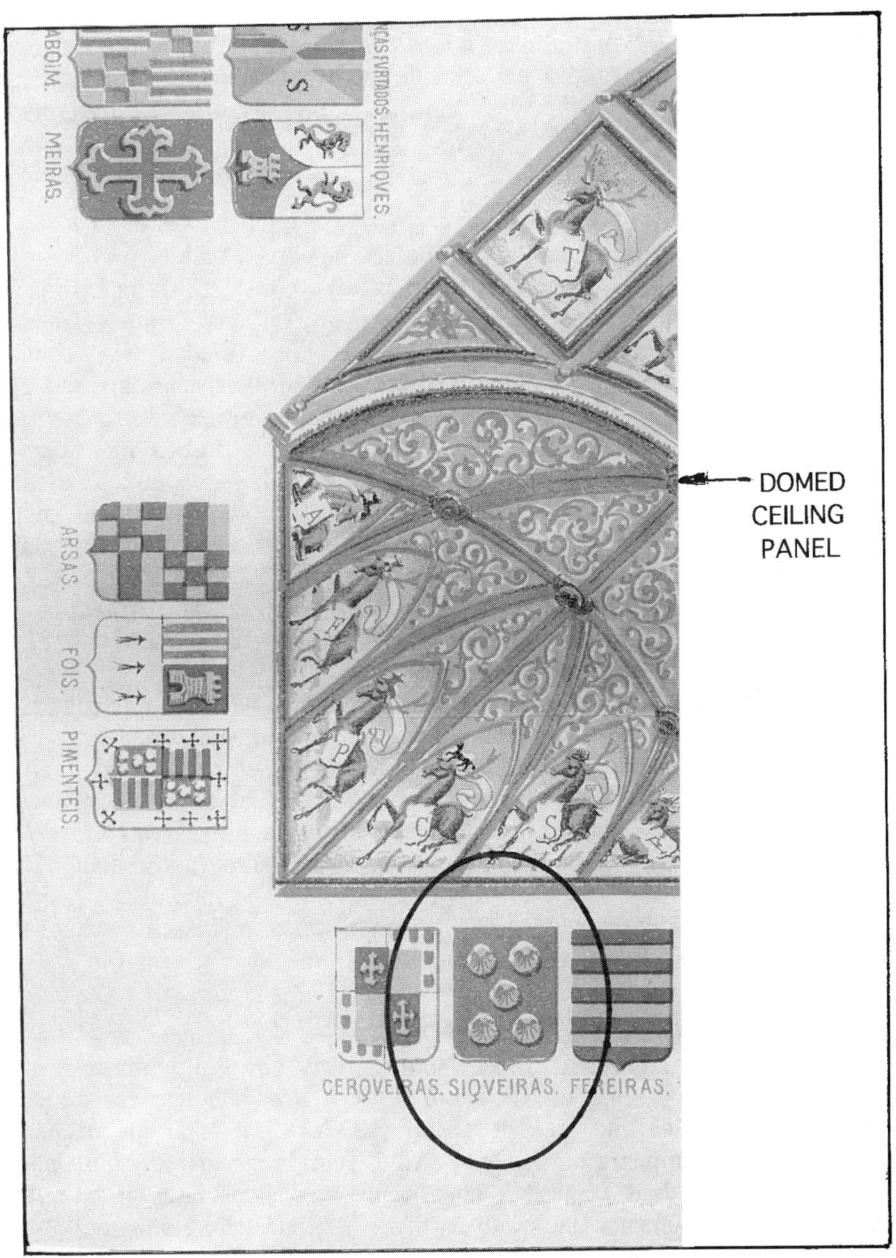

Siqueira's Coat of Arms
as it appears on the ceiling of the
Great Hall, National Palace, Sintra

panels, which if cut out and attached, would form the dome shape. Page 20 shows part of the panel with the Coutinho's coat of arms, and Page 21 shows the one with the Siqueira's. My grandmother was the last living member of the Siqueira family.

LUIZ (LOUIS) AUGUSTE VALET (1848-1905)

My maternal grandfather, Luiz Valet (spelled Vallet until the Portuguese abolished all double letters), was born 1848 in Lisbon, Portugal, son of Leandre Domingo Valet of Amboise, France (died 1869), and Henrietta Louise Chapuis of Lisbon (died 1867). They were married in Lisbon, 1837. Luiz had a brother, Carlos, and a sister, Madelena. The two brothers ran their father's successful import/export business, with Luiz in Lisbon, and his brother in France and Switzerland. They imported manufactured goods and textiles from England, and exported southern European goods to England and South America. The family was quite well off. I am reproducing on pages 24 and 25 one of Luiz's passports dated Lisbon, April 7, 1870, which records one of his business trips to Brazil and Argentina. We have two oil portraits of him showing a friendly man with an intelligent face and dark hair, see page 23.

I have a number of portraits and drawings of Luiz's ancestors indicating that they came from southern France and Switzerland.

In those days they did not have typewriters, and all correspondence was handwritten. Luiz kept a bound blank book into which he or his secretary copied by hand every business letter he sent out. The letters are in Portuguese, French, and some in English. If we could decipher the scribble, we would have a good idea of the scope of his business ventures. He died in 1905, when my mother was 14 years old. She had many fond memories of him.

ELLEN JANET HOARE (1863-1912)

My maternal grandmother, Janet Hoare, was born in Hampreston, southern England, one of 12 children of a beer wholesaler, James Hoare (born 1834) and his wife Ruth (1832-1872). A copy of her birth certificate appears on page 26. All 12 children married, but only my grandmother had a child. The family was close and my grandmother took my mother back and forth to England where she got to know her 11 aunts and uncles well, and where she learned English as her first language. My mother was very fond of her aunts and uncles. She kept a record of everyone birthdays as shown on page 27. A copy of my grandmother's passport appears on pages 28 and 29.

My grandmother originally wanted to be a teaching nun, but the order of nuns that she wanted to join required that a girl first travel

Ellen Janet Hoare Valet

Luiz Auguste Valet

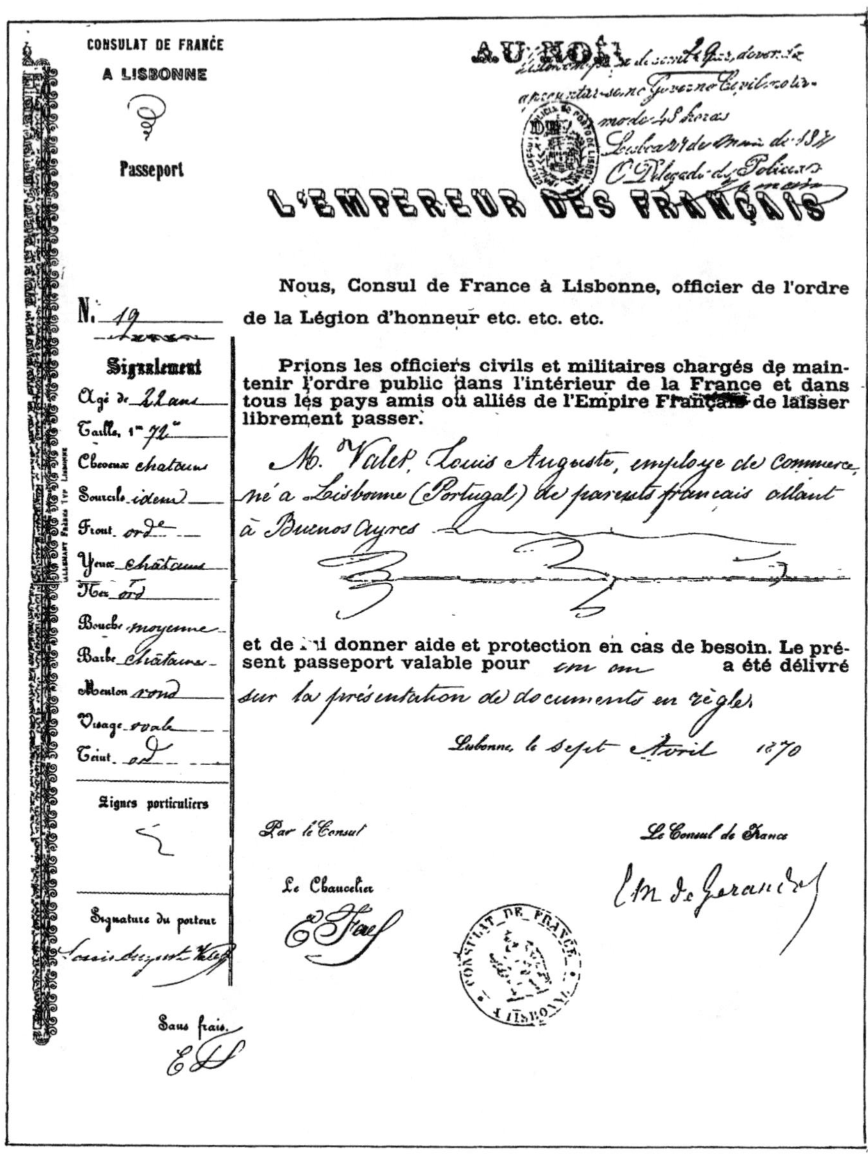

French Passport for Luiz Auguste Valet,
Dated: Lisbon, April 7, 1870
Original Size: 10 x 13 inches. Page 1

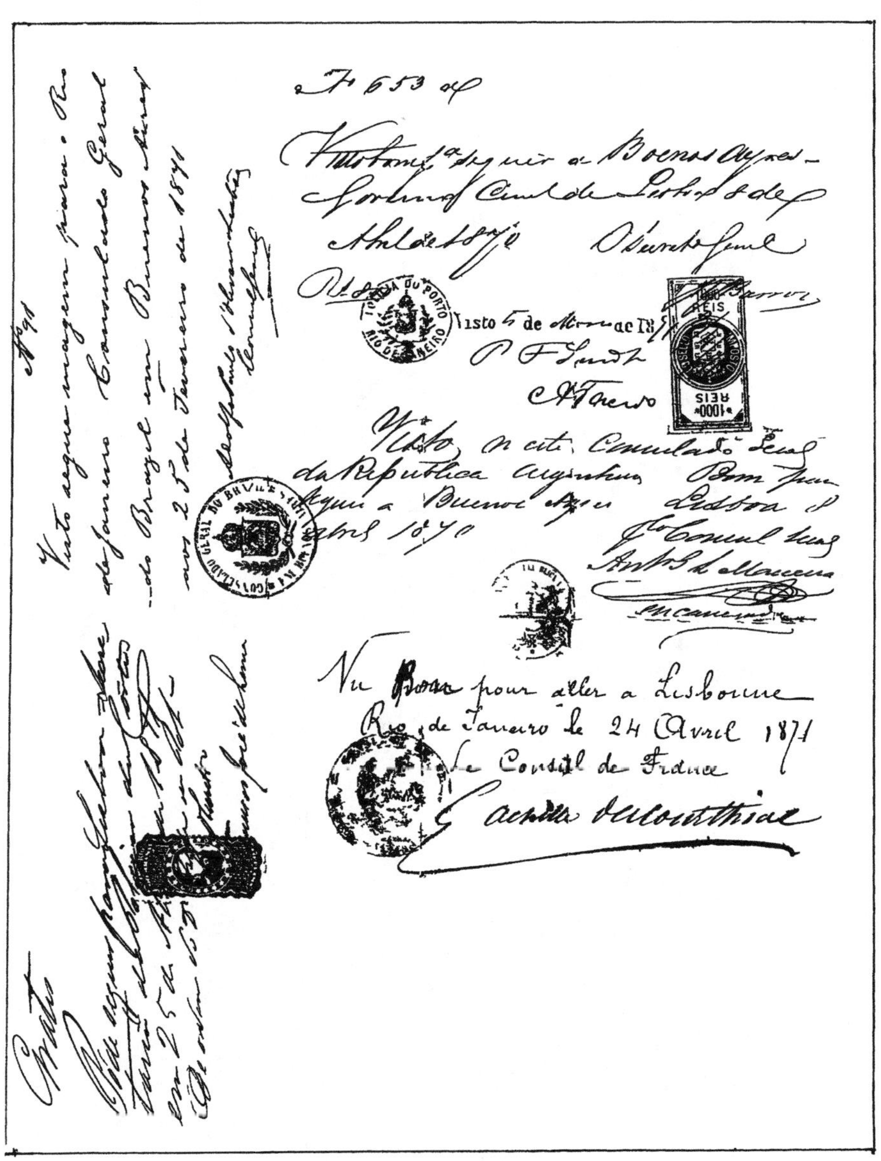

French Passport for Luiz Auguste Valet,
Page 2

P 902403

[Printed by Authority of the Registrar-General.]
B. Cert.
S.R.

CERTIFIED COPY of an ENTRY OF BIRTH.
Pursuant to the Births and Deaths Registration Acts, 1836 to 1929.

The Statutory Fee for this Certificate is 2s. 7d. If required subsequently to registration, a Search Fee is payable in addition.

Registration District				Wimborne					Insert in this Margin any Notes which appear in the original entry.
1863. Birth in the Sub-District of			Wilchampton		in the	Counties of Dorset and Hants			
Columns:— 1	2	3	4	5	6	7	8	9	10
No.	When and Where Born.	Name, if any.	Sex.	Name and Surname of Father	Name and Maiden Surname of Mother	Rank or Profession of Father	Signature, Description and Residence of Informant	When Registered.	Signature of Registrar.	Baptismal Name, if added *after* Registration of Birth.
207	Twenty First April 1863 Fern Down Hampreston	Ellen Janette	Girl	James Hoare	Pruth Hoare formerly King	Grocer and Beer Seller	Pruth Hoare Mother Fern Down Hampreston	Fifteenth May 1863	Thomas Beckingham Registrar.	

I, William Haskell Short, Superintendent Registrar for the District of Blandford, in the County of Dorset do hereby certify that this is a true copy of the Entry No. 207 in the Register Book of Births No. 7 for the above-named Sub-District, and that such Register Book is now legally in my custody.

WITNESS MY HAND this 26th day of July, 1938.

Wm Haskell Short
Superintendent Registrar

CAUTION.—Any person who (1) falsifies any of the particulars on this Certificate, or (2) uses it as true, knowing it to be falsified, is liable to Prosecution.

Ellen Janet Hoare's Birth Certificate

Dates of birthdays

My Grandfather — James Hoare was born on the — 15th of July — 1834

" Grandmother — Ruth Hoare " " " " — 8th of Feb. — 1832

" Auntie — Julia Maria " " " " — 16th of Aug. — 1854

" Uncle — Alfred James " " " " — 4th of June. — 1856

" Auntie — Laura Isabella " " " " — 25th of Jan. — 1858
  +May 2. 1895.

" Uncle — Francis William " " " " — 21st of Dec. — 1859

" " — Harry Montagne " " " " — 12th of Sept. — 1861

" Mother — Ellen Janette " " " " — 21st of April — 1863

" Auntie — Frances Olivia " " " " — 15th of Dec. — 1864

" Uncle — Christofler " " " " — 11th of June — 1866

" " — Edwin James " " " " — 11th of July — 1867

" Auntie — Lillian Louisa " " " — 19th of April — 1869

" " — Lucy Augusta " " " — 30th of Aug — 1870

" Uncle — Maximillian " " " — 25th of Feb — 1872

My father — Luiz Augusto " " " " — 25th of Dec — 1847

" Uncle — Carlos Luiz " " " " — 13th of Sept — 1845

And I — Louisa Germaine " " " " — 13th of July — 1891

My Mother's Record of Family Birthdays

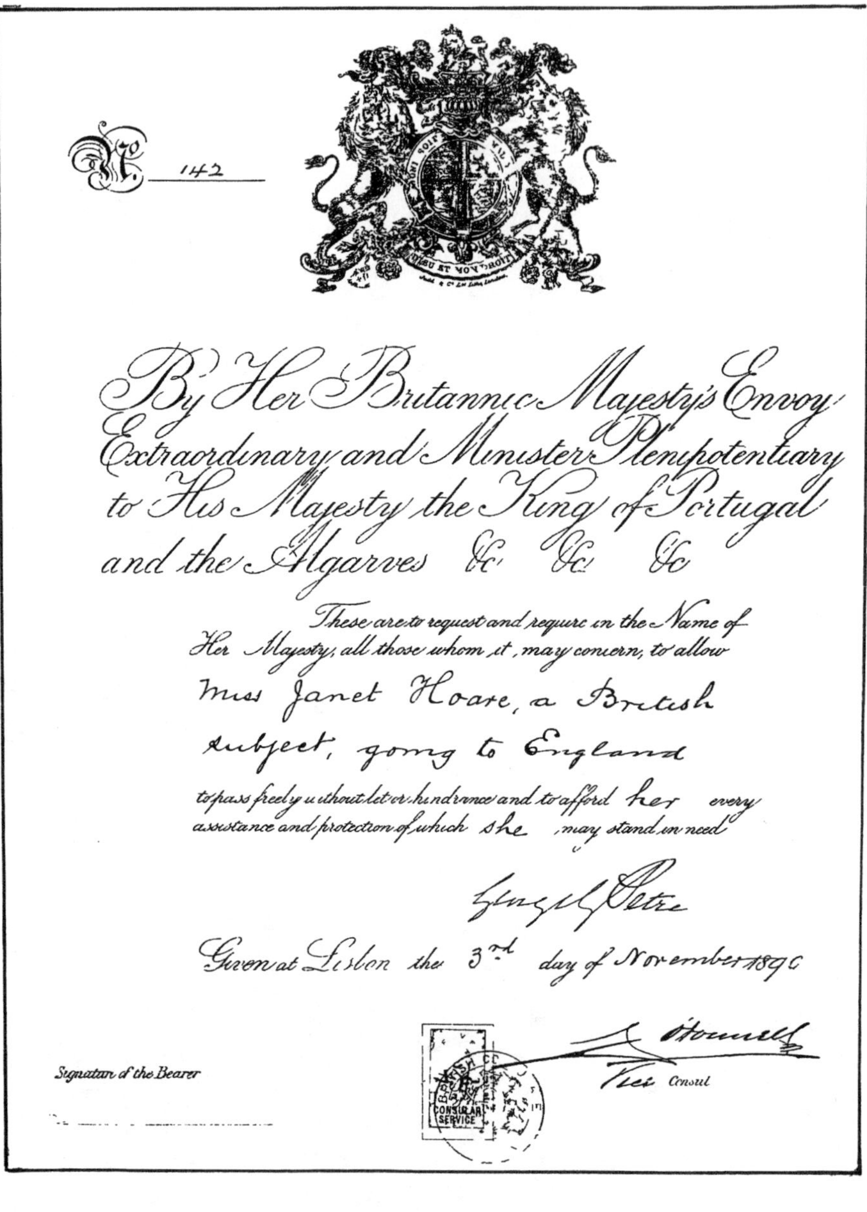

English Passport for Janet Hoare
Dated Lisbon, November 3, 1890
Original Size: 10.5 x 15.25 inches, Page 1

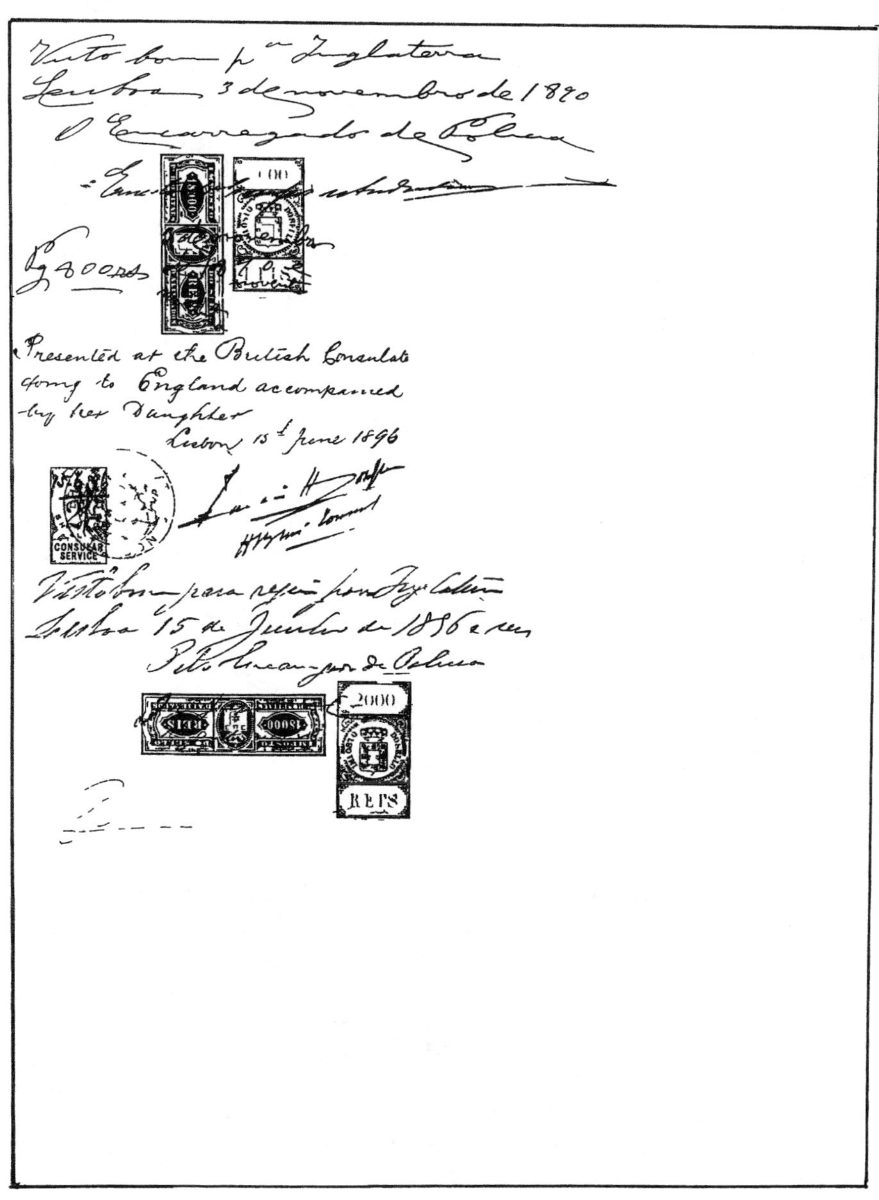

English Passport for Janet Hoare
Page 2

throughout Europe for a year before admission to the order.

Traveling throughout Europe was at the time considered a necessary experience for an educated person.

The system required a young person to obtain as many letters of recommendation, as he could, from people who knew him in his home town, to friends in foreign countries. His "tour of the continent" then consisted in his visiting these foreign friends. In a time without telephone, radio or television, recipients of such letters were usually delighted to sponsor a foreign visitor for several weeks and make sure that he saw the sights and learned something about the country. My father obtained most of his letters of recommendation from his professors in Lisbon, to professors at several of the great universities in Europe, which explains his intimate knowledge of those institutions.

In her travels, Janet came to Lisbon where there was a very lively English colony. My grandmother was naturally drawn into the social swirl. My grandfather, although a Frenchman, also partook in the social activities of the English community, where he met my grandmother. They were married and my mother was born in 1891. My grandmother had always wanted to be a teacher, and now that she made her home in Lisbon, she became the English teacher in the Lisbon Girls High School.

LEANDRE DOMINGO AUGUSTE VALLET

Leandre Vallet, my mother's grandfather, was born in Amboise, France, and was married in France to Henrietta Louise Chapuis of Zurich, Switzerland. I have a copy of the marriage certificate of Henrietta's parents, Jean Jacques Chapuis of Lausanne to Marie Bagel of Zurich on May 10, 1810 in Pully, Vaud, Switzerland, near Zurich. Jean's parents were Albert No Chapuis and Anne Fontenay; and Marie's father was Jean Conrad Bagel of Zurich.

Leandre and Henrietta settled in Lisbon where my grandfather and mother were born. Leandre ran an extensive business in southern Europe. A handbill issued by his Madrid store shows four models of room stoves, see page 31. Each such stove burned one or two small charcoal bricks a day, depending on room size. I have a copy of Leandre's 31 page will, notarized at Amboise on January 31, 1869 written in French. He was quite rich.

SINTRA

The State of Sintra contains a granite mountain range that rises between Lisbon and the Atlantic Ocean and forms the most western land-point in Europe. On the top of this mountain range lies the

Fabricante de Chimeneas de toda clase, poseedor de cuatro privilegios esclusivos de invencion para los nuevos aparatos calorificos y ventiladores destinados á calentar con ventaja y economia toda clase de habitaciones y del Aparato aspirador á aire libre para la ventilacion y evitar los humos de todas las Chimeneas que tengan esa grave incomodidad.

Caloriferos fumivoros condensadores portatiles sin Tubos.

Estos elegantes aparatos tan útiles y economicos funcionan sin tubos, tienen la importante ventaja de trasladarse en todas las habitaciones que se quieran calentar; su sistema es completamente fumivoro y solo se gasta para ellos carbon vejetal, se guarnecen con este combustible en proporcion de su tamaño, y duran asi de 8 á 10 horas resultando de estos un calor sumamente agradable é higienico, ofreciendo una economia de un 30 % sobre todos los demas aparatos de su clase.

Caloriferos Vallet á aire caliente con Tubos.

Estos sencillos aparatos de modesta invencion han obtenido un estraordinario suceso en todos los sitios en que han sido aplicados, su sistema de poderosa ventilacion satisface á todas las condiciones del higiene, asi como la gran economia que procuran sobre el combustible no caro unos que pueden sobre su parato pueden facilmente servir para calentar á la vez varias habitaciones.

Caloriferos Sifones con Tubos á represion de aire caliente.

El sistema reforido de este aparato esplica facilmente la estraordinaria valor que procura, estos se pueden aplicar con la mayor ventaja á toda clase de utilidades é industria que se desee; Palacios, cafés, teatros, colegios, iglesias, hospicios, oficinas, administraciones publicas, estuf jardines, almacenes, manufacturas &. &. &. elevando su prodigiosa calor de 40 á 50 grados por cada 300 varas cubicas con solo 5 á 6 libras de carbon de coke, solo combustible con que se deben alimentar todas las 6 á 7 horas.

Aparatos aspiradores á aire libre para evitar los humos y ventilar las habitaciones.

Estos aparatos fijos aspiradores de reciente invencion privilegiados por S. M. se colocan en las salidas de las chimeneas y evitan perfectamente los humos de todas aquellas chimeneas que tienen esa incomodidad, ayudando ademas con ventaja los malos olores y el sobrante de calor de las habitaciones.

Handbill Advertising Room Stoves
Leandre Vallet, Madrid Store

State Capital of Sintra, sometimes spelled Cintra, renowned for its natural beauty by many poets, including Lord Byron, who did wonders for the Sintra tourist trade. The cool summer mountain air attracted the Portuguese royal family who made it their summer residence for six centuries.   Sintra boasts three royal palaces within its boundaries. During the reign of the King, only nobility and selected members of the upper class were allowed to own land and houses in Sintra. My great grandparents bought a summer house half a block or so down the hill from the National Palace, that was the Queen's residence when the King was not in town.When the King was around, the Royal family lived in the Pena Palace, built on the highest peak of the Sintra range,   an   unbelievable   19th   century   conglomeration   of Moorish, Gothic, Manualine, Renaissance, and Baroque, which would send Mr. Disney into a drooling spell. The Great Hall in the National Palace is the largest room in the country and used for such special state occasions as Wellington's negotiation of the armistice after his victory over the French at Vimeiro, the first of Napoleon's local defeats, referred to in the history books as the Convention of Sintra.

PIANIST TO THE QUEEN

When my mother organized her music school in Washington, she advertised herself as "Pianist to Her Majesty, the late Queen Maria Pia of Portugal."   My mother was the first woman graduate of the Royal Conservatory of Music in Lisbon. This was an event that could not have escaped the attention of the Queen.   The Queen's life in those days was not what one might envision today.   There was no telephone,   radio, television, or air travel.   Entertainment was home-made,   by the Queen's staff or by an occasional visitor.   The Queen must have been glad to invite the distinguished young lady from down the block to come up to the palace for a visit. Her piano playing must have delighted the Queen and her staff. I can visualize my mother walking up the block to the palace, every week or even more often, where she would be welcomed to entertain the Queen and her staff for an hour or so. The Queen and her probably became good friends. It was an experience that my mother carried in her heart all her life.

European governments seem to be more personally interested in the achievements of their citizens than the US government. When later my mother gave her concert in Berlin, the Portuguese Ambassador was invited and attended, but there was no representative of the US government there. The same thing happened when she gave a concert in Washington at the opening of her music school.

When I received my Doctor's degree at the Technical University of Berlin, the University insisted on inviting the US Ambassador to the party. The invitation was ignored, nobody answered the invitation or came. The Germans could not understand that.

My mother loved to tell me stories about Sintra where she grew up. Without electronics, everybody had to work together hard to provide community entertainment.

THE LURE OF AMERICA

Lisbon had a very active social life where everybody made every effort to know everything about everybody else. In that merry-go-round, my mother and father met and got married in 1912. I came along a year later.

My father had two sisters who tried to adopt me. My mother was unhappy because she thought I was being spoiled rotten, and she was not being allowed to raise me as she saw fit. When my father came up with the bright idea to immigrate to America, she was all for it, to get away from her in-laws.

WASHINGTON

My mother was never truly happy in Washington. I thought we had a good life in our house on Evarts Street. My mother had met a big Irishman who ran some committee at our St. Martin's Church and who operated a butcher and grocery store a block or so south of our church. She started to patronize his store, but after a while he told her she did not have to lug her purchases home as she was doing. He said he would call her at ten am every morning, take her order and his truck would deliver it at noon. And that's how my mother did her shopping. If the butcher had an especially nice piece of meat one day, or a watermelon, or a cabbage, he would place it in my mother's box, and she was always delighted with his selections. My mother was a wonderful cook. She told me, if you don't have much money, but you can allow yourself one luxury, you should at least eat well. The grocery store grew with the years, moved, became a supermarket, moved again several times, became a much larger supermarket, but they always called at ten, and the truck always delivered at noon, the rest of her life.

At that time, the mailman came twice a day, and all other needed services were provided. My mother had no need to leave the house except for social purposes. Yet there was something missing in her life. She complained to me about the lack of servants. If you needed a postage stamp or had to mail a letter, you had to do everything yourself. In Portugal she always had servants to do these little things. However, you had to watch your things carefully, because the servants would steal everything they could.

My mother could not forget the happy times at Sintra. She sent to Portugal for a Sintra native dress, like the one she and her friends wore to festivals as is the custom all over Europe. The dress was brightly colored, with red, white, and green stripes. I have a photograph of her wearing it, see page 35. I don't know what happened to the dress.

BERLIN

When I was in the eighth grade, my mother decided that she would like to start teaching music and had to tune up to a professional pitch. At that time my father was established in a Berlin summer program for American students and had good connections in Berlin. Furthermore, at that time Berlin was considered the cultural capital of Europe. All the foremost artists of the world would spend some time each year in Berlin. My mother decided to go to Berlin for two years, study with the foremost pianists of the world, and give at least one public concert. My sister, Helen, and I were placed in boarding schools. I was sent to Meersburg to a Christian Brothers boarding school, and my parents found a girls boarding school for Helen, run by nuns, right in Berlin.   Helen, five years younger than me, loved her boarding school and had practically no trouble learning German. My mother visited her every week end.

On my short vacations, my mother and Helen would visit me in Meersburg (a twelve hour train ride). On my summer vacations, I would go to Berlin and spend the time with them.

My mother was quite successful in her retraining program in Berlin which ended with a well attended public concert and excellent newspaper reviews. Armed with these trophies, she took Helen and went back to Washington, where she organized her successful music school. I was left behind where, in my parents judgment, I was doing very well.

BERLIN'S SIDE EFFECTS

Berlin Americanized my mother. When she left Lisbon, her heart remained in Sintra. She often compared her life in Washington with what it had been in Portugal. For a Portuguese at that time, Berlin was considered the best of Europe. If you had a choice, it was not London or Paris, it was Berlin. In Berlin, my mother could compare life in the best of Europe with Washington. No matter how you look at it, Berlin is not perfect. There was something about Washington that was missing in Berlin. When my mother returned to Washington, she never looked back any more, not at Berlin, not at Lisbon, nor at Sintra. The music school was her new life.

Louise Coutinho
in   her native Sintra dress

THE   COUTINHO   MUSIC   SCHOOL

My mother organized her music school located between 19th Street and Connecticut Avenue, just north of Dupont Circle, in a building occupied by a dance studio and teachers of other arts. My mother had friends teaching violin and singing, and she could call on teachers she had on standby for a variety of instruments. She taught piano and held a recital every month for the parents of the pupils of the studio. The programs were printed and she made her pupils feel that they were performing in a concert hall.

My mother had several pianos in her studio, but all her students loved her old baby grand that she had had in Evarts Street. She would only let students play on it as a reward when they excelled in their lessons. When we still lived on Evarts Street, she had tried to teach me on her baby grand, and I learned to read music and play mechanically, but I do not have an ear for music. In exasperation, my mother finally gave up. In those days, I would rather build a radio crystal set. carve wood, or go out and play with my friends on the block. Among her students, my mother always favored the boys and pushed them harder than she did the girls.

My Mother's goal was to discover and encourage professional musicians and to send at least one student a year to the Peabody Conservatory in Baltimore. There were years when she did not succeed, but then there were years when more than one student was accepted. That year she walked on air. My mother thought it was very important to teach her students how to act on a stage in public. Today, I see artists on television and am amazed at how many lack basic stage manners.

She gave a number of concerts in Washington. My father knew people in the embassies, and he would go around and distribute tickets to his friends of rank. Enough of them would come and make the concert an event that would be reported in the newspapers.

She also played at weddings and acted as master of ceremonies. This often got her name in the newspapers too, and provided publicity for her music studio. My mother had a contract with the Board of Education in Washington that awarded credits to music majors in the City's high schools, who took class lessons in her studio. Her photo appears on page 37.

She was an active and respected member of the Washington music establishment, a group whose objective was to bring an orchestra and opera to Washington, and that eventually was responsible for bringing the Kennedy Center to the Nation's Capital, putting it on an artistic level with London, Paris, or Berlin.

Louise Coutinho

FATHERLY VISITS

When my father came summers to Berlin, he would visit me in my room at the most unexpected time. He would scold me thoroughly for keeping such a messy room and rant on and on about how studying engineering instead of medicine or law was such a waste of time. Then he would take me out to dinner in one of Berlin's most expensive and fancy restaurants. He would tell me about the history of the place and how the Crown Prince and other notables had held their parties there.

My father did not want his American students' Berlin experience to be restricted to their classrooms, so he took them on trips to see all the major sights. Sometimes he took them on trips through Berlln's manicured environment of lakes and wooded waterways. On these trips he would take me along. His students would immediately accept me and tell me what a great man and wonderful teacher my father was.

HELEN'S TURN

Since my father could not sell me on a medical career like his father had, he turned his attention to Helen. She was admitted to and graduated from Marquette University Medical School. Then my father got her admitted as an intern at Gallagher Hospital in Washington which has the reputation of providing interns with the best medical education. The truth is that Gallagher, as the free District Hospital, is overcrowded and the doctors overworked. On Friday and Saturday nights there are regular savage fights in the slums of Washington, and occasionally Helen would have ambulance duty. At stops, she would sit on the street curb and joke with the local kids while the paramedics were rounding up the victims of gun shots and knife wounds. She would arrive home in the wee hours of the morning with her clothes completely drenched with blood from digging out bullets. I really felt sorry for her. Whatever she was doing, it wasn't woman's work.

After my mother died, my father bought a new house, had the basement of the house remodeled as a doctor's office and Helen took possession.   But she had a real problem.   Her patients were all neighbors, nice people she knew and liked. She was helping them, doing something she liked to do, how could she charge money for that? She never sent out a bill. Some patients noticed and just left some money on the table, but it was not enough to pay expenses.

As a solution, Helen joined the Army. The Army provided her with a new patient every 30 minutes and paid her a salary. Those were the best days of her life. After her tour of duty, the Army insisted on sending her to Texas. She wanted to stay in Washington with my father, so she quit.

After the Army, Helen looked for a local job and decided that the patients at St. Elizabeth's needed her the most. St. Elizabeth's is Washington's mental institution and Helen was the only medical doctor. All the others were psychiatrists. The place was full of old people just sitting around, with nothing to do. Helen would buy and bring in toys and other gadgets to keep her patients busy. Everything she brought in would be stolen by the staff.

At the time the custom in Washington was that if a mental patient had spent all his money and was about to die, he would be sent to St. Elizabeth's. Doctors don't like to sign death certificates. The management of St. Elizabeth's appeared to believe that their job was to expedite death as much as possible, and Helen's job was to sign death certificates. Helen felt her job was to treat sick patients, extend their lives and make them as comfortable as possible.

There was an ongoing clash between Helen and the hospital management until they finally retired her. The small pension was sufficient for her to live in my father's house and engage in her hobby of dispensing free medical treatment. The whole neighborhood thought a lot of her. She took care of my father until he died at age 92.

One summer evening she was in a rocking chair on the front porch of her house smoking a cigarette, when she suffered a heart attack and fell to the floor, dead.

DREAMS AND REALITY

As a young man, my father was impressed how his father, as a successful physician, moved around at ease among the upper class in Lisbon. The rewards of a successful medical practice are inspiring.

There was another factor in my father's set of values. He told me once that he remained a university professor because it was a job where he was his own boss. He did what he wanted to do, when he wanted to do it, and there was nobody telling him what to do. This was another quality he admired about his father's medical practice.

My father had no idea what it took to get there, to attain the position of a successful physician servicing the upper class. My father did not witness what his father did treating the natives in the tropical jungles of Goa, Angola, and the Canary Islands There my grandfather acquired the hard way, the hands-on education that allowed him to demonstrate in the hospitals of Lisbon that he knew how to treat tropical diseases better than anybody else, and that is why he was successful and accepted.

There is another of my grandfather's qualities that my father missed. To be a successful physician one must be a good business person. My father was not a good business man. He dissipated my mother's inherited wealth with his unrealistic ideas on the New York Stock Market.

My mother was a good business person, as she demonstrated in running her music school.

Helen was a sensitive, kind, generous, self-sacrificing, deeply religious person. She would have made a good mother. She did not have the disposition for digging bullets out of Friday night slum warriors. She was not a business person. She hated it when her mother curled her hair and dressed her in pretty clothes. She ignored her hard headed mother's advice and sacrificed herself to the dreams of the father she loved.

MY FATHER'S WORLD

EDUCATION

My father was a kind, meek mannered little man, born in Portugal. He was only an inch or two taller than my mother who was a small woman.   He had a dark, Portuguese complexion, black hair, brown eyes, slender figure, and some very strong convictions, see page 42.

Before World War I, it was the custom among well-to-do families in Portugal to provide their sons with as much local education as they could take, then let them travel travel throughout Europe for a year or two, and after that they were on their own. Any wealth the family had was inherited by the girls. My father had two sisters, so he had no inheritance to look forward to. On the other hand, when a man married, all of his new wife's wealth belonged to him.

After he concluded his university studies in Portugal, my father spent his travel time at some of the major universities of Europe. He froze in the fire-place heated rooms at Oxford. He was enchanted with the centrally heated rooms in Berlin as well as with the friendly and supportive relationship between professors and students at the university. Of all the universities in Europe, Berlin made the best impression on him.

FIRST JOB

When my father returned to Portugal and started to look for a job, he found that one of his former professors had been named Prime Minister. He liked my father and made him his secretary. In this position my father got to know many important people in Portugal, some of whom became his life-long friends. In the active social turmoil of the capital city, my father met and married my mother in 1912. I was born a year later.

My father's family background was aristocratic, his family had been friends with the King. Although my father was well entrenched in the republic which had been proclaimed in 1910, he was deeply dissatisfied with the way things were going. He decided he could not live with the new republic any more.

Dr Joaquim de Siqueira Coutinho
(about 1935)

THE MOVE TO AMERICA

In 1916 my father managed to find himself a job at the Portuguese Embassy in Washington and he immigrated to the United States. After he found a house for us in Georgetown, my mother and I came over the following year.

PAN AMERICAN UNION

My father had no intention of staying at the Portuguese Embassy. He soon found another job more to his liking as head of the Brazilian Desk at the Pan American Union (now Organization of American States).   In this capacity, he made several fact finding trips to Brazil. On one occasion he explored the then still unknown upper regions of the Amazon River and prepared the first maps of that area.

At this time he also got himself a part time job at George Washington University teaching Portuguese. This was the first university course in Portuguese taught in the US. With the cooperation of two other professors, he wrote a Portuguese Grammar that remained the standard text for teaching Portuguese in the US for many years.

THE SCHOOL OF FOREIGN SERVICE

My father's work at the Pan American Union brought him into contact with Dr. Constantine McGuire, one of those shadowy, behind-the-scenes, Washington consultants that make things go around. McGuire was an expert on foreign affairs and felt that the US needed an academy to train foreign service officers who would be on a level with their British and French counterparts. He submitted a proposal to Georgetown University to organize a School of Foreign Service (SFS). He discovered a bright, young Jesuit priest, Father Edmund Walsh, whom he proposed for Dean. He enlisted my father as a charter member of the faculty, and my father helped him assemble the rest of the faculty. My father spent the rest of his working life associated with the SFS. Today, McGuire's contribution to the founding of SFS is forgotten. That's the way he wanted it, he wanted to leave no tracks.

CATHOLIC UNIVERSITY

My father also taught economics at Catholic University for a number of years while the Rector, Bishop Shehan, was planning to build the Basilica of the Shrine of the Immaculate Conception, one of the largest cathedrals in the world. After the building contract was let, Bishop Shehan turned the job over to Monsignor McKenna, his secretary and my father's boss. McKenna made my father the building superintendent during the building of the crypt. Sometimes my father would take me to work with him. I was about eight years old at the time and I had a lot of fun jumping from one pile of stones to the other. Later, after they installed some of the alters, some visiting priests would want to say mass there, and I would have to serve as alter boy. I really did not know the Latin responses but I mumbled my way through, and the priests did not seem to mind.

When he worked at the Pan American Union, my father made friends with the Director, Dr Oliveria Lima, an extremely rich South American, who had filled his palace with all those expensive artifacts and treasures which rich people buy when they don't know what else to do with their money. When he died, he left all this, together with a bundle of money, to Catholic University to start a museum. At this time, the crypt of the Shrine was just about completed. The vast space under the church-to-be was empty. My father took possession and set up all of Lima's treasures on display in the crypt, in best museum style. He was appointed Director of the Museum, a job he held until his retirement.

My father was always concerned with students who looked as if they were not going to make it. During the school year, he held open house every Sunday afternoon in our living room. About seven to ten students came regularly. My mother served tea and cookies. Sometimes I would eaves-drop from an adjoining room and listen to my father tutoring his students. He was remarkably patient with them

GETTYSBURG

My father never had a car and never learned to drive. He had a weekly pass for the city transportation system, but whenever he could, he walked. My parents had several friends who were always anxious to give us a ride in their new automobiles. The rides I remember most were our Sunday summer excursions to Gettysburg. It seemed like everybody always wanted to go to Gettysburg. My mother would prepare a basket with sandwiches, cookies, and drinks, and would also take a couple of blankets along.

I just remember the beautiful sunny summer days when one of our friends took us for a ride. Usually there were other kids in the party. The grown-ups talked about getting to Gettysburg, but in all the years that I was in grammar school, we never got there. We always got a flat tire on the way. There was always a meadow or some woods along the side of the road where my mother would find a spot to spread out her blankets and food. While my father and his friend would be changing the tire, we city children would have a grand time running in the open meadow until it was time to eat. Then we would ride home while the grown-ups would be making plans for going to Gettysburg next week if the weather was nice.

JUNIOR   YEAR   IN   EUROPE

My father always felt that there was no substitute for being exposed to a foreign culture. Every year there were always a few students at Georgetown who were two or three credits short of the number required for graduation.   My father got himself appointed as a Visiting Professor at the University of Berlin and started a program taking these marginal students to Berlin where he would conduct the courses that they were missing. Georgetown granted credit for these courses, and the students were able to graduate at the end of the summer.

Later he organized a full "Junior Year" program at the University of Madrid. This was a nationally advertised program, not just for Georgetown students. Georgetown signed a contract with the University of Madrid providing for the Georgetown junior year courses to be offered at Madrid, taught American style, that is, attendance would be taken and periodic quizzes held.. The course material would be identical to the courses at Georgetown. Before the course started, students were required to take a month's intensive instruction in Spanish. Courses started out in English, gradually Spanish was introduced, and by Christmas the courses continued in Spanish. The courses were given by English speaking Spanish university professors who were paid by Georgetown, under my father's supervision. Georgetown granted full credit for all such courses. At the end of the term, my father organized a month's tour of the highlights of Europe. The program was a great success and attracted students from all over the country. It was imitated by other US universities. Some now even have their own buildings in Europe.

PAUL   YU-PIN

Paul Yu-Pin was a most   progressive   archbishop of Nanking, China. His appearance was most surprising for a Chinese. He was a very tall broad shouldered man, such as they only have in northern China. He studied and was ordained in Rome. In addition to the normal facilities of a Catholic archdiocese such as churches, schools, hospitals, and welfare facilities, Yu-Pin published two newspapers, ran three radio stations, and a number of model farms to demonstrate modern farming techniques to Chinese farmers. He was the number two man on the list of the of the most wanted criminals published by the communists.

As the communists approached Nanking, Yu-Pin appealed to the

Pope for help. The Pope assigned the task of saving Yu-Pin to the Jesuits. At that time the international trading community was boycotting all Chinese ports and there was no way for people to get in or out of China. Except one, the Portuguese Colony of Macau. Portugal was the only trading nation that had not signed the Gold Treaty. The Chinese had to export gold to pay for their imports, so they kept their border with Macau open. The Jesuits had no connections in Portugal, the Order had been banned over 200 years ago because of insisting on telling the king how to run the country. Then they realized that my father still maintained friendly relations with friends in high places in Portugal and assigned him the task of rescuing Yu-Pin. My father organized a secret escape route through Macau and was able to get Yu-Pin and all his priests and nuns and everything they could carry out to Lisbon.

Yu-Pin was concerned about how to keep all his priests and nuns busy. He organized a Chinese Institute in Washington, associated with Harvard University, for the study of Chinese affairs. My father was the Secretary of the Institute, that is, he ran the place.

The Archbishop and a few members of his senior staff visited my father at his house in Washington. My sister fed them tea and cookies. The Archbishop had a lot of fun playing with our son Roy, then just four years old.

The Chinese Institute did not provide enough jobs for Yu-Pin's staff, so he moved to Taiwan and organized the Catholic University there.   This has been a great success and provided more than enough jobs for Yu-Pin's people. Yu-Pin was made a Cardinal. He died in Rome during the Second Vatican Council.

My father was awarded a medal by the Pope, another by the Portuguese Government. Georgetown awarded him its Axacan Award consisting of a gold medal and a beautiful illuminated sheep-skin prepared in Portuguese by Father Fadner. He must have worked on it for months. None of these awards specify why they were granted. A photo of the Cardinal at my father's house is on page 47, and a photo of Helen, my father with his newly awarded cross around his neck, with my wife Eleanor and myself, at the Portuguese Embassy in Washington at the award ceremony, is on page 48.

FRANK   FADNER, S. J.

Another good friend of my father's was Father Fadner. He had been one of my father's students and at that time became one of my father's life long friends. He was a brilliant young priest who followed in Father Walsh's footsteps. He became an outstanding authority on Russian affairs and so valuable to the university that he was retained in the same Jesuit community all his life. When Father Walsh died,

Cardinal Yu-Pin with Roy and my father
at my father's house, Washington

My sister Helen, my father Joaquim, my wife Eleanor, and myself; Award of the
Portuguese Cross to my father, Portuguese Embassy, Washington

he became Dean of the SFS. He was also an excellent artist. He produced a number of large religious paintings, but his specialty was illuminated manuscripts in the style of the old monks.

RETIREMENT

After my father retired, he would receive occasional visitors such as Father Fadner or Constantine McGuire. The two men would sit in the living room, sip tea, and talk about geopolitics and related subjects for hours. I began to realize why my father had wanted so badly for me to study medicine or law. He would have loved to have a good talk with me, but with me being an engineer, we had nothing to talk about.

This became clear to me when Grumman was delivering F-14 fighter aircraft to Iran and the US counted the Shah of Iran among its best friends. At that time my father told me that the Islamic world was on the verge of a major revolution which was going to threaten the US in a serious way.   I thought that my father was nuts. It took the downfall of the Shah, the capture of American hostages in Iran, and the Gulf War to convince me that my father really knew what he was talking about. Now I faced a new puzzle. If my father and his fellow scholars at the SFS knew in advance of the coming of the Islamic revolution, how come the US Government did not know about it and take timely preventive measures to protect our national interests?

MY FATHER SAYS GOODBYE

My father was a people person. As a professor at the School of Foreign Service, Georgetown University, he was more concerned with the progress of his individual students than any other professor that I have ever known. In response, many of his students remained his personal friends throughout their lifetimes.

In 1950, two years after my mother died, my sister, Helen, graduated from medical school. My father bought a nice, roomy house in a central part of Washington and had the basement remodeled as a medical office. My father and sister lived there for the rest of their lives.

At that time, only a few years after World War II, public accommodations in Washington were difficult to find. Many of my father's former students, now military or foreign service officers stationed around the world, would come to Washington on business, only to find that there were no accommodations available. They would call up my father for help. He turned the house into a dormitory. He bought a number of cots and could accommodate 22 men at a time. The house was often full.

The place was run like a fraternity house. Helen stocked the refrigerator. Each guest made his own breakfast or other meal, washed his dishes and helped clean the kitchen. Everybody felt at home. In return, they told my father about their personal observations on foreign affairs throughout the world.

I remember that for many years after the need for the emergency dormitory had past, there were still many visitors to the house each day. It seemed that no out-of-town graduate of the School of Foreign Service, now a military or foreign service officer from around the world, would come to Washington without paying my father a visit and making a report on his experiences. There was not a day when the house was not full of visitors.

When I retired from Grumman Aerospace on Long Island, my father was 80 years old. The number of his daily visitors was dropping dramatically. I was looking for a new job and decided that I should stay close to Washington. I decided that I did not want to be in Washington, because Helen was taking good care of my father and I did not want to interfere. I just wanted to be close by, if needed. I found a job at Aberdeen Proving Ground, just two hours from Washington, that seemed just right. My wife, Eleanor, and I visited my father regularly.

My father and I had never been close. He had wanted me to study law or medicine. I realize now that he wanted me to study something that we could both talk about. I studied engineering, and that left an intellectual gap between us.

I gave him a copy of my doctor's theses that had been accepted at the Technical University of Berlin. My father had been a visiting professor at the University of Berlin and was acquainted with their requirements for a doctorate. He knew that my theses had to be a sound scientific document. He kept it on a coffee table in the living room. I caught him a few times trying to read it. It was obvious that although he recognized the German words, he could not understand the engineering concepts involved, I felt sorry for him.

As the years passed, the number of visitors dropped off. Eventually, there was only one regular visitor, now as feeble and ineffective as my father, the Rev. Frank Fadner S,J,, a former student in the early days of the School of Foreign Service, a man of such exceptional talent that he was retained at Georgetown all his life and who served for many years as Dean of the School of Foreign Service. He died a year or so after my father.

At age 92, my father being without friends, and especially without enemies, Helen would find a medical reason three or four times a year to send my father to the hospital for two or three weeks. My father enjoyed going to the hospital. He loved the attention that the doctors and nurses lavished on him. He would roam the corridors of his floor. In a few days, he would know every patient by name, his family history, and their afflictions and prognosis. Eleanor and I would visit him three times a week. We normally would bring flowers. After we left, he would take the bouquet apart and go around the floor giving a flower to every patient who did not have any.

On one such visit, my father took me out into the corridor so we could talk privately. He said, that although we two had never been close, I had always been a good son, I had raised a nice family, and he was very proud of my engineering accomplishments. We then shook hands and returned to his room.

The next morning he underwent a test requiring anesthesia. After the test,they could no revive him. The doctors were perplexed.There was no medical reason for his death.

Without friends, without enemies, and without the capability to do any useful work, my father saw no reason to continue to live. He willed himself to die. Although I was mystified by the little ceremony in the hospital corridor the evening before, I now realize that my father was saying goodbye.

BURIAL

My father died in 1978 at the age of 92 at Doctor's Hospital in Washington. There was no medical reason for his death. He was under anesthesia undergoing a test and never woke up. He was almost totally blind and deaf. Almost all his friends were dead. Worse, all his enemies were dead.

I made arrangements for the burial service to be held in the Chapel of Georgetown University. I asked Father Fadner to conduct the service. Father Fadner arrived totally drunk. Two husky Jesuits, each one holding tight to an upper arm, dragged Father Fadner to the alter and, between his spells of sobbing, prompted him through the words of the mass. After the mass, the two big Jesuits carried him out of the Chapel. It surely was one of the most pathetic burial services the world has ever seen.

MY FATHER, THE SPY

At the end of my father's burial service, I was approached by a well dressed older gentleman who introduced himself as a retired Colonel, Intelligence, US Air Force. He told me that during the time that my father was spending summers in Berlin, the University of Berlin had a working agreement with the University of Latvia for the exchange of professors and common research projects. My father obtained papers in Berlin admitting him to the University of Latvia, behind the iron curtain.

He had no trouble getting in, the Russian guards recognized his papers.   At Latvia, he   got himself assigned to a geography research project and received papers allowing him to travel all over Russia. He spent the rest of the summer doing just that, and wherever he went, he bought maps and postcards. Because of his close association with Father Walsh, the Russian expert, my father knew exactly where to go and what maps and postcards to buy. When the summer was over and he was leaving Russia, the Russian guards stopped him and suspiciously inspected all his material. He identified himself as a member of a joint Latvian-Berlin geography research team and said he needed these materials for his continuing research in Berlin His papers were all in order. The Russians finally let him go.   When he arrived back in the US, he turned all of this material over to the US Air Force.   The Air Force had never seen anything like it. The Colonel told me that all the initial Air Force reconnaissance flights over Russia had been planned using my father's maps and postcards. He said that the Air Force Intelligence community considered my father a real national hero.

LINDEN, VIRGINIA

MRS. ANDERSON

When I was still in grammar school, my mother had among her Washington friends, a pianist, named Lavinia Anderson, who was married to David, a vice president of a local bank. The Andersons had a daughter, Peggy, a few years younger than myself, and a car, something unusual in those days.

Lavinia was born and raised on a farm in Linden, Virginia. Her father had passed away, but her mother still ran the farm. Anderson was also her maiden name. In that little corner of the earth, many people were called Anderson, and all of them were Episcopalians.

Lavinia delighted in driving her family and ours to her mother's farm for a nice weekend. Her mother, Mrs Anderson, was a practical woman and charged every one $ 1.00 a day for room and board. The arrangements were so attractive that my mother would park my sister, Helen, me, and our cat Blackie, for some summer months at a time, at Mrs Anderson's.

MR. ANDERSON

The two-story farm house was very large, I never knew exactly how many rooms it had. The farm had been laid out by Mr Anderson, a graduate Civil Engineer, who built the house and all the outlying buildings himself in his younger days. He was the County Road Commissioner and the teacher at the one room Linden School at the bottom of the hill. He knew everything there was to know about each one of his students and their families. Sometimes the bigger boys would bring their guns to school so they could shoot a squirrel or rabbit for dinner on their way home. Squirrel pie was a greatly appreciated delicacy in the area.

The Linden School graduated many students who went on to high school and then to college and became distinguished citizens of Virginia. The Andersons had a network of good friends in high places throughout the state.

When Mr Anderson died, they closed the school and bought a bus to drive the kids to a new, grand, central school in Front Royal, some seven miles down the road into the valley. With the loss of a local school, most people with grade school children moved out of Linden.

THE SHENANDOAH VALLEY

Linden lies on top of the ridge of the Allegheny mountain range that forms the eastern side of the Shenandoah Valley, on the pass from Washington into the valley. There is a stone marker on the side of the road that states that the valley was discovered by its first settlers from this point. The beautiful Skyline Drive runs south from Front Royal along this ridge for over a hundred miles. Every few miles there are overlook lots where you can park and enjoy the magnificent scenery of the valley, the winding Shenandoah River, and the Blue Ridge mountains on the other side of the valley. Many people believe that this is the most beautiful mountain scenery in the eastern United States. The valley is so rich and productive that during the Civil War people believed that whichever side controlled the valley would prevail.

THE LINDEN COMMUNITY

The village of Linden at that time consisted of a US post office, a general store, and a one room school house down the road. The road went off to one side to the farms along the mountain range. Mrs Anderson's farm was one of the closest to this point, she was within walking distance to the general store, which sold ice cream. That was a great treat in a place where there was no electricity or refrigeration. The only utility was the party line telephone. A single line was strung along the road and connected all the little farms. Each farm had its own distinctive ring, a combination of long and short rings that you generated yourself by turning the crank on your own phone. Whenever a call was made, everybody in Linden would rush to their phones and listen in on the conversation. This kept everybody up to date on what was going on.

FARM LIFE

In addition to the farmhouse, Mrs Anderson had a barn, a smoke house where she smoked her own hams, a spring house, a chicken coop, and a roomy two seater out house. The water pump was just outside the kitchen door. The spring house enclosed a space where a spring ran out of a rock, A large tub caught the cold water, and the spring house acted as a refrigerator.

The farm house had a wide, covered porch along its entire front, with a rocking chair for everyone. In the evening after work, it was great fun watching people walking along the road going to the store, and trying to guess what they were going to buy. When they came back, we would try to confirm our guesses by the shape of the packages that they carried.

Mrs Anderson kept a cow, several pigs, and many chickens. She grew vegetables and corn for sale. She had apple, peach, and cherry trees. Early every morning a man came around in a truck and collected milk and vegetables from all the farmers and took them to market in Front Royal. The only things Mrs Anderson had to buy were things she could not make herself, like flour, sugar, salt, coffee, kerosene, needles, thread, buttons, cloth, and the like. She made all her own clothes.

There was a group of men in Linden who made their living by going around to the various farms as day laborers at a dollar a day, meals, and a doggie bag. Mrs Anderson hired one or more of these men whenever she needed help, such as in plowing, seeding and harvesting the corn, slaughtering a pig, or chopping wood.

Except for these heavy jobs, Mrs Anderson did everything herself. Farm life kept a woman busy. It was hard work, but Mrs Anderson did not consider it a burden. It was the means by which she maintained her cherished independent lifestyle. She went about her tasks with an enthusiasm that made us kids want to help her whenever we could. She caught, killed and plucked her own chickens, baked bread and pastries, grew and canned her own vegetables, preserved fruit, made jellies and relishes, and planted and took care of lovely flowers around the house. Occasionally, all of us would go into the woods adjacent to the farm and pick blackberries.

There was a big, wood burning, iron stove in the kitchen that also produced hot water and heat in the winter time. The living room had a big fire place, and the dining room had a Franklin stove. The rest of the house had no heat, in winter you just had to dress warmly when you went to bed.

Mrs Anderson had been a school teacher and was well educated, her interests included national politics and foreign affairs. There was a lot of good reading material available. Aside from her sewing machine, she had a piano and played well. She played a little every evening, and often we would sing along by kerosene light. Peggy, Lavinia's daughter, was often with us. She eventually became a professor at Swarthmore College near Philadelphia, married another professor, and had her own family.

SUPPERTIME

Mrs Anderson was a good cook, and for a long time I never realized that we were having ham or chicken every day, it was always a different dish. One day we had a delicious piece of liver. I thought nothing of it, but Helen asked: "Mrs Anderson, where did you get this liver?" There was no butcher shop in Linden, Mrs Anderson replied: "Why, your mother sent it up in the basket." Helen froze. She said:

"The liver is for Blackie ! It's cat food !" Suddenly, I did not feel so well myself.

Mrs Anderson laughed and said: "Trust me, that was a fine, fresh piece of beef liver." But everybody knows that BEEF liver is not edible, you only eat calf's liver. At that time, the stores did not sell dog or cat food. Beef liver, at less than ten cents a pound, was among the cheapest meats you could buy, so that is what my mother bought for her fussy Sir Blackie. Mrs Anderson had a tough job explaining to us the difference between beef and calf's liver. Not quite convinced, we finished our meal without our usual enthusiasm. To our surprise, Blackie did not seem to mind that we had eaten his liver dinner.

PROHIBITION   IN   LINDEN

During prohibition, Linden was the center of another industry. The dense forests surrounding Linden protected many moonshiners. It was well understood around town that if anyone approached a working still, an accident would happen, and you would be killed. The local Federal officers had a high respect for the moonshiners and never went near a working still.   However, they had a grand time raiding newly abandoned stills, which they did with great fanfare and publicity.   These events provided great entertainment in Linden. Both moonshiners and cops sent their kids to the same one room school house, and their families were on speaking terms.

LINDEN   TODAY

Today, the automobile has reduced the seven miles between Front Royal and Linden to a short drive. Linden has become a fashionable suburb of industrialized Front Royal. The bootleggers vanished with prohibition, and the small farms have been replaced by large industrialized farms. A bit of America has been lost.

Our relationship with Mrs Anderson started before I went to high school in Europe, and continued after I came back; until Mrs Anderson died. I took Eleanor up there before we were married, and we also went there with our son Roy when he was four years old.

After Mrs Anderson died. David and Lavinia continued to spend week ends at the farm. One week-end when they arrived, the doors to the house were open. Everything inside the house had been stolen, the piano, sewing machine, furniture, dishes; the place was bare. Heartbroken, Lavinia sold the farm.

I sometimes think back to Linden where an educated community of farmers, bootleggers, and Federal cops lived and let live in harmony, where they all sent their kids to the same one room school house where Mr Anderson, a graduate Civil Engineer, taught civics and religion.

BERLIN

MY MOTHER'S DREAM

My mother's dream was to become a professional pianist. However, the move to America, having children, and housekeeping chores prevented her from engaging in any substantial professional music activities.

When I was in the eighth grade, 13 years old, and my sister, Helen, eight, my parents decided to do something to satisfy my mother's dream. Because of my father's connections as a Visiting Professor at the University of Berlin, Germany, and Berlin at that time (1927) being the artistic and cultural center of Europe, my mother decided to go to Berlin to acquire a professional touch to her music. At that time, my mother acquired another child, Louis, age 7, whose parents were related to my mother and who had both recently died in Baltimore. Louis was my mother's godchild.

PACKING-UP

My mother, Helen, Louis and I moved to Berlin in October, 1927. All four of us were listed on one US passport.

The preparations for the move had been a big operation, but I don't remember the details. I overheard my parents talking about selling the house. I know that all our household goods were put in storage because I now have many of the things that I remember being in the house on Evarts Street.

My father had built himself a study in the basement. It was a large room with book shelves on all four walls, from the floor to the ceiling, and they were full of books. The place was locked to keep me out when my father was not in his study. My father could not live without his books, so he must have made arrangements for a place to live and where he would have access to his books while my mother was in Berlin.

PREPARATIONS   IN BERLIN

My father had been working summers for several years at the University of Berlin, and during his stay in the summer of 1927, he made arrangements for my mother to come over. He rented half of a large apartment with a piano for us, located a conservatory for my mother and schools for us children. Through his university connections, he was able to make arrangements with a group of ladies who promised to look after and take care of my mother. Berlin was ready for us when we arrived.

TRAVELING   TO   BERLIN

I have no recollection of leaving Washington. The ship was fun. It was the SS Muenchen, run by the North German Lloyd. You rented deck chairs and they served you bouillon every mid-morning at ten a.m. The dining room was the most impressive and grandest room I had ever seen. You could have all you could eat, it was great ! The next thing I remember, I was on the train, riding into Berlin. The train came in the back way, all you could see was the dreary backs of five story adjoining buildings.

My mother had no problem at all finding our apartment. The taxi driver knew exactly where it was. I often wondered how my father found his way around in all the foreign places he told me about. One day he accidentally spilled the beans; he took a taxi !

GEOGRAPHY   LESSON

I had no idea where Germany was, and how far we had traveled. I just followed my mother.

In school, they taught me that the earth was round, actually a big ball. This was very difficult for me to accept. I could see that it was flat.   I also learned that the earth had five continents, and each continent had a number of countries. All this had no meaning for me. I studied geography like I studied all my other subjects - to pass the tests. I did not necessarily believe what they taught me.

On the ship, one day was like the next, the ocean did not change. I had no concept that we were moving. Only on the train, on the short ride to Berlin, could I look out the window and see that we were moving.

The most powerful indicator that you are in a foreign country is the food. However, in our Berlin apartment, we spoke English and my mother cooked our meals Washington style as she always had. She created a little bit of Washington for us in the middle of Berlin. It took a little while before I was convinced that we were in a foreign country.

LIFE   IN   BERLIN

My mother's life in Berlin at first did not change all that much from what it had been in Washington. She was taking courses at the music conservatory, and trying to practice when she got home, but she still had three kids to take care of. I helped out by doing most of the food shopping. I would buy something at the butcher's by pointing to it then holding my hand out with my money in it and letting the butcher help himself.

I did know something about arithmetic and complained to my mother that the butcher was overcharging me. My mother told me that that was to be expected. When you are in a foreign country and don't speak the language, locals feel that they have the right to tax you for being in their country. I guess she was right. The only country that I have been in and not been cheated is Switzerland. Prices are high, but they do not cheat foreigners.

SCHOOL

School was the first thing that really made me realize that I was in a different world. Although it was a boy's school, it was not like St.Martin's in Washington.

Classes started at eight a.m. There were five classes each day, including Saturday, until one p.m. Tuesdays and Thursdays, classes were held from two to four p.m. Each class was on a different subject and taught by a different teacher. There was a five minute interval between classes, except at ten o'clock when the interval was fifteen minutes and they served us hot chocolate. Most boys brought small sandwiches from home to eat at this time.

The boys in my class had had two years of English and could speak a little. Most teachers could speak well. They all delighted in practicing their English on me. As a result, I learned little German. Helen and Louis did much better at learning German at their schools.

My worst subject was Latin. It was being taught in German, a language I could not understand. I had no idea what was going on.

BICYCLES   IN   BERLIN

When you come from Washington, the first thing that strikes you about the street traffic in Berlin is the number of people on bicycles. I thought it was funny when we had to stop at a red light. The whole width of the street was packed with several rows of bicycles. Behind the bicycles were one or two cars.

This situation has changed. The last time I was in Berlin, the streets were full of cars, and there were few bicycles.

A   CASH   SOCIETY

There were so many things in Berlin that were different from Washington that you soon realized that you were in a foreign culture. Berlin had no checks or credit cards. Almost all business transactions were on a cash basis.

Sometimes my mother would send me to the bank, and I would

observe other people transacting business. I was amazed at how many people came in with, or took out, big stacks of 10,000 Mark bills ($ 2500.- at that time). In the stores you would see people paying for their purchases with bills taken from big wads of money they carried in their pockets. It made me feel quite safe in Berlin. My mother agreed, and she let me roam around freely, as I had done in Washington.

Big companies, such as utilities, had accounts at the Post Office. You paid your bill in cash at the Post Office to the credit of the account of the utility company. My mother paid her conservatory tuition this way.

The nearest thing to a US check was an account at the Post Office. It was easy and convenient to transfer money from your account to another account. The Post Office was the biggest bank in Germany.

If you sent a postal money order to an individual who did not have an account at the Post Office, the mail man would bring the money to his house.

BERLIN   CITY   LAYOUT

Since my mother let me roam the city at will, I found out a few interesting things about Berlin. The city was developed under the watchful care of the Kings of Prussia who were very concerned about what their capital looked like. Except for the palaces of the very rich on the outskirts of the city, everybody in Berlin lived in an apartment or condominium. The houses are all five stories high and join one another. Empty lots, other than parks, are very rare.

No European city has an organized layout plan of streets, street names, and a house numbering system like Washington. In Europe, additional streets were added to a city as the city grew, generally along transportation routes. There was no master plan. In Berlin, where all houses were five stories high, and cross streets went off at all sorts of angles, it was almost impossible to tell one street from another. You had to memorize all kinds of little details. Luckily, there were foot policemen all over the place, and they always seemed glad to give me directions. Most of them spoke a little English.

Most necessities were available within walking distance of our apartment, but if we wanted to go somewhere special, like to a specific theater, museum, or department store, Berlin had an excellent public transportation system of street cars, busses, subway, city railway system, and taxis.

The standard Berlin house is built around a generally square court yard. The apartments in the front, that is, with windows overlooking both the street and the courtyard, are the expensive ones. The apartments in the back, that is, with windows overlooking only the court yard, are cheaper. Each court yard has a shed where you can park your bicycle.

Berlin is the only city I know that has no exclusive neighborhoods. Rich and poor are distributed throughout the city, the rich in the front apartments, the poor in the back ones. The children of both rich and poor play together in the court yards, never in the streets.

Berlin has its own house numbering system. You start on one side on one end of the street and number that house one. Then you walk down that side of the street and number the next house two. You keep numbering the houses on that side of the street until you reached the end of the street. Then you cross the street and keep numbering houses on that side until you get back across the street from your starting point.

Looking for a number, you sometimes walk a couple blocks down a street until you realize that the number you are looking for is across the street, sometimes near your starting point. The authorities try to help out a listing the numbers of the houses on each block on the plate with the street name, but this plate is usually attached high on the building on the corner, hard to see, and sometimes you forget to look for it.

I explained to my classmates the system that we had in Washington, odd numbers on one side of the street, and even numbers directly opposite on the other side. They would not believe me.

EXPRESS   POSTAL   SERVICE

Berlin had an excellent in-city express postal service. To obtain this service you had to cross out the address of the recipient with a heavy red crayon. Post Offices were located conveniently throughout the city and each Post Office was connected to a central station by a pneumatic tube. When you mailed your letter at your local post office, they would dispatch it immediately by pneumatic tube to the central station. There, it would be transferred by hand to the pneumatic tube to the receiving Post Office. It would be delivered as soon as a messenger was available. Practically all letters would be delivered in less than one hour.

One wall of the central station, where all the pneumatic tubes were processed, was a glass panel, so the public could watch the process. I was fascinated by it and spent hours watching the postal workers servicing the pneumatic tubes.

SPECIALTY   SHOPS

Aside from the big department stores, Berlin's business took place in small specialty shops, some of which were chain operated. These shops were well distributed throughout the city. Berliners liked to say that their city was a big collection of villages, and this was true to the extent that no matter where you lived, you had a complete collection of all required specialty shops within walking distance. Since the introduction of the automobile, this is no longer true, and most of these local specialty shops today no longer exist.

Some of the more obvious ones were the baker, whose bread and pastries were of a quality unknown in the US where these products are mass produced in large wholesale bakeries. The butcher shop windows displayed the cross section of sausages with amazing artistic designs. The number of different kinds of sausages was inconceivable. Hares (very large rabbits) and venison was usually on display. . (The Germans used their forests to produce meat.)

There was the milk-butter-cheese store, with some twelve tubs of butter and margarine behind the counter, each tub at a different price. You bought the quality of butter that you wanted. It would be formed with a paddle by hand into a little round patty, with a nice little design on top, sized to fit the round butter dishes that they used in Berlin. You had to bring your own milk pail to buy milk, pasteurized or unpasteurized. Unpasteurized milk had to be boiled before consumption, but many people believed it tasted better.

The vegetable store sold fruits and vegetables, and one type of drug store sold only medicines, while another kind sold soap, perfume, cleaning materials and the like. The barber shop was the place where many men stopped to get a shave every morning on their way to work. They paid for their shaves by the month. There was a bank, a bar, and a movie house every few blocks. The coffee shop sold coffee, but also coffee by the cup. There were no seats, but some tall round tables where four people could stand and drink their coffee.   All trades, from shoemakers to knife-sharpeners had their own little shops.

There was the local cafe, where they sold coffee and a piece of pastry, and supplied you with local and national newspapers. You could sit there and read the papers all afternoon. Some cafes had a dance floor and provided dance music in the evening. You could ask any lady in the place for a dance. There was also a local restaurant. When most Berliners went out for dinner, they made an evening of it and stayed at the restaurant until bedtime, usually talking with other customers and drinking beer.

SANTA CLAUS IN BERLIN

It was Christmas time in Berlin. The stores were all festively decorated with manikins of Saint Nicholas Here and there some musicians played Christmas carols.   Berlin at that time had about three and a half million prosperous people and some fancy department stores.

While our landlady, who lived in the other half of the apartment, watched Helen and Louis, my mother and I for several days went out on shopping excursions. We found a nice Christmas tree, we bought a turkey and all the trimmings, and in particular, strawberries and whipping cream. I was very impressed, I had never seen strawberries at Christmas time before. We also bought a lot of toys for Helen and Louis, and some things for my mother and me. Except for the tree and the food, we had to hide all the stuff that we brought home in a borrowed room. I put up the Christmas tree in our living room.

CHRISTMAS   PREPARATIONS

My mother and I had to work in secret in the borrowed room wrapping all the toys and presents. This was my first experience in preparing for Christmas. Although 13 years old, I was not quite sure about Santa Claus.

After Helen and Louis went to sleep on Christmas eve, my mother and I decorated the tree and placed all the toys and presents under its branches. Then we closed the door. In Berlin all rooms have doors. We finally went to bed.

CHRISTMAS   MORNING

On Christmas morning, Helen and Louis were up early, all excited. They wanted to see what Santa Claus had brought. My mother let them into the living room. They saw the decorated Christmas tree with all the wrapped presents underneath. They screamed with delight and ran to the tree. They each grabbed a toy with their name on it and tore the wrapping paper off as fast as they could. After they handled the toy for a few minutes to see what it was, they ran to my mother to show it to her. She acted surprised and delighted that the kids were happy. Then they ran over to me and showed me their new toys. But I had already seen them. My mother had let me pick out most of the toys for Helen and Louis. I had watched her buy them, and I had wrapped them, and knew who they were for. One look at the pile of presents under the tree and I saw that the kids did not receive any toys other than what my mother and I had bought. Suddenly, with a heavy heart and against my natural instincts, I realized that I had to act like my mother, act surprised and happy for them.

That is when it hit me like a ton of bricks. Yesterday, at age 13, I had said that I did not BELIEVE in Santa Claus.   Suddenly I KNEW that there was no Santa Claus.

TRUTH

There is a world of difference between BELIEVING and KNOWING. I was shocked as never before. I felt a great loss, the whole world around Santa Claus came crashing down No matter how well intentioned the stories are, that grown-ups tell you, and how useful they are to society, they are not necessarily true. I decided that in the future I would have to rely more on my own intellect to decide what was true.

The strawberries and whipped cream calmed me down quite a bit and brought me back to the real world.

SECONDARY EDUCATION, STELLA MARIS, MEERSBURG

SEARCHING FOR A SCHOOL

Six months after our move to Berlin, my father came from Washington to discover that taking care of three children and associated housekeeping was distracting my mother from her studies at the conservatory. Something had to be done quickly.

My parents found a girls' boarding school run by nuns right in Berlin where they placed Helen. At her age, she learned German quickly and loved the place. My mother visited her every weekend.

My father used his Jesuit connections to find a suitable boarding school for Louis and me. He found a Jesuit boys' boarding school in Innsbruck, Austria. Innsbruck is a famous resort high in the Alps, renowned for its world class skiing facilities.

Six months in the German school system had taught me something about European secondary schools. There are three types. The literal translation of the German names is meaningless in English, so I will call them classical, semi-classical, and technical. The classical schools are heavy on Latin, Greek, and ancient literature. They actually teach you to speak Latin ! They tolerate math, physics, and science. The semi-classical schools are still heavy on Latin, but they are also serious about foreign languages, math and physics. The technical schools are heavy on math, physics, chemistry, science, English and French. All types of schools require religious instruction.

EUROPEAN SCHOOLS

The European school system consists of two subsystems: popular and academic. The popular schools consist of eight years of grammar school. After that, boys and girls go into an apprenticeship or to a trade school. In the academic subsystem, students leave the popular grammar school after the fourth year and transfer to a secondary school. This is a traumatic time point in many well-to-do German families when their kids fail the entrance exams to the secondary school system. The only solution is a very expensive private school.

Secondary schools run nine years, school years five to 13. The degree you get, "maturity," makes you an intellectual and, if you want to, admits you to a university that is more like a US graduate professional school where they only cover professional subjects. Most students do not remain nine years. After six years in a secondary school, for example. boys were formerly required to serve only one year in the German Army, instead of two, and many students drop out at this point. This six-year degree of "minor maturity" admits you to a technician's school such as nurse, bookkeeper, photographer, or to a business school, or to a teacher's college for popular schools.

BERLIN EXPERIENCE

In Berlin I attended a semi-classical school, except for religious instruction. Religious instruction is mandatory in all schools in Germany. There were not enough Catholic boys in my grade to form a Catholic class, so we were sent to a nearby technical school for instruction. There I met boys from all three types of schools. The boys from the classical schools were snobs. They really didn't know any better. The boys from the semiclassical schools were more tolerant than those at classical schools, but still had a superiority complex. The boys from the technical schools seemed to be more open minded and quite human.

In semi-classical schools, they start Latin in what we call the fifth grade. Later, they derive German grammar from the Latin. It is much easier to blame the complex German sentence structure on Latin than to try to explain it on a logical basis.

When my father suggested that Louis and I go to a nice Jesuit boarding school in beautiful Innsbruck, I knew that the Jesuits ran classical schools. I was having serious trouble trying to learn Latin that was being taught in German, when I could not speak a word of German. Adding Greek to Latin created a situation in which I could not survive. I revolted. I shouted. I cried. Luckily, my mother stuck up for me. Finally, my father realized that he was outvoted.

A more thorough search discovered a boys' technical boarding school run by the Christian Brothers in Meersburg, a town in southern Germany. We all went to Meersburg to inspect the school and the town.

MEERSBURG

Meersburg lies on the Lake of Constance, the second largest lake in Central Europe, bordering on Germany, Austria, and Switzerland. It is about 10 miles wide and 80 miles long, the headwaters of the Rhein River. The north shore is German, the eastern end Austrian, and the south shore Swiss. Except for the high mountain regions, many people consider the area to be the most beautiful in Germany, but it is

The Meersburg Fortress

completely unknown to American tourists. During the season, the place is overrun by Swiss tourists who come to enjoy the excellent local wine and pastries.

There is a 200 foot cliff along the water in Meersburg. On the west end of the cliff there is a 1250 year old fortress from the time of King Arthur, built on the ruins of an old Roman fortress, dominating the town and overlooking the western portion of the lake, see page 67. The Meersburg fortress is the only fortress in Germany that was never damaged in combat, although it was besieged in several wars. There was a secret tunnel that went down to an underwater cave in the lake and provided a route for resupplies.

There are three additional newer buildings on the cliff, all about the same size: the palace of the Prince-Bishop of Constance, who resided in Meersburg; the public school, formerly the bishop's stables; and our 300 year old school, Stella Maris, originally built by the bishop as a seminary to train priests. The view from the water is breathtaking, see page 69, but the view from the school, overlooking the lake and the Swiss Alps is spectacular. It took several years before these superlatives made any impression on me. I did notice, however, that the place was clean.

The school building had always been used as a college. In the course of time, heating and plumbing facilities had been installed. We toured the classrooms, dining hall, dormitories, washing facilities, and other rooms. The place was civilized and comfortable. The high point of the tour was the beautiful baroque chapel. The school had a large and well equipped gym and a full sized foot-ball field. Physical Ed included swimming in the lake.

My parents had a conference with the Bothers and decided that Stella Maris would be satisfactory for me. Louis was too young to be admitted in Meersburg, but the brothers had an other school in Illertissen, Bavaria, that accepted boys of his age, so he could go there.

This plan pleased my father. He worried a great deal about my education because he believed that American schools did not lay sufficient emphasis on foreign languages and knowledge of foreign cultures. (This was before World War II.) Now a boarding school in the very center of Europe seemed to resolve his concerns.

I was about to be left alone on my own with the Brothers, of whom only one, the English teacher, could speak a few words of broken English. I was about to cry, but my father slipped me more pocket money than I had ever seen before, and the shock of it kept me from crying. We said our good-byes, but I deliberately did not promise to be a good boy.

View from Meersburg Harbor, Left on the hill: Meersburg Public School
Right on the hill: Stella Maris - In the Harbor: Water Transportation to:
Constance, Switzerland, Austria

MOTHER AND HELEN RETURN TO WASHINGTON

Having her children well located in boarding schools, relieved my mother of much responsibility and she could now dedicate all her time to her studies at the conservatory. After two years, she felt she had achieved her goals. She gave a public concert in Berlin and received rave reviews in the newspapers.

With these trophies, she and Helen returned to Washington. Louis and I were doing well in our schools, so we were left behind in the hands of the Christian Brothers.

LEARNING   GERMAN

My first problem was learning German, of which I knew only a few words that I had learned in Berlin.   In the German language, cuss words are the only words that are spoken loudly, distinctly, and used as individual words. Everything else is mumbled. I had no idea what these words meant. So the first words I learned were cuss words. I assembled quite a vocabulary. So when I would meet a Brother, in the hall or elsewhere, I would smile politely and greet him with a cuss word. He would be shocked, take me aside and talk to me nicely in a language I did not understand. Since he really could not not make me understand, no matter how hard he tried, we would have to go find the English teacher who would try to solve our problem, and in the process try to teach me a few good German words.

THE   GERMAN   MENTALITY

I not only had to learn German, but also the German mentality. A classmate would ask me where I came from, and I would say "Washington." He would say, "Where's that?" I would answer "Washington is the capital of the United States." He would say "You're crazy ! Everybody knows that New York is the capital of the United States."

Another subject was sports. I had been a baseball fan, and knew all the statistics. In Europe they play a kind of soccer that they call football.

I would be asked what football teams we have in the United States. I would try to explain baseball. I would be told that the United States is a very large country and has a large number of good football teams. I was just stupid and didn't know anything.

Faced with such mentality, I soon learned to first find out what they thought, and then agree with it. I lost my interest in baseball, and did not think it worthwhile to learn anything about their football.

While striving to keep my "Americanism" submerged, I became a creature of German society. To be successful in school, to be treated by the teachers as they treated other boys, I had to think and act like a German. In my school and social life, to earn people's trust and respect, to make friends who did not think I was queer, I had to be a regular German boy. I acquired the cultural background, the linguistic capabilities, sense of values, and prejudices of an educated German. The story of my boyhood is not one of a typical American boy, as you will notice in some of the following accounts.

GERMAN   TABLE   MANNERS

One of my behavioral problems that the Brothers tried hard to correct was my table manners. Later I was to learn that the German middle class is unforgiving with respect to table manners. It is a matter that is taken very seriously, if you do not have correct table manners in Germany, you will be considered a barbarian.

In Washington, I was brought up to eat with the fork in my right hand. To cut meat, I would temporarily transfer my fork to my left hand, cut the meat with my right hand, then take the fork in my right hand so I could eat what I had cut. When not in use, my left hand was on my lap.

Germans eat with their fork in their left hand, holding their knife in their right hand at the ready. Occasionally, when there is nothing to cut, they will eat with the fork in their right hand and their left hand will be held in a loose fist on the edge of the table. Under no circumstances can the left hand be placed on one's lap, as was my custom.

There were always Brothers walking up and down the aisles in the dining room. Every time a Brother passed in back of me while we were eating, he would take my left hand from my lap and place it on the edge of the table. Seconds after the Brother left, my hand would automatically go back down on my lap.

Finally, a Brother was stationed in back of me during meals. Every time my hand dropped to my lap, he would place it on the table. This went on for some months until I was able to able to keep my left hand on the table during an entire meal.

It was unacceptable to eat any food with your hands at the table, except for pieces of bread and morsels of meat on chicken bones. The latter was permitted if the following formula was followed. Someone at the table had to say: "The Queen of England takes chicken bones in her fingers, so it is permissible for us to do the same!"   Then everyone at the table would be allowed to pick up his chicken bones in his hands. I have observed people in Meersburg, Freiburg and Berlin following this custom, so at the time, it was a widely practiced tradition.

Except on a picnic, Germans never eat a sandwich consisting of two slices of bread. They use open-faced sandwiches with one slice of bread covered with meat and/or cheese, and eat it with a knife and fork. I mentioned this to my wife, who is of German extraction, but she would not believe me. On a recent trip to Germany, she asked the wife of one of my friends if this was true. The lady was shocked at such a question. She replied: "Of course, one must always use a knife and fork at the table!"

Generally, Germans say to one another, when sitting down for dinner: "It's dinner time" or "Have a good appetite!" Many families shake hands all around, or at least with the mother, before sitting down for dinner.

The rules are more relaxed on the street. The Germans do not have those long rolls on~which we serve frankfurters. When you buy a frankfurter from a street vendor, you get a frankfurter to hold in your right hand, and a round roll for your left hand. It is funny to see people walking down the street, taking a bite from each hand, especially if they are carrying something pressed between their upper arm and their body .

I have noticed that McDonald's has recently invaded Germany. I have never been in one and wonder how the Germans cope with a McDonald's hamburger. My middle class friends will not set foot in one, as they will not eat in a place that does not provide table service. They are upset that their grandchildren patronize McDonald's.

McDonald's seems to be sensitive to some local preferences. In Germany they serve beer with their hamburgers. Beer in Germany has almost the same status as milk and is untaxed. This is a touchy subject, the German population will not tolerate the taxation of beer!

German table manners may have been static in my time, but I think that the future belongs to McDonald's!

SURVIVING   IN   CLASS

Classes were dull when you didn't understand the teacher. But in math, when the teacher wrote the problem on the board, I could copy it and do the problem. As time went on, I did more and more of this. Then I discovered that the Germans had a "Karl May" series of illustrated boy adventure books, similar to our "Tom Swift" series. I soon could "guess" my way through such a book, and I think I learned to read German through this exercise.

After about a month I started to understand a little of what the teacher was talking about, although I could not yet express myself. At that time, language was not my only barrier. The Germans had their own script, and I had to learn my a- b- c's all over again. After World War II a stroke of enlightenment struck the German nation and they decided to join the human race and start writing with Latin letters like everybody else. Today, most Germans no longer can read German script.

DISCIPLINE

I had read a few books about cadet life at West Point and dreamed of living under such a system of discipline. I soon discovered that West Point could learn a thing or two from the Christian Brothers. At St. Martin's, my grammar school in Washington, when the bell rang, you finished playing and then lined up at your convenience. In Meersburg, when the whistle blew, your reaction was instantaneous and you were in line before the Brother finished blowing the whistle.

FATHERLY   INSPECTIONS

After about a year, although I was speaking badly broken German, I was getting satisfactory grades in all subjects. My father, who worked summers in Berlin, visited me once a year and made sure I was making progress.

Stella Maris ran from school years seven to ten. I lost two years when I was admitted to year seven, but after two years the Brothers let me skip a year. My grades went down a little, but they soon started to go up again, and after a year I was at the head of the class, including good grades in German.

My father had been insisting that I study medicine. In Germany, two years of Latin are required for admission to medical school. Although I disagreed with my father, I thought I had better take precautions. Stella Maris offered two years of voluntary Latin in the two upper grades. I told myself, that the most stupid person in old Rome spoke fluid Latin. You did not have to be smart to learn Latin. You did not have to think hard, the way you had to when solving math problems. It was just memory work that anybody could do. With my working knowledge of German, I no longer faced the problems I had had in Berlin. So, for the record, I took two years of Latin.

ALTAR BOY

During vacation breaks I was the only student who stayed at the school. The Brothers had mass every morning, and since I was the only boy available, I was appointed altar boy. The trouble was I did not know the Latin responses, but I quickly became an expert mumbler as I had done years before in the crypt of the Shrine in Washington. The priest here also did not seem to mind, so my position as vacation altar boy seemed secure.

The job of altar boy gave me some comfort. When you are in a strange land, and everything is different, your bed, your pillows, the food, the language, the sounds, and you cannot communicate with anybody else, the Latin words of the mass were exactly the same as at St. Martin's in Washington. I would close my eyes and listen intently, and imagined that I was back home!

THE BOY BISHOP

The old school building itself, with its four foot thick walls, was crying to be explored. The Brothers never went up into the attic, or down into the basement. I discovered a little room in the attic, with some toys in it, and a window looking down on the altar in the chapel. I showed it to the Brothers, and they became intrigued. One of them did some research and found out that about 250 years ago a local princely family had a monopoly on providing the men to be the Prince-Bishops of Constance, at the time, a tremendously powerful political position, whose domain included great parts of Switzerland and the German State of Baden-Wuertemberg, until Napoleon secularized these lands and dissolved the diocese.

At the time of the Prince-Bishops, it happened that the only male heir in the family was a three year old boy. In those days one did not have to be a priest to become a bishop, so the three year old boy was consecrated Prince-Bishop of Constance. He was raised in our school building, and during religious services he was brought to the little room I found, so he could watch the priests at the altar.

DECORATING THE ALTAR

Our chapel was one of those beautiful, light, fluffy, gold trimmed baroque affairs that I have found in abundance only in southern Germany. Our patron saint was Stella Maris, and her feast day was December 8, a great holiday at the school. I decided to decorate the Stella Maris altar with colored Christmas tree lights. The Brothers did not know what I was talking about, they had never seen colored electric lights, but told me to go ahead. At that time, the Germans decorated their Christmas trees with real candles, only a few super cautious souls used white electric lights. I also cut some branches off a pine tree and did a nice job of decorating the altar, The brothers had never seen anything like it and were enchanted. From then on I was in charge of decorating the chapel on feast days.

BUILDING A BOAT

In the cellar I found a well stocked complete carpenter shop and decided to build a boat. I found a suitable plan in a technical magazine, and then measured the large windows so I could size the boat so I could take it out through the window. Building the boat took a long time, and I had lots of visitors, the Brothers would come down to watch my progress. When the boat was finished, it was too heavy for me to lift. I organized a squad of Brothers to maneuver the boat through the window, lower it some 30 feet to the ground, and carry it down the 200 foot cliff to the lake. I now think it must have been quite funny, this little kid bossing a squad of Brothers in broken German, on how to handle a heavy boat. But at the time, nobody laughed..

The Brothers had a shack at the beach for changing clothes, and I took a heavy chain and lock and fastened the boat to a foundation strut of the shack. We had a lot of fun with the boat. The younger Brothers all came down for a swim, and the boat was the main attraction.

One sunny day we came down to play with the boat and it was gone.! Somebody had cut the heavy chain and stole the boat. The Brothers were as devastated as I was. The boat was never found. I prayed hard that the boat would spring a leak while it was in the middle of the lake and sink, drowning the thief, but we never received a police report of such an event.

MAKING   FRIENDS

The boys at the school all came from small towns or farms where there were no secondary schools. After about two years I made good friends in class and they would invite me to go home with them during the holidays. One such friend came from Todtnau, a small industrial city in the Black Forest. His father was the baker, and he had 4 brothers and a sister. The oldest brother would take over the business, the others had to look out for themselves. At that time everybody still worked in the bakery. My friend and I would deliver bakery goods all over town. We also played on the town's football team, and hiked all over the beautiful mountains.

There was something about Todtnau that I cannot forget. At Sunday mass, the men would sit on one side of the aisle, and the women on the other. The collection was taken up by the prettiest girls in town.

Frank's father sometimes had business in Freiburg, a large city on the other side of the mountains, and he would take Frank and me for the beautiful ride over the mountains. I fell in love with the city of Freiburg. I had been in cities before, Washington, New York, and the Brothers had taken us on monthly excursions that included such Swiss cities as Zurich, Bern and Basel, but I had never seen anything as harmonious and friendly as the Freiburg cathedral, the red stone university with its green copper dome, and the municipal theater. The whole city looked like something out of a fairy tale book.

MY BICYCLE

After the Brothers got to know me, they allowed me to have a bicycle. It changed my life. A bicycle is the most cost effective toy that you can give a boy. He will get more hours of fun per dollar than out of any other toy. A bicycle gives the boy mobility, it opens up the world for him. It does not pay to buy a cheap bicycle.

In my early boyhood in Washington, few boys had bicycles. Because of the heavy automobile traffic, bicycles were prohibited on city streets, they could only be used on the sidewalks. This took all the real fun out of having a bike, not being able to go places with it. As a boy in Washington, I had mobility without a bike, we had street cars.

Things were different when I went to Stella Maris. There, all the boys from well-to-do families received a bicycle for their tenth birthday. The boys at my boarding school could not bring their bikes with them, but they talked enough about them to make me, at age 14, feel left out. My mother sent the Brothers some money. They bought me a strong, sturdy bike and taught me how to ride it. I did not have much use for it when school was in session, but during week ends and vacations, it was a dream come true. I was no longer constrained to the immediate walking area around the school. Now I had mobility!

There was little traffic on the roads, many more hikers and bicycles than vehicles. The main vehicles were the postal busses delivering mail and people, and they always had the right of way. Bus service between all the little towns was excellent. In Germany, all the mail boxes are yellow. and so are the mail trucks and busses. You saw those yellow postal vehicles everywhere.

The area just north of the Alps was known to the old Romans as the "Regio." It is an area in the central part of Europe that is seeped in history. There are many books available about the region and the historic events that took place there. The area was safe, and the Brothers let me roam wherever I wished to go. I just had to tell them in advance where I was going. They often made suggestions of interesting places that I should visit. My bike opened up this world for me, but I can mention here only a few of those things that impressed me the most.

MEERSBURG

A thousand years ago, Meersburg, with a population of 2000, was an "Imperial City," at that time as large and as important as Paris. It was not subject to any prince or state; it only owed tribute or taxes to the Emperor of the Holy Roman Empire.

It was a walled city. In addition to the fortress walls, there were two sets of city walls. In one war, the outside walls were breached and the enemy broke in. During the night, the fortress released its kegs of wine, and the invading soldiers all got drunk. The next morning, the defenders were able to throw out all the drunken invaders and repair the walls, which were never breached again.

Meersburg has another little known claim to fame. The "Siegfried Lied" or "Siegfried Song" is the legend of the Germanic peoples. It has the same status among Germans as the legend of King Arthur has among the English. Three copies of the Siegfried Lied, prepared in the middle ages, are known to exist. One of them was found in the attic of the Meersburg fortress.

The fortress now includes four large rented modern apartments My mother told me that having people live in a place is the .best way to prevent deterioration..

The southern exposure of the Meersburg cliffs yields an excellent wine that is almost completely consumed locally. Wine is taken much more seriously in Europe that in the United States. The local legend explains the good wine with the story that the old Romans had excellent paved roads and a transportation system that allowed Jesus Christ to come and visit the Lake of Constance to admire its beautiful scenery As evening approached and Jesus walked along the lake, looking for a place to spent the night, as a stranger he was turned away everywhere, until he came to Meersburg. This was a cosmopolitan place were travelers were always welcome. They spoke good Latin, so it was easy for them to entertain Jesus with their good wine. Jesus felt that he was so well treated in Meersburg, that when he left the next morning, he promised the Meersburg people that their wine would always be the best in the area. And that is the way its has been.

The centers of the upper and lower parts of town are connected by a steep business street. At the midpoint of this street, there is a fountain commemorating the 167 survivors that escaped the bubonic plague that devastated the area in the fourteenth century.

Sometimes, there would be a heavy fog on the lake and you could not see more than ten feet. At those times the ships would navigate by the sound of their bells. The ships maintained their schedules, regardless of the weather. High up on the cliffs of Meersburg, we could hear the bells distinctly and could tell when a ship was approaching and landing at the harbor. I still vividly remember those foggy days and the sound of those bells.

PREHISTORIC   CAVES

A few miles in the cliffs along the shore west of Meersburg, there were three stories of prehistoric interconnected caves carved high into the cliffs overlooking the lake;   accessible only by a long 20th century staircase. Because of the age of these caves and associated findings, some local experts believe that the human race originated in this area. It was a great thrill for me to explore these livable caves, with the crude drawings of animals on the walls.

SALEM

Another near-by attraction was Salem, where there was an imposing school building where formerly, for centuries, the former princes and kings of England and most other European monarchies had been educated. Our Meersburg class went there on an annual hiking excursion to visit the chapel, an exquisite golden baroque creation, decorated with sculptured marble angles with oversized foreheads.

I was surprised to learn that almost all the princes and kings in Europe were educated in the same school, where they all got to know one another and developed similar ruling philosophies. Add this to the fact that their home states had been parts of the Roman Empire and, excluding England, inherited Roman law. Except for the local language, western European countries are all very much alike. If you do not know the language, it's is very difficult to tell one country from another, excerpt maybe for Portugal, the oldest country in Europe. Practically cut off from the rest of Europe, the challenge for Portugal was the sea. In Portugal, the word "empire" meant control of the trade routes that covered the world like a spider web, not control over land. Portugal has a character of its own.

CONSTANCE

Across the lake from Meersburg lies the city of Constance, thirty minutes by ship, which ran every half hour during rush hours. Constance was a large city, where I could buy nearly everything I wanted. It also had a great history.

Constance was the seat of the Council of Constance, 1414-1418, convoked on the initiative of the Emperor of the Holy Roman Empire to solve the problem of the three popes. All the bishops of the Church were assembled and decreed that they, the Council, derived their powers immediately from Jesus Christ, overturning the constitution of the Church by establishing the superiority of the Council over the pope. The Council then proceeded to dispose of the three popes, one elected at Avignon, one at Rome, and the third one elected by the Council of Pisa to replace the two who refused to relinquish their offices. The Council of Constance then elected a new pope and installed him in Rome where his successors still officiate today.

A new Council Hall had to be built for this event, large enough to accommodate all the bishops. Today it is a tourist attraction.

FRIEDRICHSHAVEN

In Meersburg, an event occurred every Tuesday morning at ten o'clock that was of extreme importance to me. From our classroom windows, we could see the Zeppelin airship flying majestical over the lake and the Alps on its way to South America. It flew scheduled weekly flights in all kinds of weather, but I only remember the sunny days.

The hanger where the airship had been built and where it was maintained was located in Friedrichshaven, a city on the lake about nine miles east of Meersburg. As soon as I had the confidence that I could ride my bike that far, I set off for Friedrichshaven.

I was enchanted by the great hangers. Aside from ocean liners, they were the biggest things I had ever seen. The slick Zeppelin close-up was just overwhelming. This was something you had to see for yourself, it can not be described in words, like the vastness of the ocean, or even festival fireworks. I walked all around the airship and fell in love with it. I was reminded of a stereoscope set I had as a small boy, that described the building and operation of the Zeppelin.   Then as now, I decided that I wanted to work on airships when I grew up.

Later, the Zeppelin Company built a larger airship that caused great excitement in Germany. The christening of the airship was discussed in the newspapers. It was going to be a gala affair. Hitler had just assumed power and was strutting high.   Everybody, including the newspapers *just knew* that the airship would be named   "ADOLF HITLER." The great day came and the airship was christened the "HINDENBURG." Hindenburg was the President of Germany and a great national hero.   But naming the airship after him at that time was a forceful slap in the face to the obnoxious Nazi bureaucrats. It was intended to tell the world that not everyone in Germany was a Nazi.

The horrible accident and burning of the Hindenburg in Lakehurst, New Jersey, was a terrible blow for me. However, it was the jet engine that spelled the death of the large airship. All the luxury, space, and comfort of a airship can not compete with the rapid transportation of a jet airliner, no matter how tightly you squeeze them in.

Friedichshaven was also the location of the Dornier Airplane Company. In those days, aircraft engines were not very powerful and the main challenge for aircraft designers was to provide enough power. About 1930, Dornier built a giant flying boat, the DO-X, with 20 (ten back to back) engines along the wing span. It made sight-seeing flights around the lake with 100 persons aboard. It landed on the lake at Meersburg several times where I saw it. It was the most fabulous flying machine the world had ever seen up to that time.

Someone told me that Dr. Dornier was very interested in young people and very approachable, that I should go to see him. I did and told him that I would like to work on Zeppelins. He told me to study statics, there was a great shortage of statics engineers. From then on, my objective was to study statics, although I had no idea what that was. Dr Dornier and I exchanged Christmas cards for the next ten years. With the help of my bike, I had found an objective which guided me for the rest of my professional life.

SAINT GALL

With my bike, I explored all the little Swiss towns on the southern shore of the lake, and made some in-land excursions, like to the great monastery of Saint Gall, where the the abbot had the rank and power of a bishop. He could train and ordain priests. I could not spend enough time admiring the wood carvings.

The monks liked to chat with kids visiting the monastery and tell them stories. I gathered that because of the barrier of the Alps, the great chain of monasteries in northern Europe was founded by Irish monks, followers of St. Patrick. For centuries, these monasteries reported to Ireland, not to Rome. They did not know who the pope was. Ireland reported to Rome by sea.

Each monastery was assigned a large territory to develop and civilize. At that time, land was the major form of income producing wealth. Each large, ornate monastery was actually the headquarters for a large civilizing operation. The monks built, maintained and serviced many chapels and churches throughout their territory. In those days, the sanctuary of a church behind the altar rail was reserved for the priests and their helpers. The body of the church was usually the only hall in the area and was used as a classroom and even for social gatherings, such as wedding parties. In these local churches, the monks taught the local kids religion, Latin, the three R's (reading, writing, arithmetic); and they taught the grown-ups the same things and added various trades and crafts, such as farming, animal husbandry, good building practices, and other subjects needed to build a civilized society in northern Europe. Clever children were taught arts and crafts, such as music, drawing, design and woodcarving. This organization explains why you see so many large and beautiful churches in small villages, they were extensions of the monastery, the people did not build them. Eventually, the monks developed a trail over the Alps, and the pope sent bishops to the larger towns and lands not developed by the monks.

In school at Stella Maris, we learned more about associated history. With the fall of the Roman Empire, there was no central government any more. The Germanic speaking area, for example, broke up into about 300 independent principalities. The preferred way of increasing the holdings of a principality was through marriage of ruling princes. After the Reformation, some marriages required that one party convert to another religion. The religion of the ruling prince determined the religion of the population of the principality. There was no such thing as religious freedom. When a new ruler with a new religion took over a principality, all the people in the territory changed their religion to conform to that of their new ruler.

This struck me as odd. In history class, I took a closer look at Martin Luther and St Francis of Assisi. Luther did not like the methods that the pope was using to raise money to build the new Vatican, so he started his own religion. He would not have gotten away with that in southern Europe.

St. Francis recognized that the Church needed changes. With the pope's permission, he changed the church from within. He probably would not have received any support for such a project in northern Europe.

I, therefore, felt that the Church in northern Europe was different from the Church in southern Europe. In southern Europe, the Church is like your skin, if your don't like its color, you can tan it, or paint it, but you cannot exchange your skin for a new one. In northern Europe, the Church is like a set of clothes. Changing religions is like getting a new set of clothes.

THE BROTHERS ON A BIKE

During school sessions when I could not ride my bike, a Brother would use it when he had to go on a errand in town. He would always ask me if he could use it. The Brothers always wore cassocks with a little white 4x6 inch tag hanging down from the front of their collars, like the French priests did in the time of St. John de la Salle, founder of the Christian Brothers. I thought it was funny, the way the Brothers rolled up their cassocks so they could ride the bike. They had almost as much fun with it as I did. I think they foresaw some of this when they bought me the bike, so they made sure it was a good one.

GOOD BYE,   STELLA MARIS

When I graduated from Stella Maris, I had a good command of the German language, good grades in all my subjects, and fitted well into German society. I still had to complete grades 11 to 13 of secondary school before I could be admitted to a university.

The Brothers wrote my mother a letter, saying I had three options: I could continue to board at Stella Maris and take the ship to a secondary school in Constance. It was a short trip, and many people commuted daily. The Brothers would supervise my homework and keep me out of trouble. This would be their first choice.

Another choice would be to transfer to Illertissen, where Louts was, and the Brothers had a school that included the three upper grades. The third choice was a priest they knew in Freiburg, who ran a home for out-of-town boys who attended the upper grades at local schools.

Since I had been so impressed with Freiburg when I visited there with my friend Frank and his father from Todtnau, I immediately selected Freiburg. It was a decision that I never regretted.

THE BROTHERS VERSUS HITLER

The Brothers were rabid anti-Nazis who disapproved of Hitler and predicted doom ahead. The Brothers made us read the daily newspapers, but I still didn't know who Hitler was, and looking around me at the well-oiled German economy, I could not foresee any doom ahead. But a short time after Hitler assumed power, the Nazis closed Stella Maris and threw out the Christian Brothers. My respect for the Brothers grew tremendously.

Religious personnel were treated worse by Hitler than he treated Jews. Hitler knew that he could never win the absolute allegiance of religious personnel, they were already committed to their own God. Although some religious personnel were convicted of sneaking money out of the country to support their foreign missionary activities, condemning the entire order to the gas chambers was an act of extreme brutal violence. I was later told in Freiburg by reliable sources that some of my old Meersburg teachers had been seen sneaking from one safe house to another, fearing for their lives. One third of the people who died in Hitler's gas chambers were Christians. A large percentage of them were killed simply because they were religious personnel, both Catholic and Lutheran, just as Jews were killed just because they were Jews.

I think that the Christians who died in Hitler's gas chambers should be canonized as saints by the Catholic Church.

SECONDARY EDUCATION, NEUBURG TECHNICAL SCHOOL, FREIBURG

SAINT BERNARD'S HOME

The Black Forest is a mountain range which extends in a north-south direction for about a hundred miles, defining the eastern border of the Upper Rhine Valley. About halfway between its northern and southern ends, there is a spectacular east-west pass through the mountains. At the western end of this pass, a mountain thrusts itself into the Rhine Valley. At the foot of this mountain, in a great wide semi-circle, lies the beautiful city of Freiburg, the informal capital of the Black Forest.

A road from the city winds itself up the mountain to several outlook points. A short distance up this road is Saint Bernard's Home, just high enough above the Valley floor to provide a grand view of the city, especially at night when all the lights are on, and the cathedral and its tower are illuminated.

Saint Bernard's was a home for out-of-town boys attending the upper grades in the city's schools. The place was run by a priest, Father Vogelbacher, who was also a professor of religion in several of the city's schools. The Brothers at Meersburg had made arrangements with Father Vogalbacher for me to transfer from Meersburg to Saint Bernard's. It was less than a ten-minute walk to the school I was to attend. I could have taken my bike to school, but it was more fun walking with a number of my fellow students.

The creature comforts at Saint Bernard's were superior to Meersburg's. The place was bright and airy. The food was good, but maybe I had just become more accustomed to German food. For breakfast, we always had hot soup. My favorite was ox-tail.

Otherwise, discipline was very similar to what it had been in Meersburg. We slept two boys to a room. Our rooms, closets and desks were inspected once a week, and everything had to be orderly and in its place. We had two hours of supervised homework every day, and during this time we had to do home work and could not just read any old book. We had a nice open deck where we did 30 minutes of physical exercises every day. Everything was done by the clock, tardiness did not exist.

At times we would be hit by a card craze, that is, we thought that playing cards was the most important thing in the world, and would play every opportunity we could. All the boys would be in on it. This would include study hall, where we   would have to pass the cards secretly underneath our desks.

I no longer had the problems I had in Meersburg, of language, of table manners, and of adjusting to German ways. I spoke the language well and was fully Germanized in every respect. I was accepted like everybody else, and was able to make friends easily. The other boys at Saint Bernard's came from good families, and I was able to get along well with them. The tough academic curriculum of the Brothers was at least half a year ahead of Freiburg, and permitted me in the first few days of school   to step to the head of the class. Nobody thought   of me as a foreigner, and I was able to stay at the head of the class as long as I was in Freiburg.

FREIBURG

Surrounded on one side by mountains,   Freiburg is an ancient university city and   market place where the north-south route along the Rhine valley crosses the east-west road through a pass in the mountains. It looks more Disney-like than Disney Land itself.   The great red stone cathedral has one of the highest towers in Europe, the peak is made of see-through stone lacework. It is the only cathedral tower in Germany completed in the middle ages.   The religious services attract a "standing -room only" crowd. The choir sounds like it has 150 voices.

The Freiburg cathedral, page 85, like all stone monuments of this type, is constantly being eroded by the weather. A team of some 15 expert stone masons work full time, all year around, replacing stonework that has eroded. The cost of this operation for stonework maintenance exceeds $ 500,000. a year.

The old red-stone university with its great green copper dome is most impressive, as is the municipal theater. Freiburg has a feature seldom found in ancient walled cities, a very wide main street. This street was the former ancient market. Now it is the place for the smart shops to display their fancy wares. In other walled cities, land was too valuable to be used to make wide streets.

As a market town in ancient times, Freiburg was not significant. In the early middle ages, Freiburg and a great part of the surrounding area were part of Austria. The area was called Western Austria or "Vorderoesterreich". The Archduke of Austria, Albrecht VI, married a lady from the area, Countess Matilda, and he decided he should do something to develop the area. He finally decided that what Freiburg

The Cathedral of Freiburg

needed was a university. There were no Austrian universities west of Vienna at that time. With the cooperation of the Bishops of Constance and Basel, and of the pope, the new university was founded in 1455. The Bishop of Basel became its first rector. The steady stream of educated people produced by the university since that time has made the area one of Germany's most desirable living and working areas.

Today, no cars are allowed in the old city, it is a giant festive shopping and entertainment mall, although a lot of people live there too. Around the circumference of the city, where the old city wall was, there are a number of underground parking lots. If you know where you are going in the city, you can select the nearest parking lot to your goal, it is all very convenient. There is a light and festive atmosphere about the place that is quite striking.

WHY EUROPE ?

In Meersburg, my major concern was to assimilate myself with my new environment. I had little energy left to examine the environment itself, which I accepted as given. In Freiburg, I arrived fully acclimated, and had plenty of energy to analyze my new environment.

My father had been telling me that schools in Europe were superior to those in the United States, that they taught more languages and more about foreign cultures. He also made it plain, and was more insistent as the years went by, that I was going to study medicine (and be a physician, like his father), or law if I flunked out.

I remember much talk in Washington about the local practice of medicine. Johns Hopkins in Baltimore was always mentioned as a good medical school. But it seemed that all the great doctors in town had studied in Vienna.

My father had not selected Germany as a place for me to go to school. He had chosen a Jesuit boarding school in Austria. I had revolted against the Jesuit program of Greek and Latin, taught in German, which then I could not understand. My parents had to find another school quickly, and discovered Stella Maris in Meersburg. The fact that Meersburg was in Germany was incidental. At every opportunity, my father bugged me that I should plan on studying medicine. I decided to study the European school system and learn all I could about it and compare it with the American system. I came to the conclusion that I was in Europe to prepare myself for admission to a first line European medical school, but not because the school system was that much better than the American system. I understood that an American high school diploma would not prepare me for

Gargoyle, The Cathedral of Freiburg
Sense of humor of engineers in the Middle Ages
Wicked gargoyle is thought to attract and keep evil
outside of the Cathedral and thus
protect the holy places inside.

admission and possible survival at an European medical school.

THE AMERICAN SCHOOL SYSTEM

I thought a lot about what my father could have against the American School System. American schools have evolved in response to the most pressing problems that we have with the children in our schools today. These children represent a mixture of races, nationalities, cultures, political and religious systems, some of which have been at odds with each other for centuries. American schools are responsible for the conversion of these children into good American citizens, who respect one another and who work together on projects for the common good.

One feature that the American school has developed to cope with those problems is its program of extracurricular activities. I do not believe that such programs exist to such a degree anywhere else. Groups of students are assigned responsibility for a project that is publicly visible, and often in competition with similar projects in other schools.

The High School Marching Band is an outstanding example. The integrating formations, that the children must perform while marching and playing music, is truly amazing. A misstep by any one member of the band ruins the formation. Success, especially when high schools compete against one another, depends on each individual, performing his difficult task with exact precision, in cooperation with fellow students.

High school sports demand the ultimate performance of individuals, regardless of cultural background. Students are accepted on sport teams based on what they can do, seldom for any other reason.

The system requires that parents of students with diverse backgrounds sit next to each other in the stands, and cheer for the same team. Out of town games and performances may require the expenditure of funds, requiring parents to consider these events very seriously. This process will help parents to lose some of their prejudices. In many small towns across America, the high school football game is the most important social event in town.

The high school system has also had an effect on industrial peace. In some small towns, a worker, his foreman and his boss may all have gone to the same high school and and may have had the same English teacher. Such men will have no trouble talking to one another, and are less likely to make trouble for one another's groups.

THE ROMAN EMPIRE

It is difficult to understand old European institutions without a little knowledge of the Roman Empire. For many centuries, the Roman

Empire consisted of most of Europe and North Africa. The Romans were very successful in imposing their culture throughout the Empire. They invented law, Roman Law, which was enforced uniformly throughout the great nation, and that, except for England and minor modifications, mostly due to the French Revolution, is still the law of the land in European countries. The Romans also invented citizenship. The Romans introduced a uniform language throughout their Empire. Correct, classical Latin was spoken from the shores of the Atlantic to Asia Minor. You could not tell what part of the country a man came from by his speech. The fifty gods in the Pantheon in Rome were the only ones recognized in court, the ones that would support your oath.

The Christian God was not included, because He would not recognize any of the other gods, and Christians were outside the law. This changed in the year 300, when Constantine became a Christian and Christianity became the official religion of Rome.

After many centuries of cultural uniformity and complete freedom of movement in such a large area, you could not tell the difference between a citizen of Iberia from one from Italy, North Africa, or Asia Minor.

One of my former students at the Polytechnic Institute of New York, who came to work at Grumman, married an airline stewardess. At that time, an airline employee and his relatives could fly free on all airlines. For the first three years of their marriage, before the children started to come, my friend and his wife took their annual vacations to various parts of Europe. I asked him for his observations, and he said, "If you don't understand the local language, you cannot tell where you are. All Europe looks the same. If you have seen one great city, you have seen them all!" Such is the imprint of Rome!

After many centuries as the greatest, most powerful nation the world had ever seen, the Empire peacefully expired, and gave way to the "Dark Ages." Nobody knows why.

THE RISE OF THE UNIVERSITY

There is remarkable uniformity in the European university system today. There were many operating schools left over from the Roman Empire, commonly called "stadiums." Some of these became large and famous. For example, in the ninth century, Salerno, Italy, became widely known for its school of medicine.

The first two generally recognized universities are Bologna in about the year 1000, and Paris in 1100. Bologna was a school of law and business, training the executives for the explosive expansion of trade in the Italian port cities. In the year 1200, there were 10000 students in Bologna, most of them from out of town.

Early in the eleventh century, the Archbishop of Paris introduced a beautiful new certificate which he gave to each applicant for the priesthood after he had been examined and passed all the requirements for ordination. Recipients soon found that this certification was widely accepted as qualification for a teaching position. The certificate became very popular, and many applicants for the certificate had no intention of becoming priests.

When the Archbishop found out about this, he changed the name on the certificate to: "License to Teach," and charged a fee for the examination and certificate. The operation was so successful, that he changed the name of the examining board to: *University of Paris.* The university eventually developed three independent parts:

1. An examining and licensing board presided over by a rector. They did no teaching.

2. Groups of teachers that prepared students for the examinations. Colleges were first boarding houses for out of town students, but later teachers moved in and started to teach there. Eventually, the most visible sight at a university was its federation of colleges..

3. Students' unions. A majority of students came from out of town. The unions assured that they found room and board at reasonable prices, often at a college. Books were very scare, and the union regulated the price. They also assured that the teachers taught the students the material they needed to pass the examinations.

The standard university eventually had five faculties: philosophy, theology, canon law, civil law, and medicine. The university has always maintained itself as professional school. The requirements were accepted throughout Europe and maintained through the centuries. The standard European degree has been a "License" certifying that the bearer has been examined and has done work and acquired skills equivalent to those required for ordination. While I was still in Europe, I met several Frenchmen who had graduated with a "License" from a French university.

Since all the examining boards were all appointed by the Church, they all recognized one another, that is, they accepted one anothers' academic credits at full value. A student could move from one university to another with no loss of credit. Europeans have always associated travel with education. Few students stayed at one university for their entire course of study. Teachers also moved from one university to another, providing another standardization effect. Until some 200 years ago, Latin was the common language at all universities.

Like all such organizations, the university required a reliable source of funds. At the time, the only form of wealth that produced income was land. The founders of a university usually donated a sizable parcel of land, but usually not enough. Other sources of income had to exploited.

Parish churches were sometimes extensions of monasteries. The universities followed this pattern and became the patrons of many churches around their area. The university supplied the priests for a church, and in return collected a percentage of the church's income.

Much of the time in the middle ages, the rector of an university had to be a bishop. In an era without much of a government, and with his substantial land holdings, the rectors of universities assumed the status of independent princes and the universities became sovereign states. Students became citizens of the university-state while they studied. The matriculation ceremony was and is the most festive academic ceremony of the year and makes incoming students citizens of the university. There was and is no public ceremony when a student receives his degree.

Many of these elements still exist in European universities. Even today, local police are not allowed on the campuses of European universities. When a disorderly student in town is arrested by the police, he is usually turned over to the rector. To control disorderly behavior on campus, the rector calls for the assistance of a fraternity that is not involved in the disorder.

Since the university was a professional school, it admitted only fully educated, mature individuals. These admission requirements were formalized in a spirit of cooperation with the secondary school system, that was also in the hands of the Church.

A curriculum of elementary and secondary education. spanning 13 years, was laid out and culminated in a "Maturity" degree. This program includes all academic, liberal arts, and general education subjects that educated Europeans are exposed to. Above this level, there is no general education in the humanities.

In addition to the examination in academic subjects, award of the "Maturity" degree requires the formal certification by the religion teacher that the individual is "mature."

Both the Church and the universities. for centuries after the breakdown of the Roman Empire, owned large parcels of land, which provided for their financial support. At about the beginning of the 1800's, Napoleon Bonaparte revised the map of Europe and secularized the lands of the Church and the universities. He created as many new nations as he needed to provide each of his relatives with a kingdom.

Napoleon had no desire to destroy the sovereign university. An agreement was reached, where the state would provide support for the university, but would not have any control over it. This concept is known in Europe as "Academic Freedom." The university alone recognizes what the professional needs to know, and the professor, in cooperation with the students' union, is the only one who determines the contents of the curriculum. Hitler tried repeatedly to violate this Academic Freedom by forcing the German Universities to include political indoctrination in their curriculums, but he did not have much success.

Today, educational reform is the number one priority of every European government. It is acknowledged that the present system provides an excellent education for a small elite. Today, however, the technological revolution requires that a much greater proportion of the population be much more educated. Continued technical progress in a United Europe depends on greater education. European leaders are all searching for new ways to make the benefits of greater education available to more people

AMERICAN VS. EUROPEAN SCHOOL SYSTEMS

On the surface, the European school system appears to be the simpler one. The old universally accepted "Maturity" degree, awarded after 13 years of elementary and secondary education, provides admission to a professional school (university) anywhere. In rare cases, a university course may be full, and admission is by grades, the applicants with the best grades are admitted first. There is a minimum of red tape.

In the United States, a high school diploma is awarded after 12 years of primary and secondary education, and is followed by four years of undergraduate study at a university. Applicants to a university are evaluated on the basis of their academic grades and their extracurricular activities, the latter serving as indicators of their personality characteristics. Professional (or graduate) school follows the completion of undergraduate studies.

Because of the emphasize on extracurricular activities in high school, the treatment of academic subjects suffers. This deficiency is corrected in the first two years of undergraduate study. The 13-year European "Maturity" degree is equivalent to the US high school diploma plus the first two years of college, a total of 14 years. However, the US school system includes extracurricular activities, a feature that most Americans approve of.

The length of American graduate or professional schools depends on the subject matter, as in Europe. A Master's degree in most subjects can be earned in one or two years. Law school requires three years. A medical degree requires four years of undergraduate premed and four years of graduate school.

Comparing the German requirements for a medical degree with the American ones, we find that Germany requires 13 years for a "Maturity" degree, and six years for medical school, a total of 19 years. In the United States, it takes 12 years through high school, four years of undergraduate premed, and four years of medical school, a total of 20 years. The last two years of premed plus the four years of US medical school are the same as the six years of German medical school.

There still remains the question of whether European doctors are better than American ones, as my father seemed to believe. If any one nation has better doctors, it should be reflected in that country's longevity, a fact that would be well known throughout the world. I have concluded that my father's dreams for me were based on sentiment and not on fact.

The last two years of American undergraduate university study deserve a closer look. In response to the rapid technological advances in recent years, the universities have responded with new programs in every field. You can get a degree in almost any subject you desire. Nothing like this exists anywhere in Europe. Furthermore, a system of scholarships, loans, and work programs assures that everyone who wants to go, can go to college, although tuition costs are high.

STARTING   SCHOOL

On the first day of school in Freiburg, a warm and sunny day, classes were organized on the playground. I joined a group of boys in whose class I would be placed. A teacher came up and said that there were too many boys for one class, half of us should step over here, and half over there. Almost all the boys knew one another, so they knew how to group themselves into an "A" class and a "B" class. I looked them over carefully and decided to join the "B" class. It was the most important decision I have ever made !

By law, in the Black Forest area, the large farms may not be sub-divided, they are passed on from father to oldest son. Other children have to fend for themselves. Traditionally, they are attracted to the clergy or the army.   Today, however, the Black Forest is moderately industrialized, so there are other opportunities for young people. The system makes Black Forest farmers relatively prosperous. The place is very clean, well kept, and attracts lots of tourists.

Our Alleghenies are covered with deciduous trees. As the mountains age, the deciduous trees make way for evergreens. The Black Forest is very old, as far as mountains go, and the deciduous trees are gone. They are covered with very dark evergreens, that at a distance, look almost black.

The boys in the "A" class were all second or younger sons of rich Black Forest farmers who wanted to become officers in the German Army. They all thought that they would have a better chance of being selected if they had a good Nazi record. They were all leaders in the Nazi Youth Movement, some of them of very high rank. They believed that Nazi party work was much more important than school work and they were always in trouble at school. If I had joined their class, I don't see how at age 18 I could not have become an extremist like the Nazis were, and I do not know what else would have become of me.

The "B" class consisted of 28 boys who came mostly from Catholic professional and business families in town. In class, we sat two to a desk. .The boy who came and sat next to me, Max, was a tall, very pleasant, out-going boy, son of a dentist. We became immediate friends. Max's friend was Herman, they both grew up together. Herman was a year older than Max, and a year ahead of him in school. Max's father and Herman's father had both served together in the German Army in World War I, and the two families were very close. Herman also became my friend, and we became an almost inseparable three-some most of the time I was in Freiburg.

Max was an only son at home. His older sister was a married dentist, and his older brother represented a German steel manufacturer in Mexico.

Herman was the oldest of five children, four boys and a girl. With time, I became an adopted member of Herman's family.

SCHOOL

School was in session from eight am until one pm (five hours) from Monday through Saturday, and two hours on Tuesdays and Thursdays afternoons, for a total of 34 hours per week. Then we had two hours of homework, six days a week, so we spent at least 46 hours a week on school and homework. Homework was taken very seriously at Saint Bernard's.

Standard academic courses like mathematics, physics, chemistry and languages were taught right out of the book. We had a fully equipped gym and learned to use all the equipment. Physical Education included physical exercises, football, field sports like races and swimming. Voluntary non-academic courses included such things as music, art, and the theater.

The courses that let you know that you were in Germany were History and German. These courses described the development of the German nation and instilled pride in these accomplishments. In discussing these courses with my teachers, I was told that their purpose was to make us "bearers of culture." In English, the term "Carriers of the Flag" sounds more appropriate. It is not too different from the objective of the American school system, namely, to provide the nation with good citizens.

Neuburg Technical School

In two of the following chapters, I recount some of the important highlights of these courses as I remember them. I think that they are of interest, because they influenced me as much as they influenced my classmates, which is what they were supposed to do. Because of space limitations, I have omitted much material, and I am not sure that my memory is as good as I think it is.

Based on their history, Europeans think differently from Americans. Around 1933, one of our teachers, in an off-the-cuff discussion, explained to us that the current German Government was illegitimate. As a soldier in World War I, he had sworn an oath on the Kaiser. Such an oath works two ways. The Kaiser promises him good government and protection, and he promises to obey the Kaiser. The Kaiser cannot abdicate his responsibilities without the soldier's permission. A plebiscite should have been held. At that time, the German people did not think that they had really lost the war. Then there was the question of payment of reparations which nobody in Germany approved. There was no way the Kaiser could have lost such a plebiscite. The Treaty of Versailles is an illegitimate act of violence

HISTORY   CLASS

German history starts with Charlemagne (also known as Charles I, or Charles the Great) who dreamed of reactivating the Roman Empire, one state, one religion. Eastern Europe would not cooperate, neither would the Orthodox Church. Charlemagne settled for northwestern Europe and northern Italy. He had himself crowned "Emperor" by Pope Leo in 800 A.D.

He had three sons, Charles, Pepin, and Louis. After his death, the sons divided northern Europe in more or less three equal parts: France, Lotharingia, and Germany. Over the years, France and Germany picked Lotharingia apart, and today, all that is left as an independent country is Luxembourg.

The successors to Charles became the Kings of France, and the successors to Louis became Kings of the Germans, so called because "Germany" was not yet defined. They kept the dreams of Charlemagne alive, and developed the concept of the Holy Roman Empire of the German Nation, which included the territory of the German speaking peoples in north-western Europe and the lands in Italy that Charlemagne had acquired. To become Emperor of the Holy Roman Empire, the King of the Germans had to go to Rome and be crowned by the pope. This was no mean task, considering the barrier of the Alps, and not all German kings were successful.

The Holy Roman Empire left its mark on history. The concept of one state, one religion was strong. The German nobles derived their power from the King, but the King, once crowned by the pope, derived his powers directly from God. This is expressed in the formula: "Carl, by Grace of God, Emperor,... ...."

At first, the German King was elected by the major nobles in Germany, following the Roman tradition of electing emperors. By 1200, agreement had been reached on an Electoral College of seven nobles, three bishops and four lay princes. The bishops were chosen because, having no heirs, they could be relied upon to support national policies, whereas lay nobles might be more influenced by dynastic considerations. The Holy Roman Empire was eventually dissolved in 1806, just a little over a thousand years after Charlemagne had been crowned in 800.

A serious challenge to the Empire and the concept of "one Empire-one religion" came from Martin Luther. In his debate with the Swiss theologian Zwingli, Luther realized that the abolition of communion also abolished the need for ordained priests and bishops, and this would affect the Electoral College with its three bishops. He modified his doctrine to retain the belief that when a person receives communion from the hands of an ordained Lutheran minister, he receives the true body and blood of Jesus Christ. However, the bread and wine do not become the body and blood of Christ until the moment that they are administered to a recipient. This doctrine was sufficient to require the continuing existence of bishops with the extraordinary power of ordination. This act of putting national interest ahead of religion places Luther on the list of German national heroes.

Otherwise the Holy Roman Empire was spared serious external attacks for a thousand years; the Emperors had little to do, and their power atrophied.

The new century of 1800 brought Napoleon's sweep over Europe and the reorganization of the territory of the Holy Roman Empire from small principalities into larger kingdoms. It is remarkable how willingly the Germans accepted Napoleon's reorganizations. But Napoleon was careful, where appropriate, to draw his new state borders to coincide with old tribal borders. The German population saw this as a move towards an overdue national unity and accepted it.

In their striving for greater national unity, the Germans have always been intrigued with the French. The King of France had never let his country split up into little pieces (Monaco is an exception). Everything was run from Paris. The University of Toulouse, for example, was an office of the University of Paris at Toulouse. The admiration by the Germans for things French is indicated by such things as:
- The intensive study of the French Revolution to justify the development of "democracy" in Germany

-The acceptance of the French (metric) system of weights and measures to promote commerce among the various German States

-The imitation of Versailles at Potsdam by a French speaking German king, Frederick the Great.

The two largest states in Napoleon's Central Europe were Prussia and Austria, ruled respectively by Frederick the Great and Maria Theresa. These two states conducted a series of wars for dominance among the German States, and Prussia won. Although Napoleon had passed away, the French were still making demands the Germans could not live with, and Prussia, 1870, declared war on France and dragged all the other German States along, except Austria. Prussia & Co. won, and its Chancellor, Bismarck, organized the victorious states into a new nation, Germany. This nation was now ruled by a board of the kings of the participating states, with the King of Prussia as the Chairman and title of Emperor or "Kaiser." None of the participating kings had a written constitution, and Bismarck started a movement to correct this deficiency.

World War I started as an accident in 1914. However, both sides, France and Germany, were well prepared and the whole thing quickly ground down to a stalemate. Probably the intervention of the United States tipped the scales in favor of the Allies. But probably the biggest mistake that was made was the imposition of reparations on Germany by the Allies making the Germans pay for the damages sustained by the Allies during the war. Something like this had never been done before, and it resulted in no end of ill feelings. The US Senate thought so, too, and refused to ratify the Treaty of Versailles, the Treaty that ended the war.

I have a little booklet "Hearings before the United States Senate" entitled "The Nature of Revolutions." It says, revolutions never start when a people are down and out, when life is a matter of survival. There is not enough energy in the system to produce trouble. Revolutions occur when things that were bad, are getting better, but in the opinion of some people, are not getting better fast enough. There is enough energy in the system to cause trouble, to feed discontent, and a revolution may erupt.

A succession of brilliant German Chancellors after World War I successfully negotiated a step by step reduction in reparations. The last Chancellor before Hitler, Bruening, of the Catholic Center Party, very highly respected among the Allies, negotiated the end of reparations. However, Bruening was not allowed to enjoy the fruits of his labors. An event now took place, that was beyond the imagination of reasonable men.

I WAS THERE !

In 1922, a decade before Hitler, Germany went through a disastrous inflation, when money lost all its value. Most everybody lost everything they had and were left penniless. Through hard work and a measure of discipline, things got a little better every year. Now, with the end of reparations payments, everybody expected a jump in improvements in their lives.

This was the kind of situation described in my US Senate booklet, "The Nature of Revolutions" that could lead to a revolution. However, in Germany at that time, the devil himself took over in the person of Adolf Hitler. Even William Shakespeare could not have thought of a more devastating dramatic tragedy than the one that was about to begin. And I had a front row seat!

Among the candidates for Chancellor in 1933, Hitler made the most extravagant promises. People did not know much about him, the only way they could judge was by the performances of the Nazi party in the legislatures on the federal and state levels. Both the Catholic and Lutheran Churches were dead set against him, but they did not have that much ammunition. In the election, Hitler received 46% of the popular vote. He quickly formed an alliance with the German National Party, which had received 6%. Now Hitler had 52% and could force President Hindenburg to appoint him Chancellor.

It was not a normal change of a European Government. It was something nobody could have expected, it was something only the devil could have thought up. Hitler moved in with a real BANG! It was a spectacular military takeover of an unsuspecting nation by two well trained and equipped armies, namely the:

SA - Strum Abteilung (Attack Forces) with brown uniforms

SS - Schutz Stafel (Security Troops) elite troops in black uniforms.

Left wing political parties in Europe, such as the Social Democrats and the Communists, have long had private armies to hold torch parades and demonstrations, fight one another, and riot. Hitler's armies were disguised as innocent, normal left wing party armies, but secretly, they were something entirely different. They were armed and trained as well as any national army, and in World Was II served in the same combat capacity as the German Army. In addition, they included political departments that had units corresponding to every unit of the German Government. Something like this had never existed in Europe before, it was much more sophisticated than anything the Communist Party had. The Nazi armies were trained and capable of taking over a country as large as Germany within hours.

These Nazi armed forces, using surprise and speed, replaced every federal and state executive, legislative, and judicial body in Germany in a matter of hours. Hitler's preparations for the takeover had been secret and complete down to the smallest detail.. It was done so fast that the regular Armed Forces of Germany could not respond. When they got ready to move, they could no longer find their civilian chiefs, and found themselves faced with a new Nazi civilian bureaucracy that had replaced the old one

Fear gripped the nation. It was beyond belief that such an unscrupulous and immoral monster could be at the controls in Germany. For some days, you did not know who was friend or foe. People talking on the phone were afraid to use names, they referred to other people by their initials. Fear kept the aggressors in power, everybody was scared to do anything.

I had supper with the Persons the day of the Nazi takeover. Karl had spent the day with the Rev. Dr. Fehr, the National Chairman of the Catholic Center Party. Suddenly we noticed that the two men had disappeared. We told ourselves that they were safe, but Karl's family did not know where he was.

The Nazis naturally wanted everybody to go back to work and they established a calm which gave people a chance to catch their breath. Eventually everybody went back to work   Displaced government workers found other jobs.

With the cancellation of payment for reparations, Hitler found himself floating in money. Although Hitler had nothing to do with the end of reparation payments, this event contributed greatly to his success. The immediate expansion of the Armed Forces gave the country a vital economic boost. On the surface, Germany eventually appeared to be a peaceful and prosperous place to live and work.

The annexation of Austria gave everyone a jolt, but Austria was German territory and it had been a contender with Prussia for leadership in the old German federation. Many Germans agreed that the annexation of Austria was justified and in line with the old German goal of unity among German speaking peoples. Hitler's expansionist ambitions were well known, and many people had fun guessing what his next adventure would be.

I was staying with the Persons one beautiful weekend, sleeping on the living room couch. I woke up Sunday morning and turned on the radio. Karl heard the radio and walked in to listen. Hitler was announcing that he was taking over the Rhineland..

The Rhineland is a plain between Germany and France that the Germans have traditionally used to invade France. The French side is heavily fortified. The German side, in accordance with a provision of the Treaty of Versailles, is demilitarized. There were no German troops or fortifications there.

For months, Hitler had been "secretly" moving troops, dressed as policemen, into the area. Such a large operation can not be done "secretly." Everybody knew what he was doing.

While Hitler was talking on the radio, his troops were exchanging their policemen's uniforms for Army ones.

Karl says to me: "Hitler is declaring war. He is saying that nothing that the Allies do or say will stop him from his expansionist plans." I said to myself: "The Roman Empire looms again."

ADVANCED GERMAN CLASSES

These classes covered all other topics that an educated German should know about his cultural heritage. The course started with a survey of German and foreign, modern and classical literature. German authors, more so than non- German ones, have always recognized a responsibility to translate their share of the great works of other nations into German. This provides access in the German language to a library of great world literature not available in any other language. For example, the translation of Shakespeare into German is excellent, and Shakespeare is much more readable in German than in English. There have been some successful efforts to translate German Shakespeare into English. Homework consisted of assigned reading and book reports.

The literature survey led to a discussion of the theater from the time of the Greeks to modern times, and its role in religious instruction in the middle ages. I became sufficiently intrigued to buy a subscription to the Freiburg Theater which included a performance every month, that I attended regularly. The shows included a range of classical and modern plays, musicals, and opera.

A good portion of our homework was dedicated to writing compositions, one due every three weeks. The subject matter was generally given, but once in a while they let you choose your own title. The teachers selected appropriate compositions or parts of thereof for further analysis and discussion in the classroom. Here the writing would be critically examined for grammatical and other errors, sentence structure, elements of good writing, and effectiveness of presentation. Short sentences were preferred. Compositions had to have an opening, body, and a closing.

I have always been good at writing compositions. At that time, five and ten cent stores were still unknown in Freiburg, until they opened one. We were assigned the task of writing a composition on the desirability of such stores. The Germans were all opposed to such stores because they thought such stores would threaten the existing order. I was the only student who wrote in favor of such stores, based on my American experience. My composition was so witty and well written that it was read in all the upper classes of the school.

Although everybody disagreed with what I wrote, I still got full credit and an "atta-boy" for writing well.

Another major topic of study was the development of the German language, and its influence on national unity. Old German probably goes back to the time of Christ. It is studied as you would a foreign language. There is little similarity with modern German. Literature is scarce, only a few poems and songs exist, but they include the Siegfried Song and all the other old known legends of the Germanic Tribes. We had to memorize and recite a poem in Old German, but I quickly forgot it.

There is substantially more literature available in Middle German, mostly poems and love songs. Many words are similar to modern German and could be understood, but it is difficult to read. The forms of the letters are different, and there are no spelling rules. A word may be spelled a different way every time it is used. Several of our teachers were quite enthused about Middle German, because it is the common inheritance of the German speaking peoples that pulled them all together into one nation. These teachers felt that every cultured German should be conversant with Middle German. Much of German romantic history of the middle ages is written in Middle German. We had to memorize a number of these poems.

Many of the poems of the era express a yearning for unity among the Germanic peoples. A good example is Germany's national anthem, "Deutschland Ueber Alles" (meaning: Germany Above All Things). The song was an appeal to the splintered German speaking principalities to unite into a "Germany". The term "Germany" was at that time a geographic concept and a political dream. The Nazis managed to rewrite history and give this song an ugly meaning, at first: "Germany Above All Nations"; then:"Germany Master of all Nations."

The use of Middle German gave way to the consolidation of the many German tribes into five major ones based on a geographical basis. Eventually, each tribe developed its own distinctive lifestyle and dialect. The five major German Tribes are; the Saxon, Franks, Allemans, Suabians, and Bavarians. We studied in some detail the lifestyle and dialect of each of these tribes. Lifestyle included layout of farms, villages. houses, barns; the festivals, dress codes, inheritance codes, preferred foods, and many other such things. Each dialect has its own words, grammar, and irregular verbs. People speaking one dialect usually cannot understand a person speaking another one.The dialects represent a force in partitioning rather than unifying the German speaking people.

Martin Luther, when sent to jail for two years, decided to translate the Bible. There were already about one hundred translations of the

Bible available, but all of them into a dialect, and therefore each enjoyed limited readership. Luther decided to correct this situation. For each word that he translated, he sought a word out of the five dialects that he thought most people would understand. His translation was a mixture of all five dialects. It turned out to be a huge success, because so many people could understand it. Luther's Bible German became the language of educated people, the "high" German spoken today. It is the greatest force for the unification of the German people. It is called "high" German because most of the words are taken from dialects spoken in geographically "higher" parts of the country.

SUMMER TIME

With the start of summer vacation, Father Vogelbacher closed Saint Bernard's Home for the season, and he left for the summer. There was no place for me. By this time, Father Vogelbacher knew me well, and he also knew the families of the friends I associated with outside of Saint Bernard's. In these circumstances, I was allowed to rent a room with board in the home of a teacher, one block from my school. I ate with the family.

On the surface, I appeared to be a free agent, but I realized this was far from the case. I was only free as long as I behaved myself and kept up my grades in school. The families of Max and Herman were watching me as one of their own, and Father Vogelbacher and Dr. Person worked at the same school. I am sure Father Vogelbacher received regular reports how I was doing. Furthermore, my father visited me every summer at unexpected times and thoroughly inspected my living and studying accommodations.

I spent my summer days with Max and Herman, usually with our bikes. When they don't go somewhere with their parents, kids in Europe do not stay home during summer vacations. Everybody gets on their bikes and goes somewhere. Europe has a system of Youth Hostels, spaced about a day's hiking apart. They usually have a boy's and a girl's dormitory. You have to bring your own sheets, and over-nighting cost about $0.12 in my time. Most Hostels served a simple hot dinner for about $ 0.25. They were closed during the day.

Max, Herman, and I explored the area around Freiburg thoroughly. The roads in the Black Forest were always a challenge. Riding down the steep roads was a lot of fun, but going up was something else. The farthest we got was to the Swiss city of Basel. They were having some kind of European food convention in the imposing Baseler three story convention center. None of us had ever been at a convention before. We discovered that they were giving out small free samples of food at each booth. We started at the top on the third floor and worked our way down. At each booth we got a free sample. It was very good food. When we got to the exit on the ground floor, we had had a fine meal. For the rest of my life, I have always associated Basel with fine free food.

In Freiburg there was a large square that we had to cross when we were going into town from Saint Bernard's. Along one edge, there was a large cage with about 20 little monkeys. I could not walk by without stopping a few minutes to watch the little animals at their antics. Feeding them was forbidden, but I think they got to know me anyway.

The square was surfaced with asphalt. It was such a large beautiful area, we could not cross it without trying out some bicycle tricks. If there were enough of us, we would play tag on our bikes. It was a rough game, but nobody ever got seriously hurt.

My room was on a third floor, with a window out on the main street. Herman lived two blocks away. Often, after supper, if he had finished his homework, he would come to the street below my window and whistle a favorite passage from the "Skater's Waltz." I would blink my light as a signal that I heard him. We would then go walking through town together, mingling with the crowds and admiring the store displays. Sometimes we would go browsing in a bookstore or gift shop, but we never bought anything. On rare occasions, we would stop at a bar and have a beer. If things got dull and it was not too late, we would get Max and all go to a movie. We almost always headed for home before bedtime, since there was no getting out of going to school the next morning.

I did not dislike beer, but none of us were heavy drinkers. The Brothers in Meersburg taught me to drink beer. We were having lunch in the woods during one of our monthly excursions. A Brother offered me a sip of his beer. I nearly choked on it. All the other boys laughed at me. They had all been weaned on beer. The Brother considered my performance unmanly. After that, on every appropriate occasion, I was fed a small quantity of beer, until I finally learned not to detest it, and eventually to like and enjoy it like the other boys did.

Nobody in my class had a girl. We never talked about girls. We acted as if they did not exist. We had only men teachers. I suppose, there was an underlying philosophy of everything in its time. Eventually, all the boys in my classes in Meersburg and Freiburg got married and had children. Nobody got a divorce.

THE ARCHBISHOP AND THE FLAG

Immediately after Hitler's take-over, things were pretty quite. What do you expect in a country with a group of armed SA or SS soldiers at every intersection?

The cathedral in Freiburg had been built by the city in the middle ages, and then turned over to the Church to conduct services. In the turn-over contract, there was a clause stating that the city reserved the right to fly the city flag from the cathedral tower. The day that Hitler assumed power, a Nazi committee, with the intent of causing trouble, called on the Archbishop with the demand to fly the Nazi flag from the cathedral tower.

In Germany, this was a preposterous demand. When the state secularized all the Church's property in Napoleon's time, it agreed to provide some support to the Church, but not to exercise any control over Church doctrine or activities, in an agreement similar to the one on Academic Freedom concluded with the universities. The Catholic Church is very sensitive on this point, as are the universities. The Catholic Church always flies the Papal flag as a sign of its independence from the state, never the national flag like it does in the United States where the separation of Church and state are well established principles.

Contrarily to all expectations, however, the Archbishop received his Nazi guests cordially, he greeted them in the best Freiburger tradition with an excellent Black Forest "Schnapps" and told them that he was well aware of the city's ancient rights and that they must be respected. He invited them to go right up the tower and hang out the Nazi flag. They did just that, but the fun of it did not last. Climbing the steep, narrow, circular steps up that tall tower twice a day, to hang out the big, heavy flag and take it down again in the evening, was hard work. After a few days, the Nazi flag flying from the cathedral tower, was never seen again.

This incident made the Archbishop's reputation. Whenever thereafter there arose a crisis between the Nazi State and the Catholic Church, the Archbishop of Freiburg would be called in as peacemaker.

This incident also convinced Karl and his friend that it would be safe for them to come home. They did, but Karl was dismissed from his jobs in the legislature and as Professor. He found another teaching job, at a lower rank, in a secondary school in Karlsruhe, a city some 70 miles north of Freiburg. He moved his family from the beautiful new house he had built in Freiburg to an apartment in Karlsruhe.

MAX MUELHAEUSLER

Sometimes on Tuesdays and Thursdays when we had school in the afternoon, Max would invite me to go home with him to do our homework together and to have dinner. On these days we got out of school at four pm, and if we did our homework right away, we would have the evening free. We would do our homework in Max's room, and by the time we were finished, it would be time for dinner.

Max was a fussy eater. Like most people in Freiburg, he did not like much meat. The local preference was for meat every other day. Their food of choice was pasta, such as spaetzli, noodles, spaghetti, pan cakes, waffles, and a dozen or more home made pasta forms. Spaetzli, noodles and similar foods were generally home-made. These pasta foods were served drenched with a syrup of cooked fruit, like apricots, plums, peaches, pears, apples, berries, and others. These people consume less meat, but eat a lot more fruit than we do in the US.

Sometimes the meat you expected on your dinner plate would be replaced by a thick slab of cheese. A special summer time treat was a dinner of a large soup plate heaped high with strawberries, with sugar and plenty of whipped cream. Lots of bread and butter were served to top off all meals. Dinner was unthinkable without first a plate of soup. In the summer, a cold fruit-based soup was popular.

After dinner, sometimes Max and I would play chess. Neither one of us was very good at it. Max's hobby was drawing and painting. He was also a very fine skier. In World Was II he was commander of a German ski unit in northern Norway.

Max's father was the son of a dentist who had earned his DDS degree at the University of Pennsylvania in Philadelphia. He liked to tell me stories about his student days in the United States. His practice was conducted on a personal basis in his big house. On the way out, his patients would have to pass through a room where Max's mother was holding court. Every patient received a cup of coffee or tea, a piece of soft cake, and was subjected to a thorough inquisition. She knew almost everyone in town and everything that was going on. She was very kind to me, always concerned that I got enough to eat. Max's father was also a painter and did some beautiful portraits and landscapes. He was also a hunter. The Germans use their forests to produce part of their meat requirements. Max's father leased a parcel of land from a village half way up an adjacent mountain which gave him the exclusive right to hunt on that parcel. He built himself a small cabin there, which had all the comforts of home and where he could overnight. Weekends, in the season, he would go hunting, usually with one or two friends, and always come back with a deer. which he would deliver to a local butcher. Local butchers in Freiburg all have fancy displays of wild animals and sell them for local consumption. The conventional local Christmas dinner is venison.

Sometimes Max would invite me for dinner, only to discover that he did not like what his mother was cooking, especially if it was a meat dish. He would then call up Herman to find out what they were having for supper. If he liked that better than what his mother was preparing, he would tell Herman that the two of us were coming over

Dr Max Muelhaeusler
attacks a 16-inch   Dutch Pan Cake
Leiden, Holland, June 1999 while visiting
his grandson at college

to his house for supper. If the dinner that Herman's mother had prepared did not stretch enough to feed everybody properly, she brought out the cold cuts and jams, and we filled up on sandwiches.

The boys in my class were all well adjusted individuals, and Max was a good example. Max's father was a well respected citizen with satisfying hobbies. His mother could not have been a more contented woman. His two uncles, an aunt, and a sister were successful dentists, respected citizens that led contented lives. Max's only ambition was to continue in this tradition, and he knew exactly what he had to do to get there. The immediate problem was to get good grades so he would be admitted to dental school. Furthermore, he had satisfying hobbies, painting and skiing, which he cultivated for the rest of his life.

Max got married and had two boys and a few years later, twin girls. One boy was born a short time after our Roy. We sent him all of Roy's baby clothes, all things that were unavailable in Germany. They were put to good use in Freiburg. Later Max told me that he had a friend in Poland who had a baby. Baby clothes were unavailable at that time in Poland, so Max sent him Roy's baby clothes. In the meantime, Max's friend has passed the baby clothes on to another family. Roy's baby clothes have seen a lot of the world.

Max became a successful dentist in Freiburg. He rented a suite of offices downtown and ran a business like practice. He made a lot more money that either Herman or I. He and his wife visited us once at our home in Garden City, New York, when they took a tour of the United States.

HERMAN PERSON

When I went home with Herman, the first thing he would do was to turn on the radio to some music he liked, then sit at the piano and play along with the radio for about half an hour. He was a fine musician. All five Person children had received the same private music lessons, but only Herman really played well. It was his way of relaxing. After his concert, he would raid the refrigerator. He would make sandwiches for the two of us, a thick slice of farmer's bread covered with Ringsheimer-liverwurst at least a quarter of an inch thick. It was the best liverwurst I had or have ever eaten.

Herman followed in his father's footsteps. He became a member of of the State Legislature, President of the State Legislature, and finally Governor of South Baden. His sister, Elizabeth, who I helped with her English homework, has visited us three times in Aberdeen, the first time with her husband, and after he died, with a friend who was a woman physician with whom she was taking a tour. The last time she came alone.

MY SUBSTITUTE FATHER

Herman's father, Dr.Karl Person, was a Professor of Physics at a secondary school in Freiburg and a delegate of the Catholic Center Party in the Baden State Legislature. While I was in Freiburg, he was elected President of the Baden State Legislature. He was a pleasant man of medium height, with a typical round face of the people of that region and with a shaven head, traditional of his generation. He could put you immediately at ease. He knew how to ask a lot of questions and in a few minutes, know your entire life history. He had a way of making you feel important. He was the second son of a large farmer in Ringsheim, a small farming community near Freiburg.

Karl did everything he could to make me feel at home, at his table and in his house. Many times, when an errand took him into town, he would take Herman and me along. Usually we would end up in a cafe' where he would treat us to coffee and pastry. He loved onion pie, the old German version of Italian pizza. Herman's mother would examine my clothes, and if she found a hole or a button missing, she would fix it.

The Persons bought much of their food from the farm in Ringsheim; sausages, smoked meat, farmer's bread, wine, etc. It was all much better than anything available in the stores. They had a maid and ate well.

Karl had to deal with the Nazis and the Communists in the State Legislature. He would come home and tell us stories about how he maintained order in the Legislature. Some stories were really funny. One time, an issue came up for a vote, and the Nazis had not been paying attention. The Nazi leader called over to Karl: "What's going on?" Karl replied: "Those lousy Americans are trying to steal our art treasures again !" That time the Nazis voted with Karl's Center Party.

When the Nazis assumed power, Karl lost his positions in Freiburg and moved to Karlsruhe. Just before all this occurred, I had graduated in Freiburg and enrolled in the Technical University of Berlin. On many of my vacations, I would return to the Persons in Karlsruhe. I always felt at home with them.

After the Nazi defeat in World War II, Karl got jobs in Freiburg as the President of the Baden State Legislature and as the Director of a secondary school. He moved his family back into his beautiful house in Freiburg.

The tasks that the Baden State Government had to face at that time were formidable. The long boundary of Baden borders on France. The French captured all industrial equipment that they could move, and all the factories and production facilities in Baden were mere shells. There was a deluge of refugees fleeing from the Communist East Zone. There was not enough food nor housing to go around. Money was devaluated by a ratio of ten to one. Taxes on real estate were multiplied by a corresponding factor. Almost everyone was unemployed. It was a real disaster.

Karl was in the middle of all this. After two years of intense struggle, Germany emerged as a modernized nation, smelling like a rose. Karl was awarded an Order of Saint George by the pope.

When things calmed down, the US State Department invited a number of top German political figures to the US to learn about our government. Karl was assigned to the University of Kentucky in Lexington, an environment the State Department thought was similar to Freiburg. There he studied the US constitution and related subjects. After the course, the members of the group were given three weeks to travel as they wished in the United States. Karl was not feeling well and decided to come and spend his three weeks with us in Garden City on Long Island near New York City.

During his first few days with us, I took him into the city and introduced him to various professors at several universities and to a few officers of some German clubs. The German clubs did it !   The clubs received him with the greatest hospitality. For the rest of the time that Karl was with us, he would take the commuter train to the city every morning, there the clubs would make a big fuss over him, and in the evening he would return just in time for dinner.

This experience of learning first-hand about the German-American community was important for a German politician. One on the great mistakes that Hitler made was to assume that the German American community was so large and strong, and so loyal to Germany, that it would never allow the US to declare war on Germany.   Three thousand miles of ocean blurs the vision. Karl had always felt that Hitler was wrong, and now he learned first hand that "German"-Americans are Americans and not Germans.

Karl returned home, not only with an education on the US Constitution, but also with a real intimate knowledge of the German-American lifestyle. He passed away a few years after he returned home. In Ringsheim, his birthplace, they renamed the school the Karl Person School. A section of the school library is dedicated to his memory. It contains his personal papers, newspaper and other articles and records.

I am certain, that under Karl's guidance, starting at the impressionable age of 18 and 3000 miles away from my own parents, I developed some of the characteristics which have led to whatever success I have had in life. I am so glad, that on my first day in Freiburg, I selected the "B" class in school. On one of his European trips, my own father went down from Berlin to Karlsruhe to visit Karl and to thank him for taking care of me. I understand the two men got along very well together. I guess the question of my studying medicine did not come up.

"CARE" PACKAGES

The terrible conditions in Germany that I described on page 110 attracted international attention. Several social service agencies in the US did a thriving business selling "CARE" packages for delivery to individuals in Germany. (CARE = Cooperative for American Relief to Everywhere) The US Post Office reduced parcel post rates to Germany to $.22/lb to encourage the shipment of "CARE" packages.

As a sideline, Eleanor and I went into the "CARE" packaging business. Through Eleanor's father, we were able to buy staples wholesale. I bought a canning machine and a supply of cans, so we could can all bulk staples. We had no plastics at the time, and cans were the lightest air and water tight containers available. Our canning machine attached the tops of the cans with a professional seal.

One side of our living room was lined with barrels and containers with packaged or canned staples. To prepare a package, we just had to go down the line and put a unit from each container in our package. In this manner we processed sugar, salt, powdered milk and potatoes, lard, salami, coffee, tea, chocolate, flour, dried fruit, and what nots.

All of our pocket money went to finance this project for two years. It was a small gesture in saying thanks to all the friends who had been so kind to me while I was in Germany.

The impact of a "CARE" package with its supplies of simple staples is impossible to appreciate by people who did not endure the deprivation of the terrible two years in Germany. While studying in Berlin, I bought my books at a bookstore near the University and established a nice relationship with the store owner. During the crisis, I sent him a "CARE" package. Many years later, I visited Berlin and thought I would go into the store and say hello. The shopkeeper I had known had died, but the business now was being run by his son. He remembered the "CARE" package, and fell all over himself telling me how good it had been. He offered to give me any book in the store. He introduced me to his younger sister, who was working in the back office. She just looked at her brother, she could not imagine what hewas talking about. She had been too young during the shortages. A "CARE" package had no meaning for her.

I am glad I could help when I had an opportunity to do so.

FUN AND GAMES AT THE MATURITY EXAMINATIONS

The maturity examinations held at the Neuburg Technical School in Freiburg, March 1934, were the most incredible, unscrupulous, and tragic in the history of all Europe. I would not have missed them for anything.

The local law provides that maturity examinations be conducted by a Board of your teachers acting under a Chairman who has to be a senior professor in another city. Most examinations are oral and cover the material presented in the last three years of the upper grades. Formal dress is required, but students just wear their best suits.

The customary procedure is for members of the Board (the teachers) to conduct the examination of their own students and to recommend grades. The function of the chairman is to preside at the examination, to assure an orderly procedure, to assure that the Board members do their jobs properly, and to resolve disputes. The entire Board votes on all grades awarded. Our examination started out differently, because of the personality of the Chairman.

The Chairman of the Board was Dr. Klein, a senior professor of physics in a secondary school in Karlsruhe, and also the Chief Judge of the Nazi Party Court System for Southwestern Germany. He appeared in his resplendent brown senior officers uniform, breast loaded down with medals. In no time at all, he had the rest of the Board (our teachers) completely intimidated. They huddled defensively in their morning coats and white ties in the back of the room, while Klein dominated the front.

The "A" class was scheduled to be examined in the first week of March, the "B" class in the second week.

The examination started on schedule. The first student was a high ranking leader in the Hitler Youth who had demonstrated unusual leadership qualities. He could not answer the first question. After half a day of intensive questioning, he had not been able to answer any question Klein had asked, on any subject. Klein excused the student and postponed his decision.

The performance of the second student was the same as the first one. And the third.

It became obvious that the examination could not be concluded in one week. The "B" class was told that their examination had been postponed.

Every student in the "A" class was examined for about half a day and could not answer any questions on any subject. At the end of the examination Klein flunked the whole class.

The "A" class revolted. They broke up the furniture in their classroom and set if on fire. The fire department put out the fire, the police department cleared the building and stopped all traffic within three blocks around the school.

The boys in the "A" class, as leaders in the Hitler Youth, commanded numerous squads of semi-military Hitler Youth in the city and they were looked upon as serious threat. Fighting in the streets between Hitler Youth and the police would be a national disaster. The school authorities and the police were thoroughly scared.

Two weeks later, in a heavily guarded school, the examination of the "B" class started. The atmosphere was tense. Our teachers huddled in the back of the room, in their morning coats and white ties, scared like a bunch of sheep.   Klein, standing majestically at the front of the room, watching everything very carefully, could not completely hide his fear and nervousness.

Klein announced: "We'll start the examination with mathematics. I will take students in alphabetical order. The first name on the list is: COUTINHO."

I walk to the front of the room. I try mentally to ignore his uniform. He has clear blue eyes. skimpy blond hair, his face not really unfriendly. He looks like he is more scared than I am, I have my US Passport.

Klein says: "I see you come from America !"
"Yes, sir."
"How do you like it here?"
"Its been great, sir. So far."
"H'mm. I can examine you on anything
   you have had in the past three years."
"Yes Sir, I am aware of that."
"Good. I'll give you a break. I'll let you pick a subject !"
"That's not a break, sir. With my luck,
   I always put my foot in it. You pick a subject, sir."
"H'mm. Can you derive the equations
   for compound interest?"
"No, sir. We studied that a long time ago, sir."
"What if I help you ?"
"That depends on how good your help is, sir."
"Young man, you will find no fault with my help !"
   He gives me a small hint.

The hint triggers my memory. I went to the blackboard, picked up a piece of chalk, and within the next five minutes, completely covered the blackboard with equations, just like they are in the book. The room was so quite, you could have heard a pin drop, only the chalk squeaked. I finished, put the chalk down and looked up. Klein looked like he had never seen a performance like this before, he was stunned. His mouth was still open. Finally he said:

"My help was pretty good, wasn't it ?"

"Yes, sir. Adequate."

"Sit down ! I'll call on you later !"

The ice was broken ! The teachers in the back of the room were all laughing !

The rest of the examination proceeded in an orderly manner. As the mathematics test continued, when a student did not know the answer to his question, Klein would turn and ask me. In every case, I was able to answer the question correctly. After seven such additional questions on various subjects, he said I had answered enough questions and he would give me an "A."

I hit the limelight again in the German test which included the writing of a four hour composition. I requested that I be allowed to write my composition in the Latin script instead of the German. My request was turned down and I was told, that if I wanted a German diploma, I would have to comply with all requirements. This put me at a handicap compared to boys who had grown up with the German script. For me, the German script was much more difficult to write than the Latin. I could see no significance in the German script that was derived from Middle German that had been dead for centuries, and that separated Germans from all other civilized peoples who wrote with Latin script. I was a little upset, and in my determination to show them, I sat down and wrote my composition very, very carefully in German script.

The result was sensational ! Nobody could find any fault with my composition, it satisfied all requirements. This had never been done before. I got an "A" in German !   In Germany, nobody gets "A" in German !   Today, when I go back to Freiburg for a visit, everybody still brings this up. I did the impossible!   IN GERMAN SCRIPT !

In English I got a "B" because my American accent was not acceptable to the teacher who taught what he believed to be "high" English.

The examination of the "B" class was concluded on time and with good feelings on the part of Klein and everybody else. Everybody had passed. The graduation exercise was scheduled to take place in two weeks.

In the meantime, the "A" class may have flunked academically, but they were not stupid. They had good political pull, and knew how to use it. Although Klein and the Director of the Neuburg Technical School had senior status and tenure, they were fired by the State Secretary of Education. All students in the "A" class were awarded their maturity certificates. As head of the class, I was supposed to give the address at the graduation ceremony. A boy from the   "A" class was selected for this honor. The "A" class had won on all fronts.

The place was still in turmoil. The local authorities, who could not conceive that the "A" class had won and who did not have the political sophistication of the "A" class, were still living in terror of a worst case scenario. They were convinced that the "B" class would be outraged because the "A" class received their certificates, and in their anger would join with the "A" class and use their resources of semi military Hitler Youth squads to cause some real trouble. They were having vivid nightmares. The neighborhood was overrun with fire department and police personnel. They were really scared. But nothing happened; the "A" class had already achieved everything it wanted !

At the graduation ceremony, a plain clothes policeman sat in back of each graduate. I sat in the front row at the center aisle and could be seen by all the people that could see down the aisle. During the German National Anthem and the Nazi "Horst Wessel" song, everybody was supposed to stand and render the Nazi salute. I remained seated. The names of the graduates were announced, but diplomas were not handed out, we were told to pick them up at school the following week.

At the close of the ceremony, we were immediately escorted out of the building by the policemen who sat in the back of us. Outside, many people came up to me, shook hands, and told me I was right to have remained seated during the Nazi songs.

After the war, Klein found himself in jail, jobless. penniless, all pension and property confiscated, facing a Denazification Board. He appealed to Dr Karl Person for help. Karl wrote me that Klein had not been a true Nazi, that he had just gone along like most people. He had basically been a good man. He suggested that I write a letter to the Board, stating that Klein had conducted our examination in an orderly manner. He said such a letter would be recognized by the Board and would help Klein. I wrote such a letter immediately. It arrived a day after Klein had died in jail.

The members of the "A" class who survived the war returned to Freiburg and were denazified. They met in a reunion with the members of the "B" class, where everybody was accounted for. They all became hardworking, productive, good citizens of Freiburg.

I have a festive booklet published on occasion of the 50th anniversary of the Neuburg Technical School, 1907-1957. It lists all of the graduates by class. The 1933-34 class is missing. Max went to the school to investigate. He was told something about the loss of records because of war damage. Max pointed our that there still were a number of graduates of the 1933-34 class in Freiburg who could supply the missing data. Nobody was interested.

As far as the official record is concerned, the class of 1933-34 at the Neuburg Technical School never existed.

SHOP   WORK

Technical universities in Germany require one year of shop work for graduation, six months of which have to be completed before the start of the second semester.   The universities have an agreement with suitable firms that offer an approved program of shop work to technical university students.   A student may work as much as a month in any one department, but not less than two weeks.   He must keep a work book describing the work done, and the book must be evaluated and certified by the management, and subsequently evaluated for credit by the university.

I graduated from secondary school in March and the university did not start until October, so I had six months to do the initial part of my shop work. Since I was well established in Freiburg, I decided to do my shop work there, where my friends could help me find a suitable shop.   We found an university-approved plant, B. Raimann GmbH, manufacturers of wood-working machines in St.George, a nearby suburb of Freiburg. The plant employed just over 600 people. It was founded, owned and operated by the Raimann family for well over 100 years. They had a nice display of retired metal working machines that were over 100 years old.

The firm was very paternalistic.   It owned a large parcel of land adjacent to the plant. Any employee was allowed to use about 1/2 acre as a garden. Groups of men combined their adjacent lots to form a good size farm. They rented heavy farming machinery as needed and ran a profitable sideline. Working hours were from 6 am to 2:30 pm to give employees time to work their sidelines. All the men I met there were members of families that had worked there for generations. Later, after I got to know people in the plant, several foremen invited me to their homes. They all had nice new houses with plumbing and all modern conveniences, large vegetable gardens, a couple of pigs and a yard full of chickens. If they were ever unemployed, they could survive nicely on their own.

My first assignment was a month in the foundry where castings are made.   Many parts of a machine are castings. The foundry was an enormous hall, over three stories high, dominated by three huge blast furnaces three stories high along the back of the building.   The furnaces were serviced from a walkway on the second story level in the back. The windows in the room were kept dirty to subdue the light so the men could make better estimates of the temperature and fluidity of the   molten steel, which they did by the color of the liquid steel that varied from bright orange to dull red.

Many machine parts are cast, from small 2-inch levers to the 15 foot housings for large machines. Most castings require some machining, such as removal of the stand-pipes and fillets where the two parts of the mold meet, the drilling of holes, and machining of mating surfaces.

The work in a foundry follows a weekly cycle. On Monday and Tuesday, molds are made. Wednesday, they are set up in position so they can be filled. Thursday, the steel is poured. Friday, the molds are broken open, the castings are cleaned and delivered to the machine shop for further processing. Saturday, the sand and boxes are cleaned and everything made ready for making molds on Monday.

The castings are made by pouring molten steel into a mold. The mold is made by packing sand and binder around a wooden model of the casting. The sand and binder are packed so tight, the mold is as hard as concrete, as it has to be to keep its shape when the heavy molten steel is poured in. The sand is packed tight around the model with a hydraulic jack hammer like the ones you see men using in the street to tear up concrete pavement.

I was issued a jack hammer and told to go pack some molds. A jack hammer does its business at one end, but has to be held at the other end. The handle feels every bit like the hammer. I felt as if every bone in my body was coming loose. It was pure torture. I guess I was expected to quit, but I was being closely watched by a group of young fellows who had grown up operating jack hammers and were just waiting for me to quit so they could have a good laugh. I ground my teeth and vowed to stick it out until I collapsed. Somehow, I survived.

The air in a foundry is laden with coal dust that has a way of getting into your pores. I would come home and take a shower. It would still be early, but I would eat my dinner and go to bed. The next morning, my pajamas and my bed sheets would be black.

On Wednesday, the molds were set up in long rows and attached to sloping troughs that brought the molten steel to the molds. The molds are in two pieces, so the model can be recovered. They have a stand-pipe at a critical location: when the molten steel appears in the stand-pipe, the mold is completely filled.

Thursday was pouring day. The furnaces were rather fussy devices, as are all high temperature tools. The loading consisted of about half scrap steel of unknown composition. Samples of the molten steel were taken and analyzed as soon as the steel melted. The composition was never just right. It took several wheel-barrels full of rocks from the various piles behind the foundry to attain the desired composition. It was giant-scale chemistry.

Spiking a furnace was a spectacular sight, creating a huge ball of bright sparks reaching all the way up to the ceiling. The molten steel, radiating luminous bright orange, would gush out into a giant movable cauldron. The cauldron was mounted on hinges so it could be tipped to pour a controlled molten steel flow into the trough that fed the molds.

After the excitement of pouring the steel, and letting it cool off, the molds were disassembled and the castings cleaned. They were then routed to the machine shop where the stand-pipes were cut off and other machine operations done as necessary. On Monday, we would start making molds again, for the pouring next Thursday.

After my month in the foundry, I was assigned to the machine shop and had an opportunity to observe various types of machine operations. A hallowed tradition among German machinists is that each man be required during his training to make a perfect steel cube by hand. I was given a shapeless piece of steel and a hand file and told to make a perfect cube. At first, I went to work full of confidence. As the days went by, the resistance of the steel was stronger than my persistence. At the end of my time, my block did not even resemble a cube, much less a perfect one.

Next, I was assigned to the blacksmith's shop. The "shop" was a shed, along the back of a building, open to the elements on the other side. The forges were up against the building, radiating intense heat. On my first hour in the shop, standing between the intense heat from the forge and the normal temperature of the Freiburg climate, I immediately developed the worst cold in my life.

The blacksmith was a friendly, sympathetic man. When drunk, he was an amazingly proficient artist;   he could make the most complicated part by eye within 1/16 inch of the requirement. When sober, he could not even hit the anvil with his hammer.

He had one side of his forge lined with bottles of beer, warming them up. He only drank hot beer. He introduced me to hot beer to cure my cold. I can't say that it cured my cold, but it sure did make me feel much better, able to stay at work and come back the next day.

A blacksmith makes parts out of bar stock, in a fraction of the time that it would take to machine them. At the time, my blacksmith was working on an order of rims for the 2-foot flywheel on the company's industrial bandsaw. The rims had to be almost perfectly round. It must have taken a great deal of skill to make them, but watching him, there was nothing to it. In addition to the rims, there was a steady stream of special jobs.   It was on these that his inventiveness showed that he could just about make anything. He had me hammer out a few pieces, but I made my usual mess. The steel would not stay hot long enough for me to finish my job. You have to be very fast, and every blow has to be hard and right.

Most of the time I held the blacksmith's work for him, and he did the hammering. This saved him some time, which we then spent in drinking another bottle of beer while he told me some stories. He got paid a basic wage for which he was expected to make a certain number of parts. If he made more, his pay went up, by a maximum of 25%. He always made his maximum pay. Almost everybody in the plant made their maximum pay. This incentive payment plan was the same as the one that they had at the Raimann plant in Freiburg.

After I got over my cold, he still kept me on a diet of hot beer. It helped me to survive the most severe environment to which I had ever been exposed.

My next assignment was the the wood working shop where they made the models of castings used for making molds. Packing the sand around the model is rather rough and the wood models do not last long. They have to be replaced periodically.

The wood working shop was almost as frustrating as trying to make a perfect steel cube. Wood is easier to work. I was given little jobs and managed to louse them all up. However, the men were all good natured about it. They turned out beautiful work.

My last assignment was in assembly. I helped a man assemble bandsaws, one of the main products of the company. Here I was actually of some assistance and helped him save time. So he had time on his hands and took me around the shop and showed me all the other assembly operations that were being done. The biggest machine that they made, and that was the company's pride, was an exclusive design of their own, a so-called "finish and glue machine." This was a monster, some 4 x 4 x 15 feet. At one end you dumped in relatively straight pieces of unfinished logs, about nine inches in diameter and three and a half feet long. The machine automatically processed the logs into finished strips and glued them together into a panel. The panel dimensions had to be preset in the machine, namely, thickness: 1/2 to 1-1/2 inches; width: 12 to 36 inches; and any length up to 15 feet. The finished panels came out of the opposite side, as beautiful finished pieces. As long as I was there, all of these machines that they produced were exported to Russia.

After my six months expired, I submitted my workbook to management for evaluation and certification. To my surprise, they gave me an outstanding recommendation. I had felt rather inadequate, surrounded by men of such superior skills. The management, however, had had other students in the plant before, and I was being compared with a group of my peers.

I had learned a great deal, starting with how a company that is over 100 years old treats its people. The company was still concerned with its employees after working hours. In addition to its garden program, it sponsored a bowling league, a football team, and several singing clubs. One such club was exclusive, it admitted only foremen, and all foremen in the plant belonged. I learned what it takes to make a product, and about the many skills involved. I got a good glimpse of what goes on behind those factory walls. How can I ever forget my jack hammer, my cube, and the hot beer?

When five years later I applied for my first job at Grumman in New York, they required that every engineer coming out of college first work a year in the shop, before being admitted to the engineering department. Coming from a foreign university, I was extensively interviewed, including questions about my shop work. I was then admitted directly into the engineering department. Grumman gave me full credit for my German shop experience.

I left Raimann with a lot of good feeling. Now it was time to say good-bye to my friends, get on my motorcycle and head for Berlin..

PROFESSIONAL EDUCATION
TECHNICAL UNIVERSITY OF
BERLIN

THE FOREIGN STUDENTS' HOUSE

Driving into Berlin, at that time the fourth largest city in the world, on a dark October evening, after a long ride from Freiburg on a motorcycle, the uppermost thing on my mind was finding a place to sleep. I had made a reservation at the Foreign Students' House, a dormitory described in a university bulletin which I had.

The place was nice. The rooms were large and airy, and there were several lounges for social purposes. No food was available, but that was not necessary as there were several small and attractive eating places along every block in that central part of Berlin at that time.

Location was a small problem. The House was on the campus of the University of Berlin, which was a 10 minute bus ride from the Technical University. However, the busses ran every few minutes, and I decided that the sociability at the House with the other foreign students was worth the trouble of the bus trip. There were girl students there. I decided to stay there for my first year.

My stay at the Foreign Students House provided a wonderful introduction to the city of Berlin. It would have been impossible for me to learn as much about the city if it had not been for the advice and companionship of my fellow foreign students at the House.

PETER WALSER

Students were assigned two to a room in order of registration. My room mate was Peter Walser from Chur, Switzerland. Peter was a Calvinist and in his last year of the study of Theology. He came from a family of Calvinist ministers. His grandfather had been the Dean of the School of Theology at the University of Geneva, and had spent his last university year in Berlin studying Theology. The high point of his year in Berlin was when he saw Bismarck. Peter was going to have to be satisfied if he saw Hitler. Peter's father was the Protestant Pastor in Chur, and also had spent his last university year in Berlin.

Peter was a well rounded person and we had many things in common. He was especially glad that I was a Catholic as he wanted to learn as much as possible about the Catholic faith. As our first project, we decided to compare the Catholic and Protestant Bibles. He had a Protestant one and I had an authorized Catholic one. We took turns reading to each other portions of the Bible until we had covered the entire book. Our conclusion: both books are identical, except that the Catholic version is annotated to explain the meaning of some words.

Our next project was an attempt to determine the difference between the Calvinist and Catholic faiths.

After winning its independence from Austria almost 800 years ago, Switzerland had no princes who imposed their religion on their subjects, it was the only country in Europe with religious freedom. The theologians had a ball. The Calvinists were one of the larger groups to come out of this movement.

It was during the Renaissance that the glories of Roman and Greek literature were rediscovered and enthusiastically analyzed and accepted, including the Greek mathematical concept of perfection. The theologians applied this concept to the Hebrew/Christian concept of "God, the Father" and to the Christian doctrine of salvation.

In the Calvinist view, Jesus Christ elected to save mankind through his passion and death on the cross. This was God's ultimate, perfect gift of love and salvation for mankind, a gift so infinitely great that any act of man in comparison is insignificant and meaningless. The only response open to man is to believe and accept this gift. If a man truly believes that Jesus Christ suffered and died to save his soul, he will be incapable of doing evil.

In the older Catholic doctrine, the Hebrew/ Christian concept of God is that of a caring and loving Father. Nobody said that He was perfect. The best that can be said about His creations is that they work. There is a difference between a thing that works, and one that is perfect. The concepts are often confused.

God is an immaterial spirit. A spirit is a real thing that man cannot visualize. There are many useful things in our lives that we cannot visualize, but we give them a name and forget that we do not understand them. In mathematics, the square root of minus one is such an entity. We call it "i" and it becomes a very useful number. We also know how to make and use electricity, but don't know what it is. It is the same thing with spirits. God, souls, angels and devils are all real.

Before God created man, he created other spirits who he endowed with some of his own characteristics, including a free will. Many of these spirits decided to serve God, to follow His will. These spirits we call angels. Other spirits decided it was more fun to do evil. These spirits we call devils. They roam the universe, and especially our world, tempting men to do evil, so they will gain control of their souls when they die.

When God created man, he gave him an immortal soul and endowed him with a free will. Except for Jesus and his mother Mary, no man is perfect. There are devils always tempting all of us, and we all fall sometimes to a lesser or a greater extent.

Jesus Christ endured His passion and died on the cross to atone for the sins of man, since with these sins on his record, his soul could not be admitted to the companionship of God. With his free will, man must decide for himself between good and evil. To participate in the sacrifice of Jesus, an individual man must repent his sins, avoid evil, and do good works. Christ's sacrifice opened the door for redemption which allows a man's soul to enter the companionship of God when he dies. The Catholic Church recognizes as saints those individuals who have performed exceptional good works.

Peter and I were quite proud of these analyses.

One of Peter's classes was being taught by the foremost Catholic theologian in Europe. Peter was enthusiastic about the lectures, and took me along to two of them. I could not understand what the man was saying. Peter tried to explain, but finally gave up. So much for theology.

Another project we undertook to broaden Peter's experience was to visit churches of different faiths. Berlin is such a large city, it has sizable communities of peoples of different nationalities and religions. We were always recognized as students at such churches, and graciously welcomed. To my surprise, I generally recognized fellow students from the Technical University participating in the services, sometimes even preaching in a language I could not understand.

I later visited Peter during a summer vacation at his home in Chur. Chur is the last stop on the Swiss Railroad, the highest station in Europe. It is a beautiful resort city. In Roman times it was a Roman Province with special privileges. Because of travel difficulties, the Roman Governor had the authority to appoint his own successor. There was a Roman Governor in Chur, governing as the personal representative of the Emperor of Rome, 500 years after the fall of the Roman Empire. The area has its own language, Romansch, a derivative of Latin, Switzerland's fourth language. Latin is still the spoken language in some of the remote valleys of the area.

The area is quite rugged. Peter showed me two wild mountain streams, the White Rhein and the Red Rhein, and where they merged into the Rhein River. The Catholic cathedral is perched on the highest hill in Chur, dominating the city. As Peter was showing me around, I noticed the Bishop's name on a confessional, and remarked to Peter that I thought that was rather unusual. He answered: "Why not, the Bishop is a priest!" I said to myself: "Another piece of Swiss wisdom. A bishop is a priest first, and a Church administrator second."

One of the glories of Berlin is its museums. Within a few minutes walk from our Students' House, there is an island in the Spree River. All buildings on the island are museums, it is called Museum Island.

The Germans started to search for archeological antiquities at least fifty years before anybody else. They sent teams to south eastern Europe and the Middle East to scour and dig for antiquities long before there were any restrictions on the removal of such treasures from their home countries.

In one of the museums of Berlin there is a small-sized model of the ancient Greek city of Pergamon with a beautiful white marble temple on a hill dominating the city. The Germans dismantled this temple which is in perfect condition, and rebuilt it in Berlin. They built an attractive shielding structure around the temple, with a glass ceiling to admit daylight. The effect is breathtaking. There is nothing like it in the World.

Another unique experience is the entrance to the ancient city of Babylon. To reach the main gate, you have to walk about 50 feet down this 15 foot wide path, bordered on both sides by 20 foot high walls of two foot square lucent blue tiles. On the top of the walls, there are provisions for guards to watch you and your belongings as you walk along this entrance way, and to decide whether or not you are a safe person to admit to Babylon. (This exhibit was destroyed in the war.)

One of the most beautiful items in the Berlin Museums is the large life-size, 3500 year old bust of Queen Nofreteta of Egypt. She was the wife and co-worker of King Amenophis IV (Echnaton). She took an active part in the formulation of royal policy. Echnaton, as all kings of Egypt, was considered a god. He thought a lot about this, and made religion a serious topic of discussion at his court. He finally came to the conclusion, that he was not a god, that he was no different from any other man. He also decided, that there had to be a god, and that there could only be one god. Echnaton concluded that that one god had to be the sun, since all life depended on the sun. He started a new religion to worship the sun. This was the first time in recorded history that man recognized the existence of one god.

The Egyptian priesthood practiced a multi-god religion and opposed Echnaton with considerable power. Nofreteta had seven daughters, but no sons. When Echnaton died without a son, the priests practically disposed of his dynasty. However, the religion of the one god survived underground and spread beyond the borders of

Egypt. It is speculated that it inspired Abraham. The historical timing and the geographical proximity of Egypt and Judea would support this possibility.

After Peter went home, I visited the museums with other fellow students. In our mathematics exercise class, every two students were paired to help each other out with our problems. I was paired with a Persian student. His father was head of the Persian railroads. I went with him to visit the Persian Museum. We found a life-size section of a Persian palace on exhibit, including several rooms. The walls and ceilings were completely covered with beautiful inlayed woods of different colors. My friend said that was exactly what his house and rooms in Persia looked like.

Together with New York, London, and Paris, Berlin is one of the few cities of the world that had an entertainment industry. There was a three-ring circus that performed the year round, except during the summer months when it was on tour. There was a zoo and an aquarium, two opera houses and 17 theaters. In the entertainment district, there was no curfew. The bars, movies, casinos, restaurants, cafes, night clubs, dance halls, and cabarets, all jammed one next to the other, were always open 24 hours a day. The thick crowds of people on the street were thickest at three to four am. I imagine that today some of this has changed. People now have television.

The cabarets were famous for their disparaging jokes about the public authorities. They provided entertainment for the entire city. It was said that even Hitler was not sure that he had a firm grip on power until the cabarets started to make fun of him.

I had a students ticket that provided me with a performance a month at a different theater (one opera) for ten months.

Berlin had a number of world class fancy department stores, but I hardly ever had occasion to go near them.

REGISTRATION

The day after I arrived in Berlin, I went to the Technical University to register. My papers were all in order. I told them I wanted to study "statics," as Dr. Dornier in Friedrichshafen had advised me. I was told "statics" is not a field of study. It is part of a "subject" such as "airplane design." I said, OK, I'll study "airplane design." They said, "airplane design" is a third year "subject." Incoming students have to register in a "course" such as "aeronautical engineering". I compromised and registered as a student in a course in "aeronautical engineering." I received the number A/216.

In examining my papers, they found that I had had a lot of chemistry. They said it was enough and gave me credit for

Berlin Technical University, Main Building
Before substantial damage in World War II

chemistry.   Later I found out that chemistry was the only class that had girls.

MATRICULATION

The Matriculation ceremony at European universities is the most festive occasion of the Year. A great hall is bursting full of people, there is music, an academic procession with professors in colorful academic robes, speeches, ... the works. Berlin, on the other hand, prides itself on its spartan procedures. There is no assembly, no music, no robes.

Incoming students were ushered 20 at a time into the Office of the Rector and lined up. The Rector went down the line and asked each student his name, where he came from, what he was going to study, and a couple of other trivialities. Then he shook hands and welcomed the student to the University and told him if he ever had any trouble whatsoever, or otherwise needed any help, the first thing he should do was come and see him, his door was always open for us. We were then, fully matriculated, ushered out into the hall. As long as I was in Berlin, I never saw the Rector again.

DEPARTMENT OF NAVAL ARCHITECTURE, MARINE ENGINEERING, AND AERONAUTICAL ENGINEERING

Aeronautical Engineering was a new course at the University. It had been organized by the professors of Naval Architecture who applied their knowledge of hydrodynamics of ships to the aerodynamics of airships and aircraft. They were a tight knit little group that had developed their traditions and practices at the Academy of Naval Architecture a long time before the Academy was incorporated into the Technical University about a hundred years ago. After incorporation, they retained their traditions and practices to accommodate the special needs of students of Naval Architecture. Ships have long hulls, and students learning to design ships are provided with long 12 foot drafting tables and other equipment that students cannot be expected to provide at their own expense, such as splines, duck weights and long straight edges. Splines are long 1/2 inch high strips of wood, varying in thickness from 1/16 to 1/4 inch, that can be bent to into a long, fair curve. A duck weight is a heavy piece of lead with a hook on it to keep the bent splines in place. A ten foot, three inch wide and a quarter .inch thick graduated steel straight edge is used to draw a long straight line and mark off distances along the line.

To provide facilities for design instruction, the Department had a number of its own drafting rooms with 20 to 25 students assigned to each room. The students for each room were carefully selected to yield a good mixture of junior and senior students. The administration of the rooms was provided by a fraternity, the "Spline," ("Latte" in German), that assigned students to rooms, patrolled the rooms, and was responsible for order and security. Use of the rooms and the equipment in them was necessary to do the design problems, there was no way to study Naval Architecture, Marine Engineering or Aeronautical Engineering unless you were a member of the "Spline."

The drafting room was our work place. All students would arrive about eight am, put on their white coats, and stay until after five. We would leave (without our white coats) to go to classes, laboratory exercises, lunch, and personal business, otherwise we were in our white coats at our drafting tables. Outside the drafting rooms, we always wore suits and ties. The days were not long enough for us to do all our work in the drafting room, so we usually had to take some home with us. I was assigned to Room H 217.

The problems of the Naval architects were too large to be removed from the long drafting tables, so the professors would come to the room to review progress. Whenever that happened, all the students in the room would gather around the table of the reviewee, listen in on the conversation, and kibitz, given a chance. Sometimes we could get the professor to discuss other subjects of interest.

The system gave the younger students some insight into what the older students were doing, and a better understanding of why they were required to take the basic courses they were taking.

THE ENGINEERING CURRICULUM

In the first half of the twentieth century, the engineering community organized itself into five branches: civil, electrical, mechanical, chemical, and mining/metallurgical. Within each branch, there are specialties such as design, analysis, manufacturing, materials handling, operations, and similar functions.

With the increase in technical knowledge, and especially with the advent of the computer, engineering procedures in the second half of the twentieth century underwent a refinement driven by such new specialties as electronics, quality control, system safety, human factors, dynamics, logistics, space technology, and other similar high technology disciplines.

If you select a branch of engineering and a specialty, and list for that specialty the scholastic disciplines required, you will get a short list of top courses, each one at the top of a diagram of courses that looks like a Christmas tree. Each course in the diagram is a prerequisite for a course above it, and itself will require a number of courses beneath it. This study plan has no give, it is not a matter of opinion. All courses listed are prerequisites for higher level courses.

The courses listed for a specialty will almost always consume all the available time, there is little time left over for electives. Such required courses will be about the same in every engineering school in the world. In the above breakdown of the engineering profession, the Berlin Department of Naval Architecture, Marine Engineering, and Aeronautical Engineering is a school of mechanical engineering, design and analysis.

THE   STUDENTS

Because of the limited number of spaces available in the Department's drafting rooms, incoming students could be carefully selected. The "Spline" exercised this responsibility for accepting students as part of their job of assigning drafting tables. The result was that students of the Department were considered an elite among the university community.

Most students were sons of officers in the German Navy and intended to become German Naval officers themselves. German military schools are all post graduate schools, they do not have academies like the American West Point or Annapolis. Officer candidates come from the regular university system

The university requirement for a year's shop work was revised for students of Naval Architecture and Marine Engineering to "practice" for at least six months at sea. As a result, these students had been all over the world, and most had been in the United States. Some had spent more time in New York and knew more about the city than I did. They were very well informed on international affairs.

As a prerequisite for attendance at a German university, students had to be members of a Nazi organization. The members of the "Spline" belonged to, and were leaders of, an elite SS organization stationed at the University. The unit had a command car at its disposal, one with a siren and blinking red light. Family cars were still scarce in those days, and none of the students were good drivers. They were really concerned about driving in Berlin traffic. So when they had to go somewhere, they just put on the siren and red light, and that stopped traffic two blocks ahead of them and cleared the way.

German universities are self-governing bodies, in particular, local police have no jurisdiction on a university campus. In case of disturbances, rectors have traditionally called on reliable fraternities for police duties. In such cases in Berlin, the Rector called on the "Spline" for help. The "Spline" felt it had to be ready to assist the Rector in case of demonstrations. It organized squads of five big guys to hold one of our heavy steel straight edges and use it as a ramming rod when charging an opponent. There had been numerous demonstrations at the University before Hitler, and experience showed that four or five such squads abreast charging at a body of demonstrators quickly broke up the crowd and effectively disbursed it. That heavy steel straight edge proved to be a wicked weapon. This status, plus our separate drafting rooms and white coats, did much to reinforce our "elite" standing on campus.

At 3:30 every afternoon, it was coffee time. We stopped working and gathered around a corner table to solve the world's problems. One subject that came up repeatedly was: How realistic is our training? We admitted that the exercises taught us how to think, but nobody believed that the approach to problems and the exercises had any relationship to the way things were done in industry, or that the problems themselves were realistic. I remember these discussions well, because when I started my first job at Grumman Aerospace in Bethpage, New York, the engineering department operated almost exactly like the Berlin drafting rooms, and the work was very similar to the problems we had to do. Within my first hour at Grumman, I felt immediately at home.

Another popular subject at coffee break was politics. I was so fully Germanized that nobody considered me a foreigner and my presence in no way inhibited the discussions. Everybody, except me, hated Hitler fiercely. I was the only one who on occasion approved something he did. I remember one discussion on Hitler's plan for national automobile expressways. I thought it was a good idea. Everybody else was dead set against it, because Hitler proposed the idea.

We all knew that a war was coming. They knew that they would have to fight, and that many of them would die. They knew the strength of Germany's adversaries. Yet, although they personally opposed Hitler, they looked forward to serving in the military and they worked hard at their para-military SS duties. This incongruity reminded me of "The Charge of the Light Brigade," the Noble six hundred, see page 131.

It was a great experience to work in a Berlin drafting room. I was the only American at the Technical University. There were only six others at the University of Berlin, we all met for Thanksgiving Dinner at the US Embassy. I was the only American ever to have

THE CHARGE OF THE LIGHT BRIGADE
By Alfred Tennyson

THE CHARGE OF THE LIGHT BRIGADE
Alfred Tennyson

Half a league, half a league,
Half a league onward,
All in the valley of Death
    Rode the six hundred
"Forward the Light Brigade!
Charge for the guns!" he said
Into the valley of Death
    Rode the six hundred

"Forward, the Light Brigade!"
Was there a man dismayed?
Not though the soldier knew
    Some one had blundered
Theirs not to make reply,
Theirs not to reason why,
Theirs but to do and die
Into the valley of Death
    Rode the six hundred

Cannon to right of them,
Cannon to left of them,
Cannon in front of them
    Volleyed and thundered,
Stormed at with shot and shell,
Boldly they rode and well,
Into the jaws of Death,
Into the mouth of hell
    Rode the six hundred

Flashed all their sabres bare,
Flashed as they turned in air
Sabring the gunners there,
Charging an army, while
    All the world wondered

Plunged in the battery-smoke
Right through the line they broke;
Cossack and Russian
Reeled from the sabre stroke
    Shattered and sundered
Then they rode back, but not,
    Not the six hundred

Cannon to right of them,
Cannon to left of them,
Cannon behind them
    Volleyed and thundered,
Stormed at with shot and shell,
While horse and hero fell,
They that had fought so well
Came through the jaws of Death,
Back from the mouth of hell,
All that was left of them,
    Left of six hundred

When can their glory fade?
Oh, the wild charge they made!
    All the world wondered
Honor the charge they made!
Honor the Light Brigade,
    Noble six hundred!

been a member of the "Spline." In the next few subchapters, I will refer to some of my courses and describe the lasting impression they made on me.

MATHEMATICS AND PHYSICS

My major concerns during my first two years were mathematics and physics.   There were three mathematics teaching activities; lectures, exercises, and a short, intensive review course just before the final examination.

The University enrollment was a little over 3000, 1000 of which were foreigners. The annual registration was about 1000. All of these new registrants were required to take mathematics. The auditorium had 600 seats. They were all taken 30 minutes before the lecture started. When the lecture began, all aisles were packed with standing students. It was hard to hear and understand the professor, and you could not ask questions.

You did not have to go to the lectures, no attendance was taken. To get credit for the course, you either had to pass three quizzes during the term, or a more difficult quiz at the end of the term, or a very difficult exam at the end of two years. I figured that my best chances would be to attend classes regularly and take the three quizzes during the term. Unfortunately almost everyone else thought so too, and everything was very crowded.

To make things worse, in typical Berlin fashion, almost all the lectures were over my head. The best I could do was to take notes and come back to my drafting room and have an older student explain it to me. I was not the only one with this problem, nearly everyone had it, and in all subjects.

Then we had math exercises twice a week. We met in groups of twenty students, and they allowed each two to work together. The instructor distributed sheets with ten problems. He went around the room to explain the problems and how to solve them. He tried to make sure that everybody understood each problem. These sessions were excellent and really helped me understand the lectures and pass the quizzes.

Physics was a little better than mathematics. We had a beautiful new physics building, and the auditorium had seats for everyone. Albert Einstein was one of the professors in the Physics Department, but at that time his star had not yet risen, and he was just another professor. My professor was Dr. Heinrich Hertz, the nephew of the famous *Gustav Hertz,* the former University professor who a generation ago gave his name to the engineering dimension "one hertz equals one cycle per second."

Physics instruction is based on the demonstration of controlled experiments.   They had a spotlight focused on the experiment such that the shadow was displayed on a huge screen. The equipment was so designed that you could see in the shadow all the moving elements of the experiment on the screen.   You could also see and hear the professor. It was an an ingenious arrangement and a good course in physics.

To get credit for the course, you had to go to the laboratory and perform 20 experiments per term.   They had small booths with everything set up and a short label of instructions, such as "Measure the specific weight of the sample." They gave you three hours. Otherwise nobody would talk to to you or explain anything.   You were expected to know the layout, the test procedure, and what to do. The experiments all involved the measurement of a physical characteristic. You had to come up with a number at the end of your experiment. You either had the right number and could go home, or your number was wrong, and you had to come back and do the experiment over until you got it right.

I got the right number on all my experiments on the first try, but most other students did not, and many found the experience very difficult and trying.

Mathematics and physics influenced my thinking for the rest of my life. Mathematics is the only science that is not based on empirical data. The physics laboratory made me aware of what it is that I really know, and what is an assumption or a matter of faith. It gave me meaning to the maxim: "You know what you can measure."

ELEMENTS OF DESIGN

The first part of this course was straight forward, we were taught how to prepare engineering drawings. Then we were each assigned a small device and asked to prepare two drawings; a final assembly drawing with a bill of material and notes, and a manufacturing drawing of a part of the device. My assignment was to design an automobile jack.

Design instruction is different from instruction in other disciplines, much more student participation is required. In design you start with a blank sheet of paper on your drawing table and on your own, you find out all you can about the device you were told to design. Then you draw everything you know about the device as a proposal on your sheet of paper. You analyze if for strength, performance, handling. appearance, and other qualities it should have. After you have given it your best efforts, you take it to class where the professor and your fellow students will subject your proposal to a thorough critique. They will offer you many helpful suggestions for improvements. The professor will summarize all suggestions that have merit for you to take back with you to your drawing table for consideration.

Back at your drawing table, you reanalyze your design in light of all these helpful suggestions and incorporate all the improvements that fit. Sometimes you will just have to start all over again with a new clean blank sheet. When you have done your best, you take your new design proposal back to class and repeat the procedure. Eventually, after several such cycles, the professor will decide that your design is good enough and will accept it. That will give you credit for the course.   I went through this procedure with the design of my automobile jack. Our drafting room kept a library of the works of all former students. I found there the design of an old jack. I copied some of the design features. The older students in my drafting room were also of great help. There was competition between drafting rooms as to who could produce the best designs, and I was as much the representative of my drafting room as I was working on my own project. I was quite proud of my final assembly drawing. The note called for red paint on the body and black on the handle. I also learned a great deal critiquing the work of other students.

Although Berlin invested a lot of time in design instruction, the result was not perfect. One of the students in our drafting room was assigned the task of designing a clock. He searched through our library and found a clock somebody had designed years ago. Checking the mechanism carefully, he found that the clock ran backwards.

Another imaginative Greek student in the Chemistry Department received high praise because he developed a new compound. A few years after he left, another student checking his work found that every chemical experiment had been rigged, and the new compound was a fake. The University authorities would have withdrawn his diploma, but he was already beyond German jurisdiction. I thought that he had demonstrated extraordinary mastery of the subject, to have hoodwinked all his professors, and should receive a metal.

Design is such a difficult subject to teach, there are few schools of design, and few professors. Hence, most design is taught on the job. It takes ten years for a man with a university design background to become a proficient designer, longer if he has no university training. As a result, companies tend to feel that they have a lot invested in their designers and like to keep them on the job.

LINES DRAWINGS

The drawing of a ship's lines required the entire length of our 12 foot long drawing tables. A ship's hull lines drawing defines the dimensions of the inside of the hull in three views, from the side, top, and back. The lines are drawn for cross-sections through the hull, taken at some convenient intervals, such as 10 or 20 feet.

In the shipbuilding industry, the hull lines are enlarged to full size and reproduced on the floor of a large loft. The ships ribs are manufactured on the loft floor, to match the cross-section lines of the ship. To preserve the high accuracy of the lines, the Romans thousands of years ago engraved their hull lines on a polished marble slab. All traditions in the shipbuilding industry are very old.

The problem is to locate a point in space on the double curvature of a ship's hull when you only have a two dimensional sheet of paper to work with. To visualize double curvature, take a sheet of paper and bring the top and bottom edges up within a couple of inches apart of each other, leaving the center of the sheet in a graceful bow. Now take the two sides of the sheet at its bottom point, at the center of the bow, and try to bend the two sides together like you did with the first two edges. The paper will not yield. To form a metal sheet into double curvature, you have to stretch it on a die.

In the side view of the lines drawing, the horizontal grid lines are called waterlines, and the vertical grid lines are called stations, measured from some convenient zero point. A lengthwise cross-section through the hull is shown for every width line. In the top view, the width of the hull is shown for every waterline. The back view, against a background grid of waterlines and width lines, the cross-section of the hull is shown for every station.

Any two of these views would be easy to prepare. The problem is the third view, which defines the double curved surface of the hull in space. Every point of the hull line in one view must fall on the hull line on the two other views at the same grid locations. You do it by trial and error. You get one point done, and at first, four or more neighboring points will not go into place. It is a tedious, frustrating job. You wear out several erasers, erase holes in your paper, and start over.

All the students in the drafting room come around to look at your work and offer suggestions. The professor comes by occasionally to check your progress. There is no such thing as a perfect job. When the professor says that your drawing is good enough, you get credit. I had to prepare a lines drawing of an airplane in the best naval architectural tradition. It took me five months, almost full time.

When I first came to Grumman and learned that their first contract had been for Navy floats, I wondered where they had gotten their lines. I investigated and found out that they bought them from a seaplane manufacturer. Later, when the company started to build an airplane, instead of a lines drawing, they first built a small model and tested it in a wind tunnel. They enlarged the dimensions of the model to get the dimensions of the airplane. At that time, airplanes were small enough that this procedure was adequate. In modern times, naval architects have also built models and towing basins, but the scale between models and the real thing is too large to permit reliance on basin test results for design purposes.

At about that time (1935) in the United States, there was a similar problem, namely with automobile fenders, which are double curved surfaces. Every fender was a little different, just enough so that a skilled mechanic required considerable time for initial installation as well as for replacement.

In the 1950's, an engineer in the automobile industry developed a set of second degree mathematical formulas for locating a point on a double curved surface. Such points could now be located with any desired degree of precision. This permitted the design of fair dies, but the fenders were still not interchangeable because the steel contained too many impurities. No two pieces of steel sheet would stretch in the same manner. A great quality control effort, the greatest such effort the world has ever seen, was undertaken in the automobile/steel industries, to produce a homogeneous sheet of steel. The effort was finally successful and it became possible to mass produce interchangeable fenders.

At Grumman, our linesman, Bob Locke, now had his computer do the work and engrave airplane lines full size on a set of large white enameled aluminum sheets. To get the exact dimensions of the outline of an airplane at any station, an engineer places a sheet of vellum over the lines on the respective aluminum sheet and with a sharp pencil, followes the groove of the station he desires.

AERODYNAMICS

Aerodynamics was taught like mathematics. There were lectures, exercise sessions, a small wind tunnel (a larger one was planned), and three quizzes per term to get credit. The professor was Dr. Hoff, who was also the Director of the German Research Institute for Aerodynamics, the German equivalent of the National Advisory Committee on Aeronautics (NACA), of which Col. Charles Lindbergh was Chairman, and which was the forerunner of the National Aeronautics and Space Administration (NASA).

Hoff took a personal interest in each student. He believed that a war was coming and he advised us to obtain a reserve officer's commission while there was still time. He cautioned us to take good care of ourselves. He said that Germany might lose the war, in which case educated young men like ourselves would be sorely needed to rebuild the nation. He himself was trapped in Berlin at the end of the war when the Russians marched in and committed suicide

The exercise session took place once a week for three hours in groups of less that twenty students. There were two monitors. They distributed sheets with ten problems and came around the room to help each student to understand and solve each problem. One of the monitors was Gunter Buchmann, with whom I made friends and who I will discuss below.

AIRPLANE   DESIGN

This was the toughest course at the University. The professor, Dr. Herbert Wagner controlled the admission to his course carefully. He invited potential students to come to his office and take a three hour examination in his conference room to demonstrate that they had the background to understand his lectures. The test was such that students failed on their first two attempts. He would advise them on what to study for the next test, since most of the students who still had the courage to come back, generally passed the test on their third try.

In the Berlin atmosphere, where easy courses were despised and we prided ourselves on doing difficult work,   Wagner's methods were looked upon with deep respect, and his students wore invisible halos.

As a foreigner, I was not entitled to be included in the full initiation ceremony, but Wagner interviewed me for some 30 minutes and then gave me a test which I completed on my first try in some three hours. I was then admitted to his class.

The lectures consisted of load and stability analysis of all types of metal aircraft structures.   Statics was used to determine the distribution of loads in metal aircraft frameworks. This is what Dr. Dornier in Friedrichshafen had in mind when I visited him.   However Wagner went further into associated stability problems, shell design, and elasticity. Most of this material was not yet available in any published book, so I kept a neat notebook. Later, when I was able to continue this work in elasticity at New York University, we had a new book, or rather, a series of three big and heavy new books on The Theory of Elasticity by the Russian Professor Timosenko. The books were published by a Joint Engineering Societies Fund for publishing worthy professional books that had no chance of making a profit and could not be published commercially. To everyone's surprise, these books were an immediate hit in the engineering community and a complete sell out.

To get credit for Wagner's course, you had to complete three exercises, each one taking about three months to complete. You had to lay out a substantial part of an aircraft structure, such as a wing-fuselage intersection, analyze your design and prove that it was safe but not overweight, and prepare a manufacturing drawing of some major detail such as a large fitting. You were free to choose what you wanted to design and suggest it to Wagner. If it was acceptable, he would agree.   One of the problems I selected was the engine attachment structure on an airship. I had to layout a portion of the airship framework and the attaching structure which supported the engine. I finished the job by preparing a manufacturing drawing of the fitting that held the engine on the supporting framework. It took me three months and all the help I could get from the other students in my drafting room. When I was finished, I thought that Dr. Dornier of Friedrichshafen would have been proud of me.

This was the most difficult, but probably also the most useful course I ever took.   Almost everything in the course was closely applicable to the work on my first job at Grumman in New York.

Wagner left the University to join the German war effort. He invented the wire-guided missile, which is still being used today (2000) by the US Army in its most advanced tanks. He was captured by US troops at the end of the war and brought to the US. He was assigned by the Army to work at Grumman and lasted some three weeks. I think Grumman was afraid that he was going to shake up the place and got rid of him. During this time, Eleanor and I had him over at the house for supper. He was a delightful guest.

After Grumman, he went to California as a consultant to the aircraft industry located in that state. As soon as his status as a prisoner of war was lifted, he returned to Germany and became a professor at the University of Aachen.

THE   OIL   LABORATORY

The curriculum required students to take a major laboratory exercise. There was an aeronautical laboratory in the planning stage, so in the meantime they told us to take the mechanical engineering laboratory.
I found out that this laboratory had mainly to do with the properties of steam and the generation of electrical power. I had to take a laboratory, but the properties of steam did not interest me, so I looked for something else.

The Western Nations had cut off part of Hitler's oil supply, and the German Air Force was operating on scarce aviation fuel made from coal. This intrigued me, and I discovered that the process of manufacturing aviation fuel from coal had been developed right here in the Oil Laboratory at the University. I decided it would be far more interesting to take than the mechanical engineering laboratory. I knew that there would be trouble getting in, and that I would have to take an admissions test.

Sometime before all this happened, a Berlin weekly published a series of four excellent articles on the development of oil. I had kept these articles and now studied them carefully to the point that I almost knew them by rote.

My first application for admission to the Oil Laboratory came back with the remark: "Of course not, the Oil Laboratory is only for advanced students of chemistry." With some perseverance, I finally got to Dr. Heinze, the Director of the Laboratory, and told him how much chemistry I had had in Meersburg and Freiburg. He finally agreed to give me an admissions test.

The test, in typical Berlin fashion, was a pleasant two hour chat in the Director's office. Dr. Heinze went right down through the material in my weeklies. He was surprised at my answers. I told him I read a lot. I answered and elaborated on every question. There was no doubt regarding my qualifications.

The laboratory requirement was to perform 20 experiments, each requiring a full day. I decided to dedicate a summer vacation to working full time at the laboratory. It was more relaxed than the physics lab, there were no booths or isolation. I was given an opportunity to study and discuss what each experiment was all about. Other students came around while my tests were in progress and made sure that everything was in order. It was all straight chemistry, there were no miracles. My four years of chemistry in Meersburg and Freiburg gave me all the background I needed.

I kept a neat notebook, recording everything I did. When the summer (as well as the Lab) were over, and I got my reviewed notebook back, it was graded with an "A".

Some 20 years later when the German Air Force began looking for an airplane for its new post war organization, Grumman tried unsuccessfully to sell Germany its F8F Bearcat. A team of military and civilian experts visited Grumman. The civilian experts included two professors from the TU Berlin. Professor Edgar Roessger recognized my name. He told me that I had left a permanent mark on the University. He said that I had been carefully watched by the faculty when I applied for admission to the oil laboratory. I was not expected to pass the admissions test, and when I finally completed the laboratory with an "A," they found it to be unbelievable. They then carefully analyzed the laboratory's program, and decided that it made a fine addition to an aeronautical engineering curriculum. Today, when they have a particularly brilliant student, whom they want to offer an additional challenge, they recommend that he take the Oil Laboratory instead of the aero engineering one. Quite a few students have done this over the past 20 years, and it had worked out very well. However, so far, nobody has completed the Laboratory's program with an "A."

A few weeks after I completed my work at the Laboratory, Hitler came to see the place. It was all very hush-hush; except for the people in the Laboratory, nobody knew that Hitler was on campus. The Laboratory was on a far end of the campus with an entrance to a public city street, where a discreet access could be maintained.

Minutes after Hitler left, his visit was the talk of the campus. I went over to the Lab to get the story first hand. Hitler had made a good impression. He was restrained, relaxed, polite, friendly, easy to talk to, cracked jokes. He listened to the technical presentations attentively, asked intelligent questions, summarized what he had learned accurately, and thanked the staff of the Lab graciously for their fine work in support of the Air Force.

It was difficult for me to believe what I was hearing. This was the first time since I had been at the University that anybody had said anything nice about Hitler. I also realized that this was the only time that I had, and probably would ever have, an opportunity to talk to people who had had personal contact with Hitler.

LOUIS de OLIVEIRA

On page 57, I wrote that Louis de Oliveira, whose parents had both died in Baltimore when he was seven years old, was my mother's godchild, and that she had brought him into the family. She took him along with us when we moved to Berlin. He was too young to be admitted to Stella Maris where I was, but the Christian Brothers had another boarding school in Illertissen, Bavaria, that ran the full nine years of secondary school, and that admitted Louis. My father visited him every year, as he did me.

While I was studying in Berlin, Louis graduated with good grades. He was a tall, well built and well mannered young man, with light brown hair, blue eyes, a longish face, and spoke German well. My mother sent me some money to get him a ticket to come home and for any other immediate needs he might have. Louis and I had quite a meeting. Louis did not want to go home to Washington, he wanted to go to Portugal and join the army.

Louis had become a victim of Nazi propaganda. Unless you lived in Germany for a sufficient length of time under the Hitler regime, you cannot understand what happened. The Nazi system was painstakingly carefully designed by the devil himself, it was something beyond the thought processes of a normal human being. Louis had spent nine years in a Christian Brothers boarding school, a hotbed of anti-Naziism. Yet you cannot isolate boys completely from what is going on in the outside world. There are newspapers, radios, vacations, brothers and sisters, and other contacts.

The Minister of Propaganda, Gobbels, was, after Hitler, the second most powerful man in Germany. Every person in the country was obligated to belong to a Nazi organization. At meetings of such organizations, the brainwashing was intensive. Nazi doctrine, even more so than that of the communists, sought to deify the state, and to establish the purpose of life as service to the state. Somehow, Louis got infected by these devilish concepts. He viewed America as a place where everybody was chasing the dollar, that was no place for him. Portugal was a small country he could understand, the place his parents came from and where he would be accepted. The army provided an immediate opportunity for selfless service to the state.

I was up against a stone wall. Three thousand miles away from home, in desperation, I appealed to the Persons for help. Karl had been a boy's school teacher all his life, I could think of no better person to advise Louis. I had Louis go spent a week with the Persons.

Karl pointed out to Louis that it would only take him a month to get back his fluency in English, and with his education, he could get a good job in America. Or he could even stay in Germany. He was qualified for a good job right here. Karl made no impression. Louis was not looking for a job, that's not what he wanted. He wanted to be of "service to the state." Karl ended up as frustrated as I was and finally advised me to let Louis go to Portugal. He said, Louis could always change his mind in Portugal and decide to return to the United States.

Mrs Person was an angel. I sent her some money and she stretched it to buy Louis a complete new outfit, a new suit, new shoes and socks, new shirts and undergarments, a new suitcase.

I wondered what my father had observed when he visited Louis annually. I suppose he checked his grades, his health, his adaption to his environment (how he was getting along with the food.) I doubt that he ever inquired about his ambitions, about what he wanted to do in life.

Reinforced by Karl's advice, I bought tickets to Lisbon and gave them to Louis, together with the rest of the money that my mother had sent me. It was enough to sustain him in Lisbon for several weeks.

Thank God for the Persons. I don't know how I could have made such decisions all by myself, three thousand miles away from home.

My father continued to visit Louis every year, as long as he spent his summers in Europe, until the early 1950's when he retired. He showed me photos he had taken of Louis and his family. Louis married, had a nice wife, two pretty daughters, a nice house. He wrote to my mother regularly. After she died, he wrote to my father, and after he died, to my sister. After my sister died, I found Louis's address among her papers and wrote to him twice. Both letters came back marked "Addressee unknown."

The real loser in all this was my mother. She never saw her beloved Louis again. I think she would have been very proud of the young man that I sent off to Lisbon.

THE MAYBACH MOTOR COMPANY

I selected the Maybach Motor Company in Friedrichshafen on the Lake of Constance in 1935 as the place for my next period of shop work. Maybach was a famous name in Germany at the time because of their very expensive luxury automobiles. They only built about 150 cars a year, but each one was tailored to a customer's specification. Every car was different. Field Marshal Goering, Commander of the German Air Force, was the only member of the German Government who owned one. The automobile department was small. The company was fussy who they sold cars to. It was a public relations operation. They sold cars to make friends with people who could help the Zeppelin operation, either politically or financially.

Maybach was a member of the Zeppelin combine. The objective of the combine was to design, manufacture and operate Zeppelin airships. The combine consisted of a number of companies whose objective was to make products useful in airship manufacture or to make money to help support the airship operation. One company made aluminum. It was the first company in Germany to make aluminum, and it did so to supply the material for the airship framework. Another company made the gear boxes for almost all the cars manufactured in Europe. Still another operation was a lumber company.

Gasoline engines were in their infancy when the first Zeppelin airship, the LZ-1, flew its first flight on June 1, 1900. The Maybach Motor Company was founded to develop and build engines for the Zeppelins. All Zeppelins airships, except the last one, the LZ 129, "Hindenburg," were powered by Maybach gasoline engines.

About 1930, it appeared that the diesel engine was going to be superior to the gasoline engine for airship operation. Maybach started to develop a direct injection diesel, the most efficient of the diesel types. Normal diesel engines contain a hot spot that helps with ignition. A direct injection diesel relies solely on compression. The combustible gases in the piston chamber heat up as the gases are compressed. The compression is set so high that the temperature reaches ignition without the assistance of a hot spot. The saving in fuel is appreciable. Unfortunately, the direct injection diesel proved not to have the flexibility required for airship take-off and landing and the Mercedes-Benz regular diesel was selected for the "Hindenburg". However, Maybach was able to find another market for its 750 HP direct injection engine.

Some Northern European railway systems were experimenting with replacing their long trains that ran once or twice a day, with rapid single cars that operated throughout the day, providing street-car type service between cities. The Maybach diesel engines, with standard electrical transmission, proved to be very satisfactory for this type of service. This type of transmission was too bulky and heavy for airship use.

In addition to diesel engines, Maybach also built several sizes of gasoline engines. The largest one was the 550 HP engine for German tanks. Then they built truck engines in various sizes. Their smallest ones were the automobile engines.

I was rotated every two or three weeks through various manufacturing and assembly operations. Most interesting were the assembly operations. Engines are assembled as individual units, not on an assembly line. Mechanics were paid by piece work. They were allotted a certain amount of time, such as 25 hours, to assemble a small engine. If they did the job in less time, they still got paid for 25 hours, up to 125% of their base pay. Almost everybody in the plant was earning their maximum pay.

The first few days on an assembly job, I just watched where the parts went as an engine was assembled. Then I got to the point where I could hand the mechanic the right part to go on next. Finally I was able to perform some of the easy assembly operations myself. As a result, the mechanic and I were able to assemble an engine in record time. With all this time on his hands, the mechanic would take me around the shop and introduce me to his friends who would explain to me the operations that they were performing.

Engine test is the last operation. Every engine is tested individually on a test pad which has a dynometer to measure power output. Most gasoline engines pass their test without incident. Every once in a while, an engine is deficient in its power output, and an engineer is called. The engineer arrives with a special stethoscope around his neck that has a metal bar as its tip. He holds the bar at various parts of the engine, while listening carefully. Eventually he will look up and say something like "Number two bolt on number three piston rod is loose."

They then take the engine off the test pad, disassemble it, and sure enough, the designated bolt is loose. They reassemble the engine, put it back on the test pad, and this time the engine passes the test.

Every time there was a problem with an engine, the engineer with the stethoscope would find the trouble and prescribe a solution. There did not seem to be anything about gasoline engines that they did not know about.

This experience was instructive for me. I had toyed with the idea of doing some work with engines. Now I realized that engine engineers had to have a very acute sense of hearing. My musical ear is so bad, that my own mother gave up trying to teach me how to play the piano. I realized that I could never become a good engine engineer.

My observations in the diesel department were just the opposite of the ones in the gasoline engine department. When a newly assembled diesel engine did not produce the required power output, a whole team of engineers would come and stand around looking at the engine. Finally, they would decide to take the engine apart and inspect every part. Sometimes they would find something wrong and would correct the problem. Sometimes they would exchange parts, because that had worked on a previous faulty engine. After doing everything that everybody could think of, some engines would suddenly mysteriously perk up and pass the test. In contrast with gasoline engines, nobody seemed to know what they were doing. I decided to stay away from diesel engines.

As required, I kept a notebook of all my work, observations and experiences. I received a good recommendation from the company management and full credit from the University.

My stay in Friedrichshafen had been an enlightening experience. Ever since I was a small boy, I had dreamed of working on Zeppelin airships. The Maybach plant was located next door to the Zeppelin hangers. During lunch break it was a few minutes walk to the hangers and I could just walk in through a back door. It was summer, 1935, and they were just putting the finishing touches on the "Hindenburg" that was soon to start regular scheduled service from Friedrichshafen to New York (Lakehurst, NJ). The "Graf Zeppelin" left every Tuesday promptly at 9:30 a.m. for South America, and returned the following Sunday. (It had started this service in 1931.) I was enchanted by the beautiful big ships and the giant hangers.

The terrible accident and fire that destroyed the "Hindenburg" in May, 1937, and ended airship transportation service, forced me to rethink my objectives. After some deep thinking, I came to the conclusion that although Zeppelin airships were beautiful, it was not the machines, but what you could do with them that was of interest, and what you could do with them was flying. It was flying that was of interest, not the machines.

Wiley Post and Harold Getty made the first instrumented and scheduled flight around the world in July, 1931, marking the beginning of a new era. They demonstrated that all the elements were now in place for the airplane to provide regular, scheduled air service. The airplane could now do anything that the airship could do, but had the potential for higher speed and did not need such large, expensive hangers and large take-off and landing crews. I began to see that the future belonged to the airplane. Dr. Dornier, my early advisor, had been an early associate of Graf Zeppelin, but had become an aircraft designer. I began to see the airship as the forerunner of the airplane. It had solved all the problems of "how" to fly, while engineers were perfecting the airplane. I decided that airplane design would require "Statics" as much as airship design, and went back to my studies.

THE SYLT GLIDING AND SOARING SCHOOL

With aircraft fuel in short supply in Hitler's Germany, the German Air Force was very careful in allotting fuel for training purposes. Aspiring student pilots were required to learn as many flight skills as possible on equipment other then fuel burning aircraft, such as gliders and flight simulators. The first step in this program was the glider training. Gliding schools, in special cases, earned the same University credit as shop work without the requirement for a workbook. I qualified as a student of aeronautical engineering. A certificate of attendance from a gliding school was recognized for credit. This gave me an additional incentive for attending.

My friends recommended Sylt as the best gliding school. Sylt is a little island lying like a needle in the north-south direction in the North Sea, about 15 miles long and less than a mile wide, except in the middle where the west side widens to form an arm some five miles long and meets the tresseled railroad line coming from the mainland. Sylt lies ten miles off-shore and parallel to the Danish-German coast. The northern tip of the island is a few miles north of the continental German border and is the most northern point of Germany.

The eastern side of the island is a fine, wide sandy beach. There is a small town on the island, Westerland, a couple of villages, and several large, fancy hotels. The west side of the island is a sheer cliff, about 150 to 200 feet high. In good weather, the steady winds from the east hit this cliff and create a steady updraft, several miles long.

It is one on the best gliding and soaring sites in the world. The students at the school were all aspiring German Air Force Officers. I was fully accepted and got along very well with them.

The school had four classes, A, B, C, and Silver C. To pass the A test, to which I aspired, you had to fly five straight flights, four in excess of 20 seconds, and one in excess of 30 seconds. One thing the course taught you is how long 30 seconds can be. The Silver C requires you to soar continuously for five hours. It is the highest certification you can get in soaring.

Much time was spent waiting for your turn at a glider. You watched your classmates make mistakes and resolved not to make the same errors. My first lesson was to sit in a glider facing the wind and keep the wings level. It does not sound like a big deal, but it is similar to riding a bike. One or the other of the glider's wings kept falling to the ground. Then, all of a sudden, I caught on and did it naturally. After that, I had to practice releasing the tow line.

The gliders are towed into the wind by a long wire rope pulled by a winch. The gliders rise as the winch pulls them into the wind. At an optimum height, the student is supposed to release the tow line and fly in a straight line to the ground. During his first flights, he is supposed to stay in the air for 20 seconds. All students failed the first few times. This bothered me. The task seemed so simple, why could not these smart boys pass the first time? I watched very carefully, so I would do everything correctly.

Finally it was my turn. I confidently take my seat in the glider. I examine the tow release mechanism, it seems OK. Suddenly they start pulling me up. Suddenly I realize I am alone, all alone. No instructor around. I have to make decisions by myself. I look down, yee gods! Am I high and going up fast ! I must be already past my optimum point. I release the tow line and prepare for a long straight glide. Instead, the glider goes **plop**, and hits the ground **hard** !

An instructor comes over and informs me that I had released the tow line about a quarter of the way up. The flight control system was never engaged. Go back and start over.

It all went so fast ! But after several more trys, I was finally able to release the tow line at the right height and stay in the air for 20 seconds. But flying a straight line was another problem. My gliders insisted on bearing right or left. It took my full concentration to follow the center line.

Thirty seconds does not sound like much more than twenty seconds, but it is 50% more. That means that the optimum release point is about 50% higher. The last few seconds of the flight are the most tense, they are the longest seconds of your life. I made it by the skin of my teeth.

The school was a wonderful experience and I got my University credit. Evenings, we would go swimming at the beach. I made a lot of friends standing in line. Unfortunately, after we disbanded at the end of the course, I lost touch with all of them.

During the time that I was at the school, Field Marshall Goering, Commander of the German Air Force, and his wife, Berlin's most acclaimed opera star, came for a short vacation at the beach. He could not leave without paying our school an official visit. He watched some fancy soaring and seemed pleased with his visit.

GOOD   FRIENDS

I made two good lifelong friends in Berlin.   One was Gunter Buchmann, an assistant to Professor Hoff and my mentor in the aerodynamics exercise sessions. Gunter was an only child, son of a secondary school teacher in Berlin. His father had passed away and Gunter lived with his mother in a nice, roomy apartment.

Gunter had a nice circle of friends, both boys and girls. He belonged to a small informal group that met at a bar every Tuesday evening, and he started to take me along. There were two nice girls in the group. I was surprised and shocked when one of the boys announced that he was going to marry one of the girls. I just never realized that students could marry, I thought you had to have a job first.

Gunter would also have parties at his mother's apartment. They had a large living room with a piano in it. We would move the chairs out into the next room, roll up the rug, and have a perfect dance floor. Gunter was a proficient musician and spent the night banging away at the piano. Sometimes one of his friends would bring and play a violin.   Gunter's mother would keep herself busy serving refreshments. These were wonderful little parties and we all had a ball.

Gunter picked up an exotic friend at the University, Captain Fuat Uglu of the Turkish Air Force. He was a lot of fun, and we became good friends.   When Fuat's graduation time approached, a problem surfaced. He had his thesis, "Establishing an Aeronautical Industry in Turkey," all nicely written in Turkish, and he didn't know enough good German to translate it into that language. The thesis had to be submitted in German. I was glad to help him out. I moved in with Fuat for a week, he had a sofa in his room. We worked from early morning until late at night. He explained to me the contents of his thesis, paragraph by paragraph, in broken German, making full use of hand gestures, and I was able to type it all up in good German.

While washing myself with Fuat in his bathroom, I was amused to see him washing the inside of his nose. He laughed at me and explained that the Arabs have a desert tradition where the horses stir up a lot of dust that gets into your nose. So you must wash out your nose carefully every morning. It also prevents colds and similar diseases. He said, we in the West would be much healthier if we would wash our noses every morning.

He returned to Turkey with his degree and occasionally he would write me a letter or postcard. He got married and eventually became a general. In the last postcard that I received from him, he offered to bet me that he still had more hair than I had.

After the end of World War II, there was no aeronautical work to be had in Germany, and Gunter signed a ten year contract with the Government of Indonesia to establish an aeronautical school at the University of Jakarta. After his ten years were up, conditions in Germany were still not to his liking, and he asked me for help. I got him a job as an aerodynamicist at Grumman where I worked. He had married before he went to Indonesia and now had a little boy. Gunter was happy at Grumman and became a senior aerodynamicist. He remained until he retired and then stayed on a few years as a consultant.

Gunter's son, Peter, became enchanted with surfing, and went to school at the University of Southern California where he could practice his hobby. He then got a job in California. After Gunter stopped working, he moved with his wife to California and enjoyed the California climate for a few years. Eleanor and I visited them several times, whenever a business trip took me to the area.

DANCING IN BERLIN

I joined the International Students Association because all the other foreign students seemed to belong, including all the foreign University of Berlin girl students. Some of the girls were very pretty. The ones from South Africa stood out as surprisingly blond, tall and strikingly beautiful. It was also one of the few places that was completely free of Nazi political indoctrination.

The Association had a number of activities. One was the monthly meeting. The preparation of a program would be assigned to the students of a given country. The presentations would briefly touch on race, geography, political organization, economy, religion, and other such weighty matters, but then settle down to a solid program of songs, dances in ethnic costumes, maybe some fairy tales and poetry.

A large proportion of the members of the Association were girls. The girls ran many activities and had as much to say about anything else as the men. I had never dealt with women on this scale before. I had met some girls at the International Students House when I first came to Berlin. I had been taught by nuns at St. Martin's Grammar School in Washington. Aside from that, the only women I had contact with were the sales girls in the few stores I patronized. I had always gone to a boy's school with men teachers. I had never thought seriously about girls, my preoccupations had been with boy's games and hobbies. These girls now at the Association were out going, friendly, and competent. I decided to approach them in a business like manner and keep all relationships at an arms length. This scheme worked out fine.

Many members of the Association were talented musicians. Almost all social and business meetings of the Association ended by pushing aside the furniture to create a dance area, or moving to another room. Light refreshments would be available, the music would start up, and an impromptu dance just naturally ensued.

At first I had a problem with these meetings, I could not dance. The problem was easily corrected with a series of weekly visits to a dance studio. They taught the one-step, the tango, and the waltz. I did not think much of the one-step. I never learned the tango right, although at the time it was Berlin's most popular dance. But I practiced and practiced the waltz and it became my favorite dance for the rest of my life.

I soon discovered that in back of the social meetings, there was a serious purpose. If a foreign student had a good two year record, and through no fault of his own, his means of support collapsed, such as his father died or there was a revolution in his country, the Association would grant him a full scholarship to complete the rest of his studies in Berlin. We did not have many students to support, but there were a few and we required a reliable source of income.

We raised money by staging an annual dance. Berlin had at the time a row of five interconnected grand ballrooms in the block between the Zoological Gardens and the Budapester Street. Each ballroom was decorated in gold and white baroque style, over three stories high, the height of elegance. Each had a grand stage and a row of boxes along each side, at the second story level. The Association rented all five ballrooms for its dance, one of the few organizations that could do so. We hired the five top dance bands in Berlin and sold 10000 tickets at ten Marks each. Luckily, many people who bought a ticket never came, but the place was still jammed.

In line with the dance's international flavor, we invited the international community, that is, all the embassies and consulates in Berlin to rent a box, that we then decorated with the flags of the respective country. All countries cooperated, except the UnitedStates.

We still hung out the American flag on an empty box. It was all a most elegant and colorful sight.

It was a big operation. In addition to the bands, we had to deal with vendors who supplied the bar, food, refreshments, waiters, the stage and cleaning crews, ticket takers, cloak and sanitary rooms, security, and others. We pre-approved all prices charged at the dance. The Association had been dealing with these vendors and crews for years, and knew them all well, but we still had written contracts. Since I spoke German better than most other students, my job was to review these contracts and make sure that they specified correctly the services we desired.   This became an issue whenever we wanted something different from what we had the previous year.

Dress requirement was for formal, either a tuxedo or white tie/tails, and patent leather shoes. The ladies all wore long dresses. The dress requirement at all Berlin functions were strictly enforced, there were no exceptions.   In order to participate in the social life of the University, it was absolutely necessary for a student to own two formal suits: a tuxedo, a pair of tails, and patent leather shoes.

The dance was held on a Saturday evening, 9 p.m. to 2 a.m. At 2 a.m. we would close four ballrooms, send the bands and other help home, and everybody still anxious to dance would adjourn to the open ballroom with a student band that would play until 8 a.m.

Although members of the Association were assigned specific operations to watch and make sure that everything went smoothly, we still had plenty of time to dance and enjoy ourselves. I always had a great time. All the girls from the Association were there, we had no lack of dance partners. I never saw two girls dancing together, as I have seen in the United States. I would help closing up and would never leave before 9 a.m. I would feel silly walking home Sunday morning in my tails in broad daylight when everybody else was going to church.

As was the custom *only in Berlin,* every successful dance was repeated all over again, the following week.

BERLIN TODAY

Berlin today is a very different place than I have described in this book. In my time, the Technical University had 3000 students, of which 1000 were foreigners. Today, in the Year 2000, the University has almost 40000 students, of which 6000 are foreigners.

The large residential area on the north side of the campus that was leveled during World War II has been taken over and developed by the University.

RETURN TO WASHINGTON

PACKING UP

Mid-April 1938, I was at my drawing table at the University in Berlin planning how to best acquire all the chits required for admission to the final examination. I was still missing a few pieces, in particular some two months of shop work. I was interrupted in this exercise by a telegram from my father informing me that my mother was very sick and I should come home immediately. So I dropped everything that I was doing and started to pack up to go home.

I had acquired a lot of treasures during my long stay in Germany. Probably my most expensive item was my motorcycle. Then my camera and my darkroom equipment. My typewriter. My books. My collection of photos and stamps. All this had to be stored until my return.

Or was I coming back? I had to think this out carefully. My father did not approve of the study of engineering, he had made it clear that he considered it a waste of time. I was being supported by my mother from the profits of her music school. If she were to become disabled or die, would my father support my continuing study of engineering? I had to plan for the possibility that I might not come back to Berlin.

For a quick round trip, I had to travel light. For the case that I did not come back, I took along my "statics" workbook from my aircraft design class, a few quiz papers that has been graded "A", and a list of all the courses that I had taken, certified by the University. Everything else I had to store quickly.

I had been renting a corner of a large garage to store my motorcycle. I told the people there that I would not be back for a while. My landlady was most helpful. In the reception area of her large apartment, there was a clothes closet she was no longer using. She helped me pack all the clothes that I was not taking, and all my other belongings in this closet. The closet was full to the brim.

The students of naval architecture in my drawing room all went to sea as part of their required shop work. The channels for applying for such sea duty through the University were well established. I applied for service on a ship to New York and return, with leave in New York to visit my family. I was accepted as an Assistant Engineer on the SS Europa, one of the two largest and fastest liners on the New York - Europe run.

My father sent me the money for the trip.   I received it on May 5, see page 153.   I wrote a letter to the University explaining my sudden mid-term departure, and said a quick good-bye to my friends.

SS *EUROPA*

The crew of the SS *Europa* was used to having technical university students come aboard for their required sea duty. I was issued a set of seaman's papers and welcomed aboard in a routine manner. I reported to the Chief Engineer, and he assigned a seaman to show me around. I was assigned a nice inside cabin in the crew quarters, and when not on duty, I was free to roam the tourist class. I ate in the crew dining room, which was open 24 hours a day, because men were going on, or coming off duty, at all hours. You just went in and could have breakfast, lunch or dinner at any time as you pleased.

In an age before transatlantic air transportation before World War II, the SS *Europa* and its sister ship, the SS *Bremen*, were the queens of the seas.   They were the largest ships afloat. They were the ultimate in glamour, comfort, and speed.   There was nothing else like these two ships.

My world was the engine room, an immense cavern dominated by the four giant turbines, each one more than three stories high. A peep hole in the turbine wall let you look inside, so you could gasp at the roaring fire.   Engineers used the peephole to check the color of the flames, an indication of temperature, when they were adjusting the turbines to change the speed of the ship. Each turbine drove a screw through a shaft that was some two and a half feet in diameter and almost half as long as the length of the ship, supported at points about about 50 feet apart. It was a real technical marvel. In addition, there were many pumps and other machinery that provided for the environment in the ship.

Duty consisted of an hourly tour to inspect every piece of operating equipment. We had to read and record all the gauges (run, pressure, temperature) and check that there was no vibration, noise, smoke, leakage, odor, etc., to assure that everything was operating properly. The ship carried a supply of spare items and the crew was trained to replace almost any piece of equipment that failed.

I watched as they started up the ship. Almost every member of the crew had a job, monitoring or adjusting a piece of equipment. When the ship got underway, we had watch duty. I would go around with the duty officer and observed how he read and recorded his gauge readings and inspected the area.   A complete round tour took about three quarters of an hour. On the last two days I was on the ship, they let me do the work while the duty officer watched.

THE AMERICAN EXPRESS COMPANY INC.
ROKIN 88-90
AMSTERDAM

E 1528 A 5000—6—37

AMSTERDAM, 4th.May 193 8

Mr. John de S. Coutinho

Technische Hochschule H 217

BERLIN-CHARLOTTENBURG.

In accordance with your letter of
Ingefolge Ihres Schreibens vom

we have posted to
haben wir auf

your Dollar-
Ihr

account the following items:
Konto folgendes gebucht:

	Value / Wert	Debit / Soll	Credit / Haben
Received for your account from Mr.J.de S. Coutinho, Washington cheque	4/5		$ 230.--
telegram-charges & stamp on note	"	$ 1.25	======== u.u.r.

Please note that Mr.J.de S.Coutinho
advised us that the amount of the
above cheque enables you to come home
and visit your mother, who is very sick.
In accordance with his request we
informed you by telegram of the arrival of
the money, as per copy of our telegram
attached.

THE AMERICAN EXPRESS COMPANY INC.

Summons to Come Home

I was assigned an important job when we stopped at Southampton to take on passengers. The homes of the rich and famous there are all located on a hill overlooking the harbor. The prevailing winds blow over the harbor and cool off this privileged area. If a ship in the arbor generates any smoke, it will blow right into the homes of the beautiful people. That is not allowed, and any ship that generates smoke in the harbor faces a fine of $ 5000. My job, while we were in Southampton harbor, was to sit in a comfortable chair on deck and watch the smokestacks. At the first sign of a trace of smoke, I was to call the engine room so the engineers could adjust the turbines. I spent a relaxing afternoon in the sunshine and never detected a trace of smoke.

After duty hours, I was free to see the sights. It was easy to get lost on the ship, so I never went anywhere alone. There were plenty of seamen my age on the ship, and I made friends with a number of them. We would go in small groups to the tourist class. Generally we would have a beer in one of the bars. They always had dance music. Sometimes we could entice one of the younger female passengers to dance with us. We all had a good time.

I kept a neat workbook describing the engine and auxiliary rooms, and the tasks I had done. It was reviewed and approved by the Chief Engineer with a favorable recommendation. I submitted it to the University and was granted full shop work credit for the time I was on the ship.

I went to the Captain's office to say goodbye. He told me to stay in touch, and that whenever the ship was in the harbor, I should come back for a visit.

I was released on leave. I was issued a pass, see page 155, which allowed me back on board anytime. I remained a member of the crew and could go back to Germany and Berlin anytime I pleased. I was also given a nice report card, see pages 156 and 157.   I think the secret of my being so well treated on the *Europa* was my language. Through my daily association for four years predominately with students of naval architecture, I had picked up some of the idiom of the German marine community. The way I spoke could not be faked, it was considered a more reliable identifier than my looks or my passport. I was immediately accepted on the *Europa* as a high class member of the   German marine community

Leaving the ship was somewhat of a thrill. I had observed all the commotion with immigration and customs that the passengers had to go through on the giant pier that sticks out into the Hudson River from 12th Avenue. After all the excitement was over, the pier was completely empty.   There were no guards around, no passport

NORDDEUTSCHER LLOYD — BREMEN

ZAHLMEISTER

SCHNELLDAMPFER
„EUROPA", May 17. 1938

New York

To whom it may concern.

This certifies that the bearer

Assistent-Engineer John de S.Coutinho

is a member of the crew of the S.S. "E U R O P A".

Zahlmeister des Nordd. Lloyd
D. „Europa"

Crew Pass

NORDDEUTSCHER LLOYD
BREMEN
—

Dampfer **EUROPA**

156 Reise 193*8*

Führungs-Bericht

über den Ingenieur-Assistenten *(überzählig)* *John Coutinho*

für die Zeit vom *10. Mai 1938* bis *17. Mai 1938*

Allgemeiner Gesundheitszustand: *gut*

Charaktereigenschaften:

   Führung: *sehr gut*

   Pflichtgefühl: *sehr gut*

   Nüchternheit: *stets*

Leistungen:

   im Wachdienst: *gut*

   im Arbeitsdienst: *wurde nicht zum Arbeitsdienst heran-*
gezogen.

Zu welchem Dienst besonders herangezogen? (Kühlmasch., Elektr., Nachtdienst usw.)

Herr Coutinho zeigte im Wachdienst großes Interesse

Besondere Fähigkeiten:

Allgemeine Bemerkungen: *Herrn Coutinho wurde Gelegenheit gegeben*
sich in den Turbinen-Heiz- und Hilfsmaschinenräumen gründ-
lich zu informieren.

New-York, den *17. Mai* 19*38*

O. Scharf
Kapitän

H. Eints
Ltd. Ingenieur

Bemerkung   Über die an Bord Ihres Dampfers bediensteten Ing.-Ass. ist dieser Bericht laufend alle halbe Jahr bezw auf Reisen nach Ostasien Australien und der Westküste Süd-amerikas nach Beendigung jeder Reise und in allen Fällen bei Versetzung bezw Abmusterung an die Nautische-Technische Abteilung des Norddeutschen Lloyd Bremen einzureichen

SS "EUROPA" Performance Report

TRANSLATION

**NORTH GERMAN LLOYD
BREMEN**

SS EUROPA
156th VOYAGE, 1938
PERFORMANCE REPORT

For Assistant Engineer (supernumerary) *:* ....John Coutinho

For the period:..........................May 10, 1938 to May 17, 1938

General Health Condition:.. very good

Personal Qualities:

    Behavior...excellent

    Sense of Duty ....excellent

   Sobriety.. consistent

Performance:

    On Watch Assignments .... very good

    On Labor Assignments..........................was not
    called to any labor assignments

In what duty did he perform best?
   Mr Coutinho showed great interest in watch duty

Special Skills:

General Remarks: Mr Coutinho was given an opportunity to
thoroughly acquaint himself with the turbine and auxiliary
machinery areas.

New York, May 17, 1938
  /s/ O. Scarf   /s/ H. Tints
   Captain   Chief Engineer

control, no customs, everybody had gone home. I left the ship by the crew exit and walked all by myself with my suitcase through that great empty hall and out a small unlocked door onto 12th Avenue. Nobody saw me. I returned to the United States of America without the benefit of an official welcome from the US Government.

THE TASTE OF AMERICA

The pier was close to 42nd Street. I remembered enough of New York City to know that I had to walk along 42nd Street to 7th Avenue, and then south on 7th Avenue to Penn Station on 34th Street. There was a train from New York to Washington every hour during the day.

On my walk, I came to a big drug store, the likes of which I had not seen in eleven years. I went inside and headed for the soda fountain. I asked for a chocolate soda.

If you have not been deprived of ice cream sodas for eleven years, you cannot understand my elation. It was a heavenly treat. I drank the soda and ate the ice cream as slowly as I could, to make it last as long as possible. It was so delicious. It was a little bit like being in heaven. I scraped the bottom of the glass carefully. I considered ordering another one, but decided against it. It was too much of a good thing to overdo it.

I left the drug store and continued my walk to Penn Station. Half way to Washington, I had another great culinary experience. A man came through the train selling ham and cheese sandwiches and coffee. There is no such thing as American white bread in Europe. Most Americans, who only go abroad for a short period of time, never notice it. They think European bread is good. But when you have not had any American bread for eleven years, things are more basic. While I was away, my mother sent me some American goodies, like peanut butter, candy, ketchup, and mayonnaise. There is nothing in the world like Heinz's ketchup and Hellmann's mayonnaise. But my mother never thought of sending me a loaf of bread. I never knew I missed white bread until I returned to the States.

My train sandwich, again, made me feel like I was in heaven. It was just like the sandwiches my mother made for me when I went to St. Martin's Grammar School, before I went to Europe. Like my soda, I ate the sandwich very slowly, relishing every little bit. It gave me a great lift to realize that I was finally coming home. What a wonderful welcome!

I arrived in Washington in the best of spirits. I walked through that grand old Union Station waiting room and took the street car home.

CONDITIONS AT HOME

My sick mother and my sister Helen had moved into my mother's studio, leaving my father with all his books to shift for himself in the family apartment. He seemed to be doing very nicely all by himself.

My mother's studio was on the third and top floor of a building facing 19th Street, the fourth building north of Dupont Circle. The back of the building was on Connecticut Avenue. "Avenues" in Washington run at angles to "streets." Connecticut Avenue is at a slant with 19th Street and the center lines of the two streets intersect at the center of Dupont Circle. My mother's large studio was therefore a short block long, being located between these two converging streets. It had a small kitchen and bathroom in the back, and my mother had screened off a dining area.

My mother had her bed in front of the pianos so she could instruct her pupils from her bed. She was still giving lessons to a few of her favorite pupils. Helen, who was a premed student at American University, slept on a cot in back of a screen in the rear of the studio. She had put up another cot for me in back of another screen.

My mother had hired a friendly young black woman, Wilma, who acted as nurse, cook, housekeeper, and jack of all trades. My mother had taught her how to cook all my favorite dishes, and there did not seem to be anything that Wilma could not do. The supermarket, that once had supplied my mother on Evarts Street, still called, but only made deliveries once a week.

In a Washington tradition, the block in front of the studio was patrolled by a friendly black warden who lived on tips. He would not let anybody park on the block except those who had business there. My mother's pupils could always park almost next to the front entrance door. He watched your car, and kept undesirables away from the block. He was available to get a cab, to run errands such as taking a parcel to the post office, even to move around the pianos or other heavy furniture in the studio. He was very helpful.

Helen had been looking out of the window and saw me coming up the block. She ran down to greet me. My mother was most elated to see me. She was so weak she could not get out of bed. Helen called my father and he came over in a little while. Wilma prepared a fabulous dinner for us. We ate on small individual portable tables spaced around my mother's bed.

A MIRACULOUS RECOVERY

After my arrival, my mother immediately started to get better. Within a week, she was sitting up in bed. Wilma was feeding her bouillon and beef tea (Brovil). She wanted to know all about my studies in Berlin. She asked a lot of questions about her own lady friends in Berlin, that I was not able to answer. We relived the time we had spent together in Berlin, especially the Christmas with the strawberries. My mother had lived in Berlin in a different world than the one I lived in; her's was around the Music Conservatory, and mine was around the Technical University. We still had plenty to talk about.

Every day she got stronger. After two weeks, she got up and sat in a chair. At the end of a month, she was ready to go out.

She told me she had a routine for spending an hour whenever she had some free time in her schedule of lessons. She would go downtown to Woodward and Lothrop's (Woodies), one of Washington's best department stores, walk around for a while, and come back. That's what she wanted to do again on our first outing.

Our block warden quickly got us a cab, and it seemed in minutes we were at Woodies. My mother was immediately greeted by the salesgirls as a long lost queen. They were all excited about seeing her; they took her into a back room where they were all talking at the same time. In a flash, the news went through the store that my mother was back, and the sales women from all over the store came to greet her. She knew them all. After half an hour or so of merry making, I decided that my mother had had enough and eased her toward the door. We managed a quick get-a-way in a home bound taxi.

On the way home, my mother explained to me how department stores work. Say they buy 100 dresses at $50 each, that is $5000. Store expenses amount to 40% of sales or $2000, so they have to take in $7000 to break even. Sales of a new dress will at first be brisk, but will eventually slow down. Suppose 50 dresses are sold at $100 each for $5000 before the slowdown occurs, the store will then reduce the price by 20% and sell 25 dresses at $80 each for $2000. Now the store has reached its $7000 objective and still has 25 dresses left. These dresses could be given away and the store would not lose any money. Instead they put them on sale at 50% off, this is now pure profit for the store.

At this point, the salesgirls will hide some of these dresses in a back room. They would watch for their friends and good customers to come through the store and would take them into the back room and offer them the dresses hidden there at bargain prices.

My mother told me that after going through the store a few times a week for several years, she knows the store's merchandise and prices as well as the salesgirls. She also knows the salesgirls and their family histories. She watches as new dresses are put on sale, how they move, and how the price comes down. She can predict if and when a dress is going to be sold at 50% of retail. She needs good clothes to conduct her monthly recitals and occasional public appearances, but she has never paid over 50% of retail for a dress, and usually much less when invited into a back a room.

My mother was very excited and pleased with our little excursion. As she got stronger, the two of us made other outings. We went back to Woolies several times. She wanted to buy me a new suit, but I refused. The one I had was quite decent, and I could not carry an additional one back to Berlin. She took me on short visits to some of her friends. She was quite proud, walking down the street with me and introducing me to her friends. She was a small, slender, English type woman and did not look her age. I was several inches taller than my father who was a few inches taller than my mother. My mother's friends were invariably surprised, that she had such a tall son.

We went to the movies several times and ate a few dinners in one of her favorite restaurants, while Wilma took care of Helen and my father at home.

Helen spent her days at American University and usually came home with lots of homework. My father would come in the late afternoon, and Wilma would serve dinner for the four of us. Normally, my father would stay until it was time for him to go home to go to bed.

My mother called her pupils back, and soon she had a full schedule of classes. She appeared to be fully recovered. My father told me it was time for me to go back to Berlin and get my degree.

DR. FRENCH, MY MOTHER'S PHYSICIAN

Dr. Bernard French was a graduate of Johns Hopkins Medical School and one of Washington's most prominent physicians. He had a lucrative practice and was a member of several District Medical Boards. In those days, doctors had their offices in their homes and made house calls. They came by street car. French had a car and a driver that delivered him to the door of the house of his sick patient. The driver would park in front of the house and wait for him, or park nearby where he could watch the house. As soon as French appeared at the door, the driver would come right up and take him to his next call.

After I arrived in Washington, French developed the habit of dropping in every evening to see my mother and chat for a while as his last call of the day. Sometimes he would come very late, close to midnight, but he never missed a visit. After my mother was able to get out of bed, she started to make coffee in anticipation of French's visit. Then she started to bake a cake. So we always had a fresh cake and coffee waiting when French arrived. My mother's prize was pineapple upside down cake, we all loved it.

French was always full of stories of funny things that happened during the day, not only of humorous patients, but also of political happenings at his high level Board Meetings. These were relaxing social visits and French enjoyed talking to my father. He stopped sending a bill for his visits, but I saw my father slipping him a $100 bill every once in a while.

I told French that my father had told me to return to Berlin to continue my studies. French told me very forcefully that I could not go. He said that remission of uterine cancer is never permanent, my mother did not have long to live. He went on to say that I was doing very well keeping her happy, and should keep it up. My mother depended on me, if I were to leave, she would die.

RESERVE OFFICER'S TRAINING CORPS (ROTC)

My mother did not want to keep me cooped up in the studio and devised ways to get me out. My first errand was up Connecticut Avenue to a flower stand to buy flowers for the studio. My next assignment was to supply the ice cream for desert. Also a couple of blocks up Connecticut Avenue there was Schwarz's Drug Store that had a giant soda fountain. It was one of the few places in the city that sold black raspberry ice cream, my mother's favorite.

After talking to Dr. French, I realized that I would have to stay in Washington an indeterminate period of time, and had better find something useful to do. I thought of Professor Hoff's advice in Berlin that it was time to obtain a Reserve Officer's commission and get settled in the military before hostilities started. After some investigation, I found that the War Department ran an ROTC Officer's Candidates School for Government employees. The Commanding Officer of the School was Major Andrews who, I discovered, had been a former student of my father's. We became immediate friends, and with these credentials I was admitted to the school.

The four year ROTC program is conducted at many universities in the US and students are commissioned as officers upon graduation. The War Department program consisted of two parts: correspondence and drill. The four year ROTC classroom material was provided as correspondence subcourses. You did not need to take four years to complete the course, you could work at your own pace.

The drill was conducted twice a week after working hours in the

War Department parking lot. The drill consisted of exercises such as formation marching with simulated guns, calisthenics, running, jumping and climbing over various barriers, and standing in front of a squad and shouting orders as loud as you could. My impression was that the drill was designed more to increase our physical fitness than to teach us military skills. A number of points were granted for each drill attended, and you had to earn as many points as the ROTC program required at the universities. It was a physically exhausting experience, and I felt sorry for my fellow students who had to go to work the next day.

I realized immediately that this course offered me an opportunity to brush up on my English. I did not know most of the technical terms, and had to look them up in the dictionary. I think I nearly wore out the dictionary. I worked very hard on this course, but felt that it was worthwhile because of the English I was learning. As a result, I got good marks on each subcourse, mostly in the high 80's, low 90's. For each subcourse competed I received a certificate like the one on page 164, for "Map Reading." My grade here was 89%, and I received fifteen hours of class room credit.

MY   FATHER'S   FRIENDS

My father always liked to introduce me to his friends. I remember that when I was still in grade school, he made a big fuss about introducing me to Father Sheen at Catholic University. In the following years, Father Sheen became Bishop Sheen and a nationally prominent radio personality.

On pages 43 and 50 I have already mentioned Dr. McGuire and Father Fadner. Then there was Dr. Max Munk, a German and professor of aerodynamics at Catholic University, world famous in the industry because of his study of the drag of wing tips. My father admired him very much as a scientist. I also met Dr. Louis Crook, head of the School of Engineering at Catholic University.

GETTING   AROUND IN   WASHINGTON

In those days, 1938, everybody rode the street cars. My father walked whenever he could, but if it was too far, he took the street car. He had a weekly pass for unlimited street car travel. I observed that among all my father's prominent friends, only Crook had a car and knew how to drive. All the others had street car passes and took the street cars.

My mother always took a taxi. She explained to me that her time was too valuable to waste waiting around for a street car. In

ARMY EXTENSION COURSES

Certificate of Completion of Subcourse

This is to certify, That _________ Mr. John de S. Coutinho, _________

_____ 1508 - 19th Street, N.W., Washington, D.C. _____ has successfully
(Address)

completed Subcourse No. _10-7_, _____ Part I - Map Reading _____
(Title of Subcourse)

Extension Course of the _______ Quartermaster _______ {*School
                                                       {*~~Department~~

(19_38_-19_39_ Announcement) with a rating of _89%_ Hours of credit _____15._

Date _____ December 5 _____, 19_38._

_____ JOHN G. BURR, _____
(Name)

Lieut. Colonel, Field Artillery,
Instructor.
(Grade, Organization, etc.)

[SEAL]

APPROVED

~~By command of~~ For the Commanding General:

_____ Ellery Farmer _____

ELLERY FARMER
Colonel Infantry
~~Acting Chief of Staff~~ ~~Adjutant General~~

W. D., A. G. O. Form No. 152
July 1, 1933

*Strike out word not applicable

U S GOVERNMENT PRINTING OFFICE 3—10173

Army Extension Course Certificate

Washington at that time, empty cruising cabs were in abundance. On a main street, you just stood at the curb, raised your hand, and in less than a minute an empty taxi would stop for you.

The taxi fares were also very reasonable. The cabs had no meters, they charged by the zone, 30 cents a zone for one to three passengers, plus five cents tip. If there was more than three persons in a party, you had to take more than one cab. The street car fare was ten cents a person. My mother's studio was in zone 1. Almost all the places she ever wanted to go to were all located in zone 1.

SUMMER JOB

I decided to get a temporary job in the aeronautical industry. My father had me go talk with Dr. Munk, the self-styled expert in all things aeronautical.   Munk and my father put their heads together and decided that my English was inadequate for any kind of a job in the aeronautical industry. I should get a job in a store or a gas station where I would come in contact and speak with many people every day for about a year, until my English improved to the point that I could work well in an engineering office.

In this dilemma, Professor Crook came to the rescue. He had been born and raised on a large farm in Cabin John, now a suburb of Washington. He had rebuilt the large barn into an office, a machine shop, and a small wind tunnel. He believed that there was a place in aeronautics for a thin wing airplane, and he was in the process of designing and building one. He hired three students during the summer vacation to help him. He took me on as one of his helpers during the summer. I made a deal with him that I would keep a workbook and that he would certify it so that I could submit it to the Technical University in Berlin for credit as shop work.

I spent a very pleasant summer with Crook and two other advanced students in Cabin John, discussing aerodynamic theory, manufacturing parts and models in the shop, and testing the models in the wind tunnel.

At the end of the summer I submitted my workbook, covering three months of work, to the University. I only needed two months of credit and did not expect full credit because the workbook was written mostly in English, with German explanations here and there. To my surprise, I received full credit and a prized chit, see page 166. We needed one of these chits for each required subject for admission to the final examination.

This chit was difficult to get. Most of the other students I talked to complained bitterly that they only received partial credit for their

Technische Hochschule Berlin.

Praktikantenamt der Fakultat
fur Maschinenwesen

Bestätigung für die Meldung zur Diplom-Hauptprüfung

in der Fachrichtung ……… Luftfahrzeugbau ………

Herr cand. ing. John Condinho *Matr.-Nr.* A/216

hat zufolge der bisher vorgelegten Zeugnisse und Werkarbeitsbücher die Mindest-

vorschriften über die praktische Ausbildung erfüllt.

T. H. Berlin, am 6. 2. 39

Hauner

*Eine erneute Vorlage der für diese Bestatigung eingereichten Belege ist bei der Meldung zur Diplom-Haupt-
prufung nicht mehr erforderlich Weitergehende Praxis wird fur die Gesamtbeurteilung bis zum Meldetermin testiert.*

500 3 38

German Shop Work Certificate

TRANSLATION

Berlin Technical University
Office of Practical Training
Faculty of Mechanical Engineering

CERTIFICATE for the partial admission to the

final examination in course *Aircraft Design.*

Engineer Candidate *John Coutinho,* Registration No. *A/216.*

has complied with the minimum requirements for practical training

by virtue of the reports and workbooks submitted to date.

Berlin Technical University. February 6, 1939

/s/ Hanner

Translation of German   Certificate

workbook. I finally figured out that what your workbook had to show was what you had learned, over and above what they taught in class. You got credit only when you learned something. If your workbook only showed that you spent time at a facility, you got no credit. I spent a lot of time   preparing my workbooks. I described the facility, the product and how it was made, and exactly what I had done. I think that this type presentation showed what I had learned, and was the reason that I always got full credit.

THE SAD, SAD SAGA OF LOUIE CROOK

Before 1927 when I was still in grammar school and we lived on Evarts Street, I remember my father sometimes coming home all excited, and then the dinner conversation would revolve around what the Chief Justice of the United States had said to Louie Crook that day.   I could not understand a word of it and regarded the whole conversation as normal grown-up nonsense.

Much later, 1940, when I was already working at Grumman, it was lunch time and I opened my copy of LIFE magazine. What a surprise, to see a full page portrait of the pleasant face of Professor Crook! The legend under the photograph explained that Crook had won his case for patent infringement against the United States Government in the United States Supreme Court, and had been awarded damages of TWENTY MILLION DOLLARS, plus 5% interest for twenty years!!!

I was aware that Crook planned to sue Bendix for $50,000,000.00, but was waiting to settle his case against the Government first, because he felt it would strengthen his case against Bendix.

Crook, in his laboratory in Cabin John, where I had worked, had invented the spark suppressor like the one you have in your car. It allows you to operate your radio in a car while the engine is running. Crook is a good example of a small inventor in modern society. If you invent something really useful with a large potential market, the big companies will attempt to steal it from you and you will spend the rest of your life fighting them in court. Your productivity will be lost, and you may also lose the benefits from your invention.

Unfortunately for Crook, a guilty US Government Agency is not authorized to pay for damages it might have caused in performing its mission. To collect his Supreme Court Award, Crook needed an Act of Congress, that is the only way our Government can generate the money to pay such bills. Crook had no influence in Congress and no way to collect his award. He died a few years later and left his Supreme Court award of TWENTY MILLION DOLLARS to Catholic University. The papers may be worthless, but they make a fine contribution to the museum.

A   PEACEFUL   SUMMER

My mother made a remarkable recovery in the summer of 1938, or so it seemed. French still came to see her every evening and watched her carefully. But she was up and about. She carried a full schedule of music lessons, but did not hold any recitals or make any public appearances. Then she had an amazing idea: the family needed a car!

Helen had graduated from Holy Cross Academy and had a nice circle of girl friends from that school. One of these was Anna Grace Small whose father was the president of the Clinton First National Bank in nearby Clinton, Maryland, and who owned a Ford Agency in Washington. Anna Grace worked at the Agency, and Helen asked her to pick out a nice used car for us. Anna Grace did that, and taught me how to drive it. I taught my mother and Helen how to drive, and we all got our driver's licenses. My father remained loyal to his beliefs that a gentleman did not drive cars.

My mother even had specific ideas of what we should do with the car. She called up Lavinia Anderson to make sure that they were going up to Linden for the weekend. Then she got Wilma to pack a nice picnic basket, and for the first time, the family went on a weekend outing in our own car. I drove, my mother sat beside me, my father and Helen sat in the back. It was a little more than an hour's ride. Mrs. Anderson had not changed, she was still bubbling over. David and Lavinia were already there. It was a glorious reunion.

We made several more excursions to Linden during the Summer. I took Anna Grace out several times in our car. Helen took some summer courses at American University and continued to struggle with her premed books. My father took off as usual to teach his summer courses at the Berlin University.

I was doing well at my summer job in Cabin John, and also at the Officer's Candidate School. I was scheduled to be be commissioned in February, 1939.

JOB   HUNTING

With my mother doing so well, I felt I should find something else to do after finishing my summer job with Crook. I decided to get into the aircraft industry. I discounted Munk's advice about my inadequate English; I had done fine at the Army School and at Crook's, I did not anticipate that the aircraft industry would be more particular.

I talked to many people, but the most helpful was McGuire, with whom I was able to establish friendly relations. He knew a lot about the aircraft industry which was located mostly in California. But there were a few companies on the East Coast. McGuire was finally able to get me interviews at Martin in Baltimore and Grumman in New York. Both companies offered me jobs. The big question of my inadequate English never came up.

McGuire recommended that I accept the Grumman offer, because Martin had a department of 500 engineers and it would be too easy for me to get lost in the crowd. He believed that, Grumman being much smaller, my chances of being noticed were much better. Martin was closer to Washington, but New York was not too far, it was perfectly feasible for me to come home weekends.

The interview itself had an influence on the decision. The interview at Martin had been courteous, but short and perfunctory. It was quite different at Grumman. I recall well the details of my interview with Bill Schwendler, Chief Engineer. Since I was coming from a foreign university, the interview was very thorough. Schwendler was a structural designer and he looked through my design workbook page by page. He did not understand the German text, but he did the formulas and sketches, so with a few running comments from me, he was able to fully understand the contents of the workbook and recognize that it represented advanced work. Then he quizzed me about my other courses, especially my practical work. The interview lasted over two hours.

At the end, Schwendler told me that when Grumman hired engineers out of college, they first put them to work in the shop for a year, but in view of my practical experience, he would take me right into the engineering department, at $25 a week, that was what they paid a man right out of college with a Master's degree. Schwendler also explained that they had no room for me at the time, but that they were building an extension to the engineering department and would have more room in February. I explained to Schwendler my involvement with the Army Officers Candidate's School, and that I would be finished in February. That would be a good time for me to start. We agreed that I would report for work in February.

When I reported all this to McGuire, he was impressed with Schwendler's interview and felt that I would be well off at Grumman.

LIMITED   FLIGHT TRAINING

After Crook closed his laboratory in Cabin John in the fall and went back to work at the University, I had more time and a car to investigate what was available in Washington and surrounding area. I found a private airfield, Capital Airport, in Bladensburg. The operator, Ed Stitt, gave flying lessons. He had three Piper Cubs for use by his students and for rent.

I took his beginners Flight Training Course. This was quite different from the gliding I had done. When you have power at your disposal, you are in a different league.

My basic problem was the weather. Ed would only give lessons when the air was relatively calm. I went to the airfield many times thinking that the wind was not bad, only to find that in Bladensburg Ed thought it was too windy. I finally soloed on December 1, and Ed awarded me the certificate shown below.

I had to take a medical examination. I flunked the depth perception test. The US Department of Commerce notified me that I did not qualify for a commercial pilot's license. I decided I was not cut out to be a pilot.

The Capital Airport is now (Year 2000) long gone. It has been replaced by the suburban streets and houses of a Metropolitan Area.

(Coutinho's Flight Certificates)

STRUCTURAL AIRCRAFT DESIGN, GRUMMAN

FIRST   DAY

With the advent of fall, my mother's health started to deteriorate. She had to cut down on her teaching schedule and spend more time in bed. She followed with interest my job hunt, and was delighted when I was accepted at the Grumman "airplane factory."

My father was disgusted. He went around mumbling that he had not raised his son to be an engineer to operate machinery in a factory. I overheard my mother saying that factories have offices where engineers work, and that some engineers make as much as $5000 a year. That statement put a temporary damper on my father's concern, and gave me a personal goal. For a long time, my ambition would be to become an engineer who made $5000 a year. At $25 a week, or $1350 a year, I was on my way.

I finished my course at the Army Officers' Candidate School and was commissioned as a Second Lieutenant in the Army of the United States on February 18, 1939. I had committed myself to start at Grumman in February, so I started to make plans to move to New York on February 28.

In saying goodbye to my mother, she told me to be sure to tell her if I ran out of money.

The Grumman plant was in Bethpage on Long Island, an hour's train ride from Pennsylvania Station in New York.   Coming from Washington, it was a dreary six hour train ride before I could report to Bill Schwendler on February 28. He assigned another young engineer, John Meirs, to help me get settled.

The first order of business was to find a room for me. Grumman kept a list of local rooms for rent and Meirs obtained it. There was nothing available in Bethpage, which is a small place. The nearest town with any signs of life is Farmingdale, where Meirs lived. We decided to look there first. On the Grumman list there was a room for rent near where Meirs lived. The room was in a big house owned by Mrs. Otten and her family. She was a nice person and said that I could join the family in the evening and listen to the radio shows. I could see nothing wrong with the room and took it. I stayed there three years until I got married.

The next question was transportation to and from work. Meirs had a car and lived around the corner. He agreed to take me to and from work until I got my own car. Meirs and I became good friends. He was a graduate of Princeton University. I tried to find out where the other Grumman engineers had gone to school, and I was surprised to discover that almost all of them came from the foremost universities in America. I was in excellent intellectual company!

SEATING ARRANGEMENTS

The extension on the engineering department was not yet completed and the engineering department was very overcrowded, so there was a problem of where I could be accommodated. The department had a Frieden Calculator on a mobile cart so it could be moved about the department to where it was needed. The cart had a drop leaf. They raised the drop leaf and offered it to me as a makeshift desk. For a seat we found an unused waste paper can, which we turned upside-down and behold, I had a nice round seat! So that is how I started to work, sitting on an upside-down waste paper can and doing my work on the drop leaf of a calculator cart. If my father could only see me now!

Working on the calculator cart leaf had some advantages for a new man. Every time somebody needed to use the calculator, I would be displaced for a few minutes. This got me talking with the men that needed to use the calculator and provided me with the opportunity to get to know most of the other men in the office and what they were working on.

The were 27 engineers at Grumman at the time and I received the "Permanent Number 602," a number assigned to each employee in the order in which he is employed.

CRUNCHING NUMBERS

I was assigned to help Connie Sweetzer, a graduate of MIT and an exceptionally fine piano player. He explained that Grumman was designing and building the XF4F-1 (Wildcat) in a Navy competition with a number of other companies, where each company was designing and building its own airplane; (see page 174). The Navy had issued a specification for a new carrier fighter aircraft, outlining exactly what the new airplane had to do. The Navy paid several competing companies to each build such an aircraft, and the company whose aircraft best met the specification would be awarded a production contract. Grumman's future depended to a large extent on us winning this contract.

Sweetzer's job was to analyze the proposed wing of the XF4F-1, that is, make sure that it would be strong enough at all critical flight conditions at least weight. He was writing a report that would be submitted to the Navy "for approval." The calculations in his report, such as those that I would be doing, would be checked by another

F4F Wildcat, 1939

engineer, and then by the Navy. The Navy would check the report carefully, and if they found anything wrong, they would send it back for correction. If they found nothing wrong, they would "approve" it and Grumman would get paid for a "work package" which included the design and analyses of the wing.

Sweetzer had calculated all the loads over the wing for all required flight conditions in accordance with a Navy specification. He then divided the wing span into 20 inch segments, calling each segment a "panel." He calculated the load over each panel and applied it at the center of the panel (panel point). He identified in each panel the various load carrying structural units: this permitted him to systematically calculate the applied stresses in each unit of the proposed structure.

He then calculated the strength in each proposed structural unit. For each unit, the strength of the structure had to be just a little bit greater than the applied load, otherwise the design would be overweight and would have to be changed to reduce the weight. These calculations, for each unit of structure at each panel point, required tens of pages full of numbers. The procedure was exactly as we had been taught in Berlin, where I had sweated for months to develop an understanding of this procedure and was now well acquainted with all aspects of the analysis. The Grumman engineering department also had long drawing tables, splines and duck weights around, just like the drafting rooms in Berlin, although Grumman was more crowded and there were girlie pictures on the walls. From my very first hour, I felt very much at home at Grumman.

Sweetzer showed me the pages of his report that he had completed, page after page full of numbers, and they made perfect sense to me: I recognized what the numbers represented. Sweetzer gave me a few pages to fill out. He had the arithmetic all set up. For weeks on end, I sat on my overturned trash can and happily crunched out pages of numbers.

Sweetzer and I got along well. Eventually, he gave me portions of the analyses to do. I became thoroughly acquainted with all aspects of his report.

When they built the actual wing, I went out into the shop to watch. I was stunned. Because of my experience with gliders and Piper Cubs, I associated flying with real light weight flimsy structures. Here they came with heavy sheets of aluminum, heavy steel fittings, and other heavy structural parts. I stood there and said to myself, "They can't expect this thing to fly. They can't be serious!" I just had no feel for the power of a 900 hp engine.

I examined an individual piece of structure and discovered that it was built in accordance with the numbers in my report. I looked at the hundreds of other pieces of structure that made up the wing and realized that every piece of structure had been made according to my numbers. Weight is such an important consideration in aircraft design, that every part has to be carefully designed so that it is just strong enough at minimum weight. The XF4F consists of 30000 structural parts, and every one of these parts has to be just strong enough at minimum weight. To perform these calculations, I and my associates completed thick reports of pages full of numbers.

The XF4F was being designed in competition with other aircraft. The weight affects its performance. If Grumman is not very careful in controlling the weight of its design, a competitor may win the production contract with a lighter airplane.

Grumman had a rough formula for estimating the benefits of weight reduction. One pound of structural weight increased airplane gross weight by six pounds (weight growth factor) because of the provisions necessary to carry that pound around. A pound of gross weight was worth $100/year in commercial aviation. This gave us a guide on how much we could spend on machining to save an ounce.

My shop visits opened my perspective as to the role of crunching numbers in airplane design.

It was a great day at Grumman when the news came, that Grumman had won the F4F production contract. (The X for "experimental" is dropped on production aircraft.) Thousands were built by Grumman, Eastern, and General Motors.

TRANSPORTATION

On my *"EUROPA"* trip, I met an elderly couple, Mr. and Mrs. Bulck, who were coming to the US to visit their son, Emil, at Oyster Bay, Long Island. They gave me his name and address and told me to go see him sometime if I was ever in the area.

Oyster Bay is not far from Farmingdale, and both towns have stations on the Long Island Railroad. One afternoon, I decided to go see Emil, and found that he owned a large gas and auto repair station, had a lovely wife, Olive, and two small children, a boy and a girl. We became quite friendly.

My biggest personal problem at the time was the lack of a car. And here I had stumbled on Emil and his auto business. He found a ten year old stately Packard, that looked like it had been in funeral parlor service, and sold it to me for $50. It ran well and provided me with reliable transportation for a couple of years.

NEW YORK UNIVERSITY

I was rather proud of having attended the Berlin Technical University, at that time considered to be a top university everywhere in the world except in the United States. In practically all my social contacts, I would be questioned why I had to go to Germany to study engineering. I decided I had better acquire a US degree to stop this talk.

I discovered that New York University (NYU) was one of the few institutions in the country at that time that offered degree courses at night and on Saturdays. Furthermore, it listed a "Guggenheim School of Aeronautics" associated with its College of Engineering. I went to NYU to investigate.

I met Dr. Alexander Klemin, Head of the Guggenheim School and one of the most remarkable men I have ever met. Klemin examined my credentials even more scrupulously than Schwendler at Grumman had. Klemin then proceeded to examine me thoroughly in my various subjects. He had other professors talk to me. I had a two and one half hour interview with the professor for aeronautic power plants.

When the evaluation was over, Klemin offered to admit me to the Graduate School and award me 12 credits towards a Master's Degree, the maximum amount of credit allowed by the University for credit earned at a sister institution. Klemin laid out a plan of courses on Saturday morning and Tuesday evening that would lead to a Master's degree in a year and a half. I accepted.

The Tuesday evening classes on Elasticity were conducted by the Mathematics Department at Washington Square. I took the commuter train from Farmingdale to Pennsylvania Station, and then the subway to Washington Square. On the return trip, I would come back with another student who was an instructor in mathematics at the University and working for his doctorate. He often could not understand the instructor's objectives, which I, as an engineer, intuitively recognized. On the other hand, the mathematics sometimes got very complicated, and I had trouble following it. This part was very easy for my friend and he would explain it to me very well. Our interchange of viewpoints, my engineering versus his theory, helped both of us get a lot more out of the course.

On Saturday morning, I had four hours of courses. I drove my car to Forest Hills and parked it in a lot next to a subway station. Then I took the subway to University Heights. I stayed in school Saturday afternoon and did all my homework. This schedule kept me up to date on all my school work. When I finished my homework, I would leave my car in the parking lot and take the train to Washington and go visit my mother. Classes in the technical subjects at NYU were no different from what they had been in Berlin.

CITY PEOPLE, WHO LIVE IN THE COUNTRY

The Grumman people. who lived in and around Farmingdale, developed an active social life. Those were the days when the automobile had just become a reliable vehicle and city people were beginning to live in the suburbs. More and more people who worked in New York City moved to outlying communities. They called themselves "City people, who lived in the country."

One popular event, staged by Grumman people, was the monthly square dance at the hall of the Episcopal Church. You did not have to bring your own girl, and I attended regularly. I met several nice girls there.

Grumman was quite concerned for the welfare of its employees and sponsored a number of activities to keep them happy. Probably the most expensive one of these was the cafeteria, that served really good food. One day, years later, we had invited company for dinner at our apartment, and Eleanor was not feeling well. I bought eight dinners at the cafeteria for take-out. Eleanor just had to heat and serve them. Our guests obviously enjoyed this meal and had no inkling that it was not home cooked. I would not have tried this deception anywhere else except with the Grumman cafeteria.

Grumman sponsored a baseball club that later became the champions of the East Coast Industrial League for many years, a band, a bowling league, a golf club, a card club and a tennis club. I joined the tennis club, but I was such a lousy player that I dropped out. I should not have done so, because tennis playing slowly died out and the members turned to playing cards at their monthly meetings. I could have held my own in such an environment. For a while, I joined a group in the company that went horse back riding in Bethpage State Park.

Another special feature of Long Island was its beaches. One of these, close to Farmingdale, was Jones Beach, the pride of Robert Moses, New York City Park Commissioner, who only built the best in the world. Jones Beach had everything, it could not be improved

The Grumman crowd and their Farmingdale neighbors constituted an active and lively community and there was always something to do.

WAR BREAKS OUT

In September, 1939, war broke out in Europe. Although far away, it affected me directly. Three facts decided my fate:
- It was now impossible for me to return to Berlin to finish my studies and get my degree.

- I was well in line to receive a Master's degree from New York University, I would no longer need a Berlin degree.
- I held an Army commission, and the Army probably would not let me leave the country.

In view of these facts, I decided that there was nothing to be gained by my returning to Berlin to get my degree. I already had a fine engineering job which could not be improved by having a Berlin degree. A Master's Degree from NYU would serve me in the future just as well. Furthermore, I had been getting along fine without any of the personal property that I had left in storage in Berlin. It caused me no trouble to consider it lost.

It was Grumman policy to release reserve officers as they were called into service, but they made an exception when I was called. Schwendler wrote a letter to the Adjunct General, and there were several telephone calls between the Army and Grumman. It ended up by the Army giving me the choice of resigning my commission or reporting for active duty. After considerable soul searching, I resigned. I sold my soul to Grumman for the duration of the war effort.

A friend of mine in Grumman engineering, Second Lieutenant Harvey Leach, US Marine Corps Reserves, was called to active duty. He sold me his Ford for $150. It was a good car and lasted me until several years after the war, when I was able to buy a brand new Hudson.

MY MOTHER DIES

After moving to Farmingdale, I returned to Washington every week to visit my mother. The six hour one way train ride created a heavy schedule, and it seemed that I never got a chance to really rest up. Under these circumstances I began to go see my mother every two weeks. My mother died in October, 1939, on one of the weekends when I did not go to Washington.

On each visit I was able to explain to my mother a little more about my job and my new life on Long Island. She got a good laugh out of the story of my sitting on an overturned waste paper can and working on the drop leaf of a calculator cart. She seemed to understand my story of how you design an airplane for critical design conditions at least weight. She liked the things I told her about Grumman, and she told me that many people have trouble finding work applying what they learned in college and doing something that they liked. She thought that Grumman was a fine company and advised me to stay there. She was always concerned that I had enough money. At first, on $25 a week, taking a weekly train to Washington, and buying a car, things were pretty lean. My mother gave me three checks of $50 each during that time. After I received my first raise, I became financially independent.

As the months passed, her condition grew worse, eventually she was restricted to her bed. She cut back her teaching schedule to a few favorite students a week.

Her burial service was held at St. Mathews Church (later Cathedral), the same church where President Kennedy's burial service was held. She was a devout Portuguese Catholic and very much at odds with the Irish Catholic priests that serve in American Churches. (Portugal is the only western country that has it own Patriarch.) I do not know what her trouble was, somehow we never got around to discussing religious questions. She discovered a French Catholic priest at St. Mathews, and found that the Portuguese Catholic and French Catholic viewpoints were quite compatible. We all attended services at St. Mathews, although that was not our parish church.

Both my father and mother were public figures in Washington, and the huge church was almost full at her burial service. There were three bishops in the sanctuary.

My mother was buried in the Catholic Section of Cedar Hill Cemetery on Pennsylvania Avenue, in Maryland, just outside the District Line. Our family plots are in Section 27, Lot 181,on top of a hill with a beautiful view overlooking the nation's capital. Dr. French picked the site.

GIRLS

Grumman had a busybody Chief Production Engineer, who I shall call Shorty. He had a pleasant, good tempered wife and seven children. He had his nose into everything.

He did not like the cut of my German suit when I came to work. He took me to a large men's haberdashery in Hempstead, the nearest large town, to get an "American" suit for me. The store had a large collection of suits. With the help of the salesman, I picked out a nice conservative one.

Shorty hit the ceiling. He said that the suit I picked out was just like the one I had brought from Berlin. He pushed the salesman aside and picked out a real loud suit for me. When I put it on, he declared that now I was a real "American" engineer.

For years thereafter, whenever we had visitors in the engineering department, he would call me over with my stupid suit and be in his glory, telling everyone how he had helped me buy this new suit and make an "American" out of me. I could not have been more embarrassed.

Shorty really went out of his way to embarrass me. When I was first employed at Grumman, Shorty found an opportunity to carefully examine the translation of my birth certificate. In Portugal, family relations are of utmost importance. Portugal is a small country and at that time, practically all business was conducted on a family basis. People tried to do business exclusively with relatives or relatives of relatives. They would load up a child's birth certificate with the names of as many relatives as possible in the belief that they were opening future doors for their kids. Until the proclamation of the Republic in 1910, birth certificates were prepared by parish priests who knew the history of everybody in town and could be relied upon to keep the records straight.

Shorty said he counted fourteen names on my birth certificate and thought it was hilarious. At times when we had visitors and I was not wearing my stupid suit, he would call me over and ask me to recite the names on my birth certificate. Shorty acted as conductor as everybody was required to laugh heartily. Again, I could not have been more embarrassed. I had to make a decision between putting up with this type of harassment or looking for a new job. Grumman seemed to be more important.

Shorty also had a inside line to the Farmingdale High School teachers' community. He exerted a great effort in matching young Grumman engineers with pretty high school teachers. He also picked out a nice girl for me. She came from Albany, New York, from a nice family. I was good to her, within my means. Shorty must have told her that I had the potential of making $125 a week. She understood him to say that I was making $125 a week, and she expected me to entertain her as if I was making $125 a week. She had her mother and aunt come down from Albany to look me over. They were nice people, but I could not go through with it on my $25 a week, less than she was making. In a small town like Farmingdale, it is not easy to avoid a girl who smells $125 a week on you. I felt sorry for her, she took it very hard.

I made friends with a young man of German extraction who delighted in practicing his German on me. One nice Sunday afternoon, he invited me to go to a German picnic with him. My friend went to see his girl friend, Ann Burkarth, who was at the picnic with her family. Ann had a sister, Eleanor, who was one year younger than she was. I was introduced to the Burkarth family and found them to be very congenial. We had a good time. At the end of the picnic, I asked Eleanor if I could drive her home, and she agreed.

WITH ELEANOR IN NEW YORK CITY

Eleanor was a beautiful, pleasant girl, easy to entertain. That summer we took full advantage of Jones Beach. Afternoons, we sunned at the beach, towards evening there were inviting restaurants for leisurely dining. On Saturday evening there was a live show in the amphitheater.

Eleanor was employed by the Liberty Mutual Insurance Company in Hempstead where she was the office manager and underwriter. She graduated from a business school and from the Liberty Mutual Underwriter's School, both in New York City..

Most of the year we would usually go Saturday afternoons to New York City. The City was our playground. When I started to work at Grumman, New New York City was a vastly different place from what it has became today in the year 2000. At that time, independent suburban communities, based on the automobile, did not exist. There was no such thing as a shopping mall. Most people in the outlying areas of the City depended on the City's down town department stores for their heavy shopping. The Times Square area was a vast entertainment complex. Thirty-fourth street between 7th and 8th Avenues was an almost solid block of first run movie houses, each one trying do outdo the other with a blaze of lights. Few people had cars. It was still the time when young people in the outlying areas of the City would spend a nickel for the subway to Times Square, to walk around in the streets and mingle with the crowd for the fun of it. Sometimes they would buy an ice cream cone.

It was therefore natural that when I was faced with the problem of what do you do when you take a girl out, my first thought was to take her to New York City. The Times Square area at that time had many nice restaurants with a dance floor and a three-man dance band. We would go to one of these for an early dinner and a few rounds of dancing before going to the theater.

In the basement of the Times Square Building, a firm called "Le Blanc Grey" opened at 7:15 pm every evening to sell leftover unsold tickets to all Broadway plays at $1.25 each. You could sometimes get front row seats to a popular Broadway play, but generally, we got good seats to a good play. After a nice dinner, we would go there and get tickets to a play to top off the evening

I bought season tickets to the Metropolitan Opera. I kept that subscription all the years we lived on Long Island. We have seen all the operas in the book several times. New York City provided many other attractions, such as Radio City with its live shows, ice skating rink, and New York's Christmas Tree. Then there was the Metropolitan Museum of Art and other great museums. The number of New York attractions is almost limitless. We often took our out-of-town visitors to the sight-seeing platform at the top of the Empire State Building for a bird's eye view of the City. We made a one time special outing to go see the Statue of Liberty. We did not go to many bars or nightclubs.

Shopping in New York City department stores was most convenient because they delivered anything to your home anywhere in the Metropolitan Area. Nobody carried packages. Macy's package delivery service was one of the best, it was a cornerstone of their good service and was expanded to serve other department stores. Eventually the delivery service changed its name to United Parcel Service.

To get to the City, I would drive the Packard to a parking lot next to a subway stop in Forest Hills, and take the subway to the City. We would mingle with the crowds and admire the store windows. There were some works of art that were in the "must see" category, like the block long row of Macy's display windows along 34th Street featuring automated figurines illustrating Christmas fairy tales.

At Christmas time, the toy departments in large New York stores were an inspiration.   Many had special restaurants in the toy departments during the   season that served fun meals.

I also took Eleanor to Washington a few times to meet my father and Helen, and to Linden, when we were all there with Lavinia and David. Eleanor got along real well with all these people.

These were the activities that filled our Saturdays. On Sunday, Eleanor   invited me to her house for Sunday dinner with her family. Her mother was a very good cook and Sunday dinner was always superlative. In addition   to her older sister, Eleanor had a brother, Charlie, one year younger than herself, whose main objective was to sneak out of the house, away from his sisters, and join his buddies outside. Then she had two little sisters, Elsie and Inge, seven and eight, whose idea of fun was to wrestle me to the floor and jump all over me.

Eleanor's father, August, was a friendly man, a florist who had been trained in St. Gall, Switzerland, and who the ran the "City of Glass," a huge complex of green houses in Farmingdale that were owned by Bloomingdales, one of New York's elite department stores.

THE NEW YORK WORLD'S FAIR, 1939/40

The New York World's Fair provided us with entertainment every Saturday for almost two years. I bought season tickets, so we could go whenever we pleased.

Most foreign pavilions tried to show what it was like in their countries. Many had restaurants serving their native food.   I was especially interested in countries that served peanuts as a staple.

The Fair was designed by the best human minds in the world to show what our world would be like in 50 to 100 years. It was a supposed to be a great view into the future. The biggest thrust was on individual transportation: small   cars racing on roadways at various elevated levels through the cities. We watched enchanted for hours at the fantastic, monumental, animated displays by Ford and General Motors. But as I can see now, some sixty years later, none of these predictions have come true. On the other hand, things that have come true, were completely unforeseen. No space vehicles were on display at the World's Fair. In 1940, the world scientific community had no inkling, that in less than 30 years, the US in 1969 would safely send two men to the moon and back. Our world today, shaped by the computer and the jet engine, was inconceivable in 1940.

The New York Worlds Fair was great entertainment, and it left us with a beautiful park and a new baseball team and stadium. But it did little to influence the direction of future technical progress.

LONG ISLAND

In the early 1900's, Long Island was an unusual geographical formation that earned it the title: ***Cradle of Aviation.*** Before Long Island was "discovered," aviation in the US was restricted largely to race tracks.

In July, 1908, a Frenchman, Henry Farman, brought his airplane to Brighton Beach Race Track to give New York its first air show and won great acclaim among local enthusiastics. A group formed the New York Aeronautic Society and selected the old deserted Morris Park Race Track in the Bronx as their field. They tried, unsuccessfully, to build several planes, and finally decided to buy one they were sure would fly. They turned to Glenn Curtis, and the first sale of a commercial airplane in America was transacted.

Curtis delivered the plane to Morris Park in June 1909, and the machine was promptly christened the ***Gold Bug***. Curtis felt, however, that the Bronx was no place for flying. They got out a map and studied the surroundings of the City and discovered Long Island. Curtis and several others drove out there and were greatly pleased to find the large, level, grassy stretches of the Hempstead Plains. At that time, Curtis was also anxious to make an attempt to win the Scientific American Trophy for the first flight of 25 km (15 1/2) miles, and the Hempstead Plains seemed like an ideal location for the flight. In the early hours of July 7, 1909, Curtis took off in the Gold Bug to win the $10000 prize. Such prizes did much to accelerate the advancement of aviation at that time.

In addition to being a natural flying field, the Hempstead Plains possessed an ideal geographical location, strategically placed near the largest city in America. Thus they became a focal point for the development of aviation, the zero milestone for most of the great flights which were the steppingstones of progress in building the history of aviation.

Most flying activities around New York were settling near Mineola, and the field became known as the Mineola Air Field or Hempstead Plains Aviation Field. The Wrights came and attracted a number of enthusiastic followers who clashed with the Curtis disciples. Each group formed its own sect and there was violent animosity between them. Many others came and gave their time, money, and efforts to design and build the earliest craft. They made fundamental contributions to the development of aviation.

Harman bought a French Farman and set his sights on winning the Country Life in America Trophy for the first flight across Long Island sound. He tried four times, each time he was driven back by turbulent air conditions. Finally, he made it and was so touched by the acclaim he received that he donated a perpetual trophy to be given by the President of the United States to the pilot making the most outstanding contribution to aviation each year.

In 1911, during the Second International Air Meet, Postmaster General Frank Hitchcock established the US Airmail Service at Nassau Boulevard. He swore in Pilot Earle Ovington as Airmail Pilot No. 1 and handed him the mail. Ovington took off in his Bleriot monoplane and flew with the mailbag between his knees to Mineola, about six miles away, where he dropped the bag near the Post Office.

Lawrence Sperry witnessed Farman's first flight at Brighton Beach in 1908. He returned home to Flatbush full of enthusiasm and immediately started to build his own plane. In those early days, one of the basic problems was how to stabilize the airplane. The planes of the time were treacherous and unstable, the pilot could never relax in flying or his ship would go out of control. The number of fatalities among flyers was a powerful force in deterring public acceptance. Most inventors were trying to solve this problem by aerodynamic means. Sperry took another approach. He built an "automatic gyro stabilizer" which he later developed into an autopilot.

In 1913, the French Government posted a prize of $10000 for the best method for stabilizing an airplane. Sperry arrived in Paris alone with his machine and hired a mechanic to help him put his airplane together. There were 80 contestants, but 79 did not have a chance. On July 2, 1914, as Sperry approached the judges' stand at low altitude, he had his mechanic crawl out on the wing tip, and he himself stood up and flew past the judges with his hands high in the air. Here was a machine that could fly itself, nothing like it had ever been seen before.

Sperry brought his prize home to Long Island, but the war clouds were gathering over Europe. His "automatic gyro stabilizer" was classified as a military secret.

During World War I, the great pilot training centers were located in

Texas and California, because of the good weather there most of the time. However, most American flyers passed through Long Island before going to France. There was much industrial activity on Long Island. It was one of the great wartime airfields.

In 1919, the Navy completed the first Transatlantic Crossing by air. During the war, three great tri-motor flying boats were built by Curtis in Garden City for the long range bombing of Germany. However, the armistice came before the planes were completed. The Navy continued the project, and on May 8, 1919, all three ships took off from Jamaica Bay, planning to fly to Southampton via Newfoundland, the Azores, and Portugal. Only one ship arrived at its destination. Later that same year, the British paid us a visit by air in their new dirigible, the R-34. These transatlantic flights inspired Orteig, a wealthy hotel owner, to post a $25000 prize for the first non-stop flight from New York to Paris.

The first non-stop transcontinental flight was made on May 3, 1923, by two military pilots, Macready and Kelley, flying from Long Island to San Diego. When their water cooled engine started to run dry over the mountains, Kelley, without parachute, climbed out on the nose of the plane and poured coffee from his thermos into the radiator, enabling them to complete the last leg of their journey.

Several famous pilots of the day were on Long Island making extensive preparations for a Transatlantic flight. There was much stirring on both sides of the Atlantic. Of the six attempts to fly the Atlantic in 1927, only Lindbergh reached his announced destination. His success was heralded with an ovation unparaelled in the history of New York City.

These Transatlantic flights in 1927 were the last great flights which may be classified as outstanding sports achievements. Their success depended on a combination of personal skill and luck, they were conducted with inadequate technical means, and the capacity of both the machine and the human operator was stressed to the very maximum.

A new era was in the making. There were engineers on Long Island designing equipment to make the airplane the master of the air space. The new era started with Wiley Post demonstrating in his "round the world flight" a machine that was adequate for the job. Technical adequacy and professional competence replaced luck and extraordinary personal skill. The fair weather aerial circus performer graduated to all-weather full-time, airline pilot, providing peoples of the world with safe, fast, efficient air travel and our country with air supremacy in World Was II.

Among the aviation organizations that prospered on Long Island was the Grumman Aircraft Engineering Corporation. At the beginning of World War II, Grumman was at the right place with the right product at the right time and the right management. The company grew very fast and made a significant contribution to the War effort.

After the War, Long Island found itself the last large undeveloped open space adjacent to New York City, and a magnet for real estate developers. Professional flying, now completely mature, was limited to three huge airports, Kennedy International, LaGardia, and MacArthur, where tens of thousands of air travelers are accommodated daily. The open fields, that were once the cradle of aviation, were taken over by the housing and shopping mall developers.

THE ENGINEERS' FORUM

A young engineer who sat next to me for some time and who was also a reserve officer in the Army, told me about the Engineers Forum of the American Society of Mechanical Engineers (ASME). The Forum held monthly meetings in the Engineers' Societies Building on 39th Street in New York City. The Forum discussed non-engineering topics of general interest to engineers, and my friend found it to be an outstanding educational opportunity.

My friend was called up by the Army, so I had to go to the Forum alone. I found it to be everything he said it was, and more. I made many friends there.

The Chairman of the Forum was Adolf Ehbrecht who owned a medium size small parts manufacturing plant in the Bronx. He let me run some of the meetings. I had to pick a subject, invite the speaker, take him to dinner at the Engineers' Club before the meeting, bring him to the meeting, and introduce him to the audience.

As a newcomer in the New York area, I was fascinated by the parkway and bridge system. I was looking for a speaker to enlighten me on parkways and found that there was only one man in New York City who could talk on parkways: Commissioner Robert Moses. Moses ran a tight ship, and would not let anyone else talk on parkways because they might say something that might endanger his source of funding. In New York City there are so many agencies like schools, hospitals, police, etc. fighting for available funds, that Moses was very protective of his share.

I wrote a nice letter to Moses on ASME stationery, inviting him to come and speak at the Forum. (This is one of the real benefits of Society activity, you get to use stationery that usually gets some results.) Moses wrote back saying that he was busy that day, but he was sending his Chief Engineer, William Shapin. That was OK by me.

I took Shapin to dinner and afterwards he gave us a memorable talk. He explained that Moses believed that that community would best survive that had the best means of access and egress. This led to the concept of the restricted access four lane highway with no traffic lights, right into the heart of the City. With Moses also being Park Commissioner, the concept blossomed into that of a "shoestring park."

Next came the problem of where to build such a "shoestring park" with available funds. The Rockefeller family had built a private, two lane, restricted access, toll road along the less inhabited parts of central Long Island to take them quickly from the City to their elaborate homes on Eastern Long Island. Moses was able to buy a large part of this right of way, and it became the Grand Central Parkway, the first such parkway in the world leading right into the center of the City.

To talk about bridges, I recruited Dr.Steinman, author of the book "Builders of the Bridge," who worked on the George Washington Bridge over the Hudson River and on the modifications of the Brooklyn Bridge. He told us the following stories.

Bridges are among the longest lasting structures that men build, and often become the landmark of the area that they serve. Bridge builders are therefore very aware of their responsibility to build beautiful structures. Roebling, the inventor of the wire rope, built his suspension bridge towers with masonry, as in the Brooklyn Bridge. Later, engineers built steel towers, but encased them in masonry to hide the steel and uphold the tradition of a masonry tower. This was the plan for the George Washington Bridge. Steinman realized that they were going to run out of money before they got around to encasing the towers. So they designed the steel towers esthetically so that they did not have to be hidden. Sure enough, the project ran out of money before the towers could be encased. The naked towers have stood the test of time, they have been fully accepted by the public. Since then, no suspension bridge tower has been encased in masonry.

Steinman showed a set of slides of the most beautiful bridges in the world. The audience was fascinated. The auditorium was full with about 200 men sitting on the edge of their chairs. It was so quite you could have heard a pin drop.

After the end of the War, we became interested in the Marshal Plan, where the US, for the first time, was spending millions to aid foreign countries, in this case, to assist Europe in repairing the damage incurred in the War. The success of this plan depended to a great extent on the cooperation of the US engineering community. The Forum held many meetings on this subject.

The US Engineering Societies, in cooperation with several universities, organized committees for various tasks. One of these early tasks was to develop a plan for monitoring Germany to assure that no secret preparations for war or revolt were taking place. A plan was drawn up to monitor the local consumption of electric power. If there was any sudden large increase in electric power consumption anywhere in the country, the committee was ready to investigate the reason. Any weapons manufacturing coming on line would require sudden large local amounts of electricity.

A major problem in modernizing Europe was teaching Europeans about US industrial production techniques. Teams of European engineers were brought over to the US to observe our operations, and teams of US engineers were sent to Europe to supervise the introduction of American techniques. This was the beginning of a development which, today in the year 2000, takes up a large portion of the US budget.

A professor, active in this process, explained to the members of the Forum, the difficulties involved by telling us the following story. Ten Eskimos from ten Arctic villages were selected for a trip to New York, where they were taken to the zoo and shown an elephant. They could not believe their eyes. They touched and felt the elephant all over, expressing their wonder. On the way back to their hotel, and all that evening, they talked of nothing but the elephant. They did this for ten days. Then each man returned to his village, and was asked what he had seen. He tried to describe an elephant. His fellow villagers laughed at him and accused him of spending his time in New York in a drunken brawl. They continued to tease him about the elephant, so that after a time, he himself had some doubts.

After a year, he was invited to a reunion in Eskimo land with his nine pals who had been with him in New York before. All had had the same experience in their villages, and had begun to doubt their experience in New York. But now they all reassured one another that they had really seen an elephant. Bolstered by this support, he returned home, only to be laughed at again.

Every year the team had a reunion and in each successive year, they were less sure that they had seen an elephant. Eventually, they all agreed that they must have been dreaming, that elephants do not exist. This is the type of mentality that US engineers had to cope with in their attempts to rebuild Europe. Europeans considered American production techniques as the   Eskimos considered elephants.

A group of small European manufacturers was invited to tour small US companies. As their bus turned to pass through the parking lot of a medium size machine shop in New Jersey, the bus riders all broke out into an uproar. They yelled, this was not the place that they wanted to visit, they had been promised to see a small manufacturer. The tour leader tried to tell them that this was a small manufacturer. The Europeans could not believe him. They pointed to all the cars that were being made here. The tour leader explained that all the cars belonged to the workers, who used them to come to work. This was inconceivable for the Europeans. In their minds, you either walked to work or rode a bicycle. Workers did not have cars. Eventually, they had a fine tour of the plant.

A notice of an Engineers' Forum meeting from this time period is shown on page 191.

I made many friends at the Forum.   A group of us from Long Island felt that the industrialization of Long Island had reached a point that it could support an ASME Section. First we organized a Long Island Sub-Section of the Metropolitan Section, that a few years later became the ASME Long Island Section. I served for many years with this group, including my turn as Chairman. My incoming Chairman's Message is reproduced on pages 192 and 193.

From the Engineers' Forum, I was promoted to the Metropolitan Section Executive Committee. One project that I undertook was as Editor of the Bulletin. Originally, this was an 11 x 17 inch sheet, printed on one side with the monthly program of the Section. There were usually eight meetings a month by the various technical groups in the Section. I filled the empty side of the Bulletin for some 10 years.   I went to several selected meetings each month and wrote a report on the meeting in an effort to increase interest and attendance. This project taught me a good deal of discipline. I had to write enough to fill two 8-1/2x11 inch pages, and have my copy ready by the printer's deadline, every month. The Bulletin was distributed to 6700 members and if I made a spelling or grammatical error, I heard about it, loudly. It taught me how to write.

THE   ENGINEERS   CLUB

New York City in the 1930's and 40's was a center of engineering. Many engineering consulting firms had their offices in lower Manhattan. Most of the engineers lived uptown and came to work by subway. In the evening, after supper, many would come back down to midtown to the Engineers' Club on 40th Street, back to back with the Engineering Societies Building on 39th Street.

The Club had eleven stories. In the evening, all rooms would be packed full of men playing cards, poker, billiards, and similar games. It was difficult finding an empty seat.   They also actively traded information about jobs.   Everybody knew what companies were getting the new jobs, and the men followed the work from one company to another. The companies were all concentrated in a small

THE AMERICAN SOCIETY OF MECHANICAL ENGINEERS

METROPOLITAN SECTION – ENGINEERS' FORUM

THE WORLD ENGINEERING CONFERENCE

Do you approve of the Marshall Plan? If you do, as an engineer you will realize that its final success depends on the rebuilding of Europe's destroyed production facilities. The key phase of the Marshall Plan is therefore an engineering problem, and it requires the full cooperation of engineers both in this country and abroad. We American engineers, traditionally preoccupied with the domestic problems of developing our great continent, find ourselves overnight in the international spotlight, where we are suddenly expected to repeat our production achievements, this time on a global scale! We have won the precious ball, and the fate of western civilization depends on how well we carry it!

In view of this situation, the Engineers' Forum takes pleasure in offering its facilities for a discussion of the World Engineering Conference. This organisation is the only international association open to engineering societies all over the world, and affords them the opportunity to formulate common ideals, coordinate action, and exchange technical information in a world forum, in the interest of world peace. You are cordially invited to attend this meeting and to contribute your ideas.

John de S. Coutinho
Chairman

Thursday, March 11, 1948, 7:30 p.m.
Engineering Societies Building, Room 1101,
29 West 39th Street, New York 18

ASME Meeting Notice

Long Island Sub-Section

The American Society of Mechanical Engineers

Member Engineers Joint Council and Engineers' Council for Professional Development

BULLETIN

SEPTEMBER 1964

CHAIRMAN'S MESSAGE

Your Personal Problem: Money

As a young engineering graduate, your starting salary lies within a limited range, there is not much that you personally can do about it. The "average" engineer will then receive annual increases for a number of years. At first his annual income will increase at a linear rate, then the slope gradually will taper off until at some point between fifteen years after graduation and age 40, the slope will be zero. In today's fast moving world, at age 40 the "average" engineer is approaching technological obsolescence. There are no more raises, and if he doesn't watch his step, jobs will be harder and harder to find.

The "average" is a mathematical abstraction, it does not exist in reality. The "average" person in this country has no sex. As individuals, we know that we are something special, and we pride ourselves in being on one side or the other of the "average."

Many engineers continue to get raises after age 40. Occasionally, the raise rate even increases with the years, especially for those men who assume top management positions.

Several studies indicate that your personal rate of salary increase at age 40 and above depends on what you do during the first five to ten years out of college. Once your rate of salary increase starts to drop off, it is practically impossible to do anything about it. You, and you alone in your first few years out of college, determine what salary bracket you are going to grow into at age 40 and above.

None of this applies to men of superior intellect, such as Einstein or Steinmetz. Such men will always find their place, regardless of the system. This discussion is for people who are not too far from the norm, like you and me.

Industry's Problem: People

An analysis of the employer's problems discloses a perplexing fact: a lack of men over age 40 to whom, with justification, raises can be given! A company stays in business only if it makes a profit. Most companies would like to expand and make more money. Our country has enough available investment capital, and there are many jobs to be done. Most wide-awake employers see many opportunities which they cannot exploit because they do not command the necessary top-flight engineering manpower.

In our competitive system, employers are glad to give raises to creative and imaginative engineers who will help them make more money. Any employer will take a chance on a good looking young college graduate; but employers assume that by the time an engineer reaches age 40 he has had ample opportunity to demonstrate in what salary bracket he belongs!

I believe that industry has few problems which could not be solved by a greater number of creative and alert top-flight engineers and executives. There are many books available exploiting the theme "There's Plenty of Room at the Top." Why don't more engineers of age 40 and above qualify for these good available salaries?

Your Personal Growth

With all these excellent jobs available for men of age 40, how do you apply?

As a young graduate right out of college, you cannot compete with top older engineers, age 45 to 65, who are running industry. But you can strive to be the best in your class. Not necessarily the one with the highest college grades; but the one who does the job which best satisfies your employer and his customer. You can continue this effort, so that at age 30 you are the best in your age group.

If you persist, you should arrive at age 40 at the head of the line. After that, you've got it made; you have acquired a habit which is too hard to break.

Graduate Education

We all like to associate "education" with "college". This is the easy way: you pay your money and you get your "predigested education" handed to you on a silver platter, complete with certificate verifying that you have been exposed to learning (not that any has been absorbed!)

Lets face it: today, formal education and graduate study are prerequisites. Without them, you are not even in the running. Some companies expect their engineering employees to take at least one graduate course a year for the rest of their professional lives. They do this because they want to survive as top companies, and you cooperate if you value your job. But your raises after age 40 no longer depend on your graduate degrees!

ASME — Your Self-Help Organization

Unless you were born wealthy, or have a rich wife, nothing can change the fact that you are on your own in a highly competitive world. Nobody but you yourself is going to look out for you. The time-honored solution for men in this predicament is to join together for mutual assistance and group therapy. Although few people think of ASME in this light, the Society offers a young man many opportunities for self-help. This has been one of the roles which ASME has played in the formulation of my own career, and now that you (or your representatives) have elected me Chairman of your Section, I want to share my secret with you. Our programs and activities are designed to help you to help yourself, as they helped me throughout the past twenty-five years. Our program holds one of the keys to your future success - if you cooperate. I say this because I do not know anyone who has been associated with our ASME activities for any appreciable length of time and who has not achieved some additional measure of success.

Our New Program Format

In an effort to streamline our activities, we have reorganized our program. Once a month there will be an ASME Evening Symposium, on the second or third Thursday or Friday of the month. The meeting dates are all published in the center fold, so that you can reserve these nights for the entire season. Each evening there will be a dinner followed by a number of simultaneous technical sessions and a civic affairs forum. You do not have to come to the dinner, you are welcome to attend the sessions only. This is the modern supermarket idea; there will always be something of interest to you going on; you can pick the session you want to attend after you get to the meeting. All you have to remember is the date and the time!

In addition, we are planning two meetings in Suffolk County for those who live in that area, and also two all-day Saturday symposia which will include plant tours.

The Technical Sessions

Many high level observers of today's engineering scene are deeply concerned with the overspecialization of engineers. Major engineering systems are designed by teams of geographically widely dispersed firms who were competitors before they became

(Continued on Back Page)

ASME Bulletin, Chairman's Message

CHAIRMAN'S MESSAGE

(Continued from Front Page)

associated on the current project, and who intend to compete again after completion of the current association. Often, they simultaneously compete on parallel projects.

This working arrangement imposes special personal responsibilities on the engineer. Complex management systems keep him in his place. He may be denied many channels of communication across company lines with other engineers whose work interlocks with his own in a most sensitive manner. The succes of the project may depend on the engineer's ingenuity in developing an understanding of the technical interface problems involved, in spite of the communications barriers placed around him. The component designer must develop a greater awareness of the quality and performance requirements imposed by system operation. On the other hand, system engineers need to develop a better understanding of the inherent limitations of component performance. From a company viewpoint, these considerations are fundamental for maintaining a competitive position.

The importance of a strong competitive position cannot be overemphasized. The economy of Long Island is changing. At one time this area constituted the "cradle of aviation" with a growing defense industry. Defense today is being replaced by high-value commercial product lines. The engineer is expected to assume considerable leadership in the creation of these new products. To qualify for this assignment, he must be flexible, alert, recognize new opportunities and be able to help develop new needs and markets.

Your Program Committee has assembled a coordinated program which will present some significant aspects of a few selected modern or advanced systems. These presentations will give you authoritative broad visibility in a fraction of the time that it would take you to acquire the same information in any other way. Participation in the discussions will broaden your understanding of the problems involved.

The Civic Affairs Forum

An area of dynamic growth such as Long Island, stands to benefit from any reduction in the existing serious time lag between development of a feasible and useful technical concept, and its implementation. The engineer is responsible for the technical concept, not for its implementation. Those responsible for implementation are often not aware of the availability of feasible technical concepts, and of their potential benefits. It follows that one of the civic responsibilities of the engineer is to make known the availability of new and useful technical concepts whose implementations would benefit the public welfare.

The Peace Corps, and the War on Poverty, are variations of this concept on a broader level. To quote the late President Kennedy: "We have the capacity to make this the best generation in the history of mankind - or the last!" Such is the impact of the engineer on society.

The speakers at these forums are selected from different fields and include civic leaders who are not engineers. We hope that these forums will contribute to the solution of some of Long Island's important technical community problems.

These forums should also be attractive to ladies. The Program Committee invites you to bring your wife to the forum, while you attend a technical session.

Need for Wider Participation

Most of the active men in the Section are associated with either of two companies, Long Island Lighting and Grumman. Although these are two fine companies, the Section should have a broader base. Men from other companies are cordially invited to join our committees and participate in our work.

Our Success Depends on You!

Your Program Committee has assumed considerable risk in developing the new program format. We took the risk because we believe that doing so would be in your interest.

Success at our first meeting on Friday, October 16, is critical. If the attendance at this meeting does not warrant it, it will be most difficult for the Program Committee to continue with this new scheme.

Please lend me your support and take advantage of this opportunity. Send in your reservations now for October 16, and plan to attend the entire series. Bring your wife, if you can, and some of your engineering associates. Put up our program on your plant bulletin board and help us with our publicity.

You cannot get full benefit by just attending one meeting, you must participate regularly. As in any other educational activity, what you get out is proportional to what you put in. However, the benefits available here cannot be obtained elsewhere; I assure you that it will be worth your effort.

John de S. Coutinho
Chairman

Long Island Section
American Society of Mechanical Engineers
Post Office Box 568
Hicksville, New York

ASME Bulletin, Chairman's Message, page 2

area downtown and nobody had to move when they changed jobs. It was a way of life. Engineers formed practically a closed community in the City, with the Club as their headquarters. Today, in the year 2000, almost all engineering firms have left New York City, and the Club is closed. The Club's dining room on the eleventh floor was one of the most beautiful and ornate public rooms in New York City. I entertained all the speakers, that I invited to speak at the Forum, in this room.

ANTICS IN THE ENGINEERING DEPARTMENT

The Grumman Engineering Department consisted primarily of young men. One day, Schwendler had to go to Washington on business. It was a beautiful day, and the bright sunshine outside our large windows seemed to impede our will to work. Somebody threw a spitball, accurately. The reaction was loud and instantaneous. Within seconds, spitballs. erasers, even tennis balls were flying back and forth with loud shouts of gutter humor. It was very similar to the outbreaks we had in our classrooms in Meersburg when there was no Brother around. At the height of this disturbance, Leroy Grumman walked in looking for Schwendler. Everybody froze and Grumman walked out. Everything was quiet for the rest of the day.

The next day, Schwendler called each man individually into his office, to get a description of what happened. It was determined that Johnson had been the ringleader. We were then told that Johnson was appointed Administrative Engineer and personally responsible for maintaining order in the Engineering Department. If there was ever another such outbreak, Johnson would be fired.

Some engineers liked to make fun of the shop by releasing fake drawings of parts which were impossible to make. Several years later, when a much larger extension to the engineering department was built, serious conflict broke out between the shop and the engineering department. Any engineer caught in the shop got half of his tie cut off. The engineering department retaliated by cutting off the shirttails of any shop man caught in the engineering department. Schwendler went into action real fast and somehow quelled the conflict. Those of us who were not involved had a good laugh.

Later, during the war, when women had been admitted as a permanent feature to the engineering department, an ingenious engineer built a hydraulic spitball cannon out of rejected parts he rescued from the scrap heap. The contraption was amazingly accurate up to 100 feet. He would place it on the floor and aim it under the drawing tables at a good looking female calf some 40 feet away. The engineering department would be very quite, everybody would be working away very industriously. Suddenly, some woman would jump high in the air, holding her leg and screaming at the top of her voice. This was not a demonstration against our lovely female "engineering aides." They were all competent and good workers, and we admired them. Several engineers showed their deep respect for them by marrying them.

XF5F-1, SKYROCKET

The Navy advertised for a new carrier based fighter, superior to the F4F, and Grumman responded with a proposal for the XF5F-1. The basic problem at that time was that with the available aircraft engines, you could only pack so much power into an airplane; this defined its performance limits. Grumman took a dramatic step and put two of the biggest available engines (12000 hp each) in the XF5F-1, to be the first ever twin engine carrier based airplane.

Sweetzer was still busy with the F4F structure, and I was the only one available for the XF5F-1 wing. I now worked for Pete Erlandson, a graduate of Princeton University and Chief Structural Engineer, who reported directly to Schwendler. I was getting places.

The preliminary design group placed great emphasis on technical innovation, designed to win competitive contracts. The twin engine configuration, with engines mounted on the wings of an airplane with a tail wheel, gave the pilot vastly increased visibility, see photo on page 196. It also put large loads on the wings. To cope with these loads, the designers selected a "box beam" structure, that is, two beams, and load carrying upper and lower skin covers between the beams. This was the lightest possible arrangement, but there was a problem: we had no structural formulas for such an arrangement. Structural formulas apply to "Statically determinate" structures, like those with one beam. Two beams are "statically indeterminate" and to solve the problem mathematically, you have to rely on additional elastic equations, such as I had in my course in "Elasticity" at NYU. This requires the highest level of mathematics and is best avoided. All this had been very thoroughly discussed in my statics class in Berlin, and I had had a difficult time understanding what it was all about. At this time, I wanted to proceed with the design of an airplane, and not get lost in applying higher mathematics.

I had some deep discussions with Erlandson, Sweetzer, Meirs, and other helpful engineers, and developed the following plan. We knew that the bending stresses in the box beam covers would be a maximum at the beams, and a minimum at the center of the box, like a clothes line hanging between two poles. The difference between a theoretical straight line stress distribution in the cover, and the actual distribution shaped like a clothes line, is called "shear lag," see the sketch on page 197. I found that by using one of Meirs' templates, I

XF 5F-1 Skyrocket, 1940

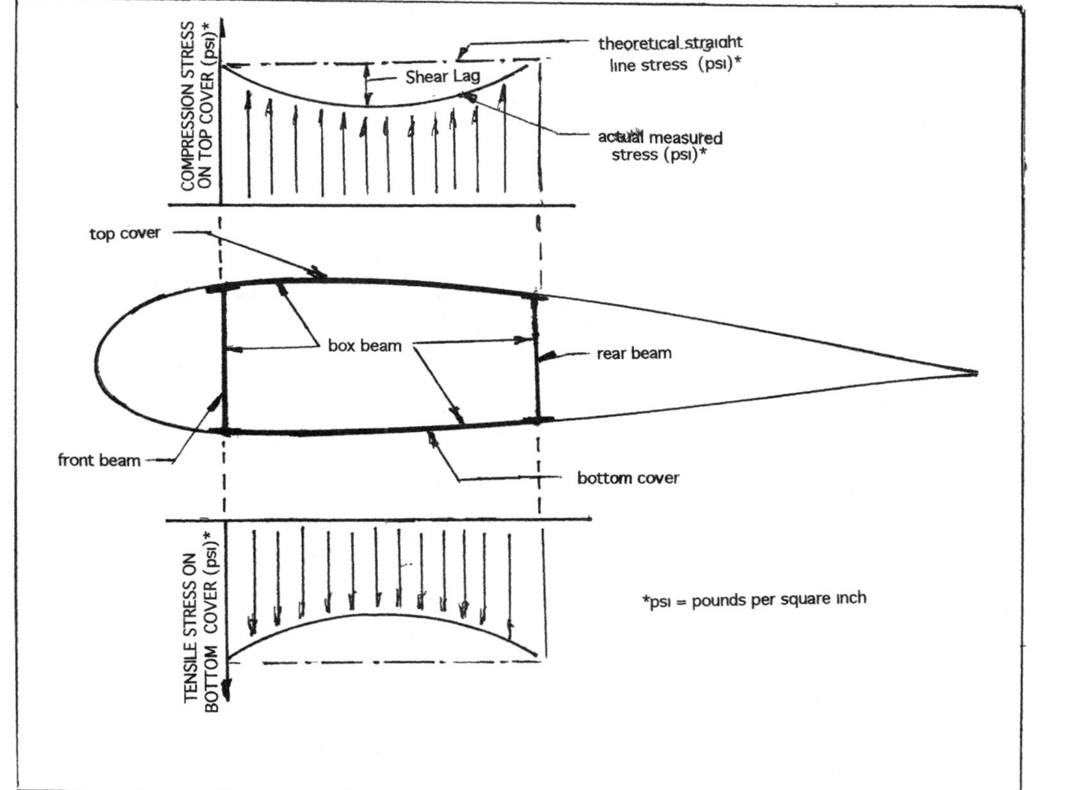

XF 5F-1 Wing Cross Section - Bending Stresses in the Box Beam

could draw what I thought was a reasonable curve of the stress distribution in the cover. I called it the Meirs' Curve. I suggested that we use this curve to calculate design stresses. Later, after the static test, we could then compare the assumed Meirs' stresses with the measured stresses. If there was no large difference, we could adjust the design stresses so they would be compatible with the measured stresses. If the difference between the Meir's Curve and the measured stress was too big, we would have no choice but to redesign and retest.

It was a good thing I gave the Meir's Curve a name. Several years later, I found young engineers using the same method and talking about the "Meirs' Curve." With a name like that, it had attained respectability.

I presented my plan to Schwendler and he gave me the go-ahead. I prepared a stress analysis report that was submitted to the Navy for "approval," and that was approved without question. Then I prepared and submitted a test plan, that was also approved.

A static test at Grumman is a big deal. A large area is roped off in the huge test hanger. All the engineers and managers in the company, at one time or another, come to stand around in back of the rope and watch what you are doing. I put up a blackboard and marked my progress for them. They established a pool, taking bets on when failure will occur.

As the static test progressed, I was absolutely amazed. They had taught me how to run a test in Berlin, but with little test pieces. This was real big stuff. I had a row of twenty huge hydraulic actuators over the span of the wing, simulating thousands of pounds of air load. And it worked, just like it said in the book. I kept loading up the wing, holding the load for three minutes, dropping the load, and the elastic wing came back exactly to the zero position every time. You can't see the failure when it occurs. I had to watch for the beginning of permanent deformation in the wing. When the permanent deformation reached 0.02%, that point was designated as "failure." It is very disappointing that you can't see something "break," or make a "big bang." But this was engineering, not fireworks.

The Navy Inspector signed my test log, certifying that the test had been conducted in accordance with the previously approved Test Plan. I wrote a description of the test in a Test Report that was submitted to the Navy for "information." The Navy does not have to approve reports of tests that are conducted in accordance with an approved test plan.

SHEAR LAG AT NYU

At this time, I was scheduled to select a subject for my Master's thesis at NYU. I thought my analysis of the XF5F-1 box beam would make a fine subject. I approached Klemin with this proposal, and he was pleased. He said he welcomed such a theses written in industry rather that a rehash of research being conducted at NYU.

I submitted a series of partial reports as I wrote the thesis, and they were all approved without comment. Finally, I submitted my final thesis, and it was also approved without comment. Klemin was delighted. He had me write a condensed version that he had published under the title of *A Practical Method of Allowance for Shear Lag*, in the Journal of the Aeronautical Sciences, October, 1942. It was also published in the series Contributions from the College of Engineering, 1942-43, No. 35, New York University.

I satisfied all the requirements for a Master's Degree on schedule in February, 1941, but had to wait until the Graduation in June before I received my diploma. I no longer had to refer to my experience in Berlin.

My thesis earned me a solid reputation at NYU. Several years later, after Klemin had passed away, I was offered a position as instructor at the University. It was an attractive offer, but having been released from the Army to work at Grumman, I did not feel free to accept the offer.

XP-50

The XF5F-1, with its twin 1200 hp engines, turned out to be the fastest pursuit airplane in the world. It was entered in Navy competition with the F4U-1 Vought Corsair. The Navy had never had a twin engine airplane on a carrier and they did not know what problems they might have. The Navy chose the Vought airplane.

Grumman sold the XF5F-1, subject to some modifications, to the US Army Air Corps. Catapulting, arrested landing, and tail wheel provisions had to be removed. The Army wanted a "triangular" landing gear with nose wheel. A nose wheel structure and nose wheel had to be added, see page 200.

My job was to analyze and to test the proposed nose wheel structure and nose wheel. By this time, this kind of work was routine for me, I knew exactly what to do. A static test is always a big deal, as I have explained, so I decided it required a little bit of showmanship on my part. I gave the static test much thought. I decided that I needed a fancy test fixture that would entertain my audience. I searched the company's stock rooms and scrap heaps for actuators, other hydraulic elements, and pieces of steel of the right size that I could weld together for my test fixture. I did not have to buy anything. Everything worked, the test was a huge success. The audience had a good time, and the Navy inspector (acting for the Air Corps) signed my test log. I also wrote all stress reports, test plans, and test reports.

XP 50, 1941

After the test, Erlandson told me that I had been very clever in developing the test fixture and running the test. I had done so very cheaply and saved the company a lot of money that they used to buy two heavier and stronger tracks in the test hanger. (The tracks are embedded in the hanger floor and are used to hold test fixtures in place, they have to hold heavy loads.)

The XP-50 was faster than the XF5F-1, it became the fastest pursuit airplane in the world. It belonged to the Air Corps. In a test flight over Long Island Sound, an engine failed and broke apart, the airplane was lost in deep water. The pilot was saved by the escort helicopter. By this time, all Grumman people were busy on other jobs, and Grumman did not have the resources to recover the XP-50. It was a considerable loss to our National Defense.

MARRIAGE

My friends at Grumman told me that I could not get married until I was making $50 a week. I finally got there. In December, 1941, I got a raise bringing my pay to $50 a week.

In the meantime, Bloomingdales sold their greenhouse business in Farmingdale, and Eleanor's father moved with his family to the Catskills. He was a native of Southern Germany and a "mountain" person. He had spent his vacations with his family in a German community, Big Indian, in the Catskill Mountains. When Bloomingdales sold the greenhouses, he went to the Catskills to buy an appropriate business. He found a small resort for sale, the Catskill Mountain Lake House. The property included some 10 acres and held a good size lake with a row boat. The clientele were all Germans, mostly prosperous storekeepers from 86th Street in New York City. At that time, 86th Street was as much like Germany as any place outside of Germany could be. Both sides of the street were lined with stores selling German wares. You only heard German spoken in the stores and on the street.

When her father moved to the Catskills, Eleanor found herself a room in Hempstead near her work. On holidays, Eleanor would go to the mountains to spend the time with her family. Ann also had a job, in Farmingdale, and she decided to stay there when her family moved away.

With $50 a week in my pocket, a few days before Christmas, I took a large box, about a foot cubed, and packed it full with walnuts. Each walnut was carefully wrapped in Christmas paper. An engagement ring was also wrapped in Christmas paper, it looked just like another walnut. I sent the package to the Catskills by bus.

The whole Burkarth family had quite a time unwrapping walnuts. They almost gave up a couple of times, but Eleanor egged them on.

Finally, Eleanor unwrapped the last "walnut," and it was the container that held the ring.

I received a phone call from her, saying that she was taking the next bus to New York, meet her at the bus station.

Our major job now was trying to find an apartment, there just weren't any available. We also had to think of furniture. One of our senior designers, Lloyd Skinner, advised me that he had been very well treated at Georges, a large furniture store in Hempstead. We went there and were attended by a very nice lady, Mrs. Hebron, who was also an interior designer. We told her our story, and she volunteered find an apartment for us. In the meantime. we looked at her furniture. We told her how much money we had, and she put together a package of Haywood Wakefield blond birch furniture for us.

She finally found an apartment for us. It would not be available until September, that was still several months in the future, but lacking anything else, we took it. The apartment was in a nice complex, Bennett Gardens, directly in back of the property of the Hempstead Elks Club. Mrs. Hebron supervised the men that restored the apartment for us, it looked like new when we moved in. With the blond furniture and wall colors she picked out, the place was an interior designer's dream. At no later period in our lives have we lived in such elegant surroundings.

The availability of the apartment set the the wedding date for us, September 12, 1942. The wedding was held in the Church of Our Lady of Lorreto, the Hempstead parish church. There were many of our friends in the church. Eleanor's family came down from the Catskills, and my father and Helen came up from Washington. After the wedding, we met at a fancy Swedish smorgasbord restaurant (Dahlstroms) for a wedding feast. Never since in my life, except in Europe, have I seen such a layout of smorgasbord. The restaurant was surrounded by a lovely garden, where we took our wedding pictures.

After the festivities, Eleanor and I left in my car, duly decorated by Charlie, with "JUST MARRIED" signs and stones in my hubcaps, for our initial destination, Niagara Falls, the standard destination for honeymooners in those days. We had two weeks time. I had to be careful with the gas. It was rationed on the East Coast, and I had to get out of the rationed area as fast as possible. As far as money went, I had plenty, $200. Wherever there was one, we stayed in Statler Hotels, they gave you a discount if you made a reservation from out of town. I called and made a reservation from a public telephone before I got into town. The double rooms at the Statler were usually $6. On our return trip, I made a reservation at the Statler in New York City for a $6 room, and they put us up in a $22 room at the $6 price, among the best rooms in the hotel.

We made the rounds at Niagara falls, and then decided to tour Canada: Montreal and Toronto. In these cities, Eleanor liked to walk through the department stores. In Montreal, the Church is a one half scale imitation of the Vatican. The Vatican is not as impressive when it is little. In Toronto, we stayed at the Royal York, at that time the largest hotel in the world. I was amused when the bell boys very politely called Eleanor "mam ."

On the way through the Canadian countryside, we saw people picking big peaches. I stopped and bought a small basket. They were the most delicious peaches we have ever tasted.

On the way home, we stopped in Pittsburgh and visited Eleanor's Uncle George, her father's brother who brought him over from Germany. He owned a bakery. We were fed coffee and pastry and told to come again. We have never had a chance to do so.

We arrived back home in our new apartment with less than a quarter of a tank of gas and with $10 between the two of us.

Our best friends at the time were Marie and Cappy (Elio Caprioglio). Cappy was the landing gear designer at Grumman. Until they had their first baby, Joann, we had Sunday dinner together at Anselmi's Restaurant in Bethpage, and then went over to their house for the afternoon. In the summer. we often went to Jones Beach.

ASME   PUBLICATIONS COMMITTEE

Because of my work on the Metropolitan Section Bulletin, the ASME Vice President, Region II, Harry Kessler, appointed me the Region II Advisory Member on the Publications Committee. After several years in this capacity, I was elected a Committee member and eventually Chairman.

The Committee oversees the Society's publications activities. At that time, the Society published more pages of technical literature than any other organization in the US, except the American Chemical Society. It was a major American publishing enterprise.

The problems with the Society's magazine, Mechanical Engineering, were always a subject of discussion. We were constantly trying to improve it. Circulation was about 60000. We were always concerned with making the design of the front cover more attractive. We discussed what we could do to attract more advertisers. I started a campaign to increase the type size to make the magazine easier to read by our older members.

The ASME is modeled after the British Institution of Mechanical Engineers (IME) and many of our procedures are patterned after the British. The type in Mechanical Engineering was selected over 100 years ago to be the same as in the Journal of the IME. Its not easy to overturn a 100 year tradition. The longevity of engineers has increased over the past 100 years, and there are more older engineers now than there were in the past.   After much deliberation, it was decided to increase our type size. In the same month that Mechanical Engineering appeared in its new larger type size, the Journal of the IME also appeared in the same new larger type as its American counterpart. That's how things work.

Another of our considerations was the second class mail distribution of Mechanical Engineering. We wanted our membership to get the magazine as quickly as possible. In New York, second class mail could sit around for weeks until a clerk was available to send it out. Our printer had a set of trucks which delivered the magazine to smaller post offices throughout the US, as far west as the Mississippi River, where second class mail would be processed more quickly. The operation had to be monitored continuously.

The <u>Transactions</u> contained all the technical papers that were presented at Society meetings and that were considered to be of "permanent value." They were distributed to all members.   My discreet surveys disclosed that most recipients did not read them. We broke the <u>Transactions</u> into four specialty Quarterlies and distributed them on a subscription basis.

A special problem was the Journal of Applied Mechanics (JAM), that had the reputation of being the most authoritative Journal in its field in the world.   I considered it a house journal for MIT (Massachusetts Institute of Technology), since I only saw papers in it from professors at MIT. In order for a professor at MIT to advance, he had to publish technical papers, this was considered proof of his competency. Acceptance of a paper in JAM was a certain way to get advancement.   I determined that almost no working engineers read the JAM. I therefore suggested that ASME drop its publication. The Council of the Society discussed this matter for over two hours. The decision was that JAM was like a garden where budding scientists could develop into "Einsteins," and we need more "Einsteins," the growth of the engineering profession depends on them. It is therefore an obligation of every engineer to continue to support the JAM. My proposal was denied. It was an interesting experience.

I was, however, able to reorganize the editorial board so that it would accept papers based on merit from any university in the world, not just MIT.

One of our international best sellers was the ASME Boiler Code. This was a stack of documents six feet high. Its development was a piece of real Americana.

About a hundred and some years ago, some 2000 people a year were being killed by boiler accidents or explosions in the US. A group of ASME members formed a "Boiler Committee" and investigated every boiler accident occurring in the country. After analysis of the accident, they wrote a set of instructions on how to design a boiler so that such an accident would not recur. With time, they gathered quite a bit of data, and started to publish a "Boiler Code," that is, instructions on how to design a boiler and associated equipment so that it would not fail in service in known accident modes. Over the last hundred years, the Boiler Code has been updated after every accident/explosion that has occurred in the US.

Today, the Code covers the smallest boilers for home and shop use to those in the largest power plants. Every boiler in the civilized world today is designed in accordance with the ASME Boiler Code, not only is it a local government requirement, but you cannot buy insurance on any boiler not inspected and certified to be in accordance with the ASME Boiler Code.

The Code is available in several languages. The western European countries, in particular, resent it that they have to comply with an US Code. However, nobody else has data going so far back in time. There seems to be little appreciation that empirical data cannot be fabricated by "scientific methods." It has to be collected in time on actual devices.

In 1980, I was one of the two past Chairmen of the Publications Committee to receive the ASME Centennial Medal.

RUNNING FOR ASME VICE PRESIDENT

I was nominated by the Publications Committee for ASME Vice President. It was mandatory that there be at least two candidates for each office, so the Nominating Committee could select the best one.

I was engaged in a friendly discussion with the Nominating Committee when somebody broke in and asked me where I was born. I answered "Portugal." That was the end of the interview. ASME did not tolerate any foreign born officers. (Maybe that has changed.)

There was a sequel to this comedy. For a number of years, committees nominating a vice president, would invite me to run on their ticket. Since I was a sure loser, I guaranteed that the other candidate would win. It was a great lesson in "democracy."

CROYDEN M. JOHNSON

Johnson was a draftsman who applied for work at Grumman at about the same time that I was hired. Grumman had lots of work that he could do, but had no room for him. The Navy required a set of ink drawings on cloth for the last airplane of a contract. These permanent cloth drawings were traced from the paper drawings that we used.

Johnson pointed out that he needed no supervision to produce tracings. He offered to work in the space that Grumman had evacuated in Farmingdale, and be paid 25 cents a square foot of drawing.

Grumman set him up with a drafting table in Farmingdale and he went to work. His tracings were of high quality, and Grumman sent him more. Working day and night, Johnson could not handle it. He asked if he could hire a draftsman to help him, and Grumman agreed. When the extension on the Engineering Department was completed, Johnson moved in, with two employees. He is the same man I mentioned in on page 194.

As the quantity of tracings allotted to Johnson grew, he hired more people. Grumman also did not have enough engineers, so they started to give some engineering work to Johnson. Johnson hired more people. Before anybody noticed, almost half the people in the Engineering Department were working for Johnson. Grumman started to look over these people, and those that satisfied certain requirements, were transferred to the Grumman payroll. That's how Grumman enlarged its engineering department so quickly. Eventually, Grumman only hired engineers who had worked a year for Johnson.

Johnson was looking around for something more permanent than little surplus engineering jobs. He took over the job of preparing the technical manuals that had to be delivered with each airplane. This was a job that engineers did not like to do, we were all relieved when Johnson was assigned this task.

Johnson's men became specialists in writing technical manuals. Johnson hired more people and needed more room. Grumman could not give it to him, so he built himself his own building across the street. He put in a four color press and produced the best looking technical manuals in the country. Eventually, he had some 250 people in his new building.

He had a library with all the technical manuals produced in the US. If an engineer had difficulty with a design problem, he could go over to Johnsons and study the technical manuals of other companies and see how they solved similar problems. Johnson made sure that Grumman had technically the best manuals in the country.

LEROY RANDLE GRUMMAN

Leroy Grumman was one of the great Americans that I have known. He graduated 1916 from Cornell University with an engineering degree and joined the Navy to become a Naval aircraft test pilot. He was one of the few men in the country at that time who believed that the aircraft carrier was to become the Navy's next main battle ship.

After his Navy tour, in 1920 Grumman joined Loening Aircraft in New York City, manufacturers of fighter aircraft for the Army and

Navy, and of "air yachts" for playboys. In 1929 Grover Loening sold his business to Keystone Aircraft who moved it to its plant in Bristol, PA. Many of Loening's former employees elected to stay in New York and on Long Island. Grumman teamed up with former Loening employees Jake Swirbul, also an engineering graduate of Cornell, who became his General Manager, and Bill Schwendler, a graduate of NYU, his Chief Engineer, and started the Grumman Aircraft Engineering Corporation in 1930. They had 21 people and a contract to build spare aircraft floats for the Navy.

At the beginning of World War II, the Navy accepted two new aircraft carriers, but still had no aircraft for them. They asked Leroy Grumman to build as many F4F airplanes as he could, as fast as he could. Grumman put his plant on a 24 hour basis, and asked workers to work as much time as they could. Many men brought in cots on which they slept when they were tired, and they worked when they were awake. The cafeteria remained open 24 hours a day. It was heavily subsidized and served very good food.

As the planes rolled off the assembly line, they were given a short flight test, and flown out to the carriers that were waiting off shore near Long Island. As soon as they had their full complement of aircraft, the carriers set sail for the Pacific. They arrived just in time. These Grumman F4F airplanes were the ones that won the Battle of Midway, the turning point of the War in the Pacific. For most pilots, this was their first time in combat. The kill ratio for the F4F was 1:30, that is, 30 enemy planes were shot down for every F4F lost. Later in the war, the kill ratio for the F6F was 1:40. No other airplanes in the world have approached anything like this record. The F4F and the F6F proved in combat that in their time they were the the best fighter airplanes in the world. Toward the end of the war, in March 1945, Grumman broke the world's fighter aircraft production record by building 664 military airplanes per month in one facility.

Building airplanes of this superior quality was not done by accident. When I started to work at Grumman in 1939, I was taught that the company was in the business of building the best carrier based aircraft in the world. They added, that if we built the best airplanes available, the Navy would have no choice but to buy our airplanes. In this case we would have no money worries. I found this constant striving for the very best to be true throughout the company. It was very much in line with the task of designing carrier based aircraft, which are much more difficult to design than Army aircraft because they have to carry the heavy provisions for catapulting and arrested landings. Yet the Navy required the same performance as the Army. On the F3F, Leroy Grumman invented the retractable landing gear to reduce the drag and increase the speed to allow a heavier Navy aircraft to compete with a lighter Army airplane. Grumman airplanes are easy to fly and pilots like them. For many decades, they have been the choice of the "Blue Angels", the Navy's crack demonstration team. An admiral during the war said: "The name Grumman on a plane or part has the same meaning to the Navy that "Sterling" on silver has to you."

During the war, our pay was frozen at prewar levels. Grumman developed an incentive pay plan based on the number of pounds of aircraft delivered per month. The bonus was significant, it almost doubled my pay. The criteria affected everybody in the plant equally, the floor sweeper as well as the foreman. The long line of men out for a smoke outside the back door disappeared.

I have evaluated many plants throughout the United States, and one thing I always looked for is cleanliness. I associated cleanliness with quality. Grumman was one of the cleanest plants I have ever seen. They had a committee of foremen that inspected the plants every month, and the dirtiest department was awarded the "Dirty Betsy," a life-size witch doll riding a broomstick. The losing foreman had to display the doll over the entrance to his office for a month. Quite often, the presentation was made by Jake Swirbul, General Manager.

British industrialist, Nevil Shute, in his 1954 autobiography "Slide Rule" describes how he and a few friends started an aircraft engine manufacturing plant and how it successfully grew to where it employed 1000 people. At that point he realized that his friends were no longer capable of managing such a large plant. A different type of person was needed. He dumped his friends and hired a new management team. They were successful and the company grew to where it employed 10000 persons. At this point, his team no longer had the capability to properly manage the company, and he had to change his team. When it reached 20000, he realized that company management requirements were over his head, and for the good of the company, he had to go. You cannot expect someone who is good at managing a small company to also be capable of managing a large one.

But Leroy Grumman did it. He was a remarkable man. At the beginning of the War, the Grumman Company grew rapidly from 700 to 40000 persons. At the end of the War, when the Navy canceled all its contracts, Grumman reorganized his company at the 4000 person level, and it grew gradually to a peace time level of 25000. I shall describe some of the practices that he used in this process to shed light on his extraordinary qualities.

Grumman Aircraft was the only aircraft company of its size that was not unionized. It was not the fault of the unions, they spent over $10 million in attempts to unionize the company, but only received negligible number of votes every time a ballot was taken. Grumman management retained full control over the running of its plants as demonstrated in the episode described in the third paragraph of this heading.

Toward the end of the war, the Navy started to cut down on its procurement. I remember when they canceled the Vought contracts. There were long protests in the local newspapers. However, an editorial in Collier's, then a popular weekly, pointed out that it made good sense for the Navy to cancel a high cost producer when they saw the end of the war approaching. The editorial quoted a price of $ 90000 to $ 107000 for a Vought F4U at different plants. The editorial said, what it did not understand, was how Grumman, in the high cost area of Long Island, could provide a competitive aircraft, the F6F, for $ 35000. I knew that figure to be true.

At the beginning of the war, Congress passed a law that required the defense industry to go on cost-plus and not make more than 10% profit. Grumman refused to obey, pointing out that cost-plus required Government inspectors in all departments of the plant to assure that the company was not overcharging the Government, and that the administration of cost-plus added an unacceptable increment of cost to the final product.

Leroy Grumman pointed out that the Navy had the cost data for the entire industry, and he was willing to negotiate a "Fair Fixed Price" for his airplanes. Grumman reduced the "Fair Fixed Price" by 10% and called it the "Target Price". He reduced the "Target Price" by 10% and called it the "Objective." The Company proposed to sell aircraft at the "Fair Fixed Price" and higher cost at no profit, at the "Target Price" at 10% profit, and at the "Objective" at 20% profit, with a straight line relationship between these points. The Navy accepted this scheme. The first contract was delivered close to the "Objective" price, and Grumman collected nearly 20% profit. On the next contract, the "Objective" was made the "Target," reducing the price again by 10%. This reduction was made in all subsequent contracts, with Grumman always coming in under the "Target," and usually close to the "Objective," thereby collecting nearly 20% in profits. The Navy was delighted. The US Price Administration Board took Grumman to court for making more than 10% profit, and they lost. In two and one half years of wartime production, Grumman reduced the cost of the F6F from $80000 to $35000.

Whenever possible, assemblies were built by teams that were responsible for quality and cost. There was lively competition between the teams in devising ways to cut costs while maintaining quality. The system made everybody in the plant aware of the need to cut costs.

Grumman paid a great deal of attention to quality of personnel. I was the only engineer hired in the year 1939. The next year, three were hired. Shorty visited their universities and talked with their professors before they were hired. When it appeared that they would have to hire a lot more engineers, they started to recruit Johnson's men. Later, as a permanent solution, they appointed Al Wilder as Director of Engineering Personnel. Wilder visited top universities, made friends with top professors, and met the good students. No engineers were hired, except those from universities on Wilder's list, who had top recommendations from their professors and who Wilder had been watching for at least a year.

Grumman had the same concern for shop workers. When I started to work at Grumman, the only way persons could get jobs in the shop or other departments was to have a relative in the plant vouch for them. I knew of cases where seven members of a family worked at Grumman.

Later, Grumman hired the principal of the Bethpage High School to form a committee of Long Island high school principals. A student had to be recommended by his teachers and the principal of his high school to be accepted at Grumman.

Unfortunately, Grumman and his cohorts could not find capable successors of the caliber needed to run such a large and specialized Company. When they passed away, the Company was unable to get another airplane contract after the F-14, nor another space program after the Lunar Module. It made money by building wings for Boeing. In desperation, it finally merged with Northrop.

Leroy Grumman, by his accomplishments, was a giant among men.

XTBF-1 AVENGER (DEVELOPMENT)

The Avenger was a torpedo bomber that arrived on the scene at the right time. First production deliveries were made in January, 1942, the month after Pearl Harbor and the US Declaration of War. It proved to be one of the most successful airplanes of World War II, used in the Mediterranean in support of the battles for North Africa, and then in the Pacific.

The Avenger had a crew of three men. The pilot was the commander. A gunner sat in a carriage in the top back on a circular track. The seat rotated automatically to the direction that the gunner pointed his gun. The third man was a gunner at the very back end of the tail, gun aiming aft. The plane carried one torpedo in its belly.

I was assigned as the stress analyst for the fuselage structure. I knew exactly what to do. The job involved stacks of pages full of five digit numbers, ending up in a stress analysis report and a test plan that had to be submitted to the Navy for approval, and a test report for information, signed by the resident Navy inspector who will have witnessed the test. I was now an expert in analyzing an aircraft structure and preparing these documents.

While I did the fuselage, Tommy did the wing. I had great respect for Tommy. In checking a report, he did not recalculate all the numbers like the rest of us. He would read the report and identify the critical numbers. Then he would devise some other model for calculating them without going through the detailed calculations. If he got the same numbers as in the report, he would sign off on it. It would usually take him less than a day. I was not yet able to do such independent thinking. I required a week to check a technical report. One issue to which I gave much thought was the thickness of the outside skin of several large side panels. One of the strict rules in our department was that we could not use a skin thickness of less that 0.032 gauge, because it was difficult for the shop to handle, it buckled easily, it was difficult to dimple, and any number of other reasons. My numbers indicated that the next lower gauge of 0.020 inch skin would be adequate, and would save a significant number of pounds. There was no use talking to anybody in Engineering, as they all went by the rules. I went to the shop and talked to a number of foremen that I respected. I asked them, was it worth the additional trouble of 0.020 skin to save a few pounds. They all agreed that it was. I specified 0.020 for the skins of the side panels. Nobody in Engineering caught me. As the airplane was being built, engineers and managers came down to the shop to admire the construction. Nobody noticed the thickness of the skin panels. I was the only one that knew that the side panels of the TBF were of 0.020 gauge, a size that the shop could not handle.

The Avenger was designed to launch a torpedo at a speed of 150 knots (sea-miles per hour) and escape in a three-gee pullout. One vertical gee is equal to the gravity of the earth, it is a force and could also be expressed in pounds like your weight when you are sitting in a comfortable chair. Gees are used in the aerospace community as standard units of measuring forces generated by flight maneuvers, such as pullouts. You can feel a horizontal gee when you accelerate your car. When you stop suddenly, you will be thrown forward by gee forces.

The 150 knot requirement was established by the Navy as the highest speed at which a torpedo could be launched from an aircraft and still go straight after it hits the water.

During the static demonstration test, the Avenger wing failed at one point two-gees, far below the required three-gees. This was a disaster.

In my structures course in Berlin, Germany, we were taught that wings in flight were subject to combined torsion and bending. The torsion is small compared to the bending. Most engineers were not aware of this;   they left a margin of safety on bending,   and this generally took care of the torsion. Nevertheless, most wing failures occurred because torsion had been neglected. This was part of a major research project in Berlin, and we were given the the formulas for combined torsion and bending that had just been developed there. This material had not been published anywhere, neither in Germany nor the United States.

Tommy had not been aware of the torsion. In our post-test discussions, I presented the torsion-bending formulas that I had in my Berlin workbook. I was told to redesign the wing-fuselage intersection, to work as many hours a day as I could, including weekends. I worked 12 hours a day for about a month.

Nobody bothered me, they left me completely alone. This was most unusual for Grumman, where everything was carefully checked.

Grumman design practice required that weak points be designed in the structure at easily accessible locations, so that they could be most readily repaired in case of failure. My most easily accessible location for a weak point was the wing-fuselage attachment. The stress calculations would normally require bolts of a non–standard size, and I would have to specify bolts of the next larger available size. I now had to design the attached structure stronger than the bolts, to keep the bolts as the weak points. This and similar conservative practices required me to design the structure for six-gees, instead of the specified three-gees. Doubling the strength in this fashion does not double the weight. Because torsion was involved, some configuration changes were necessary. Otherwise only a few other main structural members had to be reinforced.   I watched the weight increases carefully, and they were acceptable. Such practices, of squeezing every bit of performance out of every structural member, resulted in the Navy referring to Grumman as its "iron works."

When I was finished, I took my drawings down to the shop, without anybody checking them, and they were immediately incorporated on the aircraft.   When the shop was finished, I was told to conduct a static demonstration test.

Both Erlandson and Schwendler were watching me conduct the test. When the strength of the wing exceeded three gee and went up to four, Erlandson got all excited and started to climb over the rope and come to see me. Schwendler held him back, assuring him that I knew what I was doing.

I was elated when the wing failed at 6.7 gees (start of permanent deformation, about 30% below actual rupture.   Measured by instrumentation, you cannot see anything.) The Navy released the aircraft for production and for three gee flight.

After the test, Erlandson seemed to forget about the 6.7 gee. He had probably reviewed my reports very carefully, as was his custom, and noticed that there had been no significant weight increase. The additional strength had been achieved by rearranging the structure, not by adding weight. He complimented me on running the test, but never mentioned the gees. The Navy was only concerned that the airplane survive three gees, that it was good for 6.7 gees did not seem to interest them.

TBF AVENGER PRODUCTION

At the conclusion of the XTBF-1 design, I decided that I had learned the skills of a stress analyst, it was time to move on. The most logical thing would be to stay with the TBF and transfer to production engineering. Unfortunately, that was Shorty's territory. And I had another problem. The Chief Draftsman (Engineering Department Administrator), was Walter Novak. We had become good friends, and I knew that he would resent my leaving the Engineering Department for Shorty's benefit.

I braced myself and went to see Shorty. He was very friendly. He said, of course, I could stay with the TBF through production. I told him about my relation with Novak, and asked Shorty not to tell Novak that I had asked for this assignment. Shorty assured me that he would never tell Novak any such thing, he would tell him that there was no one else available and he needed me for the job.

As soon as I left Shorty's office, Shorty went over to Novaks and bragged about my asking for a transfer to his production team. Novak would not talk to me for almost a year.

The XTBF-1 had been built in very cramped quarters in Plant 1. Grumman had built a new plant, Plant 2, by far its biggest plant, for TBF production, see page 214. The plant was so big, it took me a full ten minutes to walk quickly from one end to the other.

The Assistant Foreman on the XTBF-1 had been Joe Moldashl. Joe and I moved into the almost empty huge plant. We were the only two persons in the plant that knew anything about the TBF.

The Engineering Department was empty, except for a plush front office. It was occupied by a nicely dressed gentleman. He said his name was Jack, and he was the Engineering Supervisor. I was to report to him.

I convinced three members of my design group to join me. I gradually filled up the rest of the department with female "engineering aides" supplied by the Plant 2 Personnel Office. Eventually I had 40 people in the group.

After I got to know my people, I appointed Wilma Holdorf to

Grumman Plant 2, Bethpage, N.Y. 1941

my Assistant Group Leader to do my administrative work. (I wanted to keep my men on engineering work.) Holdorf had degrees in mathematics and interior decorating, an unusual combination. She was quite good looking and the only female assistant group leader at Grumman. Shorty was so jealous, he could hardly control himself. He really let me have it every time we met.

Airplanes are not like mature consumer products. On a batch of 20000 automobiles, the first car is exactly like all the others, up through the 20000th car. In a contract of any number of aircraft, say 200, every airplane in that batch will be a little different. Many changes will be the result of cost cutting efforts. The user always has many ideas for improvement. I had to hear all these people out, decide which suggestions had merit and implement them.

I took a notebook and made a tour of the plant every day after lunch. I talked to every foreman and every mechanic that was making or installing TBF parts. The men knew I was coming, and if they had something to tell me, they would wait for me. I always made a careful note of any good suggestions they had. It became known throughout the plant, that if a note was in my book, eventually it would be taken care of. Everybody was very aware of the need to cut costs, and almost every day, I received some good suggestions.

I was the original source for all technical information in the plant - for the shop, for manufacturing engineering that provided the tooling, for planning and scheduling, for purchasing. When we got into high production, 72 offices required information from me.

The basic document that I issued was the engineering drawing that included a bill of material and other notes as required. I also put out a set of memos when needed. I recognized that there could not be any excuse for anybody in the plant not being able to do their job because of the lack of engineering information.

At first, I made weekly reports to Jack, but he never had any advice or took any action. After about two months, he disappeared. I don't know what happened to him. After that, I had nobody to report to, and did not report to anybody. I am sure that Shorty and others were watching my performance carefully and were always ready to jump in and gleefully take over at the first sign of a foul up. But as long as everything was on schedule, or ahead of schedule, nobody bothered me. I felt like a little king, with the absolute control of such a huge plant in my hand. It was fun. (Eleanor has a different story, about what a grouch I was at home.)

We produced the first TBF in eight months, which was some kind of a record, considering we started from scratch. I had a number of visitors from other companies who wanted to learn about Grumman's "production miracle." I showed them the plant and told them how I operated. They would not believe me. They had never met anybody before with such unlimited authority. They left convinced that Grumman was holding out something from them.

The first squadron of 17 Avenger production aircraft attacked a Japanese fleet in the Pacific early one evening. All planes flew in on a straight run at 150 knots to launch their torpedoes, intending to escape in a three-gee pullout. All aircraft were shot down, and the Japanese were able to avoid all the slow torpedoes. One hundred and fifty knots was too slow a speed for such an attack. All crews ejected and were observed swimming in the water. Japanese carrier fighters came and shot them all dead, that is, all except one. One pilot found an empty orange crate floating in the water. He turned the crate over and stuck his head in it. Japanese do not shoot at orange crates. He was picked up the next morning by a Navy rescue squad. He had an exciting story to tell.

The Navy was quite upset by this fiasco. One pilot investigated, how the Navy had arrived at the requirement that a torpedo could not be launched from an aircraft at more than 150 knots. He found that the Navy had run tests at increasing speeds until they reached 150 knots. At that point, *their funds ran out,* the tests were terminated, and so nobody knows what happens at higher speeds.

The pilot decided on his own to run his own test. His flight plan called for an attack on a moving target at 450 knots with a six-gee pullout. He selected the speed and maneuver so he would be safe from anti-aircraft fire. In such a test, he would lose his airplane in structural failure, but so what, these aircraft were useless anyway.

He approached his target at 450 knots, launched his torpedo and pulled out at six-gees. The torpedo went straight as an arrow and hit the moving target. He looked at his wings expecting them to be bent all out of shape, but they looked OK. He flew back to his carrier and the Avenger underwent a scrupulous structural examination. The aircraft was in perfect condition. The Navy was mystified.

Grumman received a letter from the Navy inquiring what had to be done to the Avenger to release it for six-gee flight. The letter was routed to me for reply. I was no longer working on the TBF, but I referred to my stress analysis and static test reports that had already been furnished to the Navy, stating that the prototype had been designed for six-gees, and in its static demonstration test had survived 6.7-gees. The Avenger, as configured, could be released for six-gee flight without further action. This was pure DUMB LUCK. Nevertheless, it was a big day in my life.

The Avenger became an extraordinarily successful airplane. Grumman built 8000 and General Motors 12000, a total of 20000 copies. It helped to win many battles and clear the Pacific area of

Japanese forces.

Military forces in combat have to do their jobs with the equipment at hand, even though the equipment may not have been designed to do such tasks. The Avenger was called upon to perform many such tasks for which it was not designed, because it was available. One such aircraft attempting to destroy Japanese communications facilities in the Pacific was shot down, but the pilot survived. The pilot was a US President to be, George Bush.

DR. ALEXANDER KLEMIN

Dr. Alexander Klemin was Chairman of the Guggenheim School of Aeronautics at New York University (NYU) from 1926 until his death in the early 40's. He was an old-timer in the aviation business. He was the successful expert witness for Montgomery, who had been sued by the Wright Brothers when he invented and patented the aileron. The Wright Brothers twisted their wings and shifted their body weight to guide their airplane into a curve as the birds do. Montgomery recognized that you would not be able to twist wings as airplanes got larger. He put a set of ailerons, that is, small air flow control surfaces that moved up and down in opposite directions, at the tip of the trailing edge of each wing. Klemin convinced the court, that this device was "new and useful," the legal definition for a US patent.

As the principles of aeronautical engineering became recognized, he became professor of aeronautical engineering at New York University. He taught his courses in the mechanical engineering department. His quarters in 1924 were cramped and crowded and he could only accommodate a limited number of students.

He had a remarkable insight into technical subjects. He was brash and would not tolerate any nonsense, but he had a sense of humor. He was an advocate of helicopters that were highly unreliable at that time. He was fond of saying: "There is a no more honorable way of losing money than by investing in the helicopter business."

He was pals with Harry Guggenheim from the old days when flying was a sport.   Harry was one of the sons of the Guggenheim family that had made its fortune in mining in the western US. Harry's generation was in the business of finding ways of spending some of that money in doing good works. Klemin convinced Harry to get his father, Daniel, to put up a new building on the campus of NYU and to sponsor three professorships. The new Guggenheim School of Aeronautical Engineering opened in 1926, offering instruction on a par with other branches of engineering. It was an immediate success.

The new problem in aeronautics was that weight was a prime design parameter. Say it takes ten men to design for performance, it takes almost ten times that number to design for performance at minimum weight.   Klemin knew this, that a healthy aircraft industry would require large numbers of engineers, as no other industry had ever required before.   He convinced Harry to persuade his father to establish the Guggenheim Fund for the Promotion of Aeronautics to fund Guggenheim Schools of Aeronautics at seven additional universities, namely, Cal Tech, MIT, Michigan, Washington, Stanford, Georgia Tech, and Akron.

When later President Roosevelt perceived war clouds on the horizon, I heard him on the radio challenge the aircraft industry to start producing 50000 aircraft a year. At that time there were only some 12000 airplanes in the entire country. But the Guggenheim Schools were in place, educating large numbers of engineers who could step into the rapidly expanding aircraft companies as group leaders, to provide direction to engineers of other disciplines and integrate them into the war effort.   The American aeronautical capability was an important contributor in changing the balance of power of the Western Allies, leading them to victory in World War II. By 1950, virtually every senior engineer in the aircraft industry was a graduate of a Guggenheim School.

The great numbers of available aeronautical engineers after World War II enabled the United States to take the lead in air transportation. American airplanes now are dominant in service in all countries of the world. One American company advertised its product with this riddle: "What American word is used in every language of the world?" Answer: "Boeing."

Dr. Klemin was a man of vision, who used his gifts to initiate the establishment of a nation-wide system of education for large numbers of engineers that contributed significantly to the Allied victory in World War II, and enabled the US today to take the world lead in air transportation, and even to touch the moon. He was one of the men who changed the world for the better.

THE FLIGHT SAFETY FOUNDATION (FSF)

Klemin and the Guggenheims recognized that national governments had limited powers to assure the safety of international flights. The process of negotiating and ratifying international treaties is expensive and time consuming, and such treaties are difficult to change and update. To provide a more efficient and responsive system to assure international flight safety, Klemin got Harry to get his parents to found the Daniel and Florence Guggenheim Flight Safety Foundation at Cornell University (Short Name: Flight Safety Foundation, FSF). This is a private organization that monitors and disseminates information on flight safety, but itself has no enforcing powers.

The membership of the FSF consists of the safety officers of all major airlines and aeronautical equipment manufacturers in the world. At the closed and secret annual meetings of the FSF, all accidents and mishaps that have occurred in the world since the last meeting, are reviewed and analyzed by the personnel who investigated the accident, and corrective actions are discussed. All new flight safety procedures, equipment, and flight personnel training programs are reviewed. The FSF is a "bottom up" organization, where personnel responsible for flight safety educate one another, and then take actions that they feel are necessary when they return home. Secrecy of the proceedings is an absolute requirement to prevent lawyers from identifying individuals who did the investigations and subpoenaing them to testify in damage suits. The objective of safety personnel is to identify defects and correct them to provide safe operations, not to be diverted by legal procedures.

Later, when I was the Chief of the Reliability and Maintainability Section at Grumman, I represented the company on the FSF. I was invited to present a paper on the reliability of aeronautical equipment. From that time on, I was the FSF's expert on reliability.

About that time I also presented a paper at the New York Academy of Sciences on "Failure Effects Analysis," an analytical procedure that I developed at Grumman, to assure during the design phase, that a device would meet its reliability requirements when built. The Academy published my paper in its *Transactions* and awarded me a gold medal. The FSF received a copy of this paper, evaluated it, and sent a copy to each of its members around the world. Today, the procedure is universally used throughout the aircraft industry.

I once talked to the chief pilot of a small, progressive country with a well respected international airline. He told me that his country had more people than jobs. His socialistic government felt responsible for providing jobs for everyone. His government felt it needed the airline to enhance its international prestige. The airline was overloaded with personnel. His pilots were extremely well trained, responsible and safety conscious. The airline was small enough that he knew each pilot personally and could monitor his performance. He had no money for the computerized safety systems of the major airlines. However, his safety record was as good or better than those of the the big international airlines. He came to the FSF meetings to check if his safety procedures were still adequate, or if he had to improve them or buy new expensive safety equipment.

By such education of responsible safety personnel, the FSF provides for flight safety in international air transportation in an area where national governments have limited regulating powers.

As an international organization, the FSF would like to hold more of its annual meetings in different countries throughout the world. However, there are few facilities outside the United States that can accommodate such a large technical meeting. So the FSF schedules only every fourth meeting in a different country. During the time that I was associated with the FSF, an annual meeting was held at the Castelana Hilton in Madrid, Spain. Like many of the other American members, I took Eleanor along. The women had a ball. They took tours of the city, viewed the great churches, museums, and department stores. They also took a side trip to Toledo where they make fancy inlaid silverware.

However, large technical meetings in foreign countries present special challenges. The entrance to the meeting room in Madrid was flanked by two long tables, covered with green felt that reached down to the floor. Our secretaries from New York laid out on the table copies of the papers that were scheduled for the next session. They kept all the papers that were to be handed out on the floor under the tables, in back of the green felt. One morning, they came down and all the papers were gone. Nobody could figure out what anybody in Madrid would want to do with all that specialized technical material.

Almost everybody in Madrid goes walking up and down the boulevards between five and seven every evening. The crowds are as thick as in New York during rush hour. But in New York the people are going to and from work, in Madrid they are out having fun.

One basic rule that was strictly enforced on foreigners to impress on them that they were in Madrid, was that you could not find, anywhere in Madrid, anything to eat for dinner before nine pm. All tourists complained loudly about it, and the Spaniards just smiled. I hope that by now McDonald may have come to the rescue of American tourists there.

On Friday afternoon we held our important wrap-up session that had to be concluded on time to allow people to catch their planes home. The hotel was given explicit instructions, verbally and in writing, that lunch could not exceed one hour. The hotel manager smiled, but he knew differently. This was his chance to impress a large number of Americans and other foreigners with the treasured, traditional pomp and ceremony of the grand Spanish dinner customs. These were developed in olden times for the entertainment of Spanish nobility that had nothing else to do. They were not appropriate for busy flight safety specialists who had other problems on their minds and were concerned about catching their planes. It took two and a half hours before they let us out of the dining room. It wrecked our Friday afternoon technical wrap-up session, that many people had come to Madrid for. It was too bad that there was not a McDonald's nearby.

THE INTERNATIONAL HANDBOOK
OF AERONAUTICAL ENGINEERING

After Klemin retired from NYU, he organized a panel of international experts to write a new *International Handbook of Aeronautical Engineering,* with himself as editor. He invited me to write the chapter on *Detailed Stress Analysis.* I did so. At that time, NACA - Langley was just completing its research program on shell design, and I was able to capture all this new material. Klemin was delighted.

Unfortunately, Klemin died before he had gathered all of his material. Mrs. Klemin appointed another illustrious university professor to finish the job. He accepted, but he was a busy man, and let the project drop.

I should have taken my material, expanded and reworked it a little, and published it as a book. I think it would have made a fine little book. I only thought of this option after it was too late and I had discarded my material.

XF6F-1, HELLCAT

After the TBF production line was well established, I made another job change. I felt that the job I had done on the TBF had been exceptional. Wages had not yet been frozen, and all of my people had received excellent raises in pay. In contrast, I only received the minimum $2 per raise period. Shorty was playing games again, and I could not live with it.

I went to see my friend Novak, with whom I was again on speaking terms. He was surprised and shocked. He said that my pay was completely out of line compared to other men in my class.

I had observed that design engineers were the ones who were calling the shots. I told Novak that I wanted to get into design. Novak agreed to accept me in design engineering and promised to adjust my pay. I made him promise me that he would not tell Shorty that I had asked for this transfer. Subsequently, Novak told me that he had had a fierce fight with Shorty, in which Shorty had tricked him into admitting that I had asked for this transfer. Novak said he was sorry.

Novak assigned me to the XF6F-1, see page 222. I was given the job of designing the engine attachment fittings. I could not help but think back to Berlin, where one of my design problems had been the mounting of an engine on an airship. I now had a stress analyst who helped me by doing the number crunching.

My major means of communication had suddenly become the engineering drawing. I had had a good course in engineering drawing in Berlin, but as a stress analyst, I did not have to prepare any drawings. The first engineering drawings that I prepared at Grumman

XF6F-1 Hellcat, 1943

were those of the torsion-bending XTBF-1 wing redesign where everybody just assumed I had all the skills necessary to handle the job. While on TBF-1 production, I supervised many "engineering aides" preparing engineering drawings. Now, Novak put me in a job requiring engineering drawing rather than number crunching. Actually, based on my Berlin training, I had no trouble expressing my ideas on engineering drawings. I am always surprised when I run into technical people who cannot read engineering drawings, which happens quite often.

Everybody liked my engine attachment fitting, and I was assigned to the XF6F-1 cockpit section. The airplane specification called for a six pounds per square inch (psi) pressurized cockpit. The company felt that this feature required extra time and could not be done within the delivery schedule. Grumman agreed with the Navy that the pressurization feature could be added at a later date. I was told to design the cockpit section with all the necessary provisions, so that pressurization could be added later.

I had to figure out how to do that. I had to identify all the provisions for pressurization that had to be included in the unpressurized version. The only way I thought I could do that, was to design the cockpit for pressurization, but then leave out all of the elements not needed for structural integrity. Nobody noticed I had to go through this exercise.

One of my problems was the flat firewall between the cockpit and engine sections. A flat surface is very difficult to pressurize. It required a number of heavy vertical stringers to take the load. These stringers would be very difficult to install at a later date on a production aircraft. I decided to install them in the unpressurized aircraft.

At this time, the Martin Company in Baltimore had developed a method for transferring drawings photographically and in true scale, from one white painted aluminum sheet to another. Grumman bought the process from Martin and assigned Novak to exploit it.

Novak developed a plan for preparing engineering drawings without dimensions on a white painted aluminum sheet. For sheet metal parts with flanges, the flanges would also be shown in their flat pattern. Novak picked me to design the fin attachment bulkhead of the XF6F-1 and to prepare the drawing on a white painted aluminum sheet. I developed all the details for what was really a new system of engineering drawings, based on precise drawing to scale, and eliminating all numerical dimensions. It became the Grumman standard.

I only drew the left half of the bulkhead, thinking that they could turn over the photo negative to get the right side. This was a mistake. The negative was on a glass plate, and when they turned over the plate, the thickness of the glass distorted the dimensions. All other drawings after mine showed full bulkheads, both right and left sides.

The engineering drawing was reproduced on other white painted aluminum sheets that were sent to the shop. The shop cut out the flat patterns of each part and used them as routing templates, templates for drilling holes, and for making forming blocks. Formerly, most of these parts had to be drawn and dimensioned separately. The method was particularly effective with parts that had to be shaped to fit the curved contours of the aircraft. It was a real revolution in providing engineering information to the shop and must have saved oodles of money.

Much later, when the F6F was in production, it became obvious, that the cockpit pressurization requirement would never be implemented. I walked through the shop one day and noticed all the firewalls with those now unnecessary heavy vertical stringers. I went to the engineer in charge and told him that the stringers were now unnecessary, that he could save five pounds by replacing them with lighter stringers. According to the Grumman Engineering Manual, an ounce of structural weight saved, is worth $100 per aircraft per year. Five pounds, then, should be worth $8000 per aircraft. Nothing happened.

I went to see his supervisor, but nothing happened. I went to see everybody involved in production engineering, but nothing happened.

I pulled a set of drawings, and went to see Schwendler. Schwendler had a lot of respect for a saving of five pounds. Things happened very fast and I was treated to the best performance of hollering and fake Indian dancing that I had ever seen Shorty put on. He kept shouting at me: ***"Keep out of production engineering!"*** But I saved five pounds on the F6F and Schwendler was pleased.

The F6F went out to join the Wildcat in the Pacific War. Its performance characteristics were superior to those of the Japanese Zero in every classification. Grumman built 12000. It is impressive that no changes other than eliminating my firewall reinforcements, were required in the airframe.

XF7F-1   TIGERCAT

The Tigercat was another Grumman attempt to pack more power into an airplane. It had two 1800 hp engines and was the company's second attempt to build a twin engine carrier based airplane. This time, the company was almost successful. Two squadrons of F7F Tigercats were on board a carrier in San Diego, ready to leave for the Pacific theater, when on August 14, 1945, the Japanese surrendered.

After the XP-50 accident, the Grumman Research Department continued to work on the concept of a twin engine carrier based aircraft. Charles Mack, head of the Department, prepared a dynamic analysis of a carrier landing of a twin engine airplane. He came up with some surprising results. An airplane is an elastic structure, and when you put such heavy concentrated loads, such as an engine, out on the wing, the elastic response to a shock load, such as an arrested landing, may be something you do not expect. Mack's analysis showed that when one wheel touches down first, the critical wing loads occur on the other side of the airplane. Mack submitted his analysis as a doctor's thesis to NYU.

I was assigned to the central portion of the fuselage, the so-called "tank section," because it included the fuel cells. This was the time of the battle for North Africa. The TBF's were returning to their carriers bullet ridden, big gapping holes all over their structure, and streams of fuel pouring out of their fuel tanks. Fuel tank removal required too much time and was not an option. Such planes could not be taken down into the hanger deck because of the fire hazard, and there was no room to store them on the flight deck that was already full. Eighty five TBF's had to be shoved overboard.

Also at that time, we received an analysis of a captured German Messerschmidt. One of the items stated that the fuel tanks could be removed in 25 minutes. This item was marked with a red pen and a note that read: "Coutinho, please note." Schwendler was the only person in the Engineering Department who used a red pen.

I resolved, that on the F7F, it would be possible to remove the fuel tanks in no more than 15 minutes.

I designed the fuel tanks as bullet proof, 5/8 inch thick neoprene bladders, mounted along the top edge to a flat plate which extended over the upper longerons and was fastened to them by quick removable fasteners. A door on the bottom of the aircraft provided quick access to detach the hoses. The space above the upper longerons was enclosed by a fairing that was attached by Dzus buttons for quick removal. A door in this fairing provided access to fill the fuel bladders.

To remove the fuel bladder from the airplane, the hoses had to be disconnected at the bottom of the aircraft. This took minutes. Simultaneously, the upper fairing had to be taken off, the fasteners on the longerons had to be removed, and a hoist attached to the center of the plate. The bladders could now be pulled up and out of the airplane. I had a team of mechanics do this as soon as the aircraft was built, and they did it in less than 15 minutes.

The empty space above the upper longerons was a beautiful, empty, easily accessible space for mounting all kinds of equipment, and especially for running the control lines for the rudder and elevators. I had the fight of my life to protect this space against all engineers who wanted to install their equipment there.

The flight control group had a special reason for wanting that space. They always had priority in selecting the shortest, clear route for their cables and pushrods. The control system "break-out" force is an important fighter aircraft characteristic. It is the force required to overcome the static friction in a control system at rest, that is, the force required to initiate movement of the stick. At high speed, very small movements of the stick are required to control the flight path of the airplane, and the lower the break-out force, the quicker a pilot can respond to the need for a flight path correction. The flight control group tried to design their lines so that the static friction in the system would be a minimum.

There was little room between the fuel bladder and the outside skin, not enough room for a good traditional ring-stringer framework. My supervisor at the time was Lloyd Skinner, the Project Engineer of the XF7F-1. He was one of the best aircraft designers in the country. He recognized that my fuselage panels in the tank section presented an unusual problem. He spent several hours with me every day as we brain stormed one scheme after another, for two months until time ran out on us. Neither one of us was proud of our final result. One feature of our design was that we ran the control cables between the bladders and the outside skin along the center of the fuselage.

On one of the first test flights of the XF7F-1, it was a very hot day and the pilot reported that he could not operate the rudder and the elevator. We had a beautiful airplane in the sky that could not land.

The pilot made a pass close to the control tower, and one observer blurted out; "Hey, that gal looks pregnant!" We immediately concluded that the fuel bladders had expanded with the heat and clamped the control lines between the bladder and the outside skin. The pilot was told to go fly out over the ocean and dump most of his fuel. He did so, and then the controls worked fine. He came back and made a fine landing. I solved this problem by running the control lines inside a plastic tube in the area of the bladders.

After completion of the fuel bladder tests, I was assigned to the tail section of the XF7F-1, on which no work had yet been done. The airplane specification required a carrier based airplane to make 100 arrested landings on the Navy's simulated carrier deck in Philadelphia. This simulated deck consisted of a big ring painted on a runway, its diameter equal to the width of a carrier deck. Across the center of the ring, that is, across the runway, was an arresting wire, attached to a standard Navy arresting gear like they have on carriers.

The business of Navy test pilots was to break off the tail of test aircraft when landing in this circle. They were expert in picking up the wire a few inches from the ends, and making the hook travel while engaged in the wire to the center of the runway. This movement was not smooth, the hook would jerk savagely along the wire, putting shock loads on the tail of the aircraft like from a giant sledge hammer. All this happened in a minuscule fraction of a second. New test aircraft seldom survived 30 landings, then they were reinforced in a test-fix-test cycle until they survived the required 100 landings. It was an expensive and frustrating experience.

I was told that Grumman was tired of this procedure, that I was to design the XF7F-1 so it would survive the 100 landing test on its first try. No excuses would be accepted. Grumman management was very serious.

The XF7F-1 failed on its 89th landing.

I went to Philadelphia to inspect the damage, and was able to design a simple reinforcement to strengthen the damaged area. On the next series of tests, the XF7F-1 survived 100 landings without any structural damage. Actually, I was pleased that the fuselage had failed in the first test at 89 landings. The airplane was almost good enough. If it had survived the 100 landings the first time, nobody would know how strong it really was. I could have been accused of being responsible for an overweight design.

With the sudden and unexpected end of the War, the Navy had no further use for the F7F's and turned them over to the Marines. The Marines were used to making do with the Navy's castoffs and were delighted to get a brand new aircraft. It was used in Korea to good effect. The Marines put a radar in the nose and I had to redesign the cockpit section to accommodate a radar operator. The Tigercat became a successful two man night fighter. A total of over 400 units were built.

ROY ARRIVES

The Japanese surrendered on August 14, 1945, and Grumman closed its plants until further notice.

At about 10 o'clock in the evening, Eleanor asked me to take her to Mercy Hospital. We had made a reservation for this date some seven months before. We had to drive through the center of Hempstead. The town center was full of people celebrating and dancing in the street. We got lots of confetti all over the car. Once we got through the center of town, it was only a few minutes before we got to the hospital.

They gave Eleanor a nice room in the new maternity wing. They gave me a comfortable easy chair. We did not have too long to wait.

Roy arrived at two am on August 15, 1945. He weighed nine pound four ounces, he was a very big baby. Eleanor nursed him for nine months.

In those days, Eleanor was allowed to stay a week in the hospital. Since Grumman was closed, I spent most of the day with her. She had quite a few other visitors.   The girls from her office came in full force, (and brought a bottle).   They were having a merry old time when the head nurse decided that this was not behavior conducive to a hospital atmosphere. A squad of nurses rounded up the girls and threw them all out. Then they put up a big sign, saying that visiting hours were from 10 to 12, and 6 to 8, no more that two visitors in a room at any time. Somehow, they let me stay most of the day.

We rearranged our apartment to make a place for our new baby. Every room had special accommodations for him. Bennett Gardens proved to be a good place to raise a little boy.   The apartment complex covered the whole block of Elks Street, that terminated at both ends, so there was very little traffic on the street.

Since Eleanor was nursing Roy, she had no idea how much milk he was getting. I bought a baby scale and weighed Roy before and after every nursing session. I plotted daily milk consumption by weight and weight increase per day of baby. Eleanor studied these curves carefully, and was gratified by Roy's progress. He gained weight quickly and was walking by nine months. He was our engineered baby, see page 229.

There were a number of children in the apartment complex. After Roy got bigger, he had no shortage of little friends. Across the street from the apartment was an almost empty lot, the only building on it was the Hempstead Elks Club, with its back toward Elks Street. There would generally be one or more mothers in folding chairs out in the lot watching their children. Somebody had built a sandbox. Eleanor could always leave Roy for a few minutes in care of one of the other mothers when she had something to do.

We took regular weekend trips to the Catskills and to Washington to show off Roy to the rest of the family. Roy liked riding in the car. Sometimes when he could not go to sleep at night, we would take him for a ride, and with the motor running, he would go to sleep.

The best baby sitter that we ever had was Eleanor's brother Charlie. He was released from the Navy and came to stay with us until he decided what he was going to do. Eventually, he found a carpenter's trade school in New Jersey that he liked, and he moved to New Jersey. But in the few months that he was with us, he was the most agreeable house guest that we had ever had. He and Roy hit it off just right.

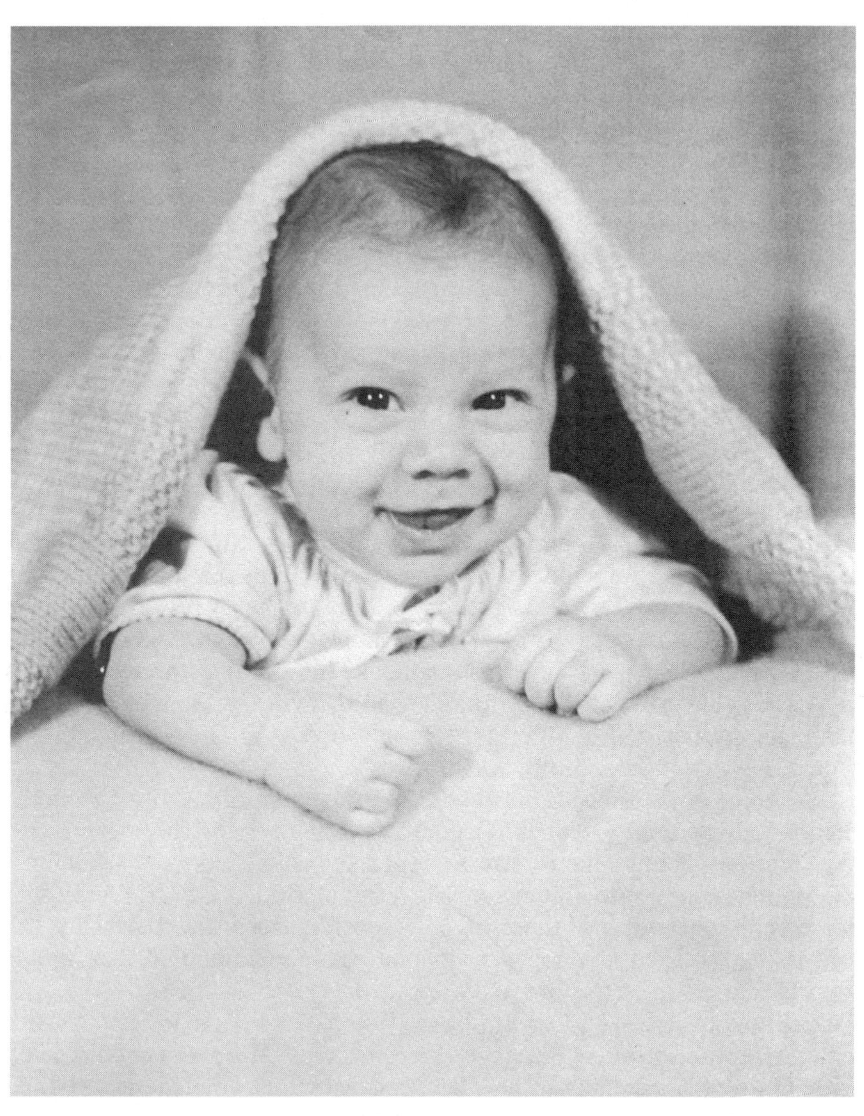

Roy Coutinho, age 3 months

PUBLIC RELATIONS WITH THE NAVY

Design group leaders who submitted reports to the Navy for approval were required by Grumman to go to Washington once a month and make contact with at least the personnel that had approval authority for their reports. Grumman wanted us to understand what the Navy needed and preached to us that "we had to get in bed with the Navy." Grumman did not have a Washington office like other companies, but believed that direct contact by responsible individuals was better than correspondence through a third party.

At that time, I was attending meetings of the American Institute of Aeronautics and Astronautics (AIAA) with some regularity. Fatty, who was Chief of Structures at the time, asked me to make friends with Clete Baum at these meetings. Baum was the Navy official who approved Grumman stress reports and he was giving Grumman a hard time by rejecting or holding up approval of reports. This was serious, because Grumman got paid for a design work package only when the appropriate stress report was approved.

I had met Baum before at AIAA meetings, and had no trouble making friends. Sometimes I would go to Washington the evening before my business date, so I could be at the Navy Department, Bureau of Aeronautics (BuAir) when they opened at 8 o'clock. In those cases, when I was in Washington in the evening, or when I was in Washington for two days, Baum would invite me sometimes to his home for supper with his family. He had two sons and a daughter. In return, I would take him out for lunch.

After I got to know Baum better, I asked him about the Grumman reports. Apparently, the Grumman engineers who came to Washington about their stress reports, only talked to Baum's subordinates, never to Baum himself. Baum said that Grumman was not complying with a number of new specifications that the Navy had issued. I notified the right people at Grumman, and all Grumman reports started to get approved without delay.

Baum introduced me to his boss, Ralph Creel, and to his Division Chief, Captain Walter Keen. I also became close personal friends with both of these men. They both occasionally invited me to their homes where they introduced me to their families.

I discovered that Creel originated the system of stress analysis, structural demonstration, and reports submitted for approval that we used. He had also sent a Navy Commander over to the CAA for two years to introduce the system for civilian airplanes and transports. He had a number of Air Force officers assigned to the Bureau to learn the system. I thought that Creel was a genius and that his work was a major contribution to the design control of structurally safe aircraft. At that time, I was chairman of the Honors Committee of the ASME Aviation Division, and I nominated Creel for the Spirit of Saint Louis Award, a gold medal that was the highest ASME award in the aviation field. The award was presented to Creel in the Grand Ballroom of the Waldorf Astoria Hotel in New York City, during the 1967 National Transportation Conference. United States Senator C. Peel, the Senate's transportation expert, gave the address.

Keen and his people were highly regarded in BuAir, and as a result of my association with them, I became a personage in the Bureau. I was the only non-Navy person walking freely in and out of the front office. Men I did not know, would stop me in the hall and tell me about their technical problems, and request my advice on what they should do, as if I were an old friend. With some 3500 people in the Bureau, none of these men who stopped me had ever talked to Baum or Creel. Since I knew Navy policy from my close association with Baum and Creel, I was often able to help these men.

I remained close friends with Baum, Creel and Keen for the rest of their lives.

THE GRUMMAN CORPORATION REOPENS

Some weeks before the end of the War, Grumman asked its people to write on the back of their time card if they intended to leave the company at the end of the War, or if they would like to stay. One hundred and twenty six said that they intended to leave.

With the end of the War, Grumman closed all plants and sent everybody home, except for a few top managers who had to make decisions. This gave those who thought that they would not be called back, the earliest opportunity to find other jobs. People were told that they would be called back by telegram at the end of three weeks.

There were two exceptions, namely the 350 senior engineering specialists on Schwendler's staff who would be difficult to replace, and Leroy Grumman's list of the 250 people who had been with the company during its first ten years. Since I was on both lists, I was able to enjoy an unexpected vacation taking care of Eleanor and our new baby.

The company had to guess at what jobs the Navy would continue in peace time, and determine what personnel it needed for these jobs. The F6F and the TBF would surely be canceled. However, work would probably be continued on projects under development such as the XF8F-1 Bearcat and the XF9F-1 Panther. Grumman called back a total of about 4000 people.

This was not an easy exercise. In such a severe cutback, a large number of higher level jobs are eliminated. But the people that held these jobs were good people that the company would want to keep. These men had to be called back to lower level jobs. It also had to be a mix of people at all levels, from foreman to floor sweeper.

Before the end of the War, Grumman had been giving some thought to what it would do just after the War. One problem was how to keep the big stretch presses busy. These presses are used to stretch aircraft skins over a mold into double curvature sheets. They are big, expensive machines, representing a large investment, and it did not appear to be good practice to let them stand idle.

Someone came up with the idea of building an aluminum canoe.

At that time, the Grumman plants and equipment were all owned by the Navy and could not be used for any other purpose than performing Navy contracts. (For insurance against eviction, Grumman retained ownership of the runways.) There was an unused six lane bowling alley in the basement of Plant 2. Grumman had built it in case some emergency prevented workers from going home and they had to remain in the plant. The bowling alley would provide some means of recreation. However, it was never used and remained locked up tight, nobody except a few top Grumman executives knew that it was there. It provided an ideal hiding place for the development of the canoe, beyond the eyes of the Navy.

The Grumman canoe with its light weight of almost one half that of a wood-and-canvas canoe, and water tight compartments, was an immediate worldwide success. It was available in four sizes. Manufacturing the canoe kept the stretch presses busy and provided many jobs. Grumman had no idea of the cost of the operation, but it did not want to drive the wood-and-canvas people out of business. They set the price of the Grumman canoe at 115% of the cost of an Old Town canoe of the same size. Old Town was the best canoe in America at the time. At first, Grumman manufactured more canoes than could be sold, and at one time had a backlog of 40000 canoes in its warehouse.

To separate its military and commercial businesses , Grumman built a new plant in upstate New York to manufacture aluminum canoes. This facility is still operating today.

The canoe project kept the big stretch presses busy and many men occupied until Grumman and the Navy agreed on the scope of Grumman peace time projects.

XF10F-1   JAGUAR

When I returned to Grumman, the company had received a contract for the development of a new carrier based aircraft, the XF10F-1, Jaguar. I skipped working on the XF8F-1 and the XF9F-1, and was assigned to the XF10F-1. This was a big and heavy single seat airplane, designed to accommodate a giant jet engine and afterburner combination being developed by Curtis Wright to produce 10000 lbs

XF 10 F-1, Jaguar

of thrust. See page 233.

The XF10F-1 was another bold Grumman experiment, it sported the first American variable sweep back wing. (The world's first was the German Messerschmidt.) The sweep back of the wing could be varied in flight from 13.5 degrees at low speed to 43.5 degrees at high speed.

The low speed performance of the XF10F-1 turned out to be outstanding, but at high speed, the variable sweep wing became the subject of an intensive research program. The new technical information gained in these flight tests was exploited in the successful designs of the variable sweep back wings of the future F11, F111, and F14.

The Curtis Wright engine was a disappointment, never producing more than 6300 lbs of thrust. It was replaced by the Westinghouse JOY, that provided 7200 lbs of thrust and promised to yield 11600 lbs of thrust when the afterburner became available. Unfortunately, the afterburner never materialized. The second aircraft was half finished when the project was canceled. The unfinished structure provided a scarce structural test specimen; the test community had a real ball with it. The aircraft was also never carrier qualified, and I never had the pleasure of nursing it through 100 arrested landings in Philadelphia.

I guess I had established my reputation with the XF7F-1 arrested landing test. I was assigned to the XF10F-1 tail section that included the arresting hook.

The engine was mounted at three points in the fuselage mid section. The removable tail section started just aft of the rear most engine mount attachment, and covered that portion of the engine, that is, mostly the afterburner, that stuck out behind the mid section. The tail section was pulled over the exposed portion of the engine like a glove over a finger.

There were several structural engineering problems associated with the tail section. The tail section had to be removed quickly to get at the engine, so the attachment to the mid section had to be of the quick disconnect type. However, the arresting loads were heavy, and on the lower longeron I ended up with a longitudinal bolt, 7/8 inch in diameter, easily accessible and removable.

The empennage, including rudder and elevator, were attached at the rear bulkhead and introduced appreciable air loads. On the bottom of the same bulkhead, I mounted the arresting hook with a 1.25 inch bolt. The XF10F-1 had a tricycle landing gear with a nose wheel, but in an arrested landing, the tail was likely to bang down on the carrier deck, so I added a bumper on the bottom of this bulkhead.

During the first six months, I was alone on this job. I attended the weekly design engineering meetings regularly, but nobody asked me any questions and I had nothing to say. There was much serious discussion at these meetings, primarily about the swing wing mechanism, and any contribution I could have made was never missed. What kept me busy was making sketches of every fitting and structural member in the tail section. I worked out in detail what I wanted at every joint and prepared a rough stress analysis. I ended up with a large pile of sketches.

As a matter or course, I always checked with manufacturing engineering and always had them look over my proposed designs. They usually made good suggestions.   Normally, manufacturing engineering was understaffed, and could not give me much time. On this occasion, however, my friend Jerry did not have much to do, and reviewed my sketches thoroughly.

Aircraft sections, like a wing or a part of the fuselage, are assembled in a "jig," a heavy steel fixture which holds the attachment points in place, so that when the various sections are joined together, the attachment points will match one another.

An aircraft structure consists of many parts. The airframe also supports many pieces of equipment. All of these parts are assembled in a jig on schedule. There is not enough room for everybody to get to their work location at the same time. Several men are always vying for the same work space. It is a loud, hectic operation, involving many people around a jig.

Jerry suggested that I break down my tail section so that each of the four skin panels, upper, lower, left, and right, could each be assembled with their stringers, ring segments, and equipment, in its own jig, located where there was plenty of room. The main jig would then be used to hold the front and rear bulkheads and the four longerons in place. The four skin panels would then only need to be riveted along the edges in the main jig for complete assembly. This work would require two members of a riveting team to be inside the tail section, eliminating all the normal hectic pushing associated with jig assembly. I agreed to go along with Jerry's ideas.

Jerry searched the scrap lot for suitable parts for my main jig. He made use of old jigs that were built for other purposes. He ended up with a tall, giant, bolted monstrosity which cost him next to nothing but which did the job. The only location he could find for it was the broad main intersection in Plant 5. You could no longer walk straight through the intersection with that thing in the way, but there was still plenty of room to walk around my giant jig.

Grumman management had their offices on the top floor of Plant 5, overlooking the runway. Instead of walking along the corridors of the upper floor on their way to the lunch room, they walked through the shop to see what was going on. One day, their path was impeded by this monstrous jig that they had to walk around. They inquired discreetly who was responsible for it, and were told "Coutinho." They then dubbed the structure the "Coutinho Tower."

As soon as the design of the front sections of the fuselage was completed, some design engineers were released and assigned to me. Within a few days, I had a group of ten design engineers and a stress analyst. I parceled out my sketches to them and had my team working without any loss of time.

The Coutinho Tower was empty for many months until my drawings were released and the shop got around to start building tail section parts. Every day, Grumman management made some comments about the Coutinho Tower, not all of them complimentary.

I was in the shop watching when they took my rear bulkhead out of its jig. They laid it on a cart and took it to the weighing station, and I walked along with it. At the start of the design, when this bulkhead was still only a single straight pencil line on a piece of paper, the Weights Department had allocated 63 lbs to the bulkhead. Now, after all these months, they put the bulkhead on the scale and it weighed 62.5 lbs. I added another imaginary feather to my cap.

One day, two bulkheads and four longerons appeared in the Coutinho Tower.   Grumman management must have felt very relieved, and now awaited a show of heavy, hectic, activity around the jig. The next day was rather disappointing. The skin panels were in place, and only two teams of riveters were at work. On day five, the jig was empty again. This they could not believe.

The Coutinho Tower stood its ground, empty, for many months. When the project was canceled, Jerry had his crew disassemble it and cart it away. Since it had been a bolted structure, the work only required a few hours. The next day, when the Grumman management went for lunch, the monumental Coutinho Tower had disappeared. That day at lunch, Grumman management really had something to talk about.

ALAN JOINS THE FAMILY

Our traditional project engineers, Stall and Skinner, were both engulfed in the mechanical problems associated with the swing wing. The acting project engineer, who ran the weekly design engineering meetings, was a new man who I shall call Dummkopf. He was an old time pilot, but also had an engineering degree. I don't know where Grumman picked him up.

Dummkopf spent most of his time in the flight hanger, waiting around for a chance to fly an airplane on company time and expense. He was generally unavailable in the engineering department when needed to help make decisions, provide guidance, or give advice. All design engineers despised him. He (or any body else) had never talked to me or given me direction about the design of the XF10F-1 tail section.

On or about September 4, 1950, Dummkopf came to my office to talk to me for the first time.

The Navy had just acquired a new carrier with a canted deck, that is, a deck canted at a small angle to the centerline of the ship. This made it possible to move the command tower to one side off the deck, and make more room available for the runway, which was a very desirable thing.

Dummkopf was concerned that the new canted deck might have some new unknown design feature that would make it difficult or impossible for the F10F-1 to land. The new carrier with the canted deck was scheduled to make a short one day stop at Philadelphia on September 6. Dummkopf asked me do go to Philadelphia on that date, inspect the carrier, and determine if they had made any design changes to the deck that would prevent the F10F-1 from making carrier landings.

I told Dummkopf that Eleanor was expecting a baby on September 6, and that I could not go.

Dummkopf told me that a baby's projected arrival date is only an estimate and never a sure thing, and that women in an emergency have the ability to hold back a birth for a day or two. He ordered me to go to Philadelphia and forget about an estimated birth arrival date.

I argued with Dummkopf to the limit of my ability, but he would not listen. He said he could not send anybody else, that I knew more about arrested landings than anybody else in the company. (I had written a statistical analysis of arrested carrier landings with the help of my statistician, Nat Lichter, that was the basis for the Navy's new landing gear specification.) Dummkopf insisted that this was not a matter where we could take chances. It was an absolute necessity for the company to know that the F10F-1 could land on a carrier with a canted deck.

So I went to Philadelphia on September 6, 1950.

The lady in the apartment above us took Eleanor to the hospital while I was away. Roy was with his grandparents in the Catskills.

On the carrier in Philadelphia, I observed that the arresting gear was identical to that on all older carriers. I could see no changes on the flight deck, it looked just like any other carriers, except that it was wider. I also discovered that the Navy has an engineering unit that determines what aircraft can land on what carriers. This information is important when the fleet is operating with escort carriers that have smaller flight decks. This unit had the F10F-1 listed as being capable of landing on all big carriers. The Navy does not buy carrier aircraft that cannot land on their carriers.

I wrote my trip report and stated that Dummkopf's concerns were a non-problem. I had been sent on a wild goose-chase.

Dummkopf, who was really useless, was desperately trying to impress Grumman management that he was concerned with the quality of the company's products. It was sham show.

When I went to see Eleanor at the hospital, she would not talk to me. She remained mad at me for a long time. On the other hand, she lavished all her loving attention on Alan. He was a big, responsive baby who weighed eight pounds, twelve ounces at birth, see page 239.

I started to weigh Alan to chart milk consumption and weight. This had been so helpful when Eleanor had nursed Roy. But now Eleanor would have nothing to do with the charts. She and Alan developed their own close relationship, and she could just feel how Alan was thriving. She nursed him until he got his first tooth and started to bite her.

BOYS WILL BE BOYS

There was no air test facility on the East Coast big enough to accommodate the high speed XF10F-1 swept wing flight tests. Dummkopf and a few of his crew were sent out west to find a suitable facility.

One evening, they discovered a brothel a short distance down the road from their motel. They got all excited and decided that this had to be investigated.

The madam was delighted to greet such new eager faces on expense account. She did her utmost to see to it that that the boys all had a good time. In fact, they had the time of their lives.

When they arrived back at Grumman, they could not restrain themselves from bragging about their exploits out west. The entire engineering department was titillating. That is when I decided that the leader of the group should be called "Dummkopf."

Dummkopf was getting more and more frustrated because the men in the flight hanger would not place an airplane at his disposal, so he could go flying on company time and at company expense. He finally went to see Schwendler. He gave vent to his frustrations and told Schwendler to reorganize the company. He ended his tirade with the ultimatum, that if Schwendler did not cooperate, he would have to leave the company. Schwendler told Dummkopf that he had made some good points. But taking his viewpoints, and those of all others concerned into account, it would appear that the best solution would be for him to leave...... right now!

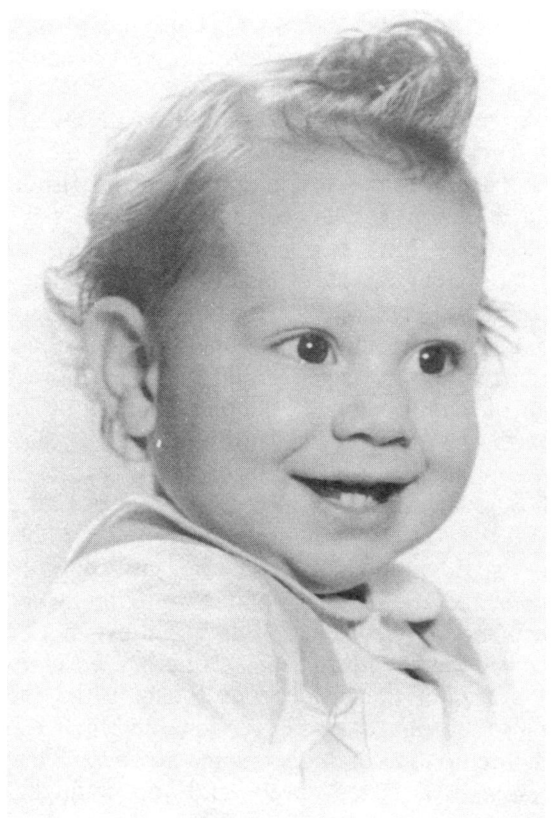

Alan Coutinho, age 10 months

RAM JET FEVER

In the mid-1940's, BuAir realized the need for an Air-to-Air Missile (ARM).   But BuAir was not authorized to procure missiles, the ammunition people did that. To solve this dilemma, a new term was invented: "Pilotless aircraft." It was effective, but it did not last long. BuAir had its charter changed and became the Bureau of Naval Weapons (BuWeps), and "Airplane" contracts became "Weapon Systems" contracts that included missiles. ARM became the hot topic of the day.

Before BuAir became BuWeps, Grumman was awarded a contract for a Pilotless Aircraft. This was a monstrous missile, some 24 inches in diameter and 18 feet long. It was too big to be airborne, but was a step in the right direction. It was designated XSSM-N-6, Rigel.

The Rigel came in two parts, the missile section (warhead, guidance, fuel tank, engine, etc.) and the booster. The engine was a ram jet that could operate only at a speed of at least Mach 2. To accelerate the missile section to its operating speed of Mach 2, a booster had to provide a thrust of 90000 lbs for four seconds.

The concept of a ram engine is simple. There is no compressor and few moving parts. A ram jet has an outside shell, that is, a straight tube of constant diameter, and an inside body whose diameter varies over its length. As the air flows in the tube and over the inside body, the diameter of the inside body increases, making the gap through which the air is flowing, smaller. The air is compressed, becomes hotter and moves faster. At the point of maximum compression at the end of the inner body, when the air is hottest, hot fuel is injected into the airflow, ignited, and at Mach 2 the hot gases expand against the ram and the rear of the inside body, pushing the vehicle forward. This push against the ram can only be done at Mach 2 or higher, it is an unique characteristic of supersonic airflow. This engine was successfully tested in a Texas desert, and you could hear the roar of the engine for three miles.

I was assigned to the fuselage airframe. All the sketches of ram jets in the literature show the inner body floating in the center of the outer tube, but nowhere is there a description of how the bodies are attached. I decided to attach the inner body with a series of posts at 0, 90, 180, and 270 degrees. I tried to get design approval from my supervisors, but they were non committal. Probably, they did not know what effect the posts would have on the airflow, the subject is not discussed in the literature, and they were not going to stick their necks out. So when the engine test in Texas was a success, I felt relieved.

In those days, the solid propellant grains in rockets of the size of our booster tended to crack. The important feature in a rocket is that the grain burns evenly. A crack increases the burning surface area, increasing the pressure, and the rocket disintegrates. For the case that a solid propellant booster might not be ready in time, Grumman decided to sponsor a back-up development of a liquid fuel booster. Arrangements were made with a prominent chemical engineering company, M.W.Kellogg Chemical, and I was appointed liaison engineer. The engineers from Kellogg were nice people, they never tired of telling me what a fine company Kellogg was. Chemical plants that they built 75 years ago were still producing productively.

I explained to them that we needed a liquid fuel booster that put out 90000 lbs of thrust for four seconds, and that could not weigh more than a solid propellant booster. The proposals that they prepared one after the other looked like they were designed to last 75 years, and weighed 50 times our allowable weight. I tried to talk real nice to them, just like I talk to Roy and Alan when I want them to do something for me. It just did not register. They could not conceive that one of their designs should only last four seconds. In the meantime there occurred a dramatic increase in the reliability of large solid propellant rockets, which made Grumman confident that they could use such a solid propellant booster for the Rigel. Grumman rescued me from my dilemma by canceling the contract for the liquid fuel booster.

Twenty five Rigel Pilotless Aircraft were built and delivered to the Navy for testing at the Naval Missile Test Center, Point Mugu, California. However, at that time, great advances were being made in solid fuel rockets. They were smaller and lighter than a ram jet with the same capability. After the Rigel, few ram jets were built.

Nevertheless, the flight tests at Point Mugu were very productive, especially with respect to supersonic flight. These data were useful on subsequent missile designs, especially on the Polaris.

In view of the new functions performed by electronics, and the greatly increased size of the power plants, an interesting and heated discussion broke out in the industry. Who should be prime contractor, the electronics, the power plant, or the traditional primes, the vehicle people? Grumman became the sub-contractor to Bendix, who was prime on the Eagle. I attended a few organizational meetings with Bendix, but was otherwise not involved. The project was later canceled for lack of funds.

CHARLES A. VILLIERS

Throughout the 1940's, the hottest topic in the aeronautical community was ARM. The meetings of the newly organized American Rocket Society were all overcrowded. Grumman wanted to make sure that they did not miss anything. They signed a consulting contract   with Charles A. Villiers, one of the country's most visible rocket scientists and President of the American Rocket Society.

Villiers showed up for work one morning and I was assigned to keep him company. He was an impressive, flamboyant big man with wavy silver hair. Nobody told me what to do with him.

Villiers was a great pontificator, skilled at giving glowing speeches to spellbound audiences. He started off by trying to convert me into an enthusiastic rocket engineer. I figured that what Grumman wanted from him was advice on business opportunities in the rocket industry.

I explained to him that Grumman was big company, and we had to make known his ideas to a large number of busy executives, who would then take appropriate action as might be indicated. The best way to proceed was for him to tell me about one of his recommendations at a time, and I   would   write a report for distribution among Grumman management personnel. Villiers did not like this   discipline at all, but he went along with it. He dictated, and I wrote the reports. He signed them. They were read by Grumman management personnel.

I described to Villiers some of the projects that we   had at Grumman, and he immediately became fascinated with the XSSM-N-6 Rigel Ram Jet. I told him about the fiasco we had with Kellogg, trying to develop a liquid fuel booster. He immediately made this topic the subject of his immediate study program. He was convinced that you could build a liquid fuel booster of that size that was lighter than a solid fuel booster. With his guidance, I wrote Report No. P/A 1401, Investigation of a Liquid Fuel Booster Rocket, FL 66000, June 26, 1947. This report described the procedure for designing a liquid fuel booster that was lighter than a solid fuel booster.

This report was written after Grumman had made the decision in favor of a solid fuel booster for the Rigel, so it had no influence on booster selection. But if I had had this knowledge earlier, the Rigel might have had a liquid fuel booster, at least as a back up.

I tried to get Villiers to identify business opportunities for Grumman in the booming rocket industry, but he had his mind on solving scientific problems. Some of the reports that we wrote were:

P/A Report 1204, Water Launching of Rocket Missiles, July10,1947

P/A Report 1407, Firing Test of a 500 lbs Thrust Liquid Fuel Rocket Motor, Part 1, Test Plan, June 7, 1948

P/A Report 1403, Proposal for the Design and Development of a Liquid Fuel Rocket Booster, October 14, 1948

P/A Report 1404, Variable Thrust Ram Jet, not dated.

The Villiers consulting contract eventually expired. He left, telling me that he had had a most enjoyable and enlightening learning experience. I felt that he was   going to be a good advertisement for Grumman in the rocket industry.

GERMAN   ROCKETS

The German Peenemunde Rocket Facility was captured by the Russians towards the end of World War 2. They divided the captured material with the US Army. This material was split up and sent to various US companies for evaluation. Grumman got the drawings for the V-1, V-2, and the Wasserfall. Since I could speak German, the drawings were assigned to me for evaluation.

During the last part of the War, the V-1 was in production and used to bomb London. The V-2 was a more effective V-1, in an advanced state of development, also designed to bomb London. The Wasserfall was a most sophisticated and much larger missile, still in the first stages of planning, designed to bomb New York. I received no analytical, planning, manufacturing, or other type of information other than the engineering drawings. I also did this review after working on the Rigel and learning about the spectacular progress that the US was making in the rocket sciences.

The drawings were all straight forward engineering, at the state of the art. There was nothing on the drawings that could not have been reproduced at Grumman, and I could not see anything that we could learn from them. I wrote a report of my findings, and Grumman submitted the report to the Army when they returned the captured material.

THE GERMANS ARRIVE

The Guggenheim family built a very large beautiful mansion on Long Island.   As successive generations developed other interests and moved away from the family home, the family donated the empty family home to the AIAA. The AIAA rented it to the US Navy.

The German scientists that were captured by the US Forces at the end of World War II were brought to the United States and assigned in groups to various Government facilities throughout the United States. One of these groups was assigned to the Guggenheim Mansion on Long Island. These men were distributed to work at various Long Island industrial plants. Grumman received three such men, namely: Herbert Wagner, my former aircraft structural design professor in Berlin, R. Lippish and Joe Hubert, both from Messerschmidt.

Wagner had lost his wife, but had his five year old daughter with him. We invited them over to the house for dinner one evening, and the little girl had a grand time playing with Roy. For some reason, Wagner did not like it at Grumman, and after three weeks, he was transferred to California. There he opened a consulting business and eventually got married again. As soon as his "prisoner" status expired and he was free to do what he wanted to do, he went back to Germany and became a professor at the University of Aachen.

Lippisch also did not like it at Grumman and was transferred to another company in Philadelphia.

Hubert just wanted to get back to Germany, to his wife and three sons. I finally talked him into staying. He brought his family over and finally got everybody settled on Long Island. He was an outstanding aerodynamicist, and eventually became Chief of Aerodynamics at Grumman, a better job than he ever had in Germany. His three boys all did well at college in this country, and all got married here.

HOUSE   HUNTING

With two little boys added to our family, our cozy apartment in Hempstead became rather crowded. We needed a new house in a new neighborhood.

No new housing had been built during the War, but now, five years later, things were reverting to normal. The Levitt Brothers were covering large areas of Long Island with their excellent prefabricate houses that they sold to veterans for $6990.

Every Sunday afternoon we took a ride through the neighboring towns around Hempstead, looking for new developments. We eventually found a nice house in a community south of Hempstead. The salesman told me that I had to be making $8000 a year to live in this neighborhood. At that time I could not imagine how I would ever make as much as $8000 a year, so we continued our search.

We finally decided that we would like to live in Garden City, but there were very few empty lots available in that town. We found a large empty parcel on the west side of town and decided to wait until some builder would begin to develop that parcel. Sure enough, one day a sign went up, announcing that a builder was going to develop that land. We contacted him right away, and learned that most of his proposed houses were already sold. We had our choice of the two or three that were left, and picked 32 Dartmouth Street, Garden City, N.Y. 11550. See page 245. It was a nice house and yard (65 x 100 ft), only the first floor with its two bedrooms was finished, the rest of the house was unfinished and kept me busy for the next 21 years that we lived in the house. Alan was just one year old when we moved in.

I had a 1000 gallon oil tank buried in the front yard, thinking I would always have half a tank in case of an emergency. However, the oil company refused to fill the tank and would only deliver half a tank at a time when the tank was almost empty.

The Coutinho Residence, 32 Dartmouth St., Garden City, N.Y.

The boys liked to play on the basement floor, but it was cold on the bare cement. I put down a wood floor, and made the basement more livable. Over the years, I finished the basement, complete with a corner bar.

The house came with a nice staircase to an empty attic. I had the back side of the roof raised, that gave me room to build three additional bedrooms and a bathroom on the second (attic) floor. The whole neighborhood came out to watch the roof raising operation, (it only took an afternoon, the guys knew what they were doing). A number of my neighbors hired the crew to raise the roofs on their own houses.

I added an enclosed porch to the back of the house, and in good weather, we always ate our meals out there.

The house was in a good location. I took Old Country Road, a two lane highway, to work at Grumman. It took me 15 minutes. Then, with the rapid growth of Long Island, they widened the road to four lanes, built lots of stores on either side, and with time, put up 35 traffic lights. My time to get to work increased to at least 30 minutes.

We also had excellent train service to New York City, but I could drive to Forest Hills, park in a lot next to a subway stop, and be in the City in less than a hour. Both boys went to high schools in New York City, and they took the train, like almost all the men in Garden City. With trains running every half hour, they had more freedom to participate in extracurricular school activities than the Garden City kids that had to rely on the school bus with its fixed schedule.

THE ALUMINUM STARTING GATE

I wondered why Jake Swirbul, the Grumman General Manager, and avid aviation fan, held the position of New York State Commissioner for Race Tracks. So one day I asked him.

Swirbul told me that running a large company like Grumman brought him into contact with a number of State offices where he sometimes had a difficult time negotiating what was best for Grumman employees. To   make things easier for himself, he got himself appointed as a State Commissioner. As such, he can walk in and out of the Governor's office when he needs to, and he is on a first name basis with the Governor. It makes doing business with State officials much easier.

In his capacity as Race Track Commissioner, Swirbul observed that the crude steel starting gates in general use were heavy, and when they were drawn across the race track after a start, to clear the track, they left deep ruts across the track which represented a hazard for the

Aluminum Starting Gate at Belmont Park Race Track
Walter Novak standing at Stall 6

horses who had to run over them.   He felt, a good looking aluminum starting gate would be much lighter and would not leave such large ruts when it was rolled off the track.   Swirbul contacted Novak and asked him to design such an aluminum starting gate, and he asked one of the foreman, who had a shop in his house, to build it.   Swirbul wanted a valid cost figure, so no Grumman resources could be used. Novak asked me to prepare the stress analysis.

Novak and I went to the nearby Belmont Park Race Track several times to observe how starting gates were operated, and what the design requirements were. We met with a starter who provided us with quite an education on the lore and operation of race tracks. The starter is the boss of the race track up until the start of a race.   He observes the behavior of the horses in their starting gate stalls and talks to them until they stop squirming. When the horses are finally all still, he opens the gates and lets the race begin.

We added a requirement of our own, that our starting gate could be towed over the public road system. This meant that the height had to be limited so the gate would pass under bridges. Most of the design work was done at Novak's house, although I did some of it at home.

The photo on page 247 shows the finished starting gate at Belmont Park Race Track, with Novak in front of it. Page 249 shows the gate in operation.

The gate was used at Belmont Park, towed to Saratoga for a season, and towed back to Belmont. On its way to Saratoga, it was towed midday like a regular big truck up New Hyde Park Road, half a block west of our house on Dartmouth Street in Garden City. Saratoga was then a fashionable watering place. Eleanor and I went there to assure that the gate was functioning properly. While we were there, we visited the spa and took advantage of the natural mineral springs.

Our gate was much better looking than the steel gates. As a result. it was only used for the most prestigious races. With the big wheels that we provided, and weighing less than half the weight of a steel gate, it left negligible ruts on the race track when pulled off after a start.

The only problem with the aluminum starting gate was its cost, $ 30000, as against $ 10000 for a welded steel gate. Thirty thousand dollars was a lot of money at that time, it would buy you a great big house in a nice neighborhood.

Steel gates are used for five or six years and then they start to rust. They receive a nice coat of paint and are sold to foreign tracks for $ 5000 to $6000. The use of a steel gate is less than $ 1000 a year.

Our gate was hand made, the cost could be reduced appreciably by serial assembly. However, steel welding is a much cheaper method of assembly. Aluminum does not rust, so the life of an aluminum gate

Aluminum Starting Gate in Action, Belmont Park Race Track

would be much longer than that of a steel gate. However, no matter how we analyzed it, we could not compete with the cost of a steel gate at $1000 a year.   Swirbul checked our numbers carefully and became convinced that he could not sell an aluminum starting gate at our price. Nevertheless, it was a fun exercise. I am sure that our aluminum gate is still in operation somewhere, since its owners maintained it like a jewel.

ALAN   HAS   NEPHRITIS

At age three, Alan came down with a mysterious disease that Dr. Millet, our Garden Ciaty physician, called "Nephritis," a rare children's kidney disease, often fatal. He said that he had about one case a year, it occurred mostly in small boys, and there was no cure. It was absolutely necessary to keep the child quiet.

We borrowed a hospital bed from Grumman and put it up in the back corner of our living room.   The bed came with several attractions, such as the cranks that would raise or lower the bed, or only the head or the foot part, or the center (knees) part. In no time at all, Alan was a master at operating all the cranks.

The hospital bed proved to be no help at all in keeping Alan, our perpetual motion machine, quiet. The only way I could keep him quiet for a few moments was to hold him on my lap. It only took him a few minutes before he squirmed himself loose.

Millet sent us to a very expensive specialist on Park Avenue in New York, who confirmed Millet's diagnosis of acute nephritis and said that Alan was on the road to recovery.

Millet came to see Alan every week. One day, he stepped into the living room while Alan was standing on the top of the bed's headboard, with his arms outstretched so his hands were touching the room ceiling. Millet looked at me and asked: "Is this the way you are keeping this child real quiet?"

After eight months, Millet pronounced Alan well again.

RAISING   TWO   BOYS

Eleanor and I were blessed with two intelligent and super active little boys. It took all the help we could get from our church, the schools and universities, and even the military to raise them into responsible and productive American citizens.

When our son Alan was three years old, we lived in a detached house on a moderately busy street. One of our greatest worries was protecting him from running into the street in front of an approaching car. I decided to build a fence around that portion of our back yard that included the big swing and the sandbox.

Alan helped me build the fence, as he did with all my shop work.

1970 Family Reunion in Finished Basement,
32 Dartmouth Street, Garden City
Left to right, front row sitting on the floor: Roy Coutinho, Dan
Henry; Inge Henry*, Eleanor Coutinho, Ann Spencer*
Center row: Kim Henry, Kelly Hall, Eleanor's Parents, Marie and
August Burkarth, Elsie Hall*, Robby Hall, Robert Hall, Hilda
Burkarth, Linda and Karen Burkarth, Dennise Henry
Rear row: John Coutinho (dark, behind bar), Charles
Burkarth**, and Alan Coutinho
*Eleanor's sisters   **Eleanor's brother

He was interested in every little detail. The last job we did was to install the gate. He was intrigued with the gate, it was great fun opening and closing it. Then I got out my lock and installed it on the gate. Alan was inside the compound and now watched carefully. When the gate would not open as before, he tried with his hands to open the lock. After a minute or two, when that did not work, he ran back to his secret hiding place and got out his little screw driver that he kept hidden there. He tried very intently to force the lock open with his screw driver for about fifteen minutes, until he finally realized that he could not open the lock. He then threw himself face down on the ground, his little hands pounding the earth and his feet kicking the air, while screaming his little head off.

Two days later, convinced that Alan was safe in his foolproof compound, I went out the front door and caught him about to cross the street. He had figured out a way of getting his shoes sideways into the mesh of the fence and climbing to the top, then rolling down on the other side. It was unbelievable.

One of the most helpful organizations in this process of molding our boys was the Boy Scouts of America. One of the activities in the Boy Scout Program is camping. From Garden City, where we lived on Long Island, about an hour's car ride to the east, the Boy Scouts had a beautiful camp called Camp Wauwepex. In the center was an almost round lake, about one half mile across, and surrounded by deep forest. Each troop went there for two weeks. Individual scouts were also accepted, they formed temporary troops with such visitors. Our two boys went out with their troop, and then stayed the entire summer. We visited them every weekend.

The camp had a stage at the bottom of a hill, with the spectators sitting on the hillside. The boys put on a show every Saturday night for the parents. Lighting was poor. Somehow, Roy organized a giant searchlight, built a platform in a convenient tree, and became the stage lighting manager. The searchlight was a tremendous improvement. After Roy's tenure, Alan inherited the job and the Coutinho family had a monopoly on stage lighting for the next eight years. The job, up in the tree, carried a great deal of prestige at camp.

When they outgrew the Scouts, both boys became Assistant Scout Masters and Counselors at camp. Roy became head of the Rifle Range. When a troop came in for target practice, he gave them a half hour talk and demonstration on how to handle and use a gun. He did this very well and we were real proud of him. Then he supervised the kids on the range, issued ammunition and helped each kid to shoot properly.

Alan became the Assistant Chief at the Trading Post.   This was a

Oil Painting of Eleanor Coutinho
by Victor White, 1946

real store with real money transactions. Much later, when he took a college course in business administration, he would tell me how the professor described the procedures that they had followed at the Trading Post.

Roy was smart and one of my concerns was to get him into a great university. This meant that he had to have a good high school background. I sent him to Xavier High School in New York City, a Jesuit high school. After Regis, also a Jesuit high school, Xavier is the toughest high school in New York City. It is a military high school. Roy graduated sixth in his class, meaning that he could go to any university he wanted to. The boys always wore military uniforms and had military drill and exercises. Roy was very proud of his uniform. When we took him to the doctor's in Garden City for a medical examination, he insisted on wearing his uniform.

At Xavier, Roy joined the Ham Club and the Drill Team. He would spend all kinds of after-school hours at the Ham Club. We had excellent commuter train service to the city, and he could come home any time he wished.

Roy's problem was Latin. Eleanor became the world's best Latin tutor and together, they were finally able to meet all of Xavier's requirements.

Roy decided to go to Engineering School at Columbia University in New York City as a resident student. He would be away from home, yet he could come home by subway/commuter train any time he wanted to. He joined the Ham Club, the Drill Team, and Navy ROTC.

In those days, hams worried about their antennas. The Columbia Campus contained a number of 15 story buildings. Roy strung wires between the roofs of these buildings to give himself a much better antenna. He got elected Executive Officer of the Drill Team and had to make arrangements with teams at other universities for competitive matches. Wherever he went throughout the country, he usually had to deal with former members of a Xavier Drill Team.

Summers, Roy worked in the Electrical Department at Grumman, making electrical cables. He noticed that Grumman discarded pieces of cable that were too short to make a required cable. Roy attached proper ends to these cables, stamped a fictitious number on them, and sent them on down the line. The fake cables hit inspection and fireworks erupted. They never found out who did it.

When Roy graduated from Columbia, he was granted a year and a half leave by the Navy to get a master's degree. He enrolled in the University of Pennsylvania at Philadelphia where he earned his degree in electrical engineering before reporting to the Navy. While on duty in San Diego, he decided to get married to a nice girl, Judy, that he had

Alan, age 2, and Roy, age 7

worked with at the Ham Club at Columbia. Roy was the Radar Officer on an old destroyer in the Vietnam War. They were cruising up and down the Vietnam coast bombing targets as requested by the ground forces. The shots were amazingly accurate, but every time the ship fired a broadside, the old radar would fail, and Roy would have to repair it. For weeks on end, Roy was on duty 24 hours a day and had to catch his sleep at odd moments. After his tour of duty on the destroyer, Roy was assigned to the Beach Jumpers in Vietnam. Roy today is a Director at AT&T. (That is one grade below vice president!) He and Judy have two daughters, see page 265.

Alan became a problem at the end of the fourth grade. He was going to a Waldorf School, same as Roy did. Waldorf Schools develop the whole person, do not give grades. Alan had analyzed his world well. He knew that grown-ups were funny, but he had to put up with them. School was a place to have fun with other kids during recess. Class work was again something he had to put up with, but he felt a deep responsibility to keep the class entertained. I'm sure that the teacher's meetings consisted mostly of quoting the funny things Alan said in class. He had a very funny remark for anything that happened, and everybody loved it. Every year we received glowing reports about his personality development. At the end of the fourth grade, we were told that Alan could not read, was deficient in every subject, and had to repeat the grade. I blew my top.

I started looking for a boarding school run by a Catholic male religious order. I found that they all admitted students only if they passed an entrance examination. I took Alan around to a number of schools, and he flunked all of the entrance examinations. Some schools told me he did not even qualify for first grade.

Alan liked me and would do anything to please me. I took a fifth grade arithmetic book and we started to do the problems in the book. We worked together four hours every night after I came home from work, and ten hours every Saturday and Sunday. At the end of the summer, Alan could do any problem in the book.

Our local Catholic school offered a three week summer course in remedial reading. I had a little talk with the instructor. Alan took three courses, one after the other. At the end of the summer, he could read.

We hired an English teacher to come in and work with Alan. After two weeks, Eleanor decided that she could do better than the teacher and took over the job.

In the fall, I took Alan around to a number of boarding schools to take the entrance examinations to the fifth grade. He passed them all. We selected a school run by the Salecian Order in Goshen, New York, that started with the fifth grade. We visited Alan every week

Alan and Roy all dressed up for
Aunt Elsie's wedding

end. At the end of the school year, he was promoted to the sixth grade. He ranked 28 in a class of 30.

At the end of the school year, the Salecians closed the school, the facility was needed for other purposes. Alan was transferred to Mt. St. Michael in the Bronx, run by the Marist Brothers. This was fine with us; Alan now had a clean record. He graduated from Mt. St. Michael in the upper third of his class.

He elected to go to La Salle High School, a Christian Brothers day school in lower Manhattan, because some of his pals were going there. He lived at home and took the commuter train to the city, as Roy had done. He did not have to take Latin, and again graduated in the top third of his class.

He selected Manhattan College, also a Christian Brothers institution, again because some of his pals were going there. This was a resident school. At this time, he also acquired a motor cycle, which increased his mobility. Manhattan had a working agreement with Mt. St. Vincent, a girls' college a mile or so up the street. The boys went to Mt. St. Vincent for liberal arts courses, and the girls came to Manhattan for technical courses. In this process, Alan met a nice girl, Meg, and the motor cycle came in handy for rides between campuses.

Alan joined the Air Force ROTC at Manhattan and became the unit photographer, to avoid having to do drill and other dumb things. He knew he had to be good to hold this position. On one occasion, a general came to inspect the unit. The general was in conference with the colonel and other officers when Alan barged in and called for a time out to take a picture. He lined up the general and other officers, took his pictures, thanked them kindly, and rushed to his darkroom to develop his pictures. When the conference was over and they opened the door, here was Alan with a set of professional quality photos for each officer. The general was delighted and shook hands with Alan.

After graduation from Manhattan, he was granted a year's leave by the Air Force for graduate study. He enrolled in Fairleigh Dickinson University and earned a Master of Business Administration degree before entering on active duty. Alan married Meg and served several tours in the Air Force. He ended up at Andrews Air Force Base as commander of the unit which maintains the Presidential Fleet, reporting to the White House. He also took care of the aircraft of any heads of state that visit the US. On page 261 is a photo of the Pope thanking Alan's group for taking care of his airplane. Alan is standing directly behind the genuflecting airman.

Alan decided that his job was the top job a non-pilot could have in the Air Force, and it was time to move on. He is now Vice President of a company that advises businesses on the use of the Internet. He is still active in the Air Force and holds the rank of Lieutenant Colonel.

Ensign Roy Coutinho, US Navy Reserves
Cadet Alan Coutinho, US Air Force Reserves

Meg and Alan have three boys, see page 263.

FAMILY VACATIONS
Catskill Mountains

Before we were married, at every chance we had, we would drive up to the Catskill Mountains where Eleanor's parents had a resort, the Catskill Mountain Lake House. This included some weekends and our regular vacations. There was always enough work to keep us busy.

As the war effort intensified, the resort business dried up. In the neighboring town of Fleischmanns, there was a florist business whose owner was drafted into the Army. Eleanor's father took over the business for the duration of the war until the owner returned. Charlie, Inge and Elsie were still at home and were put to work in the greenhouse. When Eleanor and I came up for a visit, we joined them. On holidays, especially at Easter, we spent most of our time delivering flowers up and down the valley.

After the War, Eleanor's parents moved back to the Lake House and most of their old customers came back. After we were married, we continued to go up to the Catskills whenever we could to help out.

Fort Lauderdale

The first family vacations we had that are worth writing about are those that we started to take at Christmas time in Fort Lauderdale, Florida, when Alan, our smallest son, was almost four years old, after he recovered from nephritis.

Our Chief Draftsman, Novak, had been taking his vacation for some time in the winter at Fort Lauderdale and recommended the place to me enthusiastically. I was concerned about taking two small boys in a car on such a long trip, but Novak reassured me, telling me that the roads were good, with lots of motels and service stations along the way. We also felt that the sunshine would be good for Alan after his illness. Novak made reservations for us for the Christmas holidays.

We arrived in Fort Lauderdale at about nine p.m.. and it was raining cats and dogs like nothing I had ever seen before. Novak had made a reservation for us in a large apartment in a garden complex that occupied a full city block.   Most of the area was lush green grass and palm trees. In a corner of the lot was a fully equipped children's playground.

We were charmed with the place. The next day the weather was warm and beautiful, not a cloud in the sky. It remained that way during our entire stay. We went out to buy a Christmas tree, turkey, and all the trimmings.

Our first excursion was to the beach. Getting there and back was a

Pope John Paul II thanks the 89th Air Force
Maintenance Squadron for taking care of his airplane,
Andrews Air Force Base

bit of a bore. We had to cross the Intercontinental Waterway and the bridge was usually up to let the boats go through. The ten minute ride took over half an hour in the hot sun. In Fort Lauderdale, the entire beach is public, there are no structures between the ocean and Highway A1A, only tall palm trees. The sand is courser than on Long Island, but this did not interfere with the boys building sand castles.

Santa Claus found us on schedule, and after the excitement, we went to Church at St. Anthony's. They had a spectacular soprano singer, a marvelous creche, and a beautiful service.   Then we came back to our apartment for our Christmas dinner.

Fort Lauderdale is a moderate size city with just about every type of amusement you might want: movies, restaurants, marinas, amusement parks, theaters, and a dolphin show. It had the most beautiful shopping center that we had ever seen. We made them all. One year we saw "The King and I" with the Broadway star Yul Brynner playing the role of king. We visited the Novaks and went out to dinner with them. We met them year after year, they became real Floridians.

On New Year's day we went to Miami for the parade. There is always a championship football game in Miami on New Year's Day, preceded on the day before by a parade. The parade has many large automated floats and many of the best high school bands from a large part of the southern US. On the way home we had to pass through large good-natured mobs of college students demonstrating in favor of the New Year. However, there were a few years when the college students got violent, and the police responded with tear gas. One year, we got a little whiff of it.

I did not like the heavy traffic on the way to and from the beach. I found a nice apartment, a short block from the beach, which I reserved for the next year.

Pompano Beach

The following year while driving around the area, we found Pompano Beach, a few miles north of Fort Lauderdale. Here we learned the story of Mr Kester, who before the Great Depression worked for an electronics company in New Jersey. He invented the neon light and made a lot of money. He quit his job and moved to Pompano Beach. When the Depression struck, he was the only man in town with money. He bought the local bank and a large part of the real estate in town. One parcel of interest was the property about 100 yards wide and three or four miles long on A1A along the ocean.

Kester, who was single, built a row of sturdy cottages, including all of the furniture, about 75 feet apart, along this property facing the

Joe, Mike, and Jimmy - Alan and Meg's boys

ocean. The cottages were roomy, included a full kitchen, two baths, and two to four bedrooms. The rest of the property was neatly covered with grass and many palm trees. Every morning, a crew of men would come through the property and clean up everything.

Kester had died when we found the place, but it was run by his two nephews. One ran the bank, the other took care of the real estate.

We rented one of these cottages year after year, and the boys always had a grand time. They could run and play games in the large grassy area, climb the palm trees and pick the coconuts which I found hard to cut open. There was the ocean across the street, but they could only go over if Eleanor or I went with them.

A few miles north of our cottage there was a lighthouse and a fishing boat marina. The fishing boats would come back about four o'clock. We would go see which boat had the most attractive fish, and would buy one for $1 or $2. We would bring it home and Eleanor would wrap it in aluminum foil and bake it. I have never, before or after, ever tasted such good fish.

We would pack all of our Christmas presents, tree and other ornaments and other supplies in two large steamer trunks and ship them ten days ahead of time by freight to Pompano Beach. When we got to Florida, one of the first things we did was go to the freight station and pick up our trunks. We had everything we needed for a good holiday.

One of our main activities was to get the boys professional swimming and snorkeling lessons. I tried to take them to a lesson each day. Roy also took a scuba diving course. Since we lived next to the beach, Roy was assigned the job of getting up at five am to check the weather, read the temperature and check the water condition to determine whether or not the group could go out that day. Usually the group could go and would have a great time. Roy would come back and tell us all about the beautiful underwater coral reefs he had seen.

I think these sessions paid off. When Roy went to his first Boy Scout camp, all the boys had to pass a swimming test. They had to swim back and forth the length of a pier. When we got there, lots of boys were thrashing around in the water, getting nowhere. When Roy had his turn, he gracefully dived into the water, took two strokes, and the instructor stopped him and told him that he passed. I did not see him do this to any other boy.

There were a number of different kinds of amusement parks in the area, and with time I think we visited them all. We also drove several hundred miles over the keys and ocean highway to Key West, the most southern city in the United States. We went to the beach there, the most southern point in the US. Key West is a charming old city,

Kathi and Lara
Judy's and Roy's daughters

also known for its giant turtles. We saw the boats bring them in, most measured about 18 inches in diameter. The weather in Florida was not reliable. Most of the years the days were warm and sunny, but not always. One year when I had accumulated a months vacation, we invited my father and sister to come along. We had one of of Kester's largest cottages, there was plenty of room for all of us. But that year, the weather did not cooperate at all. It rained most of the time, and when it did not rain, it was stormy and the ocean was full of Portuguese men-of-war, so it was impossible to go into the water. People were standing around the entrance to their quarters saying: "Am I paying $200 a day for this?"

When the boys started college, they developed more interest in girls and lost their interest in family vacations in Florida.

Acapulco

I was disenchanted with Florida, since the weather was unreliable. I only had a limited number of vacation days and had to make each day count. By studying a map and weather patterns, I found that Acapulco, Mexico, was in a zone where you could be almost certain of good weather. So for the last few years of my working career, Eleanor and I went to Acapulco for our Christmas vacation.

Acapulco is a port city in an unexcelled location on Acapulco Bay. The word "Acapulco" is derived from the Spanish for "pure water." In the old days, freight cargoes from Spain to the Orient would go to Veracruz, then overland to Acapulco, and then across the Pacific to the Orient, and vice versa. Acapulco has an Archbishop and a cathedral. We liked our hotel with its swimming pool on the beach. We had a beach front room with an unsurpassed view.

Texas

While I was working for the Army at Aberdeen, MD, I was assigned by my office for a year to the Corpus Christ Army Depot to work on helicopters. Corpus Christ is the Army's largest helicopter overhaul facility I took Eleanor along, and almost every weekend we took a trip to some place of interest in in nearby Texas, such as San Antonio where the Alamo is located.

I learned a lot about Texas history, such as the story about the Yellow Rose of Texas and the Battle of San Jacinta. I saw a Yellow Rose displayed all over Texas, so I became curious and investigated the story.

After their their victory at the Alamo, the Mexicans under their President, General Santa Anna, wanted to consolidate their gains. Santa Anna, with an army of 1200 men, marched into Texas. The Texans raised an army of about 1000 men under Sam Houston. Both

Houston and Santa Anna marched their armies for months up and down either side of the Jacinta River, eying each other. The Mexicans took a nap during siesta time each day.

On August 31, 1843, a very hot day, when both armies were opposing one another at the town of San Jacinta where there was a bridge, Houston and his men sneaked over the bridge undetected during the siesta hour. Houston had sent the Yellow Rose, a prostitute, to sleep with Santa Anna. Houston's men surrounded the Mexican army, and on signal, fell on the sleeping Mexicans and killed 630 men, wounded 206, and captured the rest. The battle lasted 18 minutes. The Yellow Rose kept Santa Anna in his tent until Houston appeared, captured him and sent him to Washington.

To get its President back, Mexico surrendered almost half of its territory, namely, Texas, New Mexico, Arizona, Nevada, California and part of Colorado. It was one of the significant battles in world history, and outside of Texas, hardly anybody knows about it. Houston went home to become elected President of the Republic of Texas.

Hawaii

Several years ago, my boss Mox and I were assigned to a two week job at Fort Staffer, Hawaii. Mox decided that since Fort Staffer was only 30 minutes up the mountain from Honolulu, we might as well stay in town. He picked a hotel on Waikiki Beach. Toward the end of our two week tour, Mox's wife and Eleanor flew out to join us. We each still had a week's vacation. Through the Army Recreation Office, I obtained a car and a room at the Marriott Hotel on Maui. There are five big hotels in a row at the beach on Maui. It was the most opulent place we had ever seen. The dining room of the hotel next door was built around a natural 15 foot waterfall. We ate there several times.

Lindbergh

I had heard that Charles Lindbergh had lived and been buried on Maui. I found out how to get to his grave and decided to go there. The road was not just unpaved, it was covered with sharp rocks. The few 4-wheel drive trucks that we encountered seemed to try to drive me off the road. We were about half way there, it was raining heavily, and I got a flat tire. Reluctantly, I gave up and turned back.

I went to the rental agency where I had gotten the car and reported a flat tire. The man laughed and said that I must have been on the road to Lindbergh's grave. He said, everybody in a regular car on that road gets a flat tire. When Lindbergh lived in the United States, he had no privacy. He finally moved to this remote corner of Maui to protect himself and his family. His neighbors on Maui liked him and did everything they could to assure his privacy. One thing was the road, they would not let the State improve it. Instead, they designed the sharp rocks surface to assure that anyone using the road would get a flat.

With our trip to Hawaii, Eleanor and I have been to 49 States of the Union. We have never been to Alaska.

Houseboats

Some time ago, Alan found a new vacation destination. He rented a houseboat on Lake Cumberland, Kentucky. In subsequent years, he invited Eleanor and me to go along.

Lake Cumberland is a man made lake, a little over 100 miles long, created by a dam in the Cumberland River. The mountains come straight up right out of the water, there are only a few places where there is a little shore, and this is where they rent the houseboats. There are a large number of small coves along the main lake. It is unspoiled and beautiful.

Alan rented a houseboat with more sleeping bunks than we needed, a full kitchen and dining facilities He also rented a power boat for water skiing, and he brought his two hydrobikes. These consist of a bicycle structure without wheels, mounted on two pontoons. The pedals drive a propeller. Hydrobikes can go about ten miles per hour.

Eleanor and Alan's wife, Meg, prepared much of the food in advance. Careful planning was required, because once you leave port, there is no place to buy anything.

The weather was beautiful and we had a wonderful time, swimming, water skiing, and hydrobiking. At night, we would park in a cove and tie the boat with ropes to a tree on each side of the cove.

I was very proud of my grandsons. They ran the boat. Each boy knew what he had to do, and they worked together like a well oiled team. They were always alert and ready to take action if something had to be done. Nobody had to tell them anything.

Switzerland

When Alan was in his last year of high school, we took him on a Christmas trip to Europe, primarily to Switzerland and Germany. Roy was away at college. In Switzerland, we went to Zermat at the foot of the Matterhorn, and Alan wanted to go skiing.   We rented a pair of boots and skis for him. He took the cam railroad up the mountain, while Eleanor and I went to a cafe' to have some coffee and pastries. When the last train came down, Alan was not on it. The people at the railroad station told us not to worry, the kids always find a way down. If Alan does not show up in three hours, they'll go looking for him. We went to the parking lot and sat in our car. In about two hours, Alan shows up. He had not realized that he had a round trip ticket. He said that all he had to do to get back was to walk downhill, and he fully expected to meet us at the car in the parking lot.

In Geneva their were a number of formally dressed Chinese staying at the same place as we were. At that time, Chinese were an unusual sight for us. I guessed that they had business at the League of Nations.

Christmas in Germany

Although I had spent many years in Germany, there are many little things that you forget.   One was, how the Germans celebrate Christmas. Christmas is practically a three day national holiday. The first day is Christmas eve, and the next two days are the two days of Christmas. These three days are taken very seriously, and practical everything, that is, anything you might need, is closed.

We arrived in Freiburg in the early evening of Christmas eve and looked for a nice place to have supper. I drove all around town, and every restaurant was closed. I decided to go to the railroad station. I remembered that these stations have nice restaurants that are open 24 hours a day. The station was closed, no trains were running, there were no services available.

I started to look for a hotel. I went to all the places that I knew, and they were all closed. I started to make a systematic search, street by street, and found a small hotel that was open. Rooms only, the dining room was closed. We took a room.

The hotel clerk told me about a bar that might be open and where we might be able to buy something to eat. Alan and I went there. It was a sleazy little joint, but we were able to buy some greasy fried sausages, French fries, and soft drinks.

We spent Christmas day with my friends in Freiburg as noted in the following paragraph on Freiburg.

The day after Christmas, my plan was to drive to the Frankfurt Airport, turn in our rent-a-car, and take shuttle flight to Berlin. The shuttle flights run all day, this is a walk-on operation and they do not issue reservations. We would not need a car in Berlin. So we arrived at the Frankfurt Airport, and everything was closed.   There were no shuttle flights to Berlin. The car rental agencies were all closed. All restaurants were closed.

I decided to drive to Berlin. I called the hotel, where I had a reservation, and told them that I would be very late. They said that they would wait. The next day, the day after the three-day Christmas, was a normal working day, and I turned in the car at the Berlin office of the rental agency.

Freiburg

We spent Christmas day with a former classmate, Herman, who was now Governor of South Baden. He had five children, one girl and four boys. The kids were amazed that Alan could not speak German. They had never before met anybody who could not speak German, and could not visualize that such people existed.

One boy could play the trumpet well and he had played it that Christmas morning from the top of the cathedral tower. Alan could play a little trumpet, so they lent him another instrument. The girl played the piano, the other boys each had a different musical instrument. Alan knew all the pieces that the German kids knew and played along on the trumpet. We had a very musical Christmas that afternoon.

Meersburg

In Meersburg I showed Alan where I went to school and took him on a tour of the old fortress, built around 730 AD on the foundations of a Roman fort. It is the only fortress in Germany undamaged, although it was attacked in several wars. It is still inhabited, it contains four modern apartments, but the great hall and the other rooms on the tour are in their original condition. I told Alan, this is the kind of place where King Arthur lived and conducted his Round Table.

Heidelberg

In Heidelberg, we toured the university and I told Alan about some of the great men who had worked here. Eleanor said the place needed a coat of paint. During our tour of the castle, I pointed out to Alan the dormitory building, called the English House because of its architecture, where the prince kept his 300 girl friends. I commented that the people in this part of Germany are too busy to plot wars. You can tell a lot about the character of the people in a country by the great structures that they build.

Berlin

We had to drive through the Russian Eastern Zone to get to Berlin. I was warned to obey the speed limits, not to stop the car, and to stay on the road. It was dark when we arrived at Check Point Charlie, the entrance to Berlin. The big plaza was brightly lit up and surrounded by towers with machine guns pointed at us. The car and baggage search and personal examination took over two hours until we were allowed to pass.

I took Alan around the university and showed him the other sights, including the Palace of Charlottenburg. One room is full of Chinese porcelains. The manufacturing of porcelain in former times was a Chinese State secret, and the export of such information from China was a crime punishable by death. Queen Charlotte was very fond of these porcelains and she managed to import 300 Chinese porcelain workers to Berlin and to found the Prussian State Porcelain Factory which today still makes some of the world's best and most expensive porcelain ware. I showed Alan how the Palace was designed for people who were more concerned with business than pleasure. They were more likely to want to expand their empire than to make love.

Los Angeles

My job and professional activities required me to travel occasionally and if the place was interesting, I tried to make a vacation out of the trip. One time, I was chairman of an engineering research conference at the University of California in Santa Barbara. I decided to drive out to California and to take Eleanor and Alan along.

We drove west via the southern route, stopping along the way to see the sights, such as the Grand Canyon and Las Vegas. At the Grand Canyon gift shop we saw a pair of longhorns that we bought and that now are on display in our apartment. Alan helped the salesgirl take them down from the wall and he carried them into the back room where she could wrap them. Senator Goldwater was in the room and came over to admire our longhorns. He and Alan had a nice chat.

In El Paso we decided to go over the border to Juarez, Mexico, and spend the night in the Cameo Real, then one of Mexico's first line tourist hotels. We were assigned a very large room with massive Spanish style furniture. However, I could not help observing that the concrete work in the hotel and sidewalks was badly cracked.

While I was at work in Santa Barbara, Eleanor and Alan explored Los Angeles, including Disney World, the movie studios, and other wonders. The old Mission of Our Lady of the Angels contains some remarkable paintings of Our Lady and other Saints created by Indians whom the monks had taught how to paint.

Muir Woods

At the end of my conference, we drove north to San Francisco. The northern part of the highway follows the top edge of the cliffs along the Pacific Ocean. It was spectacular.

From San Francisco we made an excursion to the Muir Woods where there is a stand of giant Redwoods. These evergreens are over 4000 years old, the oldest living things on earth. They were already 2000 years old when Jesus Christ walked on the earth. The place is awe inspiring. The trunks of these trees are some 20 to 30 feet in diameter, and they are well over 100 feet tall. The road goes through the trunk of one of the trees, they have chopped a hole in the tree big enough to drive a small truck through it.

In a little clearing there is a brass plaque stating that the signing of the papers establishing the United Nations took place here, Roosevelt, Churchill, and company attending.

The Northern Route East

On the way east, we took the northern route and visited several National Parks along the way, such as Yosemite, Yellow stone, and Rocky Mountain. In South Dakota we saw a road leading to an Indian reservation which had a sign reading: "Please do not laugh at the natives!" In Chicago, the Museum of Science and Industry was a real experience.

Colorado

Another successful vacation that I was able to associate with a business trip was when I was sent to attend a conference on electronic systems design at the University of Colorado at Boulder. This was a three day conference, Monday through Wednesday. I made arrangements to visit Martin-Denver on Thursday and Friday, as Martin was building the boosters for the Apollo, and there were a number of questions that I wanted to clarify. Eleanor and I flew to Denver some four days before the conference and were able to drive through the northern part of the state, from east to west and back again, both times through the Rocky Mountain National Park, before the conference started.

After the conference, we moved to Denver and I visited Martin. The man in charge of the aspect that I wanted to discuss was Tommy, an old friend. We concluded our business by Friday noon, and Tommy took Eleanor and me for a ride in the Denver City Park, a large area where they keep a herd of buffalo. We hunted buffalo all afternoon, but never found any.

We then went through the US Air Force Academy at Colorado Springs. and through the southern portion of the state from east to west and back. We saw some beautiful mountains, and a number of old historic mining towns like those you see in old western movies.

Family Get-Togethers

With our family so scattered geographically, we developed a plan for get-togethers. At Easter we rented a cottage at Oglebay in Wheeling, West Virginia, famous for its Christmas lights, and at Thanksgiving we got a large apartment at Seven Springs, a ski resort in the mountains of western Pennsylvania not far from Pittsburgh. Some years there would be snow at Thanksgiving, and the kids would go skiing. These places are approximately halfway between where my boys live, and Aberdeen where Eleanor and I lived.

These places have swimming pools, dances, and all sorts of entertainment facilities. We always had a good time together. On the occasion of our 50th wedding anniversary, our children surprised us by putting on a play at Oglebay, with Eleanor, me, and our two sons as the main characters. The play started with my courting Eleanor, then went on to describe all of the many mistakes that I have made, and all the bad luck events that have occurred in my life time. Everybody thought it was hilarious.

ADJUNCT PROFESSOR OF AERONAUTICAL ENGINEERING

In 1951, Professor Nick Hoff, Head of the Department of Aeronautical Engineering and Applied Mechanics at the Polytechnic Institute of Brooklyn, who I had known for years from affairs at the AIAA, asked me to teach their course on aircraft structural design. I did so for nine years. After four years, I was awarded the title of Adjunct Professor of Aeronautical Engineering.

This was a required spring semester, senior year, four credit course, two hours of lectures and four hours of exercises. Hoff wanted me to organize the material myself, based on my industrial experience. Attendance in the class was about 30 students. Brooklyn Poly was a highly technical university, and all the boys were expert in manipulating differential equations.

I could not fail to think back at my own Berlin experience, but I could not conceive how Berlin's four years of intensive design instruction could be compressed into a single semester. But there were certain principles that I remembered. A basic rule was that you learned by doing an exercise, not necessarily by attending lectures.

I started by telling them:

"This course will be different from anything you have had before. Many of the courses that you have had were prerequisites for this course, and we will make use of that material. In design we will start off with a clean sheet of paper, this is something that will disturb you. It is something you will have to get used to. You have to begin by laying out some concepts and ideas on your clean sheet. Then you analyze your design with the tools that you have learned in your other courses. Normally, unless you are very experienced, the analysis will show that your layout has deficiencies. You will have to go through several cycles of design changes and analysis before your layout will be satisfactory. In this class we will only have time to go through the first cycle.

"We are going to start out with the drawing of an airplane. If you

are knowledgeable, you may lay out any airplane you like. For those of you with less experience, I have prepared a simple drawing of an airplane, and you may copy it to get yourself started.

"You will be required to prepare three reports and three drawings as follows:

Reports: 1. *Airplane Technical Data*
2. *Air Loads on the Wing*
3. *Analysis of a Fitting*

Drawings: 1. *Drawing of an Airplane*
2 *Lines Drawing of the Front Portion of the Fuselage*
3. *Layout. A Portion of the Structure that*
         includes a major Fitting

"Drawings and Reports have to be submitted on schedule, because of the way I grade them by comparison. When I compare two reports, I can usually tell which is the better one, and which student has a better understanding of the technical problem. After I have reviewed them all, I line them up in order of quality, the best ones at one end of the line, the worse ones at the other end. If warranted, I like to give the three best reports and drawings an A, and the three worse ones a C, unless any one is so bad that I have to give it a D, but I try to avoid that. All reports in the line between an A and a C get a B. I feel that if you do these exercises, these drawings and reports will reflect what you have learned, and there is no need for a final examination. I have taught aircraft structural design to many incoming young engineers at Grumman, and evaluated their progress, without having to give them a final examination.

"Report 1 and Drawing 1 contain the type of data that a designer knows, dreams up or assumes, and which we need to get started. I will help you to get this material together.

"One of the unique characteristics of an airplane is its airfoil (double curvature) shape. In practice, this shape must be held to within a 0.005 inch tolerance. In preparing Drawing 2 you will learn how to use a set of second degree curves to control a double curvature shape.

"I cannot give grades for reports that are not submitted on time, because I will not have anything to compare them with. Using my judgment, such items will get a C or a D."

The faculty watched my grading system carefully. Since I came from industry and had no academic teaching experience, they expected my grades to be different from theirs. Everyone was surprised when my grades were completely in line with those given by other instructors.

I was challenged by the students on everything I said that was not established practice at Poly, but I could not think of a better way of preparing them for a job in the aircraft industry in one semester.

I had trouble with one genius. He was so smart, he never had to do any work. He did not attend all classes. The day before an exam, he would browse through a book for a short time. Then he would take the exam and get an A. In all his four years, he had an A in every class, except mine. Although I beat on him as hard as I could, he prepared no reports or drawings. I flunked him. The faculty was fascinated, nobody had been able to cope with him before. I did not hurt him much. He took a make-up course and received his degree six months later.

Almost all the boys had their eyes set on getting a job in California where the big aircraft manufacturers were located. These were all boys from nice families in Brooklyn, who lived at home. I pointed out what it would mean to their family life to live 3000 miles from home, especially if they got married and had children. What were their mothers going to do? Nobody had ever pointed out these things to them. Some of the best ones came to Grumman every year, and were quite successful. Many others found jobs on the East Coast.

A fraternity took a survey to determine who was the most popular professor. I came in number three. A few weeks later. the AIAA Student Section held its Annual Meeting. I was the invited speaker. After dinner, we had a beer party. Other professors came and stayed for one glass of beer. I stayed until closing. I took a carload of students and dropped them off on the way home. In the car, they discussed the survey, and told me that if the survey had been held after the AIAA party, instead of before, I would have been number one. This goes to show you that among men, the thing that counts is how well you can hold your beer.

FLIGHT CONTROL SYSTEM ANALYSIS-GRUMMAN

F8F-1 BEARING

When Villiers left, Cappy (Elio Caprigolio), now head of the Flight Controls Design Group, invited me to join his group . His group was expanding rapidly, and he was in need of analysts. The first task that he assigned to me was the F8F-1 bearing.

This bearing was located in the rear of the outer portion of the wing and supported the bell crank which held two push rods, the one that operated the elevator, and the other that was driven by the hydraulic system. The loads were very high, and there was not much room because the wing was quite thin at this point.

This bearing failed after 25 flight hours in Naval service. Grumman, at that time, was conducting the F8F-1 flight test program, and the bearing in these tests was also failing at about 25 hours of test flight. Grumman received a letter from the Navy stating that the bearing had to be fixed so that it would last as long as the rest of the flight control system.

Cappy gave me a copy of this letter and told me to go do whatever was necessary to comply with its directive. He said that nobody knew what was meant by the term "last as long as the rest of the flight control system," nor how we should go about complying with the Navy directive. In other words, I was being given a task that no man had ever done before. I decided that it should be fun.

I assumed that the control system life was equal to aircraft life. Component failures and replacements are tolerated on an aircraft and a control system, and do not detract from aircraft or control system life. Such component replacements cannot be performed on a bearing.   Bearing life should therefore be equal to aircraft life.

I had done some work on predicting airplane life and still remembered a little of how I did it. I sketched out a scheme on how I could predict the life of the F8F-1 bearing. I was not concerned about what Grumman would accept, but I was worried about the Navy. I went to Washington several times and talked to them about my ideas. You cannot expect approval from them in a developing case like this, but if some of your suggestions are unacceptable, they will find some way of letting you know. The important thing is to let the Navy know what you are doing, so that when you submit a report for approval, they will already know what is in it. Surprises are intolerable.

I wrote a technical report predicting a life of 4000 flight hours for the F8F-1 aircraft. I submitted the report to the Navy for approval, and in due course, the report was approved. Now I had to demonstrate that the bearing would survive 4000 hours of operating life.

I obtained copies of the ongoing Grumman flight tests and extracted the load history on the bearing. I counted the number of times a load of a given size and duration occurred. I arranged the loads according to size and duration and eliminated the no-load time periods. The result was an active loading spectrum of about 400 hours. This was tedious work, it took me and two assistants six weeks to complete this task.

To demonstrate that a bearing would function satisfactorily in the F8F-1, it would have to survive the 400 hour load spectrum. I assumed that such a test would run six hours per eight hour work shift, and we could run two shifts a day, including weekends. At 12 test hours a day, we could complete a 400 hour test spectrum in 400/12= 34 consecutive days. The number of six hour test periods would be 400/6 = 67. Each such six hour test period would be a mini spectrum consisting of 1/67th of all the loads in the master spectrum, such that the application of 67 mini spectra would be equal to one 400 hour master spectrum, or to 4000 hours of service life. One mini spectrum would be equal to 4000/67 = 60 hours of service life.

I got together with the testing group and we designed a fixture to apply the mini spectra to the bearing.

I had been going to Washington periodically and keeping the Navy informed about what I was doing. Now I wrote a formal Test Plan that outlined this demonstration scheme, and submitted it to the Navy for approval. I received a letter of approval in a short time.

We built a test fixture, and the first thing I did was test the F8F-1 bearing. It failed at about 25 hours of flight time. This was remarkable, my test plan and and test fixture were thus vindicated. It was worthwhile writing another report to the Navy for information.

I now became a bearing designer. I studied bearing design manuals and redesigned the bearing using all the tricks in the books. I was able to achieve some improvement, my redesigned bearings survived 40, 60, 70 flight hours, but it was very frustrating when you are trying to reach 4000 hours. I put the books away and started looking for suitable materials that were not recommended for bearings. I finally found a very hard stainless steel. This bearing finally survived 400 hours in the test fixture. It was installed on the production aircraft, and no reports of failure of this stainless steel bearing were ever received over the service life of the F8F-1 aircraft.

This job had required skills greater that those of a stress analyst, it required innovative thinking. Consider that the Navy reported that the bearing was failing in 25 hours of service. Then I independently demonstrated a bearing life of about 25 hours in my test fixture. This was an awesome demonstration of the power of mathematical thinking.

Cappy was not in a position to provide technical guidance, he was busy with his design group. His concern was to satisfy the Navy. He knew that I was keeping the Navy informed about what I was doing. As long as he did not get any negative signals from the Navy, he was content to let me operate on my own.

F8F-1   BREAK OFF WING TIP

Grumman built the F8F-1 in high hopes that it would become the Navy's standard carrier based aircraft like the F4F and the F6F. It did turn out to be a fine airplane with excellent flying qualities, easy maintenance, and all that. However, at that time, extraordinary advances were being made in electronics, and the Navy's operating range was increasing rapidly. The Navy was thinking in greatly increased ranges, and the F8F-1 range was suddenly inadequate.

Every airplane has a limit on the maneuver load that a pilot may exert, but there is no way of policing the pilot. In some flight conditions, he may exceed the limit. Manufacturers, therefore, must provide a generous margin of safety between the pilot's limit and the failing (ultimate) strength of the aircraft.

In the discussion of the F8F-1 problem, someone suggested that if a device could be developed to guarantee that the pilot could not exceed his limit, the margin could be reduced, that is, the limit could be moved up, closer to the ultimate. This would provide the F8F-1 with the capability for an increased range, like for instance, with the addition of external dropable fuel tanks.

The discussion then considered how this could be accomplished. After due consideration, it was agreed that the best way to accomplish this goal would be to design a break point in the wing, some three feet inboard from the tip. The tip would then break off when the pilot exceeded his limit sending an unmistakable signal to the pilot that he had exceeded his limit and that he should abort his mission and immediately return to base.

I was assigned the task of designing a device to release the wing tips on the F8F-1, whenever the pilot exceeded his maneuver limit.

The wing that close to the tip was quite thin, about three and one half inches thick. The loads were also quite high. I studied all the available kinds of break mechanisms, and none would fit in that space.

I also discovered another requirement. In a rolling pull out, the load on one wing is higher than on the other, but both wing tips had to be released simultaneously. There was no way I could do this mechanically, it had to be done with an electrical signal.

. After much soul searching, I finally came up with a bright idea. I might be able to blow off the wing tips cleanly if I attached a strip of explosives chordwise to the bottom skin, and detonated the explosives by a strain gauge attached to the upper longeron. These strain gauges would measure the load on the wing. I also could design an electric circuit that would simultaneously blow off the wingtip on the opposite side.

There was nobody at Grumman that knew anything about explosives and could help me. I made arrangements to visit Dupont in Wilmington to get more information.

The engineers at Dupont were most cooperative. They studied my drawings and said the concept was perfectly feasible. For the explosive charge, they recommended that I use a 20 inch length of "Primacord." Primacord is a fuse that burns almost instantaneously. It was developed to set off simultaneous charges that were located some distance apart, like when you want to move part of a mountain and set the charges maybe one half mile apart.

Primacord is a plastic tube filled with a fast burning compound. When it is set off, it exerts a moderate lateral force along its length. The US Army used it in World War II in Europe. The old roads there often have trees along the sides, impeding the passage of big Army vehicles. The soldiers would walk along the road and wrap a couple of rounds of Primacord around each tree. They tell me it was a sight to see, when they set off the Primacord, all the trees along the road for a mile or two would all fall over together. The Dupont engineers were sure that if you can fell a tree with Primacord, it has enough, but not excessive, power to blow off the F8F-1 wing tip as shown on my drawing.

I ordered some Primacord, and it was delivered by boat to Freeport, Long Island. It was against the law to transport it across state lines. I then had to find a secure storage place at Grumman.

I cut off a few 20 inch lengths of Primacord and fired them after working hours in various locations of the test hangar. I expected the windows to rattle and stationed observers throughout the hanger to detect any undesirable effects. You could hear the noise, but there was no measurable change in air pressure 20 feet away from the explosion. It was no worse than a large Fourth of July fire cracker.

I built a test section of the wing, with a break joint three feet inboard from the tip, and installed a 20 inch length of Primacord some two inches outboard of the break joint, on the outside of the skin. I fired the Primacord, and the tip blew off clean, no ragged edges or deformed ribs.

I designed an installation which provided for both wing tips to blow off when either one was broken off, and for the system to be disarmed when the landing gear was extended. The system was active only after the pilot pulled up his landing gear in flight.

I had the parts all made and was ready for installation in an airplane, when I hit a solid wall of resistance. Erlandson, Chief of Structures, objected to the use of explosives built into an aircraft structure. He would not give on the principle that aircraft structures and explosives did not mix.

I had worked for Erlandson for many years. He was a man of high intelligence, honesty and integrity. But explosives were a subject outside his frame of reference. I ran into this condition several times later in my career, and I will relate further below cases when the facts lie outside of a person's experience, and that person will be incapable of recognizing the truth. I'll call this condition the "Erlandson phenomenon."

One day, Erlandson had to go out of town on business. At the beginning of the day, Bob Hall, the Chief Engineer, called a meeting of all the people involved, other engineers, shop, flight test, the test pilot, etc. He asked me to explain what I had done, what was the status of the project, and what I wanted to demonstrate with the proposed test flight. I did so. I explained that explosives required special handling, but so did many other items on our airplanes. Hall, a former test pilot, asked a lot of questions and determined that nobody was concerned about my use of explosives, that all the parts were available and the shop was ready to make the installation in time for a test flight before dark, that an airplane was available, and that the test pilot was willing to make the test flight that afternoon, before Erlandson got back. Hall said GO!

I never saw the people in the shop move so fast. You could just feel that everybody wanted the test to go on and be a success. The airplane was ready in plenty of time before dark, and the pilot took off.

The pilot landed half an hour later and reported that in a rolling pull out, both wingtips had blown off simultaneously. An Engineering Order was issued, calling for the installation of the system on all production airplanes.

I wrote the installation instructions and had them checked out carefully. Kits of the parts and the installation instructions were made up and issued for the many aircraft already in service. The Navy decided to classify the instructions "CONFIDENTIAL." When the package was delivered to a field unit, the installation instructions were separated and locked up in a safe, and the parts delivered to the shop without instructions. The shop was told to do the best they could when installing the device. The mechanics had no idea of what to do with the kit, they had never seen anything like it before. They did not know how to handle explosives. They installed the parts where they thought they would best fit.

Many wing tips were blown off while the airplane was still on the ground. One wing tip would come off, but not the other. Others would be blown off just after the pilot took off and retracted his landing gear. Many men were hurt, two were killed. It was a disaster!

Grumman was appalled. There was no appeal to Navy Security. Grumman had no choice but to withdraw the field installation and the production order. The great dream of making the F8F-1 the Navy's new standard carrier based aircraft was dead.

Although the project was not successful, the experience taught me that I was capable of operating on my own, that I was no longer dependent on my Berlin and NYU note books. I had come up with something new, something that had worked when the instructions were available and followed. I could solve engineering problems that went beyond what I had learned in school.

THE JAY CEE (JC) MANEUVER

Supersonic air is different from subsonic air. We ran into a number of surprises when we started supersonic flight. One of the first ones was the JC maneuver. A test pilot was flying along minding his own business in the low supersonic range, when the control stick suddenly with great force started to whip back and forth through its entire range, practically knocking out the pilot's teeth and causing him to yell out as loud as he could, "Jeezzes Christ!" This flight condition was aptly dubbed the "JC maneuver," and I was told to fix it.

Vibration analysts consider a system consisting of three elements: a mass, a spring, and a damper. The flexible aircraft structure is considered a spring. The mass and spring can only be changed by adding weight, which is against the rules in aircraft design. This left me no choice but to do something about damping.

A damper is the opposite of an engine. An engine puts out useful energy. A damper destroys energy. Most commercial dampers, like the shock struts on your car, consist of an oil filled cylinder enclosing a piston with a hole in it. As the piston moves in the cylinder, the oil flows through the hole in the piston, from one side to the other. Forcing the oil through the hole consumes energy and heats up the oil. This heat is dissipated in the environment and is energy lost.

A review of all available dampers disclosed that they all use an oil which was unsuitable for use in a flight control system at the operating temperatures of an aircraft. A non-oil using damper was required.

This was something new. I researched the literature, without success, until I found an illustration in a physics book, showing that the movement of a copper plate in a magnetic field generated a load which impeded the movement. Here was something independent of temperature, it looked like a concept that I could use.

I constructed a device consisting of a 12 inch copper disc rotating in a frame which held permanent magnets all along both sides of the edge of the disc. It was a perfect damper. When you turned the crank that drove the disc to rotate slowly, there was no resistance on the crank. If you turned the crank fast, there was strong resistance.

I had no design data. I changed the number of magnets on my device systematically and measured the force on the crank for various disc speeds. This gave me a nice performance design formula.

The test aircraft had been completely instrumented, so the aerodynamics section was able to analyze the JC maneuver and provide me with a reading on the amount of damping required to suppress the maneuver. I designed a small 6-disc device to comply with this requirement, the discs rotating in rings of permanent magnets at their rims.

Grumman was big on flight simulators. A flight simulator is a fully equipped and operational cockpit that, instead of being in an airplane, is mounted on a ground based fixture that moves it in response to control system commands, through three dimensions as if it were in an airflow, just as if the cockpit were in a real airplane. The aerodynamics section had a three dimensional flight simulator for each airplane we built. They had duplicated the JC maneuver on the flight simulator. I installed my damper in the flight control system loop in the flight simulator, at the foot of the control stick. The aerodynamics section could no longer reproduce the JC maneuver in the simulator.

We next did the same thing on a real airplane, with the same results. The pilot could no longer get the airplane to vibrate in the JC maneuver. Grumman never had trouble with the JC maneuver on any of its supersonic airplanes.

My next problem was to find a manufacturer for the unit. Purchasing sent the design out to a large number of instrument companies. They all came back with ridiculous prices of $17000 to $20000 per unit. To minimize slop in the gears, I had used close tolerance gears. I now presumed that the instrument companies were fearful of a design calling for a train of close tolerance gears. I asked purchasing to find a precision gear manufacturer. They found a nice small company in New Jersey that bid $650 per unit. They redesigned my unit and made a number of improvements. It worked fine in the airplane. They found additional commercial uses for the damper and advertised it widely in the technical press. I had fun for many years looking through technical magazines and finding my little damper still being advertised.

BUZZ

"Buzz" is another deadly vibration encountered when entering the supersonic flight range.

A prominent aircraft company in California developed two aircraft it was ready to turn over to the Navy. It scheduled a flight demonstration and invited all the top Navy brass to attend.

The first few minutes of the air show were spectacular, with all the admirals and captains watching carefully. Then the pilot, who wanted to demonstrate his airplane to the best advantage, started a run of maximum speed in front of the dignitaries. He was just about in front of them when the aircraft disintegrated in flight.

The pilot had no reason to anticipate this danger in a maximum speed flight. This run was a normal conclusion to a flight demonstration.

The next day, the demonstration of the company's second airplane was held over water, with the dignitaries on shore watching the maneuvers. After his air show, this pilot went into a maximum speed run over the water, and when he got approximately abreast of the spectators, this airplane also disintegrated. The news of these tragic events spread quickly throughout the aircraft industry.

The Grumman aerodynamics section was able to reproduce this flight condition on its simulators. The condition was a high frequency, violent, low amplitude oscillation of the tail section that drained the strength out of the structure. It was labeled "buzz." I was assigned the task of designing a device that would suppress buzz.

Again I had three elements to work with, mass, springs (structure), and damping. Changes in mass and structure were out of the question, especially in the most weight sensitive area of the the tail. I had to consider damping.

A basic problem was where to apply the damping. In an intensive and long discussion between the aerodynamics, structures, and vibrations sections, every likely element of the tail section was examined. It was decided that the rudder hinge was the most flexible element where buzz was most likely to start. I decided that in this case, which involved a small device, I had to use an oil operated damper. Space limitations prohibited the use of any other device I could think of. The increase in undesirable control stick break out forces were small and existed only at cold operating temperatures. After due deliberation, the aerodynamics section finally agreed to let me proceed.

The company's best hydraulic design engineer was assigned to me. We developed a little rotary damper to fit into the rudder hinge.

Aircraft structures are built as stiff and rigid as we know how to build them. When I use the word "flexibility" here, I am referring to extraordinary small values. To establish a zero point on a test fixture so we could measure flexibility of this small size, was a real challenge. I had the assistance of one of the world's best test engineers, a fellow named Shepherd. He came up with the design of a test fixture using a length of the heaviest 24-inch high I-beam of structural steel as a base. The curve of damper performance that he produced was completely believable.

We installed the damper on the flight simulator and it worked fine, buzz was completely suppressed. We installed it on an airplane, and it successfully suppressed buzz in flight.

We had one problem we could not lick. Our little damper leaked oil while suppressing buzz, both in the simulator and in the airplane. Almost the whole hydraulics section worked for months, trying every trick in the books, but we could not stop the leakage. We were really at our wits end.

At that time, a salesman called on me and said he had a new device he wanted to show me. He explained in great detail how North American had spent over $ 500000 to design a test stand to support the development of a little damper that they put in the tail of their airplanes. He showed me the damper and its performance curve. They looked just like ours. But there was no evidence of leakage. The salesman never used the word "buzz," and he was vague on what the damper was supposed to do. He did not intend to make a sale, he was just killing time showing off his little gadget.

I asked him if I could borrow his damper for a few minutes and he agreed. I called Shep, gave him the damper, asked him to verify the performance curve and the leakage. He came back 20 minutes later, gave me back the damper, said the performance curve was exactly the same as the one for our damper, but there was no leakage.

I handed the damper and its papers back to the salesman and told him, we would take 600 units. He was speechless.

Grumman was one American supersonic airplane company that had no flight trouble with buzz.

The XF9F-2 (Panther) was the first airplane to benefit from this research. It was Grumman's first jet, equipped with the British Rolls Royce Nene jet engine, and the first aircraft in the world to fly at supersonic speed in level flight. This accomplishment was recorded in the *New York Times* in a small 1/2 inch high column on the lower half of a back page. Some three months later, the same newspaper reported, in large print and with a large photo of the airplane, on the top of the front page, that a British airplane had just completed the worlds's first level flight at supersonic speed. Since then, I have lost confidence in the ability of the *New York Times* to report reliable news.

THE BIRTH OF THE POST-WAR GERMAN AIR FORCE

In the late 1950's, the Allied Powers decided that it was time for Germany to have its own air force. The President of the United States appointed the US Air Force to advise the Germans and assist them in finding a suitable US airplane.

The Air Force decided that the most important function of an air force was developing new airplanes, that flying was the easy part. The development of a new aircraft is a unique, high-tech, long and difficult task that requires special skills. This is what the US Air Force believed that the Germans had to learn first, and they selected the Lockheed F-105, which was still in development, to turn over to the Germans.

The US Navy disagreed. They felt that you had to learn to fly first, and learn about the performance and maintenance of aircraft, before you started to think about developing a new airplane. They selected the Grumman F8F as the ideal aircraft for the Germans. Its range was perfectly adequate for the European Theater. As a carrier based aircraft, its short take-off and landing distances made it suitable to be used at small airports all over the country. Its performance and maintenance requirements were well established by several years of service in the US Navy.

Since the Air Force was acting under a Presidential directive, the Navy had no way of making its views known. Arrangements were made with Grumman to invite the Germans for a plant visit and expose them to the F8F.

The German mission consisted of a General, Commander of the German Air Force, ten of his officers, and five civilian experts. They were received by Schwendler, with me as interpreter at his side. I heard and understood everything the Germans were saying to one another, even when then talked in code. My time with the "Spline" in Berlin, with its military connections, stood me in good stead.

Grumman threw its doors open, to all the shops and labs, and gave them a fine flight demonstration. I gave lectures in German on the performance and maintenance requirements of the F8F.

I received personal calls from several admirals encouraging me to make every effort to assure that the Germans would select the F8F.

The Germans were perplexed. Grumman was a Navy facility. To

their knowledge, navies operated ships, and air forces flew airplanes. What was a navy doing here with aircraft? They simply could not believe what they saw. (Shades of the Erlandson phenomenon!)

At dinner, on their last day at Grumman, we all sat at one long table, the Germans on one side, the Grumman people on the other. The German General sat in the center of the table, Schwendler was sitting opposite him, and I was next to Schwendler.

After dinner, the General asked Schwendler: "Do you really have the resources to meet our requirements?" Schwendler smiled and said: "I think so." Bedlam erupted on the German side of the table. Every man on the German side exclaimed loudly: "He only thinks so, he is not sure!" I tried to explain that the word "think" has a slightly different meaning in English than it has in German. In English, it is definitely positive, in German, it leaves some room for doubt. The Germans told me that they had been speaking English for years and that they understood perfectly well what Schwendler had said. The Germans decided to follow the advice of the US Air Force and build their new air force around the Lockheed airplane.

I wonder what the German reaction would have been, if I had told them that the US Navy not only operates a navy, an air force, but also an elite army, the US Marines.

RETURN TO BERLIN

One of the civilian experts in the German Air Force Mission was Dr. Edgar Roessger, Director of the Institute of Aeronautics at the Technical University of Berlin, who I have mentioned on page 139. I invited him home for dinner and he met Eleanor and my two sons. I explained to him why I had to leave Berlin suddenly in 1938 and have always regretted that I did not have a Berlin degree. He invited me to go back and get a Doktor-Ingenieur degree. He said they would give me credit for my Master's Degree, Professional Engineering License, and professional experience. I told him that I had four weeks of annual leave and could spend a month a year in Berlin. He assured me that he could work out a schedule for me on this basis.

My application for readmission was based in part on a certified list of all the courses and exercises that I had completed in Berlin. But all the files in Berlin that were needed to verify my list had been destroyed in the war. However, they continued to search surviving filing cabinets, until they found a test paper which I had written and that agreed with my list. On this basis, I was readmitted to the University.

It took me five years, spending a month a year in Berlin, to earn a Doktor-Ingenieur degree.

I needed a few credits. I studied at home, then went to Berlin for the last few sessions of the class and the examination. In a few cases, this was not sufficient for credit, and the professor would invite me into his office, where he would question me for an hour or so. In all cases, I was granted the credits I needed.

The main job was the thesis. By this time I was working on the Lunar Module and selected a problem I had solved for Cape Kennedy, namely, how much testing of a new space craft is needed, until it is ready for launch. The format of the thesis was prescribed by the University.

At that time, Roessger was friends with Stark Draper, Professor of Aeronautics at MIT and the two universities were working on a number of common projects. People from Berlin were coming over to MIT with some regularity. They had to change planes at JFK to get to Boston. They would notify me that they were coming, and I would meet them at the airport for an hour or two, while they reviewed whatever progress I had made on my thesis. This scheme worked out fine.

The final exam was set for Tuesday, June 30, 1970, Room 1036. I was scheduled for two exams, thesis and comprehensive. The exam was conducted by two professors, Roessger and Professor Koelle who had been von Braun's chief engineer at Huntsville, but had returned to Germany. They started off by telling me that they had read my thesis and recommended four changes. The changes were all improvements in language or clarity and I accepted them without hesitation.

They said we could put the thesis aside and proceed with the comprehensive. They gave me a problem, which I analyzed and figured out how to get a solution. As soon as they saw that I was getting to a solution, they gave me a new problem. They kept this up for two and a half hours and just about covered the entire scope of aeronautical engineering. We were all having fun.

At the end, they asked me to leave the room for a few minutes. I went out into the hall where Eleanor and Dr. Peters, my thesis advisor, waited. These two had been waiting for me for almost three hours and they were getting rather apprehensive. A normal examination lasts only about three quarters of an hour, they could not imagine what was going on behind that closed door.They greeted me as if I had been long lost.

After a few minutes, I was called back into the examining room and told that I was receiving an "A" (sehr gut) for my thesis, and also an "A" on my comprehensive exam. Eleanor, Peters and I had a festive lunch in one of Berlin's better restaurants.

A REVOLUTION IN DESIGN CONTROL

POWER OPERATED FLIGHT CONTROL SYSTEMS

In the development of new military aircraft in the early 1950's, the greater weight, the higher speed, and the greater required flight-path accuracy became more than a pilot could handle with his own strength and senses operating a manual flight-control system. To solve this problem, the flight-control design group developed a power-operated flight-control system. With time, they would develop automated target acquisition, flight path, and weapons delivery, with the pilot serving as the monitor. One look at the complexity of these devices and the whole thing became anathema to Grumman management, which included pilots who were extremely safety conscious. Various sophisticated, costly aerodynamic devices were tried, but nothing worked.

Grumman management decided that they needed a second opinion. They wanted an investigation on whether a power-operated flight-control system was really necessary, conducted by somebody who was unbiased, that is, somebody who knew nothing about the subject. I was selected to conduct this investigation. The only qualification that I had for conducting the proposed investigation was that management knew me and had faith in my opinions.

In my discussions with the flight control design group, I quickly concluded that power-operated flight-control systems were necessary. However, there was a serious problem that needed attention.

Aircraft structural systems, with which I was acquainted, have two measurable design parameters, strength and weight, which are easy to measure. Strength can be used as a parameter of safety. But a power-operated flight-control system consists of many subsystems, each with its own traditions and design parameters. These subsystems include the artificial feel system; mechanical parts such as push rods, cables, gears, springs, and their mountings; instruments and their wiring; hydraulic parts such as pumps, actuators, dampers, reservoirs and lines; electrical parts such as motors, actuators, sensors, and wiring; pneumatic devices such as air speed indicators and other flight instruments; and a myriad of other parts. These subsystems had no safety parameters in common. It was overwhelming,

The designers of any one of these subsystems had their own traditions and criteria for safety, and no two designers had the same concept of system safety requirements. There was no central design control. I found this condition to be unacceptable.

I reported to Grumman management that I found that power operated flight control systems were necessary, but that we had to develop a measure of safety, similar to the structural margin of safety, that would indicate to what degree power-operated flight-control systems were safe.

Grumman management accepted my report, and told me to develop a measure of safety for power-operated flight-control systems.

RELIABILITY RESEARCH

I now had to find a safety parameter that applied to all components of a power operated flight control system. I did a lot of reading. I finally discovered a report by Robert Lusser of the US Naval Missile Test Center. Lusser had been Chief of Reliability at the German Peenemunde Rocket Facility and was captured by US Troops at the end of World War II and brought to the US. The Germans had had trouble with the V-1 when they were bombing London. Lusser took a statistical approach and used the "probability of success" or "reliability" as his parameter of interest. He found that the reliability of a system equaled the *product* of the reliabilities of the system components *(product rule.)* This was a new design rule that changed our approach to system design.

In further research, I found a report by Carhart of the Rand Corporation on the reliability of electronic piece parts. Carhart assumed that the distribution of failures of a component over its useful life was exponential. This gave him equations for reliability as a function of failure rate and of time, and for mean time between failures (MTBF).

The introduction of large electronic assemblies consisting of small piece parts posed a new challenge: nobody knew how to test them. E.J.Nucci, reliability engineer in the Office of the Assistant Secretary of Defense, realized that Carhart's proposal provided a method of measuring the reliability of electronic equipment. He organized the Advisory Group on the Reliability of Electronic Equipment (AGREE), consisting of a number of outstanding electrical/electronic engineers, to write a test plan for electronic equipment, using Carhart's formulas. They did a superb job of classifying operational environments for electronic equipment, and proposed test plans for each environment. Their report was published by the Assistant Secretary of Defense in 1957 and is known as the "AGREE Report."

Nucci aggressively flooded the military engineering community with the AGREE Report. In response to the full page seal of the Assistant Secretary of Defense on the cover, the report was taken quite seriously. Even reliability requirements for non-electronic equipment were discussed and specified in terms of the AGREE Report, that is, the use of *time* to measure reliability.

This use of time to measure the reliability of components under an operational spectrum was a remarkable innovation. The AGREE Report provides for representative samples of mass-produced small electronic parts, to be tested on a continuous basis under a spectrum of applicable operational environmental conditions. When a part fails, it is replaced with a new part, so that the number of parts on test is constant. The length of time that a component survives the loading spectrum is a measure of its reliability.

I joined the American Society of Quality Control (ASQC) because it was the community most interested in reliability technology. I met there almost everybody in the country who was interested in reliability and was able to test my ideas and make sure I was on the right track. I determined that Lusser's product rule and Carhart's reliability analysis enjoyed universal acceptance in the United States.

The application of the above procedures to an ongoing design would be similar to the work done by a stress analyst on structures. It involves a Navy specified and funded work package, with technical reports submitted on schedule for Navy approval. I had to find a way to get the Navy educated so that they would specify a reliability work package in their contracts and train their people to read and accept technical reliability reports as submitted.

I was confident that Grumman would accept whatever I recommended. My basic problem was to get the Navy to specify a reliability program. Grumman would accept any reasonable program that the Navy would specify and fund.

EXTENT OF A RELIABILITY PROGRAM

We counted the number of parts in a 1950 airplane, there were about 30000 parts. Then we counted the number of parts that had a failure history in our failure rate data bank, and noted about 300 parts. We concluded that 29700 parts on the airplane never failed in service, since we had no reports in our failure rate data bank. These were linear parts designed in accordance with a mathematical model. Our reliability program had to be concerned with the 300 non-linear parts for which a mathematical model did not exist.

The linear parts were assigned a reliability of $R = 1.0$ and thereby eliminated from further statistical analysis. This assignment was contrary to general statistical practice. The value of 1.0 is approached asymptotically, that is, you never actually reach it. I rather felt that linear parts belonged to a different population, developed in accordance with deterministic models that do not approach a target value, they are already there. By this reasoning, I removed the 29700 linear parts from statistical consideration.

All of my initial work in establishing the Grumman reliability program was done without the assistance of a statistician. At this time I was besieged by aggressive statistical reliability consultants who offered to help Grumman set up its reliability program. They told me that it was a task that I was not qualified for and could not do myself They gave me the impression, that Grumman was the only company that did not employ consultants for this purpose. I felt that every statistician in the country was trying to get a contract with an aircraft company as a consultant to establish a reliability program. I politely showed them to the door.

Not having had statistical assistance in establishing its reliability program may be the reason that Grumman appears to be the only company that effectively used the useful concept of $R = 1.0$.

I attended the meetings of the American Society for Quality Control (ASQC) regularly. During a recess at an annual meeting of the Society, I went to the bar for a drink and started to talk to the man next to me, a well dressed, dignified gentleman. It turned out that he was a professor of statistics at a British university.

I took my keys out of my pocket and held them over the bar. I asked him to watch me carefully and dropped the keys. I picked them up, held them over the bar again, and asked him, "What will happen to my keys if I drop them, just as I did a moment ago?"

He replied, "They will fall."

I asked, "What is the probability that they will fall?"

"Very high?"

I said, "Come on now, you are a professional statistician, give me a number."

"It is very high, but I can't give you a number."

I asked. "Is it $R = 1.0$?"

He gasped and said, "Oh no! It can't be 1.0, there is no such thing!" After three drinks, we agreed, that I was formulating the problem so that it could not be expressed in statistical terms. We parted friends.

In BIMRAB, that I will discuss below, I had the opportunity to review the reliability reports of other companies. They would have documents about three inches thick with equations that went on for page after page, including all the parts in a system. Most parts were listed with very high reliabilities, very close to one. I felt that these reports were a waste of labor, compared to my reports, which were quite thin.

I found that there were some non-aircraft companies that had excellent failure rate data bases. One was Consolidated Edison

Company of New York, with its one million man-holes in Manhattan and lead shielded underground cables which rats loved to gnaw through and create short circuits. Another one was Caterpillar with its tractors all over the world, subject to ingenious applications for which they were not designed. The Caterpillar system was manual, but they had a tough Vice President in charge of failure reporting who made sure everybody took it seriously. Bell Labs had just laid a new transatlantic telephone cable with amplifiers every fifteen miles. All components in the amplifiers had an operating history of at least twenty years without failure. Bell Labs did not have a "reliability" activity, this was all considered regular engineering work.

I did not find any statisticians involved in non-aircraft reliability work, but I only contacted a few large companies, just enough to convince myself that I did not have to be a statistician to organize a reliability program

NAVY PROBLEMS

In 1956, the US Naval Aviation Safety Center (NASC) in Norfolk, Virginia, was allotted a new, modern mainframe computer, into which it entered all its flight accident data. The possible new outputs were truly wondrous. Correlations of accident related issues could now be made, something that had never been done before.

In its enthusiasm, the Safety Center called a meeting in Norfolk inviting the entire aircraft industry, the Air Force, the Army, and the Civil Aeronautics Authority (CAA), to come and admire its new "toy".

The Safety Center's presentation showed different types of accidents caused by defects in various types of equipment. Contractors were asked to study this information and use it to design safer airplanes. The problem was urgent, the cost of accidents was rising rapidly, and the Navy did not have the funds to replace the aircraft it was losing in accidents.

I had been invited to this conference as representative of the Grumman Company and because I had done business with the Safety Center before. I stood up and stated that aircraft are designed to comply with the specifications called out in a contract. Naval procurement procedures did not allow for deviation from the specifications. I said that if the Navy was generating new safety insights and information, that that data had to be processed and incorporated into Navy specifications before contractors could respond. I suggested that a joint Navy-industry committee be formed and charged with the performance of these tasks.

Rear Admiral Allen Smith, Director of the Safety Center, agreed with my comments and asked me to organize such a committee.

ORGANIZING A NAVY-INDUSTRY
ADVISORY BOARD

I went to BuWeps to see my friends (see page 230). After I told them what had happened in Norfolk, Captain Keen took me in to see Rear Admiral Coates, Assistant Chief for Research, Development, Test and Evaluation (RDT&E), Bureau of Naval Weapons (Bu-Weps). I repeated what went on in Norfolk, and that Admiral Smith had asked me to organize a committee. I asked him to be chairman. He asked me what I expected him to do. I told him, identify the best brains among the executives in the Navy-associated aircraft industry, put these men on the committee and preside at their meetings. Admiral Coates agreed to do that. I told him that I would make up a chart of the proposed committee organization, and he could fill in the names. I also organized a group of division heads in Bu-Weps that I could call on for advice and guidance.

With the guidance of this advisory group, I drew up an organization chart. I had served on the By-Laws Committee of the Metropolitan Section of the American Society of Mechanical Engineers (ASME), and as a founding member of the Long Island Section of ASME, I had written the by-laws for the new Section. I took these by-laws and modified them for the Navy environment. I laid out a Board of 12 top industry executives and Bu-Weps division heads, to meet twice a year and establish policy. I established an Executive Committee of six men, with Bu-Weps employees as chairman and secretary, to meet as often as necessary. I tentatively set up four committees, on electronics, flight controls, power plants, and maintenance. The committees included both industry and Navy personnel, with a Navy employee as chairman. Their job was to analyze accident and failure data and develop specification requirements for equipments to make them less accident and failure prone, and to establish reliability requirements for their specialized equipment.

Such specification changes were something that affected the entire industry, so I could not leave the matter in the hands of a few industry representatives. I provided for an annual conference where the committees would report what they were doing to industry and other Naval, Army, and Air Force organizations. This would provide industrial organizations, that had no representation on the committees, an opportunity to make an input or express objections. The conference also gave us an opportunity to find new members for our committees. Conference proceedings were to be published and provided to each attendee at or after the conference. I suggested that the committee be called the Bu-Weps/Industry Material Reliability Advisory Board (BIMRAB).

NAVY ACTION

When I was finished, I prepared a package that my advisors in Bu-Weps approved and submitted it to Admiral Coates. He went along with everything I proposed and sent the package to the Navy Legal Affairs Office. Several days later, the package came back approved.

Admiral Coates had also been working. He assigned a Bu-Weps employee, Frank Snyder, to be BIMRAB Secretary. He had a list of men he wanted to appoint to the Board, the Executive Committee, and to the chairmanships of the four committees. He called a meeting of the Board that approved the proposed BIMRAB structure and the plans for the annual conference.

Snyder did the leg work. Reporting to the Executive Committee, he found a hotel, sent out invitations, organized the registration, published all the papers in a bound volume available at the conference, and arranged for security by the Marine Corps. He kept all BIMRAB records. Most of the papers were provided by the committees, reporting on their work. The rest came from the Executive Committee.

The conference accomplished everything expected. There were three admirals present. Industry was well represented, as were the Army, Air Force, CAA, and NASA. The committees were doing some excellent original work that added to the excitement. Many people wanted to join the committees. We had no lack of manpower.

ADMIRAL POWER

Changes in specifications and inclusion of reliability requirements in contracts was something that was strongly resisted by the rank and file of the conservative Bu-Weps bureaucracy. Reliability was considered "just another passing fad."

With the years, from 1959 to 1973, the BIMRAB conference presentations became more sophisticated, analyzing the Navy's operational problems and suggesting solutions. It attracted more and more admirals every year. The conference program was designed to make admirals want to come back next year, and bring their friends.

The first year there were three admirals. By the time of the sixth conference, there were thirty two. This was a good fraction of the total admiral corps in the entire Navy! There are few events where you can see thirty two admirals together.

The admirals were getting a good basic education in reliability engineering and Navy schools were starting to teach courses in the subject to incoming Bu-Weps supervisory officers. This finally started to have an effect on the thousands of civilian employees in the Naval procurement system who objected to the incorporation of reliability requirements in specifications. They started to realize that the next Commander, Bu-Weps, would be no different than the present one, and that it was time for them to change. The conference was well attended by representatives of the Army, Air Force, and CAA, and had a similar effect on these services.

I spoke with many Air Force officers at these conferences, most of them lieutenant colonels, a few colonels. They were all well informed on reliability techniques and enthused about their work. Such a group indicated that the Air Force generals thought much like the Navy admirals. The Army representatives had different problems. They were more statistical oriented and worried about problems like the reliability of their huge quantities of ammunition stored for long lengths of time, and the fatigue life of large, heavy gun tubes that wore out in battle and were difficult to replace under combat conditions.

THE   COMMITTEES

The committees were the creative heart of BIMRAB. Within their scope of expertise, they analyzed the Navy's reliability problems and developed original solutions that were effective. The chairmen of the committees were Bu-Weps officers who had the authority to put committee recommendations into effect. The committees made contributions over a wide range of equipments that were presented and discussed at the annual conferences before they were put into effect.

INDUSTRY RESPONSE.

With the publication of comprehensive reliability design requirements by Bu-Weps and the other services, there arose a problem in the industry, how to respond? What had to be done to satisfy the requirements? I have explained the techniques proposed by Lusser, Carhart, and Nucci, but these techniques were known only to a small group. The news of technical innovations, developments and practices is normally spread in professional circles by publication in technical journals and conferences sponsored by scientific or engineering societies.

In response to the AGREE Report, the Institute of Electrical and Electronic Engineers (IEEE), the American Society for Quality Control (ASQC) and others sponsored the *Symposium on Reliability and Quality Control of Electronic Equipment.* The IEEE was primarily interested in developing testing procedures of small electronic piece parts to comply with the AGREE Report. The ASQC was concerned with developing statistical sampling procedures for the acceptance of mass produced parts.

I felt that the *Symposium* was not addressing the challenge posed by the new reliability specifications developed by BIMRAB as discussed above. As a member of the Aviation Division of the ASME, I was encouraged by the Chairman, Dr Bob Dillaway, to organize a multi-Society design oriented reliability conference. I invited the American Institute of Aeronautics and Astronautics (AIAA) and the Society of Automotive Engineers (SAE) to join me. They accepted my invitation.

I wanted to break "reliability" away from "quality control" and associate it with "design engineering." Quality control personnel and design engineers perform different functions and have little in common. Since "maintainability" was recognized as a design engineering discipline, I decided to call my conference *The Annual Reliability and Maintainability (R&M) Conference, cosponsored by ASME, AIAA, and SAE.* A volume of the papers presented was distributed to all attendees and deposited in all major technical libraries.

The combination of "R&M" was generally accepted. I was concerned that Grumman suppliers had every opportunity to learn how to comply with the new reliability requirements. I organized and was Chairman of the 1963, 64, and 65 Conferences. This enabled me to build up a strong team that carried on the conference after I gave up the chairmanship.

Attendance at our first Conference was a little over 200, and increased with each year. In the tenth year, the attendance reached 1000. During those ten years, the *IEEE/ASQC Reliability and Quality Control Symposium* moved more and more toward design, so that after ten years there was not that much difference between the two conferences, and they decided to merge into the *Reliability and Maintainability Symposium (RAMS),* which is still being held today. I served for many years as the ASME representative on the RAMS Board of Directors.

Through these conferences, the principles of reliability engineering were made available to all working engineers who had a need to know. Practically all aeronautic engineering schools started courses in reliability engineering, some even developed doctoral programs.

The local sections of the ASQC also provided strong programs in reliability engineering. I spoke at many such sections all over the country and participated actively in the programs on Long Island, where there were many aerospace suppliers. There was a monthly meeting dedicated to reliability. Starting in 1962 the Section held an all day *"Annual Quality Control-Reliability Conference and Technical Exhibit"* on a Saturday; originally at Hofstra University in Hempstead, Long Island. They chose a Saturday because they did not want any attendees who were not willing to give up a day of their own time to learn something useful. Initially, attendance ran between 100 and 200. The Section published a Transactions including most of the papers presented. These conferences were a remarkable professional activity, where pioneering engineers were teaching their fellow engineers, everybody trying to help out others. Other ASQC sections throughout the country had similar programs.

Through these activities of engineering societies, design engineers in industry learned the techniques required to comply with the new military reliability design requirements.

DISSOLUTION OF BIMRAB

After 14 years of spectacular BIMRAB operation, the Board observed that reliability engineering had become standard operating procedure in the Armed Forces and in industry, and was a required subject in aeronautic engineering schools. It appeared that nothing more could be achieved by BIMRAB, and the Board dissolved itself. Snyder deposited all the records in the Navy's archives.

BIMRAB wrote the specifications that established reliability engineering as contractual requirements on all aircraft operating systems. The concept that reliability was "just a passing fad" was no longer tenable.

BIMRAB had been like a fireworks show. It was a burst of energy at a critical time in the development of electronics, jet engines, power operated flight control systems, and space flight. Dazzling progress had been made in a short time, that changed the design engineering culture in the Armed Forces and in industry. When the job was done, BIMRAB fizzled out gracefully.

I have written a paper entitled "Navy Buys Computer, Discovers Reliability" which describes the extraordinary achievements of BIMRAB in greater detail. The paper is published in the Air Force journal *Air Power History,* December, 2000. As a result of BIMRAB, all Grumman contracts now include reliability requirements and funding. I never forgot what I was trying to achieve.

FAILURE   RATES

In order to apply Carhart's equations, I needed failure rates. I went to see Lou Jones, Assistant to the Admiral at NASC. Lou recognized that the only place I could get failure rates was from the Navy. Lou started to ask a lot of questions wherever he went and soon the topic of failure rates became a hot subject of discussion all over Bu-Weps. I noticed that almost all incoming mid-rank officers at Bu-Weps would be assigned the task of designing a system to produce failure rates.

The system that evolved was simple and made use of our new

computers. If a mechanic needed a new part to replace a failed one, he went to a stock room and filled out a preprinted postcard with the number of the part he needed, the tail number of the airplane he was working on, and checked off a block describing how the part had failed.   Whenever such a new replacement part was issued, the stockroom clerk requisitioned a new one by stamping the date and stock room identification on the postcard and dropping it in a mailbox. The postcards went to the US Navy Aeronautical Material Research Center in Philadelphia where the data were punched on IBM cards for further processing. I made arrangements to get copies of all the cards pertaining to Grumman airplanes. This was a good list of all replacement parts issued.

There was another minor source of spares when the stockroom did not have a part in stock. Most facilities had a "hanger queen" from which they took scarce parts. However, the Grumman Service Representatives were alert to this situation and reported almost all irregular requisitions to me. They also reported cases where the mechanics would repair parts without taking anything out of a stockroom. Other sources in the Navy were able to give me flight time by airplane. With these data, I was able to calculate replacement data.

This was not yet a failure rate as required by Carhart's equations, but it was a good approximation of it. The Grumman Service Representatives were very alert on everything that was going on in the field and they supplied me with additional data that enabled me to construct a serviceable, approximate failure rate data base. We had so many airplanes in service, that I soon was processing 8000 IBM cards a month.

In my BIMRAB activities, I had the opportunity of exchanging failure rate data base information with other aircraft companies, and mine was always the best. There were a number of reasons for this. Many managers do not realize that empirical data must be collected the hard way from actual field operations. They think it can be created analytically. They have not had the personal experience to relate themselves to field data. In this respect, Grumman was different.

Early in 1930,   when Grumman delivered its first production squadron of F3-F to a carrier, Jake Swirbul, Vice President and General Manager, went along for two weeks to make sure that everything went well. At the end of the two weeks, he decided to stay a month.   In the meantime, a stream of messages demanding immediate delivery of replacement parts and calling for engineering design changes was being received at the plant. Parts were often taken off the production line to comply with these requests, and all requested parts were shipped by air.

When the month was over, Swirbul decided to stay another month. He stayed a total of eight months, until appropriate engineering changes took effect and the demand for replacement parts abated.

When Swirbul got back, the first thing he did was to install Roger Kahn as Service Manager. Kahn was a little man, one of the sons of Otto Kahn, President of New York Citibank, filthy-filthy rich and an enthusiastic aviator. Kahn acquired an F3-F, had it painted red, and toured the world, hopping from one carrier and Naval Air Station to the next, generating a stream of demands for replacement parts and engineering changes like Swirbul had done. His proclaimed goal was: KEEP THEM FLYING. The one thing that he would not tolerate was a Grumman airplane at a Naval facility on sea or land that was not flight ready.

Kahn tolerated no back talk from anybody, he was worse than the toughest drill sergeant in the Marine Corps. He was the most feared man at Grumman. His orders for replacement parts had the highest priorities in the company, as had his recommendations for engineering changes.

When I organized the reliability program and asked management for resources to establish a failure rate data bank, Kahn recognized the implications and gave me his full staunch support. Swirbul also saw that I was attempting to do in the design stage what he had done on his carrier excursion. I had his full blessing. In these circumstances I could afford to spend a lot of time and effort organizing my failure rate data bank, it was the basis for my reliability analysis.

STATISTICS

Lusser's product rule introduced statistics into the design control function. Statistical thinking is different from traditional engineering thinking which is deterministic with the objective of designing a product that works. Statisticians think in terms of an ideal distribution of events that they can express and manipulate in mathematical terms. I took an excellent two-semester statistics course that was broadcast on nationwide TV weekdays from six to seven am. The basic service that a consulting statistician can provide you with is to recommend the most suitable distribution that fits your case. This may not be enough for engineering purposes.

Carhart's equations assume that the operating lives of components are distributed exponentially. I have plotted the distribution of the lives of a good number of components. None have ever been exponential. But I have no other means of analyzing this material. Since the actual data were similar to the exponential, I am willing to accept the assumption that the distribution is in fact exponential for the benefit of being able to use the mathematical equations. However, I must always keep in mind that the statistical results are always an approximation.

An additional advantage of the exponential distribution is that it only has one variable, time. It therefore takes the least amount of time to apply. All other possible distributions have two or more variables. In our reliability program, the analyst supports the designer, when he is trying to decide between several possible configurations. The reliability engineer must keep up with the designer and give him reliability estimates for the various configurations that he is considering. If the reliability engineer cannot keep up with the designer, the reliability activity is useless. At this point, speed is essential. The reliability estimates for competing configurations must all be prepared in the same manner. The accuracy of the absolute values is not that important at this time. Using a equation with two or more variables does not provide any additional useful information. We used the exponential distribution as the preferred distribution in design engineering.

SYSTEM ENGINEERING

System engineering is performed by a designer, with the reliability engineer providing support. A new complex system, such as a power-operated flight-control system, will consist of a number of components

Linear components (see page 290) are designed in accordance with a mathematical model. They will never fail when operated within the conditions for which they were designed. *Non linear components* are those for which no mathematical models exist. They are designed by trial and error, based on experience.

During the design of a system, component specifications will be drawn up and released to a manufacturer, who will make the component and demonstrate in a qualification test that the component complies with the specification. All linear components should pass their qualifications tests.

Probably none of the non-linear components will pass their qualification tests. Manufacturers will scramble and do their utmost to improve the components, but in all likelihood, they will not be able to get the components to comply with all the requirements of the specification. Under the pressure of time dictated by the schedule, non-complying non-linear components will be accepted anyway.

Both linear and non-linear components will be assembled for an integration test to demonstrate that the system complies with the system specification. Since the non-linear components do not comply with their specifications, the assembly will not work. This is the first time that the designers have seen the assembled hardware and they become very inventive. They recognize the faults in the system and will want to start over with the project, but time will not allow that.

An intensive effort, calling for great inventiveness and ingenuity, will be made to get the system to work (not to meet its specification). The effort will continue until time runs out and the system as-is will be accepted. On some systems, work will continue after delivery of the first units, sometimes even during the entire service life of the unit.

FAILURE MODE, EFFECTS, AND CRITICALITY ANALYSIS (FMECA)

In 1955, the Navy was the first agency to specify a "failure analysis" in its *General Specification for Design, Installation, and Test of Aircraft Flight Control Systems* and I was the first contractor to respond to this requirement. My analyses were applicable to the F14 and the E2A.

In the analysis, each component of the system is in turn isolated and every possible failure mode of the component is tabulated. The effects of each failure mode and the probability of its occurrence (unreliability) is listed, based on the information in the failure rate data bank. If the unreliability of the component is greater than its apportioned reliability, it must be redesigned until the requirement is met, or provisions included to counter the effects of the failure.

This analysis is comparable to a stress analysis in structural design. It assures the customer that the reliability requirement of the system is met. The name of this type of analysis has gradually grown to Failure Mode, Effects, and Criticality Analysis (FMECA).

The analysis applies only to non-linear components, subject to random failures (exponential distribution). The analysis must be prepared while the designer is laying out his system since the analysis assures the reliability of the proposed component. The release of the drawing of a non-linear component should be signed by the analyst who prepared the FMECA.

The FMECA report should only refer to the delivered item and no space should be wasted on "how" the design was developed. I never had enough manpower to do a complete reliability program on any airplane. I could only hit the high spots. My major challenge was to identify the major problems, and in each case, how far in depth to go.

In 1963 I wrote a technical paper on "Failure Effect Analysis" and offered it to the ASME. It was rejected "as just another one of those Navy fads like 'Zero Defects' with no permanent value." (Shades of the Erlandson phenomenon) I then offered the paper to the New

York Academy of Sciences. After presentation, the paper was selected for publication in the Academy's *Transactions,* and I was awarded a big Gold Medal that became Eleanor's favorite piece of jewelry that she wore for years.

OVERSTRESS TESTING OF ELECTRONICS

We took a page from the structures manual and established a test-to-failure program for electronic equipment, based more on judgment than on science. A device is tested functionally under increasingly severe steps of combined operational loading: shock and vibration, and, when indicated, heat and humidity. Drop tests simulate the shock of aircraft landings on a carrier. Vibrations are created by the engines and by air turbulence over the wings, and are distributed by the elastic airframe structure, that acts as a spring, throughout the aircraft. Heat represents the environment in non air conditioned aircraft compartments that can under some conditions become very hot. Humidity occurs regularly when aircraft, flying at high altitudes, become soaked with cold at low temperatures, and then land in a hot and humid environment.

When a failure occurs during testing, the design engineer is requested to redesign the failed element so it will not fail again under that loading. Designers are clever at fixing such elements at small increases in weight, once they have seen and understood how the element has failed. Often, just changing a wire size will result in a jump in reliability. Sometimes designers will find a better configuration for the element at less weight.

The procedure is repeated until the device operates under conditions of combined loading; shock, vibration, heat, and humidity that represent good margins above the intended service conditions. The method is remarkable. One of my men, Jake Bussolini, wrote a technical paper published by the IEEE, entitled: "The Application of Overstress Testing to Airborne Electronics," where he reported that we had increased the reliability of devices by factors of over five to one in less than 200 hours of testing. Devices tested by this procedure seldom failed in service.

Such tests are expensive and engineers must be careful not to overdo them. Sometimes there are no parts available for testing to failure, and the testing phase to increase reliability cannot be applied. At other times, there may be no parts at all available for testing. However, the lessons that designers learn in a test-to-failure program are invaluable and provide knowledge that can not be obtained any other way. Engineers, who constantly compare analytic predictions with results of tests-to-failure, develop a feel on how much they can rely on analytic predictions.

NAT LICHTER

After my program was well established, to make sure I had not missed anything, I hired Grumman's first statistician, Nat Lichter. He was very intelligent with impeccable statistical qualifications. We learned from him that statisticians come with a handbook of statistical methods and have a tendency to reformulate engineering problems so that they can be solved by the statistical methods in their handbooks. The results usually were less than satisfactory for engineering purposes. It took two very painful years to reeducate Nat until he became a valuable contributor to the company, and could use statistical methods to solve engineering problems without reformulating them.

DORIAN SHANIN

Our Grumman Chief Engineer, Bob Hall, was an enthusiastic sailor and participant in the Bermuda Races. One of his close pals in these races was a man named Strong, of the firm of Rath and Strong, Consulting Engineers, Boston.

Rath and Strong issued a fancy invitation to executives in the New York area to an all day session in an exclusive New York hotel where their reliability engineer, Dorian Shanin, would explain the intricacies of this new subject of reliability to executives. Orders from our front office directed Fatty and me to attend.

I knew Shanin well, I had met him many times at meetings of the ASQC. He was one of the men on whom I had tested many of my ideas. I had spent many hours talking with him.

At lunch, Fatty maneuvered himself into the seat next to Shanin. He pumped Shanin for his qualifications, and was impressed when he found out that Shanin was a consultant to 106 distinguished American companies including General Motors. He invited Shanin to come to Grumman for a week and evaluate my reliability program.

I agreed with Shanin that he would spend the next five Mondays at Grumman. The first two Mondays I would spend showing him what we did. The third day I would let him interview project engineers and program managers. On the fourth day, I proposed to take him to the Navy Department. On the fifth day, he could make his report to Grumman management.

I was warned by my friends that consultants use such visits to convince company managements to hire them, and that I was going to have Shanin as my next boss. I disregarded this advice. I had known Shanin for several years and knew him to be an honest man.

The first days went well. Shanin was impressed. He said that he had never seen such a complete and well organized reliability activity. On our third Monday, I took him around to talk to our project engineers and program managers. They all gave him a good report of how well I worked with their groups.

On the fourth Monday, we went to Washington. As my first stop, I had selected an old friend, Rear Admiral Coates, now Chief of Naval Research. Coates wore his uniform and all his medals, something you only saw at special occasions at that time in Washington. I introduced Shanin and left the room. Later I found out that Coates had told Shanin how we had had a failure in the flight control system of one of our early warning airplanes, and how the whole fleet was grounded for three weeks. He described the rapid response of Grumman to analyze and fix the failure and get these airplanes back on station. He said that there had been a big hole in the US Atlantic defense system during these three weeks, and that if the US had been attacked during that time, it could have been disastrous for the East Coast. He told Shanin not to say or do anything that might impede the cooperative way that I worked with the Navy.

Shanin was a vivacious man, always with a lot to say. When he came out of Coates' office, this was the first time that I found him speechless.

I left him with a Navy official with whom I worked. He was to tell Shanin what he thought about the service that I provided to the Navy. Then he was to pass Shanin along to a string of other Navy men who would also brief him.

In the afternoon, I picked up Shanin and brought him back home. He said it had been a new experience for him, looking at things from the customers viewpoint.

On his next visit to Grumman, he presented his report to Management. He told them that this was the best and most complete reliability program he had ever seen, and he could not make any recommendations for improvements. He had also determined that the Navy was very satisfied with Grumman's performance. As his reward, Grumman awarded him a contract to present a 24 session course on statistics in the Engineering Department.

MY RELIABILITY PROGRAM

The program that I evolved consisted of the following functions. When the program was in place, my group was designated a section, the Reliability and Maintainability Section of the Engineering Department. We either performed these functions, helped others to do so, or assured that others performed them.

The program applied to all parts on an airplane that were non-linear, that is, their reliability was less than one and they were listed in our failure rate data bank.

1. Mission analysis. A reasonable description of how the system will be deployed. (routine job)

2. Reliability requirements to enable the system to meet mission requirements. (routine job)

3. Configuration Analysis. For each competing system configuration, all critical characteristics should be determined, including a reliability estimate. The competing configuration with the best balance of characteristics to meet mission requirements, should be selected, not necessarily the one with the best reliability, as long as the reliability meets or exceeds the requirement. (imaginative routine job)

4. Reliability apportionment. The system requirement is apportioned to lower level subsystems and components, according to the product rule, establishing a reliability requirement for each element of the system. (routine job)

5. Establish a good failure rate data bank. (difficult job)

6. Using Carhart's Equation, estimate the reliability of all lowest level piece parts and components, and working up; through all assembly levels, to the system level. (routine job)

7. When estimates do not match requirements, work with designers to make repeated changes until requirements are met. Allotted apportionments may be changed, as long as the product rule is observed. (difficult job)

8. FMECA. A paper demonstration that subsystems and systems meet their reliability requirements. (difficult job)

9 Test parts and assemblies to demonstrate that they meet requirements. If they don't, redesign until they do. Use test-to-failure to improve specimen reliability. (very difficult job)

10. Integration test. As soon as hardware is available, demonstrate that subsystems on higher levels meet requirements. If they don't, and they hardly ever do on first try, make design changes until they do. (most difficult job)

11. System qualification test. Demonstrate that the prototype meets all requirements. This is a go/no-go test. If the prototype does not qualify, and it hardly ever does on first try, it must be redesigned until it does. (very difficult job)

12. Production test. Demonstrate that production units are as good as or better than the qualified prototype. (routine job)

13. Management of parts that failed in service and are returned for investigation. (routine job)

THE REVOLUTION IN ACTION

The impact of the revolution in design control is best illustrated by an example.   The product rule, the concept of distributions, and the limitations of the AGREE Report were very difficult to understand and apply.

When the E2-A proposal first appeared on the scene, I determined that no one had prepared a reliability mission analysis, so I sat down and wrote one.

The E2-A was a carrier based early warning "defensive" weapon, therefore the number of aircraft that could be accommodated in an "attack" fleet had to be limited.

I assumed that a battle fleet would consist of three carriers, and that each carrier would carry four E2-A's, that is, a total of twelve in the fleet.

An emergency scenario called for early warning surveillance for 24 hours a day for at least a week. Five E2-A's would be on station at one time, flying equally spaced in a huge circle several hundred miles around the carriers. This would provide early warning extending to another circle several hundred miles further out.

In addition to the five aircraft on station, another five would be in maintenance being serviced to take off to relieve the aircraft on duty at the end of their six hours. It cannot be assumed that they would be flight ready before their scheduled take off time.

If an aircraft on station were to fail, the radius of the circle it was flying would have to be decreased and a spare aircraft dispatched. The range of early warning would be decreased for the time it would take for the spare aircraft to get on station. This situation would be acceptable.

If two aircraft were down at the same time, the radius of the circle that they were flying would have to be reduced to a barely acceptable size. The two spare aircraft would have to be deployed. This condition would still be acceptable.

If three aircraft on station were down at the same time, the amount of early warning available would be inadequate. There would be no available spare aircraft. This condition would be unacceptable.

My calculations showed that a scenario of at least three airplanes on station would require the aircraft to to have a reliability of 100 hours MTBF. This should be the reliability requirement for the E2-A. Our reliability estimate of the E2-A showed that the most optimistic estimate of the design as proposed with tube technology was three hours MTBF. If solid state electronics were used, the estimate went up to 17 hours MTBF. Using integrated circuits, we could probably meet the requirement of 100 hours MTBF.

I went to Washington and presented this mission analysis to the

Navy. They listened carefully, but said nothing. Three years later, I was invited to Washington to hear a trend breaking presentation on reliability. The speaker was a brand new Navy Commander (I could tell he was brand new from the way his three shiny new stripes sparkled.) He had just graduated from a new Navy reliability course. His presentation, on the Navy's new thinking about reliability, was almost word for word the same as my presentation on the E2-A that I had presented in the same room three years before.

On the other hand, in contrast to this success with the Navy, my efforts with respect to the electronic subcontractor, General Electric (GE), were zero. GE was sitting on 10000 pounds of electronic equipment, and I was convinced that nothing worked. To ease my concerns, GE hired one of those statistical reliability consultants who proclaimed that they were so smart, but I never saw the man. I determined that he was ineffective and had no effect on the design of the hardware.

I was making so much noise that GE decided that they had to take the strongest possible measures to shut me up. The Vice President and leader of GE/Utica requested a meeting with Grumman top management. Except for Mr Grumman, all the company's vice presidents were on hand to hear the Vice President/GE make his most eloquent presentation. He frankly admitted that they had had some minor reliability problems at first, but now they had hired this distinguished reliability consultant who had contacted me and was working well with me. The two of us had developed a plan that GE had put into effect and he was now convinced that the GE design would comply with all reliability and other requirements. He was sure Grumman would be proud of their work.

I realized that I faced one of those big-shots who believed that a fact was whatever he said it was. This was worse than the "Erlandson phenomenon."

I responded that I had never met or talked to this new GE reliability man, that we had not worked out any plan to save GE, that no necessary changes had been made in the GE design, that the whole presentation was one big lie. I said that the present status of the program at GE was that nothing, absolutely nothing worked.

I was convinced that I was going to be fired. This did not bother me. At every national meeting of the ASME or ASQC that I attended, several men would approach me with job offers. I always declined because at Grumman I was my own boss, and because my two boys were well established in local schools.

To my utter astonishment, the Vice President of General Electric/Utica was replaced.

GE organized a competent reliability group and they did some excellent work. They managed to get the maximum performance that was possible with tube technology. (I had predicted three hours MTBF for the E2-A).

The first E-2A, built with tube technology, required 30 days of preflight maintenance for take-off. Once in the air, its performance was remarkable; it fulfilled the Navy's wildest dreams. But after an hour or two of flight, and the smoothest landing that a pilot could manage to reduce the landing shock, nothing worked. Another month or more of maintenance was again required before the aircraft could take off.

The Navy wanted the aircraft badly.   They issued an order for redesign, using latest technology solid state devices. The resulting E-2B had a reliability of about 17 hours, just as I had predicted, not nearly enough for a carrier based airplane of the U.S. Navy.

At that time, the Director of the Bu-Weps Electrical/Electronics Division was Col Art Lowell, U.S. Marine Corps, who was also chairman of the BIMRAB Electronics Committee. This committee consisting of the country's best electronic engineers, provided Lowell with the best independent, expert advice he needed to do the job he did.

Lowell and I decided that the only solution to save the E-2B was to redesign the system with integrated circuits. But the industry was not ready.   Design concepts were not fully understood, and production would require expensive plant retooling.   In the late 1950's there was also a problem regarding the effectiveness of industrial reliability programs.   There was much publicity about reliability, most of it generated by the AGREE Report. Most companies were willing to hire a few reliability engineers, place them in a nice office, and let them operate as a public relations function. But interference in design was unthinkable.   Lowell visited these companies, suppliers to GE, and convinced them to use integrated circuits.

On its first few flights, the E-2C, shown page 309, with its integrated circuits, demonstrated a reliability of well over 100 hours MTBF. It has now been in the successful service of the armed services of the US and several other countries for almost forty years. It pioneered the use of integrated circuits which today has touched the lives of every person in the civilized world.

TRANSPORTATION, A SERVICE

About the mid 1960's, the Council of the ASME was disturbed by their finding that urban sprawl, slums, and metropolitan areas were all growing out of control.   In their efforts to decide on a single governing factor in this confusing picture, they decided on transportation   as   the   common   denominator   with   the   most

E-2C Hawkeye

engineering content. It was decided to organize a national conference on transportation to bring everyone associated with the subject together. I was asked to organize the conference and act as chairman.

Although I was busy at the time, I agreed to do so. With the help of the members of the ASME Council, I was able to gather around me a committee of the most knowledgeable experts in the world.

The conference entitled: *Transportation, a Service,* was held on August 28-30, 1967 at the Waldorf Astoria Hotel in New York City. The *Transactions,* a hard bound volume containing all the papers presented, had 911 pages.   All aspects of transportation and its impact on city planning and social factors were discussed. We even had a paper by Professor Constantine Doxiadis of the University of Athens, Greece, on *"The Emerging Great Lakes Megalopolis."* Doxiadis' course on the "Megalopolis" was world famous and had been attended by quite a few US Congressmen.

There are three megalopolises in the United States, the eastern one from Boston to Richmond, the Great Lakes area, and the western one from San Diego to San Francisco. A transportation design goal might be to provide a system to move people and goods from any given point in the megalopolis to any other point in a minimum of time. We have made some progress in overseas cargo transportation by using sealed air-sea-land containers from an inland point of origin to ultimate destination, rather than merely from pier to pier. But we still have a long way to go.

In the United States we have a problem with city planners. City planning is considered so important that city councils will not hire a city planner unless he has a rock solid reputation and is a mature 50+ years old. However, city planners are not effective until they are 20 years on the job. There are few planners left after age 70. A good example is New York City's brilliant Robert Moses, who held office until his late 70's.

Nothing like this conference had ever been held before, and it created a lot of excitement. Especially the Civil Engineering Schools all over the country were enthusiastically talking about it.

Unfortunately I was too busy with my other activities and could not continue the chairmanship. My successors were not able to get the same support that I had, and after two more conferences of lesser scope, the conference series was discontinued. I often think that if I had remained chairman of this conference, I might have improved some aspects of our transportation system and changed some of the world for the better.

A good example of possibilities for improvement is provided by the airlines who march so proudly in the front lines of technical innovation. The airline ticket holder must spend his own time to move from his point of origin often through heavy traffic to the crowded airport parking lot, from there walk to the back of the long line waiting at the check-in counter. Then there is another long walk to the departure gate, and the wait at the gate. Admission to the airplane does not necessarily mean take-off, often there is another wait for runway space, sometimes at large airports there may be 20 to 40 airplanes ahead of you waiting for their turn to take off. After landing, the passenger has to spend more time finding the baggage claim section, where he can wait for his baggage. Then he has to spend more time getting to his final destination. Regardless of the fabulous improvements that have been made in aircraft design, the revolution in convenient travel, of moving from any given point to any other in a megalopolis, has yet to get started.

THE CHALLENGE OF SPACE

ECHO 1

With the development of the large boosters such as we had on the Rigel to achieve supersonic flight, our next logical step was to consider the challenges of space. Grumman organized a Space Steering Group which bid unsuccessfully on the orbital Mercury capsule. They were more successful with the Echo 1, an non-active aluminum balloon, 135 feet in diameter, placed in orbit and used to reflect radio signals from one part of the earth to another. It was packed in a fancy canister that opened up in space to allow the Echo 1 to blow itself up. The design was straight forward and contained no "non-linear" parts, so I did not foresee any reliability problems.

We were all very excited when the Echo 1 was successfully launched, it was our first space venture. On a clear summer evening, Eleanor and I would go into our back yard and search the sky until we found our very little, but bright, pin-point beacon. You could just hardly see it with your bare eyes. This was really something new in world history, we had created our very own new star in the heavens!

ORBITING ASTRONOMICAL OBSERVATORY, OAO

The Echo 1 encouraged Grumman to support and build up its Space Steering Group. The group did some extensive first class space research and made an excellent impression on NASA. As a result, Grumman won the OAO contract in a competitive procurement process.

There were two problems that established the need for the OAO. The first was the need to complete an accurate map of the sky for navigational purposes. All the major observatories of the world had been working on a cooperative basis for over 100 years to map the sky, and had barely completed half the job. At that time, an airliner flying to New York from Europe could navigate no closer than 20 miles to its destination, and needed assistance from the ground to find its way.

The second problem was to provide a stabilized space platform for the study of cosmic phenomena that are obscured by the earth's atmosphere. The two problems were interlocked, the second problem had to be done so the mapping problem could be accomplished.

These   two   problems   established   new   severe   engineering requirements for a stabilized space platform. An OAO stationed over New York, for example, would have no trouble detecting a golf ball flying over Chicago. The OAO, and later the LM, became the two best engineered projects the world had ever seen.

The OAO, at 3900 pounds, was in its day by far the heaviest spacecraft ever launched. It was 80 inches in diameter and ten fleet long. It orbited 500 miles above the earth. Running the center length of the OAO was a hollow cylinder, 48 inches in diameter, for the installation of experimental equipment, such as the 36 inch telescope mirror.

The stringent stabilization requirements were met with a system of dry jets for gross position adjustments, and inertial wheels for fine adjustments. In space, if you turn a wheel in one direction, the supporting spacecraft will turn in the opposite direction. Thousands of turns of the wheel were required to achieve one turn of the spacecraft, so the position of the spacecraft could be held very precisely.

There were three batteries to provide power to turn the wheels. The batteries were recharged by two wing panels of over a hundred square feet holding solar cells generating 1000 watts when the panels were normal to the sun.

The OAO had another unique power back-up system. Electricity is generated when you move a wire through a magnetic field. The OAO was equipped with a number of the largest loops of wire that could be accommodated on the spacecraft. When the spacecraft moved in orbit, its loops cut through the earth's magnetic field and generated electricity. This had never been done before on a spacecraft.

Another problem was the control of heat. Normal spacecraft are painted half white, and half black, and the desired temperature in sunlight is maintained by rotating the spacecraft to the sun. The black part of the spacecraft absorbs heat, and the white part reflects it. The OAO was a stable platform locked on the stars and could not be rotated. Every heat source had to be provided with a heat collector that conducted the heat to a point where it could be dumped overboard.

The design of the OAO was accompanied by an intensive reliability program. I wrote a plan that was submitted to NASA with the proposal, applying the procedures that I have described on pages 304 and 305. NASA asked for a year of operational service. During the design, I found that I could not stretch my numbers that far. I realized that my numbers were conservative, and that the actual vehicle would be better than my numbers indicated, but I had no way of knowing by how much. I added a note at the bottom of a page on a report to NASA, that our goal was one year, guarantee one month. Nobody said anything.

Four OAO's were built and delivered at a cost of about $15 Million each.

Number one failed after a few orbits because of arcing in the power supply system.   The OAO became inactive and began to tumble in flight.

Number two, launched in December, 1968, was a tremendous success. It flew for more than four years and made over 20000 orbits before it was turned off. It finished mapping the sky, and scientists from all over the world were lined up with problems for it to solve. Number two was turned off because the ground support was becoming too expensive, and it was sending down more data than the scientific teams on the ground could process.

Number three encountered booster trouble on take off, and never reached orbit.

Number four was in service for over seven years. NASA appealed to the world wide scientific community for problems to assign to the OAO, but it had already solved all the problems that it was able to solve, and it was turned off.

The OAO finished mapping the sky, and answered all questions associated with the obscurity of the earth's atmosphere. It exceeded all its initial objectives. Its users regretted that it was not a manned vehicle, because a manned vehicle with the same capability would have been much more helpful.

The OAO design had been an exercise in coping with the most difficult problems of space flight. It required intensive engineering down do a level never done before. Grumman was now ready to tackle the Apollo!

REACHING FOR THE MOON

THE "LUNAR ORBIT RENDEZVOUS" (LOR)

The OAO project had been an exercise dealing with the most difficult problems of space flight. Grumman was now ready to participate in the great experience of reaching for the moon.

NASA had for several years sponsored studies on how to land men on the moon and bring them back safely to earth. Several schemes appeared feasible, but the "Lunar Orbit Rendezvous" (LOR) method finally won out. An integrated three man, three component, vehicle (Command, Service, and Lunar Modules {LM}, eventually named the "Apollo") is boosted from the earth into moon orbit. The LM is disengaged and flies with two astronauts down to the moon surface, lands and stays a bit, and then returns to moon orbit where it is reunited with the Command and Service Modules. The astronauts transfer to the Command Module and the LM is abandoned in space. Closer to earth, the Service Module is also abandoned and the Command Module returns to earth with all three astronauts.

Grumman made every effort to win, first the Command Module contract, and when that effort failed, to win the Service Module contract. Both of these contracts were won by North American Aviation of California. This left the LM contract, that Grumman had to win. There were seven other companies bidding for this contract.

THE LM RELIABILITY PLAN

The LM Request for Proposal (RFP) issued in August, 1962, emphasized that reliability would be a major consideration in source selection.

Grumman management did not understand reliability technology thoroughly, like they did older engineering disciplines that they grew up with and in which they excelled. They were extremely concerned, to say the least. They were proceeding, to a great extent, based on faith in me. I was gratified, and felt a deep responsibility on my shoulders. With my unique training in reliability technology, I was the right person at the right place at the right time. This was a matter of pure luck.

I felt strongly that a "reliability program" carried the first responsibility for assuring that the vehicle would perform satisfactorily in its operating environment and that the manufacturing processes would be designed to assure compliance with design requirements.   I had written and administered the reliability programs for the E-2C, F-14, OAO, and a number of other vehicles. From my activity on BIMRAB, I had observed what kinds of reliability programs the best companies in the US had, and I was convinced that my program was by far the best.

I had also prepared the reliability plans for the Command and Service Modules proposals, so I was well prepared to write the plan in support of the   LM proposal.   The plan I wrote discussed how Grumman would apply the procedures listed on pages 304 and 305 to the proposed LM structure.

When Grumman first received the Request for Proposal, we noticed that no "mission analysis" had been written. Whatever information was available was scattered over many documents.   Grumman was awarded a contract to prepare a mission analysis for the Apollo. My friend Tom was assigned the task of preparing the analysis. He asked me to provide him with the reliability requirement.

In my group, we gave this matter much thought and came up with the theory, that men will take risks, or can be asked to take risks, in proportion to the glory to be won by their achievement. To quantify the concept, I sent two men to the Indianapolis Race Track to determine the risk of death and injury. They came back with two numbers indicating the risks of death and injury that men would take voluntarily to win a dangerous international sports event.

We thought that these numbers might be an American characteristic, and we wanted an international confirmation. I sent two men to Mexico City to determine the risks that Mexican bullfighters take in the Mexico City Ring. They came back with numbers comparable to those that we got at the Indianapolis Race Track. We concluded that it is a universal human trait for men to take or accept certain limited risks in proportion to the glory that they can win.

The glory earned by a man landing on the moon is greater than the glory that can be earned at the Indianapolis Race Track or the Mexico City Bull Fighting Ring. We can therefore ask such astronauts to take higher risks on a lunar excursion. Accordingly, I increased the risks measured at Indianapolis and Mexico City by orders of magnitude, and established these numbers:

       Probability of Mission Success: $R = 0.9840$
       Probability of Crew Safety: $R = 0.9995$

I wrote these numbers on a piece of paper and took them in to Tom. He just glanced at them, and thanked me kindly. He inserted these numbers in his Mission Analysis, and they were accepted by NASA without any further explanation. If the LM is successful, all future spacecraft will use these numbers. As the responsible expert, I did not have to explain to anybody how the numbers were derived.

It is important to realize what these numbers mean. Let me explain what actually happened later when we built the LM. These numbers are at the top of the pyramid of the drawing tree that lists every subassembly and part on the LM. These numbers are allocated down through the various levels of the drawing tree to the lowest level. At every level, the allocated reliabilities of all the components and subassemblies on that level must equal the reliability on the top level in accordance with the product rule. In this way we established a reliability requirement for every non-linear "black box" and component of the LM.

The LM was the first manned vehicle ever built to operate exclusively in space, it was the first ever "spacecraft." It did not have to overcome any air resistance like an airplane or a missile. On the other hand, we were concerned that it not contaminate any bodies in space, nor return with any contamination unknown on earth. We were also concerned with possible damage from radiation and meteorites.

The effect of the reliability plan was felt strongly in the selection of parts at the lowest level of assembly of the LM. On page 290, I mention that a reliability analysis applies primarily to non-linear parts. On the LM, however, all parts were intensively scrutinized. All parts were rigorously tested to demonstrate that they at least met their requirements with an acceptable margin of safety under their expected operational environments. All metal parts were x-rayed. Parts were only handled, tested, and assembled in clean rooms.

This testing was the next most important impact of the reliability program. In general, there was no way of demonstrating the very high component statistical reliability requirements. We substituted very high operational environments for high statistical probabilities and designed and tested all components and subassemblies so that they would survive the very high environments at the limit of our test equipment. At the start, we generally had many failures under operational conditions, but our repair and retest program (test-fix-test) was amazingly effective in increasing the reliability of components by large factors.

In actual flight, every LM had a few failures, but because of the redundancies provided in the design, none of them affected mission success or crew safety. Every such failure resulted in the redesign of the failed part on the next vehicle.

Management demonstrated a great deal of confidence in the

reliability program when it made its earth-shattering decision to broadcast the manned flights to the moon on television with the whole world watching. It required a great deal of courage to make this decision, and it reflects most favorably on the character of the men who managed the Apollo program.

PREPARING THE LM PROPOSAL

A proposal is prepared in response to a "Request for Proposal (RFP)" and consists primarily in detailed plans to accomplish each task or "work package" required in the RFP, a description of the proposed vehicle, plus cost or manpower estimates. Proposals are graded in accordance with those features that the customer considers most important, like, for instance, cost. A contract may then be awarded to the contractor who submitted the proposal that ranks highest in the grading. There is usually not much time available between the issue date of the RFP and the required submittal date for the proposal, that in this case was in September, 1962. As a result, engineers writing a proposal generally have to work day and night, like from 8 am to 12 midnight, including weekends, to complete their work. It's a hair raising experience.

In addition to the plans for accomplishing requirements, the configuration of the vehicle must be defined in the proposal. The LM RFP included a requirement that the pilot be able to see his landing site on approach to the moon.

Lacking a prepared runway on the moon, and not really knowing what the moon surface was like, the LM would have to descend straight down to the moon surface at an approximate 90 degree angle. The design problem was to provide a pilot sitting in a seat with a view looking straight down. Since the landing site was directly under the LM, this was difficult to do. Industry conventions are hard to break.

Grumman had eight design teams in competition in secret locations working on this problem. This was a different world from when they needed an answer to the power operated flight controls problem, and I was the only one assigned to find a solution.

One of the teams eventually came up with an answer. The length of the flight from moon orbit to the surface of the moon could be measured in minutes, not hours. The pilot did not have to sit. He could stand, although strapped in, at the inside forward edge of the vehicle, and lean his head forward over the edge and look through a sloping window straight down along the outside vehicle edge to see his landing site.

Of the eight bidders responding to the LM RFP, Grumman was the only contractor to solve this problem.

Grumman had been studying the the design of space craft for several years and had developed solutions for many problems. One typical problem had to do with the hose disconnect fittings in the hypergolic fuel lines. Hypergolic fuels ignite spontaneously upon contact with one another and are very viscous. They leak at every disconnect, presenting a serious fire hazard. As a result, a drip pan had to be installed below every disconnect to catch the dripping fuel, and the drip pans had to be emptied and cleaned regularly.

A Grumman subcontractor developed a disconnect with a number four sealing surface. A normal high grade machine finish is number 125, number four is at the end of the scale and was something that could not be made. However, the Grumman subcontractor found a way of achieving a number four finish by expert hand lapping. Touching this surface by hand or any kind of instrument destroys the finish.

No number four finish is perfect, every such surface has a number of imperfections. Specially trained inspectors examine the surface under a microscope, and by extensive training, they decide when the extent of imperfections is sufficiently small that the surface will provide a good seal. Grumman had a training program for mechanics who were authorized to handle the disconnects. In its time, the LM was the only space craft without drip pans under every hypergolic fuel disconnect.

We did a lot of talking about batteries versus fuel cells. I was enthused about fuel cells. I looked forward in ten to fifteen years to be driving an electric car, stopping at a gas station once a week to refill my fuel cells with gasoline. North American selected fuel cells for the Command and Service Modules. However, the data that I had in my data bank would not support the use of fuel cells on the LM, and I recommended the use of batteries.

The Grumman proposal for the LM, as submitted, was the most careful and complete proposal Grumman had ever written.

THE NORTH AMERICAN RELIABILITY PROGRAM

After the submittal of the LM proposal, I was able to get copies of the North American Command and Service Modules reliability programs. Each was a beautiful printed book, almost an inch thick, with an attractive light blue cover. I studied them very carefully.

I was appalled by what I read. The two documents were both the same. They were written in the language of the AGREE Report. They were an accumulation of the highfalutin statistical theories that were being promoted by the many pompous statistical reliability consultants that were running around loose in those days. Vehicle requirements were stated in MTBF terms that could not be demonstrated in a test and simply made no sense. There were no procedures to assure the reliability of the hardware. There was no demonstration program.

The review of these documents provided me with two tragic insights:

1. North American did not understand what constituted an acceptable reliability engineering program.

2. NASA did not have the capability to select a good reliability program.

This was an untenable situation. How was I going to sell my excellent reliability program to an agency that talked big about reliability, but had no idea how it was achieved? My last resort was to pray for a miracle.

MIRACLES HAPPEN

I gave a technical reliability paper at a meeting of the American Society for Quality Control (ASQC) in Las Vegas. Las Vegas was an excellent place for technical meetings. The facilities were the very best, and the prices were much lower than anywhere else in the country.

One man in the audience kept asking a number of questions, and after the session, he came up front and asked me some more. He introduced himself as Jim Koppenhaven, Director of Reliability, NASA Headquarters, Washington, DC. I suggested that we go have dinner together.

At dinner, Jim disclosed no statistical bias and appeared to be truly interested in what I had to say. Apparently, this was all new to him. After dinner, we went to a bar and talked until two am. I think I gave Jim a good introduction in reliability engineering and was relieved that I had had such a successful interview with a high NASA Official. Miracles do happen.

KENNEDY SPACE CENTER, FLORIDA

Through my activities on the Aerospace Reliability and Maintainability Conference series, I managed to make good friends with several men in the reliability section at Kennedy Space Center (KSC). From my conference activities, they were acquainted and impressed with my engineering approach to reliability and induced Dr. Debus, Director of Kennedy Space Center to invite me to give a four hour lecture on Reliability Engineering in their brand new auditorium at the Cape.

I divided my lecture into two two-hour periods, with a 15 minute recess between the two periods. I have attended many such lectures, and in the second period, the speaker normally loses at least a third of his audience.

The engineering community at KSC had been exposed to statistical reliability techniques. My engineering approach was something new to them. My presentation consisted of describing the tasks listed on page 305. I was surprised when almost every one used their recess period to go back to their offices and alert their coworkers to come and listen to me. My second period addressed an overflow crowd, standing room only.

Later I was invited to come back to KSC and attended special reviews and events. I maintained my close relationship with some engineers at KSC for as long as I worked at Grumman. The success of this lecture greatly bolstered my confidence with respect to my ability to sell my engineering approach to reliability to NASA, in competition with North American's statistical approach on the Command and Service Modules.

NASA AWARDS GRUMMAN THE LM CONTRACT

After a short period of time, that seemed like a century to us who had been waiting for a decision, on November 7, 1962, NASA announced that Grumman had won the award of the LM contract. The spontaneous merriment that immediately followed this notice was soon toned down by the distressing situation that became apparent from reading the fine print of the contract.

The take-off weight of the Apollo was dictated by the capability of the boosters, which was 98000 pounds. There was no foreseeable way to increase the capability of the boosters, so any overweight on the Apollo was completely unacceptable.

The contracts for the Command and Service Modules had been awarded before the one for the Lunar Module, and North American had been successful in being allotted 70000 pounds, leaving only 28000 pounds for the LM. At that time, there was nobody there to speak for the LM. A review of the LM requirements, using standard engineering procedures, indicated that there was no way that the LM requirements could be met at 28000 pounds.

It was realized that the LM design would be a constant battle for fractions of an ounce, and Grumman was in for a struggle that it had not bargained for.

NASA INSPECTS THE GRUMMAN FACILITY

Soon after contract award, a NASA team came to inspect Grumman's facilities to assure that they were adequate to perform the requirements of the LM contract. The team was headed by Dr. Gilruth, Head of the Apollo Project.

The NASA Team broke up into groups of specialists and each

group, with its Grumman hosts, inspected the shops or laboratories of its interest.

After the site inspection, lunch was served to the NASA team and its Grumman hosts in the executives' dining room. Schwendler and Gilruth were sitting alone at one table. I went and sat next to Gilruth, pinning him between Schwendler and myself. The two men were talking about real estate, straining to make conversation. In a lull, I broke in and said. "Dr. Gilruth, what do you think about our Reliability Plan?" He said, that he had heard others talk about it, but he himself did not know anything about it. I proceeded to give him my short version of the elements listed on pages 304 and 305. I had never talked to Schwendler about reliability before, and he listened to me very carefully. When I finished, Schwendler said that my remarks described our basic Grumman design philosophy and was the way we would want to approach any job, whether we had a formal reliability program or not. Gilruth seemed pleased with the discussion.

After lunch, the NASA team met with its Grumman counterparts in one large room for a question and answer period. The Grumman people were seated in a large semicircle on one side of the room, and the NASA team in another semicircle on the other side. In the middle of each semicircle, there was a table for the team leaders. There were three seats at the Grumman table.

In view of the emphasis on reliability in the RFP, Grumman management was very concerned that NASA would ask questions about this subject. Accordingly, the three men at the Grumman table were: Joe Gavin, Vice President, in the center, Bob Mullaney, Program Manager, on Joe's one side, and myself on Joe's other side.

Grumman personnel were seated first, then a door was opened and the NASA team entered and filed into their semicircle of seats. As Jim Koppenhaven entered the room, he saw me sitting at the Grumman head table, he smiled and winked. I smiled back and winked.

The questions were all friendly and easily answered. Grumman did not know what to expect about reliability. Finally, Jim spoke up and asked how the reliability program was going to be administered. Joe said that we had submitted a Reliability Plan that we intended to abide by, that I would be the sole person administering the program, and Grumman management would not interfere with me. Jim was satisfied with this answer, and to the surprise of all the Grumman people, he had no further questions. What they did not realize, was that all the technical questions had been answered at a bar in Las Vegas two months before.

Joe's verbatim reply was incorporated in the LM contract, together with a notice of my appointment as Reliability Director, Lunar Module.

This was the high point of my career. I realized that by dedicating myself exclusively to the LM, I had to surrender the leadership of a large engineering department that I had built up, a job that I would never again be able to get. From now on, I was just going to go downhill. I just did not realize at the time how forcefully disaster would strike.

LM CONTRACT RENEGOTIATIONS AT HOUSTON

In an effort to tie down all loose ends, the LM contract was renegotiated during six weeks in November and December, 1962, at the NASA Manned Space Flight Center in Houston. The LM contract consisted of some ten work packages, most work packages were represented by three men. The Grumman team, therefore, consisted of some thirty men. Joe Gavin was the team leader.

Each Grumman team met with a similar NASA team during the day, and at five o'clock the Grumman teams reported their accomplishments and problems to Gavin, and the NASA teams reported likewise to their management. Gavin met with his NASA counterparts the following day to resolve any problems uncovered the previous day. This procedure was scheduled for six weeks in the hope that this contract would need a minimum of expensive changes during its execution.

Joe Kingfield of Grumman Quality Control and I were assigned to the Reliability and Quality Control package. Joe and I decided to split up, since our problems were different. Joe met with the one NASA quality control specialist, while I met with the other two men who were reliability specialists.

The two NASA very intelligent reliability specialists were died in the wool statisticians without any engineering experience. They opened the meeting by giving me copies of the beautiful light blue covered North American Command and Service Modules Reliability Plans, and asked me to read them. They said that they were the very best technically possible plans and had been approved by NASA top management. They were sure that I would find them to be most excellent technical plans. Because of cost considerations, NASA management was anxious to simplify the administration of the Apollo program and had decided to have only one reliability program for all three modules. Since the North American Plan was such an excellent one, I was asked to accept it for application on the LM.

I had difficulty believing my ears. I had already read the North American reliability plan at home, and knew it was unsatisfactory. When it came my turn to talk, I pointed out that the weight allotment of 28000 pounds to the LM was insufficient to design such a vehicle using standard engineering design procedures. The design of the LM was going to be a fierce battle for each fraction of an ounce. In their efforts to make their equipment as light as possible, designers had to be monitored by reliability personnel to assure that they did not go too far and that their equipment functioned as required in extreme environments. The Grumman Reliability Plan is unique and is designed to address this problem. I assumed that NASA management had not yet recognized the problem and is therefore not yet aware that the LM design needs special treatment.

I made it clear that this tragic situation was no fault of Grumman's. It was the result of NASA oversight of allotting North American 70000 pounds without any consideration of what the LM would need. This NASA oversight now has serious repercussions on the LM design.

I told them that I had already read the North American Plan and had determined that it contained inadequate provisions for detail design control and component testing and was therefore technically inadequate for application on the LM. If the North American Plan were applied to the LM, the men in the Apollo would never reach the moon and make it back safely to the earth.

I expressed my annoyance that they had not read the Grumman Reliability Plan. I told them that the Grumman Plan had been designed to assure that the LM would meet its reliability requirements, regardless of the difficult conditions in which it was being designed. There was no other plan in existence that met this requirement.

They admitted that the LM design was going to be difficult, but they had been ordered by NASA top management to establish one reliability plan for all three modules, and this was their job.

We continued to talk in circles until 12 noon, lunch time. My two companions proved to be real gentlemen during lunch. Not a word was said about our business meeting. They told me many nice stories about Houston, they were perfect hosts. After our pleasant lunch hour, we went back to our meeting room and continued to talk in circles.

At five o'clock I reported my dismal day to Gavin. He was most sympathetic, but told me to that I just had to hang in there and not give up.

This was a situation where the two sides had conflicting incompatible objectives that they could not compromise. The second day was the same as the first, as was the third. This went on for 10 days, that is TEN DAYS, namely eight hours on Monday, Tuesday, Wednesday, Thursday, Friday, and the following week again on Monday, Tuesday, Wednesday, Thursday, and most of Friday. By Agreement with Gavin, on Friday afternoon, I presented an ultimatum.

I told them that if they had not read and analyzed the Grumman Reliability Plan by Monday morning, I was packing up and going home, effectively terminating the negotiation. The Grumman Reliability Plan was an essential part of the proposal with which Grumman had won the LM contract. If the Plan is not negotiated here and now, it will go into effect as written. Grumman has no objection to that.

On Monday morning they came in, bleary eyed. They had read and analyzed the Grumman Reliability Plan and admitted that it was the toughest and most complete program that they had ever read. I now suggested, that if they wanted a common reliability program on all three modules, the thing to do was to impose the superior Grumman program on North American. They were shocked. I was told that this could not be done because the North American contracts were already signed. I pointed out that all development contracts are continuously being modified. They said that modifications always cost money and their objective was to keep costs down. It was now understood that Grumman would proceed with its Reliability Plan and so, I stopped beating a dead horse.

We started to talk about how Grumman was going to administer the plan. All of the tasks listed in the plan were analyzed in detail and listed on the blackboard. I had been allotted 29 men. They asked me how I was going to complete all the tasks listed on the blackboard with 29 men. I had to explain that 29 men was the most manpower that Grumman could allocate to me and keep the cost down within a range that could win the contract. This is a common procedure in competitive biding. As it becomes apparent that more people are needed on a job, contract modifications are made to provide them.

My statistician friends did not like this. They had long discussions with their managements. In the end, I was assigned 159 men. I was the only team leader to get a manpower increase, all the others got cuts.

Later, when the design process started in earnest, it became obvious that 159 men were not sufficient. At the height of the design effort, there were over 400 men in the reliability group.

In the end, every single provision in the LM contract was changed from one to many times. The original LM contract, signed in January, 1963, for $ 368 million, was unusual in that it was written more in terms of operational objectives rather than in terms of specific hardware, that is, it specified what the LM had to do. As a result, we went through at least four "final" configurations until arriving at an acceptable one.

DESIGNING AND FABRICATING THE LM

The LM design and fabrication program was so large, that there was no way that I could oversee the whole. Although I was in a better position than most participants to oversee activity, I still felt like I was looking through a tiny peephole in a solid high fence at a gigantic spectacle of world wide proportions. Many other participants will write about other aspects of the LM project that I know nothing about.

The project employed over 9000 people, some 7000 at Bethpage, 1400 at Kennedy Space Center, 450 at Houston, and 300 at White Sands. Of these people, some 2400 were engineers.

The LM design posed a number of unusual problems. The LM was the first true space vehicle. It operated only in low gravity space. The fact that it was not to operate in an earthly environment posed all kinds of technical testing problems. It was a no-maintenance machine with five separate applications:

     as cargo stored in a slender rocket

     as a self-propelled vehicle in space

     as a habitat for astronauts on the moon

     as a life boat in case of failure of the Command and Service modules

     as a communications center

This design was a task of national importance conducted in the full glare of nationwide publicity.

The construction of the LM was a massive job involving some 150 subcontractors and 3000 suppliers. All the systems and components had to be brought together on schedule and in perfect alignment, the first time, in a small spacecraft, smaller than the average living room. In total, the LM consisted of over a million separate parts. To control this operation, Grumman introduced a new type of document, the interface drawing, that was supplied to the manufacturers of any two components or assemblies that were to be joined. These documents were a great success in assuring that all joints were in perfect alignment the first time that an attempt was made to assemble them, including the LM joint with its carrier rocket and with the Command and Service Modules.

Our major reliability design problems were:

     Guidance and control system, Subcontractor: MIT Instrumentation Lab

     Descent engine, Subcontractor: TRW

     Ascent engine, Subcontractor: Rocketdyne

     Reaction control thrusters, Subcontractor: Marquardt

Before the Surveyor Spacecraft made the first unmanned landing on the moon surface in June, 1966, we had no idea what the moon surface was like. Some scientists believed that the moon was covered with a 50 foot (or deeper) layer of dust, and that the LM, when landing on the moon, would sink into the dust and disappear. Others believed that the moon surface was so rough and irregular that no landing was possible. The Surveyor gave us good data with respect to the moon surface and put our minds at ease.

LM RELIABILITY DIRECTOR

The Grumman Company was overloaded with work when the LM came along. The F11 Tiger and the F14 Tomcat required practically all of the company's facilities. As a result, the LM Project was located in its own brand new building, Plant 25. The payroll of the company would more than double to almost 40000 people.

Gavin's office was in the executive suite on the top (third) floor in a corner of our new building. He had a large room for himself, with windows along two sides, and a smaller one for his secretary. My office was next door. It had an unusual feature. The wall against the corridor contained a large store-size glass panel, so I could overlook the corridor and see everybody who went in or out of Gavin's office. I don't know why I had this panel, I did not ask, and nobody told me. Many visitors looked me quizzingly up and down as they approached Gavin's office.

I decorated my office with my over-sized Florida professional engineers license and a large wall map of the expansion of the United States showing how the original 13 States acquired first Florida, then the Louisiana Purchase, and finally the Mexican territories that reached to California. These two items always helped me to start a friendly conversation with strange visitors. I had a pet riddle that I solved with help of the map. I would ask, what are the most northern, southern, eastern, and western States of the Union? My visitors would concentrate on Maine and Florida, until I showed them on the map that Hawaii was our most southern State. Then I would show them that Alaska is not only the most northern State, but is also the most western and eastern State, as the Aleutian Island chain straddles the 180 degree longitudinal that divides the world into eastern and western hemispheres.

I did not like my office in the executive suite because it was so far away from the engineering department. In engineering, I always surrounded myself closely with my people so that they could always come to me with questions when they had them. Now I was enthroned some distance away in splendid isolation and was afraid that people were afraid to come and talk to me.

My job was to make sure that Grumman followed the LM Reliability Plan that I had written.

My biggest personal problem was that I was no longer Department Head. Before my promotion, the men in the Department all worked for me, I trained them, I assigned them their work, saw that they did it, gave them their raises. Now I was on the outside, watching that the work progressed in accordance with the plan. I felt like I was in a passenger seat of a car, next to the driver, making sure that he took the right road. I much preferred to be the driver.

Before we moved into the new building, I had analyzed the LM Reliability Plan and assigned tasks to various group leaders. By the time we moved into the new building, everybody was working in accordance with this plan.

Most of the work was allocating reliability requirements to lowest level components, then working with designers to assure that the requirements were met. Failure Mode, Effect and Criticality Analyses (FMECA) were prepared on all systems and major subsystems and submitted to NASA for approval.

The major problem across the board was to reduce weight. Booster performance increased by 4000 pounds during its design, and all this weight was allotted to Grumman, giving us an allowable gross weight of 32000 pounds. This was most helpful, but it was still far from enough and Grumman would still spend $100 for machining or other manufacturing process to save an ounce.

Conventional aircraft are subject to a growth factor of one to six. That means that an additional pound of weight in the airframe results in six pounds of take-off weight. This is because of the additional fuel, tank space, and structure required to carry that extra pound. On the LM, the weight growth factor was 1 to 800, that meant, every pound of LM weight resulted in 800 pounds of Apollo take-off weight. As a result, every item was carefully analyzed and tested as never before to assure reliable performance at least weight.

As soon as components were built, they were tested to failure, to measure their reliability characteristics and also to improve them. Much common sense and engineering judgment is required when testing to failure, and most engineers are afraid to apply the method. Although we never made a big fuss about it, I feel strongly that our test to failure program was one of the most effective technical innovations that made the LM a superior design.

A good example of the effort that was taken to keep the weight down is the instrument panel. Many times when a change was made in an operating system, a corresponding change had to be made in the instrumentation in the cockpit. On a conventional aircraft, the instrument panel is large enough that the instruments can be moved around a bit. This was not the case on the LM. Here the instruments in the instrument panel were arranged so that the panel weight would be a minimum. Sometimes, when an instrument was changed, the entire panel had to be redesigned for minimum weight. During the

LM development period, the instrument panel was redesigned 34 times.

There were some things I worried about because I could not do anything about them. The LM ascent and descent engines were at the top of this list. Grumman selected Rocketdyne to build both engines, but NASA wanted to develop another source. Grumman was directed to pick another supplier for one of the engines, and they picked TRW for the ascent engine. TRW had never built such a rocket engine. Furthermore, these were the first two throttleable rocket engines ever built.

I watched TRW carefully. I went there quite a few times. The first thing I look for when I go on a plant visit is cleanliness. TRW was by far the cleanest place I have ever seen.

They hired one of Rocketdyne's top rocket engineers. He was the only one on the project who knew what he was doing, and he was a tough disciplinarian. He had 150 engineers on this project, all of them going to school learning about rocket technology, but in the meantime, each man was following instructions explicitly.

A rocket engine is like a match, when ignited, it only burns once. Four rocket engines of each type were built for test, and they worked perfectly. The engines built for the LM were very carefully inspected, and operated with water, but were not ignited until they were on the moon and all the world was watching with bated breath.

After it was all over, I arranged through my connections with the ASME Aerospace Division Honors Committee to give an award to our successful TRW engine builder. The award was presented to him at a banquet held in conjunction with an ASME national meeting in Los Angeles. I could not attend, but ASME staff reported back to me that they had never before witnessed an ovation as they did at this presentation. Apparently, many people agreed that the award was well earned.

To develop my people, I liked to give assignments in terms of objectives, and let the men figure out the best way to do the job. Some men could not take this kind of supervision and usually left, but I think the good ones thrived. As a result, the department became the best management school in the company. Fourteen members of the department went on to become vice presidents of Grumman, or left Grumman to become presidents or vice presidents of other companies. No other department at Grumman has this kind of a record.

THE PRESIDENTIAL ADVISORY BOARD
ON APOLLO RELIABILITY

Concerns About Apollo Reliability

In the first stages of the Apollo design, a major management concern was the reliability of the system, that is the probability of success of the launch, flight, and retrieval provisions. The President of the United States appointed an Advisory Board to investigate and evaluate the reliability of the Apollo system. The Board consisted of the most eminent scientists that could be found in the United States.

The Board Comes To Grumman

The Board notified the Grumman Aerospace Corporation that they were coming to visit for two days to discuss the Lunar Module. As Director of Reliability for the Lunar Module, it was my job to prepare the Grumman position and give the presentation. For a two day meeting, I had to prepare for four sessions, and I figured that we could discuss five slides per session. I prepared 20 slides.

The Meeting Begins

The Board arrived on schedule. The meeting was held in Grumman's best conference room.

The first slide showed the configuration of the Lunar Module. The presentation elicited no comment.

The second slide showed the Lunar Module on the surface of the moon, one leg compressed, resting on a four foot rock. The room exploded. "Where did that rock come from?" "Why is the rock four foot high?" A million questions, everybody shouting at the same time.

At that time no probes had yet been landed on the moon, and nobody knew what the surface of the moon was like. Grumman had studied the problem thoroughly, and had made a number of assumptions that NASA had approved.

As soon as I could get a word in edgewise, I explained that the Lunar Module pilot could be expected to look for a smooth surface to land on. But at this time, we did not know what the moon surface was like, so we had to make provisions to allow the pilot to land on an unfriendly surface, including a deep layer of dust or a rough terrain. We were designing the landing gear for the worst, reasonably possible case. We hoped the pilot would find a spot where the rocks were less than four feet high. We established the design conditions for the landing gear so that if one leg hit a four foot rock, it would retract and the Lunar Module would not turn over.

The LM was also equipped with a probe that extended some three feet below the landing gear. If the landing area were covered by a layer of dust that could be blown up by the engine jet on landing and obstruct the pilot's vision, the probe would touch the ground before the landing gear and shut off the engine. (This actually happened on two LM moon landings.)

The Moon Surface Problem

The Board members did not want to listen to me. They wanted to discuss the surface of the moon. If you hold a sphere, like an orange, in a dark room and shine a flash light on it, the reflected light will be brightest at the center of the orange. The reflected light will gradually fade as you approach the side of the orange. The reflected light from the moon, however, is uniform over its entire surface, as if the moon were a disc. Each man on the Board had his own theory of why this was so. I just leaned on the lectern and smiled while the discussion went on, hot and heavy.

At lunch time I announced that it was time to eat. They quit their discussion, but started up again as soon as they sat down for lunch. They continued when we got back to the conference room. They kept it up until quitting time.

They were taken to a local motel for dinner and for the night. They continued their discussion into the night without any interference from Grumman.

The Second Day

The next day, I tried to say something, but was overruled by the Chairman of the Board. They continued their discussion, hot and heavy. The second day was a repeat of the first. My second slide, the one showing one leg of the Lunar Module on a four foot rock, was still on the screen. Grumman management was having nightmares.

I finally announced quitting time. The faces of Grumman management personnel reflected deadly gloom and doom.

The Board Findings

The Chairman of the Presidential Advisory Board took my place at the lectern with a happy face. He announced that this had been the most interesting, stimulating, educational, and rewarding meeting the Board had ever held. He thanked Grumman for its gracious hospitality He said that Grumman's approach to the design of the Lunar Module landing gear, with one foot on a four foot rock, was remarkable and an indication that, with this philosophy, they could rely on Grumman to produce a reliable manned space vehicle. Obviously, the Board had had a real good time.

It was unbelievable. Grumman personnel could not believe their ears.

I thanked the Chairman for his kind remarks, and bade the Board farewell.

Scientists and Engineers

The President of the United States does not know the difference between scientists and engineers.

Scientists struggle to discover the nature of things, their goal is to create new knowledge. By their very nature as scientists, the members of the Apollo Advisory Board were eager to discover what the surface of the moon was like. Each one dreamed of being the first to present a paper, at the New York Academy of Sciences or similar international association, describing to the world scientific community, what the surface of the moon is like. That was a first class challenge for them. The final output of the work of a scientist is a book.

Engineers use knowledge to create things that people can use. Their final product is a useful thing or procedure.

A scientist is no more qualified to evaluate the reliability of the Lunar Module than a good physician, lawyer, clergyman, or real estate broker. It is a job for an engineer.

It was just a stroke of dumb luck that the Board gave the President of the United States such a glowing report about Grumman's capabilities and progress.

CLEAN ROOMS

Final assembly of space craft is performed in "clean rooms," far cleaner than any hospital operating room. Clean air is fed in on one side of the room, and exhausted on the other, assuring a constant supply of clean air. Working personnel enter the room through an air lock, wash their hands and faces and don smocks covering their clothes and heads, and put on special boots. All components not manufactured in clean facilities are thoroughly cleaned before delivery to the assembly clean rooms.

The requirement for clean rooms was a new one for space programs. The clean room for the OAO had been a small affair, since each OAO had been assembled in sequence, and cleaning of components was done in a number of smaller converted rooms.

Because of the size of the LM, and a contract calling for 14 units, the clean room became a major project in designing our new building. The final clean room accommodated six assemblies that could be seen in various stages of assembly. The room was immense, about a city block long, a third of a block wide, and almost three stories high. Along the outside top edge of one of the long sides was a walkway from which the assembly operations could be viewed. This walkway was the most popular and interesting stop for any special visitors to the plant. The enormous room was painted white, brightly lighted, and strikes you with the impression of being antiseptically clean. You could see far below little white garbed, unearthly figures busily carrying parts to and fro and up the latters and installing them on the LM. The LM at one end of the room was almost completely assembled, while the one at the other end was just a skeleton. It was one of the most fantastic and futuristic sights on earth. I suppose that for many viewers it was the experience of a lifetime.

The man in charge of the clean rooms was an engineer and a long time friend of mine. At a conference some time in the past, it had been decided that he should be in charge of the clean room program. However, he found that the engineering department did not recognized clean rooms as being within its jurisdiction. He went to other departments, such as Manufacturing, Tooling, Facilities, looking for a home, nobody had a place or provision for clean rooms. Desperate, he finally came to see me and asked, are not clean rooms necessary to achieve reliability? I said "Sure," and set him up. After that, he went around announcing that he worked for me. He had no further trouble with his standing in the company and did a terrific job.

SIMULATORS

The use of simulators is another unique feature of air and space engineering that I found fascinating.

Simulators have been used for many years in the aircraft industry. Most simulators are a representation of an airplane cockpit. The controls are the same as on an airplane, and the visual, sound, and motion reactions are the same a pilot would experience on a real airplane. Most simulators are used for flight training, but at Grumman, they were also used to check out proposed design features.

Space simulators expanded the applications of aircraft simulators. We had two big space simulators, a LM landing simulator and a Rover simulator. The LM landing simulator was a real monster, over two stories high. You had to climb a long steep set of stairs to get to a reproduction of the LM cockpit that included all flight controls. Standing in the pilot's position, and looking out the window, you could see the vast moonscape, including your possible landing area. Several types of moonscapes could be selected. The controls let you fly over the moonscape at about several hundred feet altitude, select a landing site and land the LM where you wanted to.

The LM landing simulator was used to train astronauts to land on the moon.   As the astronauts became more skillful, they made suggestions for improving the simulator.   As soon as the improvements were incorporated, the astronauts' skills improved some more, and they had more suggestions for simulator improvements. This leapfrogging operation went on until the actual moon landing took place.   The astronauts were well trained in this simulator to   land on the moon.   The moon landings were all accomplished without the slightest difficulty.

The LM landing simulator cockpit was small and not a good place to take a visitor.   Only astronauts and special official visitors were allowed in the LM cockpit.

The Rover simulator took up the area of a large room and consisted of a small scale representation of various typical moonscapes. The Rover was a small four wheeled vehicle that responded by remote control to a control station at one edge of the moonscape and could be driven all over the moonscape. Because of the distance between the earth and the moon, a radio signal from the earth to the moon takes 1.5 seconds. When you issue a command to the Rover, it takes three seconds before you receive the notice that it has responded. If the Rover were headed towards an obstruction, you had to command it to turn three seconds before it got there. It sounds easy, but it is not.

The Rover simulator was one of our favorite exhibits, we showed it to all our visitors. They always had a good time.

Years later I learned that the Aeronautics Department of the Technical University of Berlin had installed a three second delay in their Link simulator that they used to train student pilots.   They found that by using the three second delay, they forced the student to expand his perception and that they could train a pilot in less than half the time that was required with conventional devices. There was no problem when transferring a pilot from a simulator to the real airplane.   I thought that this was a remarkable advance that would revolutionize pilot training, but I have not heard of any follow up. I have to assume that the cost of the simulator is too high and costs more than the time saved in training.

SPECIAL ASSISTANT TO THE VICE PRESIDENT

After some three years as Director of LM Reliability, the design and testing practices had become well established and supervision had become routine. I began to feel useless.   I asked Gavin for reassignment to engineering to a responsible job where I could design something useful.

Gavin agreed that the LM reliability function was progressing well and that I could be released. However, he did not want to let me leave. He suggested that I become his Special Assistant, he could see a lot of things that I could do that would save him time and make life easier for him. For example, I could attend, in his place, some of the many meetings that he had to attend, and then let him know if anything happened that he should know about.

There always seemed to be a number of high level Government, industry, or NASA consulting personnel who just had to talk to him personally, and such interviews often required travel. I could save him a lot of time if I took his place at some of these interviews.

One of Gavin's main concerns was that a million unique, specially designed parts from 3000 sources had to be brought together on time and fit together the first time that they were assembled. If any one of these million parts did not arrive on time or did not fit right, depending on its criticality, it might cause anything from an inconvenience to a mission delay. The associated paperwork was a nightmare. He wanted me to visit selected suppliers and spot check that the paper work correctly reflected the actual status of the hardware development.

Although this was not the kind of job that I wanted, I realized that Gavin needed help. I accepted the position of Special Assistant to the Vice President.

PLANNING AND SCHEDULING (P&S)

If I was to help Gavin, I had to acquaint myself with the operations of his office. One big operation was Planning and Scheduling (P&S).

All department heads had to do P&S for their own departments. This was a relatively small operation and we all used the manual Gnatt charts that are still being used for small jobs today.

With the introduction of the computer, a new system became available for large jobs, the "PERT" (performance, evaluation, and review technique) system. It enjoyed universal popularity. The system accepted data starting with the lowest level of the Work Breakdown Structure (WBS). The starting and completion points of work elements were called "events." PERT arranged events over time such that either *cost* (*manpower*) or *time consumed* was a minimum.

Gavin was an expert on PERT. He had been a member of his local school board when they built a new high school. He managed the job using PERT. The high school was finished many months ahead of schedule and several million dollars below estimated cost. Gavin recognized PERT as a valuable management tool.

The LM program encompassed 80000 events. The largest computers that Gavin could find in those days were at NASA and had a capacity of processing 20000 events. The 80000 LM events were separated into four 20000 event programs, and the interface between these smaller programs was to be done by hand. It did not work. The hand operation could not keep up with the computers.

Something had to be done, and very quickly. A new giant P&S sheet was developed, using engineering drawing vellums, three by twelve feet in size. Each line across of the short span of the sheet contained the P&S data for a work element of the WBS, starting at the lowest level, by part number. There were three lines per inch, or almost 432 lines per twelve foot sheet. To track a million parts, some 2315 sheets were needed.

The operation took place in a very large room equipped with three by twelve foot engineering drawing tables. The P&S sheets had lines the long way, and a column the short way for each item on a standard P&S sheet, indicating the status of each work element. A man could run his finger along a long line and ascertain that all 432 items on the sheet were on schedule. If he noticed a discrepancy, he could take corrective action himself, or notify the cognizant engineer, who could take corrective action or notify the Program Manager, Bob Mullaney, who reported to Gavin.

I talked with a number of P&S operators and found them to be very conscientious and aware of their awesome responsibility. Still, I could see why Gavin was worried.

CAPPY'S PARTY

On a nice sunny summer afternoon, the Cappy's invited a number of their friends, including Eleanor and myself, to a delightful party around their swimming pool in their back yard. Among their guests were Mr and Mrs Shorty who lived two houses down the block from the Cappys. I have mentioned Shorty before, he was the Chief Production Engineer at Grumman. Everything was very civilized and pleasant until Shorty saw me across the swimming pool. His face turned purple, he pointed at me with his outstretched arm, and yelled at me at the top of his voice: "RELIABILITY - RELIABILITY! ALL THAT GUY CAN TALK ABOUT IS RELIABILITY-- RELIABILITY!"

A party in Cappy's back yard is no place for such an emotional, one-sided technical discussion. Eleanor and I quickly found Mr and Mrs Cappy and regretfully took our leave.

I wondered what had brought on this outburst, I had not talked or dealt with Shorty's people for years, and I had been out of the "reliability field" for a long time. I realized that Shorty was peeved because I had made my way at Grumman without his "help," but that was not enough to justify such an outburst. The shout of "Reliability" indicated that it must have had something to do with work. Shorty insisted on being the absolute master of his domain and must have had a conflict with the independent reliability group .... and lost!

I can remember when many years ago Shorty walked through the engineering department roaring his head off because the Navy insisted in installing an additional radio in the F4-F "Wildcat." He could not see the use of putting a radio in a space that could be used for more ammunition. Shorty was convinced that he knew more about how a fighter aircraft should be equipped than the men who flew and fought with them. I knew Shorty well and could remember many of the goofs that he had pulled over the years.

I could visualize where today Shorty was unwilling to comply with some futuristic Navy specification. The reliability people who I had trained were possibly the only ones who would stand up to him. They might have told him that the Navy pays good money for a product that complies with Navy specifications, and their job is to assure a reliable and conforming product. That would really have gotten under Shorty's skin.

I trained my reliability people well.

JACK OF ALL TRADES

I did everything I could to make life easier for Gavin, especially time consuming jobs, like sitting in on meetings. Much of the work was straightening out problems with outside organizations. I maintained contact with some top NASA officials, as well as with the management of subcontractors and suppliers.

I went to Washington once in Gavin's place to listen to a top NASA management consultant tell me that this country had the technical capability to successfully build and conduct the Apollo Program. His basic concern was, did we have the management capability, the will, and the discipline to put together such a vast and tremendous task.

I told him about technical specifications, design and weight control, reliability control, test integration and demonstration procedures reporting and government monitoring procedures, planning and scheduling, quality control, and all the other bottom level procedures that were being used.

He was surprised. He had never heard of any of these procedures. I assured him that the management of the Apollo Program was in good hands.

This visit made me aware that the specialized management tools that we were using were known only to a very small part of the engineering design community. People outside our community, like this top NASA management consultant, had no means of learning about our methods and capabilities. I further decided that these procedures, that enabled us to get to the moon, constituted a national treasure that should not get lost. I decided to write a book recording our methods, to make their existence known to the general public and future generations. I started out on an outline of the book as soon as I got home.

Gavin was somewhat uncomfortable with so many new suppliers and he wanted me to visit as many critical suppliers as I could, just to see how they were doing. I felt I had to have a system for grading them. There were two areas I had to look at, management and production.

How do you walk into a strange, large manufacturing plant and within an hour or so, evaluate it's management? I decided that the *time* it takes a management team to organize itself and solve a problem is a measure of its effectiveness.

To evaluate production effectiveness, I decided to stick to the *smallest possible piece-parts* and associated manufacturing processes that I could understand. I knew enough about integration testing to beware of any assemblies where they might try to bamboozle me with big words not in my vocabulary.

Before visiting a plant, I would talk with the cognizant engineer and have him select a small part that was 100% manufactured in the plant that I was going to visit. I would note the part number.

Arriving at a plant at eight o'clock, I would ask to see the drawing of which I had the part number. They don't show drawings to just anybody, and to show me that drawing required a management decision somewhere. I figured that the amount of *time* that it took to get me that drawing was a measure of the effectiveness of their management. In a few places, I received the drawing within ten minutes, at a few others it took over four hours. All the rest were somewhere in between. During my wait, I was subject to all kinds of divisive tactics, namely "important" things that they had to show me, but I stood fast and waited for the drawing.

When the drawing came, I studied the signature block, identified the designer, and asked to go see him at his work station. I would be taken into the engineering department and introduced to the designer. I had a prepared list of questions regarding the function of the part, what other options had been considered, material selection, stresses, tests, etc, etc. The designer would not know all the answers and would have to call the assembly engineer, the manufacturing engineer, the quality control man, the test engineer, the P&S man, and others, until I had a representative production team around the designer's board. I watched them carefully to see how they interacted (or did not interact.)

After this little show, I asked to see a used Route Card for this part, and then asked to go to Route Card Station No 1. I was taken to the shop to the right machine and introduced to the operator. I showed him the drawing and asked him to tell me what operations he had performed. We discussed any unusual aspects of his operation. I then asked to speak to the inspector at that station and asked him to describe his functions. He would do so. I said that his inspection operations should be specified in a manual that should be easily accessible. Where is the manual? In some places, there was a little bookcase around the corner with all the manuals. Sometimes the manuals were kept in the foreman's office. In other places, I was told that they took up too much space in the shop and were somewhere up in the attic. In a good number of shops, I was asked, "What Manuals?"

I then proceeded to to Station No. 2, 3, etc. until I finished all the Stations on the Route Card. On my way, there were always people who wanted to distract me and show me something important that the company was developing. I stuck to my tour. These parts that I was tracking were all intended to be used in a clean room. I inspected how they were handled, packed, and stored for shipment.

After my plant tour, I was ready to talk to management and was shown into a board room which always had on display a large flow chart of the company's operation. In practically all the companies that I visited, the flow chart never agreed completely with what I had observed on my tour of the shop.

In one shop I visited, the actual managers were the Air Force Inspector and the Grumman Representative. They made all management decisions and nothing was done in the plant unless they approved it. They built a fine product. Normally, I would never voice an opinion at a plant that I was visiting. I wrote a report. If action was necessary, Gavin would take corrective action through his liaison officers. With some 3000 suppliers located all over the country, I spent a lot of time trying to cover all 48 states.

Large US Government contracts have to be split up between many states to keep as many Congressmen as possible happy. Grumman had suppliers in every state. Sometimes, I would plan to go to a location where there were at least five suppliers in proximity so that in a week, I could spend one day at each. I tried to keep good notes during my visit, and after my visit, I would go directly to my motel room. I had a small tape recorder, and referring to my notes, I would dictate my observations while they were still fresh in my mind. The next morning, I would airmail the tape to Grumman, where on arrival, it would be typed and Gavin would read it. I could then forget all about that visit and approach the next plant with a clear mind.

I changed my agenda whenever the trip had a special purpose. Gavin liked to go witness important tests. I would go on a plant visit some three weeks ahead of time, survey the layout, get a description of the test procedure and test plan. Gavin would arrive well informed, able to ask the right questions and know what to look for. He always told me that he appreciated this help.

A problem arose of how to pay some suppliers.   The US Government has a standard way of paying for supplies. Funds are appropriated by the Congress by "line items." By law, funds appropriated for a line item must be spent for that line item and for nothing else.   In contracts for supplies, the line items are broken down into "work packages" of the Work Breakdown Structure (WBS). The system assures that the money is spent on its intended purpose, and that the Government does not get charged twice for the same supplies.

A number of specialized high-tech LM suppliers had never had a government contract before and their accountants had designed an accounting system that best helped them to manage their operations. For example, at Grumman, flight test was a high cost operation, in my day it cost $10000 an hour. One Grumman accounting system was designed so management could keep close track of flight test and other high cost operations. The Navy, nevertheless, paid its bills by work package, several of which contained flight testing. This system required Grumman to keep two sets of books.

I visited these suppliers and met with their accountants. Everybody was friendly, but nobody wanted to keep two sets of books. Finally, after much talking, their accountants would set up a temporary second set of books for the LM operation.

GUEST INSPECTOR

A group of us were having lunch at a BIMRAB meeting, when I told them how I went through a plant to evaluate its operation. One of the men at the table, a Vice President of one of America's foremost electronic manufacturers, asked me if I would like to go through his plant and give him an evaluation. I said I would like to, and the next time I was in the vicinity of his plant, I called him up.

On arrival at the plant, my friend gave me a small part and a used route card. He said that he would introduce me to the workers at the beginning of the route, but then I should follow the route card by myself. He gave me a name tag and said I could go anywhere I wanted to in the plant. At noon, I should come to his office, and we would have lunch. After lunch, I could continue my tour and   then come and give him my report before quitting time.

My friend introduced me to the workers at the first station of the route card and I started asking them my list of questions. My friend did not leave, as he intended, he discovered that he was interested in the answers to my questions. In fact, he stayed with me all day. When I was through, he said that this was most revealing and interesting tour he had ever had of his own plant.

I think that what he had not known was that the competence of departments varied throughout the plant. Some departments excelled in their work and upheld the reputation of the company. Others were just riding along, concerned with not making waves.

I did not have to give my friend any evaluation. He realized what he had to do to improve his company.

THE MAKING OF A BOOK

Ever since organizing the Aerospace Reliability and Maintainability Conference series in 1963, I had maintained close personal contact with engineering personnel at Kennedy Space Center, Florida (KSC). First there was Bob Body, Chief Reliability Engineer, one of those top level people who left the program right after the initial excitement was over. He went to Australia and was replaced by Otto Fedor, who became my lifelong friend.

I told Fedor about the book I was writing entitled: *Advanced Systems Development Management*. He was very interested and followed my progress carefully. As soon as I had completed my table of contents and a set of notes for each section, he invited me to come to KSC and give a course on the book. He suggested that I stay a week (five days) and give a four hour lecture every morning. In the afternoon, I could be available for personal discussions with people that had problems, and attend some meetings that might be of interest. This was an extraordinary opportunity to get my material reviewed by experts, and I jumped to accept Fedor's invitation.

My lectures worked out real well. I could talk at length from my notes. I filled out the four hours every morning without any trouble. KSC organized a class of thirty men. They were not the same thirty individuals every day, but there was always thirty men in the class. There was nobody in the class who had any concept of the total scope of the book, but on the other hand, there was always at least one expert on every single topic in the book. The class was interested in the material and we had lots of lively discussions. They gave me many good tips. It was as excellent an expert review as I could have hoped for. I felt reassured that my total presentation was complete.

In the afternoon, I walked around the office, acting like a supervisor, talking to individuals here and there and helping them when I could. I attended a number of meetings that Fedor thought would interest me. One such session was an FMECA meeting, where it was determined that it was unacceptable to have a power failure during a launch. The solution was to get a second power company in another part of the country to provide a second source of power.

I drove to Florida and took Eleanor along. It was August, and it was HOT, close to 100 degrees! I worked in an air conditioned building and did not feel the heat, but when Eleanor left our motel room, she had to hurry from one air conditioned store to another. After two days, she had had enough. When I came back to the Motel in the evening after work, we would go to the beautiful beach just outside our door.

Fedor taught a number of courses at the Florida Institute of Technology. After its publication, he used my book in his classes for many years until his retirement.

THE SEMI-DEMISE OF COMPANY-X

Whenever Gavin or I smelled a rat somewhere, I would be sent there to investigate.   One day, Gavin stuck his head in the door of my office and said: "Why don't you go to Company-X tomorrow and see how they are doing?"

Company-X was one of the most prominent manufacturers of electronic and electrical equipment in the world. Its trademark was plastered all over billboards across America. It had an excellent reputation and its name was a household word in all except the poorest homes in America. To evaluate such a large, famous and successful international business organization in a day's time was, to put it mildly, an interesting assignment. Luckily, I had developed the tools to do just that.

Company-X was supplying the exterior radar for the LM. I knew that Gavin's secretary would call them and tell them that I was coming. All I had to do was to show up there at eight o'clock.

I arrived on time and they had the red carpet laid out. I was shown to a large conference room where top management was already assembled. They had worked hard all night to put on a good show for me. There was a long table in the middle of the room, with the president of Company-X at one end, resplendent in his $1000 hand made suit.   Along either side of the table, in descending order, were vice presidents in their $800, $700 and $600 hand made suits. Individuals of lesser rank sat around the four walls. I was shown to the seat at the bottom of the table, where I sat in my best $50 department store suit.

A beautiful model of the LM radar set was placed in the middle of the table. The major engineering drawings of the set were hung along the top of the four walls of the room.

I was given a beautifully printed agenda for the day. The president explained that in the morning we would have four presentations explaining some of the drawings that were hung on the wall. Then we would go to lunch at a restaurant down the street, that was really one of the best restaurants in the country. We would then come back and finish discussing the drawings.

The president said that he was confident that after this presentation, I would be fully informed on the status of the program and pleased that I had come.

I thanked him for his remarks, but said that my job required me to be already acquainted with the information in his proposed presentation. I had seen this model of the radar, and had reviewed in detail all the drawings hung on the walls. In fact, I said laughingly, I probably could do an adequate job myself, of giving the presentation that he proposed.

In line with my personal principle of always starting out an investigation at the lowest possible level of the WBS, I stated that I was not smart enough to conduct an investigation starting at the top level of assembly. I had to start at the bottom with the smallest possible part. I invited the gentlemen at the table to pick out a small piece-part of the radar that we could all talk about.

They just sat there and glared at me. I said, if nobody wants to pick a part, I would do so. I noticed that the antenna disc was mounted on an arm that, in turn, was mounted on other moving struts that were hinged on four bearings such that the antenna could move through 360 degrees horizontally and 180 degrees vertically. I asked, what are the design requirements for this bearing, and how was it selected? (I knew a lot about bearings, I had designed several while a member of the power operated flight control group.) I said that if they did not like my selection of a bearing, please pick something else.

Deep silence in the room. You could hear a pin drop.

I said: "Come on, gentlemen, that bearing was selected by somebody who is now in this building. Let's find him and get him in here to tell us his story!"

After some more prodding, the president mentioned a name, and that man was summoned.

A man came in, well dressed in a $300 suit. I explained what I wanted, somebody who knew what were the design requirements for this bearing, and how was the bearing selected. He had no idea, but recommended another man who might know.

Two more men came in one after the other, with the same result. There was a long waiting period between appearances. The president announced that it was time to go to lunch.

I said that we had no time to go to lunch. We had already wasted too much time in trying to find the man who had selected the bearing for the radar. This man was in this building, it was difficult to understand why he could not be found. I was going to stay here until the man was found. (My evaluation depended now on how long it took for their top management team to identify the individual who had selected the bearing supporting the radar antenna disc.)

I said that this morning, while coming here, I had noticed a McDonald's down the block. I suggested that we send somebody over there to get us some hamburgers and drinks that we could consume here while we were waiting. I would like a quarter pounder and a coke.

The president called in a man who took our orders and went out to get them. I thought it was very funny to see all these extremely well dressed gentlemen sitting around the table eating hamburgers with their hands. They could have made other arrangements for lunch. They had lunch facilities in the plant. The quick way that they accepted my suggestion to go to McDonald's, without considering any other viable options, did not speak well for the way that they made management decisions.

An hour or so after our lunch, a nervous man in shirt sleeves and tie came in. The radar set was designed in his shop. He did not know who had selected the bearing, but it was one of his men.

After interviewing two more engineering supervisors one after the other, a nervous young man came in, wearing a short sleeve shirt with open collar, carrying a three inch thick file. I asked him if he had selected the bearing holding the radar antenna disc, and he said that he thought so. He started to leaf through his file, and after some time, he found what he was looking for. Referring to his file, he said yes, he had selected this bearing. I asked him, what were the design requirements. He said that their major concern had been complying with the extremely high reliability requirements. They had searched high and low until they found a bearing with an operational history of no failures. Then they improved the material of which it was made. I asked: "You mean, you built the bearing out of the most expensive, suitable materials your could buy?"

He looked at me and said "Yes."

I told him that when I first looked at the radar, I felt as if the bearings had been taken off a five ton truck. He laughed and admitted that it looks like that. I thanked him kindly for his information and dismissed him.

I then turned to the president and told him that the 32000 pound allowance for the LM was determined by the booster capability of 102000 pounds for the Apollo that allowed 70000 pounds for the Command and Service Modules. If the LM is overweight, the booster cannot fling it into a trajectory to the moon. There is absolutely no give on the LM weight allowance.

The 32000 pounds have not been enough to build the LM by standard engineering methods. The design of the LM has been a ongoing constant battle to keep the weight down. Grumman will spend $100 on machining or other manufacturing process to save an ounce.

The weight growth factor on the Apollo is 1 to 800, that is, every additional pound on the LM results in 800 pounds on Apollo take-off weight. I estimate Company-X's four radar bearings to be at least one pound each overweight, increasing the Apollo take-off weight by 4 x 800 = 3200 pounds. I find this situation to be unacceptable.

I noticed that it was now time for me to go home. I expressed my regrets that I could not investigate other radar elements, but just looking at the model, I could see that it has not been designed for minimum weight.

The president walked me to the door. He said that nobody here had ever asked such questions as I had asked today.

In the morning, I always tried to get to my office before Gavin came in. The next morning, he was passing my office when he stuck his head in and asked: "How is Company-X doing?"

My complete report on my visit consisted of the remark:"Joe, those guys just don't know what the hell they are doing!"

Gavin made a long face and said: "Oooooooooooh!"

He went to his office, picked up the phone and organized a team to go to Company-X and determine the status of work on each work package of our contract. The team came back with a verdict of "unsatisfactory" in every category.

Gavin took this report to NASA who conducted their own investigation. As a result of their negative findings, NASA paid Company-X $10 million to buy back all of its contracts. NASA further prohibited Company-X from ever indicating in any way that it had made any contribution to a NASA program.

This nearly killed the great Company-X. Its famous trademark disappeared from the American landscape. The name of Company-X is today no longer a household word in America.

I was personally unhappy with this result. Company-X had a fine reliability group and all the resources to build a fine LM radar. The Reliability Director was a retired US Army general who I knew and liked, and who was very competent. I had been proud to co-author several technical reliability papers with the Chief Reliability Engineer of Company-X, who I regarded as a friend.

As I pointed out on pages 217/218, Klemin in the late twenties had recognized that new aeronautical requirements for minimum weight and design control dictated a vast new level of engineering. Company-X had not learned that the tools required to develop a successful commercial product were inadequate to develop an aeronautical product. As was the case with many other US companies, the Company-X management did not understand anything about reliability technology and the reliability department was merely a public relations front and had no influence on product design.

SHORTY TAKES COMMAND

Gavin's space activities in their own grand new building were somewhat isolated from the rest of the Grumman Corporation. The new plant was a basic design and development (test) facility with limited production capability. The LM contract called for fourteen copies, and to accommodate this quantity of production, the production facilities in other parts of the company had to be utilized.

Gavin had tried his utmost to engage other production facilities in the company, but they simply would not respond. Production facilities were controlled by Shorty, Vice President Production, who ruled with an iron hand. It finally occurred to Gavin that if he wanted to make use of the company's production facilities, he had to invite Shorty to join his LM team. Gavin did this, and Shorty graciously agreed to assign the necessary facilities to LM production.

One of Shorty's major managements tools was the Eight O'clock Stand Up Meeting. It was stand-up so nobody would become too comfortable sitting down. The meeting took place every working morning in Gavin's office. Each group leader reported briefly what he had accomplished yesterday, what he was going to do today, that he had all the resources that he needed to do the intended job, and that he foresaw no other problems. If a group leader did not have all that he needed, immediate arrangements were made to provide him with what he required. Every effort was made to conclude the meeting in half an hour. I was present when the very first such meeting was assembled. Shorty saw me and yelled at the top of his voice:

"What the hell are you doing here?"

I answered: "I work here!"

Shorty pointed to the door with his outstretched arm and shouted:

"Get out !"

I left quietly and went to my office next door. I realized that Gavin needed Shorty more that he needed me, and that the project was not large enough to accommodate both Shorty and myself. I packed my belongings and went next door to see Cappy. He was sympathetic and said that he had a lot of engineering problems that I could do. He accepted me as his assistant. That was the end of my association with the LM.

The hard part of the job was done; the concept, the design, the selection of suppliers, the manufacturing. What was left to do was final assembly, putting all the pieces together. They went together like a dream, the first time! Never in the history of the Grumman Corporation had a major structure been assembled with such ease. The use of the interface drawings mentioned on page 326 really paid off.

APOLLO TOUCHES THE MOON

COUNTDOWN AND LIFT-OFF

People who are not intimately acquainted with Kennedy Space Center (KSC) cannot visualize the immensity of the massive structures that are on the facility. These are built for a special purpose, the assembly, test, and launch of large spacecraft, and there is nothing else like it in the world.

Casual visitors to KSC are shown a building in the far distance and told it is the Assembly Building. In the distance, it does not look very big. Visitors are not permitted any closer. There are underground hypergolic fuel storage facilities located throughout the property and most of the area is off limits to all except authorized personnel.

The Assembly Building is used for the final assembly of the space vehicle. The big boosters are mounted in a vertical take-off position on a giant special purpose flat top tractor. The spacecraft has to be hoisted up and installed on top of the boosters. This entire operation is enclosed in the giant Assembly Building, that is so big that it has its own weather system.

The tractor itself, a marvel of mechanical engineering, transports the space vehicle, assembled in a vertical position on the tractor's flat top, some three miles to the launch site. This distance must be maintained so the blast from the boosters on take off will not damage the Assembly Building. Top speed of the tractor is almost three miles an hour.

At the launch site, the tractor positions the space vehicle next to the launch tower. This tower is as high as the assembled space vehicle and contains an elevator that brings the astronauts up to the top where there is a gangway to the Command Module. The tower also supports the lines to fuel the tanks of the Apollo spacecraft, that are now high up above the ground.

At a safe distance from the launch site, that is, at a considerable distance, there is a viewers' grandstand for dignitaries. Behind and at both sides of the grandstand there are acres and acres of level fields where thousands upon thousands of people, many of them families with children, come and park their cars and wait to view the lift-off. Many bring picnic baskets and portable radios so that they can listen in on the commentary.

With the thousand and one things that can go wrong during a

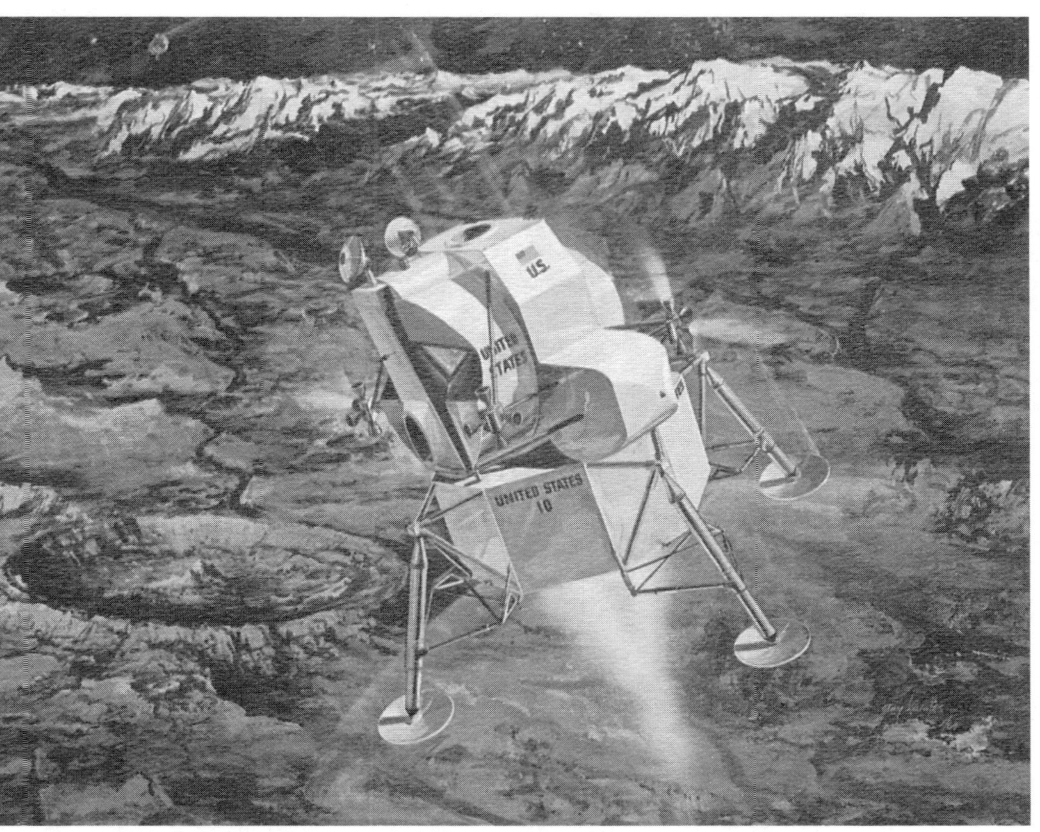

LM approaching the Lunar Surface

launch, and with the less than scientific weather forecasting, launches are sometimes delayed or postponed. The crowds are amazingly patient and come prepared. There is a carnival atmosphere and families camp around their cars and picnic, waiting for the main event. Arrangements are made for employees of KSC who are not engaged in launch operations, to witness the launch on television in the huge auditorium. You have to have a ticket to get in. The atmosphere in the auditorium is very festive, everybody is all excited. I was invited to witness such a take-off with Otto Fedor and his crew.

The countdown is the most solemn moment leading to lift-off, all activity and movement stops. You can hear a pin drop as the commentator intones "TEN...NINE...EIGHT...SEVEN...SIX...FIVE.. ..FOUR...THREE"(engine start, begin of engine roar).."TWO...LIFT-OFF!" You cannot hear the last two calls because of the overwhelming roar. The giant space vehicle starts to move upward, very slowly at first, then ever faster. All spectators think that now is the time to start applauding. You can see their arms moving wildly and that they are screaming with their mouths wide open, but you cannot hear anything above the roar of the space vehicle boosters. However, as the space vehicle ascends higher and higher, the roar of the engines decreases, until you cannot hear them all. You can still see the space vehicle as a point of light, that becomes smaller and smaller until it disappears in space.

The commentator announces that the fuel in the first stage boosters has been expended, and that the boosters have been ejected.

After a little while, the commentator announces that the fuel in the main boosters has been expended, and that the boosters have been ejected. **The Apollo is on its way to the moon !**

APOLLO TOUCHES THE MOON

On July 20, 1969, the two men in the Lunar Module (LM), Neil Armstrong and Edwin Aldrin, landed on the moon, emerged from their vehicle, planted the American flag, took pictures, wrote postcards, and walked around taking great big six-foot steps because of the low gravity on the moon. The whole world stopped for a moment, watched on television and applauded. That day, the whole world was united in spirit as never before.

On page 351 is an old NASA drawing of the "Lunar Orbit Rendezvous (LOR)" that I have described on page 315. This drawing was prepared before the Apollo contracts were awarded, and the names of the Apollo elements as shown were later changed as follows:

        Lunar Capsule became the Command Module
        Lunar Bug became the Lunar Module (LM)

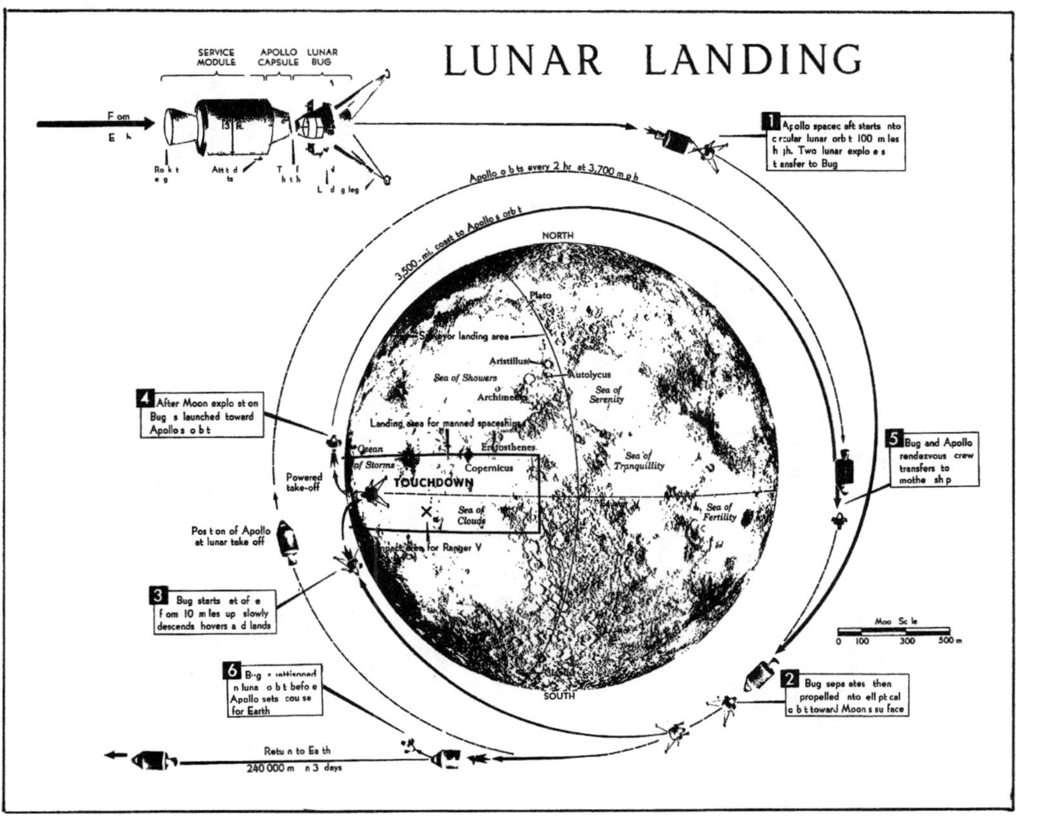
LUNAR LANDING
SERVICE MODULE
APOLLO CAPSULE
LUNAR BUG
From Earth
1 Apollo spacecraft starts into circular lunar orbit 100 miles high. Two lunar explorers transfer to Bug
Apollo orbits every 2 hr at 3,700 m.p.h.
3,500-mi. coast to Apollo's orbit
NORTH
Plato
Surveyor landing area
Aristillus
Autolycus
Sea of Showers
Archimedes
Sea of Serenity
Landing area for manned spaceship
Ocean of Storms
Eratosthenes
Copernicus
TOUCHDOWN
Sea of Tranquillity
Sea of Clouds
Sea of Fertility
Impact area for Ranger V
Powered take-off
Position of Apollo at lunar take off
SOUTH
4 After Moon exploration Bug is launched toward Apollo's orbit
5 Bug and Apollo rendezvous crew transfers to mother ship
3 Bug starts return from 10 miles up slowly descends hovers and lands
6 Bug is jettisoned in lunar orbit before Apollo sets course for Earth
2 Bug separates then propelled into elliptical orbit toward Moon's surface
Moon Scale
0   100   300   500 m
Return to Earth
240,000 m in 3 days
Scheme of the Lunar Orbit Rendezvous (LOR)

from the Command and Service Modules, and descends to the moon surface following Point (3), at TOUCHDOWN, see page 351 and 353. The LM is built in two parts, the lower half acts as a launch platform for the upper half that ascends to the moon orbit (4), see page 355, and rendezvouses with the Command and Service Modules (5). The LM is jettisoned in lunar orbit (6) and the Command and Service Modules "return to Earth" orbit in the lower left hand corner of the drawing.

The original cost estimate for this initial performance was $ 30 billion. We landed two men on the moon and brought them back safely to earth for $ 24 billion. Men worked on this project with exceptional dedication for long hours. Despite a long tradition of "robber barons" in this country, and the large sums of money involved, nobody got rich. This is unheard of for a large project involving so much money.

These statistics should help to put the Apollo program in perspective. This chapter only describes the observations of one man, looking through a tiny peephole at a gigantic spectacle of world wide proportions. Others will tell other stories. I hope, however, that by sharing my limited experience with others, I can help sustain the appreciation of the American contribution to the new Age of Space Exploration.

At the beginning of the program, it was known that this country had the technical capability to successfully build and conduct the Apollo program. The basic concern was, did we have the management capability, the will, and the discipline to put together such a tremendous task.

The personnel and commercial companies on this program rose to the challenge with a dedication beyond belief. Fierce commercial competitors worked together like the members of a champion football team, every one contributing his very best. Foreign observers who came to watch could not believe what they saw. Today, many Americans do not believe we did what we did.

Because of the weight limitation, the LM was the most carefully designed spacecraft in the world. As a result, it operated without a flaw. The American Flag planted on the moon will be there for a long time into the future.

One of the major decisions that the Apollo management had to make was whether or not to conduct the program on television. The Apollo project was not a sure thing. On page 316, I list the reliability requirements that were established for the design. It could at that time not be assumed that the reliability of the final product would equal or exceed this original specified design reliability

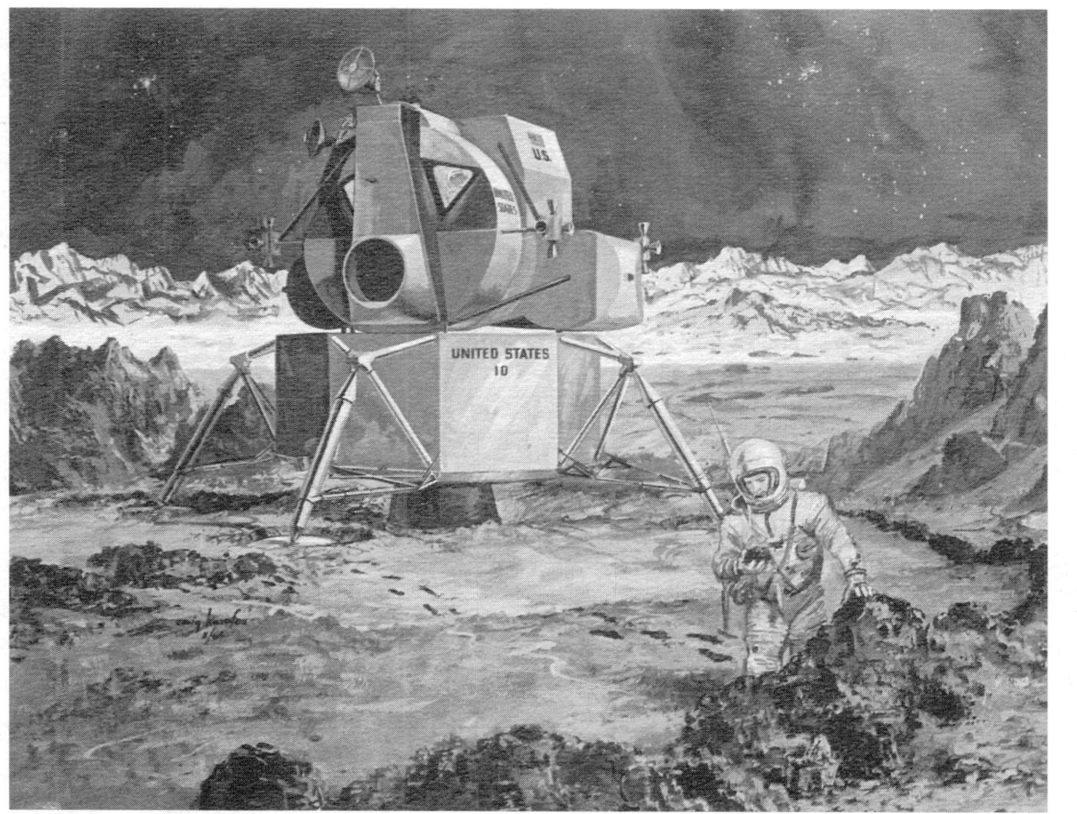

LM on the Lunar Surface; Astronaut collecting Lunar samples

requirement. Project management was faced with the problem that the Apollo flight might fail, however small that probability might be.

PROVISIONS FOR DISASTER

In the event of a disaster, when nothing more could be done to save the astronauts, Armstrong and Aldrin, radio communications with the moon would be cut off and the astronauts left either to die alone or to commit suicide. Plans were made for a clergyman to commend their souls to the "deepest of the deep" in the fashion of a burial at sea. President Nixon was to call on the "widows" to express condolences. His speech writer prepared the following short speech that he could deliver to the world:

Fate has ordained that the men who went to the moon to explore in peace will stay on the moon to rest in peace.

These brave men, Neil Armstrong and Edwin Aldrin, know that their is no hope for their recovery. But they know that there is hope for mankind in their sacrifice.

These two men are laying down their lives in mankind's most noble goal: the search for truth and understanding.

They will be mourned by their families and friends, they will be mourned by their nation, they will be mourned by the people of the world, they will be mourned by a Mother Earth that dared to send two of her sons into the unknown.

In their exploration, they stirred the people of the world to feel as one; in their sacrifice, they bind more tightly the brotherhood of man.

In ancient times, men looked at the stars and saw their heroes in the constellations. In modern times, we do much the same thing, but our heroes are epic men of flesh and blood.

Others will follow, and surely find their way home. Man's search will not be denied. But these men were the first, and they will remain the foremost in our hearts.

For every human being who looks up at the moon in the nights to come will know that there is some corner of another world that is forever mankind.

These preparations for an unlikely but possible disaster serve as a reminder of how risky was the voyage to the moon. The men in charge had extraordinary courage, knowing the risks, to put the show on world-wide television.

THE POWER OF TELEVISION

Several of my old school friends in Germany sent me telegrams congratulating the United States for the successful landing of men on the moon. .Later, in talking to them in person about the landing on

Upper half of the LM returning to the orbiting Command and Service Modules

the moon, they all used the pronoun "we" as if they had been participants. In fact, television made the peoples of the world feel as active participants. It was amazing how easily everyone throughout the world accepted the leadership of the United States.

NASA'S MOST SUCCESSFUL FAILURE

On the next to last planned trip to the moon, Apollo 13 was approaching the moon when the fuel cells in the Service Module exploded, leaving the Command Module without power. This was the biggest emergency that NASA had ever faced, and it called for the highest level of NASA action. After much to-do, level heads prevailed and it was decided to use the LM as a "life boat" to tow the Command and Service Modules back to Earth orbit. The big unknown was, did the LM have the required power reserves to do the job.

The entire procedure was televised. Everything was done openly in the eyes of the world. The astronauts were instructed in detail, what switches to turn off to conserve power. The available power reserves were continuously checked. It was high drama with the world glued to its television sets, dutiful biting its fingernails.

The world community uttered a great sigh of relief as the LM deposited the Command Module in Earth Orbit, from where it could make a standard reentry through the atmosphere and landing on Earth. Luckily, the power available in the LM had been just enough to do the job.

Or was it just luck?

My reliability plan provided that every level of assembly be subjected to a Failure Mode, Effect and Criticality Analysis (FEMCA). In this process, every element of a system is assumed to fail in turn. For every such failure, it is determined, what provisions are needed to prevent system breakdown. Such an analysis was made, assuming that the Command and Service Module became inoperative between Earth and moon orbits. The provision that was made to rescue the disabled Command Module was to use the LM as a life-boat to tow the Command Module back to Earth orbit. Due to weight limitations, just enough power reserves were incorporated in the LM so it could do the job. This was all written up in a report and submitted to NASA for approval at the time. But who reads reports submitted several years ago? Nevertheless, NASA officials acted in an emergency exactly as the LM designers assumed that they would. (See page 326).

Grumman sent North American a bill for $312,421.24 for towing the Command and Space Modules from Lunar Orbit back to Earth Orbit, see page 359. The bill was signed by Lew Evans, President of Grumman. The bill was addressed to be delivered on the USS Iwo

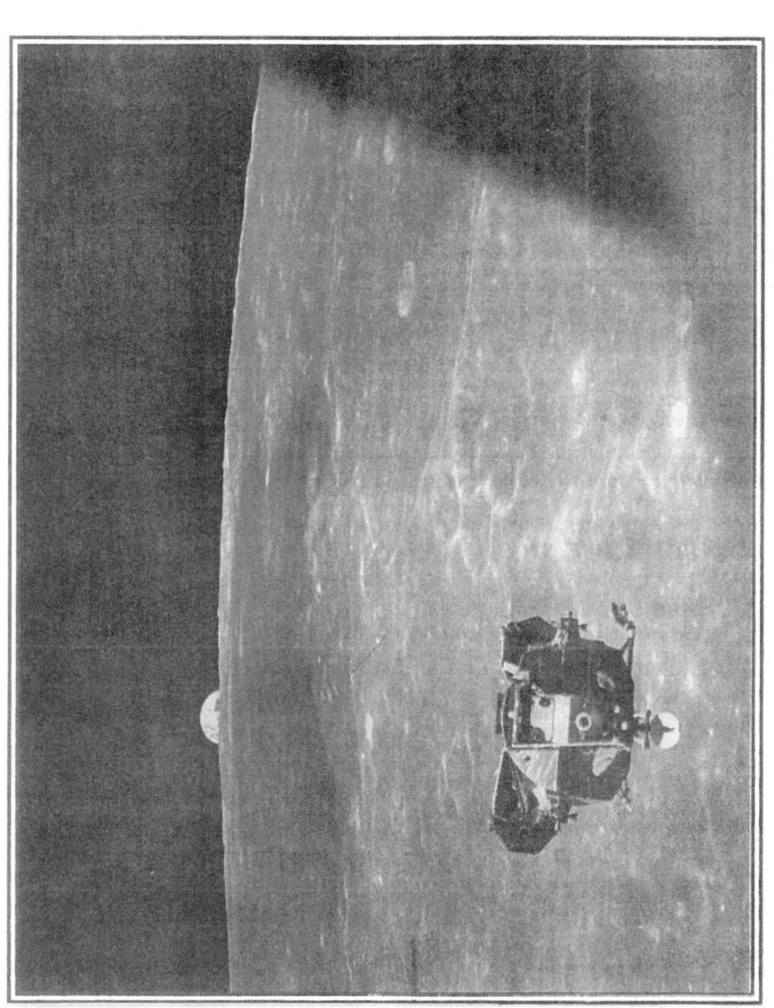

LM approaching the Command and Service Modules after the 1969 landing on the moon. Earth rising over the Lunar horizon

Jima, the carrier that picked up the Command Module in the Pacific Ocean. North American ignored the bill on the basis that it had not received payment for ferrying the LM's on previous trips to the moon.

AN UNIQUE EXPERIENCE

The Apollo program has only been one chapter in my life. But everything that came before was training that went into my performance on the Apollo program. And everything that happened afterwards has been influenced by the extraordinary experience of a lifetime, an experience that I can not forget.

I salute my many thousands of coworkers whose selfless dedication and often unrecognized personal sacrifices made it possible for America to reach up and touch the moon.

The National Aeronautics and Space Administration cordially welcomes you to the launch of Apollo 13.

Kurt H. Debus, Director
Kennedy Space Center, NASA

This credential is issued to the bearer for his sole, exclusive, personal use, and is not transferable. After launch, it may be kept as a souvenir of the mission.

Name ___________________________   № 5346

Admission Ticket, NASA KSC Auditorium

			North American Rock		LR 6.		GATE SEC D IN FEDERAL
1) North American Rock	4		CONTRACT NO.			PROMPT 1	DATE 4/13/70
2) Pratt & Whitney	4		UR B(00) B(00)				
3) Beech Aircraft	4		SUBJECT TO GOVERNMENT INSPECTION AT [X] YOUR PLANT [ ] BASE [ ] NONE		Houston		Cash
SELLER AWARDED PURCHASE ORDER			PURCHASE ORDER NUMBER				
North American Rock							

SHIP TO: Hou-MSC
VIA: IM-7, USS Iwo Jima, GOVAIR
DELIVERY REQUIRED AT BASE: None
SELLER PROMISES: Never Again

ITEM NO.	QUANTITY	UNIT	PART NO.	DESCRIPTION	LF	ACCT NO./JOB NO.	TAX CODE	UNIT PRICE
1.	400,001	MI		Towing, $4.00 first mile, $1.00 each additional mile / Trouble call, fast service				$ 400,004.00
2.	3	XWH		Battery Charge (road call + $.05 XWH) / customer's jumper cables				4.05
3.	50#	#		Oxygen at $10.00/lb				500.00
4.	3			Sleeping accommodations for 2, no TV, air-conditioned, with radio, modified american plan, with view		NAS-9-1100		Prepaid
5.				Additional guest in room at $8.00/night (1) Check out no later than noon Fri. 4/17/70, accommodations not guaranteed beyond that time.				32.00
6.				Water				No charge
7.				Personalized "trip-tik", including all transfers, baggage handling and gratuities				No charge
				Sub-Total				$ 400,540.05
				20% commercial discount + 2% cash discount (net 30 days)			(-)	88,118.81
				Total				$ 312,421.24
				No taxes applicable (government contract)				

SUGGESTED SOURCES/REMARKS (INCLUDE CWA NO. IF APPLICABLE)

RECEIVED/DELIVER: USS Iwo Jima
VIA: Air Express

REQUIRED BY / QTY / PLT & DEPT NO. / DATE

NASA(MSC)

APPROVED BY [signature]

PURCHASING/SUBCONTRACT MGMT.

Towing Bill sent by Grumman to North American

ASSISTANT TO THE DIRECTOR, VEHICLE TECHNOLOGY

ASSISTANT TO

I was now Assistant to the Director, Vehicle Technology. There is a world of difference between an "assistant to" and an "assistant." An "assistant" represents his boss in all things whenever the occasion arises. An "assistant to" is just another guy in the office.

A "director" is one step below a "vice president."

ENGINEERING DEPARTMENT ANNUAL REPORT

Cappy was Director of Vehicle Technology, and Fatty was Vice President Engineering. Cappy's office was next to Fatty's, and Fatty spent a lot of time in Cappy's office. When I reported to Cappy for work, Fatty was in there and said that he had a job that I might be able to help him with.

Fatty was writing his Annual Engineering Department Report for presentation to Grumman management. He told me that this was a very difficult job for him. Management has always given him a very hard time, every time he has presented his Annual Report. I advised Fatty to put his presentation on a set of view graphs and that his verbal presentation should consist of explaining the view graphs. The view graphs should contain facts only, no opinions.

First we made a view graph showing the organization of the engineering department, listing each section, number and kind of personnel, capabilities, job assignments, and responsibilities. Fatty's verbal comments were to describe the capabilities and responsibilities of each section and point out how they contributed to the strength of the company. Next came a view graph showing the jobs that we had in house. Then we showed the manpower requirements, by jobs, over the next three years. The manpower requirements over the next one and one-half years were fairly constant at 2000 men, but then the work started to peter out. The view graph indicated that if Grumman did not win a major new contract in the next two years, we would be facing massive layoffs in the engineering department.

This was not a "good news" report, and Fatty was very concerned about it. But I convinced him that it was objective, factual, and contained nothing that he could be criticized for. It gave management something important to chew on, that would detract them from picking on him.

That is the way it worked out. After the presentation, he told me that this was the first time that they had not given him a hard time. They accepted what he said, and there was a very serious discussion about the urgency of getting new contracts. Fatty was elated over the success of his presentation and wrote me a nice letter thanking me for the help I had given him.

FINISHING MY BOOK

Although I technically worked for Cappy, after helping Fatty with his Annual Report, I started to get all my work assignments from him. He was very friendly and supportive, and even hinted at vice presidency. I was even assigned an assistant of my own, George Breen, a very clever young man, graduate of Note Dame, with an additional MBA degree that many engineers at the time believed that they needed to get ahead.

Under these quiet circumstances at the office, I was able to turn more of my attention to my book. I noticed that at the beginning of the Apollo assembly phase, that is, after most of the hard intellectual work had been done, many of the first line members of the NASA team were leaving, for more challenging assignments elsewhere. These were the men who had the knowledge of how this vast operation had been managed. I realized that this management system had been the real secret of Apollo's success and was a national treasure that should not be lost.

The control devices used in this management system have a long development history. The first basic design control concept of this type was developed in the early 1930's by Ralph Creel and his group in the Navy Bureau of Aeronautics. These concepts were expanded by BIMRAB and similar movements, and finally consolidated by NASA on Apollo. This was the knowledge that I feared might be lost, and I decided to write a book to conserve this knowledge.

As I mentioned on page 341, I had a title for the book, a table of contents, and a set of notes for each chapter that I had discussed with a class at Kennedy Space Center. The text still had to be composed. This I did at home in the evenings. I brought this work in to the office the next morning, and Breen would go over it carefully. We had many deep discussions over the procedures. Breen made many useful suggestions, and then I had the text typed.

JOHN REARDON

John Reardon was the reliability engineer in the Office of the Secretary of Defense. I met him while attending an ASQC national meeting, and we became good friends. I told him about my book, and he volunteered to review it. He invited me to bring my manuscript to his office in the Pentagon. I arrived one morning at eight am, and he told this secretary that he could not be disturbed.

We sat side by side at his enormous conference table, taking turns reading out loud from the text, for two full days. He was a most meticulous editor. He made many suggestions, mostly grammar, and he improved my writing a great deal. However, he agreed with the concepts presented. But he made so many small changes in the manuscript that it had to be retyped.

John thought that the book was complete and very important. He said that there was not anything else like it in the technical literature.

The book was published in 1977, entitled *Advanced Systems Development Management,* by Wiley in New York. It received excellent reviews in the technical press. It survived two editions and is now sold out. Copies will always be available at the Library of Congress. The book was also translated into Russian and distributed in that country.

THE SEARCH FOR THE LEAST LOUSY
(COUTINHO's RULE)

My book promotes the very important, but little recognized, principle of searching for the least lousy adequate solution. It is unrealistic and wasteful of precious treasure to strive for perfection. As humans with limited time and treasure, we must strive for the least lousy adequate solution. This principle is very difficult to understand.

"Least lousy' should not be confused with "good enough." If you settle for "good enough," somebody else will beat you with something that is better. There is a lot of room between good enough and least lousy.

If you strive for the very best, you usually will be tempted to aspire perfection. If you know that perfection does not exist, you will be satisfied with the least lousy. It worked on Apollo and helped to put two men on the moon, on schedule and within budget.

I do not believe that NASA's first line Apollo design team was aware that they were searching for the least lousy adequate solution. They did it instinctively, because they were good. It was only after I wrote the book and carefully analyzed their methods did I discover that that was what they were doing. Successor NASA teams have not been as clever or successful.

An example will illustrate the principle. I recently watched a story on television about a Texas County that had grown so fast lately that its courthouse was completely inadequate. They received a generous appropriation from the State of $50 million to build a new courthouse.

The County hired an architect to prepare a set of plans for a new courthouse. The proposed courthouse plans were found to be deficient. They fired the architect and hired a new one. The new plans were also unsatisfactory. They repeated the process until they spent all their $ 50 million on plans that turned out to be useless. Now, the TV story reported, they had no plans and also no money to build a new courthouse. And no one would ever trust them with any more money.

They had not read and understood my book. Had they done so, they would have known that there is no such thing as a perfect courthouse. All courthouse plans are lousy to some extent. The problem is to find the least lousy plan that is still adequate.

Probably the first set of plans would have been adequate. After all, the architect was a professional. If certain aspects needed improvement, the architect could have made changes in the plans. If they had proceeded on this basis, they would now have an adequate courthouse, and if they had been careful, they probably would still have some money left over.

However, the proper procedure would have been for the County to first prepare a specification and a cost estimate that everybody with a say would agree to. This is the critical point, "agreement." Different people want different things, and the available funds will only go so far. So the strong individuals will get more, usually not all, of what they want, and weaker individuals will get less. In this give and take, everybody agrees to the best that they can get, and the resulting specification is a compromise.

The specification could then be published in one or more architectural magazines, inviting submittal of plans and cost estimates complying with the specification, for competitive selection. The County could then select the least lousy plan that best complied with its specification within its available funds.

The building contractor should be selected by a competitive procedure among bidders who submitted proposals. The guideline for selecting the winner might be to select the one who best matched the specification at least cost, not to exceed available funds.

The County would have to appoint a building superintendent to monitor the contractor's activities to assure quality of workmanship, and compliance with the specification and cost estimate. When the superintendent notices the slightest deviation from requirements, he must take immediate corrective action.   If he lets any non-compliance go too far (as is unfortunately often the case), corrective action will be impossible.   The monitoring activities of the superintendent must be carefully spelled out in the contract.

The loss of $50 million of the taxpayers' money, and of all chances of getting a new courthouse, is a terrible tragedy.   It is difficult to understand why the first architect did not give them better guidance to prevent them from squandering their money and forfeiting their courthouse.   Maybe, in an effort to save money, they scrimped on his fee.

IN THE DOGHOUSE

THREE STRIKES AND YOU'RE OUT

I was well aware that some of the work that I had done was exceptional. This raised an important general question in my mind, namely, if I was so smart, why wasn't I rich?

From where I stood, the simplest way to get rich, was to become a Grumman vice president. Fatty had hinted of that possibility, and the assignments that he was giving me, indicated that he was trying to groom me for high office. Fatty knew that a vice president had to be a well rounded person and he was looking for an opportunity to provide me with such an experience. He knew that technical capability alone was not sufficient for a vice president, you had to have other skills, including handling people other than engineers.

At that time, our Director of Engineering Recruitment, Al Wilder, retired. Fatty encouraged me to take that job. I knew Wilder well and what he did. He visited periodically all the best engineering schools in the country, made friends with the best professors, identified the best students, followed their progress in detail during their last two years, and tried to talk them into taking jobs at Grumman when they graduated.

Every year he recruited some of the best students in the country. It was Grumman policy to hire a number of graduating students every year, and to retire all those persons reaching 65 years of age, in order to keep the company from becoming overloaded with old men. Management watched the average age in the company very carefully. Wilder's activity provided Grumman with the best young engineering personnel in the country. It was a source of Grumman's life blood. His was a very hard act to follow.

Then I had some personal reservations. Wilder spent most of his time traveling from one university to another. I had done a lot of traveling as Gavin's assistant when working on the LM and I did not want to be away from home that much any more. Furthermore, Wilder was a people-person. My father and sister were people-persons. I once accompanied Helen one day to buy a pair of shoes. As we left the store, she knew the salesman's entire life history, where he grew up, what schools he went to, when he was married, how many children he had, etc. The salesman loved it. To relate to people like that was a job I could not do.

I was convinced that the best job that I could do on recruitment would be pale when compared to the terrific job that Wilder had done over the years. I would not get a very good score. I told Fatty that I preferred technical work, that I knew I was good at it, and that taking on Wilder's job would be a waste of my technical education. STRIKE ONE !

The ASME is one of the major standardization bodies in the United States, and eventually I was drawn in for some years as a member of the United States Standardization Committee that is subordinate to the International Standards Organization (IS). Most countries of the world are members, and each has one vote. Most of these countries envy us, some hate us to the extent that they blow up our embassies around the world. International standardization is a vicious form of economic warfare.

While I was on the Committee, we had one remarkable success. You can see many of those land-sea-air containers, every time you drive on an interstate highway.   The containers are loaded and sealed at the shipper's establishment.   The seal is not broken until the container is delivered to the recipient. Around the world, the sealed containers have cut down on shipping losses caused by theft at harbors and airports by a high percentage. The standard containers fit on flat truck-trailer beds, on flat railroad cars, and in air freighters in all countries of the world.   All international harbors and airports are equipped to handle them in large quantities.

This was an United States initiative, and, as a matter of principle, the rest of the world was dead set against it. It was a major job. It took a lot of patience over the years, to wear down the opposition of these small self-righteous countries, each with their own one vote, on a par with the United States.

Except for some highly industrialized countries like England and Canada, most of the rest of the world, primarily the underdeveloped part, is trying actively to push the metric system on the United States. It is not generally recognized that the main impact of this affects our standards.   The United States has the best and most complete set of commercial standards in the world, primarily because the US is the only country where such standards are established without government help. (In the US, the Bureau of Standards establishes weights and measures, and the military has its Military Standards.   There is no government agency for commercial standards.) If the US were to convert to the metric system, all of our standards would have to be rewritten, and coordinated with foreign standards of lesser quality. All production and service facilities would have to be retooled.

An important example is our system of screw threads which few people ever think about. Many metal, plastic, and wooden parts and devices   use bolts and screws as fasteners. In the US, we use the American, British and Canadian (ABC) screw threads. While I was on the Committee, the ABC system was the only system in which bolts and screws were commercially available in all sizes and grades.

Originally, each foreign industrialized country had its own metric system of screw threads. To compete with the ABC system, a major effort was made by metric countries, to set up a new metric system that all metric countries adopted, just different enough from the ABC system, so the parts would not be interchangeable. This is the system that the IS is trying to introduce into the United States. At the time that I was on the Committee, it would have been much cheaper for the rest of the world to adopt the ABC system than for the US to convert to metric.

The ABC system is used throughout the world wherever American products are dominant. Wherever an American plane lands and is serviced, ABC tools are available. The US oil industry is dominant throughout the world. Italy is a major supplier of spare parts for oil rigs. All such parts are manufactured to US standards and dimensioned in the ABC inch-pound system.

I told Fatty about these problems, and he became interested. He pulled his weight as Grumman Vice President Engineering to be appointed as Chairman of the US Standardization Committee, with me as Co-Chairman. Our first Committee meeting was scheduled. I had several ideas for the Committee to work on. Fatty asked me to write them up, and he would use them in his introductory remarks when he took over the chairmanship.

Our first committee meeting was scheduled for 9 am in Washington. Fatty decided to go the night before and stay at the Mayflower, just across the street from the building where the meeting was to take place. We decided to meet for breakfast at the Mayflower at 7:30, and I could brief him on his talk. Fatty was sharp and able to absorb such material quickly.

I had been going to Washington for 20 years, at least twice a month, and had never been late. I told Fatty that I would rather sleep in my own bed and was confident that I would be at the Mayflower with my papers at 7:30.

The morning of the meeting, I was at the airport on time. I had two choices, Eastern Airlines or American. I decided that American was more reliable and took my seat on that airplane. But the airplane would not take off. An hour and a half later, we were transferred to another airplane. Over an hour later, we were told that the fuel pump would not work. We were transferred to another airplane. I got to

Washington over three hours late.

The meeting had been in session for about an hour. I was greeted with sullen silence.

I presented the material I had prepared for Fatty. It went over like a lead balloon. STRIKE TWO !

I was no longer welcome on the committee. Fatty was no longer my friend. You cannot embarrass a Grumman Vice President in public and expect to survive. George Breen was transferred to the E2C.

After we returned home and Fatty had calmed down, he told me about his concern with the "quality of electronic design." In mechanical engineering, we employ such analytical techniques as stress analysis, weight control and similar techniques to assure that the design, when built, will comply with specifications. In electronic engineering, Fatty said that he cannot find any such predictive analyses. He asked me to look into the matter and see what I could come up with.

I already knew from my experience that I could apply the principles of reliability estimating and control to an electronic design job. I had watched electronic engineers at design work and had supervised a small design group. Fatty did not know all this. I decided to take the principles of mechanical design and quality control and apply them, step by step, to the design steps of electronic equipment. I had prepared quite a thick preliminary report and was struck by an idea for a new name for what I was doing: *Software Reliability*.

One day Fatty came around to see what I was doing and I, somewhat proudly, showed him my report. He took one quick look at it and without any explanation, got mad as hell. This must have been a preplanned trick, because he did not look at my report long enough to get any idea of what was in it. He just assumed that I did not have anything, since the assignment was an impossible job. He stormed out of my office and went to see the Administrative Engineer, Warren Allen, and demanded that I be fired on the spot ! STRIKE THREE ! This time there is no hope !

I took my papers home and reformatted them into a technical article that I submitted to the American Society for Quality Control (ASQC.) The paper was accepted for publication in the Society's Journal and created quite a stir. I received a lot of favorable correspondence. I was awarded the ASQC Brumbaugh Award with great fanfare at the ASQC Annual Meeting for "the most significant technical paper published by the Society in 1972." This Award is one of the Society's top three awards.

When later I started to work for the US Army, they knew about the paper and organized a committee to incorporate the concepts in a Military Specification. I was a member of the committee. This new

MIL-SPEC was then called out for all new systems with embedded electronics procured by the US Armed Forces. Even Grumman had to comply. The MIL-SPEC was modified several times during the next few years until it became obsolete and was replaced by a new MIL-SPEC.

BACK TO THE DRAWING BOARD

But back at Grumman, our new Chief Engineer, George Skurla, called me into his office and told me that I was being transferred to the EO Incorporation Group. This is the lowest entry-level group for draftsmen in the company. This was unjust punishment: Skurla had made no attempt to learn my side of the story like Allen had done. He did not know that a Chief has an obligation to stick up for his men.

Technical drawing is a language that designers use to communicate their work. Those engineers, who are not designers, normally can't read drawings very well and are not comfortable working with them. Neither Skurla nor Fatty had been at Grumman long enough to realize that I had been a designer and was used to working with drawings. Their sending me to the EO Incorporation Group was the closest thing to hell that they could think of. They obviously hoped that I would not survive in that environment and would quit.

When a designer wants to change a drawing, but has no time to do so, he issues an Engineering Order (EO). The EO is a 8.5 x 11 inch sheet with a sketch of the change and the necessary signatures. The shop can then proceed as if the drawing had been changed. The drawing itself is eventually changed and updated by the EO Incorporation Group.

Except for the supervisor, the group consisted of young men starting their careers. The supervisor was an older man, and we got along well. We went out to lunch together every day. I actually became a help to him. The young men needed a lot of help, and they soon found out that they could come to me when they needed clarification on a technical point. Even the supervisor came to me occasionally for technical advice. I got along very well in my exile.

The Grumman Company is the only company in the world that has the dubious distinction of having a Doctor of Engineering, a graduate of a world renown university, in the lowest possible job in the engineering department, incorporating EO's on its drawings.

REINSTATEMENT

I made it a point to go see Cappy periodically. These were hard days for Grumman. The decline in work that Fatty had predicted in his Annual Report three years ago had come to pass. Every month now,

Cappy received a list of candidates for layoff. Cappy told me that every time such a list came out, Fatty was right there asking why my name was not on the list. Fatty was not on the committee that determined the layoffs, he was not quite as big a big shot as he thought he was.

In this process, George Breen was laid off. He did not have the seniority required to stay with the company.

Cappy was aware of how I was making out in the EO Incorporation Group. He said that as long as I was not too unhappy incorporating EO's, I should stick to it, something was sure to turn up. He had a number of jobs that I could do, but every time that he mentioned it to Fatty, Fatty would not let him offer me the job.

Finally Cappy found a job that Fatty agreed that I could take. The company had established a committee to computerize the company's operations, and the committee requested the engineering department to appoint a member to represent engineering. I guess that Fatty did not think much of the idea of computerizing the company, so he agreed to my accepting this job.

I knew from my experience on the TBF Avenger in Plant 2, the importance of engineering as a source of information (data) for the operation of other company departments. The means of distributing this information was the engineering drawing with its bill of material.

I was aware that 72 copies of every drawing were made as a standard release. This told me that there were 72 offices in the company that needed some data from each one of our drawings in order to operate.

My job, as I analyzed it, involved identifying what detail data each of the 72 offices needed, and how to provide it most efficiently on the punch cards that we were using at the time. When I knew what I needed, I could reorganize the engineering department to most efficiently furnish this information. I presented this plan to the committee, and they agreed that I should so proceed.

This plan brought me into contact with the supervisors of the 72 offices in the company that needed engineering data. This was a matter of prime concern to them, since their operations was based on their receiving engineering data on time. I made many friends in this process.

I knew the engineering department well, and where and how data was generated. I designed forms for engineers to fill out so the data could be punched on cards. I did not have the opportunity to finish this job, but my incomplete instructions filled two inches in a three ring binder.

THE COMMITTEE OF TWENTY

Somehow it became known in the Computerization Committee that Fatty was trying to lay me off. I don't know how this happened, since I never talked to anyone about this matter except to Cappy. It must have been Fatty himself who did the talking, since nobody else was involved.

One of the older department heads who I was working with recalled that Grumman had a special procedure for laying off employees who had been in the company for 30 or more years. A committee of department heads had to review the employee's record and decide on the layoff. My friend organized a committee of 20 department heads and scheduled a meeting. Fatty represented the Engineering Department. (This was a special courtesy to Fatty, Cappy was my boss.)

At the meeting, a motion was made and seconded to lay me off. The chairman asked each man around the table, in turn, to present his viewpoint and state what he knew about me. Everyone, except Fatty, said that they had known me for many years, had worked with me or knew of my work, and gave me a very favorable recommendation. I had a excellent reputation in the shop. For example, when I was analyzing failure rate data as described on page 297, I was receiving some 8000 reports of failures on punch cards per month from the Navy. This number was so large, not because our airplanes were unreliable, but because we had so many of them in the field. I did not think that processing these cards required an engineer, so I picked a few older mechanics who had trouble walking, from the shop, for a sit down job in the engineering department. These men knew part numbers and associated parts, were very dedicated and did a terrific job. I was the only engineer who ever selected shop men to work in engineering. This story spread through the shops and practically made me a hero. Several similar stories about me came out in the meeting.

Fatty was given every opportunity to speak, and he had a lot to say. The other department heads listened carefully and asked many questions.

The chairman then asked each man around the table, in turn, for a short summary of his position, and then took a vote. The result was 19 to one against the motion to lay me off.

I could no longer be laid off as long as Grumman was in business. I had a good job, but the dream of a vice presidency, with its associated riches, had evaporated.

DREAMING OF A MOON STATION

During the time that I worked in Cappy's directorate, I maintained contact with my friends at Kennedy Space Center. We had many discussions on the future of our space program. We noted that most support equipment for the Apollo mission was specifically designed for that program. For example, the large control room that was packed with computers and that you watched on television during the space flights, was designed specifically to support the Apollo mission. At the end of the mission, a group of my friends at NASA and I were shocked when millions and millions of dollars worth of computers were dumped. Nobody had any use for them any more.

In 1971, we decided that what NASA needed was a 25 year program, updated every year. With such a plan in place, equipment needed for today's mission could be designed with an eye to being adaptable to tomorrow's programs.

We had to establish a goal for our 25 year plan and selected a <u>Station on the Moon</u>. Such a program would require development of 52 new technologies, such as the manufacturing of fuel and water from materials available on the moon, and less costly methods of launching spacecraft from the earth into orbit. We estimated that the job would require 1000 engineers with the technical capability available at Grumman.

Awarding a contract for 1000 engineers for 25 years is a big deal, and NASA is very cautious in such circumstances. They had to find a contractor in whom they had confidence and could trust. I had built up a good reputation at NASA, and they were aware of Grumman's technical capabilities. Specifically, they were impressed how I had organized and supported BIMBAB, and organized the Reliability and Maintainability Conference series. A member of the NASA group told me that NASA would have confidence in a Grumman team under my control, and advised me to get Grumman to submit an unsolicited proposal.

A moon station would require permanent living facilities far more sophisticated than what we had developed at the South Pole, where we maintain a permanent base to keep an eye on the Russians. The requirement for 52 new technologies would unleash a research effort that would pale the Apollo effort.

Both the Space Shuttle and the Manned Space Station had little additional technology beyond Apollo, and American-Russian cooperation in space has not been viewed by the American public as a significant advance in foreign affairs. However, the first healthy baby conceived and born on the moon, would unleash American public applause and excitement as never seen before.

RESIGNATION

I proposed to Cappy, with Fatty listening in as usual, that Grumman submit to NASA an unsolicited proposal to design and build a moon station with a team of some 1000 men in a period of 25 years, under my control.   I said that I had some assurance that NASA would consider such a proposal favorably, and that if Grumman did not want to go along with my suggestion, I would quit.

Fatty took over and using some very strong and vulgar language, turned down my proposal. So I told him that I was quitting and walked out. It was 1972. I had worked at Grumman for 34 years.

I was very aware of the fact that if I had been awarded the moon station contract by NASA, I would have had to clean out the business management and legal types that were controlling the Grumman Corporation. I probably would not have been able to do so.

The dream of a moon station is not yet dead, NASA just has to find a contractor whose performance would indicate that he can be trusted with the job. On page 374 is an article from the Baltimore Sun, dated August 18, 1987, that reports that a committee chaired by Astronaut Sally Ride recommended, in a report to the NASA Administrator, a moon station as the nation's next space goal. Since then, other similar committees have made the same recommendation.

U.S. moon base proposed as stepping stone to Mars

CAPE CANAVERAL Fla (AP) — A task force headed by retiring as tronaut Sally Ride yesterday recom mended a moon base as the nation s next manned space goal and said such an outpost could be a stepping stone to Mars

Without a bold program of sci ence and technology the United States will not regain the worldwide space leadership it once enjoyed Ms Ride said in a 63 page report

If the initiatives outlined by the task force are implemented the re port said astronauts could return to the moon by the year 2000 and could set up camp on Mars 10 years later

The moon and Mars bases were among four possible initiatives the Ride panel submitted to James C Fletcher administrator of the Na tional Aeronautics and Space Ad ministration The others are an ex tensive study of Earth s resources from orbit and stepped up explora tion of the solar system with un manned probes

Mr Fletcher had asked Ms Ride the first American woman to fly in space to recommend ideas on which he could formulate a space policy to submit to the White House

Ms Ride noted in the report s preface that the United States until recently "was clearly and unques

The moon and Mars bases were among four possible initiatives the panel submitted to NASA's administrator.

tionably the leader in space explora tion However in the aftermath of the Challenger accident reviews of our space program made its short comings starkly apparent "

The space shuttle Challenger ex ploded Jan 28 1986 killing its crew of seven The fleet has been grounded until at least next summer while the spaceship is redesigned

Ms Ride said the United States has lost leadership to the Soviets in two key areas unmanned explora tion of Mars and manned flight aboard a space station "and is in danger of being surpassed in many others during the next several years "

Clipping from the *Sun,*
Baltimore, August 18, 1987

THE DEMISE OF GRUMMAN

PROFITS

The demise of the Grumman Corporation was a national tragedy. It takes many years and much treasure to build such an aeronautical design team as the one at Grumman. It was the best in the world - at the service of the nation. The loss of this team was irreplaceable.

When I first came to Grumman, I was taught, as I mentioned on page 207, that Grumman was in business to build the world's best carrier based fighter aircraft, and that if we did so, the Navy would have no choice but to buy our products, and we would have no money worries.

In 1958, the Book of the Month Club sent me, as its selection, a book entitled *Image of America* by a French Dominican priest, Father Bruckberger, who had spent eight years in the United States studying the American scene. One of his major observations was that the business ethics in the US were much higher than those in Europe. He determined that a successful American business had four objectives:

1. Provide a product or service that people need or want
2. Provide a good place for its employees to work
3. To be a good citizen of the community where located
4. To pay its rent and other financial obligations

To my surprise, he said nothing about making a profit.

One of his examples was Henry Ford, who reduced the price of his cars so a farmer could afford one to relieve him of his isolation in the wide open spaces of the American continent, and to take his family to town and to Church. Simultaneously, Ford was paying his workers unheard of high wages.

I compared Grumman's performance with Bruckberger's four business objectives, and found that Grumman complied with all four. For example, with respect to being a good place to work, the heavily subsidized company cafeteria served excellent quality food, something I found nowhere else in my travels to other companies. And the unions, who spent over $10 million over several years trying to unionize Grumman, never got more than a handful of votes. There can be no doubt that the employees liked to work at Grumman.

The most interesting aspect of my analysis of Grumman is its attitude towards profit. They emphasize that if you make the best airplanes in the world, the Navy has no choice but to buy them, and you have no worries about money. During World War II, Grumman did over a billion dollars worth of business, and during all that time, its stock was pegged rock solid at $ 25 a share. It was $ 25 a share when Grumman had 700 employees, and it was still $ 25 a share when Grumman had 40000 employees. Nobody on the stock market was interested in Grumman stock, it did not equate with profit.

I think that Father Bruckberger's neglect to discuss profit means that profit just comes naturally as a result of complying with his four objectives. Profit is not a driving objective that you plan for. You do not adjust the four other objectives in order to achieve a predetermined profit.

UNDER NEW MANAGEMENT

A change in Grumman management was first detected during the F-14 design phase. Completing work on time became most important. Engineers who had been trained to rack their brains to assure that their designs were the best in the world, were given fixed time limits for the preparation of each drawing. At the end of that time, finished or not, they were relieved of their drawings that were pronounced "good enough" and released to the shop for manufacturing.

I was told by my Navy friends that you could always recognize a Grumman engineer by the way that he was so proud of his work. On the F-14 design, for the first time ever at Grumman, there was no design group leader who was proud of his work.

Grumman lucked out in having a superior engineering department. Al Wilder had spent his working life recruiting the best graduates from the best engineering schools in the country. The department was geared to designing aeronautical products that were the "best in the world." When forced to produce a product that was just "good enough," that product was still better than what anybody else could produce.

COMPETITIVE PROCUREMENT

The Defense Department of the United States has the unique problem of procuring high-tech materiel at least cost. This is done by competitive procurement. The formal procedure is as follows:

A Request for Proposal (RIP) is issued to interested, registered, certified qualified bidders who will submit their proposals before a stated closing date. The various proposals are evaluated by the Government and the one best meeting all of the technical requirements at least cost is generally selected as the source for the procurement.

Countries other than the United States tend to rely more on

government owned arsenals to supply their military materiel. The competitive process tends to provide the United States with superior materiel at less cost.

Competitive procurements are also used in the US for large commercial one of a kind projects that are not available in the market on a competitive basis. However, its limited use to military and specialized commercial procurement makes it practically unknown in the commercial world. Business schools do not mention the subject.

The practice of competitive procurement, however, determines the character, organization, and thinking in those organizations that practice it. It is a matter of survival. The basic truth is that if such a company cannot win its share of competitive contracts, it will not survive. It follows that such companies must therefore first be organized so that they can win competitive contracts and execute them at least cost.

REQUEST FOR PROPOSAL (RFP)

The objective of an RFP is to procure the best possible military materiel in the world. When Navy officials write an RFP, they have to know what is the best that they can ask for. They cannot ask for something that cannot be done. Before an RFP is written, it is important for potential bidders to communicate with the RFP writers and tell them about their capabilities.

When I was a design group leader, I was required to visit the Navy Department in Washington once a month and at least check in with all officials who had approval authority over my work. Many engineers did not like to make these trips to Washington, not only did they take up too much of their time, but they considered them a waste of time. I remember the loud, consistent, engineering management admonishment of the time:

"You gotta get in bed with the Navy!"

Another good case along this line was the F-14. The fuselage section between the two wings (called the wing intersection) carries the greatest load and is the heaviest structure on the airplane. To save a great deal of weight, Grumman decided to build this portion of the airplane out of welded titanium. This metal, although strong and light, is very difficult to machine and weld. Once you cut into it, it changes its dimensions. Grumman had a team of 50 manufacturing engineers working for two years designing this wing intersection. The resulting weight of the F-14 was significantly less than that of any of its competitors.

If Grumman had waited until the procurement action to spring the news of this achievement on the Navy, Navy officials very probably would not have believed it. But Grumman had kept the Navy informed of their titanium welding research on a running basis. When Grumman proposed a significantly lighter airplane than its competitors, the Navy was prepared and believed that Grumman could be expected to deliver what it promised. The RFP was written so that the Grumman advantage could be fully exploited.

After publication of an RFP, no communication between the Navy and the bidders is allowed during the selection process.

CLINT TOWL

Clint Towl was the accountant at Loening and he joined Grumman and his team when they organized the new Grumman Corporation. He was close to the founders and he absorbed their ideas.

After the retirement of the founders, Towl became president and tried faithfully to continue the policies of the founders. He had a difficult time, because the new generation of vice presidents thought differently than he did.

I invited him to give a talk at the eighth BIMRAB annual conference in 1965. He accepted the invitation and told me to write the talk. I discussed some ideas I had and he liked them. I told him that I was looking for a good title and he suggested "Fair Price, Fair Play." I wrote the paper and passed it around at the vice presidential level for review. All reviewers rejected it completely as being inappropriate. Since I had discussed the basic ideas with Towl himself, I paid no attention to them and made no changes.

Towl scheduled a review meeting of the talk to take place in the presence of Fatty, four other vice presidents, and myself. First, Towl skimmed through the paper, then read it very carefully in silence while we all sat there and watched him. I saw the hands and legs of the other men shaking in fear. I had never seen anything like this before, I could not understand it or visualize what was going on. I knew Towl as always being a very pleasant man and easy to work with. Then, Towl read the paper out loud. He stopped twice and asked me to be more forceful at these points. Otherwise he accepted what I had written. He did not ask anybody else for their opinion.

The talk went over very well at the conference. I spoke with some admirals and vice presidents of other prime contractors, and they all said that Towl had given a splendid talk and made some good suggestions.

Two things are noteworthy. First, the Grumman reviewers all rejected the paper, indicating that they lived in a different world than Towl, and secondly, the physical fear that they exhibited at the review. This would indicate that the policies of the successors to Towl were going to be different from Towl's and from those of the founders of the Grumman Corporation.

MR BIERWIRTH

After Towl retired, Grumman had a series of presidents, none of whom survived in office very long. Most of them had been Chief Engineers, like George Skurla. None were old time Grumman people, but outsiders who were hired after Al Wilder resigned. Fatty and Skurla did not know the old time Grumman people, so instead of training and promoting such people to to upper level jobs in the engineering department, they hired from the outside. These new people were the ones who were becoming chief engineers and going on to become presidents of the Grumman Corporation. The effect on moral in the engineering department was devastating.

Finally, they found a man who seemed right for the job, a Mr Bierwirth. He was rich and well educated with advanced degrees in the liberal arts and in business management. Bierwirth made sure he was backed by a Board of Directors of people with illustrious degrees from the best business management and law schools in the country. These people all had been taught that with their knowledge of the elements of the business model, they could manage any type of business. Indeed, they were superbly qualified to run a railroad, a shoe factory, a steel mill, even a high tech electronics plant. They knew nothing of the US Department of Defense competitive procurement practices.

Mr Bierwirth proved to be an inspiring leader who turned what in outward appearances was a small, pathetic, limping company into one that was galloping through the business community to great public acclaim.

Bierwirth's biggest deal was to obtain a subcontract from Boeing to build aircraft wings for their giant airliners. Wings are the most difficult aircraft structures to build and require special tools for their manufacturing. For example, the giant milling machine at the Grumman Plant at Glen Arm, Maryland, was an awe inspiring, unbelievable city block long and a quarter of that distance wide.

Grumman stock rose steadily and the company enjoyed the best reputation on the stock market and in the commercial community.

JOHN O'BRIEN

When Bierwirth retired in glory, much richer than he had been when he first came to Grumman, John O'Brien assumed the presidency of Grumman. O'Brien had been very carefully selected. He had impeccable qualifications in business management and law, and he had demonstrated what he could do in practice. In the spirit of good will, one of the first things that he did as Grumman president, was to write an open letter to all Grumman employees, telling them how he was going to follow in Mr Bierwirth's footsteps and boost the growth of the Grumman Corporation.

I maintained contact with some members of the engineering department at the time and they told me that O'Brien's letter went over like a lead balloon. They were so outraged that a few guys got together and wrote a reply. This reply was circulated in the department and universally approved. I received a copy that had been circulated and was quite tattered, so I copied it so it could be reproduced on the next two and a half pages.

I doubt that O'Brien ever saw this letter, but if he did, with his business and law background, he would not be able to understand it. Nevertheless, the letter makes several general issues clear. The first is that aeronautical engineers want to build airplanes. They may have to build the world best aluminum canoes or truck bodies when things are slow, but their objective will still be to build airplanes. They came to Grumman when it was the Grumman *Aircraft Engineering* Corporation to do *aircraft engineering.*

The letter refers to the deplorable loss of the ATA competition, which seems to have bothered the engineering department more than the Board of Directors. The letter complains about the lack of engineering management, and lists the various matters that are needed and which only a good engineering management can provide. Unfortunately, business types do not know what engineering management entails, and don't realize when there is a problem. Engineering management requires people who can make good decisions regarding what is the best technical approach to a given problem. To compete for a new airplane, a company must organize its best brains and outdo itself. This is an engineering management problem. The letter makes clear, that the gulf between the engineering department and Grumman management had become unbridgeable.

I. M. Anonymous
Grummanville, USA
10 March 1988

Mr. John O'Brien
President, Grumman Corporation

Dear Sir:

Several of us have discussed your letter of March 8 and have decided to reply, even though we know that your invitation to do so was largely *pro forma*. We have no real advice to offer, but, since you are a pseudo-parent figure, we decided to let you know how we feel.

The loss of the ATA was devastatingly demoralizing. We suppose you had to put on the best public face, but we feel that it was a disaster. We feel betrayed by those in charge of the proposal, and feel that our efforts are not being supported by a real effort in other departments. That may be unfair, but most of us are here because we love airplanes and aviation. If we wanted to work on refrigerators, we'd have gone elsewhere.

LeRoy Grumman left Loening to build airplanes, and that is why we came to Grumman. Cumulatively, we represent many thousands of years of aviation experience, and we feel neglected. Perhaps we are naive, but we feel that we could have provided useful and innovative suggestions for the ATA proposal - no one ever asked for them - nor were we able to figure out a way to provide them to the proper office.

The ATA experience perhaps best illustrates one of Grumman's biggest problems - excessive compartmentalization. Not only do we not know what the left hand is doing, we don't even know where it is. There is no "Grumman Team" - maybe there never was, but Roy Grumman, Jake Swirbul, et al would surely say otherwise if they could.

We're also tired of reading and hearing exhortations for greater efficiency. We feel that we are already doing remarkably well in an organization that often impedes our efforts, rather than encourage them. The management itself is bloated, rife with cronyism, defeats accountability, fails to define objectives, and resembles no effective model that we are acquainted with. At the technical level, project leaders are often good men, capable men, who are exasperated by the stultifying bureaucracy with which they have to contend.

Leadership is none existent, and management is obsessed with minutiae and incapable of motivating its employees. Good employees are not rewarded, nor are bad employees punished or weeded out. It is farcical.

Although it's probably good politics, we feel that "we're staying on Long Island" doesn't   make much sense. If our operating costs are such that we cannot compete, lets' go elsewhere. We'd much rather move and keep working than eventually turn out the lights in Bethpage. It had been said that all problems are opportunities, but we seem to be sticking our heads in the sand,

Other pronouncements having to do with the difficulty of securing/doing military business are beginning to exasperate us. Our competition is doing great military business. We wonder if Mundy Peale's example is being emulated, to our ultimate ruin.   We need Washington, not the other way around. Surely we can do better than to follow the miserable decline of Fairchild-Republic.

So, in our department, at least, malaise and cynicism abound. Ridiculous and unrealistic public statements no longer amuse us. Mr Bierwirth is a wealthy man who leaves Grumman with considerable additional wealth. We did not feel inspired when he was at the helm, nor do we   feel hopeful now that he's going.   We're well aware that people in your position are not like we are, and aware that one day you too will retire wealthy, while the rest of us will be left to get by the best we can. There is no "Grumman Family" now - lip service is paid to the concept, but it is dead in fact as a dodo.

So, you may say, you made lot of wordy statements and complaints, what do you suggest? Simply this:

1. Give us some leaders, and don't let number-crunchers destroy the spirit of the company.

2 Recognize and reward excellence.

3 .Encourage personal development, not just ambition. Find out what your personnel resources are and *use* them.

4. Establish a genuine feeling of cooperation between workers and managers, and eliminate the present confrontational attitudes which created so much bitterness.

5. Try to be a visible presence yourself, rather than an ivory tower type. We know you're busy. but we need you, and maybe you need us.

6. If we can't get the political support in this area that we need for our defense business, let's go elsewhere. Leave HQ on Long Island, but the rest of us can certainly move.   We'd probably like it in a more stable, traffic free location.

7. Get everyone interested in major undertakings. Encourage suggestions, and don't bury them in bureaucratic procedures. We are here to help - use us. Don't treat us like lackeys, or that's what we'll become.

8. Expect more of everyone, but reward additional efforts. 3% raises

over 2 year periods are definitely demoralizing. On the other hand, if a raise isn't earned, don't pay it. Demand excellence, especially from your managers - and demand *leadership*, not just task accomplishment.

We do not expert that you wish to read this. We expect, in fact, that it will be short stopped at a lower level, and dismissed as the work of disgruntled employees. In the unlikely event that you do read this letter, we thank you for your time and apparently sincere interest. We do feel frustrated, but we are not completely demoralized, or we wouldn't have bothered writing. We're Grummanites, and we really don't want to go to Fort Worth, St. Louis or the Coast to find jobs, but we will if we have to. We feel, and please pardon our frankness, that it's time to knock off the bullshit, and get everyone working together. We're flying IFR now, Mr. O'Brien, and we're bound to crash and burn if we continue flying blind and without direction.

Take hold of this company, Mr. O'Brien, and kick some butts - make certain they're the right ones.

Thank you for your time.

THE FINAL SOLUTION

It finally dawned on the Grumman Board of Directors that the Grumman Corporation, for reasons that they did not understand, no longer had the capability to win a competitive procurement contract. They wrote a letter to the Secretary of Defense, with attached "Grumman Corporation Strategic Statement," that was widely circulated in the engineering department and that I have reproduced on pages 386 to 389.

The purpose of the letter is not clear, it was possibly written in the false belief that the Secretary of Defense is interested in subsidizing companies that are not capable of winning a competitive procurement contract. Nothing is said of how Grumman studies the Navy's requirements and future needs, and how the company is positioning itself to help the Navy by winning future competitive contracts to furnish the Navy with the best military airplanes in the world. The "Statement" leaves the impression that Grumman is making lots of money on fancy technical doohickeys when it states:

"A continuing focus on shareholder value, through cash management and operating performance, has improved our position in the financial and investor markets, and provided access to capital for investment. Grumman is now positioned to leverage its strategy, technology and capabilities to address a challenging new marketplace and, through a series of carefully planned alliances, including acquisitions, undertake the changes needed to reposition the company for the future."

The major motivation here appears to be *profit*. This is not a letter from a man who is in bed with the Navy (see page 377). There is no recognition of the Department of Defense's (DOD) problems, that one of its jobs is to procure the best military airplanes in the world, for possible use in combat against an opponent who also is trying his level best to develop the best military airplanes in the world. Nothing less than the defense of the United States and the lives of the pilots is at stake here.   This is a serious market that demands the full and exclusive dedication of all those who participate in it.

The DOD procedure for procuring the best airplanes in the world at reasonable cost has been the competitive procurement contract. The system has generally produced good results.   However, if after awarding a competitive contract, DOD decides that the aircraft is not turning out as good as needed, or that our opponent has developed a better one, it will cancel the contract. The defense of the United States is always the overriding consideration.

The Grumman complaint about excessive capability in the aircraft industry is without foundation. Before the take-over by the business managers and lawyers, Grumman thrived in an environment of competition. The F4F and the F6F contracts were won under heavy competition.   There were eight bidders competing for the LM. Without competition, DOD can never be sure that it is getting a good deal.

The letter on page 386 is signed by Renso Caporali, Chairman of the Board and Chief Executive Officer, who started to work at Grumman in the engineering department where he stayed for a few years. I never had anything to do with him. Apparently, he decided that he could make a lot more money in management, where he learned his business management lessons well, and forgot everything he learned, or should have learned, in engineering.

I experienced the effects of outside hiring when I was building up the Reliability and Maintainability Section.   I think the company wanted to help me (their way) and give the Section more status, so they hired a retired Navy captain (engineering specialist) as my supervisor. He had no concept of design engineering, he was an expert on part numbers and how to order the right spare and replacement parts from a supplier. He had never heard of reliability technology, and could not believe anything I told him. He was disturbed that I was telling designers what to do. He wanted to know who authorized what I was doing. I told him that my job was to assure that the reliability of Grumman equipment complied with Navy specs. I watched preliminary design, and identified systems that had a reliability of less than one. These systems I followed through the design and test stages and assured that their reliability met their specification requirement.

Nobody told me what to do. He was unhappy with this explanation, and told me to stop what I was doing, until he investigated. I just ignored and avoided him. He just sat in his office in the supervisors section and never went out. Eventually, he just disappeared. I don't know if he was transferred or quit, I never saw him again. Most of my old time associates were not as successful in dealing with new supervisors hired from the outside.

Six months after Caporali sent his letter, page 386, to the Secretary of Defense, Grumman merged with Northrop and turned the lights out in Bethpage.

Grumman Corporation
Bethpage New York 11714-3580

Dr Renso L. Caporall
Chairman of the Board and
Chief Executive Officer

October 4, 1993

The Honorable Les Aspin
Secretary of Defense
3E880, The Pentagon
Washington, DC 20101

Dear Mr. Secretary:

Since 1988, Grumman's strategic plan has called for expanding our electronics and information systems businesses while maintaining our expertise in aircraft and ground transportation. In response to the DoD's recently issued bottom-up review, we are further convinced that our strategy is appropriate. I would like to share some thoughts on this with you.

We are committed to remaining one of the nation's ten largest aerospace/defense companies. However, as you know, the bottom-up review indicated that there are too many airframe manufacturers competing for too little work. The market for high-performance military aircraft has been severely diminished by the cancellation of the A-X

We can no longer justify maintaining the staff and the facilities necessary to compete for the next attack/fighter prime contract when no one knows when that competition will happen This means we will be closing high-speed wind tunnels, sophisticated flight test facilities and other laboratories that are extremely underutilized with today's workload. It also means we will review our staffing in these highly specialized technical areas

Taking these costs out of our aircraft business will enable us to offer better prices for upgrade and modification work on F-14s, EA-6Bs and other Grumman aircraft. One of our top objectives for next year is to win the JPATS trainer competition. Of course we remain committed to the production of the E-2C Hawkeye. We will maintain the staff and facilities needed to do first quality work in these areas.

Caporali Letter to the Secretary of Defense, page 1

The Honorable Les Aspin   Page 2

     However, I expect our future prime aircraft contracts will be grounded in our electroncs systems expertise -- like Joint STARS, EF-111, E-2C and EA-6B -- not in our aerodynamics capabilities. We will build on our strengths in surveillance, electronics countermeasures, airborne early warning, and computer-based information systems.

     You're well aware that since World War II electronics systems capability has been the core of our aircraft, so I'm sure that none of this comes as much of a surprise to you.

     We are determined to keep Grumman strong and healthy. I am available at any time to discuss these measures with you, and I'll keep you informed as things progress.

                                        Best wishes,

                                        Renso L. Caporali

Caporali Letter to the Secretary of Defense, page 2

September 1993

Grumman Corporation
Strategic Statement

Grumman's current strong financial position is the result of a well-defined strategy for survival, change and growth   A continuing focus on shareholder value, through cash management and operating performance, has improved our position in the financial and investor markets, and provided access to capital for investment   Grumman is now positioned to leverage its strategy, technology and capabilities to address a challenging new marketplace and, through a series of carefully planned alliances, including acquisitions, undertake the changes needed to reposition the company for the future   These actions will be taken to both expand capabilities and market positions, and to achieve the economies of scale needed for sustainable competitive advantage and increased shareholder value.

Aircraft design and manufacture have been the core of Grumman's business since its inception   Continuing production programs, together with an increasingly important series of upgrades and system modifications such as those performed on the F 14, E-2, EA-6, EF-111, A-6 OV-1 and C 2 have fueled our company over many years   Today, however, the combined effects of the collapse of the Soviet Union and major global economic shifts have triggered dramatic, structural changes in the defense and aerospace industries. An almost complete absence of new starts and prospects for minimal production over the next decade have necessitated a rethinking of our strategy for the future   In the absence of strong Government support, sustaining the complete high performance airframe design and manufacturing capabilities associated with our traditional role as a vehicle prime contractor is clearly unaffordable   Conversely we have no intention of stepping away from our Customers and the more than 1000 Grumman aircraft currently in service, since an important and sizeable market for upgrade and modification work on our own and other's products continues to exist   Therefore Grumman is initiating a restructuring of strategy and infrastructure which will emphasize, enhance and exploit our system design, development production and integration capabilities, successfully developed and honed over the past three decades   We will compete on this basis, across all platforms, aircraft conversions and aircraft components each on the basis of best value for the individual customer   This position will allow Grumman to partner on any new aircraft program, and participate as a prime contractor on those programs which, like Joint STARS, depend upon the synthesis and integration of the on board systems as the key to success

Fundamental to this shift in strategic direction is an escalation in our emphasis of Electronic and Information Systems linked together through the process and infrastructure of Systems Engineering and Integration   In addition to an extraordinary breath of systems

Grumman Strategy, page 1

Grumman Corporation
Strategic Statement
Page 2 of 2

experience, Grumman brings more than 30 years of Electronics design, manufacture and systems integration experience to this objective Spanning the range from test equipment and trainers to the more recent combat electronics this experience will be exploited to achieve dominance in surveillance systems and electronic warfare, and be leveraged to achieve a leading position in the areas of battle management systems and delivery platform integration

Information Systems, both as an embedded element of defense systems and in stand-alone management and process systems, represents another major Grumman strength, one in which we have enjoyed significant success In recent years, our credentials as an integrator of hardware and software solutions has facilitated expansion into non-Defense Federal markets This experience and the leverage accruing from internal systems development provides a firm base from which to grow Sales to Federal State and local government customers are a continuing focus, but commercial endeavors that support these markets are also of growing interest

Consistent with this central theme of integrated systems, Grumman has and will continue to focus on non traditional applications of our primary raw material - advanced technology Early on our application of aerostructures technology led to a significant position in Ground Transportation, particularly in segments of the commercial vehicle and aluminum truck body market This position is now being leveraged to achieve growth in the broader transportation market In another arena Grumman has established a lead technology position in advanced Energy Systems critical to such diverse emerging requirements as nuclear waste management space propulsion and high speed rail transport Similar opportunities exist today for development and application of a broad range of technologies to problems of national and international scope including energy, environment and health, to name but a few In each case, prudent financial and operating parameters and market understanding will provide the framework to assure economic viability and competitive advantage

In summary, Grumman s strategy is to grow by becoming the supplier of choice for high technology, integrated systems to defense, other government related and selected commercial customers We will continually refine our technology capabilities, and infrastructure to better match market demands for agility and competitiveness, so as to further enhance operating performance and shareholder value Carefully planned and executed acquisitions and other forms of alliances will become an integral part of our strategy, allowing Grumman to establish a position among the leaders over a range of markets, and thereby reducing dependence on individual segments of our overall market

Grumman Strategy, page 2

US ARMY MATERIEL SYSTEMS ANALYSIS ACTIVITY,(AMSAA), ENGINEERING PROJECTS

CHANGING JOBS

Continued from page 373 (Resignation). When I quit Grumman, I was 59 years old. Grumman had a mandatory retirement age of 65. I did not want to retire at age 65. It is that much more difficult to get a job when you are 60. I decided that I had to act quickly.

My father was 81 and lived in Washington with Helen. She was taking good care of him and I did not want to interfere. But I wanted to be close by, in case I was needed.

Most aeronautic companies that I knew about had a 65 year retirement age just like Grumman. The US Government's retirement age was 70. I decided to go to work for the Government. While I was in Government service, they abolished the retirement age and I stayed on until I was almost 80.

An old ASME friend, Bob Dillaway, was Director of Laboratories, US Army, a three star slot. He was concerned that the Army knew too little about a contractor's problems when designing a new piece of Army equipment. He wanted to establish a small laboratory where the Army would design critical elements of a new piece of Army equipment in parallel with a contractor, to determine and establish a better understanding of the problems that a contractor was up against. Bob asked me if I would like to organize such a laboratory. I said that I would be delighted. Bob decided to locate the new laboratory at the US Army Materiel Systems Analysis Activity (AMSAA) at Aberdeen Proving Ground, Maryland, that is not far from Washington.

Bob told the Director of AMSAA, Dr Joe Sperrazza, that he should strengthen his engineering capability and recommended that he hire me. He did not tell Joe about his plans for a design laboratory, he wanted to get the allocation of funds first. Joe conducted a very pleasant, long interview with me, over three hours. He tried to find out as much as he could about me. He leafed through the draft of my book and admitted, that I would strengthen his engineering capability. He hired me to organize a new Engineering Section.

I moved into a motel room in Aberdeen and we planned for Eleanor to stay a few weeks in our house in Garden City until it was sold. Then she was to join me in my motel room until we found an apartment in town.

My immediate supervisor was Pat Bruno, an engineering graduate of New York University. We both admitted that New York University had an excellent engineering school and immediately got along very well together. Sperrazza had a   doctor's degree in engineering from Johns Hopkins University. Otherwise, there were very few people with engineering degrees at AMSAA, which employed about 400 people.

SOURCE SELECTION EVALUATION BOARD

Bruno and I had long discussions as he tried to give me an overview of the work done at AMSAA. His major project was monitoring the Army's vast ammunition storage facilities and assure that with time there was no degradation in reliability in the stored ammunition. This was one of the jobs that Nat Lichter (see page 303) had been associated with before I hired him at Grumman. Bruno was surprised and delighted when he found out how much I knew about his project. He gave me a few little jobs to do and seemed pleased with the way I did them.

After a few days, Bruno told me that the Army was organizing a Source Selection Evaluation Board for an Advanced Attack Helicopter in Granite City, Illinois, a northern suburb of St. Louis, and that AMSAA had been invited to send one man. It was a two month assignment. Bruno asked me if I would like to go. I readily agreed and thanked him for his confidence.

I picked up Eleanor in Garden City and we drove to St. Louis. I rented a real nice furnished apartment there for two months. Our house in Garden City had just been sold, but the closing had not yet taken place. Alan represented us at the closing. Our real estate agent was Mrs. Peters, wife of the long time Scoutmaster of our local Boy Scout Troop to which both Roy and Alan belonged.

A Source Selection Evaluation Board (SSEB) is the initial evaluation of the bids submitted in a competitive procurement. The SSEB consists of engineers and the evaluation is purely technical. The findings of the SSEB are reviewed by a Source Selection Board that includes members other than technical personnel and makes the final decision.

Everything about the two Boards was top secret, including meeting location and personnel. Our SSEB met at an abandoned, spooky Army base north of St. Louis. Each one of us members was considered a technical expert who needed no outside help. We were free to discuss our problems with one another at the office, but not anywhere else outside the office. We were strictly prohibited from calling our home offices or any other military installation for any reason. We were prohibited from talking to any of the bidders, except with special permission. Our Board consisted of over 50 individuals, supervised by a General. These men represented the best technical experts the Army could muster. A few men were borrowed from the Air Force, Navy, and NASA. Working hours were 12 hours a day, except Sundays when the office was open six hours.

Eleanor usually drove me to work, so she had the car during the day and could explore St. Louis. She had a ball. Alan visited us once in St. Louis, and we all had a real good time.

I was assigned to the engine group. The winning bidder proposed the use of a GE engine that had been in service for a number of years and had demonstrated that it was a fine engine. However, it was fully developed and no further increases in performance could be expected. I found the Lycoming engine that was designed for the M60A2 Tank and was the same size as the GE engine. It was a brand new design which had lots of room for increases in performance. But the critical consideration, in my opinion, was the fact that Army combat helicopters operate in close formation with the tanks and are stationed and serviced, not at a distant airport, but at temporary maintenance points near the battlefield, close to the maintenance points for the tanks. Having the same engine in both the helicopters and the tanks would mean one set of spare and replacement parts, and one team of mechanics who would service both helicopter and tank engines. I was real proud of this plan.

I was permitted to meet with the representatives of Lycoming to discuss this option. The only real important issue was the design of the attachment fittings that were different on the helicopter from those on the tank. Lycoming agreed with my plan, but wanted $50 million to modify the engine for helicopter use. I was shocked. I could design those fittings myself in less than a month.

I recommended that the Lycoming engine be selected, but that the cost of design of the attachment fittings be reduced to not more than one million. The SSEB just saw the $50 million sign and got scared. I think that they could not accept the idea of using an engine, that had been developed for tank usage, in a helicopter, although the performance of the tank engine per weight and space was the same as that of the GE engine, and the potential performance was superior. They could not believe that the only thing involved was the design of the attachment fittings. They selected the GE Engine.

The Advanced Attack Helicopter was eventually named the "Apache" and several hundred copies were built. On page 393 is a

DEPARTMENT OF THE ARMY
ADVANCED ATTACK HELICOPTER
SOURCE SELECTION EVALUATION BOARD
Headquarters & Installation Support Activity
Granite City, Illinois 62040

21 JUN 1973

SUBJECT: Letter of Appreciation

THRU: Director
US Army Materiel Systems Analysis Agency
Aberdeen Proving Ground, Maryland 21005

TO: Mr. John de S. Coutinho
AMXSY-RC

1. I would like to express my sincere appreciation for your outstanding performance of duty during the Advanced Attack Helicopter Source Selection Evaluation Board from 17 February to 18 April 1973. Your efforts were a major contribution to the successful accomplishment of this Board's mission within a rigid timeframe and resulted from many long hours of conscientiously applied efforts.

2. Your professional competence, experience, initiative and cooperation contributed materially in the effective and timely completion of the engines proposed for the Advanced Attack Helicopter.

3. It is only through the competence and diligent efforts of individuals like yourself that the Army can expect to successfully select the equipment for use by its troops. You should be proud of your efforts which were greatly appreciated by all in support of this evaluation.

WILLIAM H. BRABSON, JR.
Chairman, Advanced Attack Helicopter
Source Selection Evaluation Board

CF:
Official 201 File

Letter of Appreciation
Advanced Attack HelicopterSource Selection Evaluation Board

reproduction of the letter of appreciation that I received for this service.

FORTY SIX EAST BE AIR AVENUE

Upon returning to Aberdeen from St. Louis, one of our first problems was finding an apartment. We were very successful in finding a convenient one at 46 East Be Air Avenue, close to the center of town and near the entrance gate to the Proving Ground. The building was one of a cluster of garden apartments. Our apartment was on the third and top floor and was very spacious. The single dining/living room was the largest room I had ever seen in an apartment.

Helen and my father came to visit several times, and Helen was enchanted with the place, primarily with all the space. She had never seen such large rooms in an apartment. We stayed here for over two years, until I found a nice lot in town and designed a house to fit on it.

We used the time we were in the apartment to get to know Aberdeen and the surrounding area, to look for a suitable lot in town where we could build a house. We eventually found a suitable lot in a new section called "Ramsgate," that seemed to be one of the finest developments in Aberdeen. The houses were all on one half acre lots (about 100 x 200 feet) or larger. We bought the lot at 602 Westgate Road, and later I also bought the lot next door, 604 Westgate, that I still own and that is undeveloped.

Next I had to design the house and find a builder. There were certain things I wanted in a house, and the only way to get them was to design the house myself. One thing was the basement. In Garden City, I had refinished the basement, complete with a built-in bar, and it had become a very important room in our house, where we held all our family and other big parties. I had a list of all the things that were wrong with our Garden City basement that I was going to correct, namely:

1. The ceiling was too low. Tall people hit their heads on the beam. I wanted an eight foot clear ceiling.
2. There were two poles that shortened the span of the beam that held up the overhead floor. They spoiled the continuity of space in the room.
3. The heating system took up too much valuable space.
4. The stairwell in the middle of the house broke up the room.
5. There were no kitchen facilities, we had to bring everything down the stairs.

Some of my architectural concepts were formed as a result of experiences I had many years ago. For example, many of the churches in the small towns around Meersburg that I explored with my bicycle are very ornate and frilly baroque structures with lots of gold decorations, that made a big impression on me. They were built by the rich monasteries rather than by the local people as I have explained on page 80. During one of my mother's visits, we went to the Meersburg parish church, which was a plain box, obviously built by the local community with limited funds. I made some comments to my mother about the church being such a plain box. She answered: "But it is such a beautiful box!" I have never forgot this lesson.

Before the time of Christ, Meersburg was for some centuries at the frontier of the Roman Empire and the site of a large Roman fortress. The surrounding town had about 2000 residents, it was as big and as important as Paris in its day.

When my parents left me in Meersburg, it was midsummer and about six weeks before the start of school. The brothers used the school's dormitories and dining halls during the summer as a youth hostel, while their regular students were on summer vacation. They had no place for me. They made arrangements with the wife of the local physician to take care of me until school opened. The doctor had his office and lived in the old center of town, where the houses were over 2000 years old, originally built before Jesus Christ was born. Well-to-do people in Europe like to live in old places like this. Those houses had all the then modern conveniences, like plumbing, electricity, central heating, and telephones, but the people were very careful to keep the old appearances on the outside. One item, for example, is the size of windows. Two thousand years ago, large glass panes were not available, and windows in houses were very small, as they still are on the street side of the old Meersburg houses. But in the back, the windows are large, and the rooms are bright and cheery.

The lowest level of the house was level with the outside street, the Remans had not yet introduced the "cellar." You entered the house into a big fifteen foot high room, as big as the outside dimensions of the house. It had three stalls for horses and all the facilities needed to take care of the horses and carriages. The front door to the street was a very large, fancy wood carved affair, large enough to let a horse and carriage pass. The big door had a small door built into it for pedestrians. A set of stairs led to the living quarters upstairs. I had a nice room in the attic. The doctor and his family were very kind to me.

I have never forgotten the impression I got when coming in from the street into this large room. I started the design of my new house with a layout of the basement, to be level with the driveway. I laid out the outside dimensions, 52 x 30 feet. I had the concept of a "box," with the intention of adding decorations later. Along the short north side, I laid out a two car garage and my shop. Next to my shop, along the front of the house, was Eleanor's laundry room, a small bathroom, and the stairwell. I used two steel beams with a 30 foot span to hold up the floor on the level above. This construction resulted in one big and high basement room with no poles. I put a fireplace in the middle of the south wall, and near it along the wall, provisions for a complete kitchen.

Eleanor wanted a big porch, so I put a twelve foot wide porch along the full length of the back (east side) of the house. The roof extended over the porch, and underneath the porch was a concrete patio. I provided for a similar patio, six feet wide, along the full length of the front of the house. On the north side of the house there was the concrete driveway. I added a three foot concrete walkway along the south edge of the house, so now I had concrete adjacent to the house on all sides, to divert the rain water from the foundation walls.

The thing I omitted from the basement was the heating and air conditioning plant. This was a very large piece of equipment which I could not accommodate in the basement. I designed a solid platform for it and installed it in the attic. I mounted the outside edge of the platform along the north wall, and the inside edge on lolly columns that were hidden in the living room walls and were mounted on the steel beams in the basement. The platform itself was mounted on its four corners with some vibration isolators that I still had in my tool box, and that were designed to mount jet engines on an aircraft.

The builder was very skeptical of this installation and told me that the vibrations from the heating and air conditioning system would tear the whole house apart in six months. He came to the house one day after it was finished and the heating system went on. He heard a very low hum and was puzzled where it came from. I told him that it was the heating system. He could not believe it. We lived in the house for twenty years and never had any problems with the installation.

The front patio with the entrance door was four feet above the basement floor. The front door opened on a small foyer that had six steps up into the living room, and six steps down to our basement room.

The kitchen was in the southwest corner of the house, between the south wall and the stairwell. A window in the front of the house provided a view of the street. In back of the kitchen, extending to the east wall, was the dining room.

The sleeping quarters were on the north side of the house where we had three bedrooms and two bathrooms with outside windows. With great difficulty, I was able to get an oversized bathtub. Since we left Aberdeen, Eleanor has never been happy with the bathtubs we have had to live with.

This arrangement of concentrating the sleeping quarters on the north side of the house left space for a huge living room in the center of the house. It was quite impressive when you entered the house through the front door and came up the short set of steps into such a large and bright living room.

The back porch, that I later enclosed with awning windows, proved to be a popular substitute safe playground when we had small visitors. When Roy lived in Connecticut, he would visit occasionally with his two little girls. We bought a large log cabin playhouse, five feet high, and set it up on the porch. It was a great attraction until Roy moved to Indiana. We gave him the playhouse and he installed it in his back yard there.

So far, I had a nice box of a house, but now I had to dress it up so it would fit into a neighborhood of fine houses. I placed six white columns, twelve inches in diameter, along the front of the house, holding up the front edge of the roof. It looked spectacular, and there were no complaints about looks.

I prepared a set of working drawings and sealed them with my New York professional engineers seal. (Later on I acquired a Maryland seal.) My drawings were approved without comment by the Aberdeen Planning and Zoning Commission that issued a building permit.

I paid for the house with the money we had received from the sale of our house in Garden City. I ran out of money and the builder left the house a little unfinished. I had to do some of the painting, and work in the attic and basement. With all the work I had to do on our large lot, I could not finish all the work I wanted to do on the house in the twenty years that I lived there.

As soon as the house was livable, we left our beautiful apartment at 46 Be Air Avenue and moved into our gorgeous new home at 602 Westgate Road, see page 398.

ORGANIZING AN ENGINEERING SECTION

Sperrazza issued a notice to all AMSAA that I was organizing an Engineering Section and that anybody who wanted to join should

Coutinho's House, 602 Westgate Road, Aberdeen, MD

come and see me. Practically all 400 employees of AMSAA came.

I had in my mind what Dillaway had told me about a design group, so I was looking for design engineers. There were none at AMSAA. Many of the men I interviewed and did not accept were statisticians and were upset and angry at me for the next twenty years because they knew that they were so smart and could solve any kind of problem, engineering or otherwise. They did not understand why I turned them down.

Unfortunately, Dillaway's plans never materialized. He had been Director of Laboratories for quite a few years. But with a change in the political administration, the military, who wanted that spot for a military general, prevailed, Dillaway lost his position. So my design group never became a reality. My assignments from Sperrazza and Bruno required little design work, and I could have used some good analytical engineers.

I finally decided on two men who I thought had design possibilities. One was Dr. Jim Liu, a Chinese who had just earned his doctorate under Prof. Hausmann (not his real name) at the University of South Carolina. Then there was young Nick Hagis, an engineering graduate of Johns Hopkins and former employee of Martin. Although these two men had no design experience, I felt I could work with them.

Later, I found Bob Marchetti, a mature engineer, also a former Martin employee, and an outstanding mathematician. I felt that he could be useful in support of our engineering investigations.

M60A2 FAILURE TO RETURN TO BATTERY (FRB)

One morning, Bruno came into my office and told me to come with him, the General just called and we have to go to a meeting in Washington.

On the way, Bruno told me the story. The M60A2 tank with the M162 main gun is the Army's newest, most sophisticated tank, probably the best in the world. Six hundred have been built and have been standing on a dock in Brooklyn for two years, awaiting shipment to Europe. They cannot be shipped because a defect has been discovered. In something like five to fifteen percent of the guns, the gun *Fails to Return to Battery* (FRB) after being fired. This means that the recoiled part of the gun does not completely return to its original position (called battery) so that the gun can no longer be fired.

When we arrived at the Army Materiel Command (AMC), the meeting was already in progress in a large auditorium, presided over by Major General Sammit and the Tank Program Manager (a Colonel). In the room, there were about 100 men, representatives of all the automotive industry laboratories that were working on the FRB problem. This was a very big problem, and the entire industry was involved. We listened for over an hour as one learned group after another got up and explained what they were doing, and giving lame excuses of why they, after two years, had no ideas of how to eliminate the FRB in the guns.

General Sammit noticed Bruno and me enter the room. He was getting more and more frustrated. Finally, he looked at us and said:

"Can you guys from AMSAA help?"

I answered: "General, that's why we're here!"

General: "What do you need ?"

This was a tough technical question that had to be answered immediately. Without much thinking, I answered:

"Ten guns."

The Program Manager jumped up to his feet all excited and yelled:

"TEN GUNS! From where does that guy think we are going to get ten guns?"

General to Program Manager: "That's why you have those eagles on your shoulders, so you can get people the resources they need to do their jobs!"

The General turns and rapidly goes out the nearest door, which he slams with a loud BANG! Everybody in the room is petrified, except Bruno and me. Bruno gives me a shove and says:

"John, quick! Let's get the hell out of here!"

While everybody is still dazed in their seats, we are out the door, into the car, and driving back to Aberdeen.

Before the week was up, I had ten guns delivered to me at Aberdeen. I locked them up in a "secret" warehouse and kept the key. Nobody else could get to them.

I had listened carefully in Washington to how the members of the automotive community were approaching the problem. All of them were in the midst of analytical approaches. This is what you learn in engineering school, and it is the general approach applied by most engineers to all their problems. However, as a result of my unique reliability engineering experiences, I knew that there are cases where the analytical approach has its limits, and you have to apply an empirical approach. In Washington, not a single member of the automotive community was applying an empirical approach.

I knew exactly what I had to do, and was confident that I was going to find a solution. Neither Sperrazza nor Bruno agreed, and I was sure that I could not explain it to them, they did not have the background to understand. I decided not to ever tell them what I was doing, just say that I was making progress and was sure that I was going to come up with a solution. They could not stop me because I had the General's ten guns locked up in my secret closet.

The first thing I did was to get a set of drawings of the gun and gave them to Marchetti to design a mathematical model of the gun. For a required performance, a mathematical model describes the behavior of every moving part of the gun during the period of a shot and the process of returning to battery. The results are usually shown on a set of curves.

Then I went to the Test and Evaluation Command (TECOM), across the street from AMSAA, and borrowed a real good test engineer and an instrumentation trailer. The trailer was as big as those 16-wheel jobs that pass you on the expressways. I just had to say that I was working on a special assignment from General Sammit and I got everything I asked for.

I set up one of my guns on a secret range at Aberdeen. All of my operations were done under a thick cloak of secrecy. The automotive community was very nosy, they pestered Sperrazza to find out how I was doing, that was another reason why I did not tell him anything. My test engineer instrumented the gun, as can be seen on page 402. Then I ordered a truck load of ammunition.

We had to decide on a reference point from which everything would be measured. We could not rely on shot number, which many people do, because each round of ammunition can be very slightly different. We selected a point ten feet ahead of the muzzle of the gun, where we measured the speed of the round.

Finally, we were ready for our first shot. Amazingly, everything worked. We got a nice reading at every instrument point. We compared these measurements with Marchetti's model, and every measurement agreed with the model value. This was a most important result, it meant we could predict analytically what the behavior of the gun elements was going to be on future shots. We had established "control" of the gun.

I started to shoot one round after the other, as fast as I could, always comparing the measured values with the model after every shot. The values always agreed. I intended to keep this up until I got a FRB.

Sperrazza called me in a few times to see how I was doing. I always assured him that I was making progress and was sure that I would arrive at a solution, but never told him exactly what I was doing. He was under heavy pressure from the automotive community to get me off the job, as I was not a member of the automotive community. Tanks are not procured like aircraft in a competitive procurement process. The procurement system for tanks is more like the system in other countries. Most of the critical tank features are developed in Army laboratories. The US tank manufacturer is Chrysler, who has its

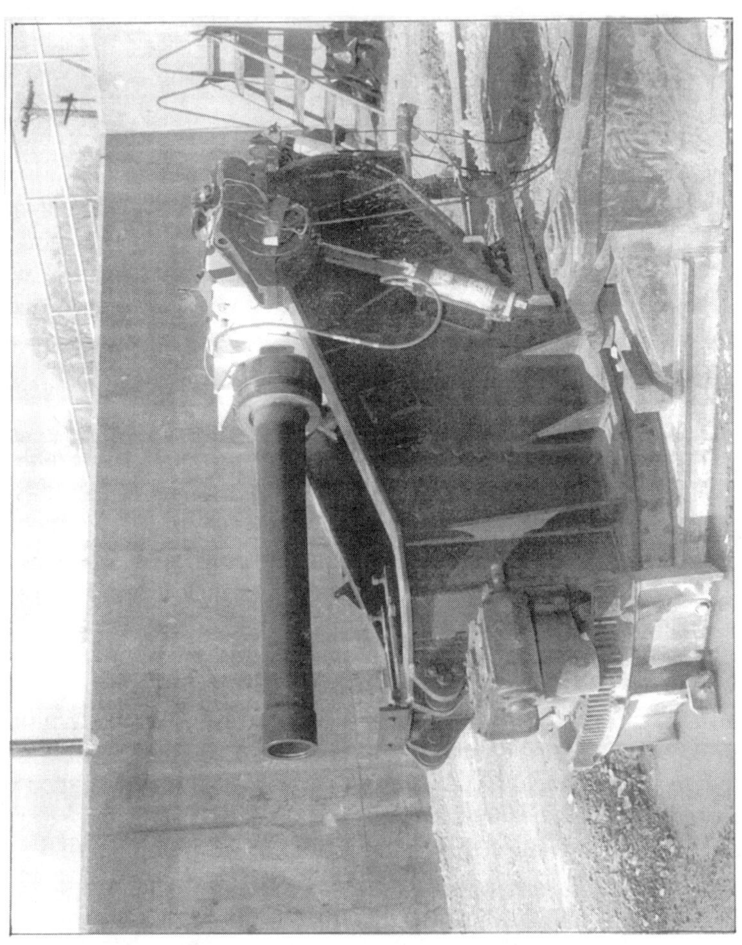

Instrumented M162 Main Gun for the M60A2 Tank Mounted in a Firing Test Stand

giant tank manufacturing plant next to the Army Tank and Automotive Command (TACOM) in Detroit. Chrysler maintains a closed shop, iron grip on its suppliers. No Army communication with any of the subcontractors is ever allowed. The General's meeting that I referred to above was most extraordinary and an act of desperation on the part of the General. My assignment of this task was an infraction on TACOM's sacred relationships. The automotive community is a closed shop, they will not tolerate an outsider working on any of their projects. I was very much of a sore point with them. Sperrazza assured me that if I just quietly dropped the job, it would not be held against me. I was glad I had established such tight security measures.

After about two months, it happened, we got a FRB! We took the gun to the laboratory and started to dismantle it. As we emptied the oil out of the recoil cylinder, we observed loose pieces of rubber floating in the oil. On further disassembly, we found that the piston O-ring had disintegrated and under the extreme pressure, extruded itself between the piston and the cylinder wall, locking the piston in place and preventing it from returning to battery.

I took a second gun and put it through the the same procedure. We obtained the same result. I was now sure that the O-ring failure was the reason for the FRB. It was also apparent that every gun would have an FRB if enough rounds were fired, not just five to fifteen percent of the guns as originally was thought. I wrote a report describing my tests and the results and sent it to General Sammit at AMC.

In a day or two, AMSAA received a message ordering Sperrazza, Bruno, and myself to appear before the Commander of the Armament and Chemical Command at Rock Island, Illinois, and discuss my report. Sperrazza and Bruno decided that they were engaged in some very important work and could not possibly go. I was told to go alone and represent them.

At Rock Island, I was ushered into a room full of some thirty colonels with angrily scowling faces, there was no doubt that I was in enemy territory. The automotive industry seemed determined not to let me, an outsider, succeed. Only the three star general sitting across the table from me, seemed relaxed and friendly.

His first concern was that that the results of the model and the instrumented tests agreed, how could that be? I knew what his trouble was. Marchetti had been able to acquire surreptitiously the Armament Command's model; and had checked it carefully. He had found a small error in it; however there was no way that the results of this model could agree with test measurements. This is what the automotive community believed to be true in general, and is what the General had been told by his men and what he also believed. Now I was telling him just the opposite. I could not tell him about the error in his model, because I was not supposed to have seen it. I knew that his engineers would find the error eventually.

The General was briefed to show that by my maintaining that model and test results must agree, I did not know what I was talking about, and he could throw out the rest of the report. He questioned me very thoroughly, and I held my own by explaining to him in detail that a properly designed model analyses the specified gun performance and in turn derives the required performance for each moving element of the gun. When a gun is built and tested, the test must show that each element functions exactly as required by the model, or the gun will not meet its specified requirements. I told him this is standard engineering design control procedure.

The General could not shake me and did not know what to believe, so he changed the subject. He looked over my test results and recommendation for a new piston O-ring. This made sense to him, and he immediately ordered a redesign of the O-ring.

The new piston O-rings were installed in the tanks and tested. They eliminated the FRB. The new O-rings were installed in all the tanks on the Brooklyn dock, and the tanks were shipped to Europe. I returned ten guns to the Program Manager, two of them slightly used.

This had been a case of me against the collective automotive laboratories of the United States, and I won.

Some months later, the Program Manager was returning from a review of tank performance in Europe and stopped at my office in Aberdeen, on his way home to Rock Island. He told me that everything on the tank worked fine. However, the tank was so sophisticated and complicated, that normal tank crews could not handle it; they hated the tank. The Army then experimented with crews consisting of college graduates who had attended four years of college, no matter what subject. These crews loved the tank and operated it well at its performance limits. However, the Army was not able to recruit many such college educated tank crews, and had to abandon the tank. It was a terrific loss for the Army.

The M60A2 tank was superseded by the M60A3 tank that turned out to be very successful and popular.

TNT PLANT EXPLOSION

On May 31, 1974, an explosion occurred at the Army Ammunition Plant in Radford, Virginia. Bruno suggested that I go take a look. I asked for a two day postponement of my trip, so I could educate myself in blast dynamics.

Blast dynamics is a subject that was first investigated by Professor Hausmann in his younger days when he was head of the Engineering School at the Johns Hopkins University in Baltimore. He divided his investigation into ten parts, and assigned each part to a graduate student as a doctoral project. One of these students was Joe Sperrazza. These ten students, after receiving their doctorates, spread all over the country. They maintain contact with one another and provide local service in blast dynamics wherever it is needed.

Sperrazza, while he was working at the Ballistics Research Laboratory (BRL) that is next door to AMSAA, educated a group of his men in blast dynamics. I went over to BRL and got myself briefed on the highlights of the subject.

I drove to Radford and took Eleanor along. It was beautiful weather and we had a pleasant trip. Radford is the site of the Virginia Polytechnic Institute and the students were all packing up to go home for summer vacation. There was a lot of activity all over town, and Eleanor had a good time student-watching.

The Board of Investigation had been in session for several days when I arrived. The purpose of a Board of Investigation is to determine the cause of an accident and to make recommendations to prevent such accidents in the future. The members of a Board must be knowledgeable in all aspects of their specialties.

I was cordially welcomed by the Board and shown how a TNT (Trinitrotolene) plant works. Such a plant is usually a square building, built over a huge water tank as big as the building itself. Around the inside walls, there are some eighteen large tubs with machine driven paddles. Raw materials and water are filled in the first tub, where they are thoroughly mixed. The mixture is then bled into the second tank, where more raw materials are added, and again thoroughly mixed. This procedure is repeated through each tub, until the last one, where the final product, after being thoroughly mixed, is poured into molds where it hardens.

The mechanism that supports each tub is attached to a cord that hangs from the ceiling. The cord runs along the ceiling to the center of the room, where the other end hangs over the operator's table with a tag identifying the tub to which it is connected. In an emergency, and in a TNT plant, the slightest irregularity in the operation of a tub is an emergency, the operator will pull the cord and that dumps the the tub into the water tank below and stops the operation of the plant. There is also a red cord at the operator's station, if this is pulled, all the tubs are dumped into the water.

In the case of the May 31 explosion, the operator saw a small flame between two tubs, and he did not have time to pull the cords, he just evacuated the plant as fast as he could. The plant was built on

DEPARTMENT OF THE ARMY
HEADQUARTERS UNITED STATES ARMY ARMAMENT COMMAND
ROCK ISLAND ILLINOIS 61201

REPLY TO
ATTENTION OF
SARVO

? 2 AUG 1974

SUBJECT: Letter of Appreciation

THRU: Commander
           US Army Materiel Command
           5001 Eisenhower Avenue
           Alexandria, VA   22333

TO: Director
           US Army Material Systems Analysis Agency
           Aberdeen Proving Ground, Maryland   21005

1. On behalf of this Command, I would like to express my appreciation
to your agency for its support to the Board of Investigation for the
explosion that occurred at the Radford Army Ammunition Plant on 31 May
1974. Dr. John De S. Coutinho, Chief of the Engineering Branch, visited
Radford on 8 and 9 June 1974, and provided much meaningful information
and background in the technical area of blast attenuation. His information was of particular value since no member of the Board had expertise
in Dr. Coutinho's area of speciality.

2. Please extend to your agency and Dr. Coutinho my thanks for the
services provided which, in part, will allow for continued and safer TNT
production operations in the future.

                           JOHN C. RAAEN, JR.
                           Major General, USA
                           Commanding

General Raaen's Letter of Appreciation

hill, and the bottom of the hill was cut to let a road pass. The operator ran for this spot and threw himself down onto the road, along the cut. The explosion passed over him and he was unhurt.

There was nothing left of the plant. The explosion left a great big hole in the ground, some 200 feet in diameter and 50 feet deep. Heavy pieces of equipment, such as large pieces of the tubs, were found over three miles away.

The Board was perplexed about the great size of the hole. I got out my equations and calculated the approximate amount of TNT required to blow such a large hole. It was a much larger amount of TNT than what the Board had assumed. The Board felt that only the last tub had TNT of the full composition and would be capable of explosion, that the other tubs would not yet have the full composition of TNT and would not explode, but only burn. However, in view of my numbers, the Board reconsidered its viewpoint and accepted the theory that under the intense heat of the original explosion in the last tub, the contents of the other tubs would also explode.

I also participated in the Board's review of the safety features built into an ammunition plant, and how to lay out and space a cluster of ammunition plants, and take advantage of geographical features. I was able to make a few suggestions in these discussions.

By the end of the second day, the Board could not think of any additional questions to ask me, and I returned home. A short time later, I received the nice letter of appreciation from General Raaen shown on page 406.

BLAST RESISTANT FENCE

The Nuclear Regulatory Commission (NRC) was concerned that its contractors did not have secure storage facilities for "Special Nuclear Material (SNM)." The need for accessibility and maintenance ruled out the use of sophisticated underground vaults such as those used for precious metals. A series of Joint NRC/DOD surveys indicated that there was a great deal of variation in the design of vaults and their penetration delay capabilities. None appeared to be satisfactory. Both agencies agreed to cooperate in evolving a comprehensive security system. AMSAA was assigned by AMC to help the NRC.

Typically, NRC contractors would have a vault or strong room with an alarm system and a single guard at night. A team of intruders, intent on stealing the nuclear material in the late hours of the night, would probably shoot the guard. The alarm system would go off in the guards' dormitory some distance away. It would take a team of guards at least twenty minutes to awaken, get dressed, get to their vehicles and respond to the alarm. By this time, the intruders, who could have made as much noise as necessary, and who would have cased the facility in advance, will have used explosives to penetrate the vault walls, will have stolen the nuclear material, and will have departed. NRC was looking for the design of a secure vault that contractors could build in their facilities and which could not be penetrated in less than 30 minutes.

Sperrazza had an idea! Somewhere in Europe, he had seen a demilitarizing plant where explosives were destroyed in an open field. The surrounding area was protected by a thick circular grove of evergreens that surrounded the demilitarizing activity. The needle-like leaves of the evergreens acted as an effective blast attenuator. In another case, he visited a demilitarization plant in Great Britain, where the blast was attenuated by a depth of rows of hanging ropes. It was therefore indicated that blast can be attenuated by a series of screens. Sperrazza asked me to design a screen that could be used as a vault wall and could not be penetrated by explosives in less that 30 minutes.

I felt that there was a significant difference between the trees and the ropes at a demilitarization plant, where there was a considerable distance between the exploding material and the attenuator, and a situation where the explosives would be attached to the vault wall. I felt we needed a screen of strong steel bars. Sperrazza agreed, and I found a supply of 1.5 inch round steel bars in a warehouse that I appropriated. Sperrazza also agreed that a 6 x 6 foot, 3 foot deep test specimen would be fine.

The next step was to prepare an engineering working drawing of the test specimen. I was the only one at AMSAA who knew how to prepare such drawings, so I got out my drawing supplies and went to work. My friends at the office had never seen an engineering drawing, much less anybody making one. There was almost always somebody around my drawing table watching me work. My major problem was to stagger the bars such that there was no clear line-of-sight through the specimen that would provide the blast with a clear path.

I found some one inch thick steel plates that I used for the top, bottom and side covers of the test specimen. I specified the location of the holes for the bars on the outside of the covers, so the bars would stick through the cover plates and could be welded on the outside. I found an excellent welder in one of the Ordnance School shops, and he did an outstanding job, see page 409. We decided to call the specimen a "Blast Resistant Fence" to divert attention from the real intended use. I specified mounting on a thick steel base and a front covering of a thin sheet of steel, so the penetration team could not see the core of the specimen. The "Fence" specimen, mounted

Blast Screen of Blast Resistant Fence
1.5 in Rods, Mostly 3.5 in Spacing.
Weight 15668 lbs

on the firing range, is shown next to its proud designer on page 411. The white square in the center of the specimen is the area where the explosives may be emplaced.

I realized that this test was the first in what could be a long series of development tests. I thought that it was essential for my possible successors in future tests to know exactly what I had done. I had to use the simplest type of components and require no sophisticated manufacturing facilities for fabrication. The concept had to be one that could be easily reproduced by NRC contractors.

Our next task was to design the test plan. To provide a credible threat, NRC/AMSAA decided to invite Special Forces, Fort Bragg, GA (the famous Green Berets) to send an expert team to penetrate the test specimen.

I painted a line on the ground, 50 feet ahead of the test specimen, and placed the target (an empty gallon paint can) 15 feet behind the specimen. The penetration team was to stay in back of the 50 foot line, while one or two members of the team carrying explosives approached the test specimen, emplaced the explosives, and returned to the 50 foot line. While emplacing the explosives, their hands could not come closer than eight inches of the specimen. The APG Safety Officer was to fire the explosives. I would measure the time with my stop watch that a member of the team or the Safety Officer was in front of the 50 foot line. The total time that was required to penetrate the specimen was to be considered the measurement of the specimen's ability to resist penetration.

The objective of the test was to create a hole in the specimen, big enough   for a man to crawl through, pick up the target (paint can) and return through the hole to the 50 foot line.

The Fire Department was asked to have an engine on standby, and the hospital was alerted to possible emergencies.

A five man team plus two officers from Fort Bragg arrived the day before the test to execute the penetration. The officers were allowed to inspect the test specimen, but the team members did not see it. The officers decided what charges to build and supervised the men getting ready for the penetration.

We had expected them to use explosives, but did not tell them. We were willing to accept any penetration method that they recommended. On their own, the team members decided that the only feasible method of quick penetration was by explosives.

They brought nothing with them, but made use of the Aberdeen shops and storerooms. They manufactured:
a. One Linear (Ribbon) Charge (9.5 lbs of C4 explosive)
b. Two eight-inch Platter Charges (14.6 lbs of C4 explosive each). The explosive charge is sandwiched between two 8-in round, 0.5 in

Test Specimen with its Designer, Set Up and Ready for Test

thick steel plates.

c. One 24-inch Platter Charge (66.5 lbs of C4 explosive sandwiched between two 24 x 1-inch round steel plates) Total weight: 199.5 lbs.

d. Eight Bangalore torpedoes, 2.5-inch aluminum electrical conduit, each one filled with 6.7 lbs of C4 explosives.

The test specimen was penetrated with five charges:

1. Linear Charge
2. Eight-inch Platter Charge
3. Eight-inch Platter Charge
4. 24-inch Platter Charge
5. Five Bangalore Torpedoes

The result is shown on page 413, which also shows me second from left and Hagis, second from right. A Special Forces team member crawled through the hole in the specimen, retrieved the target (paint can), crawled back through the hole and returned with the paint can to the starting 50 foot line. Total time, for the five charges and retrieval of the paint can, was 12 minutes.

The test was witnessed by Sperrazza and a delegation from NRC. All test operations were recorded on motion pictures.

Since this was the first of what might be a series of development tests, I decided that it should be carefully documented and wrote a detailed report: "AMSAA Interim Note F-25, Test of Blast Resistant Fence, John de S. Coutinho, May, 1979." The report includes a reproduction of my engineering drawings, the test plan, a detailed description of the charges, and a log of the test.

The 24-in Platter Charge was an overkill. An eight-inch Platter Charge with 30 lbs of explosives, would have been sufficient to create complete penetration, that could have then been enlarged as required by more Bungler Torpedoes.

On page 413, on the ground in front of Hagis' feet, there are several broken pieces of bars, about a foot long. They are broken off in shear. There are also a number of broken rod ends visible in the specimen hole. Most have straight breaks, indicating a failure in shear. A close-in blast results primarily in a shear loading. This scenario is quite different from the blast loading at the demilitarization plants that Sperrazza initially talked about.

The 12 minute penetration time indicates that much work has to be done to develop design concepts to increase the penetration time to 30 minutes.

ENGINEERING - MISCELLANEOUS

Sperrazza was a high strung, very creative individual, he was constantly thinking up more engineering problems for us to work on

Blast Resistant Fence after Penetration Test
Coutinho is second from left, Hagis is second fron right

than we could possibly do. I often wrote a report to conclude an investigation. Some of the reports I wrote and jobs I did are listed below to indicate the scope of work that we did.

Repriortizing the Weapons Acquisition Process

To establish better control over the total cost of new aerial weapons, that do not require the application of new technology, the Army was experimenting with a new procurement concept: "Design to Cost." This procedure differs from conventional "Design to Performance" in three areas:

> a. *source selection*
> b. *control of parallel developments*, and
> c. *competitive flight/cost elimination*

The new *source selection* concept had been thought out at high levels in the Army, and corresponding procedures developed. However, not all the problems associated with b. *control of parallel developments* and c. *competitive flight/cost elimination* had been recognized. The purpose of this study was to identify those problems and to suggest possible procedures for further   discussion and consideration.

Suppressive   Structures

This job was managed by the Armament and Chemical Command Unit at the Edgewood Area of Aberdeen Proving Ground. I was assigned as a designer to this job because of my ability to prepare engineering drawings.

A suppressive structure is a vented steel structure enclosing an automatic manufacturing operation involving explosives. The structure is strong enough that it is not damaged by an accidental explosion, and the blast is attenuated by the vents so that it will not damage the ear drums of a man standing 75 feet from the explosion.

I designed four different types of vents and four quarter size test specimens, one for each type of vent. All four test specimens were successfully tested by the Armament and Chemical Command.

The next task was to find an application for the new technology. The fabrication of small charges appeared to be a good candidate. Small charges are manufactured on automatic machinery in explosion proof cells with heavily reinforced concrete walls, some three feet thick. Occasionally, there is an explosion in the production line. The damage to the machinery, if any, is quickly fixed, the dents in the wall are repaired and repainted. Since the production quotas were being met, there did not appear to be any need for suppressive structures in this application.

I studied the machinery for fabricating charges, and developed a design that I thought eliminated the explosions. The Army decided that my design was too expensive and the proposal was dropped. I remembered my trip to Radford where a TNT plant exploded and left a big hole in the ground, 50 x 200 ft. An automatic TNT plant would be the ideal application for a suppressive structure. But I could not think of a structure that could survive an explosion that made that big a hole in the ground.

Over-Design of Equipment

This study was prepared at the request of General Deane who was disturbed that his Program Managers (PM's) oftentimes did not have the data required to make cost effective design decisions. The purpose of this study was to determine the extent of over-design in Army equipment and propose appropriate corrective actions. Over-design is a product characteristic which increases cost but is not necessary to meet requirements. Under-design is the lack of product capability to meet requirements.

This was a big study and I interviewed almost all Army PM's and visited many suppliers. I organized a committee to help me. All advanced systems, military as well as commercial, evolve over a period of time. Initial prototypes will always include some elements of over and under-design.

The Army prefers competitive procurement procedures to reduce costs and minimize over design, and much effort is expended on developing alternate sources of supply. However, the size of the market for many Unique Military Items is too limited and often excludes alternate sources. In this situation, the Army has developed programs such as value engineering, Design To Cost, Incentives, Production Engineering Planning (PEP), and others. These procedures are effective to a degree, but they do not have the motivating force provided by competition. A concept still missing was the systematic approach for the elimination of over-design.

Much over and under-design results from the PM's lack of continuing visibility into low level design activities. *Design is at the heart of engineering:* it is a creative, intuitive activity; yet the process remains something of a mystery to most engineers and administrators who generally are not associated with design. At present, design is the weakest link in the development process. Designers do not have the status of, nor do they communicate well with, other engineers. In establishing tight development schedules, planners work backwards from the delivery date. They recognize and allot adequate time for all activities which are incompressible: shipping, testing, assembly, manufacturing, procurement of materials, even time for unproductive paperwork, and other activities. The remaining time is then allotted to design. It is seldom enough to allow the design team to do a good job.

This condition can be corrected by more in-depth program monitoring by technically competent personnel. The personnel and skills required for such monitoring exists within Army Organizations, but they are not being used for this purpose. It is recommended that use be made of the Ad Hoc Laboratory Staff Members, who represent the laboratories and who also are currently assigned to the PM's, to perform this function. These Staff Members should be made responsible for providing independent detail monitoring of the design and development process by expert consultant personnel recruited from facilities not involved in the project, to assure that:

1. The specified technical requirements properly reflect the user's operational needs.

2. Over and under design are minimized with respect to the specified requirements.

3. Margins of safety are consistent and reasonable to provide for inadvertent overloads and inadequacies in materials, manufacturing and quality assurance procedures.

4. The specification of MIL-STD's and MIL-SPEC's, especially the boiler plate provisions, have been tailored to achieved maximum cost effectiveness.

Representatives of the Staff Members should attend all monthly suppliers' design review meetings during the design phase to assure compliance with Items 1 to 4 above. Their attendance at these meetings must be contractually provided for. *There is no other way to obtain this information in a timely manner*!

The Staff Member shall review and sign off on the Technical Data Package that includes all design, test and inspection information, and he shall certify that the above listed functions 1 to 4 have been accomplished in the most effective manner possible under the circumstances. For each Technical Data Package reviewed, the Staff Member shall prepare a "Lessons Learned" report for the PM, listing any deficiencies noted in design and systems integration models and other design and test procedures, and including his recommendations for improving the development and monitoring process. The PM shall review this report and prepare appropriate recommendations for submittal to Army Materiel Command (AMC).

I never found out what General Deane did with my report.

Incentives for Reliability

In the aircraft industry, the incentives for reliability were self evident. On page 292 we see that the Navy could not afford to replace the aircraft it was losing in accidents. On page 288, Grumman management was terrified at the complexity of power operated flight control systems. In other industries and in the Army, the incentives were not so obvious. The transfer of reliability technology from the aircraft industry to other industries was a difficult problem. By chance, I became acquainted with the following story.

During the 1970's, I met and became friends with Ed Parascos, the one and only reliability engineer at the Consolidated Edison Company of New York. At that time, one of Con Edison's recurrent problems was the "brown-out," when the electrical power supply failed in a district of New York City.

Electrical power was supplied to local districts at 4000 volts. At each district, a transformer reduced the 4000 volts to 120 volts for local distribution. The problem was that the transformers would burn out once in a while. To supposedly prevent this, a team of inspectors would cover the city daily to read and record the temperature on each transformer. In actual fact, the inspectors spent their days playing cards in a local bar, and shortly before quitting time, they would put their heads together and fill out their reports, assuring that each one had a different set of imaginary numbers. When they turned in their reports, the very large stack of papers was carefully filed but never reviewed.

Parascos designed a form that could be machine read and acquired a reading and plotting machine. When the last man turned in his report at quitting time, Parascos threw the stack of papers into the machine and in less than 15 minutes he had history curves of all the transformer temperatures over time, one curve plotted over the other. With one look, he could see if any one curve was showing a temperature higher than the others, indicating that a transformer had a temperature that was increasing above the normal range.

One day, the daily readings on a specific transformer started to rise and Parascos drew a curve of the increasing temperatures and extrapolated them to show that in two weeks the transformer would burn out. He wrote a memo to management to this effect, namely, that there would be a brown out in this district in two weeks. Management thought his memo was a great joke. Parascos became the laughing stock of the company, that is, for two weeks until the transformer burned out as predicted.

Sometime later, he found another transformer with rising temperature, and he wrote another memo. This time, nobody laughed, but neither did they do anything. The transformer burned out as predicted, and the next day, the Vice President - Operations was in Parascos' office, wanting to find out, just how Parascos had done it. Parascos became a respected member of Con Edison's management team.

He had some interesting reliability problems. Electrical underground cables in Manhattan are shielded with a lead covering to keep out the moisture. Rats loved to gnaw through the lead, creating a short circuit and causing a local brown out. Automatic measuring devices locate the the location of the short from the nearest manhole. There are over one million (1,000,000) man holes in Manhattan.

Other departments observed Parascos' success in solving field problems, and asked for his help. In one case, they complained about the difficulty of parking service trucks during the day in New York City. Parascos developed a form that designated a parking space where a service truck could park early in the morning and could remain there for the rest of the day. The form listed the various jobs in the immediate vicinity that the men could do during the day, and all the tools and materials required to do the jobs. (Some of these jobs might be of low priority and would have been on the bottom of other lists.) The planning was not perfect, and sometimes jobs had to be rescheduled for another day, but the system was better than anything they had had before.

A night team would get the trucks ready and load them with all the tools and materials needed as noted on the form. In the morning, the service teams, on arrival, would jump into the trucks and drive off to their assigned parking spaces. When a service truck came back in the evening, another team would check it out, check all the tools and left over materials against the form. Losing tools had been a generally accepted practice at Con Edison, nobody thought anything of it. During the first year of use of Parascos' form, one screw driver was lost.

Parascos also discovered that operating equipment guaranteed for one year generally had a high probability of surviving five operational years before breakdown. Con Edison had a 30 year maintenance cycle for its generating plants. Parascos found a few pieces of equipment with a five year guarantee, but there was not much of that available. He was trying to show that operating equipment with five year guarantees had a probability of lasting 30 years before breakdown.

The incentive for achieving higher reliability was saving money and providing better service. Parascos' problems were different from those in the aircraft industry, but his objective was the same. Parascos organized an annual   "International Reliability Conference for the Electrical Power Industry" that I attended and where I presented several papers. There were quite a few engineers from

European power companies in attendance, which surprised me. I learned that European power companies have a far greater number of reliability engineers on their staffs than US companies. The reason for this is that socialistic European governments own both electric power generating companies and manufacturing facilities of all sorts. If power fails, production stops, and the loss to the state is considered unbearable. Thus, European power companies have a much greater incentive to assure the reliability of their plants than do US power companies that are not responsible for comparable loss of industrial production in case of a black out.

Steam Lava Flow Deflector (SLFD)

The US Geological Survey had been observing the swelling of the north east side of the Hawaiian volcano, Mauna Loa, for several years, and expected a possible eruption of lava in the near future. The major concern was for the city of Hilo, Hawaii. The safety of Hilo was the responsibility of the State of Hawaii that had requested the support of the US Military.

Historically, volcanic eruptions of Mauna Loa have consisted of relatively slow oozing of lava, with a minimum of volcanic ash. The problem is to prevent the lava flow from entering the Wailuku watershed that includes the city of Hilo.

If the lava starts to flow in the direction of Hilo, the Air Force is prepared to bomb the cone with laser guided 2000 lbs bombs to create an outlet for the lava in a different direction. However, if the Air Force bombing is not completely successful, some lava may still flow in a direction hazardous to Hilo.

Soon after eruption, as the lava flows in a channel, the outside surface of the channel hardens as the lava cools off, forming a crust that becomes the sides of the channel or even a tube. The molten lava flows inside this channel or tube.

At its front end, the flow moves forward slowly at a speed of about two tenths of a mile per hour. This condition presents a situation where there is some time available for diversionary action. The sides of the channel or the ceiling of the lava tube can be broken into chunks that will pile up into a barrier. The lava is forced to flow in a new direction or maybe just to spread out over a greater exposed surface for cooling off, thereby slowing or arresting the forward flow. The thickness of the lava crust forms at approximately two feet per week.

The best way to penetrate an established tube is by Air Force bombing with high explosives. In this case, the possibility of duds is a potential hazard, and accuracy is questionable since identification of targets is difficult.

Once a lava channel has been formed and the lava is flowing in a hazardous direction, AMSAA proposed the use of Steam Lava Flow Deflectors (SLFD) as a possible alternative. The SLFD is a sealed, insulated container filled to a predetermined level with water, and that can be carried by no more than two men. Once an undesirable direction of the lava flow is established, a number of these SLFD can be delivered by helicopter and anchored to the ground, intercepting the lava flow. Once the flow reaches and engulfs the SLFD, the heat of the lava will cause the water-filled containers to explode, breaking up the crust which will pile up into blocks and form a barrier, diverting the flow into a new direction or spreading it over a larger area where it can cool off. The SLFD must be securely anchored to the ground so it will not be pushed aside or float on top of the lava. The containers are insulated so they will not explode prematurely.

The energy released by a SLFD, on a weight basis, is about one half that of TNT. The SLFD is preferable to high explosives since the unexploded units are completely harmless. This feature allows hand emplacement at a safe distance ahead of the lava flow, and also permits the use of a larger intercepting field of dispersed SLFD.

I participated in the preparation of an AMSAA proposal to design, construct, deliver, store, and emplace SLFD in an emergency. However, the swelling of Manna Loa subsided, and the project was placed on hold.

PROFESSOR HAUSMANN

Professor Hausmann developed the theory of blast dynamics when he was head of the Engineering School at Johns Hopkins University as I described on page 399. Hopkins had a mandatory retirement age of 65, and at that time in his life, Hausmann moved on to the Engineering School of the University of South Carolina, that welcomed teachers who were over 65.

Sperrazza signed a contract with Hausmann as a consultant to AMSAA, for one day a month. At first, Hausmann looked around at AMSAA to find out what everybody was doing. Eventually, he spent all his time in my office, overlooking all our various jobs. He made many useful suggestions. I was very happy to have an outside unbiased authority looking over my shoulders making sure I did not make any mistakes.

I used to meet Hausmann regularly at ASME meetings, and we became quite friendly.

SPERRAZZA RETIRES

Sperrazza was married to a very lovely lady who understood well how to handle him. Her father had been a builder, and she took great interest as I designed and built my own house.

On a cold winter day, she took her two little poodles to Be Air for a trim. On the way back, the big Cadillac skidded on a batch of ice on the road, the car swerved and crashed into a telephone pole, colliding at the driver's seat. Mrs. Sperrazza was killed instantly.

Sperrazza went to pieces. In a short period of time, he remarried and redivorced several women. It soon became obvious that he could no longer function as AMSAA's Director.

For some years, Sperrazza had been training a young statistician, John McCarthy, to be his successor. He asked me to help McCarthy whenever I could, but McCarthy never let me come close to him.

When Sperrazza retired, his military advisor, Colonel Al DeProspero, took over temporarily. DeProspero was a very competent administrator. He was surprised at all the work my Branch was turning out, with only four men. He had assumed we were at least thirty people strong.

One of Sperrazza's ambitions was for AMSAA to develop a greater engineering capability. When he retired, he accepted a contract to come back and give four lectures to an assembly of all personnel. Sperrazza carefully analyzed the engineering disciplines and squeezed them into his four lectures, that is, all the engineering principles that are taught in a four year engineering curriculum. His objective was to get the AMSAA statisticians to recognize this body of knowledge and start to apply it in AMSAA work.

During his first lecture, except for the men in my Branch, nobody understood a word of what he was talking about. The three following lectures were canceled.

Sperrazza went to work for one of the small consulting outfits in Aberdeen. A few years later, he died.

BRUNO DIES

Shortly after Mrs. Sperrazza's accident, Bruno had a heart attack. He was in the Harford Memorial Hospital in Have de Grace and told that his condition was very serious. Under no circumstances was he to get out of bed.

He had to go to the bathroom, it was only a short walk. He got out of bed and was half way to the bathroom when he dropped to the floor, dead.

Bruno would have made a fine Director of AMSAA as successor to Sperrazza.

CHANGE IN MANAGEMENT

After Sperrazza's retirement, one of our Assistant Directors, Keith Myers, was appointed Director. He was a classical statistician and had no use for engineers. John McCarthy, Sperrazza's choice, was still too young to be considered. He remained as Chief of the Logistics and Readiness Analysis Division.

My Engineering Branch was dissolved, nobody had any use for us any more. Engineering was out, the word itself was disreputable. I lost my office, my three good men and excellent secretary. They had to go look for somebody that needed help and where they would fit in.

I was almost seventy years old, lived comfortably in a beautiful house in Aberdeen, and did not feel like looking for a new job. I looked around and found an empty desk, moved in and waited. I had tenure, a reputation at Headquarters, and I knew that eventually something would turn up.

REPAIR PARTS FOR COMBAT DAMAGE

Before this study in 1982, the Army provisioning system did not include any repair parts for combat conditions. Studies showed that weapon system availability for combat missions can vary significantly with part stockage levels. This present study was established to develop a comprehensive list of repair parts as required by front line troops in a combat environment. The study analyzed ten of the Army's front line weapon systems. This was a very large study and involved many people in AMSAA and BRL.

A master plan was hatched, to a weapon system to an existing computerized war game, and observe what mission essential parts got damaged, so they could be stocked and replaced by front line troops. Not all damaged parts in this scenario were mission essential, only those that prevented the system from continuing its mission. It was decided that a part is not mission essential if it:

> only contributes to crew comfort
> can be substituted by improvisation
> can be readily fabricated from bulk materials
> can be drawn from kits available to the crew
> is redundant to another system, part or component,
> is common hardware.

The following generic groups are not mission essential:

flotation equipment	special tools
armored doors	automatic rammer
all lights except IR	gages
access panels	spade
winterization kit	equipment boxes

> seats, except gunner's intercom equipment
> fire extinguisher, except engine

The first weapon system selected for this study was the M109A2, 155 mm, Self Propelled Howitzer. The study broke down into a number of tasks:

- Prepare computer generated representation of the weapon system
- Select suitable computerized war game

- List of weapon system parts damaged in the war game
- Identification of mission essential damaged parts.

Prepare   A Computer Generated Representation of the M109A2

This was a BRL job. The computer representation of the outside of the weapon system is shown on page 425.   Each individual part is identified by a unique National Stock Number (NSN).   All internal parts of the weapon system were enclosed in space envelopes, each one identified by a BRL Item Number.   Lists were prepared to associate each NSN with its BRL Item Number. A computer generated representation located each BRL Item in its proper place inside the weapon system.

Simulated War Games

In a simulated war game, missiles and steel fragments are aimed along a straight shot line through the weapon system, from various directions and at various speeds. The armor and each BRL Item will have some resistance to penetration, so if any projectile penetrates the armor, it will eventually be stopped along the shot line by the accumulated resistance of the BRL Items that it has penetrated. This study resulted in a list of damaged BRL Items.

Identification   of Mission Essential Damaged Parts

The identification of mission essential damaged parts among the parts damaged in the simulated war game proved to be an impossible task, since nobody knew how to identify a "mission essential" part. There were long discussions, and many ideas proposed by the smartest and brightest people in AMSAA and BRL, but all to no avail.

Finally, in desperation, McCarthy remembered me, called me in and told me to identify what BRL Items were "mission essential" in the list of BRL Items that were combat damaged in the computer representations. Being very aware of the limitations of the statistical mind-set, I knew exactly what to do.

The M109A2 Technical Manual (TM) is a book almost two inches thick. It contains exploded views of all the assemblies in the weapon system, showing every part by NSN in its relation to adjacent parts for every assembly.   I found these exploded views on 150 pages of the TM, and made view graphs of all of them.

I went over to the Ordnance School and recruited six Warrant

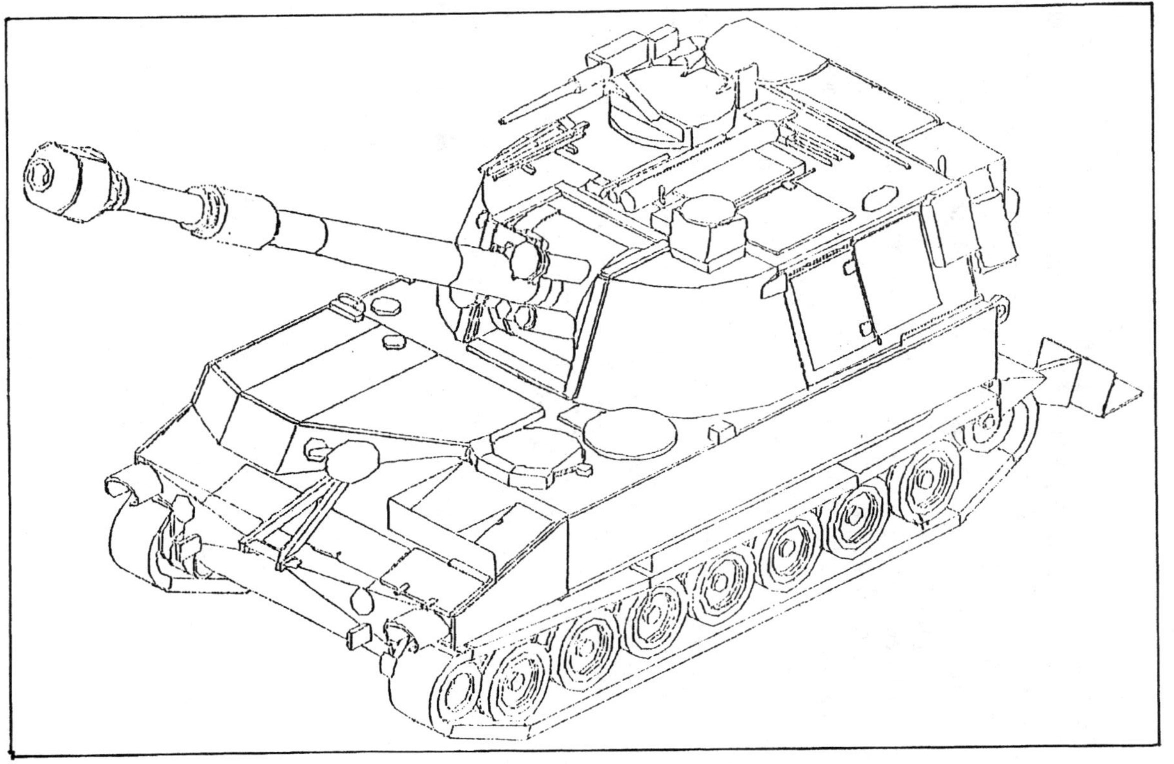

M109A2, 155 mm Self Propelled Howitzer-
Computer Generated Outline

Officers who instructed soldiers in the operation of the M109A2. These men knew the weapon system and its parts as well as the back of their hands.

I gathered my six new friends in a room with a projector, and showed them the first of my view graphs. I asked them, which of these parts would disable the M109A2 weapon system if they were damaged or failed. They pointed out the one or two parts that were "mission essential." There were no differences of opinion among the six experts during the entire exercise. I marked these parts with a red dot on my view graph.

It took us three days to review the 150 view graphs that I had, now reviewed by six professional experts.   I had a list of all the 1213 "mission essential" parts on the M109A2. I prepared a report that listed every "mission essential" part by Name, BRL Item Number, National Stock Number, TM Volume, TM Figure, and TM Item Number.

There was no way that this large number of 1213 "mission essential" parts could be stored at the front lines. Not all of these parts were likely to be damaged in combat. A computer vulnerability study is needed to determine which "mission essential" parts are likely to be damaged in combat. BRL was expert at this; they penetrated the computer model of page 425 with straight lines and those parts that were touched by a straight line were considered damaged. I prepared a number of similar reports of "mission essential" parts for other weapon systems. These reports were all used to prepare studies of the vulnerability of "mission essential" parts.

BATTLE FIELD DAMAGE ASSESSMENT AND REPAIR (BDAR)

I received a call from Dave Gilbert, our lawyer, who told me that he was organizing a team to go to a meeting in Washington, and that I should join him.

The meeting in Washington was chaired by Major General James Welch who explained that in combat, much equipment was damaged and discarded, when actually it could be repaired at or near the battlefield by clever, expedient procedures not in the Technical Manuals, and returned to a possibly degraded function in combat. At present, it is illegal to repair or service any Army equipment except by procedures authorized in a Technical Manual. General Welch wanted us to write a manual of expedient repair procedures for combat damaged equipment, to be used on a battlefield or close-by under cover.

Major Welch said that he was scheduled to retire in one year, and he wanted the manual to be available before that time so he could himself introduce it into the Army.

In order to emphasize the urgency and importance of this assignment, Gilbert decided to form a new group, whose exclusive task would be the preparation of the new manual, to be housed in a separate building to minimize distractions.

I was surprised that I was included on this team. I could not imagine that either Gilbert or McCarthy would have selected me. Gilbert, as a lawyer, did not like me as I was an engineer, it was something that he could not understand. He did not like the way I did things. Several times before this project, he told me I could not do certain things that I was doing. I felt that what I was doing was a technical necessity and disregarded his advice. Lawyers don't like it when you do that. My inclusion on this team must have been specifically requested by the Army Materiel Command (AMC) in Washington where I had an outstanding reputation as an engineer who got things done. Nevertheless, I recognized that I was the lowest man on the totem pole, and that McCarthy was carefully watching my every move.

One of the first tasks the group undertook was to agree on a name for this operation. After much discussion, it was decided to call it: *Battle Damage Assessment and Repair (BDAR)*. The word *Assessment* was considered of utmost importance since the scope of battle damage can be very large, every case can be different, and an assessment is first required to determine if and how the damage can best be repaired.

We decided to prepare two manuals, one for the new M60A3 tank, and another for all the other Army armored vehicles. The M60A3 Manual was assigned to Clay McDowell, and I was assigned the other manual for armored vehicles.

Our supervisor was a loudmouth who, as far as I could tell, made no contribution to the manuals. I believe that Gilbert thought he was a genius.

THE WORLD STATUS OF BDAR

McDowell and I worked on the preparation of the manuals without any further actual guidance or interference. The rest of the group was engaged in learning what applications of "BDAR" there might be in the rest of the world.

The Air Force had started a program of expedient repair of aircraft that were damaged in combat. The program was being conducted at four Air Force Bases. Expedient, quick repairs were developed for aircraft damaged in combat, but that could still fly back to a repair facility. For those aircraft that landed elsewhere and were still salvageable, repair teams would be sent out to apply expedient, quick repairs so that the aircraft could fly to a repair base.

Navy ships at sea are much on their own, and their crews are well trained in expedient procedures that might be necessary in case of accidents or battle damage.

The Israelis had developed an effective program of expedient battle damage repair. Israel is a small country with a good network of railroads. Battle damaged tanks were loaded on a flat car and returned to the factory where they were repaired overnight in the most expedient manner, and returned to the front lines by flat car. Generally, repaired tanks could be returned in 24 hours. However, the bulk of the expedient repair was performed near the front lines.

The most dramatic instance occurred toward the end of the battle for the Goland Heights when 15 restored tanks were returned to the battle and helped the   Israelis mount an unexpected counterattack that secured the Heights. The Arabs were always surprised when they were attacked by tanks that they knew they had disabled the day before. The Israelis readily admit that their "BDAR" program was an essential factor in their winning the war.

The German Army had been conducting live firing tests on actual combat equipment, expediently fixing the damage, and analyzing the results. They gave us all their data, and we turned it over to the Ordnance School at Aberdeen Proving Ground (APG). The results of their analysis are as follows:

"During the first two days of combat, the loss of equipment can amount to about 60%. Then, when a 'BDAR' program becomes effective, the rate of loss becomes small and the percentage of available tanks increases to 80%, because almost every loss is replaced by an expediently repaired unit. The force remains at the 60 to 80% level for an extended period of time as long as the battle continues. If 'BDAR' is not used, the entire force can be lost in less than three days." BDAR is a significant force multiplier.

The British Army had a "BDAR" Program, and the French Army had a committee studying the subject.

AMSAA published a report: "Battle Damage Repair Capabilities-Soviet/Warsaw Pact and Free World Countries" that analyzed all the available maintenance manuals of other countries to determine their capability to expediently repair battle damage.

ARMY MANUALS

The US Army is a very large organization and employs millions of people scattered all over the world. Depending on international circumstances, the Army can expand quickly by millions of people, or can contract just as fast. People are moved around a lot, to wherever they are needed. Most people are not assigned to a specific job very long, even generals are rarely on the same assignment as long as three years.

To maintain order in this dynamic environment, all Army activities are required to be performed in accordance with applicable Army manuals. Wherever you go to an Army establishment anywhere in the world, you will find everything the same. You sometimes will not even have to identify yourself, your bearing, manner, and speech will establish you immediately as a member of the Army community and your rank. People move from one location to another and find in their new location everything the same as in the one that they came from, organized and run by the same manuals.

Manuals being such important tools for running the Army, they are very carefully written, read, and respected. A first requirement is that they be written so that nothing can be misinterpreted.

Manuals are normally written first by a responsible command, then they are validated and verified by the Training and Doctrine Command (TRADOC) at one of their schools, or by some equivalent command, and finally edited, published and distributed by the Materiel

Readiness Support Activity (MRSA) in Lexington, Ky. Before assuming responsibility for publication, MRSA requires rigid compliance with all Army publications specifications.

BDAR MANUALS

The publication process for a BDAR manual turned out to be a nightmare. There was no provision in the Army publication system for anything like BDAR. I had a "Working Group" of representatives of fifteen Army commands and subordinate agencies to watch over me. We met several times during the year, but they provided me with very little guidance.

Equipment Technical Manuals sponsored by Commodity Commands such as AMC contain an equipment description, a list of all parts, and show how they go together in an assembly. Every Technical Manual is supported by a Field Manual that originates with TRADOC and tells how to use and repair the equipment. Assessment of damage and specification of repair is a TRADOC responsibility. As AMC personnel, we were not authorized to work on assessment of damage and associated repair.

Some of the equipment that could be damaged in a tank was not all AMC equipment, but was supplied by the Communications and Electronics Command (CECOM) in New Jersey and the Armaments and Chemical Command (ARRCOM) in Rock Island, Ill. These Commands had their own manuals for the equipment that they supplied and considered management of this equipment to be within their exclusive jurisdiction.

Every proposed repair (of any kind) has to be verified and validated by TRADOC. The procedure requires an actual piece of equipment to be available. The damage is simulated as far as possible, otherwise the damage is assumed. A team of soldiers must go through all the motions, exactly as described in the manual, to demonstrate that they could repair the damage by following the instructions in the manual, and that the repair was effective. No hypothetical situations can be considered. TRADOC Schools, such as the Ordnance School and Center, are usually responsible for demonstrating compliance with the verification and validation requirements.

The US Army was not organized to conduct BDAR, in fact, its manuals prohibits BDAR. Nevertheless, it was not uncommon for an officer who has had an unforeseen breakdown in the field, to order his men: "Fix that equipment by 2000 hours, and I don't care how you do it!" He not only does not care how it is done, he does not want to know. It's against the law!

Our private joke was that our big boss, Gilbert, as a lawyer, was such a staunch guardian of the status quo. But McDowell and I, under the banner of General Welch, were about to reorganize the Army!

THE M60A3 BDAR TECHNICAL MANUAL

McDowell and I worked well together. He had good friends at the Tank-Automotive Command (TACOM) in Detroit and felt he could rely on them for the data he needed for his manual. He volunteered to take care of all the red tape.

McDowell realized that at TACOM alone he would not get a lot of material, sufficient to fill his manual, but he felt it would be enough. We decided that completeness did not matter. His main objective was to break the ice and establish a procedure for preparing a BDAR manual in the Army. The BDAR Manual had to be an "idea book" that warrant officers could study for examples of acceptable procedures that had been devised for emergency situations. Such examples should acquaint the reader with the principles of BDAR. This recognition told us that there was no use in trying to write a "complete" book, that a limited number of procedures in McDowell's fully coordinated manual would be perfectly acceptable to General Welch. TACOM had a professional publishing division that prepared all of their Technical Manuals and other technical pamphlets that were then published by MRSA. They prepared all of McDowell's drawings, edited his text, and assured that he had a real professional job. All of his expedient procedures were developed in cooperation with the engineers at TACOM.   They also coordinated all his expedient repairs of CECOM and ARRCOM equipment with these commands, and arranged with the Ordnance School for verification and validation.

SOURCE MATERIAL FOR BDAR FOR COMBAT VEHICLES, M48A5, M60A1, M1, M113A, M109A1

I chose the title "Source Material" for my manual because my intention was only to collect expedient repair procedures, and let others later package them into vehicle manuals.

I also designed a box, to be placed at the head of each chapter of a BDAR manual, that stated in big block letters: "BDAR FIXES SHALL BE USED ONLY IN COMBAT AT THE DISCRETION OF THE COMMANDER AND SHALL BE   REPAIRED BY STANDARD MAINTENANCE PROCEDURES AS SOON AS PRACTICABLE AFTER THE MISSION IS COMPLETED."

I then   designed a distinctive front cover for our new series of manuals. I felt that the manuals should all look alike and be easily recognizable, and not be confused with any other group of manuals. I gave my design to McDowell, who took it to TACOM publications, where they added a few professional touches.

I had designed the format for presenting an expedient repair in a standard manner. At that time I did not know that MRSA would insist on this. McDowell took everything I did to TACOM, and they edited and polished it to a professional level. TACOM wrote up McDowell's BDAR procedures, using more or less my proposed format.

Now I needed to learn about expedient repairs. I started at the Ordnance School, where I invited a group of older Warrant Officers to a meeting. I explained what BDAR was all about and told them that General Welch had asked us to write a BDAR manual. I emphasized that this was against the rules, but it was done all the time in emergencies. I asked them to tell me what they had done to fix disabled equipment that they needed in an emergency, when it was not possible to use the Technical Manuals.

These men all recognized the need for BDAR Manuals, and they were very open in revealing the "illegitimate" repairs that they had made in emergency situations and that were not in the Technical Manuals. They had a wonderful time telling me their war stories.

This was a start, I had the beginnings of a manual with a cover, a preliminary table of contents, introductory material and a few expedient repairs here and there. Then I started to go to various Army installations, where I showed them my incomplete manual and did the same thing as I did at the Ordnance School. Eventually, I visited every major Army base in the United States. I finally got to the point where the Warrant Officers, who reviewed my manual, could no longer add additional information.

I had collected some 500 pages of expedient repair procedures when it became time to start organizing my material for presentation to General Welch. I wrote it all up in the original format that I had developed. I decided to make things easier for the people who would package this material into Technical Manuals, by having it verified and validated by the Ordnance School. This was a big job, but we had been through all this with McDowell's manual, and it was much easier for me to do it than anybody else not as well acquainted with the system.

I gave this batch of verified and validated material to McDowell to take to TACOM. They showed it to MRSA, who rejected it because it was not in the same format as McDowell's manual. TACOM offered to rewrite it in the proper format, but found that they did not have the resources to do so. They made arrangements with four Army Depots for the rewrite, namely: the Anniston, Leaderkenny, Red River and Tobyhanna Army Depots. TACOM assumed the responsibility for the rewrite of the 508 pages, and it was accepted by

MRSA for publication. I did not let MRSA publish it, because it was not a complete Technical Manual. I published it as an AMSAA report with a distinctive cover, so I could control its distribution.

PRESENTATION TO GENERAL WELCH

Finally the day came when McDowell and I were able to present our finished manuals to General Welch. He sat there leafing through the manuals, a smug look on his face.

After his inspection, he said that he was very pleased with the manuals, that he recognized that we had utilized the cooperation of a number of agencies, and he thanked us all very graciously. He further directed that:

1. McDowell's M60A3 BDAR Technical Manual be distributed Army-wide.

2. My "Source Material" Manual be repackaged into four Technical Manuals:

    a. M48/M60 BDAR Technical Manual for Combat Tanks,

    b. M109 BDAR Technical Manual for Self-Propelled Howitzers,

    c. M113 BDAR Technical Manual for Personnel Carriers,

    d. BDAR Technical Manual for Common Subsystems.

3. A field testing program be conducted.

4. AMSAA continue to cooperate with TRADOC in developing further BDAR doctrine.

5. A new revision of each manual, including all lessons learned, be issued in a year's time after original publication.

6. The responsibility for the BDAR Technical Manuals be transferred from AMSAA to MRSA when the revised Technical Manuals are issued.

SOURCE MATERIAL FOR BDAR FOR DEFENSIVE CHEMICAL MATERIAL

A request for preparation of this manual came from the AMC Office of Nuclear and Chemical Matters, Washington. They wanted a manual like my *Source Material for BDAR for Combat Vehicles*, applied to Chemical Defensive Material. I was assigned this task, and a committee of representatives from various commands was appointed to help me. The committee proved to be useless in helping me prepare the manual.

This assignment was quite a challenge. The only thing about chemical warfare that I remembered was that I had sat through a two week course in this subject at summer camp at Fort Meade after I received my commission as Second Lieutenant. I was fitted with a gas mask and had to walk through a long hall filled with harmless tear gas, without coughing my head off. Now, what I needed was somebody knowledgeable to talk to. By a great stroke of exceptionally good luck, I found Colonel William Hahn, Assistant Commander, Edgewood Area of Aberdeen Proving Ground. Edgewood is the location of some of the Army's largest chemical laboratories.

Hahn had spent his entire career as a chemical officer and now had just a few months left before his retirement. I showed him my "Combat Vehicles" Manual and told him about my new assignment. After looking through my "Combat Vehicles" Manual with interest, he was enthused about the idea of a similar volume for defensive chemical material. I spent a great deal of time with him. By the time he retired, he had thoroughly imbued me in the lore of the chemical community, and I had a good preliminary outline of what the manual should contain. I was able to talk to chemical officers and personnel on a professional level, and knew where to go to get more detail information to complete my manual.

Hahn recommended that I attend the "World Wide Chemical Conference" of Army chemical officers at Fort McClellan, and the Chemical Equipment Readiness Seminar," a refresher session for chemical operating personnel, at Pinebluff Arsenal, and gave me a list of people that I should contact at each event. The discussions I had at Pinebluff Arsenal were so valuable that I stayed for a second Seminar.

The Fort McClellan Conference appeared to be the annual meeting of the Army's senior chemical officers. It looked to me like all the chemical colonels in the Army were there. I looked up the officers whose names Hahn had given me and briefed them on BDAR and my assignment. Every one was immediately interested and spent some time in making suggestions. They would then introduce me to other officers, with whom I did the same thing. I think I got to talk to about every senior chemical officer in the US Army.

An important subject I brought up with everyone I spoke with was the definition of BDAR and its scope in a chemical manual. There are distinct differences between chemical warfare and the tank combat operations that I had been involved with.

Most chemical defensive materiels fall into two categories:

1. *Active equipment* such as decontamination equipment and smoke generators. Breakdowns which impair mission accomplishment are readily observable. The BDAR approach is identical to that for combat vehicles.

2. *Interactive equipment* such as detectors, alarms, individual protective gear, and collective protective shelters which interact with a contaminated environment. Such equipment must be fully operational when needed, that is, prior to a chemical attack. In this

case, BDAR includes expedient tests and minimum preventive maintenance procedures to assure that the equipment will be operational when needed, and expedient procedures to assure that maximum use will be made of the equipment.

Furthermore, chemical warfare operations take place in three distinctive environments:
- *Readiness operations* involving interacting equipment,
- *Operations in a contaminated environment*,
- *Support operations* in a non-contaminated environment involving active equipment.

All senior chemical officers that I spoke with agreed with these definitions. They all advised me to include anything I could that would help the soldier in the field, regardless of BDAR definitions and otherwise Army practice.

These discussions with so many senior chemical officers gave me confidence that I had an outline that the Army chemical community would accept. I knew how to proceed with active equipment in combat and support operations, this was no different from the BDAR manuals for combat vehicles that I had already prepared. Where I required additional assistance was with interactive equipment that had to operate in a contaminated environment.

This meant that I could not limit myself to the expedient repair of battle damaged equipment, but had also to provide expedient procedures for troops in a chemical environment to continue to fight and win, even though their equipment is broken down, damaged, or performs inadequately for any reason. Because of the nature of chemical warfare, this BDAR manual had to address soldiers other than equipment operators or maintenance personnel. In a chemical attack, everybody in a contaminated area is at risk. *Chemical defense is, therefore, everybody's business.*

The arrangements I made for the processing of my manual provided for it to be turned over to the Armament and Chemical Command (ARRCOM) to be rewritten in proper format, then submitted to the responsible activity for validation. Validated copies returned to ARRCOM will be assembled into a "Preliminary Draft Equipment Publication (PDEP)" and submitted to the Army Chemical School for verification. The verified copy will be sent to MRSA for publication. These arrangements left me free to concentrate on expedient repair procedures without having to worry about red tape.

I now followed Hahn's second recommendation and registered for a two week session at the "Chemical Equipment Seminar" at Pinebluff Arsenal. This was a school for senior operating personnel, mostly experienced Non-commissioned officers. The purpose of the Seminar was to assure that all Army personnel operated their equipment in the same standard manner. All chemical equipment was on display. The sessions consisted of the instructors, for every piece of equipment, first making a short review of the Technical Manual, and then reviewing the Field Manual in detail and demonstrating the prescribed operating procedures. This was exactly the background I needed to complete my manual. I now had to determine how the equipment failed or was combat damaged, and how it could be expeditiously fixed.

I lived and ate with all these other experts. I had all the opportunity in the world to discuss my problems with the instructors and the knowledgeable men attending the Seminar. I gave a lecture at an assembly session, explaining the principles of BDAR, and asking for their help. The instructors provided me with much material, and many attendees also told me many stories about their experiences. I was so gratified with what I had learned at the Seminar, that I decided to stay for another two week session. This time I knew much better how to ask my questions and also understood better what they were telling me. In this process, I collected BDAR fixes for all chemical items in the Army inventory.

A major effect of a hostile chemical attack is to force friendly forces to don protective garments which decrease personnel performance by at least thirty percent. This makes individual soldiers on the battlefield more vulnerable and decreases their relative strength to the attacking forces. Hence, special attention has to be given to expedient procedures that allow our forces to reduce their level of protective gear as soon as possible, before the enemy reduces his protective posture.

Mask fitting procedures are the responsibility of the commander and must be rigorous, *approximate fitting is not good enough.* Masks are issued by supply in four sizes. Soldiers come in all sizes in between. My BDAR procedures specified that if a mask does not fit right, use the next smaller size for a tight fit. In addition, masks should be fitted with banana oil, which comes in ampules good for ten fittings. The banana oil is squirted as a small bead around the edge of the facepiece where it forms a seal with the face. The banana oil softens the facepiece material so that it forms a good seal. Masks must be cleaned after each field exercise. *A clean mask on the battlefield is as important as a clean rifle.*

After I returned home and got this material in a respectable shape, I visited the Chemical School and asked them to check out what I had. They reviewed my draft and accepted almost all of it as written. I had to make a few corrections. My manual now filled 306 pages. I felt it was good enough to be submitted to ARRCOM.

A BDAR MANUAL FOR THE CHAPARRAL

The US Army Missile Command (AMSMI) at Redstone Arsenal, AL, had for some time, a crew preparing a BDAR Manual for the Chaparral M48A1/A2 Weapon System, but for some undeterminable reason, the writers did not appear to be making any progress. As a last resort, I was asked to go to AMSMI for a month and see if I could help them get started.

The CHAPARRAL M48A1 Weapon System shown on page 438 is a self-propelled missile launcher and consists of a M54A1 Launching System that is mounted in the M730 Carrier Vehicle. The self-propelled feature is necessary for launchers and big guns because the enemy has the capability to pin point the location of an attacker firing a round and to shoot back in a few minutes. After firing a few rounds, the attacker must quickly move to a different, safer location.

The US Army is such a large organization that in order to operate effectively, people are rigorously trained to do everything in an approved standard manner. Commanders and supervisors can always rely on their orders being executed exactly as expected, even though personnel may be newly rotated in their jobs.

The men at AMSMI had copies of the BDAR Manuals that I had prepared and had studied them carefully. However, they had determined that all of the expedient repair procedures in my manuals were officially validated and verified. AMSMI had nothing like this validated and verified material in their files. They knew this for sure, they had researched the issue thoroughly. This was probably the reason no progress was being made; the Command simply had no suitable material available that could be included in a BDAR Manual!

To introduce BDAR, I had to start at the beginning. I told them that in field exercises, equipment sometimes breaks down when it is urgently needed. Much military equipment is not as failure proof as similar commercial equipment that has been developed over tens of years and built by the millions, like automotive vehicles, and that are being constantly improved. Heavy military equipment is generally advancing the state of the art in order to stay ahead of unfriendly forces, and is built in relatively small batches of thousand units. When field breakdowns occur, there are no repair facilities immediately available, nor is there any time for standard repair according to the Technical Manual. Commanders will order their men to fix the breakdown or damage as well and as fast as they can. The men in the field normally do not have the tools to fix the disabled equipment so it is fully functional, but as long as they can fix it to perform some useful function, it will probably provide a needed service.

Everybody knows that this procedure is illegal. If an inspector

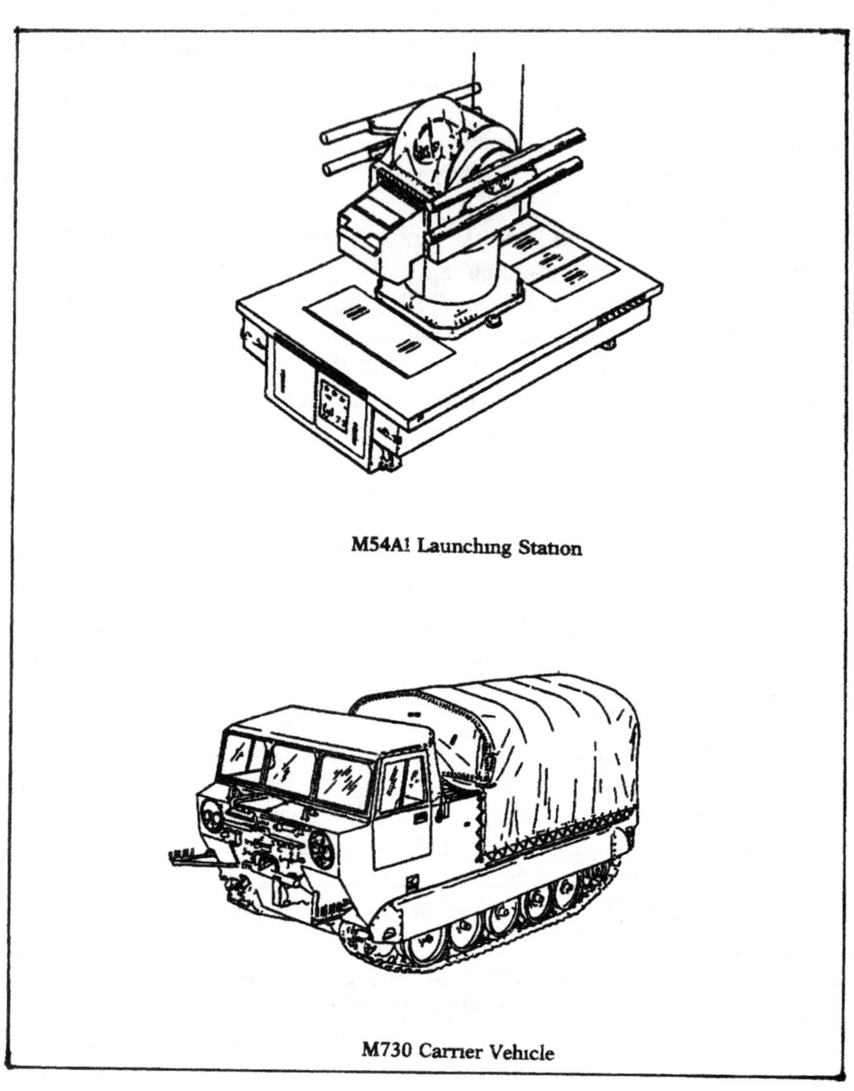

M54A1 Launching Station

M730 Carrier Vehicle

Chaparral M48A1 Weapon System

detects it, he will insist on a standard repair as authorized in a Technical Manual, regardless of time or consequences. He will have the soldiers, who performed the unauthorized repair, punished. This condition is regrettable because it hinders the Army's ability to use all its resources to win a battle. The knowledge that troops acquire in these unauthorized field repairs is such valuable information that the Army now wants to collect and use it in the training of troops for combat duty.

The ability of troops to quickly fix battle damaged or broken down equipment so it can perform some useful function in an ongoing engagement, is what the Army is trying to promote with its BDAR program.

I told them about the analysis on page 429 of the German firing tests that indicated that all of your equipment will be disabled in the first three days of normal combat. However, with BDAR, you can survive for an appreciable time in battle with 60-80 % of your force, because almost every battle damaged unit is repaired to some extent and returned to battle. BDAR is a significant force multiplier that helps the Army win battles.

You cannot sit at a desk and dream up BDAR procedures. It is not possible to reconstruct analytically the description of a piece of equipment that has broken down in a field exercise or has been battle damaged in combat. Such data must be collected by observing such equipment in the field or in combat.

Considering the large number of people at AMSMI, I felt that among all these people there should be a number of senior non-commissioned officers who had had some battlefield or field exercise experience. I proposed that we round up some of these men and encourage them to recount their battlefield and field exercise experiences. This was a difficult concept for the AMSMI writers to accept; it was contrary to anything they had ever encountered in the Army before. However, I was a persistent authority figure, and they decided reluctantly to give my proposal a try.

Surprisingly, we found quite a number of senior non-commissioned officers with battlefield or field exercise experience. After I explained the BDAR principles to them, and showed them existing BDAR Manuals, they became most cooperative and anxious to help, just as I had expected. They delighted in telling us stories of their experiences in field exercises where they had equipment breakdowns and had to to expediently repair them. They probably had never been able to talk about these experiences before. They told us what a combat damaged weapon system looked like, and how it might be expediently repaired for some useful purpose. We got a good number of BDAR procedures from them.

I then pointed out that the AMSMI writers should go to all AMSMI subordinate commands and do the same thing to get more BDAR procedures. This was a job that they did after I left.

I designed the manual cover page to conform with all the other published BDAR Manuals, and wrote the introductory material. I helped them prepare a Table of Contents.

I helped them write their first few BDAR procedures and recommended a format. I told them to check the format with MRSA and get MRSA to agree with it early in the program, otherwise MRSA might require them to rewrite the entire manual all over again when it is later submitted for publication.

I set them up to arrange for the validation and verification of their manual. These exacting review procedures they did after I left.

I was quite successful in getting them started on their BDAR Manual. They worked on it for about another year and produced a very acceptable book that was published by MRSA. It looked like all the other BDAR Manuals.

Redstone is a small place. I worked every night when I got to my motel room, so I have no recollection of the town. The only thing that I remember clearly is that I had breakfast every morning at MacDonald's.

ADDRESSING THE GERMAN GENERAL STAFF

The US and German Armies had an agreement to keep each other informed on advancements that they were making in military technology. Such an information exchange meeting was scheduled to take place in the summer of 1984 at the German Naval Base of Bremerhaven, where it was the Army's turn to report on developments in the US. I was selected to go to this meeting and give a talk on BDAR.

I was told to write my presentation, it would have to be cleared with AMC in Washington. I took my paper to Washington and met with a colonel of Austrian extraction, who was an expert in the English and German languages. He went over my paper word for word. He replaced all my English words that had two or more meanings in German with words that had only one meaning. In two days of work, we ended up with a paper where every word had an unique meaning in German, and where the meaning of no combination of words could be misinterpreted.

I was told to to read the paper word for word, not to deviate or make any extemporaneous remarks. This procedure was necessary, because we wanted the Germans to understand what we had to say, but we did not want them to arrive at conclusions based on possible misunderstanding of the text.

I studied my paper carefully so that I could practically present it by rote. I bought a new dark blue suit and a new pair of black shoes. I flew into Frankfurt and rented a car to drive to Bremerhaven. It was lovely weather and a beautiful six hour expressway drive.

The meeting was scheduled for five days, 25 - 29 June, 1984, and there were about 30 papers presented. They were not all Army papers, the US Air Force and Navy were equally well represented.

Based on my Toastmaster training, I acted as if I was speaking extemporaneously, with forceful gestures and with only occasional quick unnoticeable glances at my text. There was intense competition among the speakers as to who made the best presentation. I came in second. A Navy captain was first. When I congratulated him, he said it had not been a fair competition. He was a professional speaker who presented his material to many government agencies and congressional committees. I should discount his presentation. In acknowledgement of my performance, I received the letter from AMC shown on page 442.

Since I could speak German, I had no trouble mixing in with the upper level of officers of the German Navy, and I ate my meals at their table. I also made friends with General Pichler, German Military Representative to the US and Canada. As long as he was stationed in Washington, he invited Eleanor and myself to the Annual German Military Ball at the German Embassy.

The AMC colonel who had reviewed my paper in Washington, was also present in Bremerhaven. I think he was in charge of the Army delegation, but he was certainly most unobtrusive about it. I was with him one evening when he decided that he had to have some of that fine pastry that is unavailable in the US. We walked around the town until we discovered a nice cafe'. We made little pigs of ourselves, we each had coffee and three pieces of that pastry.

My BDAR presentation made a good impression. It resulted in the US and British Armies joining in the German Firing Tests at the German Meppen Proving Ground, firing at the latest US and British equipment. At first the US troops were unsure as to how to act after a firing, but when they saw the German troops rushing in and starting expedient repair, they quickly followed suit. The US troops eventually developed extraordinary skills in expedient repair of disabled weapons by welding techniques.

The BDAR function was eventually transferred from AMSAA to the Ordnance Center. For several years, the Center organized joint meetings every six months between the German and US Armies.

DEPARTMENT OF THE ARMY
OFFICE OF THE DEPUTY CHIEF OF STAFF FOR LOGISTICS
WASHINGTON D C 20310

DALO-PLO   9 July 1984

SUBJECT: Letter of Commendation

THRU: Director
              U. S. Army Materiel Systems
                and Analysis Activity
              Aberdeen Proving Ground, MD 21005-5071

TO: Doctor John Coutinho
              U. S. Army Materiel Systems
                and Analysis Activity
              ATTN: DRXSY-LA
              Aberdeen Proving Ground, MD 21005-5071

1.   This is to commend you for your fine performance in representing the United States Army during the 30th U. S. - German Logistic Staff Talks conducted in Bremerhaven, Germany, 25-29 June 1984. This very important forum was attended by representatives of the Defense Departments, Joint Staffs and military services of both countries.

2.   Your excellent presentation on Battle Damage Assessment and Repair stimulated considerable interest and helped lay the foundation for bilateral cooperation in this field. You will no doubt be called upon to contribute to this effort in the future.

FOR THE DEPUTY CHIEF OF STAFF FOR LOGISTICS.

J. E. ROZIER
Brigadier General, GS
Director of Plans and Operations

Letter of Commendation from Gen. Rozier

HOW TO SPOIL A GOOD MOVIE

While I was at a meeting on BDAR at MRSA, I got talking to the officer sitting next to me, and we decided that the program needed a short educational film to instruct the troops on the basic concept of BDAR. We decided to write the scenario for such a film.

When the meeting adjourned, we found ourselves a quiet, empty room and went to work. We started with a sergeant who had been home in the country on leave, but now he had to get back to his post. He and his pretty wife got into their old Volkswagen and headed for the airport, where they were to meet the rest of the family, in particular, the wife's father, who had gathered at the airport to see him off.

It was a nice sunny day. The sergeant was making good time on the isolated two lane country road when, in the middle of nowhere, the old Volkswagen rolled to a stop. Our sergeant went to the back of the car where the Volkswagen had its engine and started to troubleshoot. It did not take him long to discover that his fan belt had broken. Goodness, what was he going to do now, he had to get to his post. There were no other cars on the lonely country road. His family was waiting at the airport to see him take off. If he missed his plane, he would not get back to his post on time.

His wife was sitting in her car seat sideways, with her legs dangling out of the car in the sun. While the sergeant was deep in thought, standing next to the back of the car, but looking forward, his eye caught sight of his wife's pretty legs in the sun. He started to stare. After a few moments, he went over to his wife and asked her if he could take her stockings off. Somewhat astonished, she gave him permission to do so, and he took off her stockings very gently.

He took the stockings and rolled them carefully into a rope and made them into an expedient fan belt. He pulled the rope as tight as he could and made a small knot. He got into the car with his wife, they said a little prayer, and he started the engine. He let the clutch out very carefully, and lo and behold, the car started to move.

He drove the rest of the way slowly, but he got to the airport on time. His family had been waiting anxiously for him, and made a big fuss when he finally arrived. His father-in-law promised to take care of the Volkswagen. A much relieved sergeant flew back to his duty station.

We gave this scenario to the Army's film studio. They produced a professional film, except that they made one change. When the sergeant discovered that his fan belt was broken, he went immediately to the car's baggage compartment and took out his wife's over night suitcase. He opened it and pulled out a pair of stockings. These he used immediately to make a provisional fan belt. This sergeant obviously had been well trained in BDAR procedures. The film did not become as popular as I thought it would be.

COMBAT RESILIENCE

BIRTH OF COMBAT RESILIENCE

Although I was no longer associated with BDAR at AMSAA, the Ordnance Center invited me to attend the semi-annual meetings they had with representatives of the German Army. German officers, analyzing the results of the Firing Tests at Meppen, observed that some weapon systems, when disabled in the firing tests, could have been designed so that they would have been much easier to repair expediently than was presently the case. I listened to their stories and realized that they had made an important observation. They were talking about an equipment characteristic. After much discussion, I recommended that we call this equipment characteristic "Combat Resilience," that is, the ability of weapon systems to survive in combat with no more damage than could be repaired expediently. The Germans agreed, but could not think of a good German word for "Combat Resilience." They would think of something by the time that they got home.

I explained that design problems cannot be solved by the military alone, military/industry cooperation is required. In the US, our engineering societies provide a forum for the military and industry to meet and solve their mutual problems. For example, the Society of Automotive Engineers (SAE), one of our large engineering societies, sponsors a large military standardization activity. The SAE standardization committees all include a military officer with approval authority. Each committee initiates, writes, verifies and approves its proposed standards, and the Government issues them as Military Specifications. Such Specs are then called out in weapon system procurement contracts. The German officers stated that they do not have such a system in Germany.

I told them that I was the representative of the American Society of Mechanical Engineers (ASME) on the Board of Directors of the Annual Reliability and Maintainability Symposium (RAMS), cosponsored by ten national engineering societies. As such, I could organize sessions at the RAMS and the papers would be published in a volume of papers (Transactions) which is distributed worldwide. We could present papers at RAMS that described the need for "Combat Resilience" in weapon systems, for the need for developing contractual specifications, and for the methods of demonstrating that the specifications have been complied with.   The published papers would alert industry of the need for this new required design effort.

George Kessler, a German civilian consultant to the German delegation, said that he could organize some German supporting papers. He said that although the Germans did not have the concept of "Combat Resilience," they have been for some time designing weapon system parts so they will be less susceptible to complete breakdown when damaged. For instance, they have done much work on tires and have now developed tires that can be penetrated by several bullets and still be driven another 50 miles. After much discussion, the German delegation asked me to go ahead and organize two sessions on Combat Resilience, including both US and German papers. I did so and the Germans and the Ordnance Center found speakers and provided the technical papers for the sessions.

RECRUITING A PRINCIPAL SPEAKER

I gave a great deal of thought to who should be our principal speaker. I finally decided on the general at AMC who was responsible for BDAR, the successor to General Welch, namely now General Stalcup, AMC Director of Supply and Transportation. I wrote Stalcup a letter on ASME stationery, inviting him to talk at the next RAMS session, and suggesting that I, if necessary, could put a paper together for him.

Since I was aware of the hurdles in the delivery system of letters addressed to senior officers, I had the letter hand delivered by a high ranking friend at AMC. Apparently, Stalcup was intrigued by my letter, he asked me to come and see him. The request came through the same friend who had delivered the letter.

My appointment was scheduled for 30 minutes. Stalcup closed the door to his office after I came in. He started off by quizzing me about my background, family, education, job, engineering society activities, political views, and everything else he could think of. It was the most complete inquisition I have ever been through. He wanted to know all about our BDAR activities, our contacts with the Germans and the British, and how engineering societies, especially RAMS, operated. After an hour, I got up and stood next to the door, indicating that I would be willing to leave. He ignored my gesture and kept me standing at the door for almost another two hours.

He agreed to be the principal speaker at the Combat Resilience session at the next RAMS in Philadelphia. He asked me to write an outline for his talk, but I need not be too careful, his staff would prepare the final paper, and he would pass it around to the other generals at AMC for their reviews, to make sure that he was speaking for AMC. There was a long line of people outside of his office door looking me up and down when he finally let me out.

I wrote the paper while trying to visualize how a general thinks. He would want to explain why the Army needed Combat Resilience, that the Army needed help from industry in writing new design specifications and methods of demonstrating that contractual requirements were complied with. I also included a few jokes.

I had the paper hand carried to him, so his staff never saw it. Stalcup accepted the paper as I had written it, including the jokes. He felt no need to have his staff rework it in any way. He passed it around to the other generals at AMC. They all approved the paper with encouraging remarks, but there were no suggestions for changes.

GENERAL STALCUP AT RAMS

I met Stalcup at the airport and drove him to the Symposium hotel. Most generals, when invited to speak at such an affair, generally arrive shortly before start of their scheduled appearance, and then leave as soon as they can. Stalcup stayed the full three days and participated in several activities.

Our program consisted usually of four parallel sessions on different subjects, and you could choose which one to attend. I tried to make some suggestions to Stalcup, but he said he would make his own selections. He attended a technical meeting at every session, and several times I saw him rushing from one meeting to another within sessions. He mingled freely and talked with the attendees, especially with the members of my Combat Resilience Committee that included German and British officers. He gloried in his status as an individual. Engineering societies do not recognize rank. I have spoken with a number of presidents of large companies who told me that they engaged in engineering society activities because that was the only place they could go to and be active as individuals, and not be recognized by their rank. I think Stalcup recognized and appreciated this environment. I took him along to my committee business meetings and he was very interested in how our democratic organization worked.

When his turn came, he gave a very good presentation of the paper that I had written for him, and he conducted a lively discussion with the audience. His paper was a fine lead for the rest of the papers in the session.

THE COMBAT RESILIENCE COMMITTEE

As a member of the ASME Aerospace Division, I was authorized to appoint a committee to organize a suitable program to be presented at a RAMS meeting that is cosponsored by ASME. As such, I called my Combat Resilience Committee to meet on the morning after the last day of RAMS to plan next year's RAMS program. The Committee consisted of interested individuals such as officers from the US Army Ordnance Center, the German delegation of officers and civilian consultants, and British officers.

The Committee reviewed our presentations at the immediately past RAMS and decided that it had been a worthwhile and successful effort. There was a lively discussion and it was decided to organize another session for our RAMS next year in Los Angeles.

There arose the question, how do you get industry to respond? We agreed that first you have to tell them what your want. In this respect, I had prepared a draft specification for Combat Resilience, DRAFT AMC-P 750 XX. I asked the committee members to review and revise this draft as they saw fit. If we could agree on a final version by next year, we could present it at the next RAMS.

Another suggestion, for which I accepted responsibility, was to provide a paper on electronics. We have not had a good paper in this area before. The several other suggestions and volunteers were enough to fill two sessions for next year's RAMS.

LOS ANGELES

The meeting in Los Angeles was a continuation of the previous meeting in Philadelphia. I had been able to get US Army General Richard Chegar, Commander, 21st Support Command, as a speaker on Combat Resilience of Electronic Equipment. This Command supported all electronic equipment in Europe, and Chegar had many good ideas about where combat resilience techniques would be effective.

General Jim Dennis of the British Army came to look me over and to determine if all the good things that he had been hearing about us were really true. I don't think he was disappointed.

PLANNING THE NEXT RAMS SESSION

I scheduled a program committee meeting on the morning after the last day of RAMS. The meeting was held in an atmosphere of the highest level of enthusiasm.

Our major problem was how to get the defense industry to recognize the need to design weapon systems to be combat resilient. We had the beginnings of a specification with my DRAFT AMC-P 750-XX. We had the top military officers of three countries involved and speaking out for the need for combat resilience.

We had been telling the world about our objectives through RAMS. We believed that the engineering techniques that would be required to assure combat resilience in a weapon system would be similar to those for assuring reliability in design. RAMS was the preeminent conference in the world on reliability engineering, a subject on which there are not many conferences. There was nothing else worthy of our consideration. RAMS had a international reputation and had been conducting annual meetings for over thirty years. Its attendance was over a thousand. Its emphasis was on reliability engineering design techniques. This justified our association with the reliability engineering community in RAMS. The committee, looking at the overall picture, felt we were on the right track.

The Germans were sure that the Commanding General of their AMC would be their principal speaker next year. They had a good list of other potential speakers. The Ordnance Center and the British also had good lists of suggestions.

I went to the blackboard and started to write down the details for two sessions. Every slot on the program was thoroughly discussed before a speaker was chosen. We wound up with a well balanced program, between subjects and countries.

British General Jim Dennis was present and participated actively in the discussions. Another participant was Dave Gilbert, AMSAA's lawyer, who was very pleasant and who also took an active part in the discussions.

MILITARY REVIEW

I decided that BDAR was so important a subject that all Army officers should know about it. So I wrote an article entitled "Battle Damage Assessment and Repair" to be submitted for publication in *Military Review*, the Army's most prestigious professional publication.

I had the article written in longhand, but had no facilities to get it typed. McCarthy knew that I was involved in ASME activities and he had me carefully watched to assure that I did not spend any Government time or resources on ASME or any other outside work. It was impossible for me to get any non-AMSAA work typed.

I mentioned this in passing to Stalcup, and he said I could have anything I wanted typed in his office. We had daily messenger service between AMC and AMSAA, so he told me to address my material to his Executive Officer, send it by messenger, and he would have it typed. I sent him my article, and they did a real nice job on it.

The article was published in the February, 1988, issue of *Military Review* in English, and in May, 1988, in Spanish. Among the several complimentary letters I received, was the one on page 447 from General Solomon, Commander of the Ordnance Center and School, and the proponent for BDAR. The handwritten note to show the letter to "Keith" refers to Keith Myers, Director of AMSAA.

March 4, 1988

Dear Mr Coutinho

    Just a short note to let you know how much I enjoyed your
article "Battlefield Damage Assessment and Repair" in
February's issue of <u>Military Review</u>   I found your article
both interesting and thought provoking   As you know we here
at the Ordnance Center and School strongly support the BDAR
program   Thanks for spreading the word

                                    Sincerely,

                                      Leon E Salomon
                                      Major General, U S Army
                                      Commander

Mr John de S Coutinho
Logistics and Readiness Analysis Division
AMSAA
Aberdeen Proving Ground, Maryland   21005

Letter fom MG Salomon

MCCARTHY ENRAGED

Somehow, McCarthy found out that Stalcup's office had typed my manuscript for *Military Review.* This was something he had to investigate.

He called me into his office and asked me to explain. I told him simply that I could not find any typist at AMSAA who would type my manuscript for me, that I had mentioned it in passing to General Stalcup, and he had kindly offered to have it typed in his office.

McCarthy was dumbfounded at my statement. He asked, since when do I make passing remarks to General Stalcup?

I said, I speak to him occasionally. I keep him informed on the progress my Combat Resilience Committee is making.

"Combat Resilience" he asked, "What the hell is that?"

I explained how the concept of "Combat Resilience" had been developed at the semi-annual joint meetings of the US and German Armies on BDAR at the Ordnance Center. It is a weapon system characteristic, that is, a design problem, and we recognized that we needed industry cooperation to solve this class of design problems. We decided that presenting a session at the Reliability and Maintainability Symposium (RAMS), a large international engineering design conference that deals with similar problems, would be the best way to achieve a dialogue with industry. We have had two successful sessions so far. For our first such session, I invited General Stalcup, the successor to General Welch, to be the principal speaker. General Welch had given me his phone number and told me to call him if I ever had any kind of a problem.

McCarthy asked: "How were you ever able to contact Stalcup?"

I wrote him a letter and asked him to be a speaker at our next RAMS.

McCarthy hit the ceiling. How could I, an employee of AMSAA, write a letter to a General without going through the chain of command! Don't I know the rules?

I told McCarthy that the rules are flexible. I had called General Welch several times when I needed his advice, and he treated me very friendly. Besides, I did not approach General Stalcup as an AMSAA employee. I was a member of the American Society of Mechanical Engineers (ASME), one of the world's large engineering societies that is completely - absolutely completely - independent of the US Government and all its components, such as the US Army. Within the ASME, I am associated with the Aerospace Division that organizes technical conferences. Under the supervision of the Executive Committee of this Division, I can invite anyone, that I ascertain to be technically competent, to speak at a technical session sponsored or cosponsored by the Division. I have to comply with the directives of the Division Executive Committee, and not with AMSAA rules, since I did this work on my own time as an ASME member and not as an AMSAA employee on AMSAA time.

In my ASME capacity, I wrote to General Stalcup a formal letter of invitation **on ASME stationery,** to speak at our next RAMS in Philadelphia, an ASME cosponsored conference. If there was anything wrong with this approach, General Stalcup would have detected it and not answered my letter. Instead, he accepted my invitation and showed a great deal of interest in the subject matter.

General Stalcup came to Philadelphia and spoke at the RAMS. He stayed the full three days of the Symposium and attended technical sessions that he selected throughout the conference. He talked to a great many people at these sessions. He came with me to my various committee meetings and watched the proceedings carefully, he wanted to know how things worked. He knows a lot more about ASME, RAMS, and my activities in these organizations than McCarthy will ever know.

McCarthy was flabbergasted. He said, it was not true that I could disregard Army rules just because I did the work on my own time. As long as I was an Army employee, I had to obey the rules all the time.

I explained to McCarthy that the engineering disciplines are advancing very rapidly, and engineers must continue their education throughout their lifetimes to stay proficient. Our engineering societies were organized specifically to provide continuing education. Employers of engineers normally recognize this need in their engineering employees and support their efforts to obtain continuing education. It is even US Government policy to support engineering employees in their continuing education activities. In my case, AMSAA is not complying with US Government policy. During educational activities on their own time, Government employees are not subject to government discipline.

McCarthy replied, that I was never to contact General Stalcup again. I was not to use any AMSAA time or resources for ASME activities. Period.

THE DEATH OF COMBAT RESILIENCE

General's Stalcup's term expired and he was assigned to a command in Europe. His successor was a general who had just come over from Europe. However, he was an older man, and headquarter's activities were new to him.

McCarthy invited him to come to Aberdeen where he had each of his groups make a presentation to enlighten the General on the work that was being done. I could see that the General was leaning heavily

From   Brigadier J Dennis

Director of Production Engineering
LOGISTIC EXECUTIVE (ARMY)
Portway, Monxton Road,
ANDOVER, Hants, SP11 8HT

Tel Andover Military 2445
     Civil, Andover   (0264)82445

Dr John de S Coutinho
602 Westgate Road
Aberdeen
Maryland 21001
United States of America

D/DGEME/61/1/26

2 February 1988

My Dear John,

A small note to say how much I enjoyed coming along to, and participating in, the 34th 'RAMS' It was a great pleasure to meet so many nice people, and also to hear of the developments in America in this interesting and vital field

On a personal note may I thank you for your valuable guidance before the event, and for looking after me so well during the Symposium

I shall be 'penning' a short report to the Battle Damage Repair focus in this Headquarters, although, as I indicated on our last day I shall be happy to act as focus, as far as you are concerned, until the new chap gets his feet well under the table

Thank you once again for your kindness Please pass on my regards to Dick Gilbert

Yours sincerely, and with best regards

Jim Dennis

Letter from General Dennis

on McCarthy to help him understand the presentations.

I asked for a slot to make a presentation on Combat Resilience. I gave a short history of BDAR and of our association with the European Armies, and explained why we were now organizing sessions at the international RAMS. I presented the two sessions we were proposing for the upcoming RAMS, with the Commanding General of the German AMC as the principal speaker.

McCarthy declared that my activities, as just presented, were completely inappropriate for an AMSAA employee. (He was referring to my job description, that could be easily changed.) With the General sitting next to him, he ordered me to disassociate myself of all activities at ASME and RAMS, and advised me that AMSAA would not support any of my outside activities, such as with time off and travel expenses for meetings or conferences. This was, of course, a completely illegal order. Mc Carthy had no right to tell me what to do on my own time.

Since McCarthy, sitting next to the General, sounded like he was speaking for AMSAA, I suspected that AMSAA management might be involved in what he was saying. I remembered that the AMSAA lawyer, Dave Gilbert, had attended the last RAMS. He had attended my Combat Resilience Program Committee Meeting and had sat next to British General Dennis. General Dennis afterwards wrote me a letter after the meeting, shown on page 453, in which he sends his regards to "Dick" Gilbert.

Why would AMSAA send Gilbert from Aberdeen to a Los Angeles design engineering conference on a technical subject of which he had no knowledge? There can only be one reason: to watch me.

Regardless of the high level of monitoring of my activities, there were certain things about me that McCarthy did not know, and could not know that he did not know.

Specifically, I had a long history of leadership activity in ASME. In particular, I had served a term as Chairman of the Aerospace Division. The members of the Executive Committee had all known me for years and respected me.

I invented the term "Reliability and Maintainability" to associate reliability with design engineering rather that statistics, and organized and chaired the design engineering oriented <u>1963, 64, and 65 Reliability and Maintainability Conferences</u> to promote this concept. These Conferences were cosponsored by ASME, the Society of Automotive Engineers (SAE), and the American Institute of Aeronautics and Astronautics (AIAA). After ten years my Reliability and Maintainability Conference merged with the electronics oriented <u>National Symposium on Reliability and Quality Control</u> to form the

From   **Brigadier R A Weston ADC**

DIRECTOR OF EQUIPMENT ENGINEERING 2
LOGISTIC EXECUTIVE (ARMY)
Portway, Monxton Road, ANDOVER, Hants, SP11 8HT

Telephone   Andover Military
             Civil Andover (0264)38) ext 2442
             Switchboard, Andover (0264)32111

DEE 2/8/3

Dr John de S Coutinho
602 Westgate Road
Aberdeen
Maryland 21001
USA

24ᵗʰ January 1989

Dear Doctor

    You may recall that you wrote to Brigadier Jim Dennis on 22 November last
year He has passed a copy of your letter to me as I have now become the focus
for Battle Damage Repair in the British Army I am the engineering Director
responsible for the engineering support for tanks, guns, vehicles and Army
aircraft

    I have set up a formal committee with Terms of Reference and we held our
first meeting on 9 December 1988 One of the major topics we discussed was the
results of the live firing trials we have been involved in during 1988 with the
American Army and the Bundeswehr at Meppen in West Germany

    You say in your letter that you are discussing the current contents of
DRAFT AMC-P 750-XX with the German Army I wonder if I could ask you to let me
have a copy of the AMC-P 750-XX once it is published? Please don't worry if it
is too difficult as I can get a copy through our British Defence Staff in
Washington

    Please let me know if I can be of any assistance to you in your work or
better still do please call and see me if you come to Europe on BDAR and Combat
Resilience

With best wishes

Yours sincerely

Richard Weston

Letter from General Weston

new annual Reliability and Maintainability Symposium (RAMS), that had also become design oriented. RAMS was cosponsored by ten national engineering societies including ASME, and I served for many years as the ASME representative on its Board of Directors.

I knew the ropes intimately in both ASME and RAMS, I knew how to get things done. McCarthy had no idea of what I was doing, he had no concept of voluntary engineering society work and what it has accomplished. By cutting me out of the loop, there was no way for the good people that I had been working with, US, German, and British Army officers and their civilian consultants, to organize sessions on Combat Resilience on the RAMS program. They had no way to communicate with the right people who ran RAMS.

McCarthy thereby killed Combat Resilience, a budding program that promised significant improvements in weapon system capability to survive on the battlefield and help win battles.

What was my reaction to McCarthy's order? I was 75 years old, and it was not possible for me to get another job. My working conditions at AMSAA were rotten, and McCarthy could make them worse. I personally had nothing to gain whether or not Combat Resilience became a successful program. It was a matter of national defense, of national interest, not personal interest. I decided to obey McCarthy's order; Combat Resilience was dead.

One of the things I had attempted to do was to find a successor, a man with both ASME Aerospace Division connections and RAMS experience. Such people are very difficult to find. I did find one such man: Bob Neff. He was a clever young reliability engineer at the US Aviation Systems Command in St. Louis. I introduced him to several committees of RAMS where he did an outstanding job. I looked forward to someday turning my ASME/RAMS responsibilities over to him. Neff advanced himself by becoming one of the top reliability engineers at the US Air Force Systems Command, then still located in Washington. Neff's two teen age boys soon discovered the appeal of sailing on the Chesapeake Bay. The rest of the family, coming from St. Louis, had never seen a large body of water and soon became enchanted with the charms of the Chesapeake Bay. Neff quit his Air Force job and bought a marina on the Bay. In no time at all, he became a genuine Chesapeake water man.

On page 455 is a letter from British General Weston, successor to General Dennis, focus for Battle Damage. On page 458 is a letter from Colonel Josef Norder, Inspector General of Maintenance for the German Army, who states that he *"is at a loss to understand why this important matter still has not attracted the required attention, especially since significant impulses for the development of future defense materiel must come from BDR."*

The killing of Combat Resilience was not a logical or necessary act on the part of John McCarthy. Nobody gained anything. The US defense establishment and that of its friends were the ones who lost.

Joe Sperrazza, who founded AMSAA, and taught me that AMSAA's goal was to assure that the US won the next war, must be turning in his grave.

```
ARMY   OFFICE                    5000 Koln 51, 10 February 1988
Inspector General of Maintenance Konrad-Adenauer-Kaserne
                                 Bruhler Straße 300
                                 Tel  (0221) 3700-1
                                 Direct Dialing  (0221) 3700-2308
```

Dr John de S Coutinho
602 Westgate Road
Aberdeen, Maryland 21001
United States of America

Dear Dr Coutinho,

Thank you very much for your letter containing the best wishes
for my recovery

I was glad to learn that the management of the Symposium approved
Herr Kessler's briefing and that the Battle Damage Repair Group,
too, thought the Symposium to have been a success

Of course, I will continue my engagement for our joint matter
I am at a loss, however, to understand, why this important matter
still has not attracted the required attention, especially since
significant impulses for the development of future defense materiel
must come from BDR

I would be very grateful if you would keep me informed of your future
intentions in this matter

With best regards
Cordially

Josef Norder

Letter from Col Norder

CORPUS CHRISTI, TEXAS

THE CORPUS CHRISTI ARMY DEPOT (CCAD)

The US Aviation Systems Command (AVSCOM) was having difficulty getting its people to write BDAR manuals for its helicopters. It finally requested AMSAA for assistance.

As a result of this request, I was assigned to the Corpus Christi Army Depot in Corpus Christi, Texas, for one year to help them prepare a BDAR manual for the six passenger Attack Helicopter AH-1S (Black Hawk). The Corpus Christi Army Depot (CCAD) was the largest helicopter overhaul facility in the country.

The Depot consisted primarily of a number of giant hangers all in a row bordering the airstrip along the Gulf of Mexico. The Gulf side of the hangers consisted of a three-story bank of offices. I was assigned to an office on the third floor, overlooking the airstrip and the Gulf. This was the office where the technical writers were located. The head of the technical writers' group was Bob Indech and he did everything he could to make me feel welcome.

GETTING THERE AND SETTLING IN

My first problem was getting to Corpus Christi. Eleanor and I decided to drive, because we would need our car when we got there. We were afraid to just lock up the house and go away for a year. In particular, the grass had to be cut. We decided to let a single, senior AMSAA sergeant come and live in the house rent-free, but he would have to pay for utilities, cut the grass, and keep the place in shape. That took a load off our minds.

It was a nice drive to Corpus Christi. I located the Depot and found a good motel nearby. The first evening, we also found an attractive pizza parlor. I was ready for a good pizza and we went in. The pizzas all had fancy names that did not tell you what they were. Not knowing any better, I ordered the most expensive one. The pie was beautiful when it came, but the seasoning was so Texas-jalapeno sharp that we could not eat it. Our first meal in Corpus Christi was a complete disaster.

We decided that we did not want to spend our year in a motel. The next day we went to see a real estate agent. Parallel to the Corpus Christi coast line, about two miles out beyond the shore, there is a long, narrow island that extends from just north of Corpus Christi for over a hundred miles south to the Mexican Border. It is called Padre Island.   The real estate agent found us a furnished apartment on Padre Island, which was about a ten minute drive from the Depot, and cost a small fraction of what a motel charged.

The apartment building was eight stories high, and right on the sandy beach. All the apartments looked out over the water. Our apartment was on the sixth floor. We had a very large living room, one bedroom, and a balcony overlooking the beach and the Gulf of Mexico. It was a spectacular view. We not only saw large ships go by, but we could also see the oil rigs out in the Gulf. On the land side, the apartment house had a giant swimming pool.

I had to have a car to get to work, as I could not leave Eleanor alone in the apartment all day. She needed a car to get off Padre Island. I checked all the standard car rental agencies and was amazed at what they charged by the month.   I finally found a "Rent-a-Wreck" place that rented me a twelve year old car. It ran, and took me to and from work. It still cost a fortune, but it was a fraction of what Hertz or Avis charged.

Thus settled, I proceeded to go to work the next morning.

PREPARING A BDAR TECHNICAL MANUAL

The Corpus Christi technical writers group wrote all the technical manuals and other technical literature related to helicopters that was sponsored by AVSCOM for publication. The group consisted of sixteen persons. Except for the secretary, Rosie, all of them were graduate engineers, either mechanical or electrical/electronics. There was nothing about helicopters that the group did not know.

AVSCOM had assigned the group the task of producing a BDAR Technical Manual for the AH-1S Attack Helicopter (Black Hawk). They did not understand the principles of BDAR. They had written the existing helicopter technical manuals that included all authorized repair procedures, and they knew that any other unlisted repair procedures were unauthorized and illegal. It took a bit of explaining, and showing them some of the BDAR Manuals that I had brought along,   to convince them that the new BDAR job was legitimate.   I told them about the firing tests in Meppen, Germany, where the US soldiers became very skilled in BDAR techniques using imaginative welding repair techniques.

Each man in the Corpus Christi group was an expert on a portion of the helicopter. I sat down with him and we tried to visualize what damage to expect during a battle in his portion of the helicopter. Then   we tried to figure out how that damage could be repaired expediently in the field, so that the helicopter could still perform some useful function in the on-going battle.

In the hangers downstairs, where they repaired and overhauled helicopters, there were well over a hundred ships in every stage of disassembly. Somewhere, you could look freely at any portion of the helicopter. When we had figured out an expedient repair, we would go downstairs to the repair line and look at that portion of the helicopter and see if our proposal was realistic, if not we corrected it. There is no better way to check out a proposed expedient repair then to imagine you are installing it on a disassembled helicopter. We always checked with the shop foreman and also got his opinions on each proposed expedient repair.

The office of the test pilots was right next to ours on the third floor. These pilots were very skilled. I would watch them on the airstrip below my office   window. Every helicopter that had been repaired or overhauled was flight tested before it was returned to its owner.

To assure that a repaired or overhauled helicopter was safe at its allowable limit flight conditions, the flight test conditions had to be more severe than the allowable limit conditions. As a result, the test flights that I saw outside my window, always in excess of allowable flight conditions, were something you never see anywhere else. It was fantastic, the way they flew those helicopters.

I found that these pilots knew a lot more about helicopters than just flying them. They had a good basic understanding of each operating part of the ship. I took my proposed BDAR procedures over to their office for a critical review. They had many good ideas and gave me a degree of confidence that we were doing a good job.

DEL MAR COLLEGE

Eleanor no longer had a big house to take care of and looked around for something to keep herself busy. Del Mar College was the big college in town, although it was a two year college. Eleanor had taken some real estate courses in New York and now she found out that she just needed another year at Del Mar to get a certificate in real estate. She also had to take a course in Texas law.

TOASTMASTERS

At Aberdeen Proving Ground, I had been a regular member of Toastmasters, a club that promotes public speaking. I found that there was no club at CCAD, but there was one in the city, and I joined. They met at a local restaurant and held their meetings after dinner.

At Toastmasters, you have to give a three to five minute talk every two weeks, and your performance is thoroughly analyzed. You are trained how to walk to the speakers stand, how to stand, what to do with your hands, look at the audience, how to speak clearly, how to throw your voice so the people in the last row can hear you, how to raise your voice when needed, and all other details about good public manners. You can always tell when a speaker has had Toastmaster training.

Speakers talk about their work, their families, their vacations, their ambitions, and quite soon you know a bit about everybody else. I learned a great deal about Corpus Christi, about Texas, and Mexico. One lady, for example, was an engineer employed by the City of Corpus Christi and was redesigning the traffic light system in the city.

I made some good friends at Toastmasters. They kept trying to get me involved in other civic affairs, and had trouble understanding that I was assigned to CCAD for only one year, and that after that time, I would be gone.

They also held several socials and brought their wives or husbands. Eleanor met a lady who ran a real estate business. When she discovered that Eleanor was taking the course in real estate at Del Mar College, she offered Eleanor a job when she received her certificate. Eleanor was all enthused and was well set for a real estate career in Corpus Christi. However, when my year at Corpus Christi was up and I had to return to Aberdeen, Eleanor was most disappointed that her budding real estate career had to end in such an abrupt manner.

At my last Toastmasters meeting, my friends gave me a little gold plated statue of a man throwing a big bull over his head.

WORK, WORK, WORK

I worked very hard at CCAD. When you have fourteen people developing BDAR procedures, something new to them, and you have to talk to them individually, you always have one or more persons in line waiting to talk to you. As a result, I could not do my own checking and planning work at the office, and had to take it home with me. Every evening I would have at least three solid hours of homework.

RELAXATION

In the summer months, a half hour in our big swimming pool provided wonderful relaxation. We also managed to get away almost every weekend. I described some of our Texas experiences on pages 266 and 267.. We found that on many weekends, one of the small towns within driving distance of Corpus Christi would have a fair, and I think we visited them all.

One weekend, we ran into a chili contest. There were about thirty contestants in a big circle, each one with a big pot of their own chili over a fire. We had to go around the circle and, in turn, sample each contestant's chili, and then vote on the one we liked best. It was not an easy decision for us to make.

MONTEREY

On Thanksgiving, we had a long weekend and decided to drive to Monterey, the nearest large city in Mexico. We got lots of advice, including the address of a Holiday Inn that was a good place to stay. When we got to the Mexican border, there was a line of cars over a mile long waiting to enter Mexico and it appeared to me that it would take all day to just cross the border. I got talking to a friendly policeman, and he told me that for $10 he would take me to the admissions office behind the line. I fell for his offer. He took me to a roped off section of the customs office, where there was nobody in line.   For $20 they sent me to another office, where I got some papers for another $20. I was directed to another office to get my papers stamped for still another $20. The comedy went on until we had visited all their offices and were allowed to enter Mexico. It took us over two hours and $80 to cross the border. This was a real adventure.

We got to Monterey much later than I had anticipated, and the Holiday Inn was all out of their Thanksgiving dinners. The next day we took a professional guided tour around the city and were shown the bridge where the Pope had stood and addressed a crowd of a million people. Although the Mexican people consider themselves Catholic, there is no religious instruction in the schools or anywhere else. The Church is forbidden to perform any public activity except to conduct services in a church.

We were driven around and shown all the big fancy public buildings, and then shown some of the big factories. Monterey is a center of the automobile industry, wages averaged at that time about $10 an hour, about half of what they were in the US. However, living expenses are less in Mexico, and life in Monterey is good. There is nobody in Monterey that wants to immigrate to the United States!

I asked to see the inside of a Mexican house and was told that that was not included on the tour. I insisted, and as a special favor, we were shown a new empty house that had been designed and constructed under the supervision of the students of architecture at the local technical university. The house was now on public display and was being raffled off to raise the money to cover the building costs. This was, therefore, a Mexican "dream house," it was slightly larger and compared favorably with the amenities in a standard

American middle class home. Except for the palaces of the rich, it was probably the most sumptuous house in Monterey. And somebody was going to acquire it for the cost of a lottery ticket!

We were taken to an enormous market of Mexican arts and crafts. Some things were very beautiful and expensive. We were there for some time and it became apparent, that we were not going to leave until I bought something. We really did not have any more room at home for souvenirs, but I finally broke down and bought something that did not take up too much room, and we left.

Our next stop was at the showroom of a cut glass factory. This was a very large place and the cut glass pieces that they produced were really gorgeous. They quoted us what they called very low prices. They were probably low prices for somebody who knew what he was buying, but for us, it was just a lot of money. Here again, it appeared, that we were not going to leave until I bought something, so I bought Eleanor a beautiful cut glass flower vase that we could carry.

When the Mexicans described their institutions and government, they always referred to the "state." It was obvious, that they believed that all powers originated with the "state," except for those that the state had graciously and specifically surrendered to the people. Civic organizations that tell the government what to do did not seem to exist. I got the impression that it was not healthy to criticize the government, it was simply something one did not do. We were very aware that we were not in the United States.

OTHER IMPRESSIONS OF MEXICO

I had vacation time available and we decided to take a ten day American Express tour of Mexico. We did this at the beginning of summer. We flew from Corpus Christi to Mexico City, where the tour started.

Mexico City

The airport at Mexico City must have been designed by the Germans. The airport layout, counters, procedures, etc., are exactly as they are in Germany. Since I had spent such a long time in Germany, I recognized that German "touch" all around me.

There had been a major earthquake in Mexico City, just before we arrived. The place was still a disaster. Some buildings along a street were still standing and looked like they were in perfect condition, while the buildings next door to them were collapsed. There were big gaps in the sidewalks.

We were taken to a large hotel in in Mexico City. One feature we found in all first class hotels in Mexico was an enormous platter of cut-up colorful tropical fruit that was offered on a serve-yourself basis as the first course for breakfast. I had never seen anything as exuberant as this display before. Most of the time we just filled up on tropical fruit for breakfast, followed by a cup of coffee.

We were taken on a bus tour to see all the sights in Mexico City. The houses are all tightly packed adjacent to one another; as a result there are many parks where the people go to get a breath of fresh air. In places, the City has an European look. In some sections, you could imagine that you were in Germany.

Mexico City, one of the largest cities in the world, is built on a land mass that is floating on an immense lake in the high mountains. There is no solid foundation under the City. As a result, many heavy buildings are sinking into the earth. We were taken to the Basilica of Guadalupe to see the famous portrait of Our Lady of Guadalupe. There are three basilica around a vast plaza. The oldest one had sunk over ten feet into the ground and is closed. The second one has also sunk so far into the ground that it, too, had to be closed. The new basilica is built in the shape of a huge semicircle. The pews are arraigned in tiers, like in a sports stadium, and there are no columns, so every one has a clear view of the altar. The footprint of the new Basilica is much larger than that of the old ones, and the structure is much lighter, to lessen the pressure on the ground and minimize its chances of its sinking like the old churches did.

The portrait of Our Lady of Guadalupe is on the wall above the altar. There is a moving walkway behind the altar. To view the portrait closely, you have to go toward the back of the altar, step onto the moving walkway, and it takes you slowly past the portrait. The portrait shows the Madonna with an Indian face. It was instrumental in convincing the Indians that you did not have to be a white person in order to be a Christian. The portrait is credited with bringing about the miraculous conversion of the Mexican Indian population to Christianity.

The tour guide explained that this church is the only basilica in the Western Hemisphere. I mentioned that I had been in six basilica in the United States. The guide said that he was aware that people in the United States called some of their important churches "basilica," but that was only a local custom. Guadalupe is the only basilica in the western world that is so designated by the Pope. I have found that tour guides are fountains of misinformation. You always have to be very careful, how much of their story to believe.

The original famous Mexican Calender is carved on a very large stone, over six feet in diameter, and is on display just outside the main entrance to the Mexico City Cathedral.

In Mexico City and other cities throughout country, we visited what must be some of the most beautiful churches in the world. They were generally built in an exuberant baroque style, the art work above the altars reaching to the ceiling and brilliantly gold plated. Decorations on the walls and ceilings were all heavily gold plated. I had never seen so much gold in all my life.

I was very puzzled at the richness of these old churches in Mexico, a country that does not allow religious education and severely restricts church activity. The puzzle was solved when I found out that in colonial times, the pope had made special concessions to the King of Spain, making him the administrative head of the church in Mexico, with exclusive power to appoint all church officials, supervise the conduct of the clergy, and control church revenues. The liberal policy of the king was such that the church was able to accumulate one half of all the real property and capital in the entire country. The church was in charge of education, hospitals, charitable institutions, and orphanages. Historians of the time wrote that in certain respects, Mexico surpassed England. The new Mexican Constitution of 1917 then nationalized all church property and forbade the church from participating in political affairs.

Tropical Mexico

Our bus tour took us through tropical southern Mexico, mostly through productive farming country. We looked for heavily wooded rain forests with big trees, but did not see any. We saw some very dense high shrubs, but few trees. Lumber is a scarce commodity in Mexico. As far as we could see, all that land was planted in fertile agricultural produce.

We also looked for farmhouses and did not see any. In the tropics, almost all life takes place outdoors. People prepare their food, eat and work outdoors. They have a small, cinder block square building with a corrugated sheet steel roof, and two openings without doors. We could look into their buildings as the bus passed. We could see that there were hammocks strung in the buildings. We deduced that the buildings are used for sleeping and for protection against the heavy tropical rains. At all other times, people are outdoors and houses are unnecessary.

I could also see that here, except for work in the fields and in maintenance on farm equipment, there were no jobs available. Farms would pass from father to oldest son, and the other children would have to move on to take care of themselves.

Chichen-Itza, Yucatan

In Chichen-Itza, we were introduced to a remarkable, now vanished, civilization. Beginning in the Tenth Century, this civilization, called "Mesoamerican," arose in southern Mexico in the areas shown on the map on page 468. Our bus took us through the dense, tropical jungle to the restored ruins of Chichen-Itza, that had been laboriously carved out of the jungle.

In Chichen-Itza, only a few of the religious and public buildings are left, but they are truly monumental. The main very wide thoroughfare is flanked on both sides with these structures. Of special interest are the stepped pyramids, with an altar on top. The only other pyramids in the world are in Egypt. It is not known how the unique pyramid design originating in Egypt could have influenced the Mesoamerican Indians on the other side of the globe, or vice versa, or if they were actually two independent designs of the same concept.

The pyramids, some of which are as tall as a modern ten story building, are built of large stone blocks. The steps are about four foot high. I asked our tour guide how the older priests could climb the high blocks to get to the altar on top to perform their sacrifices. I was told that priests did not climb the steps of the pyramid, they got carried up.

These Indians had a written hieroglyphic language. but all the computers in the world have not been able to decode the meaning of the hieroglyph. It seams that every new high priest wanted to be the greatest that ever was, and on taking office, he changed the meaning of each hieroglyph so nobody could ever read anything about any of his predecessors.

They also had a system of arithmetic with twenty digits, one being a zero. They knew how to use their arithmetic. They built arches to support the structure over the openings for the windows and doors of their buildings, and they also used the arch to build bridges over streams. Their religious and public buildings are massive and required a great deal of high level engineering.

There were three classes of people: priests, nobles, and ordinary people. The priests ran the government, supervised and controlled all activity. The nobles provided the officers for the army. They had a vast commercial network of trade with other cities, and sophisticated wares were available, like fine cloth and art objects. The area surrounding the city was cleared and used intensively for agriculture.

The religion was unusual, it was based on human sacrifice. Their concept of warfare was also unique, in that wars were waged to capture the enemy's men so they could be sacrificed. Both sides were very careful not to capture each other's officers.

In some cases, however, it was an honor to be sacrificed, and people

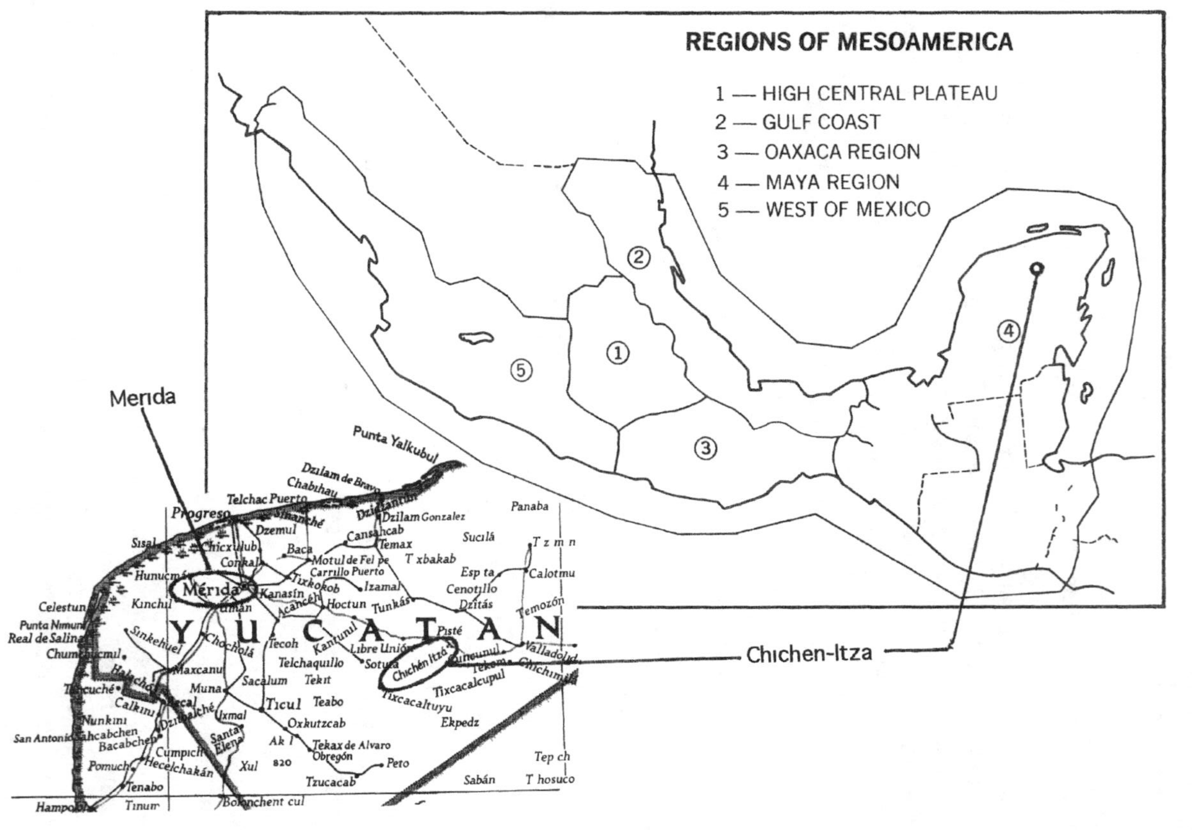

Location of Chichen-Itza'

were not afraid of death. In the center of Chichen-Itza there is a ball court, somewhat similar to our basket ball courts. Games were played with a ball against other cities. After the game, the captain of the winning team was sacrificed. As a winner, he represented the best chance of getting the priest's prayer fulfilled.

We were shown a deep well, some 20 feet in diameter, where once a year a number of young girls were sacrificed. According to the tour guide, the girls were raised for this purpose; they were not afraid of death, and they and their families looked forward to the day when they would be sacrificed.

There is no good explanation why these vibrant communities should vanish from the earth and be overgrown by the jungle. Although science may have no answers, I believe that it was because the priests lost their faith. They were intelligent men and finally observed, that human sacrifice was not effective; they normally did not get what they were praying for. Without a strong faith, they could not perform human sacrifices. They became lax in their other duties, in their control of the people, of the agricultural workers; and so the food supply dwindled, and so did the population.

I found the Indian concept of waging wars for purposes other than the control of land, enlightening. Montezuma had a large and well trained army and could have easily repelled the Spaniards, if he had only understood, what they were up to. There was no way that he could visualize that the Spanish objectives were to establish a new Europe in America.

After an interesting but exhausting day at Chichen-Itza, our bus took us to Merida to spend the night. Merida is the site of the country's second university, after Mexico City. We did not stay long in Merida, but I felt it was the cleanest city I have ever been in. From here, we took the plane to Mexico City to conclude our tour.

BACK TO WORK

Back at the office at CCAD, everybody had been working diligently and good progress was being made.

Shortly after my return, a delegation from AVSCOM came to review our progress. They liked what they saw and asked us to prepare an additional BDAR Technical Manual for the Army's other helicopter, the AH-1E/1F/1P, the two seater attack "Apache."

In the extensive discussions with the AVSCOM people, it was recognized that the Navy and the Air Force also flew the Black Hawk and could use BDAR Manuals. Because of the different maintenance environment in each Service, our Army BDAR Manual would have to be modified. This discussion led to the concept of a Tri-Service BDAR Manual. I had had extensive experience with Navy maintenance while at Grumman, and considerable contact with the Air Force during my work with BIMRAB. I felt I could revise the manual we were writing so that it would accommodate the needs of the Army, Navy, and Air Force.

The AVSCOM people were quite enthusiastic about this development as it would put the Army in a leadership position in a technical field. They left CCAD in a real upbeat mood. A short time later, we were notified that AVSCOM had agreed with the Navy and the Air Force to publish a Tri-Service BDAR Technical Manual for the Black Hawk. This would really be a "first"!

We had a problem. It had become obvious that I would not be able to complete the Black Hawk BDAR Technical Manual, much less revise it into a Tri-Service book, within my year's time.   The Commander of CCAD wrote a letter to AMSAA, requesting to have my time at CCAD extended, see copy on page 472. The AMSAA reply was negative and stated that John McCarthy would come to CCAD at the beginning of June to assess the situation, see page 473.

John came for three days. I saw him only during working hours, this was strictly a business trip. I took him around the writer's group and showed him what each person was doing. I explained how we designed each expedient procedure, and checked with the test pilots and shop foremen. I took him over to the test pilot's office and introduced him to pilots who explained how they checked me out, in a quasi validation procedure.

I took John to the shop and showed him all the helicopters in various stages of disassembly and how we, with the help of a foreman, would check out a proposed BDAR repair in a procedure that was as close to verification as you could get.
I showed him why I needed an extension of three months to complete the first draft of the manual. Then I needed additional time for the validation and verification process before we could produce a camera-ready copy. The Tri-Service Manual would take additional time.

After his investigation, John said that I had not been sent to CCAD to write a Tri-Service Manual, I could just forget that issue and the Apache Manual. He said that his contact with the CCAD writers disclosed that they were professionally very competent and that they had all learned the basic elements of BDAR, and were now fully able to finish writing the manual without any further help from me. They had gone through the validation and verification procedures many times on their own publications; they did not need any help from me here either. He ordered me to return to Aberdeen at the conclusion of my year at the end of July.

The group had a nice luncheon party for me on my last day at

CCAD and presented me with the cartoon on page 474. After I left, the group produced two excellent BDAR Technical Manuals, one for the Black Hawk with 804 pages and one for the Apache with 440 pages (It was a smaller aircraft.) The plans for a Tri-Service Manual were dropped. The Commander of CCAD wrote me the letter on page 475.

DEPARTMENT OF THE ARMY
CORPUS CHRISTI ARMY DEPOT
CORPUS CHRISTI, TEXAS 78419

REPLY TO
ATTENTION OF

SDSCC-G(MPE)   9 MAY 1986

SUBJECT   BDAR Program at CCAD

Mr. Keith A. Myers, Director
U.S. Army Materiel Systems Analysis Activity
Aberdeen Proving Ground, MD 21005

1. I understand that AMSAA is considering recalling Dr. Coutinho when his present travel orders expire.

2. This Depot is committed to supporting the Army's BDAR program by developing a group which can produce and support helicopter BDAR Technical Manuals and training materials. Dr. Coutinho is making good progress in assisting us in establishing such a group. Complications have arisen in that the Army Aviation Systems Command, the Air Force Systems Command, and the Naval Air Systems Command recently agreed that helicopter BDAR Technical Manuals should be triservice. The Army's field maintenance environment is different from those of the other Services, and we need Dr. Coutinho's background to assure that the Army's special needs are not compromised in a triservice project.

3. Recalling Dr. Coutinho is not in the best interest of the Army and will result in considerable schedule delay. I will not keep Dr. Coutinho here longer than necessary, but he should stay here until at least one triservice BDAR TM is camera-ready.

4. I would appreciate your assurance that Dr. Coutinho will remain here until I release him.

SIGNED

THOMAS M. WALKER
Colonel, AV
Commanding

Col Walker's Letter,
BDAR program at CCAD

DEPARTMENT OF THE ARMY

U. S. ARMY MATERIEL SYSTEMS ANALYSIS ACTIVITY
Aberdeen Proving Ground, Maryland 21005-5071

REPLY TO
ATTENTION OF

2 7 MAY 1986

AMXSY-L

SUBJECT   BDAR Program at CCAD

Commander
Corpus Christi Army Depot
ATTN   SDSCC-G(MPE)
Corpus Christi, TX 78419

1   Reference ltr CCAD, SDSCC-G(MPE), 9 May 84, SAB.

2. Your commitment to establishing and supporting BDAR Technical
Manuals is very welcomed. In the referenced letter your request
to have Dr. Coutinho remain until you decide to release him raises
serious concerns. Specific concerns are

    a   The original agreement was to have Dr. Coutinho available
for a maximum of one year   The one year point is 1 August 1986.

    b   The recent expansion of the effort to have a Tri-Service
Manual was not within the original scope

    c.   In a period when AMC direction is to do more with less and
reduce manpower levels, it is very difficult for AMSAA to justify
a long term full time commitment at CCAD

3   I understand a review is planned for 2-4 June at CCAD   John
McCarthy, Chief of Logistics and Readiness Analysis Division in which
Dr. Coutinho works, plans to attend this review and meet with you
privately to discuss Dr Coutinho's continued participation. My
personal assessment of the progress to date indicates that we are
moving to a point where full time presence at CCAD by AMSAA may not
be necessary   Mr McCarthy will discuss several options for continued
support, but my hope is that a reasonable date can be established
for termination of Dr Coutinho's TDY to CCAD

4   I'd like you to be assured that AMSAA has a continuing interest
and commitment to the further development of BDAR Manuals. However,
the overall responsibility for the manual development results with
the commodity command   AMSAA has and will continue to assist in
the process, but the ultimate responsibility resides with the MSC

KEITH A MYERS
Director

Keith Myers Answer, BDAR Program at CCAD

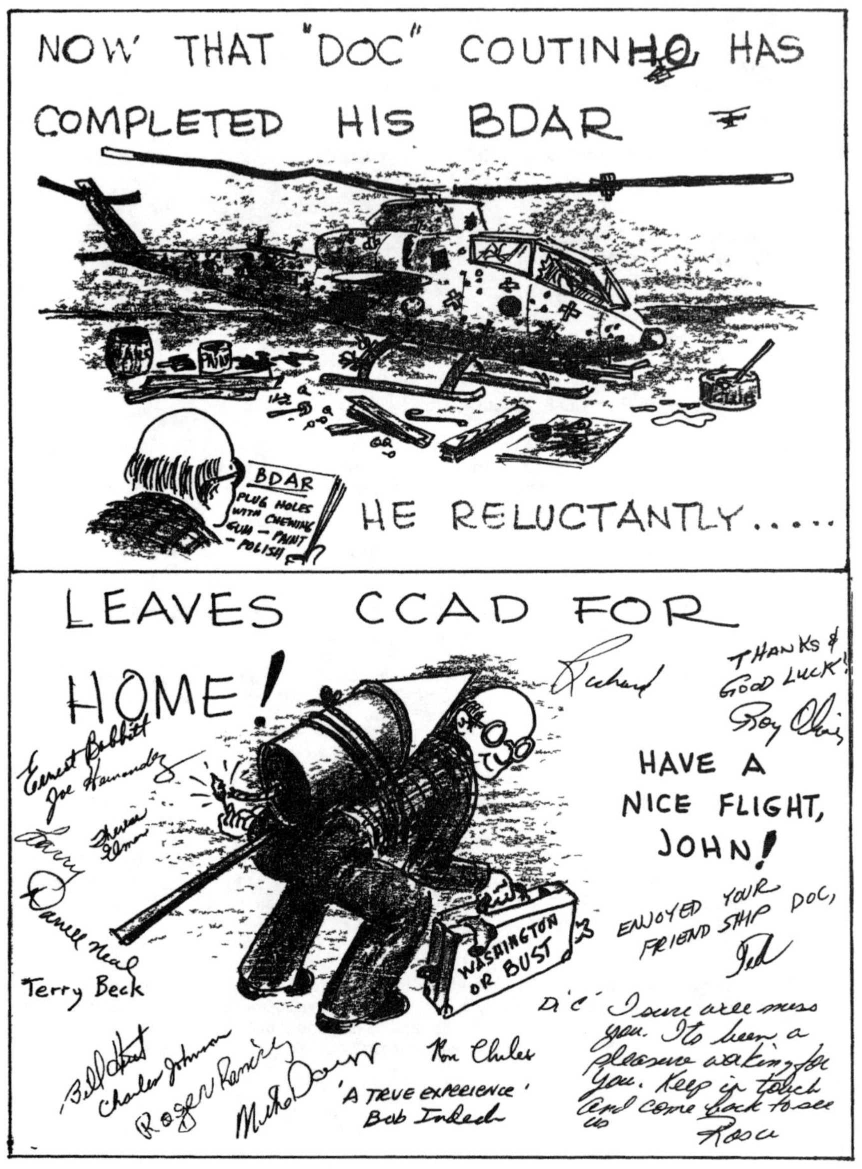

Cartoon, Coutinho leaves CCAD

DEPARTMENT OF THE ARMY
CORPUS CHRISTI ARMY DEPOT
CORPUS CHRISTI TEXAS 78419

REPLY TO
ATTENTION OF

2 8 AUG 1986

SDSCC-G(MPE)

SUBJECT   Letter of Appreciation

Director, Army Material Systems Analysis Activity
ATTN AMXSY-LA (Dr. John de S. Coutinho)
Aberdeen Proving Ground, MD 21001

1. We wish to extend our sincere gratitude and appreciation for your outstanding performance during August 1985 through July 1986 on the Battle Damage Assessment and Repair program. It is recognized that personal sacrifice occurred during your extended TDY at Corpus Christi Army Depot and that the major benefactors were the personnel of the Depot   Your contribution in coordinating a Battle Damage Assessment and Repair program for the AH-1S helicopter was invaluable as well as your technical expertise on helicopter structures

2. Again let me extend my sincere appreciation and gratitude for your enthusiastic support of this program. The extensive workload associated with this effort could not have been accomplished without your help.

3. "CCAD - Providing Leaders the Decisive Edge."

THOMAS M. WALKER
Colonel, AV
Commanding

Col Walker's Letter of Appreciation

INTEGRATED LOGISTIC SUPPORT

BACK AT AMSAA

The express-road home to Aberdeen by-passed New Orleans. To get to that city, you had to take a ten mile by-pass. It was getting late in the day, and we decided to take the by-pass and have dinner in New Orleans. We found a nice restaurant and had a pleasant meal.

When I subsequently submitted my expense report, AMSAA knocked payment of twenty miles off my reimbursement. I appealed, and after a lot of turbulence, I finally got paid for the extra mileage.

When I arrived at AMSAA, I found my desk moved into a large empty room, with only one other occupant, Ray Astor. Astor did not have any assignments, and he kept himself busy by helping out his friends. I just sat at my desk, read a book, and waited for somebody to give me an assignment, FOR THREE WEEKS !

Finally, one morning, Astor and I came to work to find half the room filled almost up to the ceiling with cardboard boxes full of documents. Astor learned through the "grape vine" that the supervision of the Army's Integrated Logistic Support function had been transferred from MRSA to AMSAA, and these boxes contained the MRSA records. Astor and I correctly assumed that we were being ordered to take over the MRSA activity.

We spent some time examining the contents of the boxes, specifically what organizations were being monitored. We found that about half the boxes referred to the US Army Simulation and Training Command (STRICOM) in Orlando, Florida, and the other boxes to Commands in the rest of the Army. Since I had a special interest in simulation, I volunteered to take on the STRICOM boxes, and Astor readily agreed to take on the rest.

INTEGRATED LOGISTIC SUPPORT (ILS)

The concept of ILS was invented by the BIMRAB Maintenance Committee in the 1960's as I have described in my paper, "Navy Buys Computer, Discovers Reliability," *Air Power History*, Winter 2000. It was a ghost out of my past. I was acquainted with all aspects of it. Since the original Navy initiative, the Army and Air Force have both developed their own application publications and the Army was now in the process of implementing the system. Astor was a retired Army Lieutenant Colonel and a Professional Logistician, and he had learned all about ILS in school.

ILS is an analytical procedure that determines all the resources needed to support a new operating system in the field. The procedure starts with a system description and a critical scenario, a failure effect analysis that establishes all the failure modes and their probabilities of occurrence that might occur in that scenario. For each failure mode, the resources required to repair the system are determined, namely, repair parts and materials, man power, tools, time, repair facilities, etc. A demonstration is required to check on the validity of the procedure. Each identified failure is simulated in an actual operating system and the simulated failed part is repaired or replaced with a new one. The required manpower and time is measured and compared with the predicted values derived in the ILS procedure. If the demonstration shows the ILS analysis to be valid, the new support system is then designed so that it will be able to support the operating system in the field operation described in the scenario.

THE NEED FOR SIMULATION

STRICOM was located in a large, new, open, well groomed industrial park, back to back to the local branch of the University of Florida. A lot of simulation design, assembly, and test work was being done at the University, and people were always walking back and forth between the University and STRICOM. Some of the experimental simulators were being built at the University.

The aircraft simulators that I was acquainted with were built around a cockpit and seat that moved up and down, up to ten feet, on a rail, and the cockpit rotated about three axes (four degrees of freedom). They were very expensive. But they were used to train pilots to fly and the expense was justified.

The Army's objectives are less sophisticated. One objective is to condition a man to perform his duties in a tank that is traveling cross-country at forty miles an hour. Such combat service is very rough. It shakes a man up to an extreme degree and completely disorients him. The Army decided that a stationary simulator would be satisfactory for this application. In one such simulator, the soldier looks out of the tank through a stationary vision block and sees how the tank is bouncing over the rough terrain at high speed, and hears all the associated noise, including the firing of his own gun. Tests indicate that a soldier subjected to this environment for one hour, unless adequately conditioned, is so disoriented that he cannot drive a car for at least two hours.

One of the Army's problems is how to condition large numbers of soldiers to fight in a tank. The original grandiose solution to this problem was provided by the National Training Center at Fort Irwin, California. The facilities are large enough to allow each brigade in the US to attend a two week training session once a year. The Center can accommodate two brigades at a time.

The first three days at the Training Center are used for settling in, getting acquainted with the facilities, assignments of tanks, and orientation classes. The last four days are spent in analyzing the results of the exercise, packing up to go home, etc. This leaves seven days for the training exercise.

The exercise consists of a tank battle against an opposing force of local professionals. The visitors never win. Every action is recorded, and in the class after the exercise, all the mistakes that the visitors have made are pointed out to the class and discussed. The visitors are there to learn, not to win.

With seven days being taken up by non-exercise essentials, a soldier receives seven days of field training a year. It was recognized that this was not enough. STRICOM developed a new plan to place a "Close Combat Tactical Trainer" in every National Guard Armory in the US. The trainers are all interconnected by a telephone wire so that they can create an image of a scenario where all the tanks are on the same battlefield, working together against a common opponent. For example, all the armories in the New England or in the Middle Atlantic States could be interconnected to form one large unit fighting a battle. The Army hopes to give every National Guard soldier at least some exposure in such a trainer every month. The trainer is a small unit that can easily be installed in any armory.

Another interesting tank simulator was the "Full Size Tank Trainer" that was being built by the University. The inside of this trainer accurately replicated all of the controls in a real tank, and the vision blocks provided a view of the motion of the tank in a scenario. The sound system provided all the sounds of battle. The simulator provided training for the members of a tank crew working together under combat conditions. The driver had all the controls to drive and maneuver the tank. The commander would detect targets and instruct the gunner how to aim the gun. He could talk to the commanders of the other tanks on the team. The gunner's job was to load and fire the gun. Several simulators could be interconnected to provide the image of all the tanks being engaged in the same scenario and working together. These simulators were intended for use in Army training centers.

THE INDEPENDENT LOGISTICIAN

How do you approach a major, successful Army Command and introduce a new technical procedure?

The first thing I did on my first trip to Orlando was to get myself introduced to all the product engineers. Then I sat down with their design engineers and learned about the products that they were designing. They knew about the Army ILS Specification, but this Spec only described "what" had to be done, like prepare a Test Plan, but it did not say "how" to do it. Some of them had written test plans for MRSA, but the review had never been completed. I finally cajoled them into writing new test plans for the required ILS demonstrations. Since there was nobody in STRICOM management with experience in ILS, I made arrangements for the test plans to come to me for review and approval. This was the way that MRSA had operated.

The test plan is a key document in any system development. The test plan describes, in precise detail, the test that must be performed to demonstrate that the proposed system meets the ILS requirements. The test plan describes the test specimen, test equipment and facilities in detail, specifies when and where the test will be conducted, exactly what data will be collected, lists the participating organizations, their responsibilities, and the resource requirements. These specifications must be sufficiently complete to provide confidence that the logistic demonstration will assure that the proposed maintenance concept and programmed support resources are adequate to meet readiness requirements. There was nobody at STRICOM who had written test plans in this detail before.

Except for Astor, there was nobody at AMSAA that I could talk to about ILS. Here I was making Army policy, and I had no backing. I went to the Pentagon and looked for somebody that I could talk to. I found Larry Hill, Chief, Integrated Logistic and Troop Support Division.

The normal procedure for me to send out any correspondence was to route it through my chain of command, where the correspondence would be reviewed, endorsed and mailed. Now I made arrangements with Larry to route my mail through his office, where his people would review and endorse it. This worked out fine. With time, I found that Larry's office, in their endorsements, were referring to me as "The Independent Logistician, representing the Deputy Chief of Staff for Logistics," a three star general. That's all the clout I needed. STRICOM developed an excellent ILS program.

FIELD MEDICAL OXYGEN GENERATING
AND DISTRIBUTION SYSTEM (FMOGDS)

I was sitting at my desk one day working on my reviews of STRICOM's ILS test plans when a man came into my office and introduced himself as the Chief Engineer at Fort Detrick in Frederick, Maryland. He said that they were developing Field Oxygen

Generating Equipment at Fort Detrick, that the equipment was very complicated, and that they wanted somebody to come in and review the program. I had been recommended as a person to do this, and AMSAA management had agreed to let me go to Frederick for this purpose.

I decided that the quickest way to check him out was to put in a travel request to go to Frederick. The travel request came back approved. I got in my car and drove to Frederick, and found Fort Detrick.

Oxygen generating equipment exists. Both the Air Force and the Navy have such systems to provide oxygen to pilots for high altitude flights, but both of these systems failed Army environmental requirements.

The Army currently supplies its overseas field hospitals with oxygen by air from the Continental US. In a major overseas conflict, 120 transport aircraft would be dedicated to this service. If oxygen could be generated locally, this fleet of aircraft could be assigned to other duties. This would be an enormous logistic advantage.

There is a problem in that once the Medical Corps releases aircraft for other uses, and the oxygen generating system breaks down, these aircraft will no longer be available for oxygen transportation. Hence, the oxygen generating equipment must have a very high level of reliability.

The Army is considering two oxygen generating systems. The first is for its stationary hospitals, the large (although small in plant size) NDI Liquid Oxygen, Production, Storage, and Distribution System, Modular, Medical (LOX). The second is a 6000 lbs mobile Field Medical Oxygen Generation and Distribution System (FMOGDS that will be located at the mobile Combat Support Hospitals (CSH) that have intensive care facilities.

The FMOGDS if too big and heavy to be located at the smaller Mobile Army Surgical Hospitals (MASH) that are the hospitals closest to the front lines, but it will refill MASH cylinders.

The FMOGDS is a big machine that automatically fills eight high pressure cylinders with oxygen at a time. It is a three man operation. The empty cylinders are indiscriminately dumped into one side of the machine. They come out fully loaded on the other side.

One of the problems is that each cylinder manufacturer has his own design, and the port locations are different for each manufacturer. The FMOGDS automatically feels the location of the ports, attaches itself to the fill port, makes sure the outlet is closed, and fills the cylinder automatically. This is a very complicated piece of equipment and presents a difficult reliability problem. The contractor had a paper design and a rough mock up, but he could not get the assembly to work right all the time.

I recognized that the situation was similar to the one I described in Chapter "System Engineering," page 300. In such projects, there comes a time when designers are just going around in circles and not getting anywhere. I knew that they were not going to solve their problem on paper as they were attempting to do. I therefore recommended that the FMOGDS be released for limited production, so the designers could see how the components of the system were actually acting. I knew, as I wrote on page 300, that when engineers see the assembled hardware, that is not working all that well, they become very inventive and usually find a way to solve the problem.

This was a new concept at Fort Detrick, and caused a great deal of concern. After much discussion, it was finally decided to proceed with limited production, as I advised. This point in a development program in the Army is called "Milestone III." The plan was to first procure up to three systems, but then as necessary, up to another seven systems were authorized. A board of four Medical Command generals was appointed to consider and decide what to do about Milestone III.

The presentations at the board meeting were made by a Lieutenant Colonel. I was sitting in the back of the room and was highly amused as the Colonel used my language to convince the four generals. After the presentations, the four generals sat around a small table whispering to each other for almost two hours. They were all physicians, and this was a difficult engineering decision which was outside of their scope of expertise. Nevertheless, they eventually accepted the colonel's recommendations, but they were obviously uneasy about it.

The board meeting closed with the signing of the Milestone III Release, page 482. I was asked to sign first, even though my name was at the bottom of the page. I signed with a flourish. Then the four generals signed after me. In their title abbreviations, "MG" stands for "Major General" (two stars) and "BG" stands for "Brigadier General" (one star).

I never learned the outcome of this project, since I retired from AMSAA before any results were known. However, I am sure that it was successful.

OUR WASHINGTON HOUSE

Another activity that was spelled "WORK" was associated with my father's house in Washington at 1890 Ontario Place, NW, in the Adams- Morgan Section of town. He bought the house in 1950 to give Helen a place to start her medical practice. One of my father's

MILESTONE III IN-PROCESS REVIEW
FOR THE
FIELD MEDICAL OXYGEN GENERATING
AND DISTRIBUTION SYSTEM

20 February 1992

NAME	COMMAND
MG RICHARD T. TRAVIS	Commander U.S Army Medical Research and Development Command
MG WILLIAM L. MOORE, JR	Commander U.S. Army Medical Department Center and School
MG FREDERICK N. BUSSEY	Deputy Surgeon General Office of The Surgeon General
BG BRUCE T MIKETINAC	Director Directorate of Health Care Operations Office of The Surgeon General
DR. JOHN COUTINHO	Logistics and Readiness Analysis Division U.S Army Materiel Systems Analysis Activity

Signature Page, FMOGDS Milestone III Release

friends, Dr. Solarski, lived and practiced medicine next door. There were a number of physicians and lawyers on the long block. It was a nice neighborhood, close to the Zoo. But it deteriorated with time and became the capital of Central America. You only heard Spanish in the streets and in the stores. Now it is getting to be a better neighborhood again. It is close to Columbia Road and 18 th Street, a booming business district.

The house is a solid stone two story row house built in 1912, of a type that they do not build any more. It had had only one former owner before my father bought it. My father and Helen had the basement refinished as a medical office. I inherited the house when Helen died in 1981.

By this time, the house needed work. I contracted with Sears to do the heavy work, like putting on a new roof, replacing the bath room and kitchen fixtures and installing a second bath room on the second floor, stringing new electrical wiring, and installing new rugs on the second floor. The place had beautiful parkay on the first floor, which I sanded and refinished. I removed all the old wall paper, and refinished all the walls, doors, and ceilings. Eleanor became an excellent wall painter. It took us practically all weekends for four years, but finally, the house was in an "as new" condition, and we rented it for fifteen years.

The basement had not been included in this renovation, so after we rented out the place, we continued to go to Washington on weekends to work on the basement. The house was built on a hill so that the rear basement wall was underground, up to the basement ceiling. This basement wall, and the adjoining floor, leaked whenever we had a good rain. All the houses on the block had the same trouble, and some of our neighbors had spent fortunes trying to get this problem repaired, all to no avail.

I covered the outside walls and the adjoining floor of the back room with a 3/4 inch thick coating of portland cement. When this cover proved to be waterproof, I finished the walls with studding and wallboard. This job took me forever, but our house is the only one on the block where the back room walls and floor do not leak. We furnished the room as a temporary kitchen, with a television, and it was a very comfortable room where we spent most of our leisure time.

In the year 2000, our real estate agent told us that real estate prices had peaked, and that we should sell the house. We would probably never again see such prices. We followed his advice and sold the house.

RETIREMENT

In 1993, I was 79 years old and decided to retire when I became 80 in the following August. However, in the spring of that year, AMSAA received a directive from AMC to reduce its manpower. In its wisdom, AMSAA offered any employee a bonus of $ 25000 if they would resign within the next ten days. For me, this meant an extra $25000 for retiring four months before I had planned to do so.

Astor was in much the same boat, although he was a few years younger than I was. We had some very deep discussions, and finally decided to both retire at the beginning of April, the last day of the ten day decision period. By this time, AMSAA had built up a good staff of ILS experts and we would never be missed.

Not having to go to work, I had to reorient the focus of my activities. We no longer needed the big house in Aberdeen, so we considered selling it. But there were still so many items unfinished. Fixing up the house so we could sell it, became my major activity. The garden also needed extensive work.

Then we had to think about what we were going to do after we sold the house. Our little family is so scattered around the country that there is no logical central family location. Many retired couples in our circumstances, move to Florida or other southern states. But Eleanor and I had spent some time in Florida during the summer season, when I worked a short time at the Kennedy Space Center. We were very uncomfortable in the hot weather and did not think we would like to live there. So after much thought, we decided to stay in the area where I had worked for over twenty years.

We looked around for a retirement community, and found that the good ones were in or around Baltimore. We finally decided on Oak Crest Village in Parkville, a suburb in and around the northwest corner of Baltimore City. Oak Crest is one in a national chain of retirement communities. We sold our beautiful house in Aberdeen and moved to Oak Crest. The place was brand new, only about a third of the buildings were finished. Now the place is built up and there are over 2000 residents.

Oak Crest is close to White Marsh where there is a large mall, a supermarket and several department stores, an entertainment center and a restaurant row. But there are may activities at Oak Crest to keep you busy. When we first came here, I took a course in

"Creative Writing" sponsored by the Baltimore County Community College. Writing about yourself is the easiest writing you can do, and the teacher encouraged us to write our "memoirs." She said that if you only write one page a day, in a year's time, you will have 365 pages. I have not done quite that well. She also said, write for your grandchildren, they are the ones who are truly interested in you.

Just about a year before we sold the house, I was completing the paint job in the basement, and I had a stroke. Eleanor drove me to the Johns Hopkins Hospital in Baltimore. The house was in good shape and did not need any more work. I recovered my speech and writing ability, but my balance is impaired and I have trouble walking.

EPILOGUE

BRUTALITY AS A GOVERNMENT POLICY

When my granddaughter, Kathi, read about my experiences at school in Germany, she advised me to add a description of the environment to help her develop a better understanding of what she read. Shortly after this discussion, Eleanor and I saw two old movies on television, "The Sound of Music" and "The Fiddler on the Roof." The action in both movies took place in totalitarian countries. Both stories ended with honorable and honest families being exiled from their homes, their property confiscated. Watching these stories, I realized, that from an American point of view, this type of action, common in totalitarian countries, was incomprehensible for Americans. Kathi's point was well taken.

The United States is different from all other countries in the world, where the norm has been for every nation or group of people to be ruled by a king, emperor, chief, or a leader, who by grace of God or other celestial favor is endowed as the source of all power. The people enjoy only those powers that the the king delegated or was forced to surrender. This condition was enforced by a cadre of nobles who served the king, and by priests, whose duty generally was to keep the population subservient and in most cases, miserable. Miserable people   do not have the energy to revolt.

In contrast to the American Constitution, the English Magna Carta, for example, is the first round list of powers wrestled from the King. All powers not listed remain with the King.

Something like America has happened only once before in the history of the world. Over a thousand years ago, and then only for a few hundred years, in Athens, Greece, man replaced the king at the center of the universe. (See: The Greek Way, by E. Hamilton, Norton). Athens was a true democracy. Its achievements in every human activity, in art, literature, science, sports, were monumental. The only blemish on its record is that for some men to live a life of leisure, at their level of technology, others had to work as slaves. It is remarkable that the history of Athens has been so admired for over a thousand years, but never imitated.

The American experience had a different impulse. The colonists came to America to create a new world, for themselves and their children. There was no material inheritance and no responsibility to previous generations. In many cases, for political or religious reasons, the colonists wanted to break their ties with the past and create a new life of their own.

There was no king in America, no power "by grace of God." What exists in America has been created by the colonists and their successors. The Constitution of the United States, unique in the world, starts with the words "We, the people." All power issues from the people, the government only has the powers specifically delegated to it in a constitution. The United States is the only country in the world where all power issues from the people.

Even the population of Mexico was very different from the American experience. The King of Spain organized groups of his subjects in Spain, equipped them with all the supplies that they would need in their new country, including plans for their new towns, and sent them off to Mexico under the protection of the Spanish Navy. When they arrived at the lands that the King had designated, they built their town and became a part of New Spain. Their relationship to the King of Spain did not change. Mexico has since become a Republic, but I have found in my travels that in the minds of the people, the King has merely been replaced by something called "The State." In talking to educated Mexicans, I find that they refer to "The State" as the source of all power, and the people only have those powers, that "The State" has delegated or surrendered to them.

In my history class in Germany, we spent several long weeks discussing and analyzing the results of the French Revolution. I kept wondering when they were going to talk about the American Revolution, that predated the French, but they never mentioned it. In the French Revolution, they beheaded the King, who had exercised his power "by grace of God," and substituted a democratic government that replaced the King and then ruled "by grace of God." All undefined power remains with the government, and the people only have the rights that the government had delegated or surrendered to them.

Except for the US Government, all the democratic governments in the world are modeled after the principles established by the French Revolution. A small indication of the far flung influence of that Revolution is shown by our measurement standards. Americans, Britains, and Canadians use the inch-pound (ABC) system of measurement. All other countries engaged in international trade use the metric system established by the French Revolution and are actively pressuring the ABC countries to adopt the metric system that is less practical.

However, rights and privileges delegated by an all powerful government can also be taken away. In totalitarianism, the state retracts all rights. People become state property. Stalin, in furthering what he felt were the interests of the Russian State, found it necessary to eliminate some state assets, namely some 21 million people. This was a bureaucratic action, and had, for Stalin, no moral scruples.

One of Hitler's major problems was how do you get a peaceful and industrious people like the Germans to make war. You have to get them emotionally all riled up, preferably hating something. The Jews provided good candidate material for this. Paint them as lecherous characters , and make people hate them. Get people to riot against them. After the fun of participating in a couple of riots, people will want more. The Jews became a great security risk.

In addition to the Jews, there was the Church. Both Catholic and Lutheran Churches had owned large parcels of land for hundreds of years. This land provided the Churches with their income. Napoleon confiscated all Church property, but the state took over the support of the Churches. Priests and bishops became civil servants and received their salaries from the state.

Hitler designed a new oath of allegiance in which he was recognized as equal to God. *Christians and Jews had their own God, they could not be relied upon to loyally follow all of Hitler's directives without question.* Many religious personnel, and even good Christians, refused to sign that oath and were branded as security risks.

Hitler had to conserve his resources carefully and made it a crime for anyone to send money to a recipient outside of Germany without Government approval. Many religious orders were responsible for the support of their missions in Africa and South America, and found ways to sneak money out of Germany. However, a few got caught and the orders were branded as criminals and security risks.

Hitler was a very busy man. The annexation of Austria in two days was a brilliant maneuver that had required a great deal of planning. Next he was engaged in the annexation of the rest of Europe to recreate the Holy Roman Empire. (The Nazis called this "the world" to conform with Roman practice.) Hitler had no plan to invade England, as she had not been a part of the Holy Roman Empire, and he was convinced that the "Bund," the US arm of his Nazi organization was strong enough that it would prevent the US from ever getting into a war with Germany.

Hitler was indeed a very busy man, and the number of his security risks was in the millions, a truly overwhelming situation. Suddenly, the gas chambers offered a quick and final solution. Nobody in Hitler's office gave it much thought, it was no big deal, considering the other problems they had. Some six million people perished in the gas chambers. Although a large part of them were Jews, about a third were Christians who could not take the Nazi oath of allegiance. While I was still in Freiburg, some of my teachers from Stella Maris in Meersburg were seen, fearing for their lives, fleeing from one underground safe house to another, seeking shelter. In the following six years of the Hitler regime, almost all safe houses were discovered and the occupants perished in the gas chambers. The Order of Christian Brothers was the second largest order of men in the Catholic Church, second only to the Jesuits. Almost all the Brothers in Germany were obliterated.

Germany had had personal registration for many years before Hitler, everybody was registered with their local police department. This is something Americans seem to have difficulty understanding. Hitler expanded this system. One of his best kept secrets was that he developed the punched card computer. Everybody, and every government agency, was recorded on a punch cards. This was a great help to him in his dramatic take-over of the German and Austrian Governments as I have described on pages 99 and 100. Nearly everybody in Germany was required to participate in some Nazi organization, where they would be extensively brainwashed. To the extent possible, the State ran your life.

MORE ABOUT MY FAMILY

During the events recounted in this book, our sons grew up and got married. Roy and his wife Judy are shown on page 490. Alan and his wife Meg appear on pages 491 and 492.

Page 493 shows myself as a Second Lieutenant in the Army of the United States, just after completing Summer Training Camp at Fort Meade, Maryland, in 1940. The next page, 494, shows Roy as a Naval Officer. Page 495 shows all the Coutinho men in a row at Mikes's wedding in Columbus, Ohio, on October 7, 2000. Underneath are photos of Mike and Joe with their brides.

Roy and Judy Coutinho

Alan   Coutinho

Margaret   Coutinho

**Second Lieutenant John Coutinho
Army of the US**

Ensign Roy Coutinho, US Navy Reserves

The Coutinho Men at Mike's Wedding
Mike and Amy   --   Christa and Joe

THE PRESIDENT'S CAT "SOCKS"

Eleanor has been working as a volunteer at the White House for over twenty years, through Republican and Democratic administrations. She drives to Washington once or twice a month with a couple of women friends, all members of the Harford County Republican Womans' Club.

Eleanor has had a number of jobs during this time, such as opening the President's mail and routing each piece of mail to the office most competent to provide an answer. Then for a while she answered the President's telephone. Lately she has been addressing the President's greeting cards. These addresses must be neatly hand written and comply with strict format rules.

President Clinton had a cat, "Socks," that was in the habit of going around the White House compound inspecting the various executive offices. Below is a photograph of Socks visiting Eleanor's mail room.

Eleanor and Socks

DRESS CODES

I was leafing through a 1938 Bulletin published by New York University and came across the photograph shown on the next page, 498. I was completely flabbergasted. The boys in the photograph are what I and all other students looked like in 1938 at New York University – and in my personal experience - at the Berlin Technical University, 3000 miles away, and at all other universities worthy of the name. This dress code for students was universal. Changes in the dress code since that time have been unbelievable, and I imagine that this has been the impetus for many other changes, both good and bad.

I remember that in 1938 I had to shine my shoes every night. I always wore a suit, jacket and pants of the same material. One of my major problems was to keep a crease in my trousers. Eventually they had to go to the cleaners to be dry cleaned and pressed. I always wore a tie, and my shirts were either white or solid blue. I never went anywhere without my fedora hat, except when I had a students' cap in Germany.   The photo on page 498 is an accurate picture of how I had to dress for school, both in Freiburg, Berlin, and New York.

The first relaxation in the dress code that I experienced was at Grumman in 1941, when the company was still small. We were allowed to wear colorful sport shirts (no ties) to the office on Saturdays when working overtime. As soon as the company started to grow in size, this privilege was retracted.

RAMBLINGS

In the description of my activities with the Navy's BIMRAB, the National Transportation Conference, and the Army's BDAR program, I showed how the scope of my influence extended throughout the country, and even internationally.   I am now attaching a few copies of unsolicited letters that show that the scope of my influence extended beyond that already described.

THE AMERICAN SOCIETY OF AMERICAN ENGINEERS (ASME)

I was a member of the ASME Publications Committee for nine years, serving two 2-year terms as Representative of Region 2 (Northeast United States) and a five year term as a Committee Member, my last year as Chairman.

The ASME at that time published more pages of technical literature than any other organization in the United States, except for the American Chemical Society. The ASME Publications Committee had all the problems of a "board of directors" of a medium large growing business. I received the letter on page 499 from O. B. Schier II, the manager of the Society, when my term expired.

1938 Dress Code at New York University

The American Society of Mechanical Engineers

TWENTY NINE WEST THIRTY NINTH STREET   NEW YORK 18 N Y   PENNSYLVANIA 6 9220

December 17, 1959

Mr. John de S. Coutinho
32 Darthmouth Street
Garden City, L. I., N. Y.

Dear Mr. Coutinho:

As a member of the Publications Committee and as its Chairman you played an important part in many questions relating to the financing and distribution of ASME publications. The several progress reports of the Publications Committee to the Board on Technology will attest to this.

In particular, you were instrumental in bringing to a successful conclusion a method of packaging the Transactions. This has resulted in a series of five Transactions quarterlies which ASME commenced publishing in January, 1959.

In addition, your presentations for the Committee during the Technology Executives Conferences were extremely valuable in bringing to the attention of our members the complexities of publishing technical literature.

For these and many more evidences of your constructive leadership the Society is deeply grateful.

Yours very truly,

O. B. Schier, II
Secretary

Letter,   ASME, Dec 17, 59

FEDERAL AVIATION AGENCY (FAA)

Mr Herbert W. Anderson was my predecessor as chairman of the ASME Aviation Division and had listened to my discussions of the emerging technical subject of reliability. He invited me to give a lecture on the subject at the Federal Aviation Agency where he worked. I did so and received the letter on page 501.

STANFORD UNIVERSITY

Henry Fuchs, Professor of Mechanical Engineering Design at Stanford University, read a couple of my articles in the ASME Journal *Mechanical Engineering*. He liked what he read, and wrote me the letter shown on page 502. I sent him more material, we became good friends, and was invited to Stanford University to give a lecture there.

UNIVERSITY OF OREGON

The Engineering Foundation is sponsored by the major engineering societies in the United States to conduct activities of interest to most societies. One such activity in my time was a series of top level engineering conferences organized to clarify a fuzzy technical area. Each conference consisted of a small assembly of the foremost experts in the country who met for a week at a remote location, to discuss the subject in an unstructured, but most thorough manner possible.

One of these annual conference series was held on the subject of "Quality Requirements." I participated for a number of years, and was elected Chairman for the 1968 Conference. I prepared the agenda, chaired the meeting, and wrote a report that was published in the *Journal of the American Society of Quality Control,* (ASQC). One of the participants, Professor Corwin Edwards of the University of Oregon, wrote me the letter shown on page 503. At that time, I was so busy that I did not have the time to follow up on his suggestion to contact the White House.

FEDERAL AVIATION AGENCY
Washington 25, D C

October 15, 1963

Mr. John de S. Coutinho
Grumman Aircraft Engineering Corporation
Bethpage L. I.
New York

Dear John

Your discussion of reliability engineering with our people yesterday is a favor valued by all of us. Judged from the comments I received this morning, your presentation and remarks were exceptionally stimulating.

The Federal Aviation Agency's Mechanical Reliability Report (MRR) System and the related data processing and retrieval functions has given us a modern capability for reliability analysis. Since we cannot use traditional or prosaic methods if the system is to be effectively used, we are particularly appreciative of unbiased and informed counsel. Thank you for giving us this kind of assistance and being so generous with your time.

Sincerely yours,

Herbert W. Anderson
Chief, Operations Analysis Branch
Flight Standards Service

Letter from FAA

DESIGN DIVISION

STANFORD UNIVERSITY

MECHANICAL ENGINEERING DEPARTMENT
STANFORD CALIFORNIA

March 1, 1966

Mr. J. de S Coutinho
Reliability Director, LEM
Grumman Aircraft Corp.
Bethpage, New York

Dear Mr. Coutinho

I have read and enjoyed your article in the February issue
of Mechanical Engineering and your paper on The Reproduction
Process. Your clear distinctions between achievement and
demonstration of reliability, and between mass-production
and space systems, have expressed less articulate thoughts
which I had.

May I please have a reprint of each of these papers, and
of other papers you might have written which would be of
interest to a teacher of design?

Sincerely yours,

Henry O Fuchs

Henry O Fuchs
Professor

HOF:et

Letter from Stanford University

UNIVERSITY OF OREGON

Department of Economics
COLLEGE OF LIBERAL ARTS

EUGENE, OREGON 97403
telephone (code 503) 342-1411

April 17, 1969

Mr John de S. Coutinho
Grumman Aircraft Engineering Corporation
Bethpage, Long Island
New York 11714

Dear John

 I have just finished a careful reading of the report of the
conference on quality requirements in which I took part   It is
an impressive job   I want to congratulate you particularly on the
last part that summarizes the general discussion.

 In reading the report I formed the opinion that your quality
engineering group ought to maintain contact with the President's
Assistant for Consumer Affairs through her White House staff   If
you see any merit in the idea, you could explore it with William
Kaye, the executive director of that staff

Cordially,

Corwin D. Edwards
Professor

CDE/e

Letter from University of Oregon

SOCIETY OF AUTOMOTIVE ENGINEERS (SAE)

Charlie Coangelo was a young, short engineering graduate, recently employed by the Long Island Lighting Company, who joined the ASME Long Island Section of which I was Chairman. Charlie's first job was to write work orders for field jobs. This was not exactly a very stimulating intellectual activity. After about a month of this, Charlie decided to go out to the field to see how they were progressing on the jobs that he had documented. At one place he came to, the men were digging a very deep, wide trench. There are some things you only learn in an engineering school. Charlie took one look at the trench and realized that the sides were not braced properly. He went to the foreman's shack and started to tell the foreman that he needed to reinforce his braces. The foreman was a great big guy. He grabbed Charlie by the back of his collar and the back of his belt, lifted him off the ground, carried him out the door and flung him some distance down the road. Charlie licked his wounds where he was scraped and bleeding, and went back to his office utterly dejected.

Two days later, the walls of the trench collapsed and killed two men. Never again did any workman, no matter how big, talk back to Charlie when he pointed out a safety infraction.

Because of his technical training, the engineer is the professional guarantor of the safety of engineered products. Almost no one else understands the engineer's professional reasoning, they are more concerned with making money. However, the engineer is usually a "hired hand," and his status is not commensurate with his professional responsibilities. I realized that the professional responsibilities of the engineer for public safety could sometimes conflict with the objectives of his employer. I wrote an article about this subject. My friend, Professor Victor Paschkis of Columbia University, advised me to publish it in the *Newsletter of the Society for Social Responsibility in Science.* I received more letters commenting on this paper, all positive, than on any other work that I ever published. One of these letters on page 505 is from Mr. Joseph Gilbert, General Manager of the SAE, one of America's largest engineering societies. He comments on a draft of this paper that I sent to Mr. Jaklitsch at the ASME. I was very pleased to get this letter. The SAE is one of the largest and most effective standardization agencies in the country. This is an activity that requires the expert adjustment of strongly conflicting special interests, such as public safety versus profits. Gilbert was well acquainted with the difficulties that engineers have in their profession, and I was delighted to receive his invitation to a luncheon meeting. Unfortunately, I never found the time to accept his invitation.

Society of Automotive Engineers, Inc.

485 LEXINGTON AVENUE NEW YORK N Y 10017
OXford 7-3340   TWX-212 867-6594
cable address SOCAUTOENG N Y

January 8, 1965
Dictated January 7, 1965

Mr John De S Coutinho
32 Dartmouth Street
Garden City, New York

Dear John

Just read your wonderful letter of September 8 to Jack Jaklitsch on the question of professionalism John, you have said better than I can just what I have felt for many years Yours is the best thinking -- by a country mile -- that I've seen on the subject

It's easy for a lot of do-gooders to talk about professionalism and the acceptance of social responsibility by the engineer To practice it is a heck of a lot harder in the light of the realities of corporate management obligations and the objectives of profit-making enterprise in this country

There's lots more that comes to mind In fact, I am bubbling over with reactions to your ideas However, because I am just about ready to get on the train for Detroit for our Annual Meeting, I had better cut it short

I really and truly would like to get together with you one of these days just to kick around this subject I would rather do it on a man-to-man basis rather than talking to you in my official capacity and having you respond in your capacity as an engineering executive at Grumman

One of these days when you plan to be in the neighborhood of 485 Lexington Avenue and have a free noon-hour give me a little advance warning so that we can arrange for a leisurely luncheon get-together

Honestly, I do want to chew this over with you

Best of the New Year to you

Sincerely,

Joseph Gilbert, General Manager

bc

Letter from SAE, Jan 8, 65

ROLLS ROYCE, UNITED KINGDOM

I wrote the lead article "Whither Reliability?" in the 1964 AIAA's *Journal of Spacecraft,* surveying the state of the art in reliability technology. I received many favorable letters regarding this article. One of the most interesting ones is shown of page 507from Frank Nixon, Chief Reliability Engineer at Rolls Royce in England. We met later in this country and he even came over to the house for dinner. We became good friends.

THE BRITISH NAVY

Commander Roy Titchen was a regular attendee at the Navy's BIMRAB Conferences where he became aware of my activities and standing in the industry.   He refers to my paper "Whither Reliability?," the same paper that Frank Nixon referred to. See page 508.

SOUTH AFRICA

Stat-A-Matrix is a company that puts on technical training programs and has, for a number of years, presented such programs to the South African military services.   When my book, *Advanced Systems Development Management,* came out, the South African military agreed to have Stat-A-Matrix present a course by that title, with me as a lecturer. I was offered the position of "Principal Lecturer" in a small team to present the material in my book, see page 509. The course was to last two weeks, and travel was by first class air. I renegotiated these terms to include an extra week of a vacation and air travel for two by coach, so I could take Eleanor along. We really looked forward to a fun vacation in South Africa. The course was scheduled for February, when it was summer in South Africa.

I submitted a leave request from AMSAA for three weeks vacation time. The leave request was denied by Security.

THE WHITE HOUSE

Eleanor had been working as a volunteer for some twenty years at the White House and was well known there. As a result of her fame, the President of the United States found out about our 50th wedding anniversary and sent us the letter shown on page 510.

ROLLS ROYCE LIMITED

P O BOX NO 3
DERBY

E EG MS
ROYCAR DERBY
TELEX 37845

E E HONE
DERBY 42424

EXT 222

OUR REF   FN.2/MB.

YOUR REF

25th August, 1964.

Mr. John de S. Coutinho,
LEM Reliability Director,
Grumman Aircraft Engineering Corp.,
Bethpage,
Long Island,
New York,
U S A

Dear John,

Further to my letter of August 20th, I have now finished reading your "Whither Reliability?" and I hasten to congratulate you on a magnificent achievement.

I started out to underline in red pencil the important highlights, but soon discontinued, as I found that I was having to sharpen the pencil at the end of each column.

For a completely balanced, dispassionate and objective review, I have never seen its equal. I admire especially the way in which you have, by reviewing the historical background, thrown light on such confused issues as statistics, AGREE, and MTBF, trying to redirect attention to the fundamental importance of basic engineering.

I shall be quoting you pretty extensively in our own Government quarters, where unfortunately some of the boffins are just catching on to the earlier ideas, now, happily, obsolescing in your country. In this connection, would you please let me know what is the pronunciation of your name which you prefer   I would be inclined to say Cooteenyo, but I would much rather get it right first time.

I shall be in the States again next January, as I have been asked to be a member of a quiz panel at the Reliability Symposium at Miami. Is there any chance that you will be there? If not I expect that I shall be spending a few days in New York, and we might meet there. I hope so.

Yours sincerely,

Frank Nway

Letter from Rolls Royce

OFFICE OF THE COMMANDER
BRITISH NAVY STAFF
Main Navy Building, P O Box 165
Benjamin Franklin Station, WASHINGTON, D C

Letters from U K to be addressed
H M S SAKER
c/o G P O London

1st February, 1965

Offic Ex 3 1940 Ext 151
Home 202 - 657 8176

JOHN DE. S. COUTINHO,
Grumman Aircraft Engineering Corporation,
Bethpage, Long Island, New York.

Dear John,

Thankyou very much for your letter of the 19th January, and for the enclosed papers. Your paper "Whither Reliability" almost completes my task for me.

Do you remember me telling you of the impending visit of the Director of our Radio Division in the Admiralty to discuss Reliability He is the Chairman of the Committee set up by the Admiralty with the following terms of reference:-

> "To consider and advise on the measures necessary to bring about a substantial improvement in the reliability of Naval Electronic Equipment bearing in mind the financial implications, and to act as a co-ordinating body with similar organisations outside the Navy Department."

They are to report to the Admiralty by April 1965

The prime purpose of his visit is to assess the state of the art of Reliability and Maintainability in the U.S. and it is quite clear that the policy and methods we adopt in the U.K. will largely depend upon what he sees during his visit.

I have organised a full programme for him in Washington, where he is visiting BUWEPS, BUSHIPS, VITRO and ARINC. He will also be visiting the U.S. Naval Applied Science Laboratory to hear the latest ideas on Systems effectiveness. What he will need after this is some common sense to bring the visit down to earth and some thoughts on the commercial aspects of reliability and maintenance. We shall be in the New York area on Tuesday the 16th March, and I would be very grateful if I could bring him to see you on that day. What I would like him to hear are the commercial aspects, shortcomings on specifications and your ideas on commercial incentives. Practical examples with results are what we need.

If you are not in New York on that Tuesday, we could probably rearrange our Mondays programme at the Naval Applied Science Laboratory for Tuesday. I will send you a detailed copy of Captain CLODE's programme. Make a note of my telephone number so that the next time you are in the D.C. area you can call me, my wife and I would be delighted if you would come and have dinner with us.

Yours

R. KITCHEN, Commander, Royal Navy

Letter from the British Navy

STAT-A-MATRIX, Inc.

TRAINING • CONSULTING

July 7, 1978

Dr. John de S. Coutinho
602 West Gate Road
Aberdeen, MD   21001

Dear Dr. Coutinho·

STAT-A-MATRIX, Inc. has been providing training programs
in Quality and Reliability in The Republic of South Africa
for a number of years now. We are currently planning
the presentation of a two-week seminar, "Advanced Systems
Development Management", which will cover a number of
items contained in your book by that title.

We would like to invite you to serve as the Principal
Lecturer, as part of a two to three lecturer team. The
program will be conducted by STAT-A-MATRIX, Inc. for
ARMSCOR at their facilities in Pretoria, Republic of
South Africa, from February 5-16, 1979.

Please advise us of your availability as soon as possible.

Sincerely,

STAT-A-MATRIX, Inc.

Stanley A. Marash
President

SAM:kc

P O Box 2152 • Menlo Park Station • Edison New Jersey 08817 • 201 548 0600

Cable Address STATAMATRIX Edison NJ

Letter   from   Stat-A-Matrix

THE WHITE HOUSE

WASHINGTON

September 10, 1992

Dear Eleanor and John:

Barbara and I have learned that September 12th
is a special day for you, and it is with great
pleasure that we send our heartfelt congratu-
lations on your 50th wedding anniversary.
We join with your many friends here at the
White House in honoring you on this occasion.

Warm regards.

Sincerely,

George Bush

Dr. and Mrs. John Coutinho
602 Westgate Road
Aberdeen, Maryland 21001

Letter from the White House

WHY A SPACE PROGRAM ?

My article "Why a Space Program ?" in the May, 1967, issue of *Mechanical Engineering* started with the following eight paragraphs.

"Modern civilized man with his electric light has little need to look at the night sky, and except when in love, hardly ever does so. But before the advent of the electric light, men were well acquainted with the sky, both day and night. Since time immemorial, many men have worshiped the sun or the moon and looked up to the stars as a source of inspiration, guidance, strength, mystery, and wisdom. Ever since man became aware of his environment, one of his basic urges, one of the greatest dreams of the greatest men to walk the earth, has been to reach out beyond the apparent bounds of our own earth and to grasp for the stars, to learn the secrets of the universe.

"Every generation, as a link in the time-chain between fathers and sons, daughters and mothers, has its special responsibilities to the past and to the future, based on what it inherits and on what is given to it to create for itself. Some generations create a system of law, others build cathedrals or pyramids, some fall on bad times and have all they can do just to keep going. We today have the good fortune to inherit a great body of scientific knowledge, and on this base we have created a technology such as the world has never seen. We are the first generation of mankind with the technical capability to reach out beyond our earth   to realize the age-old dream of our fathers. *Our cathedral was to reach the moon in 1970, and well beyond in the next decades.*

"At this point it may be well to briefly examine the purpose of life itself from a historical viewpoint. First there were a few cells in the sea, some of which developed into plants while others became animals; mollusks, fish, reptiles, mammals. From the sea, some of these species found a foothold on land and developed new forms, more suitable to their new environments. And finally, even the air was conquered by the birds, bats, insects, bacteria, and whatnots.

"It is obvious from this brief analysis that there is a basic drive in living things, not only to perpetuate the species, but also to overcome natural barriers and to adapt to new hostile environments, from the sea to land to air, by developing new forms of life as necessary. There is a will to grow in life, a will to evolve, to overcome hardship and disaster.

"Some time during this evolution, somehow and somewhere, man appeared, unique among all living things as the bearer of intelligence, created after God's own image. Man learned to control fire and to cook, to wear clothing, to build shelter, to manufacture food. He has learned to live comfortably in a once hostile environment, to inhabit the earth from pole to pole, to live for extended periods at great depths in the sea, or to fly at supersonic speeds around the world.

"Among all living things, only intelligent man today has the capability of recognizing that eventually the earth is doomed. Some day, in the far, far future, there will be a great natural catastrophe, and further life on earth, certainly as we know it, will become impossible. Does it appear to be God's will that all life should perish with the end of our earth?

"From what we can observe of the characteristics of life, of the will to overcome hostile environments, the answer would appear to be NO! For what more logical reason was man gifted with intelligence, if not to use it to protect and perpetuate life, in face of adversity and disaster, even beyond the end of this world!

"From this viewpoint, the space program is the most significant project ever launched in the history of the universe. It justifies God's wisdom in entrusting man with creative intelligence in His own image. Today there is no more important a task than our space exploration program to which a man may dedicate his life."

Unfortunately, just because something should be done does not mean that it will be done. Space programs cost lots of money. Political moneybags, who allot huge sums of money for projects of immediate benefit for their constituents, will very carefully examine space projects to assure that they contribute to such generally recognized goals as:

-National Security

-Technological Progress and associated Economic
Advantages

-Scientific Discovery

-International Competition

-International Cooperation

Historically, great peoples have not always been deterred by their political bean counters and their "virtuous" goals. The great cathedrals of Europe, for example, built for the greater honor and glory of God, required commitments that extended over several hundred years. Working on such structures is truly a form of prayer. In the United States, the Washington Cathedral and St. John's in New York City are the two largest gothic cathedrals in the world, and the Byzantine Basilica of the Shrine of the Immaculate Conception in Washington is the second largest church in the world. The City of Washington is full of gorgeous monuments that serve no economic purpose. This country just needs the proper leadership and it can accomplish any altruistic goal. As I mentioned on page 371, the leadership needed to establish a station on the moon and to execute a 25 year program, currently does not exist. The present space shuttle program with Russian participation has not generated the enthusiasm and excitement that our population would show if there were a birth of the first baby conceived and born on the moon.

In addition to its management and technical skills, our leadership has to learn how to deal with people. The Apollo operation required large numbers of highly specialized engineers in quantities which were so large as to make the operation unique in the history of the world. In a report to an ASME meeting in 1965, it was pointed out that fully two thirds of the nation's scientists and engineers were working in space or related industries. The report concluded that space and defense industries and their personnel could not convert easily to civilian markets.

Large space programs involve not only very large numbers of engineers, but provide no continuity of employment. It would appear that NASA deliberately delights in moving its big contracts from contractor to contractor, forcing the current award winner to hire large numbers of engineers for the duration of a single program. As soon as the program is completed, all of the associated jobs evaporate.

The US Government encourages the location of space and defense plants in areas of low population density, like when Grumman was asked to move from Long Island to Texas. When contracts are completed, engineers must move. Towards the end of the Apollo program, I heard stories about engineers in remote areas being laid off, without any chance of finding employment in the immediate vicinity, and because of the massive simultaneous layoffs, with no chance of disposing of their homes. They locked up their houses, loaded their families and some of their possessions in their cars, and drove off. More often than not, they abandoned their real estate and other possessions that they had accumulated during their few years of dedicated service. It can be said, that because of these conditions, the space program was to an essential point, subsidized by these specialized engineers who suffered substantial personal losses.

The rolling 25 year program, advancing one year at a time, that I proposed on pages 372 and 373, would provide for stable engineer employment. All we have to do now is to find an inspired, capable leader, and we would be on our way to finding another planet in the universe that could support life as we know it on earth.

Why a Space Program ? Because it is God's plan for mankind!

SERMONS

BY

R. WINTER HAMILTON, D.D., LL.D.

AUTHOR OF

"THE DOCTRINE OF REWARDS AND PUNISHMENT,"
"PASTORAL APPEALS," ETC.

The inductions of sound philosophy harmonize with the impressions of the man, who, feeling his own moral necessities, yields his cordial assent to this mystery of God, and seeks in its provisions his peace in the life that now is, and his hope for the life that is to come.—ABERCROMBIE'S PHILOSOPHY OF THE MORAL FEELINGS.

NEW YORK:

CARLTON & LANAHAN.
SAN FRANCISCO: E. THOMAS.
CINCINNATI: HITCHCOCK & WALDEN.

ADVERTISEMENT.

THE Author submits, with unaffected diffidence, these Discourses to the public eye. They have been written at distant intervals, and in incomplete portions, as his much-occupied time would allow. He fears that, consequently, there may be sometimes a recurrence of the same expression and thought. This may as probably be the case in the same, as in different, sermons. It might have been better if the length of a few had been curtailed. But he must frankly confess, that preparation for the press is to him an irksome task, that he was obliged to drag himself to it, and that he seldom had patience to review what was already composed. He should not have published, but he was so often requested, especially by many of his ministerial brethren, that refusal was likely to seem fastidious and perverse. Being pledged, he was compelled to proceed; but how often has he regretted that he was ever foolish enough to give that pledge! For the *doctrine* he offers no apology—it

is his joy in life, and his hope in death. The *style* will be, as usual, severely attacked, should criticism deign a notice: he must meekly bear the censure and penalty of an irretrievable offense. He can only do his little in his own way. The subjects are general, but various: though scarcely any reason, better than that of caprice, can be assigned for their selection. They were those which had been either most recently delivered, or could be most easily recalled. Nineteen years of a pastorate in one place, if studiously devoted in the faintest degree, must have accumulated an amount, out of which it is not the simplest of labors to choose. He has the hardihood to ask one thing, (though the caution can not apply to those *divining* spirits which do perfectly judge of a book without reading it,) that this volume be not thrown aside as utterly worthless until its discourses be regularly perused. He hopes he shall not be accounted an offender for a word. The whole of its value, if it may pretend any, cannot be determinable by the uncouthness of a phrase, or the infelicitous structure of a sentence. If it shall be proved that his reasonings are vitiated, and his statements are incorrect, he will bow to that judgment. Still will he stoop, if the censor be of a sufficient order of intellect to warrant a jest and sneer. Only

let him not be reproved (as he has sometimes been) in a vein of language, and with a course of illustration, which inspired no stimulating zest by containing any superior model. Be his present publication dealt with as it may, no high hope of success will lend its aggravation to disappointment. With strictest truth he can say—whatever auguries his friends draw in its favor, and whatever hopes they indulge of its acceptance—in the language of Virgil's Lycidas: "SED NON EGO CREDULUS ILLIS."

PREFACE.

Rev. Richard Winter Hamilton, D.D., LL.D., the author of these sermons, was for many years Pastor of an Independent congregation in the borough of Leeds, England. He was born in London, July 6, 1794. Very early in youth, and even in childhood, he manifested his choice for the Christian ministry, and among his playmates, as soon as able to read, one of his favorite exercises was uniting with them in reading the Bible, in singing, and in prayer. Possibly this tendency arose from the associations and relationships of life. His father was also an Independent minister, whose mother had early been a member of one of Mr. Wesley's societies, a Miss Hesketh, who is mentioned in Mr. Wesley's Journal. His mother was a daughter also of an Independent minister, who had taken Mr. Hamilton's father for his assistant. The conversation to which he listened, the exercises which he witnessed, and the natural tendency of childhood to imitate, no doubt influenced him to some extent. When referring to his childhood, he says, " No sooner was I capable of the faintest thought and observation than I aspired to the office as something mysteriously dignified ; but at that age the ambition could merely arise from bold and fearless dispositions, or from counterpart motives equally criminal and vain. The predilection was probably strengthened from the celebrity of ancestors, and the reputation of friends who gave attendance at the altar ; but while memory lingers on these indications of character and presages of futurity, I sometimes fondly hope that the divine approba-

tion originally prompted, as well as since expanded and matured them, though I wist not then it was the voice of God." The spirit and influence of his mother was powerful in forming his character. She was a woman of deep piety, of superior intellect, and of fine education. Her letters, which have been published by his biographer, manifest the depth and beauty of her religious life. She died when he was about eleven years of age; but her teachings, her example, and her prayers had been powerfully influential long before that time. When about to enter college as a theological student he drew up an account of his religious experience, in which he says: " The first impressions I had of any nature, as far as I can recollect, were those of religion; and well do I remember that when the names of a Williams or a Winter were mentioned, my heart burned with the desire to emulate my predecessors in the road to Zion, and often, at that period of life when I was most with my mother, has my heart melted within me when, with celestial fire beaming in her eyes, and animation glowing in her cheeks, she has pointed to the Lamb of God that taketh away the sin of the world, and directed my wondering eyes to the glories of immortality. Thus she led the way, and as Elijah left his mantle in his ascent to heaven, so I believe she left within me impressions too deeply graven to be wholly effaced." P. 81. When about to be ordained, he said: " A mother who taught me lessons the most interesting and important, who watched over me with solicitude most acute and tender—such a parent imprinted her instructions and hallowed her example by apparently an untimely death. I could not have entirely suppressed these recollections, for they relate to the means which were principally employed to commence within me that moral habitude which I hope neither the levities of childhood nor the inconsistencies of youth have been able to subvert.

The attractive modes of tuition which that parent adopted—her tender expostulations, her pathetic advices, and her earnest prayers—have induced an impression which, as I can never cease to remember, I hope I may never cease to obey." P. 81. Long after, in one of his sermons, he made the following beautiful allusions:

"To this moment I recall the soft, kind manner of a mother who early left her orphan child for a brighter and more congenial scene. Even now my mind returns to its perplexities when 'I thought as a child.' I can renew my objection and urge my doubt, and still do I seem to hear her gentle voice, to gaze on the

"'Rich intelligence of those dear eyes,'

while she checked the improper sentiment and relieved the painful apprehension. Her instructions are as deeply traced on the memory as her features, and as easily recalled as her tones. She told me why the Saviour must die, though the Father was pleased to forgive; and from her I learned the rudiments of that sacred science which, with all my neglect, I have never from that hour refrained to cultivate and forborne to pursue. It may be weak to say it, but if I can claim any theological taste and store, I owe it all to her. Feeble is the tribute I can pay to her excellence, nor had it been obtruded but to illustrate the principle of domestic instruction. She deserved an Augustine's narrative, a Gregory's apostrophe, and a Cowper's strain. How could thy child, blest parent, but remember thee? Ever must he retain the image of thy face, and the luster of thine example! His heart must cease to beat ere it can refuse to dwell upon that blessing and that embrace which he received from thee when thy 'soul was in departing' ere he can, after well-nigh thirty years, cease to be 'bowed down heavily,' mourning for his mother."

How far parents may influence their children for the

ministry may not be an easy question to answer. Unquestionably God selects his own ministers by his Holy Spirit. He calls them in youth or in manhood to enter upon that sacred office; yet it is not unreasonable to suppose that when he designs to call a choice instrumentality for his service he may influence the hearts of parents to make a consecration of their child in earliest infancy, and to give it such training and direction as may best fit it for that work; nor is it unreasonable to suppose that he may so mold and fashion the tastes and sympathies, even in early life, as to give peculiar qualifications for the work in maturer years. Certain it is, that among the most honored instruments whom God hath employed in his work some of them were early set apart by parental consecration, and many of them rejoiced in the holy influence of a mother's teaching and example; and little may mothers dream of the manner in which they are preaching to the coming age by the words and thoughts which touch the heart of childhood in the nursery.

There was nothing about the early years of Mr. Hamilton that manifested his intellectual superiority. He had large sympathy, affection, and generosity. His imagination was luxuriant. He had an unbounded flow of spirits and of wit, was fond of mischief and of mimicry, but was remarkably backward in learning to read. His mother patiently watched over him and taught him, but became so discouraged that at one time she said to his father, with much sorrow, that she did not think he would ever read. Probably his vivacity and buoyancy of spirits were the chief barriers. As his years increased, however, his love of study was developed, and placed at preparatory schools, he made good proficiency. His teacher wrote of him, "He is a dear boy, but he requires a tight rein." If he erred, he was frank to acknowledge his errors; and so truthful was he from

childhood that his parents often said of him to visiting friends, "There goes a child who, to our knowledge, never told a lie." From his thirteenth to his sixteenth year he was placed at the grammar school, and among other studies, he commenced the Latin and Greek languages. His religious character began to be more fully developed. A praying circle was formed among the students, in which he took part; and, still carrying within him the deep conviction that he should be a minister, he made a solemn personal consecration of all his powers to God. About this time he drew up a full and solemn covenant, in which he very clearly stated his convictions and his purposes; and the paper shows the peculiar style of writing which distinguished him in after years, as well as the deep solemnity of his spirit, and his earnest aspirations to be like Christ. Returning home, some one called the attention of his father to his ability in prayer, and he was invited to take part in family worship. His father was so much interested in his services that, though only fifteen years of age, from that time forward, whenever he was at home, he always conducted the morning or evening service. Desiring to enter into the ministry, he was admitted, at sixteen, as a student at Hoxton College, then under the care of Rev. Dr. Simpson, Rev. John Hooper, and Rev. Henry Foster Porter. Under the tuition of these eminent men his studies were directed and his ministerial character was formed. He was a diligent student, and in preparing his lectures, and in his literary essays, he easily excelled. His style was marked, as in after life, by exuberance, and his excrescences and redundancies frequently required pruning; but he was docile, deeply devoted to his work, and was esteemed and beloved by all his associates.

Very soon after entering college he began to preach, and such was the vividness of his imagination, the full-

ness of his style, and his power as a youthful, original thinker, that he drew large audiences. When about twenty years of age he received an invitation to supply a chapel in Leeds, whose society was just forming. Commencing with but a few hearers, his congregation rapidly increased, and he retained its supervision while he lived, which was about thirty-four years. Such, however, were his popularity and success that the chapel became too small to accommodate his congregation, and especially to furnish free sittings for the poor; and, through his advice and labor, a larger and much more commodious place of worship was erected, with the intention of providing some five hundred free sittings. The new chapel was opened in 1836, and the Rev. Dr. Newton, of the Wesleyan Methodists, took part in its opening services.

His life and success illustrate the power of a singleness of purpose. He lived to be a minister, and to that end devoted all his studies and all his energies, and as the result, he shone as a star of the first magnitude in the bright constellation of English ministers. "This one thing I do," was his motto, as well as that of the triumphant Apostle. How many ministers injure their prospects and destroy their future usefulness by attempting other work than the work of the ministry, fancying that a portion of their time will be sufficient for ministerial success. Doctor Hamilton did not so. He felt that the work in which he was engaged was worthy of his utmost efforts, and that it required his most constant and diligent labor; yet he cultivated all auxiliary agencies, and sympathized in great moral movements. In addition to his pulpit labors, he was one of the first members of a philosophic and literary society established in Leeds in 1831, and in 1836 became its president. His contributions were chiefly on literary subjects, and some of them were minutely and elaborately critical.

A selection from these was afterward published in a volume entitled *Nugæ Literariæ.* But of these performances he remarked that his greatest satisfaction was that they had never, in any way, interfered with either his ministerial studies or duties. He also took a deep interest in the efforts which were being made to secure the freedom of the negroes in the British West Indies, and frequently spoke powerfully and effectively at Leeds, London, and elsewhere on that question. Especially was his voice heard in clear and powerful tones when the missionaries were called to suffer persecution and imprisonment. In 1833 he complied with the solicitations of his friends and issued a volume of sermons, containing eleven discourses, and a few years afterward published a second volume, containing twenty-four discourses, generally shorter than those in the first volume. He also published a small volume of Pastoral Appeals on Personal, Domestic, and Social Devotion. They were prepared under the impression that his life was drawing to a close, although he had then reached only his fortieth year. In 1838 he issued a volume containing Morning and Evening Prayers for Four Weeks, with Twenty-seven Prayers and Thanksgivings for Special Uses. These had been prepared at the earnest request of members of his congregation, who had been charmed with the seriousness, the humility, the wide comprehensiveness, the rich variety, and the tenderness and beauty, as well as the spirituality, of these services. About the same time proposals were made in Scotland for a prize essay on Christian missions, offering two hundred guineas for the first, and fifty guineas for the second. The Rev. J. Harris was awarded the first prize for his " Great Commission,"* the second prize was awarded to Mr. Hamilton, and his essay was published in 1842, with the

* Published at the Methodist Book Concern, as an 18mo. volume, price, 50 cents.

following brief but beautiful dedication, which was addressed to his successful competitor, and which exhibits the simplicity and purity of his character: "To the Rev. John Harris, D.D., President and Theological Professor of Cheshunt College. Beloved and honored Friend: No happier event ever befell me, no prouder emotion ever flattered me, than when I found myself placed second to you. Ever believe me, Doctor Harris, yours devotedly, Richard Winter Hamilton." The title of this work was, "Missions: their Authority, Scope, and Encouragement." In the cause of Christian missions he took a very deep interest, and in 1843 he undertook a journey through Scotland, laboring zealously and successfully in behalf of the London Missionary Society. In 1844 the degree of LL.D. was conferred upon him by the University of Glasgow, and in the same year the degree of D.D. by the University of the City of New York. A prize of one hundred guineas was offered for the best essay on "The Best Methods of Extending the Benefits of Free Education to England, Consistent with the Principles of Religious and Civil Liberty." The premium was adjudged to Doctor Hamilton, and his essay had a very extensive circulation. By his close devotion to his ministerial work, the care of a large congregation, and his collateral studies and writings, his health became impaired, and by the advice of medical friends, and the entreaties of his congregation, he spent the summer of 1845 upon the Continent, addressing, at different periods, a number of pastoral letters to his congregation. From this vacation he returned with health considerably improved. In 1846 he delivered his "Lectures on the Revealed Doctrine of Rewards and Punishments." Though meant chiefly for the Congregational Library Association, they were very largely attended. The impression was decided and strong, and the discussion is marked by great ability.

This he considered the greatest work of his life. Shortly afterward he published a small volume on the Sabbath, dedicated to the Rev. Dr. Raffles, and also a memoir of Rev. Mr. Ely.

About to take a short journey on the seventh of May, 1848, he preached what proved to be his last sermon to his own congregation on "for here we have no continuing city, but we seek one to come." His description of "the city which is to come" was said to be exceedingly beautiful, and he closed it with the well-known words of Bunyan, "Which, when I had seen, I wished myself among them." Thence he attended the annual meeting of the Congregational Union in London, and read a paper on "The Literature of the Congregational Body." On the 17th there appeared on his left wrist a small spot, which he supposed to be the bite of an insect. The weather being very warm, he became languid, feverish, and sleepless; but, instead of desisting from labor, he went to Leamington, and began to write a discourse which he intended for a public service, but was obliged to desist by the inflammation, which extended through his hand and arm. He had engaged to preach for the Wesleyan Missionary Society in Rotherham. His wife sought to dissuade him from fulfilling it because of his illness, but he said he felt himself bound in honor to do the best he could. His sermon was considered a very able one, on "Other foundation can no man lay than that is laid, which is Jesus Christ;" and resting after the morning service, he delivered a spirited address in the evening. On reaching home his arm had swollen to more than twice its natural size, and the erysipelas had made such rapid progress that it had reached nearly to the shoulder.

He said to his medical attendant, "I am so thankful to get home to you again, I was so anxious to see you; but I think I have come home to die, have I not?"

Unable to preach, his affection for his congregation induced him to address a pastoral letter to his Church.
By able medical treatment the erysipelas was checked, his
arm became nearly well, his appetite increased, he was able
to sit up for several hours, and even to walk about the
house; but his nervous system was shattered, a relapse
occurred, and he sank rapidly until July 18, when he fell
asleep in Jesus, having just completed his fifty-fourth year.
During his illness his sufferings were very acute. He
said to a friend, " I have not known an hour of freedom
from pain these last eight weeks, and yet it has been the
happiest period of my life. The suffering has been
great, but the grace has been greater." Again and
again he said, "I think I have known as much of
heaven as any body out of it for the last three years."
When informed by his physicians that all hope was extinguished, and that his end was near, he said, " That is
the best tidings you could have brought me." When
the time of death drew near he inquired how long it was
probable he had yet to live. When informed it was
some hours, he expressed disappointment, but meekly
replied, " I must patiently wait." When a friend, approaching him, said, "I am sorry, my dear Doctor, to
see you in this suffering, feeble state," he quickly replied, " You should rejoice, and not be sorry; you
should rejoice. My work is done, my course is finished,
I am going home; you should rejoice." Such was the
triumphant end of a life devoted to the cause of Christ.

In his private life Doctor Hamilton was courteous,
genial, and hospitable. In 1816 he was married to Miss
Thackeray, by whom he had two daughters and one son.
She died in 1820. He remained for sixteen years a
widower, and in 1836 was married a second time to a
lady of great moral worth. His intimate friends bear
testimony to the stability and the depth and fervency of
his Christian life; yet in society his hilarity and wit

often carried him beyond the limits usually assigned to ministerial gravity. For this he was severely criticised by his brethren, but " he claimed it was as *religious* to unbend as it was to stretch the faculties of his mind, and that there was nothing in his principles or in his office to exclude him from the free enjoyment of the gratifications which are usual in such society as that which claimed him among its brightest ornaments." Notwithstanding this defense, his friends admitted that his facetiousness was sometimes excessive; that he occasionally played too much with the feelings of others; that his jests were not always well seasoned, and that he would have attained a still wider and more hallowed influence if he had repressed some of these eccentricities; yet those who knew him at home attest both the purity and the prayerfulness of his private life. He was much in his closet. " He had power with God because he was much with God;" and his family attested how fully he sanctified all his undertakings with prayer. His character at home, both as a man and as a Christian, was admired by those who were intimate in his family.

As a Pastor, his visitations were not so regular or so general as those of most of his brother ministers; but to those who were under deep religious impression he was specially attentive, and was a faithful and instructive counselor. To the sick he gave special care; and many testify to his tender sympathy, his appropriate counsel, and especially to the richness of his prayers. One of his ministerial friends, who was for years one of his hearers, says of him, " He acquired a tone of pastoral sympathy, a kind of intuition into the mysteries of human woe, that fitted him to strengthen and to comfort the anxious and distressed beyond most ministers I have known." His week-evening services were marked by simplicity, and his counsels seemed to come from a sympathetic heart, and in the administration of the Lord's

Supper he was peculiarly solemn and impressive; but it was as a preacher that he especially excelled. He had a wide range of thought, a retentive and ready memory, an exuberant imagination, and that peculiar tact which enabled him to draw illustrations not only from history and from science, but also from passing events. He was tender in his sympathies and earnest in his manner. He loved to delineate domestic scenes and household influences, and seemed to have the power to carry his audience with him as if to look upon the scenes which he described. Though full of wit, he scarcely ever made an allusion in the pulpit which provoked a smile.

He was deeply serious and earnest, and the tendency of his ministry was searching and practical. Punctuality was with him a matter of conscience. He never failed to be in the pulpit at the proper moment, as his daughter testifies, except once, when the doorkeeper forgot to call him at the proper moment; and, though the delay was but a minute, the doorkeeper declared that it was the first time he had ever seen him angry. His published sermons show his wide range of thought, his accurate delineations, his thorough discussions of his subject, the wide range of his allusions, and the earnest character of his appeals; but those who heard him say, that in his ordinary ministrations there was more simplicity and more personal address, as the " substance of his sermons, beyond his exordium, was usually more or less extemporaneous, sometimes entirely so." He was in doctrine a moderate Calvinist, and not unfrequently stated and defended his views; yet he was a great favorite among Christian societies holding other opinions. He was of a liberal and catholic spirit, and his last sermon, as we have said, was preached in a Wesleyan pulpit. On the platform he appeared to great advantage. The argumentative part of his address was strong; but l.aving laid his foundations he gave full play to his

fancy, and charmed his audience by his sallies of wit. Having a keen sense of the ludicrous, he indulged it more freely than is usual in religious assemblies. His style has been severely criticised, and, perhaps, not unjustly. His first " Occasional Sermons" that were published were mercilessly reviewed; but his style was his own. What would have been turgid and bombastic for others was natural to him. His thoughts had a wide range; he abounded in unexpected allusions; and what to others would have been unnatural, was spontaneous to him. Having been written to about the character of a young man, a member of his Church, who applied for admission into college, he replied, " How happy I am, my dear brother, that you did not inquire of me touching the quadrature of the circle or the nature of fluxions, but on a matter so simple as this." He seemed wholly unconscious of the character of his style or of its range of illustration, and when he made special preparation his discourses exceeded proper length. When a young man he was invited to preach before the London Missionary Society. He prepared his sermon with great care, and wrote it out in full, but designed to deliver it extemporaneously. Becoming embarrassed, he was obliged to produce it from beneath the folds of his gown. He was delayed a little to find the place, and then troubled with the dimness of the light, but proceeded for something more than an hour, when, to the astonishment of his hearers, he said, " And now, after these few preliminary observations, I shall detain you with the following topics of discourse." As might be expected, there was a movement in his audience; many left the house, and the preacher was obliged to curtail much of his sermon. It was full of classic allusions; history and fancy were learnedly and beautifully commingled. Some have called it a splendid poem, and yet in his introduction he says, " The sermon was designed

for popular impression." He was determined, though surrounded by learned and eloquent preachers, to sacrifice all pretension to learning and eloquence himself. His only fear is, that in attempting to renounce all ornament, and disclaim all elegance, he may have fallen into simplicity too meager, and contented himself with statements too trite. Such an estimate of such a sermon exposed him to severe treatment from the reviewers; but he evidently was unconscious of the learned and elaborate character of his performance.

The topics discussed in this volume are full of interest and importance. Man's responsibility, his constant need of divine aid, and the grandeur of the Christian life, are clearly set forth. The atonement is presented as the sole foundation of man's hope. There is no effort, as in some of the popular sermons of the day, to explain away the doctrines of man's depravity, a vicarious atonement, the work of the Holy Spirit, or future rewards and punishments. A spirit of deep piety pervades all the discourses, as well as an unquestioned faith in all the verities of our holy religion. Several of these sermons are fine specimens of exhaustive discussion, and they are marked by strong thoughts and varied and beautiful illustrations. Though the style is unusually florid, and not wholly above criticism, yet the student will oftentimes be delighted and profited by the copiousness as well as the fertility of imagination. May the work have a wide circulation, and may the blessing of God rest upon it!

With the single exception of certain leanings to the specialties of Calvinism, there is, perhaps, nothing in these sermons to which the great body of evangelical thinkers would object.

CONTENTS.

SERMONS.

I.

THE HARMONY OF CHRISTIANITY IN ITS PERSONAL INFLUENCE.

WHEREIN HE HATH ABOUNDED TOWARD US IN ALL WISDOM AND PRUDENCE.—Ephes. i, 8.

TAKE the smallest, most insignificant, most unnoticed object in nature—the particle of sand, the blade of grass, the drop of water, the worm, the insect, whatever hides in the crevice of the rock or wheels imperceptible in the eddy of the air—add to these whatever is most vast and stupendous—the mountain, the ocean, the glorious handiwork of the firmament, moons, planets, suns, vibrating in boundless space through their range of sweep and with their precision of revolution, inlaid as in a texture, marshaled as a host:—all, when presented to our eye and explained to our reason—all, when they are not raised to our powers, but when our powers are raised to them—exhibit such traces of design, such accuracies of contrivance, such wonders of adaptation, such masterpieces and models of perfection, so evidently intended for use and so efficient to the full scope of that intention, that the man who can attribute all this immense magazine of fixed consequences to accident, must believe that chance is more intelligent than order, con-

fusion more binding than system, anarchy more protective than law. So long as the human mind continues what it is—constituted to reach its conclusions by certain rules and to establish them upon certain grounds—this supposition is a too sublime abstraction for it to conceive or a too idiot babble for it to endure. Our first thinkings agree with the first dictates of religion: " O Lord! how manifold are thy works: in wisdom hast thou made them all."

There is a difficulty, which we all feel, in raising upon the frame of these remarks a higher conception. What can be greater than the material works of God? What can be more profound or more lofty than creation's depths and heights? After the most searching surveys of its ever-spreading realms—world reared above world, constellation fading before yet brighter constellation, ascending from one heaven to a higher still—what can there remain of comparison but the little and the mean? To turn from all this magnificence, must it not be to sink? Can aught but melancholy contrast await us? Can we but feel the mortifying descent? And yet, if we will let the Bible school us, we must instantly admit that the volume of earth and sea and sky is so inferior to its holy page, its sublime discovery, its spiritual excellence, that the infant's primer makes a nearer approach to the dissertations of our keenest philosophers, to the records of our most comprehensive historians, to the songs of our most impassioned bards, than the one can do to the other. "He hath magnified his word above all his name." Here we read the mystery and the good pleasure of his will. Here is the imprint of his thoughts and purposes. Here he directly reveals himself. He comes into contact, communication, negotiation, with us. He built the universe to prove that he *is*. He takes a language from it to declare to us his determinations. It is but a subservient apparatus to the scheme of redemp-

tion. Not only are the *moral* perfections of the Deity signalized in the death of Christ, but he is the brightest example of the *natural*—the power of God and the wisdom of God. And no more can his physical works divide attention with the salvation of the Gospel than the scaffolding can steal a thought from the temple, or the platform can detain a moment's interest while the train of nobles and warriors is passing over it with the kingly heir, for his coronation.

The text speaks of an abounding, a lavish munificence. It is of the exceeding riches of God's grace. With these he is thus infinitely profuse. But there is nothing of an ill-considered waste. Wisdom and prudence are seen in the supply of adequate means, in providing for probable difficulties, in guarding against probable abuses. Glorious are the gifts; but their right application is jealously secured.

The design of this discourse is to confute the charge against the Gospel that it acts with contrary and discordant tendencies. It is alleged that its effects, when received into our mind, are not consistent and proportionate, but strive with each other and draw it different ways. We would endeavor to exhibit that, though there *is a variety* in these impressions and emotions, there is no incongruity; that they are self-corrective and self-adjusting; that they are adapted, however different, to put and preserve the sinner in that state of mind which is best becoming a creature so fallen and so redeemed.

And here we may derive an analogy from the external universe. In nothing is its arrangement more obvious than in the system of checks which pervade all its departments. It is a peculiarity of its laws. By attraction and repulsion—by yielding and resistance—by a diversity of antagonist powers—by a succession of inverse movements, a reaction is constantly excited and a harmonious

result obtained. Such are the complex mechanics of nature. By contrary impulses the planets travel their orbits. By one law exclusive they must stagnate: by another, if unmodified, they would be driven from their path. Both are necessary to give the activity, and maintain the order, of their revolutions. If there were only tendency to the center, all things would consolidate into a motionless, immovable mass: if the impetus were always from the center, all things would be volatile, scattered, strewn through space: nothing kept in its place or detained for its use. And this equilibrium depends upon forces which apparently present no phenomena in common. Still is the balance completed with so much exactness that a music, beyond the fable and too perfect for our dull ear, may be generated in endless chords: its adjustment is so nice and perfect that the addition of a single atom might disturb it even to disjoint and shatter the whole.

This wisdom and prudence are manifested,

By SHOWING WITH EQUAL DISTINCTNESS THE DIVINE JUSTICE AND MERCY.

These are not rival attributes, nor can they have needed reconciliation. Justice does not arrest the hand of mercy: mercy does not restrain the hand of justice. Neither is the more prompt or slow: neither is the more earnest or jealous. An infinite placability is anterior to the exercise of both. God is not merciful because Christ has died, but Christ has died because God is merciful. Is justice the first care of his government? Mercy is earlier in its purpose than any government. In redemption they are mutually administrative: " To declare his righteousness for the remission of sins." They act with no partiality, they come into no collision. Justice is such a form of good that it exclaims, " Fury is not in me." Mercy is such an advocate of rectitude that it declares, " Surely thou wilt slay the wicked, O God."

Justice knows no enmity which mercy can calm, no frown which mercy can unbend: mercy knows no weakness which justice can help, no connivance which justice can forbid. Mercy rather than justice superintends the sacrifice of the Cross, charges itself with the awful preparations, heaps the fuel, binds the victim, grasps the knife, deals the stroke, pours the libation, kindles the fire, consumes the offering, while justice but assents, and smiles, and "makes the comers thereunto perfect." They speak with a united voice, they command with a united authority, they shine with a united glory. Neither excels. The one does not overbear the other. Their common splendor is like the neutral tint, the effulgent colorlessness, of the undecomposed ray.

The impression on the believing sinner's mind must correspond. It might be that in another proportion of these attributes our mental balance would have been endangered. Had justice been more stern, we should have been overawed: had mercy been less holy, we might have been daringly elate. We are saved, but at what a price! We rejoice with trembling. Reverence chastens trust, and trust endears reverence. We fear the Lord and his goodness. We ascribe forgiveness unto him that he may be feared. And yet this fear does not banish confidence. "In the fear of the Lord is strong confidence: and his children shall have a place of refuge." It is veneration without dismay: it is reliance without pretension.

This wisdom and prudence promote the state of mind we describe,

By exhibiting the incarnate Son of God as alike the object of love and adoration.

That Christ should be made flesh was necessary to his becoming an atonement: scarcely less that he might be the way by which we understand and approach the Divinity. He was thus made like unto us. He was born

of a woman. He dwelt among us. He had a human heart. He was beheld in a surpassing amiableness. Gracious words proceeded out of his mouth. Behold how he loved us! He mingled his tears with ours. He bore our weaknesses. He was meek and lowly in mind. And this conception of his character, his affectionate image, is most preciously retained and embodied in sacred writ. In reading those holy records which unfold his life we catch this conception, this image, as though we had actually followed him to where he dwelt, had hung upon his discourse, had sat at meat with him, had leaned upon his bosom. He still receiveth sinners. He is among us as one that serveth. He visiteth our home. He walketh with us by the way. We see him at the death-bed of our daughter, at the funeral of our son, at the grave of our brother, and his love never fails. We are assured of his entire sympathy. He is touched with the feeling of our infirmities. By unimaginable bonds he unites himself to us. "We are members of his body, of his flesh and of his bones." He calls us friends. He is not ashamed to call us brethren. He must be loved. But all these kindlier sentiments need to be chastened and hallowed. "What manner of man is this!" "We behold his glory." He is Christ Jesus the righteous. He is the Holy One, and that Just. It is he whom the seraphim adore. Let us not encroach on his glorious majesty, nor speak lightly of him. It may not always become us to press the allowance of his condescension; rigidly to enforce what his humility might suggest; to reciprocate in strict correlative every kindred name he gives us. We may hardly call him brother, however he is the first-born among many brethren. We dare not call him spouse of our soul, though he be the bridegroom of the Church. Our hearts are shocked by the appeal to the friends of Jesus, however henceforth he may call us friends. He is the Lord God whom we

sanctify in our heart and make our fear and dread. There is a style too common in speaking of him, profanely soft, familiar, undignified, which we cannot too resolutely shun. The influence of art is here to be deprecated. It perpetuates the ideas which are only to be valued as they conduct us to the measure of the stature of the fullness of Christ. "The mother of our Lord" is fixed in the expression of her earliest maternity, and he sleeps in her bosom still, the new-born babe. The sensuous of beauty is portrayed to the loss of the moral loveliness. Natural fondness is warmed in us rather than holy sentiment and lofty emotion. Our sensibilities are stolen, our instincts are excited, but adoration is suspended and reverence is checked. It is not contemplation which dreams! It is not faith which gazes! It is not repentance which weeps! Behold your God. Let us give unto Him the glory due unto his name. Let us stand in awe and sin not. Let us imitate the disciple who, when he might have reached forth his hand to the Crucified One, and have thrust it into his side, forbore, touched him not, falling before his feet at once, answering and saying unto him, My Lord and my God! Let us follow the example of the celestials, the living creatures and the elders, with their harps and their censers, bowing before the Lamb! Let us vie with all the angels in worshiping him!

Blessed admixture of emotions! It is tenderness, it is gratitude, it is complacency, without a lowering thought: it is humiliation, it is subjection, it is homage, without a disconcerting fear!

The Gospel, in its wisdom and prudence, produces this moral adjustment of our principles and feelings,

BY INSISTING MOST UNIFORMLY ON DIVINE GRACE AND HUMAN RESPONSIBILITY.

In its treatment of man the doctrine it preaches is most abasing to him, but only because it represents the

true facts of his case. It does not lay him low, but shows how low he lies. It can hear nothing of our merit. It dispels the darkness in which such a dream alone could fill the mind. We no more appeal to justice. We no more demand, " Give me the portion of goods that falleth to me." We compare not ourselves among ourselves. Sins which formerly seemed little rise up into fearful magnitude. The heart which flattered us, and which we palliated in return, is felt by us now to be desperately wicked. The God whom we had reduced in our ideas to a weak indulgence, and even connivance, is declared by himself to us as the jealous guardian of his own name and law. We are helpless as guilty. What things were gain are loss. Mercy now is our only cry. As we read that " surely shall one say, In the Lord have I righteousness and strength," *each* of us determines to be that *one.* Grace leaves us nothing but itself. It crowns itself. But while it regards us in this our guilt and powerlessness, it addresses us as moral agents. Not an original relationship is disturbed. We are dealt with according to one rule. The law must be fulfilled in us. We are not the less accountable creatures. In blessing him who maketh us to differ from another, we must not forget that he is no respecter of persons. Even we are called, persuaded, commanded, to the reception of these sure mercies. A new probation is established, a further responsibility is impressed. The Gospel is made known unto all nations for the obedience of faith. God now commandeth all men every-where to repent. In no way is any standard of obedience reduced. No principle of obligation is relaxed. And instead of grace interfering with the grounds of subjection on which man has always stood—must always stand—it augments to far more solemn issue all his original amenableness.

This is a most important result. Man is brought to

see that there is nothing but he must receive. And then his helplessness is set forth to him as a matter of blame and guilt, for which he is liable and for which there is no excuse. How correct is the poise which such constituents of principle must establish in his mind!

This state of mind is secured,

By the proposal of the freest terms of acceptance, and the enforcement of the most universal practice of obedience.

The reign of grace, though its very name supposes that it acts in consistency with moral government, necessarily must be brought to the simplest idea of gift and its acceptance. It is "the gift by grace." The manner of obtaining it does not lessen its spontaneousness, but rather illustrates it. Do we seek it by prayer? He regards the prayer of the destitute. He delivers the needy when he crieth, and him that hath no helper. Do we believe? "It is of faith that it might be by grace." Do we buy? "It is without money and without price." Do we thirst? Do we will to drink? We "take the water of life freely." Is there any reason for this grace in ourselves? We had naught to pay, and therefore our Lord frankly forgave us. "By grace are ye saved." We adjudge not our case truly until we renounce all thoughts of personal excellence: until we abjure the merit of our natural instincts and social virtues: until we see that, being evil, we have given good things to our children: that our plowing has been sin. But having been justified freely by his grace, through faith, without the works of the law, are we discharged from obedience? God now accepteth our works. They are accepted through the atonement. There is in us a new motive, a new life. It is not more a faithful saying, and more worthy of all acceptation, that Christ Jesus came into the world to save sinners, than it is a faithful saying, and to be constantly affirmed, that they who believe in

God should be careful to maintain good works. Now commences toil, watch, warfare. There is time to redeem. There is neglect to overtake. A new plan of existence opens upon us. For us to live is Christ. Works, labor, and patience constitute it. Continuance in well-doing is the only proof that we are in salvation. We show our faith by our works.

The doctrines of grace are thus demonstrated to be those of godliness; and they who view them in their coherence, will manifest in their example how united is their hold and how reciprocal is their efficiency. They will know how to be passive, and how to be zealous: when to quiet, and when to arouse, themselves. Their dependence will not torpify their activity, nor their activity elate their dependence.

This medium, so true to the wisdom and prudence of the Christian system, is maintained,

By inspiring the most elevated joy in connection with the deepest self-abhorrence.

If there be a sentiment of mind most notable in the first Christians it was their happiness. It transfused itself through all their tempers and their engagements. They found it where it was least likely to be found. They counted it all joy to fall into divers afflictions. They rejoiced in tribulation. They took pleasure in infirmities, in reproaches, in necessities, in persecutions, for Christ's sake. Look into their inmost breast. There was joy in the Holy Ghost. They were glad with exceeding joy. Their joy was full. They rejoiced with joy unspeakable. Now all this is attainable by us. The fruit of the Spirit is joy. There is the joy of faith. Do we not sit with Christ in heavenly places? Have we not come to the heavenly Jerusalem? These are gratulations and hopes which fall little short of ecstasy. But lest we should be exalted above measure, there is ever present to us our fallen nature, our long unconversion,

our indwelling corruption, our strange perverseness, our slow proficiency, our ungrateful, deceitful, unbelieving heart. God has forgiven, but we cannot forgive ourselves. We will go softly all our years in the bitterness of our soul. We remember our ways and are ashamed. We are confounded, and will not open our mouth when he is pacified toward us. It is not fear. It is not abject sorrow. It is the struggle of alternate dispositions. The heart, which breaks with grief, overflows with delight. "As sorrowful, yet alway rejoicing." Neither in the joy nor in the sadness do we lose ourselves. Both are intelligent and subdued. The one cannot soar without a recollection which stays its flight : the other cannot droop without a hope to cheer its depression. The two combined terminate in a settled calm and a perfect peace. The rapture may have passed away, but so has the disconsolateness. It is as if the rainbow arched around the eternal throne; as if that meteor of expiring tempest and breaking sunshine had now contracted itself around our soul, filling it with all the mournful and the bright associations of fear and hope, while it illuminates us with its beauty and enfolds us in its embrace.

That mean of feeling, which is equidistant from extremes, is preserved,

By displaying the different conduct pursued by the Deity toward sin and the sinner.

With that necessity which is our best conception, however it be unworthy of infinite perfection, the God of holiness has ever opposed himself to moral evil in its divers forms. It is the abominable thing which he hates. It is what he would not have exist. He resents and counterworks it. He cannot overlook it, nor pass it by. No sin was ever forgotten, or is unmarked for punishment. The death of Christ, in its respect of an atonement, is the act of divine exculpation : it is designed to clear God from every misconstruction to which his long-

suffering might be abused, to certify the exclusive basis on which his exercise of pardon can be rested, and to express, in circumstances and by means which could never be combined again, his eternal displeasure against all unrighteousness. By that authority and wisdom which belong to him, he has contrived and ordained a way by which sin, in its consequences of guilt, may be detached from the evil doer, a method of abstraction and separation, leaving the sinner, when he believes, free from those consequences, but not at all as a creature who has not sinned. Having sin, he is defiled by his sin. Though pardoned, he sees that there is a horrible perpetuity in the act. He thinks of an entail which defies calculation. His Lord and Saviour has died for him. He dwells upon the pangs, the indignities, the horrors of the cross. He blesses the substitution. He looks on Him whom he has pierced. That Sufferer bears his sins and carries his sorrows. What tribulation and wrath and anguish are heaped upon that holy head! He dies for sin! He dies for sinners! What a mystery is contained in the double bearings of that deed! To condemn sin in the flesh, and to deliver them who committed it! To make sin exceeding sinful, and to rescue them who were sinners before the Lord exceedingly! To act the foe of sin and the friend of sinners! O the divine effect of these contemplations on the soul! "Blessed," it cries, " is the man unto whom the Lord imputeth not iniquity." I might have been reserved unto judgment to be punished. It was the meet recompense. Mine iniquity is taken from me. Far as the east is from the west he hath removed my transgressions. I can the better understand its enormity now that I behold it transferred to yonder bloody tree. Strange that he spared not his own Son! But he was made sin! Justice bound him to the death! My sin is there. My guilt is upon him. Hateful, my sin, dost thou appear as thou wast never seen before!

Thou art placed thus high, thou art made thus prominent, to scare my eye, to break my heart. Die there, thou that art my bitterness and shame! I hate thee with a perfect hatred! Let me die to thee! Blessed Cross! I would know the fellowship of thy sufferings, being made conformable unto thy death!

Can the saved sinner, after such a spectacle, with the dread remembrance how his sin was taken from him, and dealt with according to its full measure of demerit and liability, sin that grace may abound, or turn grace into lasciviousness! His judgments and his sympathies are converted against it, and the contrast between the treatment of the sin and the sinner must secure a new barrier between the sinner and the sin.

This congruity of conflicting sentiments is upheld, BY COMBINING THE GENUINE HUMILITY OF THE GOSPEL WITH OUR DIGNITY AS CREATURES AND OUR CONSCIENTIOUSNESS AS SAINTS.

The holiest beings, in the view of their essential dependence and obligation, are filled with the most lowly sensibility. They cast down their crowns. They vail their faces. They see that the Infinite must be infinitely distant from them. They see that necessary excellence can bear no comparison with that which is derived and imitative. But no sin prostrates their brow. No confusion clouds their face. They are true to their high estate. They have not left their first habitation. They cannot repent. Nor do they depreciate their sphere and rank of existence. They decry not their thrones and their dominions. Their deepest humility answers to strictest truth. They confess only what they are, and adore their Creator. But the humility of the Christian is of another complexion. He knows himself the guilty and the depraved creature. He is vile. He cannot look up. He repents in dust and in ashes. He cannot forget what he has been. Still imperfect, he bewails what he

is.   For ever there will be on his spirit the memory of past guilt and woe.   His new song is a song of deliverance.   But his sinfulness is not to be avenged upon the inferiority of his nature.   That is worthy of high honor. There is nothing why man should not respect himself. The Gospel teaches him this lofty mood.   Sin is his only degradation.   His capabilities are now laid open.   The powers of his mind are braced to healthy action.   His immortality yearns within him.   He awakes to his destiny.   He is renewed after the image of Him who created him.   He cannot adequately perceive the deforming influence of sin, without placing before him the greatness it has ruined.   The voluntary humility, the reptile abjectness, to which many stoop, is at utter variance with taste, with fact, with Christianity.   Nor in our averments of Christian motive need we, ought we, to addict ourselves to this gratuitous disparagement.   If we please God—if our conscience sends back its answer void of offense toward God and man—if we have our conversation honest—there must be falsehood in the contrary charge. Jealous, as it becomes us, of our motives, knowing that, when we have done all, we are unprofitable servants, still humility requires no sacrifice of truth.   A heart right with God has a title to be seen and heard and felt in the clear countenance, the steadfast eye, the unembarrassed tone, of a manly independence.   We may have even whereof to glory, but not before God.   There must be praise where there is virtue.   But without the consciousness of self-respect neither can exist.

These remarks may be salutary in two ways : they may tend to correct the prejudice of many persons who look upon the humility of the Gospel as a groveling debasement of mind : they may incite the true Christian, clothed as he is with humility, to a fearless magnanimity —to the port and bearing of him whom integrity and uprightness preserve.

This mellowed habit of mind is supported,

BY CAUSING ALL SUPERNATURAL INFLUENCE TO OPERATE THROUGH OUR RATIONAL POWERS AND BY INTELLIGENT MEANS.

The principle of life is subtle and unscanned. But, after its kind, it is always developed in the same succession of fixed, classified manifestations. The intellectual, the highest life, follows the same law. It is known by its respective conditions. It is always and in every place, without forgetting the degrees of its expansion, the same. Having found one such creature, you have a general knowledge of all. But it is a very primary doctrine of revelation, that the work of a sinner's salvation involves the necessity that he be enlightened and purified by a power from on high. Now it might be asked, How is this influence to be ascertained? How far does it coincide with our mental constitution? By what fruits shall it be determined? Does not the opinion throw open the flood-gate of fanaticism? The answer is, "Now we have received, not the spirit of the world, but the spirit which is of God; that we might know the things that are freely given to us of God." This is the simple design, and this spirit can alone be recognized by such perception of these revealed things. "God hath not given us the spirit of fear; but of power, and of love, and of a sound mind." These are the true marks, and the existence of this spirit can alone be assured by such effects. "God worketh in you both to will and to do." He inclines our nature agreeably to its own rule of motives. No violence is done: there is choice and action. Even in extraordinary illapses, " the spirit of the prophets was subject to the prophets:" there was no overmastering impulse. Whenever the Spirit now moves in us, there is the understanding also. This wonderful, this unspeakable gift of the Holy Ghost, is imparted to us to carry out our proper nature, to lead us forward in our original

direction, to make our reason more rational, our judgment more judicious, our volition more voluntary; to allow to each power its right and to each feeling its freedom. The written word is at once the standard by which each influence must be tried and is the instrument by which a divine influence alone can operate.

It is seen, then, that the highest inspiration cannot destroy any faculty of the mind, being but its highest exercise; and that there is no denaturalizing tendency, since the mind's appropriate qualities are the only subjects and mediums of this divine impression. It enlarges *our heart.* It is the spirit of quick *understanding.* It is the law of the *Spirit of life.* All is pre-eminently a plastic power working on the fixed and regular substance of the soul, and exhibiting none other substance, however it be refined of alloy and wrought into a workmanship of beauty.

The wisdom and prudence of the Gospel discover themselves, in this respect,

By resting our evidence of safety and spiritual welfare upon personal virtues.

We must often ask ourselves whether we be in the Lord. We see no reason to deny the direct testimony of the Comforter to our acceptance. As he has brought home to us the conviction of our sins, why may he not assure us consciously of our forgiveness? Does he not witness to our adoption and with our spirit? Is not this to receive the word with joy of the Holy Ghost? But still the inferential argument is indispensable. The Spirit must attest something. That which he confirms must be already true. We cannot be called to believe that as true of ourselves which is not true at the moment of belief. No faith can make the falsehood, veracity; or the nonentity, fact. If the Holy Spirit testifies to our adoption, we are adopted. " *Because ye are sons,* God hath sent forth the Spirit of his Son into your hearts, cry-

ing Abba, Father." No direct witness can avail in the absence of holiness: the inferential argument simply respects such holiness. Then must we look, on both suppositions, to character and conduct. We may be compelled to say concerning the boaster of this assured acceptance, "How dwelleth the love of God in him?" "What doth it profit, though a man say that he hath faith and have not works? Can faith save him?" Take it any way, this must be the criterion. Only as we add to our faith virtue through every couplet of successive and rising graces, only so shall an entrance be ministered unto us abundantly into the everlasting kingdom of our Lord and Saviour Jesus Christ. The last judgment sets up the same evidence. "They were judged every man according to their works."

Such is the wholesome symmetry of practical piety: no proof of acceptance, no assurance of hope, no "yea," though we had not doubted that "the Spirit said it," is of any validity without it.

Moreover, to save the mind from those violent alternations to which it tends, the religion of Christ asserts its wisdom and prudence,

By supplying the absence of enslaving fear with salutary caution.

We know that there is a fear which hath torment—a spirit of bondage. There is a timidity of consequences. This is cast out. Who is he that condemneth? Who can be against us? We trust and are not afraid. We can think of the future, and our faith protects us from dismay and depression. Our enemy doth not triumph over us. Though a host should encamp against us, in this will we be confident. We feel that there is a boast which we may make in God. "He is able to keep us from falling. He will keep us from every evil work, and preserve us unto his heavenly kingdom. He keepeth the feet of his saints. Christ is surety for us. He will bring

forth judgment unto victory. Who shall separate us from the love of Christ? He will confirm us unto the end. The Spirit sealeth us unto the day of redemption. Our confidence of final salvation is cheerful and unfaltering. We are persuaded that neither death, nor life, nor angels, nor principalities, nor powers, nor things present, nor things to come, nor height, nor depth, nor any other creature, shall be able to separate us from the love of God, which is in Christ Jesus our Lord." All this assurance respects the covenanted purpose and declared faithfulness of God. But is there nothing to abate this confidence of boasting? Every thing that looks at the fickleness of ourselves! "Let him that thinketh he standeth take heed lest he fall." "Be not high-minded, but fear." "I keep under my body, and bring it into subjection; lest that by any means, when I have preached to others, I myself should be a castaway." "Pass the time of your sojourning here in fear." In this respect we cannot be too diffident. Our use of means cannot be too assiduous. If we are invincible, who maketh us more than conquerors? Was it ever known that soldiers who were called invincible, stood the less firmly and fought the less bravely, because their banners bore that emblazoned style? Did the ancient warriors contend the less manfully because they went into the battle with their brows filleted by victorious wreaths? The more wary was their movement, the more sensitive was their honor, the more impetuous their attack—their burst as the billow, their resistance as the rock.

THE ACTUAL EXISTENCE OF OUR DEPRAVED NATURE, AND THE WORK OF SANCTIFICATION IN US PRESSING FORWARD TO ITS MATURITY, TEND TO THAT REGULATED TEMPERAMENT OF MIND WHICH WE URGE.

Sin will be, so long as we live, a capable thing in us: it is natural, and therefore easy and ready. It is bound up with our strongest propensions. It has a deep-seated

hold in our corporeal, sentient, nature. It acts in all manner of concupiscence. It dwells in us. But there is a new and stronger power. We call it religion or grace. Sin exists and struggles: but this predominates and reigns. Paul describes the conflict. "The flesh lusteth against the Spirit, and the Spirit against the flesh: and these are contrary the one to the other: so that ye cannot do the things that ye would." He lays open his own breast. "I find then a law, that, when I would do good, evil is present with me." He contrasts his former and his present state. "I *was* alive without the law once." "I *see* another law in my members, warring against the law of my mind. O wretched man that I *am!*" The tenses mark the different times. Yet he delights "in the law of God after the inward man." Hence the contest. There are two rival principles. Yet they are not equal. That of corruption is doubtless a voluntary power, not blind nor unintelligent. But that of grace is the transcendent, and determines the superior will. Of the former the christian may make disclaimer; it is not his cherished purpose, his true bent, and, though guilty and accountable on account of it, he may still exclaim, "It is no more I that do it." His sincere, his highest, egoism cannot be in it. He seeks not exculpation. He simply declares that he cannot reach his aim, that he cannot do the things which he would, that the renewed nature is checked and vexed by the fallen nature; that the Christian's self would soar away far from all these adjuncts and provocatives of sin. Behold, then, the position of this contest. The believer is sanctified, wholly as to diffusion, but not as to degree; sin abides in him. And in proportion as his sanctification proceeds, his sin is often rendered more obvious and active. He is perplexed in this discovery. It seems the delay, and not the advancement, of his holiness. He appears less renewed than he was before. Thus, notwithstanding,

his true sanctity is promoted. It is the province of light to reveal any thing rather than itself. The depravity is not really increased. To have penetrated it is the sure method of victory over it. And now we observe that state of mind which sweetly blends extremes. How humble is the Christian kept by all the hostilities which ever beset and threaten him! How anxious is his suspense! How sleepless must be his vigilance! He is always in the presence of his enemies! It is domestic treason against which he guards! Still does he trace a spiritual volition breaking through every resistance, acquiring strength, dispersing opposition, pledging triumph! He cannot boast; he must not despond. You hear him in his lament: "The evil which I would not, that I do!" You hear him in his anthem: "I thank God through Jesus Christ our Lord!" The "depth" and the "height" of these emotions preserve him steady in his course, and help him in his patience to possess his soul!

AND CERTAIN VIEWS OF PERSONAL CONDUCT ARE SO COUPLED, IN THE GOSPEL, WITH THE NOBLEST VIEWS OF GRACE, THAT ANY IMPROPER WARPING OF OUR MINDS IS COUNTERACTED.

The works of believers are rewardable. God accepteth them and is pleased with them. He is glorified in themselves. Promise of a return or recompense is made to their acts, partly growing out of the quality of those acts, but chiefly as actual additions of happiness. He is not unrighteous to forget the work of faith and the labor of love. He covenants with us. We, knowing his word and trusting his assurance, may always have respect unto this recompense of reward. But do we boast? Is it not a constitution of grace which alone could render our deeds praiseworthy and remunerable? which can speak to us, Well done? Is it not a new, independent, and most merciful consideration and treatment of our moral

agency? It is the work of God by which we exclusively can work the works of God.

And there are errors which gain entrance and power among us by the forms of truth under which they pass. Popular aphorisms are heard, the more mischievous in that they are not wholly false. Should it be affirmed that "there is nothing good in us,"—it is true of our fallen nature, "that is, in our flesh;" but regeneration produces "a good thing which we must keep." Should it be alleged that "all which is good in us consists in divine influence," it is true, inasmuch as it is the source of all which determines "the new creature;" but true religion takes the shape of personal principles and habits, and enters the system of the voluntary, responsible, soul. Should it be asserted that "there is no meritoriousness in actions," it is true that those of the sinful creature cannot contain it, he is dead in sins and his entire life is tainted with the moral disqualification; and though the recovered sinner should obey perfectly, nothing can be of desert in that obedience: but actions cannot be indifferent, they are displacent or attractive, good or evil. There is that "which is acceptable before God." Should it be broached that "we must seek for all comfort beyond or without ourselves,"—it is true that nothing strictly original in us can justifiably or intelligently yield us any solace in our relationship to God; but the evidence of his operation on our hearts is most consola-tory, and this must be sought in our own consciousness of what we are and of what we have proved. Should it be recorded that "we must come to Christ at our last hour as at our first awakening we fled to him," it is true that we have no more individual right of access to him at one time than another; but ought we not to approach with deeper contrition and stronger faith? ought we not to draw nearer in the spirit of adoption? ought we not the more closely to resemble Him whom we have so

repeatedly implored? ought our pleadings to have acquired no more scriptural clearness, no more confidence, no more child-like trust? Are we only sinners as we were then? Are we not children? Are we not the redeemed? Surely there is much difference between the sinner's first concern and outcry, and the saint's last victory and song! And yet, the growth in grace which this shall exhibit will in nothing be so wonderful as in the humility made perfect!

WHILE THE DISTINCTIVE BLESSINGS AND HONORS OF THE CHRISTIAN MIGHT TEND TO ELATE HIM, HE IS AFFECTED BY THE MOST OPPOSITE MOTIVES.

Scripture does most vividly describe, and most urgently note, the changes wrought by a Divine Sovereignty on the subjects of its grace. They are made to differ. They know their election of God. They have been called out of darkness into marvelous light. They have been chosen from the beginning to salvation. They can appropriate that series of wonders: " Whom he did foreknow, he also did predestinate to be conformed to the image of his Son, that he might be the first-born among many brethren. Moreover, whom he did predestinate, them he also called; and whom he called, them he also justified; and whom he justified, them he also glorified." May not this induce dispositions contemptuous toward others? May it not indite a censorious style of language? May it not inspire an overweening self-importance? The people of God! The sons of God! Kings and priests unto God! This can only awaken the more ardent gratitude and more profound humility. The cause of choice is not in themselves. If intimation is ever given of the cause, it is the greater sinfulness of the object. It is some design to illustrate the freeness and power of grace in restoring the most wretched outcast. And who is this restored one, that he should glory in himself? He is the undeserving subject of all. He is a

brand plucked out of the fire. He is the chief of sinners. This is his utmost praise and claim : " Howbeit I obtained mercy." He owes, he must still owe, he must owe for ever! He has paid nothing, he can pay nothing, he can pay nothing to eternity! He is bowed down by the weight of obligations and the load of benefits; when he contrasts himself with those less favored it is only to feel that he is no better than they, though so differently treated, regarded, and blessed. The ascription of salvation must be perpetually upon his lip : thanksgiving must be the voice of his endless melody.

God abounds in this wisdom and prudence toward us, and thus " unites our hearts,"

By most strongly abstracting us from the things of earth, and yet giving us the deepest interest in its relations and engagements.

The world is placed before us as a vanity, an immense evil, a ruthless foe. The pride of life is put to scorn. But life itself is a solemn gift and trust. Household and species prefer their claim upon us. We are debtors to all. We must do good unto all. We must love and honor all men. Whatever concerns the history and condition and destiny of our fellow-creatures is our nearest interest. Our present existence is the only opportunity for seeking their salvation. Death is not only a change most serious in itself, it is serious as the termination of that opportunity: " I shall behold man no more with the inhabitants of the world." We yield to no indifference. We discriminate. We mark the points of littleness; we seize the points of grandeur. We lose our life; we gain it; we keep it. Even now our heaven begins, not only in its earnest but in its rudiment; there now worketh for us a far more exceeding and eternal weight of glory.

Such is the explanation, and such the harmony, which we would suggest of certain apparent discordances. We

have referred to the system of checks in the natural universe as an analogy. And that analogy may help us still. For really attraction is the only law. Every repulsion being only a reference to another center, it is plain that it is but another attraction. Now all differing centers are arranged in subserviency to that which is innermost of all. The natural universe is, then, one harmonious whole, and every momentary antagonism but conduces to the perfection of its harmony. There is some mighty pivot, some glorious axle, on which the whole revolves. So all the truths of salvation are not only parts of one system, but their effects upon the believing mind are common and interchangeable; and the Author of that salvation, looking upon these truths and these effects sweetly linked together, beholds in them "the things which are equal." There is spontaneous corrective and self-adjustment, all is in its level, and on the glory of the entire scheme there is this defense.

The proportion of faith is that to which we should direct our aim. There are no discrepancies in Scripture. No confusion should distort our principles. The truths of revelation, though sometimes they seem to stand apart, are all bound together, like mountain-heights swelling from the same base and commingled in the same heaven. Nor should we suffer a chaos of half-apprehended truths in our minds. As one of the chief pleasures of science consists in the perception of affinities and agreements, associating the detached and combining the remote—so Christian knowledge, next to its power in saving the soul, yields no purer joy than the comprehensive study of all revealed facts and principles, displaying their order, defining their province, and commanding their use. They are all coincident, cognate; they throw on each a mutual light, and they stand to each in a reciprocal subserviency. They are the different members of the same body; they are the varying pro-

portions of the same building. Nothing is without its function; nothing without its place. There is no extraneous, no irreconcilable, no confusing element in Christianity. It is of one : it is one. And if we be Christians, our experience will be the counterpart of it. As it works out from apparent shocks and collisions its perfect unity, so shall our experience be wrought in the same way. "In obeying from our heart its form," whatever of its influences may seem to interfere with each other, they all will be found to "establish our heart ;" as the opposing currents often swell the tide, and more proudly waft the noble bark it carries; as the counterbalancing forces of the firmament bear the star onward in its unquivering poise and undeviating revolution!

II.

THE INVIOLABILITY OF CHRISTIANITY.

———◆———

But though we, or an angel from heaven, preach any other Gospel unto you than that which we have preached unto you, let him be Accursed.—Gal. i, 8.

This " curse, causeless, shall not come ! "   Still it is too possible that man, easily beguiled, and naturally hostile, may fall into the guilt which provokes so tremendous a denunciation.   But is it not rash to point the menace farther than our race, and to give it a range among other and the most elevated orders of existence ?   It is a fearful imagining ! a stroke of eloquence in its most vehement mood and expression.   It invokes the supernatural—it supposes the monstrous ; it verges on the horrible in sentiment and feeling !   Probability is set at defiance ; a temerity, more than metaphorical, breathes through the awful vow.

It is at least a supposition very boldly conceived, and strongly mooted.   For, from what we can learn respecting these high and holy beings, they, among all created natures, would be most reluctant to interfere by such an act of impious usurpation.   Whatever information we can acquire in reference to their history and character constrains us to treat, as an elaborate extravagance, the idea that they are capable of innovating upon " the glorious Gospel," whose wonders they delightedly explore, whose triumphs they gratefully celebrate.   The " elect

angels" are beyond the reach of temptation ; their pro-bationary discipline has ceased. *This,* were it not so, would scarcely be the trespass into which they would rush or be betrayed. Otherwise there would be a second revolt in heaven, the enormity of which must make light the first, and leave it forgotten. Let but such malediction avenge such outrage, and Lucifer set not in night equally black, nor was the Great Dragon bound with links equally heavy. The later and more guilty rebels would not only reflect from their visages, and emulate in their spirits, the daring and the deception of *him* who was a murderer and a liar from the beginning : they would refine upon his cruelty, and delude with more than his guile. Indeed, he *has* " gathered this iniquity " to himself. No form of Satanic malignity, no mark of Satanic apostasy, is more descriptive and prominent than hostility to evangelical truth, in influencing its concealment, debasement, and disbelief. Too tempting was this sacrilege, hating as he did both heaven and earth, to remain unperpetrated.

And there are considerations founded on the nature of these pure and lovely creatures, which compel us to regard this hypothetical instance as extreme. They are not wholly unknown to us, nor estranged from those affections which we can appreciate. They have, ere now, put on human form, and human countenance has, ere now, shone with their radiance. We have " come to an innumerable company of angels," and they have " encamped round about " us. We can speak with precision of their temperament, we can pronounce with confidence what will or will not be their conduct.

They " do always behold the face of " God. His glory is the element of their being, the sunlight of their joy. Now they are engaged in its study, then transported in its vision, and again they strike their harps to its praise. Each disclosure of purpose, the unvailing

of each perfection, is a new occasion and source of their bliss. Their felicity retains but one character, and knows but one origin, whether their employment be contemplation, acclaim, or flight to distant worlds. And where, but " in the face of Jesus Christ," shines out " the light of the knowledge of the glory of God ? " Where, but in " the glass " of the Christian revelation, can they " behold with open face " the convergence of its brightest splendors ? Nature, by its side, is dim, and Providence but catches its reflected illumination. And will the spectators of such a scene—the six-winged seraphs, the eye-filled living creatures—renounce a Gospel to which they owe their clearest discovery of the Infinite Excellence, and, consequently, their richest fruition of the Infinite Plenitude ? A Gospel which adds royalty to their "thrones," extension to their "dominions," fame to their "principalities," and strength to their " powers ? " " Any other " would destroy the grand exhibition which this presents of the divine character, and extinguish that " glory of God " which can only " lighten " the celestial city so long as " the Lamb is the light thereof."

Their disposition is pure benevolence. As the attributes of the Deity may be resolved into love, so the godlike virtues of these spirits refer to the same principle. Since that consists in commiseration of suffering, as well as manifests itself by complacency in good, so mercy mingles with their "good-will to men." Their task may sometimes be to break seals of judgment, to discharge vials of wrath, to ring out trumpet-peals of doom—but love in all its degrees constitutes their essence and pervades their being — gives beauty to their robes, and luster to their crowns—gilds the sphere in which they shine, and attunes the harmonies which they warble. And what but the Gospel furnishes scope for its exercise, or justification for its indulgence ? What boon

can be compared with this, or what channel does there exist for such a communication of perfect love? Their benevolence but awaited immediately to follow " after that the kindness and love of God our Saviour toward man appeared." Their very nature must be reversed— their most intimate sympathies, their most tender yearnings, must be abandoned—when one of their myriads shall descend the messenger of " another gospel," or become the corrupter of " ours."

And the *offices* with which these ethereal sainted beings are invested—offices from which we derive the greater portion of our knowledge concerning their dispositions, and by which we are chiefly brought into contact and alliance with their doings—preclude the fiction, and debar the possibility of any other Gospel originating in their counsel, or receiving their sanction. He who reconciled " all things to himself, whether they be things in earth or things in heaven," and gathered together in one all of them in Christ, has incorporated in the " whole family in heaven and earth," the " angels who kept their first estate," and the " many sons whom he brings to glory."

Angels " desire to look into" these things. The " sufferings " and " glory " of Christ engage their most fixed attention. *Their* eyes are not yet open to the imposture. *They* have not yet arrived at the unworthy matters which are supposed to offend our taste, and clash with the temper of our age. To us these things may be " foolishness," they may receive our high scorn and bitter contempt; but spirits of the highest order and of a celestial residence are described to us as bending in an awe-struck attitude, as gazing with a prying research, when such themes are unfolded for their meditation. They are intent upon them, wrapt in their studies, enamored of their charms. The Gospel must forego its character, or angels must recall their admiration,

before it can suffer this insult, or they discover this vacillation.

Angels rejoice "over one sinner that repenteth." Contrite spirits and broken hearts have an attraction for them which they cannot resist. As their Lord came not to "call the righteous but sinners to repentance," so they are filled with an ardor and excess of joy in witnessing the penitent, far greater than they evince over "the just who need no repentance." Let man, the most degraded, the most disowned—the slave, the outcast—in the desert cave, on the ocean billow—chasten and afflict himself, and angels are immediately at his side with all their sympathy. From no mine can they pluck a gem rich as the sinner's heart-wrung tear, to catch and bear to heaven—nor can all the symphonies of the harmonious universe delight them as the sweet music of the sinner's sigh. But it is the Gospel which humbles our pride, softens our hardness, arouses our apathy, convinces our unbelief, alarms our fears, wins our love—and in its absence or under its mutilation, "the godly sorrow of a godly sort" would never visit a bosom. When angels, whose activities are as "the wind," and whose emotions are as "the flame," weary of speeding these embassies and spreading these tidings—when they can view the condition of the wanderer without pity, and his return without interest—then may they consent to the dereliction or perversion of that Gospel which has but, in an almighty hand, to touch the heart, and all the reflections, the upbraidings, the relentings, the soothings of genuine repentance at once seize upon it, break it, renew it, heal it.

Angels are "sent forth to minister to the heirs of salvation." They follow them to comfort them on the deep, to cheer them in the wilderness; they have "charge over them," they "bear them up in their hands," they "deliver them from all evil." They keep

the vigil while the subjects of their care sleep, and hover around them wherever they pitch their tent. But without this Gospel the hope of *salvation* could never have been cherished, the thought of it never realized, and angels would have been unbidden to conduct one expectant of the heavenly inheritance in his progress toward its possession. Its repeal would be the withdrawment of all the means and blessings of salvation; and until these offices of mercy overpower their strength or survive their disposition to perform them, the benevolent agents cannot consent to modify, or conspire to discard it.

Angels carry the disembodied soul of the Christian to heaven. They relax not their aid, they forbear not their sympathy, from the moment of his earliest repentance to that in which they convey him beyond the confines of danger and sadness. Then the glow of their benevolent satisfaction is at its warmest intensity—the completed task is the consummated reward. They love to see the spirit, enfranchised by the body's death, stretching its long-folded wing, and essaying its hitherto unconscious freedom. They stand at each gate of the new Jerusalem, as if to keep it open night and day. And while the " great number, which no man can number," receives its accession, and hastens its accumulation, no envy darkens their minds, nor stays their ecstasies. In that proportion their pleasure is enhanced, and they feel that their dignity is aggrandized. And what but the Gospel secures our " life and immortality ? " Where else is " the hope of glory.? " They must see every mansion filled, and the " nations of the saved " clustering on the everlasting hills—heaven itself too strait— and then only will they tear the Gospel from our custody, or supersede it by some idle mockery and spurious pretense.

The fact is this. The Apostle supposes a case most

violently improbable, pictures it in the deepest colors, presents it under the strongest expressions, and imprecates a cleaving curse on *his* head, of whatever order of being, from whatever region of space, who should dare to remodel Christianity, or substitute for it another system. The cited instance is set forth with this terrific power, to cut off the presumption of guiltlessness, and the hope of impunity from them who only could do this deed. Man is a creature who has always attempted to supplant or debase the Gospel. These things are "in a figure transferred" from man to angels. Even their intrusion should be resented, their rapine be avenged. How, then, can the worm of earth escape? The *greater* is threatened to deter the *less.*

This passage suggests a train of important reflections. But it is requisite to our proper pursuit of them that we be informed of that which is fenced around with these solemn safeguards. What is the Gospel? Is it the concentration of the scattered rays emitted from created objects? Is it the gathering up of the intimations which escape from the silent course of the divine government? We have not so "learned Christ." We esteem it a distinct revelation of what could not be otherwise inferred or guessed: an announcement of a salvation in which we discover, most effectually, our guilt and depravity as implied in that deliverance. Though the entire scheme and the remotest bearing of Christianity may deserve this title, yet is the Gospel most specifically its answer to the inquiry, What must I do to be saved? The doctrine of justification seems present to the mind of the inspired writer wherever he employs the term in this epistle; while its connection with personal sanctity and practical virtue is indissolubly established by all his reasonings and admonitions. He " delivered, first of all," or rather, as his "first principles," this Gospel as that "by which we are *saved.*"

This is its meaning and spirit; it is inseparable from the Gospel, and without it the Gospel is as unintelligible, as the principle of motion considered apart from its operation, or in other words, that which being at rest ceases to be. The following is the order of the reflections and conclusions which this apostolic protest seems to require, and serves to confirm.

I. The Import and Construction of the Gospel cannot be vague and indeterminate.

It cannot be reasonably doubted that the first Christians, whatever were their "differences of administrations and diversities of operations," had a "like precious faith," and a "common salvation." They coincided in "the first principles of the oracles of God," in "the principles of the doctrine of Christ." They "obeyed from the heart that form of doctrine which was delivered" them. "The form of sound words" was inculcated with the precision of a lesson, and the authority of a law. The characteristic of the Gospel was alleged to be its *truth.* This was, to the sophists of that era, a strange and novel pretension. To require faith to a testimony only so far as conformable to fact, only so far as supported by evidence, appeared to them a startling affectation. Yet this was the tone which the primeval disciples assumed —and as *history proved* what religion hallowed, we need not wonder at their port of magnanimity and valor. They "could do nothing against the truth, but for the truth." Hence their belief was definite and avowed. Neither did confusion cloud their judgment, nor strife divide their interpretation, nor suspicion canker their "singleness of heart." "Sound" and "good doctrine" they opposed to "fables;" "love of the truth" united them; they were encouraged to come to "the knowledge," and bidden to "the acknowledging" "of the truth." With this the Apostles were "put in trust;" they were "stewards of the mysteries of God." Their

power was ample; they "were teachers in faith and verity." They wore the manner of conviction the most entire and unshrinking, and justified their followers in its adoption. The language current among them was, " I know whom I have believed, and am persuaded that He is able to keep that which I have committed unto him against that day." "Hereby we know that we are of the truth, and shall assure our hearts before him." This was no conjecture, but assurance; no faltering, but infallibility. So " established, strengthened, and settled " were they, so " rooted and built up," borrowing the description from the tenacity of the root and strength of the building, that the language of the text would neither sound profane nor even forcible; it struck in with so unhesitating a sentiment, so strong a vow. They consequently affixed particular significations to what they called " the present truth," and would not brandish the curse to defend what was equivocal in its nature, or interminable in its controversy. The Gospel called up a certain set of ideas, a particular class of propositions, in their minds—they had " the full assurance of understanding " and " of faith "—they understood what they said, and whereof they " affirmed."

But such statements are frequently contested in our times. It is denied that there was uniformity of opinion, that Christianity is dogmatic, that the Saviour dictated a particular creed, that the Apostles were authorized to propound one. The following disclaimer is employed as a general abandonment of all such claim, " not for that we have dominion over your faith." 2 Cor. i, 24. But though the first sight and sound of this language might seem to leave them to any latitude of principle or interpretation, the slightest inspection of the context, and the absurdity of the contrary supposition, will refute the gloss. Paul disavows all use of tyrannic power through the means or by the circum-

stances of their religious profession. He will abstain from all such stretch of his influence and abuse of their confidence; but he subjoins what denotes any thing rather than a license for the indifference of sentiment, "For by faith ye stand." "The foundation of the apostles" was one of inspired teaching and ordinance, not that of the sinner's dependence for acceptance; and their "foundation" was held together by "Jesus Christ being the chief corner-stone." They were commissioned to "teach all nations," they were "set for the defense of the Gospel," they were the accredited representatives and organs of the ascended Messiah, they were filled with the spirit of his mission and knowledge of his will, they were in "his stead," and spoke and wrote with that awful impress and emphasis which he imparted to them when about to leave them: "As my Father has sent me, even so send I you!"

In the fixed character we recognize the true perfection of the Gospel. It is the same through all ages, not changing to every touch, and varying beneath every eye, but unfolding the same features, and producing the same effects. It is a system of particular tenets— these, it is important to recollect, are *truths*, and partake of the necessary unchangeableness of all which can boast this designation. The evidences of truth may differ, but it cannot be more or less than truth. "The word of the truth of the Gospel" has the same strict meaning, the same express design, as of old; and he who adds to it, or takes away from it, offers it an equal indignity, and does it an equal wrong.

Amid the conflicts of opinion, rife and strenuous as they are in modern days, it is an anxious inquiry, a solemn problem, *are we right?* Do we "know the truth?" The anathema which is prefixed to this discourse never could have been uttered unless the Gospel had been limited to a distinct meaning, had been sus-

ceptible of a certain interpretation. How important that we escape it by renouncing " any other Gospel ! "

How shall we know when we have attained to a just apprehension of " the faith once delivered to the saints ? " It will be easy to charge us with arrogance; it will be foolish in us to shrink from the accusation.

Is the Gospel worthy of our acceptation ? " Is it sufficiently clear and perspicuous to be conceived ? We would avoid all naked and unprotected assertions, but maintain that a believing knowledge of it may be acquired, that such a perception should be allowed a place in the mind, to the exclusion of all distracting doubt and misgiving; and that we are warranted in resting these immovable conclusions on the laws of moral certainty.

We do not make light of *scriptural investigation.* This is the basis and index of all genuine belief. We possess a divine revelation. When it is the part of science to anticipate the facts of Nature and bend them to its preconceived theory, then may it be wise and legitimate to forecast what such revelation should contain, and to measure it by that self-formed standard. The inductive principle, which is our familiar boast, is often reversed when the sacred volume is the subject. Men of any thought see, indeed, the dilemma of inconsistency into which an open violation of it would sink them; but mixing the rules of inquiry with the business of *internal evidence,* they set their assumptions against the plainest dictates and soundest criticisms. All they do is prompted by their care of the divine character and their reverence for the divine code, which otherwise would be left profanely compromised and cruelly exposed. We, however, do not fear but that God will " have pity on" his " holy name," and cannot suppose that he will " disgrace the throne of" his " glory." We do not presume to be more tenderly jealous of his honor than

himself. And taking with us " the Scriptures which are able to make wise unto salvation," we embrace all their inferences as well as facts, doctrines as well as testimonies, relying on the veracity, committed to the scope, and abiding by the conclusions, of the whole. " What saith the Scripture ? " is our only demand ; what it saith is our only criterion.

Another guide to the *discrimination* and the *selection* of *the truth* is the *moral influence* of the system which professes to constitute it. " By their fruits ye shall know them," is a test applicable to the schemes of Christianity, as well as to the character of its disciples. Such moral influence extends greatly further than acts —it reaches to the tempers and affections of the mind. If there be one form notorious for its encouragement and spectacle of supercilious arrogance, pert conceit, and contemptuous selfishness—if it should boast that the less serious the mind the better prepared it is to welcome its claims—if it may be marked by a flippant levity in its treatment of inspiration—if it has wrought every sentiment and feeling derogatory from the person and mission of Christ—if it can be proved utterly inefficient upon the habits and passions of the multitude—if it stand freezingly opposed to all generous effort toward the spread of the truth ; if it proceed to materialize the soul, and to lull it after death into a dreamless insensibility—if it extinguish each devout sentiment as it subverts all holy obligation—if its very peculiarity is irreligious indifference and captious speculation—if its effect, according to the measure of its operation, is always seen in worldly conformity, sectarian bigotry, bitter invective, and moral torpor—then we cannot doubt that it is from beneath, and not from above, nor scruple to decide that it was not from heaven, but of men. Such a scheme, denying that " there is angel or spirit," cannot be identical with that which the awful penalty of

the text was summoned to defend. Impotent, indeed, must be the threat which is raised upon a poetic machine, a mythological fiction!

To point out the tests of truth and the symptoms of error would lead us into too wide discussion: most of these are indicated by the aspect which the several systems turn on the *functions* and *characters* of our Lord's *mediation.* He, as a prophet, is slighted when the instructions of his word are denied a peremptory importance, are adulterated by tradition, or are even maintained for the purpose of rejecting his still enlightening influence. His priesthood is desecrated wherever its true expiation is reduced to a figure, or its one offering is multiplied by a superstition. The kingly authority which he wields is offended when man would mimic its prerogatives, or alter its institutions. Exalt the Saviour, surround him with all his honors, attach to him all his claims; let him be the center to which all refers, let him be the end in which all consummates; make him pre-eminent, give him glory; bow the knee, cede the heart; and there can be little room for error, and need be no fear of condemnation.

The general *concurrence* of the great Christian sections, in sentiment, will not be overlooked by them who seek for divine truth. If it exist amid so many discordances of character, temper, and interest—if it prevail under most opposite masses of will-worship and ecclesiastical domination—if it be uniformly witnessed in connection with elevated devotion and holy zeal—this identity of substance may be inferred to be the truth, while these must be its artificial, hurtful, or appropriate adjuncts. By whom has the trinity, the atonement, sanctification, with other kindred tenets, been rejected? What community and creed have abjured them? Some few, most inconsiderable for their extent of number, and only notorious by their violence of boast, may, here and

there, "contradict and blaspheme." But challenge the common and "mutual faith," "spoken of throughout the whole world"—what a unity does it unfold, what an integrity does it preserve! Combined with other causes of confidence, such general agreement will have its weight in determining us that "this is the true grace of God wherein" ye "stand."

There can be no reasonable probability that they are distinguished by the correctness of their opinions who disavow the belief of any divine influence. The fact which the Scripture assumes, the adherents to evangelical doctrine declare from the experience of themselves and others to be true, that " the natural man receiveth not the things of the Spirit of God," that he is not only inapt but inimical. Many promises are contained in the inspired volume that " the eyes of our understanding " " shall be opened," that we shall " know the truth," that the Monitor shall lead us " into all truth," that his anointing shall teach us " all things," that if we be " in any thing otherwise minded, God shall reveal even this unto" us. Now, all who profess the belief of this enlightening influence, agree in those essentials to which we have referred—if *it* be real, *this* is the result. With scarcely an exception, their opponents deny its reasonableness and existence. If any admit it, their conception of it is most unsatisfactory. Is it a process of conviction unnatural or unsound, that if all who cherish divine influence arrive at certain doctrinal conclusions, those conclusions are more likely to be just than such as connect themselves with a " despite to the Spirit of grace ? " " No man speaking by the Spirit of God calleth Jesus accursed." Every man who hath learned of the Father cometh unto Christ.

We are thankful that the true believer has a *secret persuasion,* which he cannot explain, as well as many more external, which he can. He has " the witness in

himself." This is involved in the " witness " which the Spirit bears with his " spirit " of his acceptance, but is so far distinct that it more particularly rises from the commendation of sacred and vital truth to his conscience and heart. It is so minutely applicable to his case—it is so intimately associated with his history, affecting him at all points, succoring him in all distresses—" the tried stone " of his trust, the " anchor, sure and steadfast," of his hope—that he cannot doubt of its truth until he shall despair of its efficacy. And it is remarkable that such an intuitive perception and internal impression are restricted to the consciousness of them who " hold the head ;" while in deviating from it, these parties disclaim any share of the self-closing evidence, and any toleration of an idea which they denounce to be utterly unphilosophical. But their disclaimer only goes thus far : the attestation of *others* they cannot invalidate. And, therefore, the inquirer may not inaptly argue that the positive averment of so many remains unimpaired by this negative, that such intimation to the soul is as attainable as it is desirable, and that it is the peculiar and precious " secret of the Lord," which is with them who " know of the doctrine," and are " of the truth." The impugner of the Saviour's godhead and sacrifice might spare himself the trouble of scorning and renouncing this pledge. He is absolved from the charge. But his jeer does not undeceive our judgment or disabuse our conviction. And he might more reasonably think and infer that what is the property of all from whom he differs is only withheld from himself as the mark of his error, and the punishment of his disbelief.

Unless there was this invariableness in the Christian system—if a fixed determination of its purport is impossible—we should be at a loss in what manner to follow the conduct and imbibe the spirit of the early Christians. The lofty confidence we admire in them must,

when imitated, degenerate into the vainest arrogance. Those lights and examples of the Church would only ensnare us into a mien and attitude ridiculous as profane. It would be the dwarf attempting to bare a giant's arm, a wayfaring man aspiring to a prophet's vision.

And on this supposition, instead of congratulating ourselves that we possess the *written* word, we stand in a disadvantageous position. How are we blessed in not having seen, yet having believed? We can resolve no doubt, we can obtain no certainty. Far better would it be to sit at the feet of Jesus. It could not be expedient that he should depart; the Comforter does not supply his place. Or we might have interrogated the Apostles. Their living lips might have yielded the satisfaction which their records do not secure. The oracle may still respond, but its sounds are inarticulate, and its decisions evasive.

And it is plain that there are duties urged upon the disciples of the Gospel which are sufficiently incoherent, should it be itself unsusceptible of strict definition, or should it not authorize an unequivocal assertion. If there be one obligation more enforced than another, it is to "steadfastness of faith in Christ." Nothing is more commended, nothing more earnestly and frequently impressed: "Stablished in the faith as ye have been taught." "If ye continue in the faith grounded and settled, and be not moved away from the hope of the Gospel." "I trust ye shall acknowledge these things even to the end." But if the Christian faith be vague and indeterminable, then constancy to it in any meaning, and according to any conception, must be as pertinacious as its avowal is precipitate.

The history of the martyrs, who have sealed with the prodigal sacrifice of their blood not a name or sound, but a set of opinions which they deemed a just repre-

sentation of Christianity, would appear a tragedy without a moral, were the Gospel, in sacred language, to be " yea and nay," or incapable of being adjudged. In vain did they pour out that life-stream, when it was but a risk what truth it might attest, and what cause it should subserve. It was too vast a price for a doubtful part, and too reckless a stake for an incalculable issue.

There is another spirit at work among us. It can inculcate a due firmness of erroneous opinion, it only condemns as rude and dictatorial the adoption and retention of an opposite sentiment. It is charitable, in its own favored phrase, toward all the doubting and unconvinced; it can show favor to the honest infidel, however impetuous and professed. Its contempt is reserved for those who, having, with certainly no less honesty, read the word of God and searched the Scriptures " whether these things are so," maintain their most cautious impression and uphold their most deliberate judgment. This contempt would fall strangely upon those who are celebrated for continuing in " the apostles' doctrine ;" and it might invert itself, and become apology for those whom the same record condemns. Might it not advance, in extenuation of those who were " ever learning, and never coming to the " knowledge of the truth," that they were unfettered by prejudice, and still prosecuting inquiry? and offer in exculpation of " unstable souls," that they were only seeking truth wherever it could be found, keeping their minds open and their studies unpledged, ready to obey all possible convictions ?

But the " truth as it is in Jesus," *is* contained in that word which is *truth itself ;* there it is laid up as in a casket and hallowed as in a shrine. No change can pass upon it. It bears the character of its first perfection. It is the wisdom of God and the power of God. Like the manna and the rod in the recess of the ark, it

is the incorruptible bread of heaven, it is the ever-living instrument of might, without an altered form or superseded virtue. "He who runneth may read." Nothing but clouds of unholy passion or of mental vanity can obscure it. It is only impervious to the "desires of the *flesh* or of the *mind*." "If our Gospel be hid, it is hid to them that are lost." And such is its simplicity when men read it as learners and receive it as sinners, that we can dare a contradiction to its plain interpretation, and feel that if "an angel from heaven" were so to belie it, torturing it by sophistry, annulling it by conjecture, and recasting it by prejudgment, he should suffer the "curse" which dreadly guards our faith from every violation.

This impassioned style prompts an idea beyond the intelligibleness and fixed nature of the Gospel:

II. ITS DIVINE ORIGIN AND AUTHORITY CANNOT BE CONTROVERTED.

The history of Saul of Tarsus has often been cited with happy success in confirmation of Christianity. Part of the evidence which it supplies is common to other narratives of conversion, but a greater part is of a character quite distinct. As in all it is competent to set over against each other *mistake* and *deception*, so we might in this show the impossibility of such a mind being seduced into error or tempted to imposture. If the *first*, then the most masculine mind, the most powerful counter-impression, a judgment most cautious in its use of evidence, a sobriety most jealous over each exercise of imagination, proofs always abundant and always augmenting, sign and suasion, are no presumptions of truth, no means of certainty. The Gospel is either unsusceptible of support from reasoning, or our intellect is unfitted to weigh that reasoning. If the *second*, we must transform the human being, and conceive of selfishness covetous of sacrifice, ambition intent upon dis-

honor, pleasure wrapt in austerity, hypocrisy sighing for death.

His accession to the Christian side derives much of its singularity from his hostility—hostility neither ordinary nor in the least degree controlled. It could only at any time have been exasperated into fiercer fury by the suggestion that he should soon be won to the number of the proselytes and defenders already enlisted. Had augur or soothsayer hazarded that prediction, no improbabilities could have occurred to the hearer more blind and excessive.

If any name sounded dreadful in the ear of the first Christian it was that of the young man who kept the raiment of them that slew the martyr Stephen. That name was a brand of cruelty, it was a voice of blood. It passed forth as an omen, as when nations have beheld the meteor-sword flashing above them. In vain do we search for any redeeming virtue, any exculpating circumstance, in his character and history. The ordinary palliatives of youth, temperament, inexperience, supply the actual aggravation. A rank maturity of evil contrasts itself to his youth, a phlegmatic steadiness of malignity does violence to his temperament, and an inventive redundance of aggressions more than makes up for the disadvantage of inexperience. He settles into a cool and gloating ferocity, he revolves new and more dire schemes of persecution. He can revel in the carnage of a promiscuous massacre with an unshrinking eye and unrelenting heart. He never seems warmed by a generous enthusiasm. There is none of that fine sentiment, that moral poetry which sometimes has retrieved the sallies of an extravagant zeal. His acquittal of dishonesty is the condemnation of his cruelty.

And if any conversion appeared placed beyond the limit of hope and all reasonable expectation, if any could be " too hard for God," or lying within those moral

impossibilities which he allows, because they establish his perfection of nature and rule of will, who could have wavered to pronounce that it was this? Sooner might it have been surmised that Caiaphas would have looked " on him whom" he "had pierced," and in bitter compunction would have rent his ephod, and cast his tiara into the dust. Sooner might it have been anticipated that Pilate would have worshiped that King whom neither the seal, nor cohort, nor death itself could imprison in the tomb. And even when the thousands of the populace which had insulted him in every form, spit on him in the hall, and jested with him on the cross, are " pricked to the heart," it does not impress us as so strange, nor does its announcement strike us as so unlikely, as that this stern foe should pause, that this fell monster should soften.

His earliest prepossessions would render the contingency of such an event most minute and distant. The blood of his high ancestry would rebel against the change. His education at the feet of a rabbi would confirm his attachment to " the Jews' religion," and enable him to defend it with adroitness. His sect, as a Pharisee, would induce the pride of a more strictly ceremonial consistency. Bigotry would call in public favor to its aid, for he was esteemed the champion of his nation and his faith, of his country and his God.

Persecution could not find a more ready instrument. He enters into its service with an unparalleled quickness and force of congeniality. He is formed to it at once. He puts forth all its perfect instincts and fangs. Who does not tremble as he proceeds? " Damascus is waxed feeble and turneth herself to flee." The terror, scourge, and spoiler of the Church—the pestilence withering all into a desert—the conflagration setting " on fire the course of nature," and itself "set on fire of hell" —the star of disastrous influence which, falling to the

earth, converts its waters into gall and blood—to what can he be compared ?   How long shall he be suffered to make havoc of the saints ?   Will not "God avenge his own elect?"   "Are not [his] eyes upon the truth ?"   Where sleeps his thunder?   "Judgment slumbereth not."   The rebel falls: amid his most intoxicating dream, his most applauded career—in the greatness of his way—he falls!   Jesus of Nazareth has struck down his foe.   Well has the bolt sped, true has the arrow flown.   But that light streams not to blast, that voice upbraids not to condemn, that power smites not to destroy.   O what a change has moved over his heart!   What " a new creature!"   He weeps.   He abhors himself.   "Behold, he prayeth."   The hands which " haled men and women to prison "—which a few hours ago received the fatal commission, and until this moment grasped the murderous weapon—are now penitently clasped, and suppliantly uplifted!   The knees which shook not when he was surrounded by the wailings of mothers and children whom he made widows and orphans, now pliant as the infant sinew, are bent in earnest, transfixing prayer!   The eyes, no longer bent in moody scorn, or shooting with wrathful glance, now overflow with tears.   The lips which " breathed out threatenings and slaughter," now utter the cry of shame and surrender, " Lord, what wilt thou have me to do ? "   What a conquest!   What a spectacle!   So sudden, so enduring!   " Where is the fury of the oppressor! "   It is a trophy of grace.   It is a marvel of Omnipotence.   The lamb may lie down with the lion, the sucking child may play on the hole of the asp, and the weaned child may put his hand on the cockatrice's den.

And his conversion raises not alone the argument for the truth of that faith " which once he destroyed:" we must review his mission and apostolate.   For though the doctrines he preached were precisely those of the

other disciples, and his qualifications for the office as decided, he having seen the Lord, and, therefore, being constituted virtually a witness of his resurrection, yet two things distinguish his ministry. He learned Christianity from *immediate revelation.* He was indebted to none of the " men who companied together all the time the Lord Jesus went in and out among them." James taught him not his knowledge, nor Peter enkindled his zeal, nor John infused his love. At the foot of the celestial throne he imbibed the " wisdom in a mystery," and returned to earth exclaiming, " Woe is unto me if I preach not the Gospel." In the same manner he derived his *authority* from the " Head of the body, which is the Church." So far from this investiture being proposed, or this designation being imparted, by the Apostles, " they were all afraid of him, and believed not that he was a disciple." His appointment, his instruction, were direct communications from Heaven. Now, there is a double advantage in these facts. Had the Apostles swerved from their Master's truth since his resurrection? a persecutor is caught up to the third heaven, and descends with all the lessons of that awful discipline. And the comparison establishes the important matter, that the most exact agreement subsisted between the sentiments of the earlier disciples of the Christian school and this later one—between the elder brethren and this younger one, " born out of due time." An unprejudiced witness, he could say, " Therefore, whether it were I or they, so we preach, and so ye believed." And as the *doctrine* of Christianity was proved to have remained undistorted, so this independence of the other Apostles vindicated all the parties from any collusion. It was like sending down from heaven a second original of the Gospel, and affixing to it a second seal of attestation. The vouchers were written in the same character, the impressions were received from the same signet.

From these statements we draw important conclusions, illustrated and enforced by the text. First, what must have been the *strength and satisfaction of conviction* entertained by the writer! Be it remembered that the conviction has to do with facts. It pertains to no favorite theory, no abstract science, but to occurrences which he had proved by sensible observation and perfect consciousness. Wonders had teemed around him; but his own transformation was the most signal wonder of all. Nothing without him could equal what he discerned within. True, the light which shone upon him when he was arrested in his guilty march, was " above the brightness of the sun ;" but an intenser radiance was filled his soul. True, the earthquake had set him free when thrust into the inner prison, and fastened in the stocks ; but a mightier power had laid open his heart. True, he spake words of power which cast out infernal spirits; but of more fatal possessions had he been healed. How could he doubt? He knew his cause, and he knew its trustworthy evidence. Mark now his language, and consider his responsibility! He sounds a defiance to the universe! He dares to a refutation creatures of the keenest intellect and largest power! The mind could have felt no misgiving which braves such an inquest, which denounces such a curse. Had room existed for the faintest suspicion, aye, for possible mistake, at once this language had been subdued, and its fearlessness been restrained. He would have spoken with reserve, his curse would have been sheathed in conditions. He would have trembled lest some unknown being might accept the guage, lest Heaven should avenge the quarrel. His tongue would have faltered lest, while he spoke, some oracle should burst suddenly at his foot, and falsify his assertions ; lest some angel should cross his path and " forbid his madness." And as we can thus estimate the measure and force of Paul's convictions, we

may, *secondly*, inquire what weight and credibility should be allowed them. Remember the appeal; consider the man who utters it; inspect his habitudes of mind; follow the lines of his history; try his character by any motives of selfishness and artifice; forget not the meed he loses in the danger he incurs; contrast his meekness and his heroism; combine his indignation of wrong to another with his forbearance of it toward himself; put his conduct to any test, his design to any analysis; and then determine whether *we* are not safe where *he* is undaunted; whether *we* may not decide for that on which *he* perils all; whether the anathema which *he* dares pronounce does not throw around *us* the safeguard of a divine benediction; whether *we* ought not to transfer, with whatever abatement of the verbal force and the apostolic authority, these solemn, untrembling convictions from his mind, on which they impress such strength and majesty, to our own.*

But this imprecatory language, proceeding from the present source, not only establishes the divine truth of Christianity; it is available to the proof that,

III. Its Efficacy cannot be denied.

Himself a memorable proof of what it could accomplish (and proofs only inferior multiplying on every side) no one having subjected it to more frequent and successful experiment—a witness of its energy on all characters and among all nations—Paul cannot endure that even the thought of " another Gospel " should reflect upon this. It leaves him nothing to desire. Imagination can invest it with no worthier attributes nor ampler powers. It had evinced no sign of incapacity, nor could it be charged with a semblance of failure. Sustaining the utmost grandeur of its pretensions, fulfilling the largest spirit of its predictions, only wanting " free course" to be " glorified,"—not only gone forth con-

* " Splendentia et vehementia sed rebus veris."—Augustine.

quering but "to conquer," he shudders at the rapine which would despoil and the sacrilege which would profane it.

It was not called into operation until numberless expedients of man had been frustrated. Philosophy, after a probation of ages and a felicity of opportunities, sunk dejected on her seat, and declined the reign which she had of old sought to establish over the human spirit. She cherished long and tenaciously projects of amelioration. Socrates pursued her stateliest reasonings; Plato fell entranced into her fairest dreams, and what unassisted reason could achieve, these her sons and champions must have insured. They spoke of the *becoming* and the *beautiful* in conduct; they applied the genius of their master-language in the refinements of the *necessary*, the *useful*, the *due* in obligation. They had an ambition to elevate the mind and character of man, to correct the evils of society, and to establish a condition of universal well-being. They drew their pictures of an ideal perfection, and held them up to excite emulation. It would be unjust to refuse them the praise of integrity and amiable dispositions. But they knew not the depth of the disease they undertook to eradicate. They struck no blow at the root of evil, and much less aspired to "make the tree good." The plan of each was wrecked, the world was in despair, when Christianity left the bosom of the Father in the person of his Son. From the moment it alighted on earth it has run a career of beneficence. Men have been blessed in it. By an invisible process it detaches the stain of guilt from the conscience, and pours balm into its wound. By a power no less than His "who made not only that which is without, but that which is within also," it renews the spirit of the mind. It still holds fast its youthful prime and strength. Whatever, under any circumstances, it has done, it can under any circum-

stances repeat. The sanctified instrument of the Holy Spirit, it pardons as determinately as the Saviour's voice, saying, "Thy sins be forgiven thee." It purifies as efficaciously as the Saviour's fiat, "I will; be thou clean." It adopts as truly as the Saviour's recognition, "Behold my mother and my brethren." It glorifies as authoritatively as the Saviour's assurance, "To-day shalt thou be with me in paradise." If ever a fountain, it is as at the first, exhaustless; if ever a medicine, it is the specific still; if ever a mine, it is impoverished of none of its wealth; if ever a foundation, what will not its present strength enable it to sustain? Take and learn what these Scriptures mean, "The blood of Jesus Christ cleanseth us from all sin;" "By whom the world is crucified unto me, and I unto the world;" "I will never leave thee, nor forsake thee." Ah, they have not lost their zest and emphasis! Still they breathe their sweet savor, and insinuate their soothing charm. They have suffered no diminution, they can exhibit no decay. The tree of life sheds no faded leaf; the sword of the Spirit gleams refulgent, without a spot of rust or abatement of temper.

It was well proved from the beginning. It had entered no congenial sphere. Philosophy, rhetoric, art, were conjoined to superstitions, radicated into all habits and vices of mankind. The very ruins which survive the downfall of polytheism—the frieze with its mythological tale, the column yet soaring with inimitable majesty, the statue breathing an air of divinity—recall the fascinations which it once might boast, and tell of the auxiliaries it could command. Yet these were but the decorations of selfishness most indecently avowed, of licentiousness most brutally incontinent, of war the most wantonly bloody, of slavery the most barbarously oppressive. And Christianity subverted these foundations of iniquity; and yet so all penetrating is its energy, that

it did not so much smite them as that they sunk away before it. It sobered passion by reason, and controlled imagination by truth; it excited sensibility by interest, and awed conscience by retribution; compelled gratitude by the bestowment of good, and gained affection by the portraiture of excellence. What a revolution did it accomplish in the laws, usages, opinions, and feelings of the world! It "famished the gods," (Zeph. ii, 11,) realizing the irony of the prophets in the withdrawment of the sacrifices on which they were supposed to feed; it cast down the temples; it struck dumb the oracles; the images of power fell from their pedestals; the fires of devotion went out on their shrines. It softened the ferocity and relaxed the pride of manners; it gave justice its exercise and benevolence its being. It stooped to every ill and woe. Nor was it only a proposal, but a power, to bless; not something to be thwarted by human perversity, but to melt it away. It was a practical victory, a sure triumph. It advanced without noise and pomp, but irresistibly. Its power was displayed in the might of effect, and not in the struggle of operation; in . the perfect work, without the intervention of process and delay. Like the elemental ray—immediate, piercing, renovating—or the hidden laws of nature which speed and harmonize all its most exact and beneficent results— Christianity reaches the human will, and renews the human heart. And a thousand blessings, which may at first appear derived from an independent source, are really poured forth from this: as the soft moonlight is but the reflection of the sun no longer visible, but still not uninfluential.

We may, indeed, with perfect propriety, demand what occasion has presented itself for something new? What new lights have been thrown on human powers, obligations, and destinies? What sudden secret has been struck out by the inquiries into human nature? We

wait but for the proof of its incompetency to purify the wicked and solace the distressed. That proof has never been produced. What have other systems done? What hold have they fastened on the mind, what strength exerted on the heart? What of vice have they suppressed? What of woe have they relieved? Tame the tiger with a straw! stem the torrent with a bulrush! This, this is the admirable quality of the Gospel, that it anticipates and provides for every emergency. It is projected on a scale of omniscience. Statesmen have mistaken a people, philosophers have blundered in the estimate of a generation. But its view is warped and darkened by no error: it "plucks out the secret" from the "hidden man of the heart." And it speaks decidedly for the divine excellence and consistency of Christianity, that it is prepared for the most varied circumstances, that it proceeds upon the supposition of the most critical anomalies, that it comprehends the pressure and solution of all difficulties; that it is, in short, worthy and susceptible "of all acceptation." The individual who receives it finds such an appeal to his character and testimony to his history that he is confounded, and asks, "Whence knowest thou me?" In all the intricacy of the most modified humanity, in all the womb of ever-working time, there is not a perplexity which it cannot explain, there is not a contingency for which it is not prepared. It is strong for the grapple as tender for the embrace. It is equal for all encounters and all trials. For every case it furnishes a ready precedent and a repeated counterpart. By one vast conception it generalizes man, and with as minute peculiarity it follows and unfolds all his variations. It discerns "the end from the beginning;" and to every child of Adam holds up the glass in which he may see his own natural face. It knows the heart's bitterness as if within its consciousness, and applies the soul's medicine as if itself felt the wound. It is the catholicon and

the specific—exhibiting such a comprehension of the *all,*
as though not an attention could be expended on the
individual, and such a care of the *individual,* as though
no amplitude could contain the *all.* It looks upon our
nature with the divine intelligence, and yearns for our
salvation with the divine pity.

It is not unfrequently asserted that an age of improvement requires a modification of religion; that the system
of Jesus admits of a progressiveness; that it comprises
in it an expansive tendency. There is much that is ob-
jectionable in this language—implying that Christianity
is not only elastic to every advance of society and enlargement of mind, but the subject of advance and enlargement itself. The truth is, that the doctrines of this
faith are as certain as its facts—the latter being not more
historically, than the former are inferentially, true. As
the facts are recorded under inspired sanction, so the
doctrines are deduced from them by inspired direction.
More cannot be put into the original premises and conclusions than at first intended. It is evident that when
this is done narrative sinks into allegory, and lesson into
equivocation. The Gospel is fixed in its first meaning,
and we are " shut up to the faith." But here we have
neither sense of shame nor fear of abandonment. Let
nature drop its innermost vail, let science demonstrate
its latest truth, and we do not suspect that by such blaze
of discovery and such force of conviction the character
of our religion can become obsolete, or its design superseded. Its triumph is, that it anticipates all knowledge
and all invention—that nothing of ascertained existence
or occurrence, physical or transcendental, can overtake
its originality and lessen its necessity. It always leads
the way. It affects not to be the pandect of natural
history; but, with its popular phraseology undenied,
what of its statements have any of these researches disproved ? And in its discrimination of human character,

what scheme has even approached it in its fullness and impartiality? What annalists and publicists have known the heart so well? Their failure has always been at the particular point of its success. "The Spirit speaketh expressly" all that is wanted to the knowledge of man. It is in virtue of this acquaintance with our nature, and of the remedy which is suggested by it, that we doubt not that it will outstrip every competitor, and prove that in its constitution are the impulse and germ of all amelioration. Its efficiency has been established at all times and by all experiments; it has been reduced to an unfailing principle, and we need, at the present, no more hesitate about it than we are accustomed to do when we speak of those celestial mechanics which give to the sun its center, and the planets their rounds.

Many fair promises have been made to us that if we consent to part with the Gospel the surrender shall be compensated. We are assured that the loss will not be irreparable. That all its invaluable effects would not immediately perish upon its formal abolition we can readily believe—a root would still be in the ground. Though the source of day had withdrawn, the warm glow of the sunset could not but survive for a little. But that this is due to Christianity, is a proof of its benignity, and cannot dispose us to a less reluctance, or bribe us to a less rigorous exaction, in the barter. Now, what is the Gospel? Contemplate it as an *ideal.* It draws into itself what is most tender. It assembles around it all that is fair and great. It is the model of pity. It is the archetype of loveliness. It is the perfection of beauty. It contains all the first ideas, the original principles, the virgin essences of whatever can belong to eternal worth and excellence. It has caught the earliest beam of divine irradiation which the Father of lights suffered to fall on immensity. It bathed in the fountain of life when first that overflowed its infinite

hiding-place, and has secured and turned to earth the river of those living waters. Truth has nothing more majestic. Simplicity has nothing more exquisite. Benevolence has nothing more touching. Only in this can they develop their full proportion, and obtain their unconstrained exercise. Then regard it as a *reality*. Instantly it quits the repose of abstraction. All is found capable of application. It knits itself with all the business of life, as well as with the moods of retirement from it. It dispels the guilt and fear of the sinner at the moment it breathes into him "a divine nature." It blunts the edge of adversity and tears out the sting of death. It is the guide of youth and the staff of age. It is not only a speculation, but a practical thing. Poverty makes use of it to cheer its lot, affliction reclines there its bosom of throbbing agony, and mortality soothes with it the cold sweat and ruffled disquietude of the sinking brow. All wants it relieves, all tears it dries. Ideal or reality, did imagination ever teem with such a vision, or fact substantiate and shape such a system? Then what is to be offered instead? What is the equivalent? Were it possessed of the points essential to any religion, did it "preach another" Jesus, "another" Spirit, "another Gospel"—without which declarations any religion would be vain—still we must ask, What grounds existed to require, what plausibilities could be suggested to justify, the exchange? Is the power of the only name of Jesus spent? "Is the Spirit of the Lord straitened?" Is the Gospel "decayed and waxed old, and ready to vanish away?" But still there would be a Jesus, a Spirit, a Gospel—salvation, regeneracy, good news, glad tidings. No, to add insult to injury, the better to trifle with our grief and mortification, the scheme which is to be substituted not only does not comprise such evangelical outlines, but treats them with high scorn, and throws upon them unmeasured con-

tumely—it is fabricated with a most contemptuous opposition to them. And what has it done? Having canceled all that gives a religion its vital character and moral adaptation, silenced the *saving name*, mocked the *renewing influence*, it bids us accept some *prospective* advantages. Inquiry is not yet advanced, and time is not yet ripe, but the future is its own. Its shall be the reign of mind. Its shall be the paradise of virtue. But has it no auspicious commencement? Is there no sheaf of its first-fruits? Is there no fretted line of gold to mark the orient of its day? Our text directs us how to estimate these boasted principles and effects. The substitutions of an angel would be most gratuitous, inadequate, and mean—cursed should he be if he dared to prompt, or endeavored to impose, them; therefore, how immeasurably inferior, how infinitesimally more worthless, must be the notions of man!

There appears, indeed, a desire to shock each Christian sentiment by the language which many, in these times, have prevailed on themselves to employ. Its feeblest license and most guarded restraint is derision. It might surely content them that they have reached the state of mind in which they doubt all evidence, and even presume to define the possibilities of things. There was no need to scatter taunts on those who had not arrived at the same hardihood of temperament. Cruel adventurers! What do ye propose by breaking down the landmarks which the wise and holy have always observed? Why have ye quenched the lights which have burned through ages, and to which the reverent eye of generations has so long been turned? If your souls be extricated from prejudice, if your powers of vision be disabused, enlighten and awaken not us. You cannot replace our faith, make sweeter our peace, or more abundant our joy. "From henceforth let no *man* trouble" us: we should despise and trample under foot

the succedaneum which " an *angel* from heaven " could bring !

It is a just inference from this strain of indignant deprecation, which forbids whatever could tamper with the Gospel or alter it, that,

IV. The Authority and Force of the present Dispensation of Divine Truth cannot be superseded.

The mode of discovery which the only wise God has pursued in revealing himself to man has, doubtless, ever been agreeable to " all wisdom and prudence." It has been by economies or constitutions. A particular disclosure of his will has been made under a form of external appointment and regimen. That, for the existing time, was the only medium of divine favor and human acceptance. It is no reflection on Supreme Intelligence to compare these dispensations, as it has always adapted them to the actual state of our intellectual capacity, and replenished them with sufficient information to excite the devout and benevolent affections. The twilight followed the morning star, and both heralded the sun in its strength ; but only had *that* been detained until our attention was prepared, and our eye was strengthened for the perfect day.

But all were imperfect because but preparatory. The scene was rapidly shifted, and one took the place of the other. The allowance of knowledge became more generous, and revelation hastened to its point of completion. The " sundry times " sought their " fullness," and the " divers manners " verged on their concentration. And these economies left not to others to pronounce their defectiveness. It was their own witness. They told of better things, of a " new covenant," of " a righteousness which should not be abolished." Each addressed its age with language forbearing and encouraging, similar to that which fell from the lips of Him

who was the end and glory of them all: "And now I have told you before it come to pass, that when it is come to pass ye might believe. I have yet many things to say unto you, but ye cannot bear them now."

The perfection of the Christian dispensation is, that it is *final.* In it He has spoken whose voice shall be heard no more until it "shake not the earth only, but also heaven." No other sensible manifestation can be given —the doctrine is not to be simplified, the ritual is not to be defined, to any further extent—nothing more will be vouchsafed to augment its blessings or ratify its credentials. In the fulfillment of its predictions, in the multiplication of its effects, a species of evidence does arise; but it is of the same nature which it has long appropriated, and is rather its prolongation than its renewal. We must therefore congratulate ourselves that we possess the "true light," "the perfect gift," the brightest illumination, the costliest boon. None will, in a future time, be suffered to speak of us as "desiring to see and hear the things" which they are "blessed" in realizing themselves. Christianity has received the latest touch, the highest beauty, from the hand of Him who is its "Author and Finisher." "The thousand years"—"the ages of peace," "the days of heaven upon the earth"— will comprehend only "that which was from the beginning, which we have heard, which we have seen with our eyes, which we have looked upon." The testimony is sealed, and woe to him who shall add to it, or take any thing away! We have "received a kingdom which cannot be moved." It is, therefore, the common burden of prophecy that the permanency of the Saviour's reign shall equal its glory; that the kingdom which he shall set up must last for ever; that it should receive, on his ascension, a fixed shape which neither vicissitude can affect nor time outgrow. The reasonings of the later writers of inspiration strictly coincide with this; and he

who could dare angels to " preach any other Gospel,"
argues in another passage, " If that which was *done
away* was glorious, much more that which *remaineth* is
glorious."

If the Gospel did not " remain "—if it was, like earlier
dispensations, to be supplanted—nothing would be more
foolish and impious than this denouncement of angelic
interference. We ought to "look for redemption." We
ought to be a " people ready and prepared for the
Lord." Christianity, on such a supposition, awaiting
some revision, looking for " the time of reformation," it
would become us to examine every signal, every intimation of the promised and desired event. " If a spirit
or an angel " should speak to us it might be the fitting
means of merging the present economy into one of more
consummate wisdom and grace—and " let us not fight
against God." But, being incapable of abrogation,
every attempt to displace or amend it must be necessarily most presumptuous and profane. And as the
very circumstance that the " word spoken by angels,"
though " steadfast," was inferior in weight and duration
to that " which first began to be spoken by the Lord,"
so assuredly they could not have the power, did we
monstrously attribute to them the will, to innovate
upon what the " Lord of hosts " declared perfect and
left inviolable—a trust to the Church, an inheritance to
the world, until " heaven and earth shall pass away."

The perpetuity of this system might illustrate our
probation. One transgression of the law, exposing us
to the curse, though it does not destroy our accountability, annuls any advantageous use of it. But by the
" everlasting Gospel," preached for the " obedience of
faith," we are placed in a new condition of moral agency strangely attempered by tender mercy. And it shall
be such " witness unto all nations, and then shall the
end come." But this now being proposed " to every

creature," cannot be revoked; and pledged to "even the end of the world," cannot be canceled. The oath of the Eternal Truth, the immutability of the divine counsel, defend it better than all the curses which gather to burst upon the spoiler's head.

And since the transactions of "eternal judgment" are always described as closing this dispensation, it can only be wound up by them on the event of its durability. That great and last day implies a mediatorial relation— the Gospel is the standard to elicit "the secrets of men," and Immanuel is judge.

It is obvious that such a dispensation, constituted to be co-existent with all future time, must resist every view which would impress a new form or foist a strange nature upon it. And if these views be not only foreign but hostile to its most simple elements to its best ascertained principles, then we cannot hesitate for a moment as to the decided part we must take against them. They may be announced in a manner the most sincere, humble, and devout; or with a tone exclusive, pragmatic, and condemning. They may possibly be received by the mind which had hitherto been considered peculiarly gifted and acute. They may have the temporary effect of stirring up the languid feelings, and nerving the remitted efforts, of those who have "left their first love," and neglected "their first works." They may be prized by those who cannot reconcile themselves to religious apathy, but are weary of the daily caution and struggle, self-scrutiny and self-control, which a proper disposition of piety requires, and by which alone a religious stability can be secured. Against these chimeras we have an effectual antidote in the Gospel. Was it *expedient* that Christ should go away that the Spirit might be given? Then the personal presence of our Lord, in its corporeal property, would reverse the most beneficial arrangement. Was the Gospel intended to require "spirit and truth,"

in contradistinction of external show and pomp? Then that anticipation must be unfounded which looks for the restoration of some temple-city and symbol-glory. Was the Gospel to diffuse itself as a universal good without reference to sacred haunts, a Sion or Gerizim? Then it must be a debasement to fetter it with local associations and attachments. Was the Gospel sent to deliver us from the " rudiments of the world," or Jewish economy? Then it must be to throw it back, if we would fashion it after the " pattern " of those "beggarly elements." Was the Gospel, its authority being settled by miracle, left to lean upon its spiritual worth and demonstrative power? Then it must be a confession of insufficiency to desire that the age of miracle may return. Was the Gospel decreed to " break down the middle-wall of partition " between the " commonwealth of Israel," and the " strangers " from it—the nations sacred and unclean— so that Jewish apostles, Hebrews of the Hebrews, though they had " known Christ after the flesh," according to country and lineage, would " henceforth now know him no more? " Then how wild a perversion of its intention is to be found in the theory which would preserve that people in national distinctness subsequently to their conversion, and give them allocation in their ancient land. Was the Gospel the common property of all, and did all, upon the belief of it, share the common blessing, so that none had " advantage any way," but all distinctions were lost in the intercommunity of believers? Then can it be conceived that the Jewish Christians of Pentecostal times, now amalgamated in the one blood of all nations, the proselytes of eighteen hundred years, have lost their privileges by their earlier conversion, while, as a reward for the unbelief of so many centuries, they who persist in rejecting Messiah to the last, shall be borne to " the delightsome land," and be reinstated in all their ancestral scenes and immunities? Was the Gospel

intended to teach us to "walk by faith and not by sight?" Then is it not a descent to its majesty, a falling away from its character and purpose, when it "comes with observation," when sense and spectacle are substituted for its divine light and intellectual vision? Be not "moved away from the hope of the Gospel." To these fictions "give place by subjection, no, not for an hour." The plain doctrine of Christ must not be overlaid by human fancies and conceits. The prophecies must be interpreted in accordance with its principles, and not its principles be bent to their language. Possessed of the Gospel, remember He is "faithful who called you to its fellowship." "He cannot deny himself." Let these speculations pass you unheeded by—"touch not, taste not, handle not." Be yours a consistent piety, a steady course, a zealous benevolence. All that is novel in the doctrine and the cast of Christianity must be utter deception; and you are warranted and commanded to regard them as figments and dreams. "If they shall say unto you, Behold he is in the desert, go not forth: behold he is in the secret chamber, believe it not." Such crude and spurious representations make it "another Gospel," introduce an ulterior dispensation; and you know with what emotions the very idea of this attempt filled the mind of Paul: "What carefulness it wrought in him," yea, what clearing of "himself," yea, "what indignation, yea, what fear, yea, what vehement desire, yea, what zeal, yea, what revenge!" And therefore has he recorded his interdict, and therefore has he bequeathed his curse: it stands in characters of flame, it rings in tones of alarm: "And if we, or an angel from heaven, preach any other Gospel unto you than that we have preached unto you, let him be accursed." But spoken in haste, shall it not be retracted? and uttered under excitement, shall it not be subdued? Is it an attitude to be sustained? A bolt to be launched as well as brandished,

and left rebounding until sunk and spent in the last fire? His eye does not pity, his hand does not tremble, his tongue does not falter, his purpose does not abate: "As we *said before,* so *say I now again,* if any one preach any other Gospel unto you than that ye have received, let him be accursed!"

It is an inference fully supported by the text, and naturally connecting itself with the preceding reasonings,

V. That no circumstance or agency can endanger the existence and stability of the Christian Revelation.

If the *first* proposition of this discourse be true, the Gospel cannot be set aside by any *new interpretation;* if the *second* be correct, it cannot by any *counter argument;* if the *third* be just, it cannot by any better substitution; if the *fourth* be established, it cannot by any divine appendage. But still remembering the ceaseless activity, the dark venom, of the human heart; the multiplied causes of hostility against this religion of grace, truth, and holiness; it may not be quite superfluous to bring forth a consideration which tends to "assure our hearts" that no disaster can affect, no change can weaken, the certainties of its safety.

Against Israel, when "the cry was throughout all the land of Egypt" over the judgment of the first-born, it was promised "that not a dog shall move his tongue." The completeness of their protection is thus significantly expressed. But when the security of the Gospel is to be most confidently predicted and most strongly ascertained, *supernatural power* is restrained—a curse incloses it round about, a "flaming sword," turning every way, guards this "tree of life." The treasure of all our hopes and interests is beyond the reach of harm; "neither moth nor rust doth corrupt," and thieves cannot "break through and steal." Man need not be afraid when "prin-

cipalities and powers in the heavenly places," could they be imagined adverse, might be reasonably and boldly defied !

There is a cowardice which masks an unbelief. It dwells in gloom, is restless with suspicion, " tears are its meat day and night." It trembles, and never shouts, for the ark. It portends calamity, and cannot prophesy good. The wind whispers in the ear of these faint-hearted ones but to threaten a storm; the glassy surface but curls, and they apprehend all the horrors of ship-wreck. Trust they their cause ? Lurks no doubt of it within ? Why their fears of expanding intellect and increasing knowledge ? Can the religion of light be assisted by darkness ? Can a too piercing eye be fixed on the truth of heaven ? Infidelity has often boasted loud ; but we are not, as yet, awed by its authority, or intimidated by its manner : we do not yet forego our belief in Christianity—are neither inclined to write its epitaph nor chant its dirge !

We do not mean to say that no temporary and local injury can be inflicted on this sacred cause. And chiefly is the perversion of its intentions baleful. Its *grace* is too frequently hampered, its *practice* relaxed, its *simplicity* sophisticated, its *spirituality* secularized, its *dignity* debased. The external shock has, however, more generally consolidated its strength and insured its stability. Still, it is not less imperative on us to feed the fire because the assailants cannot overthrow the altar on which it is kindled.

And how feeble are all the powers of human resistance to Christianity ! They are as the wax and the tow in the flame. Wit the most subtle, strength the best com-pacted, the aptest skill, the mightiest influence, have all been arrayed against it. The activity has always been in the ratio of the force, and both in that of the malignity. But have its enemies prevailed ? Should its friends be

disheartened? "Associate yourselves, O ye people, and ye shall be broken in pieces; gird yourselves, and ye shall be broken in pieces; take counsel together, and it shall come to naught; speak the word, and it shall not stand; for God is with us."

We have, in the first ages of the Gospel, specimens of every possible variety and strength of opposition? and in the ascendency which it obtained over them, we can exhibit the earnests of its continued and ultimate triumph. Sophistry was never more wily than that which it baffled, power more colossal than it prostrated, persecution more wasting than it survived. The second conquest is always easier from the very trophies of the first: its plan is matured, and its confidence invincible. The names which once expressed the most formidable hostility, are now but by-words of weakness and echoes of contempt; and the monarchies which shed the blood of the saints, and attached fearful notoriety to themselves by their cruel excesses, have perished, like volcanic isles sunk back to the deep from which they had been heaved; or, if in any shape they still endure, only resembling them whose fire is utterly quenched, and which just rise above the waves—a blasted mass of desolation!

And nothing short of a perfect conviction that this is the triumphant destiny of Christianity can do justice to it, or act out that devotion and heroism with which we should regard it. And what better calculated to inspire such confidence can there be, than meditation on this emphatic daring of apostolic faith and zeal? The whole array of creatures, the concentration of created power, would not constitute occasion of terror or crisis of danger; an angel from heaven would only rush upon a curse: in God we will praise his word, in God we will put our trust, we will not *fear what flesh can do!*

It is observable with what intense complacency and delight the being is regarded by the moral universe who

is engaged in the promotion of Christianity. Honors surround him, welcomes pursue him, and a chorus of benedictions bursts upon his head: "How beautiful are the feet of them that preach the Gospel of peace!" But if its herald he thus honored and greeted, however mean in himself, as loathed is its adversary, however mighty. And did an angel, though he could "set his right foot on the sea and his left on the earth," preach any other Gospel, the curse of heaven and earth should scathe him, and he should "be brought down to hell, to the sides of the pit!" But O, ye blessed ministering spirits, to whom such an act is most alien and averse, we do not dread, we cannot deprecate, your interference! By all your loyalty to truth, by all your fervor of benevolence, ye could not do it! Ye are gathered together with us in Christ! Ye sing in concord with the redeemed from among men! We will not wrong, by such a doubt, natures so pure, beings so kind; while we feel that the argumentative supposition, by its tremendous force and glaring impossibility only more plainly assumes and strongly establishes, how perfectly ye must be abhorrent of the treason, and incapable of the blasphemy!

And these contemplations tend to impress us with the purpose of Jehovah, amid all the fluctuating scenes of time. It is the Gospel which gives them their meaning. Insulated from this, they pass without coherence, and are laid without plan; they are convertible to no use, and descriptive of no moral. But the divine purpose thus explains itself. By the light it casts upon them, innumerable events become manifestly uniform and consistent. The end of all things is to perpetuate and diffuse the only remedy for human guilt and sorrow. But for this, our history would be no more drawn out, and our planet cease to roll. This is the cause of Him who hath "the government on his shoulder;" and to this trust there is universal subordination. And he hushes and

binds the elements, speaks the calm, commands the pause, that in it the voice of mercy may be heard, the appeal to sensibility may be urged, "Be ye reconciled to God." The dispensation of the Gospel—with all the state of a *reign*, the munificence of a *gift*, the fidelity of a *testimony*, the sureness of a *promise*—stretches itself out to the utmost limit of mortal interests. It shall endure coevally with man. Every breath we draw, every moment we exist, every step we take, is beneath this dispensation of grace. To us it calls, every-where it finds a voice, and it shall accent the "last syllable of recorded time." To give it an ampler theater, all nations shall be subdued unto it; and the ages are held back that it may obtain a longer opportunity. The final convulsion is arrested—the Father, who hath "put the times and seasons in his own power," checks their flight; the Saviour, "expecting until all his enemies become his footstool," is content to wait; and the "souls under the altar" refrain their importunity, and rejoice in the delay. Its trumpet of jubilee shall never be silenced, save by the trumpet of judgment; its light shall never fade, but in the embers of the last conflagration; its "joyful sound" shall never die, except in the uproar and crash of dissolving worlds; its "lively hope" shall only be buried in the grave, and under the wreck, of the universe. All things must be destroyed ere it lose its power or abdicate its claim. The massive architecture of the heaven and the earth takes it into their date, and suspends it on their durability. It lasts while they can last. It only ceases when the mountain sinks, when the ocean dries, when the poles refuse to turn, when the skies shrivel up like a burning scroll, when "heaven and earth shall flee away!" And even then its dispensative form alone is affected—its principles are invariable and indestructible—are of " the things which cannot be shaken "—and shall expand through a still more con-

genial medium and worthy economy, whose sphere is "in the highest," whose glory is "in light," and whose consummation is "God all in all!" Feeble are our present thoughts, confused our perceptions; we see every thing as from behind a cloud and in a disproportion. Our convictions are more like conjectures, and our speculations, dreams. We "know in part" and therefore perplexedly. Our conceptions are infantile, and as infantile are our minds. But we shall soon emerge from this state of crude fancies and immature ideas. Worthy sentiments and feelings will fill up our souls. Each view shall be as a ray of light striking its object, and each song be the very echo of its theme. Then shall we adequately understand why apostles kindled into indignation, and shook with horror, at the idea of "another Gospel;" and why even angels themselves must have been accursed had it been possible for them to have divulged it!

"The word of the Lord endureth for ever. And this is the word which by the Gospel is preached unto you." Amen.

III.

THE COUNSEL OF GAMALIEL EXAMINED.

And now I say unto you, Refrain from these men, and let them alone: for if this counsel or this work be of men, it will come to naught: but if it be of God, ye cannot overthrow it; lest haply ye be found even to fight against God.—Acts v, 38, 39.

The senate of Israel is now in solemn session and anxious deliberation! Though Palestine was considered a vanquished country, and groaned beneath a foreign yoke, still the council of the Sanhedrim retained a large jurisdiction. The Roman policy was very tolerant, paying a nice respect to the religious prejudices and usages of the nations which it had subjugated by its arms. Gallio most properly refused to arbitrate the differences of " words and names" belonging to a particular "law." Festus equally "doubted of such manner of questions." This assembly, therefore, kept possession of its powers, and held its regular consultations, long after the land which it adorned had lost its independence, and become a vassal in the train of universal conquest. It continued to be the high court of appeal. Its constitution was most imposing. It comprised all that was venerable in *religion*—the chief priests and presidents over the courses of the temple. It comprehended all that was elevated in *rank*—the elders and princes of the tribual states. It added to itself all that was acute in *learning*—a select number of the best lettered scribes. These seventy men

were supposed to embody the genius of the ancient dispensation, to constitute the living representatives of an illustrious succession of kings, pontiffs, seers, prophets, and bards. But how unlike, are the hoary persecutors, the fathers whom Moses, at their institution, "set round about the tabernacle," and to whom the Lord, having taken of the Spirit that was on his servant, gave the same mighty inspiration, so that they "prophesied and ceased not." "The judges are" not "as at the first," nor "the counsellors as at the beginning." Jerusalem no longer gathered her "beautiful flock." Zion no more travailed with her "precious sons." "How is the faithful city become a harlot! it was full of judgment; righteousness lodged in it; but now *murderers*." A deep and heavy cloud of guilt and doom now hung over its towers. Before this tribunal a few poor illiterate fishermen, the abettors of an improbable story, the apologists of a crucified convict, have, some short minutes since, been arraigned. But a few months have elapsed from the day in which their Leader, under the triple charge of treason, imposture, and blasphemy, was put to death with every circumstance of ingenious cruelty and accumulated infamy. His hands and feet had been transfixed with nails; the sentence of accusation had surmounted his head; while around his brows, in derision of his pretensions, his enemies had platted a fillet of thorns; and the spear of the executioner had pierced his side, and rioted in his heart. Torture had itself been racked, contempt was itself exhausted, in sharpening his agony, and execrating his name. Small was the assistance he was likely to derive from the zealots who have just been displaced from the bar. Did they promise well as the guardians of his memory, and the champions of his cause? He had been betrayed by one, denied by another, and forsaken by all. His death had struck panic into their spirits. All their hopes fled with his breath, and were

buried in his grave. It is true, that informed of his resurrection, they began to rally; and certified with a perfect demonstration of its truth, they set themselves in array. But the authorities which had decreed and inflicted the sentence were not to be intimidated. They had sealed the stone! They had commanded the watch! They make light, and speak contemptuously, of this strange report! Yet, soon the case assumed a serious complexion. The coward fugitives who abandoned their Lord, shrinking from the first signal of danger, now presented a show of defiance, and rooted themselves into a stand of resolution not to be mistaken. Nor did they act alone. Accessions, by thousands at a time, poured into the new confederacy. The city was filled with his doctrine. It intruded into the recesses of the temple. Its infection had reached the august chamber, where the "masters" and "rulers" of the nation sat in judgment. Hesitation and compromise came too late. The time for debate had gone by for ever. A strong part must be taken, an immediate blow must be struck. The course they took was to confront the partisans of this wide-spreading attestation with all that power can display to overawe, and learning suggest to confute. And what a spectacle of grave dignity, and reverend office, had they to sustain; what an encounter of crafty and malignant opposition had they to resist. How unequal the contest! How stern the inquisition! How hopeless the defense! But there, in yon now vacant space, they stood—the intrepid adherents of the crucified Galilean— whose cheeks shall never more blanch with fear, whose hearts shall never more sink in despair! They were erect and unruffled. Their air and tone agreed to their theme. They knew not to droop beneath the indignant glances which loured upon them. Their faces kindled into the expressions before which, in after times, monarchs trembled, and lions are said to have crouched.

Their's was the majesty of innocence ! Their's the armor of truth ! Their's the eloquence of conviction ! The gray-haired hypocrites were cut to the heart. They could not endure another moment the presence so holy, the bearing so undaunted, of the very men whom they had hoped to put to silence and to confound with shame. The Apostles were " put forth "—an interval was wanted to recover from surprise and vexation—and in that pause, Gamaliel rises and propounds his advice.

I. Let us examine the views which suggested, and the reasonings which supported, this judgment in its general form and influence.

The admonition of the text is really a favorite one. It is the subject of common, and almost proverbial, admiration. It receives applause as the very pattern of clear and sober opinion—of sound and discriminating *sense*. It has obtained credit for higher qualities—and here are supposed, by some, to lie the rudiments of profound political knowledge—the acuteness of the jurist, and the comprehension of the statesman. Even the springs of moral nature have been considered as open to its insight. In short, the advice has been the theme of unmeasured panegyric; and the speaker has been ranked among the foremost of those whom nations and ages love to esteem the oracles of wisdom and ornaments of candor.

And it must be allowed that it discovers a favorable contrast to the current sentiments and practices of those ruder times. Violent outrages were threatened and wreaked against the Christian cause. These it deprecated. It demanded an overt neutrality. It would not oppose principle by force. It relies upon certain tendencies in such principle to perpetuate or destroy itself. Can any thing be more incongruous than external resistance to opinion? any thing more foolish than its instigation ? any thing more ineffective than its use ?

Then may the " word of God be bound "—then may the human spirit be narrowed within the body's dungeon, and shackled by the body's chain, when the sunbeam can be severed from its source, and coerced by every accident foreign to the laws and operations of light. Persecution is so unreasonable, that whatever is adverse to it takes a strong color of probability—acquires an impress of sagacity and a semblance of truth. We have but to read the edict of Decius to extirpate the religion of our faith and profession ; and the praise of the counsel which issued from Gamaliel, by the mere recoil of the feelings may be carried to a disproportionate indulgence.

Yet, after all, this is not a lofty style of thought. It is selfish and timid. It reveals a contracted notion of things. The heart which beats in such a statement is shrunk and cold. There is but the cunning of wisdom without any of its nobler claims, and the cowardice of forbearance without any of its proper virtues. In the mediation proposed we cannot fail to mark the absence of all fine sentiment and delicate sensibility—all independence of character, all love of freedom, all overflow of generosity. A sinister policy dictates the whole ; one chilling reference to interest proves how each genial fountain of mere natural emotion was dried up in the man who could confine himself to it ; age seems to have frozen any sympathy which interest might have spared ; and if there was nothing to censure, there would still be nothing to commend.

But a cold correctness is not the fault of this advice.. The advice itself is not unexceptionable. Several objections may be taken to its principles and motives.

1. It proceeds on a misconception of what belongs to *different kinds* of truth, and of what may be *their operations.*

We all can understand that truth embraces many

particulars. It is true that the sun enlightens our planet, and that our planet revolves on its axis; it is true that straight lines crossing one another, of four unequal, must constitute altogether the same number of right, angles; it is true that certain persons have lived at such a time, and acted in such a way, exactly as history has described them; it is true that we think and feel, though no other can interfere with the evidence of our personal consciousness; it is true that the revelation of the Gospel is given, and that all its contents are certain. These diversities might be expected to operate differently on the mind, according to the degree in which they come into contact with it, affecting more or less its interests and passions.

There could be no doubt that some of the reasonings which the shrewd Rabbi urged would apply to *common error* and *truth*—those which involve physical objects and external facts, those whose perception leaves our affections and pleasurable susceptibilities in some sort of indifference. Of what can we be more sure than that *error* concerning nature, with all its train of popular delusions, shall *cease?* Does it not yield to knowledge, as necessarily as night to day? And we entertain the same confidence, that once exploded it is not in the power of error to *revive.* Who could restore the vulgar prejudice of the solar circumvolution? Who could raise to its former ascendency the foolery of certain debasing superstitions? And of what can we be more sure than that *truth,* in many of its branches—scientific and political—shall *prevail?* Does it not dispel the intellectual darkness with the same certainty that light triumphs over that which is elemental? And it is not in its nature, once known and appreciated, to *decline.* Who could annul those strong impressions which, however related to truth, are often blind to the proofs of its establishment? Who could break up that system of

observation and experiment which has created for philosophy so distinguished a rank and so proud a name?

And there are sufficient explanations of the causes which influence this recession of error and advance of truth, this impossibility of the one's restoration and of the other's failure. That can be easily *resigned* which did not touch on our moral nature; when the resignation curtails nothing that we enjoy, and checks nothing that we love. It harmonizes with our curiosity for knowledge, and our ambition of improvement. And that will be readily *embraced* which is speculatively great and attractive—truth, which makes the mind expand and the imagination glow—if it intrude not on the habit of sensual compliance, and bind not a yoke on the neck of mental pride. I have no *interest* in maintaining that colors are inherent in the substance they embellish; and, therefore, as it does not disturb a single portion of my choice or point of my desire, I acknowledge that the effect is produced by a prismatic division of the colorless ray. I have no *interest* hostile to certain problems; no stake of happiness but that which seeks the satisfaction of knowing the precise condition of the case, whatever the manner in which they are solved. Nothing to my most immediate and intense feelings is it, how many units compose a sum, how many sides constitute a figure, how many atoms build themselves up in a mass. But moral error has another hold—" men love darkness rather than light, because their deeds are evil." Moral truth may offend by its mysteriousness, its humbling representations, its holy requirements. The man who boasts that he hates error, now finds that it is " the error of *his way*," the idol of a long-cherished devotion, that he must forsake. The ardent inquirer after truth now learns that these propositions must be embraced— that man is a sinner, lost in ignorance, guilt, and pollution; that no effort, on his part, can obtain for him

knowledge, pardon, and sanctity; that God alone can impart these blessings; that they must be received with an unmixed sense of gratuitous obligation; that none are more welcome, and none are less, than others to their possession; that the salvation of the Gospel is absolutely fashioned on the principle of excluding every pretense of desert and fitness in him who accepts it, and of reserving the perfect glory to its Divine Author. These "are hard sayings." And, therefore, error constantly renews its opposition; and, indeed, in every human heart wages afresh the long-continued war. And, therefore, truth has to debate its every step, to maintain its every advantage; and though again and again established, has again and again to work the same process, and to uphold the same vindication.

Observe, then, that *moral error* is not necessarily unstable and transient. It has a coexistence with human nature, and may be traced with distinctness to that source. It is rather a part of it, its spontaneous growth, than any thing foreign which has fastened on it. It is too flattering to the principles of our depravity, too congenial to "the deceitful lusts," to lose its entail or provoke its fate. Paganism still lifts itself up in its might. Antichrist still stretches out the cup of its sorcery. If deficiency of evidence, weakness of claim, perniciousness of effect, could have counter-worked these systems, long since it must have been seen that they were not "of God;" long since must they have "come to naught." But they have often recovered the ground they had lost, and have spread themselves over lands once better favored and enlightened. The "deadly wound" inflicted on the hydra has been "healed." Its resuscitation, as beheld by the prophet, is confirmed by our experience, "it was, is not, and yet is."

And observe that there is no necessary victory to *moral truth.* It is certain that general sophistry will be

detected, that general misrule will be retrieved, that general prejudice will be dissipated; but it is not inevitable that what rebukes a self-righteous temper, humbles a vain understanding, restrains a licentious heart, shall be admitted into the convictions and affections of mankind. The thirst for knowledge, the zest of civilization, will carry us forward triumphantly toward particular results, none of which impose an interdict upon our mental dispositions and animal propensities. But Christianity meets with the inverse reception — indifference to its discoveries and distaste for its precepts. It is not only a question of historic authenticity and speculative recommendation, it is the *test of the affections.* And, consequently, it is not impossible that such a religion, simply considered in itself—encircled only by its pretensions, and protected only by its appeals—should entirely fail, and utterly perish. In many cases, as to its local habitation, it is swept away. Continents, whose depths had been pierced by it, retain no more its name. The blood of the martyrs has not seldom flowed to leave a mark for vengeance, instead of a seed for the future Church. "The kingdom of God" has been driven from them who hated its benefits and harassed its servants: the opposition has been successful. Who was "able to make war with" the beast? "It was given unto him to make war with the saints, and to *overcome them.*" Indeed, "the truth as it is in Jesus" is so pure, so refined, so ethereal, that, self-supported, it cannot survive a long exposure to the shocks, and subjection to the influences, of the present state—that under this noxious atmosphere the plant of heaven must expire! The reasoning of Gamaliel is founded, therefore, on a confusion of different matters—on a supposition that truth of every kind possesses an equal advantage for coping with the prejudice, and an equal certainty of triumphing over the hostility, of the world.

2. This counsel betrays an ignorance of the *supports* on which *divine revelation* must be rested, and of the *mediums* by which it can only be received.

A religion which is " the counsel and work of God " must always be adapted to the capacities of the creatures to whom it is addressed. A religion of this origin must always be *immediately* valuable, and as such must be as immediately credible. Its business is with the present being in his rapid passage through the day of life that is, " the accepted time, the only day of salvation." Though it contemplates the future, it does not, with a self-contradiction, draw from it the proofs necessary for the satisfaction of them to whom that future can never be disclosed. As it will require " a reason of his hope " from every disciple, so will it appear itself clad with an appropriate authority, and prepared with the instruments of conviction. If its credentials do not unfold at once to all their length—if some innermost winding of the scroll has yet to loosen—still there will always be a sufficient evolution to answer the most inquiring, and to persuade the most cautious.

Of this indispensable condition in every divine revelation, the casuist of the text intimates nothing. His advice and allegations look another way. He thinks not of examining the title of the candidate for the race, he distrusts in every circumstance of the outset, he suspends the venture on the attainment of the prize. To him it is nothing that it has *now* the aspect and presage of one that wins the goal ; it may speed toward it without receiving from him one confident judgment, one anxious look. He leaves it to itself. Durability is the only standard by which he will adjudge it. His own remaining life cannot comprise the suitable term for the catastrophe. He perhaps would have asked centuries to have made the issue sure. And had he, it would have been but a slight aggravation of the folly which sup-

poses the precise period of credibility to fall beyond any one man's opportunity whom its proposals and informations have reached of forming a well-warranted decision. For at that moment, and upon that spot, the argument had assumed its perfect shape, which *now* justifies *our* strongest faith. Christ had risen! All that was wanting was the evidence for the truth of the fact to be derived from the impression and conduct of its witnesses. It had been given! The Apostles were neither regarded by their worst adversaries as deceivers or dupes. Their recent magnanimity had wrung from them, who were their accusers and judges, another concession. As the grave had not been strong enough to detain the Lord of their faith, so they had been miraculously liberated from their dungeon. Thousands had been convinced, whose conviction was certain poverty and death. Why were not these things accounted for? Was the dungeon-gate ever known to open of itself and let go its prisoners? Was death wont to resign its prey? Did the dissolute become pure, and the profane devout, without a cause? Could any unholy error produce such an extension of piety, sweet affection, and meek heroism? To demand a momentary delay, to wish a "more convenient season," was a suicide of reason, an insult on revelation, a turning away from Him "who spoke from heaven," until that voice should be reverberated from distant ages!

We are not, perhaps, adequately impressed with our own share in this infatuation. Why do *we* believe? The reply which points to the argument of *time* may be in some way and measure right; but much deception generally insinuates itself in it. May not our assent be gained by the non-existence of any rival cause? May it not be cheaply given because greater inconvenience might attend its refusal? Has not a romantic feeling determined it? Christianity is now a *venerable* thing,

time-honored, sprung from a remote antiquity. It is *tender* — wrought into the texture of our poetry — a source of joyful and pitying tears. Its stronger features are softened down by their familiarity to our eye. Many would think it alike presumptuous to embrace it when new, and to reject it when old. Its intrinsic value is uninvestigated, and the prejudice is felt according as the date impresses the mind. The pillar of the truth repels or attracts them, not by the inscription, but by the calendar of so recent a construction, or so continued an endurance, from having risen so lately, or stood so long. When Bacon called "truth the daughter of time" he was correct as to his general extent of meaning; but facts must be invariably true, however overlaid with fable and disfigured by superstition; and Christianity, emphatically the *creed of facts* and challenging instant faith, after the lapse of centuries has neither remitted nor increased its claim.

The *disposition* of mind alone accordant with truth, is nowhere to be found in the counsel of this sage. He exhibits no love for it, nor zeal for its progress. And yet, to a properly constituted mind, truth is not less majestic and beautiful than virtue. Fair are her visions! Broad are her realms! Exhaustless are her treasures! And if we receive any dispensation of God, it must be with an esteem as well as assent—an approval proportioned to the conviction. "The love of the truth" is required that we may be "saved." Believers are, therefore, described as "rejoicing in Christ Jesus," and always triumphing in him. Had he, whose language is now discussed, been an "Israelite indeed, in whom is no guile," other sentiments must have been delivered by him. He must not only have believed the law from the "signs in Egypt, and the wonders in the field of Zoan," but have "consented to it that it was good." But is there one sentiment of a noble nature here?

One sympathy with that which, if secular, should interest the reasoning, if sacred, should engross the moral, being ?* Truth has no charm for his subtle eye and hollow heart ; he cares not how the scales may turn, so that he be not troubled to hold them, and is like a dicer throwing for others, reckless of the numbers, which cannot affect him, however they may fall !

And a false idea is supposed of the *way* or *medium* by which religious truth is received into the mind. It is argued that it must secure an entrance. A mechanical law, a physical force, seems ascribed to it. It is forgotten that mental operations are effected in a very different manner. The avenues of the judgment are not thus to be penetrated, nor the feelings of the heart thus to be won. Air, light, and water must have their scope ; but the mind—and the mind in its fallen state—presents barriers which truth, with all its energy, cannot overthrow. It is necessary to the dignity of truth that it should require another order of faculties beyond that eye and ear and sensible perception which are needed to admit the reality of the grossest, meanest thing. It is due to reason, with which truth coalesces, that it should not be invaded by that which is to become the aliment of thought and the incentive of action. If it were so, man would cease to be a voluntary agent, and there would be no more moral quality or accountable feature in his belief than when he is passive in the impression of his organs. And though the direct conclusion seems not so much dependent on the will as on the premises themselves, yet the original attention to them, the manner of regarding them step by step, are strictly responsible acts. Nor is there any complexity in these representations ; for as we enforce the cultivation of health, and only intend its means, so we urge the *conviction* of the mind, when we principally desire all the preparatives for it. " The law of faith," and " the obe-

dience of faith," necessarily imply accountability; accountability supposes volition; and these positions must endure while the letter and spirit of inspired truth correspond with each other.

Nor was this prejudice confined to him in whose proposals we now trace it. It has extended down to our times. It has received much favor from those pseudo-systems which would screen themselves under the name of philosophy. We hear that opinion is that over which man has no control. We hear of the omnipotence of truth. There is an invariable idea of force. It is to make its way.* It is to press onward. It is likened to the surge of the flowing tide. In it is heard the tread of armies. But all these statements leave out of them the " evil heart of unbelief." Is it not certain that passion may lead different persons to the contrary interpretation of the same document, and interest, to that of the same statute ? Our wish is parent to the thought; and beneath the influence of bias a change comes over us, as when the very letters of some writing wear an unnatural color to the diseased eye.

And let them pause whose sneering indifference prompts them to say, " We shall see." The blessing of Christianity is on them " who have not seen, and yet have believed." Not that these shall be denied sensible and resistless proof. Their eye shall behold the flaming pomp of the disparted sky, and final judgment. On their ears shall ring the clangor of the last trump. They shall feel the fervent heat in which the elements dissolve. Even *their* infidelity shall be quelled. Even *their* depravity shall be incapable of throwing a dreamy incertitude over these scenes. There *can* be but one conclusion, but it comes too late !

3. The counsel which we now consider evinces a *temper of mind most timid and cowardly.*

* Fit via vi.—VIRGIL.

To some the character of this lawyer presents many attractive points. They grow ingenious in its defense. They consider him as by no means to have expressed his full convictions. They commend his prudence and debating skill in turning aside the real question. They claim indulgence for him from the exasperated state of his colleagues. They have intimated that he was a Christian at heart. To this it may be replied that any earnestness in his speech is that of panic, any sobriety that of carelessness : that the profane comparisons of a Theudas, who " boasted himself to be somebody," with the humble Jesus, who shunned them who would have " made him king "—of a Judas rebelling against " the taxing " with Him who enjoined on all to " render to Cesar the things that are Cesar's "—argued an ignorance of his character and a distrust of his cause perfectly incompatible with the faintest leaning, the most latent favor, toward him.

The simple restraint upon a persecuting spirit, which otherwise would have been let loose, is the *dread of consequences.* He may have possessed some features of superiority over his brethren : natural temperament and advancing age may have stood him in service. Yet, what is the whole address but a driveling calculation ? Remove the possibility of a recoil and a retribution, and the council would never have heard of these accommodating measures, nor received this reproof of their sanguinary intentions. Let him incur no risk, and the altar of truth may rend asunder ! To set his conduct in a right point of view, we must avail ourselves of a contrast. There was brought up at the feet of this very Gamaliel a young man of Cilicia, " taught according to the perfect manner of the law of the fathers, and was zealous toward God." The proficiency of the pupil did honor to the instructor. But he could not have learned from him any moderation but the most pusillanimous.

Though he would not be taught to persecute, he would quickly see that its evil was not so much censured as its inconvenience was shunned. He would be too acute to be blinded by his master's affectation of piety, in the caveat which he pronounced concerning the danger of "fighting against God." Saul had not acquired the sycophancy of that school; he disdained artifice and compromise. So long as he continued the adversary of Christianity he was most ingenuous. "He thought with himself that he ought to do many things contrary to the name of Jesus of Nazareth; which things he also did." He forswore parley and quarter—violent in his hostility, but undisguised. His was a fearless and unblenching course. By the influence of that grace which he was always loudest in acknowledging, and of which the accompanying miracle was but the sign and emblem, he renounced his hatred to the Gospel, becoming its champion as resolutely as he had been its foe. We shudder while we pursue that bloody page of his story, but there is no imprint of dissimulation. The uprightness of his nature is now seen in all the intrepidity of Christian and apostolic zeal. It is as sustained as fervid. The synagogue of Damascus first heard the voice of the convert who had approached the gates of that city with a far different commission, and the temple-porches of Jerusalem next beheld him exposed to all the contempt and malignity of the men whom he had abandoned. But he had chosen his part, his spirit rose to it, and his cry, as he rushed into the fight of the world, was this: "*I am not ashamed of the Gospel of Christ!*" When unconverted, he knew not his preceptor's misgiving; converted, he loathed his servility. And even among his colleagues Gamaliel might have found examples of a firmer purpose. Joseph and Nicodemus had indeed yielded for a time to an unworthy duplicity. Of one we know, and of the other we may most reason-

ably presume, that "he had not consented to the counsel and the deed of them," while no such exculpation can be pleaded for the man who had far greater influence than both. His voice had not been raised to save the meek Holy One, whom none could "convince of sin." There seemed no danger, and, therefore, no impolicy, in shedding his blood. Events now wear another aspect; and only on their account would he *now* stop. But these his brethren avowed the Christian cause in its agency, in its exigency, in its agony, when it vibrated between a cross and a tomb—when each look of pity, and each sigh of lamentation, were certain of notice and resentment — then the former "went in *boldly* unto Pilate and craved the body of Jesus;" and the second, who "at *the first* came to Jesus by night," now assisted in giving that crucified corpse its embalmment and sepulture. Faith and love "cast out their fear."

But let us not be too sure that the conduct we reprobate is unknown among us. There are those who profess a middle course. They will not commit themselves to the Gospel; but they abstain from all direct opposition to it. It may, or it may not, be true. Leisure is not afforded them, power is not given them, to determine. At one time their tone is that of indifference, at another that of dislike; but in both cases it is chastised with an inward tremulousness. There is no decision. Yet may it easily be perceived that there is a purpose which they dare not gratify. With all their expressed complaisance and respect for it, they hardly endure it. O could the possibility of its truth be disproved—did they know that it was "of men"—how many mouths would open in scoffing and virulence against it! O what disclosures would innumerable hearts make of their enmity and perverseness! The decencies of an external respect would be withdrawn, each mask would fall, and an unmitigated depravity would be witnessed in contest with it. But

if it should be true! If it be certain that he who "believeth not shall not see life!" Therefore as they cannot quite invalidate it, they will not run the hazard of its sentence, nor speak triflingly respecting its vindication. Otherwise ridicule would soon have shot all its shafts, envy expended all its poisons, and hatred mustered all its onsets! They cannot dare the persecutor's fate, lest the Gospel be true; they cannot welcome the Christian's self-denial, lest it be false! It is the stronger side they seek, and about which they only care. However that may be, they exercise no impartiality in the determination. The love of sin makes them disbelieve, the fear of punishment induces them in that disbelief to waver. Their forbearance is policy, their hostility is disposition.

Hitherto we have examined Gamaliel's views and reasonings in their general form and influence; but there may be a particular truth and justice in them, when they are tried by specific circumstances, without redeeming his motive, or justifying his intention in their use.

II. Let us proceed to inquire into the testimony of fact, and the experience of history, as to the application of these argumentative principles in the present instance.

Success and perpetuity are not the necessary tests of truth. These have often been boasted and pleaded by falsehood. Many gross delusions have extended as rapidly, and endured as permanently, as Christianity. Indeed, an argument drawn from the continuance of a religion is untenable and self-destructive. For it may, after all, be subverted. To rest our faith on such a proof, is really to suspend it on what time may cast down; for any thing that can be shown to the contrary, religions may succeed each other in an indefinite series.

And the argument is not redeemed by an appeal to Divine interposition. Most truly this "teacher of the law" expresses a portion of confidence that God would

so undertake for truth as to identify himself with it, and to render opposition to it a " fighting against " himself. But it must be remembered, that its evidence of divinity is necessarily confined to the introductory stage, and that further extraordinary tokens than are necessary to authenticate that fact would be incompatible with our rational nature and moral treatment. He was contemporary with the only manifestations of omnipotence of which a religion, spiritual and credible, can admit, and for which they could be beneficial!

But when the nature of the Gospel is examined, it will not be difficult to exhibit it with most happy advantage by the lights we borrow from reasonings unworthy in their original motive, and unjust in their common reference. Its peculiarity will justify the application.

What cause has been met with such unsparing contempt, and pursued with such implacable rancor? The " holy child Jesus " was refused even the stable's shelter and the manger's rest; and driven into a distant land. His course was prefigured in these early indignities—contumely refrained not from " shame and spitting "—and all was consummated by a cross. Accordingly, his Gospel had an origin, if human estimates be consulted, the most unpropitious. It possessed not patronage, wealth, power; it had no lure to popularity, no passport to fame. It knew its own repulsiveness, but sought not to lessen the " stumbling block," or to extenuate the " foolishness." Concealment was not thrown over a feature of its aspect, apology was not heard in a tone of its appeal. Nothing in appearance, nothing in pretension, could be more perplexing to the sense, more repugnant to the taste, of mankind. Its *doctrines* put man into the relationship of a guilty, rebellious creature, and told him of a pardon through a medium which more revolted him than the sentence it remitted—of a repentance in a connection which only fomented the depravity

it should have bewailed. Its *lessons* were as strange : the classic virtues were proscribed, and the admiration which had hitherto descended upon them, was turned into all the contempt which its kind genius can know. It substituted whatever men had scorned for whatever men had worshiped ; of their loathings excited their aspirations ; and inculcated sensibility in the place of stoicism, humility in that of haughtiness, meekness in that of revenge. Its *advocates* had not a worldly polish to captivate, or a scholastic erudition to convince. Their enemies "perceived that they were unlearned and ignorant men." What reasonable hope could be entertained that a religion so beset with difficulties, so disfavored by circumstances, so singular in principles, should prevail?

The history is, however, incontestable. Christianity did spread itself over the inhabited world. The second century had not closed ere it was wrought into the temper of the times as well as diffused through the mass of the nations. It has left monuments and traditions where it is now unknown. Its enemies have written its triumphs. They were too notorious for the historian to omit them, and too interesting to remain untold by the correspondent. Could the more local and uncourtly narratives and epistles of the first ages be recovered, what an assemblage would they form of pagan surmise and consternation! What disheartenings would have been discovered in the camp, had some Christian hero entered it, and heard each "man tell his dream unto his fellow!" Christian apologists alleged as much : pitied the sculptors of unsaleable gods, and the priests of deserted temples. Now its progress and its durability do convince us

1. That it is "*a counsel and work of God.*"

Its distinctive character is derived from a crucifixion. That mode of death was a proverbial execration. It was, in the present case, made most ignominious. A

seditious murderer was preferred to the Sufferer, and thieves were put to death on either side. No insult was spared. He was scourged, He was derided, He was outraged—He sank beneath his cross; contrary to custom, his body was torn open by a lance; and the reason why it was not left on its gibbet to blacken in the sun and to wither in the storm, was a notion which connected with it uncleanness. Nor was this distinctive character at any time the subject of compromise. There was no attempt to extenuate a single part of it. The cross—long before warriors had made it a pretext of slaughter, and bigots the idol of superstition—formed the ensign of a bloodless victory, and the badge of a votive dedication. Could this stigma have been concealed, the name of Jesus might have been applauded in the Capitol, and his image have filled a niche of the Pantheon. But this was resounded, this was particularized, this was entoned, in every discourse, in every narrative, in every song. " My Love is crucified ! " was the rallying cry ; and with it the martyrs awaited the spring of the brinded monster, and saw curling around them the devouring flame. They " gloried in the cross."

It must be remembered that Christianity resorted to no subterfuge. It sought no distant realm, it reserved itself for no less inquisitive time. It asked its trial in the scene of those events of which it is but the interpretation, and claimed it at the very crisis when all was recent and to be easily decided. Close by the " place of skulls," at the mouth of the " new tomb in which never man was laid " until the remains of its Founder were deposited in it, it demanded the investigation. How unlike fraud ! How removed from chicane ! Nor was it a barbarous age; but one of professed candor, of indisputable acuteness, of characteristic refinement, of deep discourse. And the manner of the Apostles was that of perfect ingenuousness. They did not cautiously

break the intelligence. There was no policy in the slowness of communication. Nothing could exceed the distinctness, the nakedness of their disclosures. The "offense of the cross" was given a designed prominence, and not vailed with a prudential disguise.

It was indebted to no common aids of popularity. Instead of being associated with *patriotism*, it was denounced as an anti-national parricide. Instead of lending itself to the indulgence of *sensuality*, and seeking the favor of the voluptuary, it binds all its followers to a perpetual self-denial. Instead of courting *civil protection*, much less *alliance*—though truly the best guides to Governments, and the surest defense of States —it was the victim of their unrelenting hostility. Persecution was indeed a novelty in that era. Though it had always been directed against the adherents and principles of the True Revelation, yet among the "heathen who now raged" it was generally unpracticed. Their intercommunity of deities counteracted it. As the tutelary was restricted to a certain space and people, the traveler had to avail himself of the genius presiding over each strange land. But Christianity was exclusive. It had no sanction for rival claims. It followed the language of its God: "Is there a God beside me? yea, there is no God; I know not any." And what a burst of fury had it to engage! Cruelty had never devised, until now, a moiety of its tortures. It became fertile of invention. It wound still hardier nerve about its heart. The beast of the amphitheater seemed to learn its new lesson, and fire acquired a power of more lingering torture. Yet the Church was not left a waste. It grew like the grass beneath the scythe. It multiplied in the proportion of its devastation, wrought success from disaster, and found gain in loss. A few remarks will complete the argument we wish to establish: That the progress of *such* a religion, and in *such* circumstances,

proves it to be divine. Now, *first*, Christianity must necessarily be a widely and rapidly extending cause. It was not enough that it had capabilities for extension; it was indispensable that it should be extended in *fact*. For this was what the Jewish prophets foretold when every prejudice confined revelation within the borders of their land; and it was frequently and variously announced by Christ, when all probability forbade the hope that, after a few years, his name should even be remembered. So that if the Gospel did not swiftly advance and generally prevail, it would have been deficient in a particular branch of evidence requisite to authenticate it. For either then the predictions were false, or it was not the system intended by them. And, *secondly*, the progress of such a religion is but the effect of the *continually repeated evidence* involved in its *earliest stage*. We believe, at the distance of so many ages, because contemporaries of its origin believed, because they could not have believed unless they were rationally convinced, because they could not be rationally convinced unless they had adequate means and worthy grounds of conviction, because those means must have been irrefutable, or they would not have incurred martyrdom in yielding to them. Its beginning explains its progress far more than its progress ratifies its beginning. How was it able to continue but from the proofs which gathered around its commencement? How could it be suffered to pursue its course, but from the perfect equipment of its outset? Therefore, thus stands the case. Christianity, without an earthly recommendation and aid, in resistance to interests and powers the most formidable, spread itself over the globe. Its success is attributable to miracle, or it is not. If you concede the affirmative, the debate has ceased; for operations of divine power can never be put forth to abet falsehood; if you deny the intervention of miracle, then the fact

of the progress made by the Christian religion, considered in itself, and in reference to its difficulties, is an inversion of experience, a transformation of motive, a contradiction in the application of principles, an anomaly in the agency of causes, forming altogether a greater system of prodigies than all the miracles of Scripture suppose. Only this choice is left in the dilemma—whether we will call in the explicit principle of miracle, or imagine a chain of extravagances in the place of its lucid consistency.

2. Opposition to the Gospel has always borne the mark of " fighting against God."

Certain principles of a natural theology may be recognized by comparing the common course of events with the established modes of thinking and impression. By looking into the works of God and the consciences of his accountable creatures, we arrive at authorized conclusions. The elements of justice and benevolence are the subjects of clear discovery and immu-able obligation. Order and harmony are ascertained to be as beautiful in mental structure and moral conduct as in the material universe. Law is felt to be not less indispensable in the regulation of our ideas and passions than in the great binding and mobile forces of our planet, and of the firmament in which it rolls. As these are the constitutions of our Maker, we may be assured that nothing of disagreement with them, nothing of violence to them, can be pleasing to his nature, or concurrent with his will. He has given us the faculty to perceive, and the sympathy to approve, them; has placed in our minds the mirror which reflects these external manifestations. These moral rudiments conduct us to " the invisible things " of Jehovah—the moral properties of his being. But it is Christianity which gives to these views their truest precision. Without it they are very general and inefficient, though sufficiently conspicuous

and fixed to leave us "without excuse." We learn from it that the First Cause is infinitely excellent, "glorious in holiness!" It renders its devoutest homage to his *moral character.* It declares this to be the basis of all divine and human relations. "It is written, Be ye holy, for I am holy." Now, it is most observable that the enemies of the Gospel have always professed their dislike to these representations. They have felt that their best hope of undermining it was to reject them. Each step they took toward the subversion of this religion was upon the destruction of these primary sentiments. They disturbed all the foundations of peace and equity. To act their part, it was necessary to efface the impress of these principles from the minds of men; and equally, to deny the existence of their prototypes in the Deity. And was that a career which He could approve? Could He have so entangled these precious interests of individual, social, and moral man with error, that in its overthrow all must perish together? Could He look complacently on opposition to any speculation at the certain sacrifice of all these bonds between earth and heaven? In the school of infidelity there is nothing that allows virtue—it is a prejudice! nothing that respects obligation—it is an expedient! nothing that honors man—he is a machine! nothing that worships God —he is a blind impulse! It fights "against God" in taking "pleasure in unrighteousness;" in its infringement of authority, its scorn of decency, its jarring of order, its love of confusion, its license of blasphemy, its encouragement of libertinism, its relish of blood; and most effectually it makes war against him by trampling under foot that "wisdom that is from above," and which is "pure, peaceable, easy to be entreated, full of mercy and good fruits, without partiality, and without hypocrisy." So that in a most serious sense we may add, "He therefore that despiseth, despiseth not man, but God."

They who admit that there is a God, cannot altogether exclude him from the government of the world. However they may attempt to hamper this government by fatalizing causes and general laws, something of a directing mind and conscious volition must be introduced into its administration. As events are not indifferent to any mind and will, so they cannot be to the view of the Eternal; and it is impossible to conceive that he takes an interest in events which he has no power to subordinate and control. He watches not from his throne the stream of a necessarian tendency—he sitteth upon the flood, he is "mightier than the mighty waves." How can the skeptic boast that any portion of favor has been granted to his cause? Can he but confess that the universal course of things has withstood it? If Providence has a design, can he claim its sympathy and coincidence? Has not the elation of infidelity been brief, and the triumph of Christianity lasting? Has a vicissitude affected the religion of the Bible, which it did not engrave among its prophecies? Is not this the difference between the two, that the one looks for its promulgation to some uncertain chance; and that the other, with a sublime repose, knows that it is the care and trust of an Almighty superintendence and purpose? Let the opponent show where his infidelity falls in with these; when it has ever seemed the "counsel and the work of God," favorable to the tenor of divine government, and taking its rank in the scheme of divine decretion—and then, and not until then, can we excuse it from fighting "against God?" "They know not, neither will they understand; they walk on in darkness: all the foundations of the earth are out of course."

Arguing from the most general conceptions of the Creator, we should confide in his design to make his creatures good and happy. His "tender mercies are over all his works." In the care of rational creatures,

he adjusts a proportion between conduct and emotions of pleasure and pain. It is, therefore, our well-being he seeks, that is, our happiness in a particular state of mind and behavior. Benevolence, pursuing morality as its means, is consequently most godlike. But what is the predicament of all contest with Christianity? Is not the attempt pernicious? Does it promote amity? Does it breathe peace? Does it impart consolation? Does it light up smiles? Does it wipe away tears? Is it calculated to yield the mind a satisfaction? Has it been known to give the heart a relief? Can it be in accordance with a Divine " loving-kindness and tender mercy " to present to man the grave as his only shelter, and utter annihilation as his only hope? Is not this to " fight against God," who is " full of compassion," " who comforteth us in all our tribulation ? "

It might be imagined, at least, that they who trifle with our faith and strike against our profession would be influenced by philanthropic feelings. If they deride us and torture us, it will only be a severely curative process. They must awake us by a violent disturbance, by the thunder of their knocking. Now, in contradistinction, we demand, have they a reasonable—to say nothing of a benevolent — determination? What do they propose? Safety is no question between us. Happiness is not mingled in the proffered cup. If they would make us more rational, they mean to allow our animal part a more lawless indulgence. If they paint the vision of a perfectibility, they intend a disorganized community, and a dissocialized individual. They have no ambition to make man less the brute. They labor not to enlarge or brighten his horizon. They arouse him with no appeal of immortality. They infallibly sink, degrade, embitter, mock him! Why do they propagate notions so chill, so contracting, so mortifying? Have they any thing to give in exchange for a

"peace which passeth all understanding?" for "joy unspeakable and full of glory?" for a "conversation in heaven?" *It is thus they ease their pain, thus they reinforce their courage.* The plague-stricken has loved to hear the shriek of the sufferer at his side! He who walks in the dark fears to walk alone.

The bane of infidelity, even as a means of exempting men from the fears of religion, is its inability to give any *certainty*, and to inspire any *assurance.* "In the fear of the Lord is strong confidence; and his children shall have a place of refuge." It is descriptive of the Gospel, that its spirit is not that " of fear, but of power, and of love, and of a sound mind." It overcomes the sense of guilt and the dread of death. There never was the tumult of grief it could not allay. To sinking mortality it can lend the bearing of victory, turn its tear into a triumph, and its sob into a song. Unbelief, *if* it could disprove our religion, never could *certify its own.* It is a system of misgivings. Take your station by the deathbed of which it is not quite ashamed. Listen to some hollow buffoonery, or some constrained bravado. Go not to its common scene of frantic agony and despair. Seek what is more staid and unshrinking. Is this the spirit's befitting passage, if an eternity should be before it? Is seriousness incompatible with such an experiment? Is not the effort of gayety misplaced? Are we illiberal when we urge this failure of all support and holy placidity in dissolution? Can we but feel the contrast which our faith exhibits while, diverting no attention from the pain, and benumbing no sensibility to the awfulness, of the approaching change of worlds, it breathes a balm which no struggle can dissipate, and confers a dignity which none of the ghastly accidents of death—the shroud, the bier, the grave, the corruption, the reptile—can for a moment disturb? It is the religion of the dying! "Death is ours!" That which

some make their taunt we feel our glory. Infidelity here cannot prefer a claim. It has nothing for its unhappy votaries, to confirm and soothe, in the awaited extremity. And the curse of a thousand breaking, broken hearts, is its well-merited reward! "Had I not been by," said Condorcet of the expiring D'Alembert, "he would have flinched too." Combining, then, all that we know of God, he is light, truth, and goodness. If the Gospel be deceit, under his government *deceit*, without any hold of fact and motive of kindness, is the only instrument of amelioration and felicity! If infidelity be well-founded—a ray of divine light, a member of divine truth, an emanation of divine goodness—then, under the same government, it is the instrument of disorder and profanity, lust and blood ; the parent of every crime, and the source of every woe! Remember that it disparages and blots out the moral image of the Deity ; that it evidently forms no part in the scheme of Providence ; that it has no congruity with human happiness ; that it can find no justification in its motives or effects for any attempt to propagate itself; that a shaking, broken reed, only can represent its tremulous unsustaining vanities : remember that these are the very opposites to Christianity—the foils to its excellence, and the contrasts to its power—and then judge ye, whether they who abet the former, can have any thing in common with the character and design of God; whether they who oppose the latter, must not be found "fighting against " him ?

3. The Gospel, being the "counsel and work of God," and being such that none can oppose it without "fighting against " him, it follows that it "cannot be overthrown."

The Divine Being must not only always favor truth, and frown on error and falsehood, but when he has founded a moral dispensation, he will enforce it. These interests may not be visited with his sensible favor and

displacency in individuals; and even he may sometimes suffer a dispensation to be greatly affected by the hostile passions of men. "Truth is fallen in the street." But it is inconceivable, as it would be inconsistent, that he should neglect and abandon it. He has never propounded a law without the intention and means of enforcing it; and a scheme of religion, the most perfect, as being the last, cannot, therefore, but be maintained by him. He will "plead his own cause." His wisdom in its "counsel" must be vindicated. His power in its "work." must be signalized. All things will be rendered tributary and subservient. As Jehovah liveth, he must do this. His enemies must be his footstool. Every arrangement, every event, must hasten to the result of a final ascendency and triumph on the part of "the glorious Gospel of the blessed God." For that end, he will withhold no *evidence* necessary for its confirmation. *Providential succor* shall be granted, at proper intervals, in a manner which only perverseness can mistake. The "cause of truth, and meekness, and righteousness, girds the sword upon the thigh of the Most Mighty, and buckles on his bright and refulgent armor." Long since he has espoused it as his own. For this he shed his blood. For this he shone with his rising glory. For this he was installed on the throne of the universe. For this he wields all power in heaven and earth. Apparently slighted, tottering, perishing, the subject of this trust never waned in his memory, nor languished in his heart. Nor shall it cease to grow, nor fail to surround itself with accumulating strength and splendor. Like the daughter of Zion, Christianity can now "shake her hand" at her enemies. And soon she shall resemble "the great wonder in heaven"—the apocalyptic woman who had the sun for her robe, the moon for her footstool, and constellations for her crown! What is resistance offered to such a Cause of such a

Being? What are confederated powers? "He who sitteth in the heavens shall laugh!" He shall "despise their image!" Yea, he shall send out his arrows and scatter them: he shall shoot out lightnings and discomfit them. Is it his "counsel?" Hear him!—"My counsel shall stand." Is it his "work." Hear him!—"I will work, and who shall let it?" Do they, who oppose these, "fight against" him? Hear him!—"Woe unto him that striveth with his Maker." Our confidence thus lays hold of infallible pledges. "Our Gospel" is irreversible as divine intention, indestructible as divine operation, secure as divine victory. "This also cometh forth from the Lord of Hosts, who is wonderful in *counsel*, and excellent in *working*."

No other source of evidence can strengthen these convictions. They may be varied, however, by a reference to the history of Christianity. The past is an answer to fear. What has it not withstood? Manners, long since refined, must again become barbarous—nations, now civilized, must fall back into a savage state—maxims, exploded by common consent, must revive—ere it can be threatened with its ancient wrongs. It endured, it braved, it baffled them all. And it still towers high and stands firm, as the promontory rock beaten into solidity and swelled into grandeur by the tempests which rage, and the waves which boil, around it!

Gamaliel reasoned most falsely as to the test and tendency of truth; and yet he urged, however blindly and unsuspectingly, much that the believer in the Gospel may apply. And by extending some of his statements and transposing others, we can construct a moral demonstration of its truth, and draw a lively picture of its excellence.

III. LET US NOW SELECT THOSE DISTINCTIVE SENTIMENTS OF CHRISTIANITY WHICH WOULD HAVE PREVENTED THE FALLACIES OF SUCH REASONING, AND STILL ENABLE US TO CORRECT ITS ERRORS AND SUPPLY ITS DEFECTS.

The ignorance which the whole argument of the text not so much betrays as boasts concerning the *nature* of that system which Christ and his Apostles preached, is most inexcusable. Was the mind of this renowned scholar so occupied with the subtleties of his lore that it might not unbend to a theme like this? Was it not a requirement of his station to defend and direct the popular opinion? Was he not, by virtue of his office, " a guide of the blind, and an instructor of the foolish ?" If what purports to be a divine revelation has no external evidence, no decisive proof, that Omnipotence is moving in its favor, perhaps a neglect of its inspection would be justified. But when eclipse, contrary to all material law, mourned this Founder's death; when earthquake shook the house in which his disciples were assembled as the loud answer to their prayer; when tongues, ill-trained to their own language, burst into every speech of earth; when, at a word, the living died, and the dead lived; when the prison rent of its own accord and refused to hold in its gloomy confinement the persecuted disciple, as the grave had no power to retain his crucified Lord; then at least there was incentive to curiosity and ground for inquiry; there was something to rival the glories of the Jewish Church. The healed cripple, whom John and Peter brought with them before the council, was the object of universal notoriety. The council had met most numerously, " rulers, elders, scribes, and the high priest," with all his sacerdotal kindred. There was no misapprehension of the character of the cited parties, the judges " took knowledge of them that they had been with Jesus." And what was the conclusion to which they were compelled to yield? " That a *notable miracle* has been done by them, is manifest to all them that dwell in Jerusalem, and *we cannot deny it.*" After this, where appears the liberality, the candor, the ingenuousness of Gamaliel? Some time, perhaps a year, intervened between this

admission and this advice. That interval was filled up with the most public and decisive miracles. And yet he evidently remained careless and uninformed as at the first, respecting this religion, of which unparalleled signs from heaven had taken the charge and published the sanction!

Examining the contents of the Christian religion, this leader of the Sanhedrim would have found in it averments far different from his crude notions; nothing that might justify delay in acknowledging its veracity; nothing that could leave its glorious futurity uncertain; nothing that made it doubtful whether God would interpose for it; nothing that entitled men to take a negative and neutral position toward it. These are the corrections which the Gospel suggests: let us review them in order.

1. The credibility of this religion is at any given time capable of being brought to issue.

A twofold objection is raised to the reasonableness of this *immediate* claim on the questions of *space* and *time.* The *former* may be thus represented: The Gospel is the " common salvation " of men, without national exception and restriction; it is to be "made known unto all,"— how is it that it covers so few countries, and is believed by so few peoples? Let it, indeed, become universal, and we will embrace it. The *latter* may assume this form: In the vicissitude and flux of mortal things, there is a constant succession of opinions—evidence is counteracted by further evidence, and speculation swallows up speculation; we smile at the dotage of our fathers, and may be ourselves pitied by our children. Let us know the ultimatum, and then, comparing all, we can decide between them. These objections may be met in two ways. We can show that they never can be *applicable* to a moral revelation; since they may overlook whole kingdoms, and exclude whole ages. It might so be that

the conversion of the world is reserved to crown the closing years of time. Conviction is thus suspended upon what countless generations and human varieties can never behold. And this is confirmed by the present date of the objection; it is adduced after eighteen centuries. As it allows that Christianity may be true if ever it accumulate the evidence of catholicity and perpetuity—and on that evidence ought to be believed—so it admits that it may have *all this time been true,* and yet that man was *justified in disbelieving it!* And the prophetic Scriptures do most plainly express that it is in the *latter* days that " all nations shall flow together to the mountain of Jehovah's house; " that the *seventh* angel must sound ere " the kingdoms of the world become the kingdoms of our Lord and of his Christ." Besides, these objections *vitiate themselves.* For if any one has a right to withhold his belief in Christianity until all others profess it, all others must have the same right; and that right being asserted, it is obvious that all must abandon themselves to absolute infidelity. And the reservation of belief on the condition, or in the suspense, of a future religion, is equally contradictory and self-destructive. For unless each individual of the species knew himself of the last generation, and the last of that generation, he would be reluctant to certify, and tempted to doubt, and be only capable of reaching his final decision when all probation shall cease, and all conviction be an act of sense and not of mind, when " there shall be time no longer! "

Our religion is more reasonable. It has addressed every man, whom it found, from the first moment of its mission. Its evidence was always sufficient. It can always assign, what it requires all its disciples to be ready to give, " a reason of its hope." It never rolled out a credential that was defective, nor wore a character which was immature. It came forth with its full perfection. " Beginning at Jerusalem," it showed its fearless-

ness of refutation. It called all men to believe and repent. It declined no answer, it postponed no investigation; it has always said, "To-day, if ye will hear *my* voice." As salvation is a personal business, so it must be accomplished in our term of life. We have nothing to do with number and duration. We are to believe for ourselves, though not a contemporary gave us his fellowship, though not a descendant followed our example. "It is from faith to faith;" its own independent credibility elicits and warrants all our powers of confidence.

A momentary exchange, by imagination, of the era and circumstance falling to different persons of our species, will tend to prove that infidelity has always its pretext, that parties who envy each other may equally repine, and that it is the actual truth of Christianity, as *always* open to inquiry and worthy of acceptance, which holds the steady balance between them. Gamaliel, if sincere, thought that a flight of ages might satisfy all doubt, that they who should be born far onward in the history of the world must attain a settled judgment, and, perhaps glancing to *our* times, sighed for a birthright in them. *Then,* it might occur to him, would be a favored opportunity of deliberating on the problem; *then,* he might suppose, all would be decided by the mere force of events; and *then,* likewise, might seem to dawn before him a day of calm and luster, unobscured by the passions of violence and strife. Too old and selfish to risk any thing, some vision of our epoch might play upon his fancy; and under its influence he might see his own form depicted among the magic creations, his youth renewed with the transfer of his lot. He might even rouse himself to think that, were it real, he would have been faithful among the faithless, and *could* only have pursued a resolute conduct. And if he felt a passing shame, he would point to "the times that went over him and over Israel," blame his destiny, and bewail his misfortune.

But are there none of our age who affect to seek the reverse? Backward they throw "an evil eye." They regret, for all the purposes of belief, that they should live in a country and period so remote from whatever belonged to early Christianity. O could they have traversed the haunts of the first believers; mused in Gethsemane while the ground yet retained the pressure and stain of the Saviour when he agonized there; knelt on Calvary where he fainted, and kissed the blood-spots of his cross; felt the rocking of "the upper chamber" at Pentecost, and seen the cloven tongues; followed the disciples to "their own company," and "broken bread with them from house to house;" beheld the leaping lame, and the risen dead! O could they have been of Gamaliel's generation, they might have accomplished all; had they enjoyed his length of life, all this history would have been included in it; had they possessed his influence of station, they might have commanded access to every detail of fact and branch of evidence! How easy would it then have been to believe! The deeds were recent, the witnesses were at hand! And thus behold "the contradiction of sinners!" Some desire a later, others an earlier scene, of time; some speak of the same substantive proof as if it could be affected by its novelty, others as though it could be enfeebled by its antiquity; all coincide in their contemptuous treatment of the only view of truth, and share of evidence, which, in the nature of things, they can receive. No transition of times, no variation of circumstances, could alter the temper or impress the sensibility of the heart, which at any one stage of Christian history confesses its unconquerableness of doubt, and its impotence of conviction.

2. Christianity is itself a prediction of its own success. The numerous speculations of men have been forgotten, or retained, not always according to their merits. And this, probably, was the most enlarged consideration

which the adviser of his brethren now allowed. Here was ushered on the stage of public notice a class of sentiments into which he had not looked. Such a scheme might or might not succeed. But it was submitted to the eyes of enemies as well as friends; and it ought to have been tried by justice and not thrown to chance. How knew he but that the seeds of mischief, disorder, and impiety were lodged in it? If moral, as well as sensible, evidence crushed the suspicion, was it not a presumption that it contained a treasure that would repay the gaze and the acquisition? There are inventions, maxims, rules of life, means of happiness, which we are assured will last as long as earth and man. They are built on experience. They are related to utility. They bind up with them our best interests and hopes. And so, independently of other tests, we examine the principle, the bosom-genius of Christianity. We know what "glorious things" seers have beheld, and prophets have sung, concerning it; we know how the inspired mantle still waves around its form, and how the heaven-strung harp preludes its course. We see it "coming in the clouds of the prophetic heaven." But had a prediction never intimated its success, we might have forestalled that such was its right and determination. He who discovered and established it, most evidently intended it to engross the world. He could not with any consistency or truth displace it by another dispensation. It is jealous of any rivalry, and avows its purpose of suppression. Its *truth* renders all other pretensions false; its *fitness* proves all other contrivances inapplicable; its *authority* stamps all other interferences treasonous; its *grace* declares all other remedies ineffectual; its *universality* presupposes all other expedients superfluous; its *perpetuity* makes all other chances hopeless; its *unearthliness* exhibits all other projects gross and mean. Some religions have disclaimed a long duration; others have avowed

that they were unfitted for an extended scale. Far different is the announcement of Christianity. Far different is its expansive and immortal principle. Shall *it* be cramped with local shackles, or circumscribed within narrow limitations? Shall the chariots of salvation, whose speed can overtake the sin and sorrow of the world, run the little circles of a tiresome repetition, and not sweep valley after valley, and vault from hill to hill? Shall the wings of mercy, strong for a flight from one end of heaven to another, but flutter across a little country, and brood over an insignificant land? Is it a short-lived discovery? Cannot it claim a property in the deepest future? If this be not its design and scope, if it be not the religion for the whole earth, if it be not in force through all time, then it is at variance with itself. There would be a disparity between its aim and success, a struggle between its aspirations and capabilities. But such a religion may be believed. None can misapprehend its intention. Its own mouth pronounces this oracle! Its own bosom heaves with this ambition! This pledge flashes from its brow! This reward fixes its eye! This goal draws its step! It moves among the nations as something dedicated to greatness! It knows that it is the light of the world. It knows that it shall inherit "the ages to come." Confident in its career and consummation, as in its origin and motive—conscious what it shall be as well as is—it flies upon the spoil before it begins the battle, and predestines the prize ere it girds for the race.

But the worthiness of a religion may be greater than its influence; moral truth may perish in the earth : and Christianity, left to itself, must have shared that fate. We, therefore, proceed to remark,

3. That it is connected with an efficient and appropriate divine agency.

The presumption must always be that God would un-

dertake for his own cause. That interposition might be various. It might be restricted to defense and restraint. It might be employed to assuage the hostility of men, to shorten the arm of oppression, to combine circumstances and events in a favorable manner. But that would leave the evidences and doctrines of such a cause to their own unaided operation. And if they resembled those of Christianity, perfect as they are, they must fail of successful impression. Nothing could make them more cogent and distinct—it is a *subjective* difficulty. The sun may shine, and is not to be censured because the blind do not see. And so it is that this religion, from the beginning, gave the promise of an accompanying power; upon the exercise of that power rested entirely for success; and only spoke of the Spirit of Christ less emphatically than of Christ himself. That an *external* enforcement should follow a " work and counsel of God," was an idea that could occur to Gamaliel. But it is the beautiful originality, the peculiar conception, of our faith, that an *immediate* power is put forth on the *soul,* insuring its success. The Gospel already exists in its perfect truth and reason; nor can any higher quality of intelligence and fitness be superadded to it. But it is not *perceived* nor *appreciated.* " The light shineth in darkness." This power, operating within, convinces us of that guilty state and irreligious disposition under which we labor, and on account of which we need evangelical reconciliation. It assumes forms and takes directions most accurately adapted to our intellectual and moral faculties, and quite sufficient to prove that it descends from Him " who searcheth all things." It not only respects the human mind in all its springs and secrets, but in all its processes harmonizes most exactly with the principles of Christianity. It is the witness to its truth, the seal to its authority, the earnest of its blessedness. It spreads like attraction through the con-

sciousness, breaks like light upon the understanding, and distills like dew over the heart. It brings the Gospel into perpetual contact with man, "makes him willing," transforms him in "the renewing of" the mind, and brings "into captivity every thought to the obedience of Christ." This, this, insures the "counsel and work of God:" this precludes that it "shall come to naught." It is "the ministration of the Spirit." And so it receives a *perpetual sanction;* and draws out a train, along all its march, of *moral evidence and illustration.* Prejudice is turned to admiration, and enmity to love. It is hidden as an operation, it is ostensible in its effect. No contingency can render it uncertain whether the Gospel shall "return void." It shall be allowed, it shall be realized, it shall be eternally celebrated, by a "great number which no man can number." This influence is not, however, necessary to moral government and human accountability. And yet it is so abundantly promised, and is attainable by so certain a course, that they, "not having the Spirit," are as destitute of present excuse as of original claim. Nor let any conceive that the invariable thought and condescension of the Deity, in this influence, is what he will reject as unworthy of him. He assimilates it to the honors of his highest work; compares it with his noblest manifestation of prayer; "For God hath shined in our hearts, to give the light of the knowledge of the glory of God in the face of Jesus Christ."

Had the Gospel been perused by this dastard senator, he must have noticed that it made no allowance for demur and hesitation; that it regarded with no favor those who stood coldly by to see the issue; that it indulged no complacency in them who sought credit on the supposition of their neutrality:

4. It demands a positive character of decision in all whom it recognizes as its followers.

It is strange that men can claim merit in what is simply negative, and imagine that they do a good work by a course of indifference. Thousands, who boast their freedom from bigotry and their abhorrence of persecution, will urge as its ground their general toleration. They suffer others to think! They never interfere with private opinion! But where is the liberality of the sufferance, when we remember the atrocity of the resistance? Vain man! What is thy grace in forbearing to intrude on a province which thou canst never touch? or, if thou couldst, it were a sacrilegious violation? And, in the same manner, thousands express a self-gratulation that they never attacked Christianity with obloquy, nor injured the interests of its disciples. They speak of their enlightened policy in "refraining from these men, and letting them alone." But be it remembered that the very terms savor of an armistice; and that there can be no indulgence in relaxing what there is no right to inflict. Another view now unfolds upon us. The praise of this toleration between man and man we spurn. What new features of impiety does it disclose when its idea is transferred to "the counsel and work" of the Deity! It proclaims not open war with heaven! It does not take up arms against it! And what if it did? Could it fear the assault? But this is too fearful. And, therefore, men will leave the struggle between truth and error, righteousness and sin, to itself, or to other combatants; and though they take no part, they stand ready to grasp the honors of the victory. But far different is the language of Christianity. It rejects all compromise, it disowns all equivocation. It neither reserves to its professors the choice of ease, or the preservation of fame, or the refusal of death. It requires a devotion so complete, that in comparison and competition with it we must " hate father and mother, and wife and children, and brethren and sisters, yea, and

life also, or we cannot be its disciples." It had now spoken with its energy of decision to Gamaliel as it had erst to Matthew : " Follow me." The Publican left the receipt of custom, and the higher functionary should have descended from his judgment seat. If he understood the claim, he prevaricated with it ; declined to assist what he forebore to oppose ; and received the indignant answer and the just retribution which it ever hurls against the time-server and time-waiter — alike against the false friend and specious foe—" He that is not with me is against me ; and he that gathereth not with me scattereth abroad ! "

Brethren, it is temerity, it is frenzy, to " fight against God." It is not the brand and the sword of the persecutor which are necessary to do this. It may be effected by any opposition, however secret, to the mercy, the authority, and purity of the Gospel ! But other things are expected of us. An awful warfare is now in progress around us. " Without are fightings " in which *we* must close. The " good soldier of Jesus Christ " must not shrink. We " war not after the flesh." And it is he only who has " come to the help of the Lord "—who has joined in the glorious strife—that in his death-fall can exclaim, " I have fought the good fight ;" that can enter upon the rewards which are promised to him " that overcometh." These are not days for repose and voluptuousness. " The ark, and Israel, and Judah abide in tents." The battle cry is on the wind ! It is time for the host to show itself with banner and trumpet ! Let its ranks be serried, its ensigns dispread, its onsets resistless ! Take the whole armor of God ! Quit you like men ! Heaven opens amid the waving of palms and the chorus of harps ; and, rushing from the portal, is seen the white horse with Him that sitteth upon it—diadems are on his head, armies in his train—He wears not so much the muni-

tions of the Chief as the trappings of the Victor—and in " righteousness He doth judge and make war !"   Are we loyal to his cause ?   Are we fearless in our avowal? Are we " in nothing terrified by" our " adversaries ?" Short shall be the contest, we cannot fail of success; we shall hang high our trophies on the pillars of immortality ?

" Who is on the Lord's side ?"

IV.

MORAL MEANS PREFERABLE TO MIRACLE.

And he said unto him, If they hear not Moses and the Prophets, neither will they be persuaded, though one Rose from the Dead.—Luke xvi, 31.

It has been common for men in every age, and seems consonant with their very nature, to " require a sign." No " generation " is entitled to the guilty distinction of being " evil and sensual," because it " seeketh after " this kind of appeal. A preternatural display in favor and enforcement of revelation is a desirable and necessary thing. It *may* be that the demand is rather the resort of evasion than the measure of cautious research. It is certain that in the recurrence and continuity of the challenge there is sin. The temper and the occasion are possibly indicative of hypocritical pretense and willful unbelief. But there *was* a time when to insist upon miracle was most rational and laudable: " What dost thou work ? " We ought to ascertain whether it is our Creator who speaks. There ought to be proof of his direct purpose and agency. No religion can be true and incumbent but that which he ordains; and he can ordain none which shall not bear satisfactory impressions of a divine origin. He must communicate his will by a regular or arrested course of things. If in the former manner there is no notice, no warning, no absolute evidence; if by the latter way, it is his " coming forth

out of his place," and the argument is decisive. But this is not a *higher* exercise of his power, it is only a *particular*. That which can impel the operations of nature must needs be able to suspend them; or they have in the meantime become independent of their primary cause, and exceed its control. A miracle is a voluntary departure from the system established in the universe: it can only be voluntary in relation to the divine mind which established it, operating on its laws. If it be wrought in confirmation of a religion, that religion is henceforth propounded as *divine*. Unless it obtain this character of *authority*, it is impossible to commend it to man by its *wisdom*, or any other qualities of *excellence*. Nor is it conceivable in what manner the Deity could declare it to be his disclosure and dispensation, did he not thus dreadly break the silence, and interrupt the uniformity of the movements he originally imparted to his works. As these are but his *constant* volitions and processes, when altered and diverted, God is seen to interpose; and the cause, whatever it be, subjected to justify the singularity, and to receive the sanction, of the procedure, cannot but be pre-eminently and declaratively his ! *

This method and rule of evidence is adopted most professedly by every economy of inspired truth. We are only commanded to believe on the ground of its producing miraculous proof. All is suspended—its credibility of character, our duty of assent—on the competency and readiness discovered to furnish this ultimate satisfaction. Under the old law we find this species of attestation proclaimed: "Behold I make a covenant: before all thy

* "Likewise, that whensoever God doth transcend the law of nature by miracles, which may ever seem as new creations, he never cometh to that point or pass but in regard of the work of redemption, which is the greater, and whereto all God's signs and miracles do refer."—Lord Bacon's Confession of Faith.

people I will do marvels, such as have not been done in all the earth, nor in any nation: and all the people among which thou art shall see the work of the Lord." The Saviour of mankind expressed himself in a similar manner: "The same works that I do, bear witness of me, that the Father hath sent me." "Believe me for the very works' sake." "If I had not done among them the works which none other man did, they had not had sin."

It has, however, been contended that miracle is impossible in the nature of things. For not denying its abstract practicability, which would be a dispute of the divine omnipotence, certain objectors argue that it supposes a fickleness, a deviation inconsistent with perfection. Did not God, it is speciously asked, design such an arrangement, and would he break in upon it? It is a sufficient answer that this arrangement is not the effect of moral fitness but of sovereign pleasure, that there is nothing necessary or final in it, and that no pledge was ever given that it should be invariably preserved. The variation is as much a part of His eternal plan as that general regularity which it affects; and whatever is material cannot terminate on itself, but is always directed to strictly intellectual and religious results. Its subordination by miracle to some revealed system of truth and mercy lies within its most proper designs and probable uses.

And sophism has been added to cavil. Allow that miracle, it is remarked, could occur without an impeachment of divine intelligence that amounts to moral impossibility, testimony is a vehicle which is unsuited to transmit, is a confirmation unable to authenticate, it. But it may be replied, that the *report* of those parties who were warranted on the information of their senses to allow its existence, is as trustworthy as their *consciousness :* that whatever one man believes on right grounds, any other may who can ascertain that such grounds are

tenable; that it always becomes us to give credence to that whose denial would be absurd; that if we cannot doubt the *conviction* of them who were contemporary with these *extraordinary events*, and the *record* of that conviction—conviction which the rack could not terrify them to stifle or the stake to quell—then it would be the height of unreasonableness to question that they did transpire. If it is conceded that a person who saw miracle might be authorized to acknowledge the fact, then is he equally justified in narrating it; and if nothing but the *subject* of the narrative gave rise to suspicion— it being strictly sifted, and irrefragably established to be genuine—it could not be invalidated without destroying the fidelity of sensible impressions the most cautious, protracted, and multiplied.

According to these objections, *experience* is alleged to be the criterion of *testimony*, and testimony is always to be discredited when in opposition to experience. But though experience may be, in some degree, the reason why we repose confidence in others—they having been found deserving of it, and general facts vouching for its necessity and truth—yet testimony is uniformly *antecedent* to it. For it is by the perception of the latter that the former is corrected and restrained; all our early knowledge is derived from the first, and only subsequent discipline is learned by the second. Besides, what is experience? Whence know we that " all things have continued from the beginning?" What is the basis of the assertion, that the operations of nature have been, at all times and in all places, identical with each other? On what monument do we read its unvarying history? Which is the statute-book of its laws which can never be changed? Is it not the verdict of universal consent? Is it not the tale borne from father to son? Is it not the page on which generations have successively written their observations? Deny the province, abolish the

authority, of *testimony*, and you instantly shatter the foundations of all *experience!* The very same proof confirms the miraculous exception which establishes the general rule!

But we have to reason with other objectors now—the men who affect their desire for miracle, and not their disbelief of it. Without unkind suspicion, however, it may be feared that it is the same class under a new disguise. The tone of the request betrays a skepticism of its answer. They ask for what they appear to have made up their minds to treat as an impossibility. It is thus they would cover their indifference, stipulate for their indecision, and render consistent and plausible their obstinate unbelief. They must have demonstration; it must be demonstration of the most perfect kind and degree; and nothing short of it can satisfy their love of truth, and their inquisitiveness of research! They only abide the proper time, they but await the proper disclosure, and are fully prepared with their adhesion, when the fitting proofs and infallible tokens are submitted to them! They must be regarded as intelligent creatures, and expect that a due consideration be paid to their reason! They will suspend their judgment for the present, and reserve, without prejudice to their present statement, the right of another conclusion! So far nothing has occurred to warrant their admission and adoption of Christianity, their assent to its truth, their compliance with its obligation! How shall the taunt be rebuked?

There comes a voice, though it is not addressed to "man upon earth." It speaks out of heaven; and though we catch its lesson as it rushes past, it thunders into the depth of hell. And it still resounds, and remonstrates with them who, either in perverse sincerity or sneering hypocrisy, ask of Christianity "to show them a sign from heaven."

Whatever may be the imaginative description, and the

poetic machinery, of this Dreadful Tale, (and we are not expressly informed whether it is parable or history,) its lesson must be perfectly true to fact. Though these entreaties were never urged, though these dialogues were never held, though the " great gulf" be no more literally conceivable than the craving of the agonized spirit's parched tongue for the cooling drop, yet hell is not shut until a lesson is wrung from it, nor is heaven closed until its sanction is impressed upon that lesson. And what is it which is now inculcated to teach and warn us ? which we read by the glare of infernal flames, and learn by the tuition of celestial accents ? terrifically exemplified in the self-accusations of a soul irretrievably lost, but as tenderly urged by the sweet blessedness, the calm dignity, the inviolable safety of spirits coupled in their everlasting salvation—the father of the faithful placing at his side, and folding to his bosom, the spirit of this once-spurned lazar and beggar, lately received into heaven amid welcomes and escorts of its brightest and ho'iest ministry ?

And the lesson, which such awful extremes have combined to strengthen and to enforce, is this: That God has established among us a moral dispensation, confirmed at its beginning with the most stupendous proofs of his authority and purpose: that this is formed of means which are calculated to convince and impress the mind; that these means of conviction and impression are worthy of its divine character, and are adequate to their first intention: that it is an impious temerity to propose or wish any enlargement of them: that any coveted and hypothetical addition would be inapplicable and inefficient. There is now a liberty of choice, without a pretext of constraint ; a full, without being an overpowering, appeal : more information would bewilder, more argument would confuse, more light would blast and extinguish the sense of vision.

I. The ordinary means of religious conviction and impression are morally complete and sufficient.

God made this earth for a proper end: he "created it not in vain, he formed it to be inhabited." Perhaps here we may find a strong presumption that all worlds can have no just use unless tenanted by being. We only, however, can determine the condition of our own species. Man was free, and could claim a standard of decision; he was accountable, and might allege a right to a law of conduct. We think that such style of language is warranted, and that to this attitude our nature might raise itself. But nothing more could be required of justice, or belonged to the necessity of the case.

But our Maker has accumulated a revelation of another order. He has sent to us "the great things" of discovered and assured mercy. Tidings reach us of pardon and regeneration; how guilt may be forgiven and impurity cleansed. The sinner's character is drawn, that the sinner's case may be retrieved. His situation is pursued in its most exigent interests and fearful perils. All the *principles* of this revelation are deductions from so many *facts*. In its earlier portion it anticipated what should be *done* for our salvation, in the latter is the record of its *achievement*. The law we had broken is incorporated with it to show our need of salvation, and that our salvation consists in the restored opportunity and disposition of obedience. The "wrath to come" is made to flash out its "unquenchable fire," to expose the condemnation from which we are snatched, and to warn us the more to flee from it. Let it never be forgotten that the means of salvation derive all their value from certain *deeds* which were believed as about to be accomplished, or as having been accomplished: that these means are founded upon them as their authorized report

and proclaimed intention. "Moses and the prophets" constituted a phrase well understood to describe the Jewish dispensation. It compendiously expressed the measure of religious knowledge then extant. Its principles are uniform with those of the Gospel, being conformed to the same facts. Sacrifice and sanctification were taught by it in its expiations and ablutions: these were prospective intimations and types of the Saviour who should "by his own blood, enter in once into the holy place," and of the Spirit whose "washing of regeneration" carries purity through the most defiled heart. "For what the law could not do," (Rom. viii, 3, 4,) of what was it then incapable?—of justifying? at this moment he who doeth it shall live by it:—of renewing? it is the *guide* of moral disposition, and was never designed to produce it. The law could not do that which God did! He "condemned sin in the flesh;" that is, upon our nature as at present subsisting in this state of time and this scene of earth. The defeat of the law was attributed solely to the "weakness of our flesh." It had a right and a power of vengeance; but our present constituted being could not have sustained it. Our "spirit" would have failed. We should have perished from the way. Tophet must have been the sphere of retribution, and eternity would have been required for its infliction. But sin was "condemned," as most evil and malignant, "in the flesh:" on the earth it had defiled, on the nature it had ruined, and according to the existing system of things. He did it by sending "his own Son in the *likeness* of sinful flesh," and for a sin-offering. Most terrible was the resentment of the sin, in this manner of extricating the sinner! The crime was denounced, adjudged, and avenged in the very act of justifying the criminal! And yet that law, whose incapacity was declared, was only honored by the assistance rendered to it, and its righteousness is still

fulfilled in them who walk not after the flesh but the Spirit. This has been the tenor of all *gracious revelation:* it is God's call to man, not only requiring him to return, but providing the arrangements for effecting it.

The epitome of the divine truth presented in the text reminds us that, as spoken by Jesus Christ, it was speedily to receive an immense accession. He came that we might have " life more abundantly." He came to found " a ministration of righteousness " and of the Spirit which should exceed in glory. He came to ratify a " better covenant, established upon better promises." There was a peculiarity in the juncture of the announcement. The former economy had well-nigh run its race. John, the harbinger of the Messiah, was engaged in " restoring all things," or, in other words, bringing back that economy to its original intentions. His ministry was most peculiar; it seemed a living spirit, an intense power, a penetrating and consuming flame. In the desert or the palace, before multitudes or kings, he was the same. He came to honor the law, and to prepare for its dissolution. His voice was mournful as well as piercing—spoke of departing scenes and glories—and sounded as if the last blast of the Sinai trump. A modification of system was commencing: " the law and the prophets were *until* John:" and as " Moses wrote of" Christ, and to " him give all the prophets witness," so was the Baptist his special precursor and confessor— and was as " a voice crying," " He was before me," " Behold the Lamb of God." A fuller designation would now be requisite: we have not only Moses and the prophets, but Christ and the apostles. The whole is of a final character; and we may congratulate ourselves that we " are built upon the foundation of the *apostles and prophets, Jesus Christ* himself being the chief corner-stone."

We must now bring ourselves to examine these *means* in some of their distinctive features.

1. It appears that they were always submitted in a twofold shape of *sign* and *utterance.* Long before the introduction of arbitrary characters in writing, a pictorial language was employed. This seems the radix and source of all. Men read, when altars, divers washings, and bleeding victims were the letters in which revelation was composed. If, as is probable, the present style was derived from the "handwriting" of Jehovah on the mount, the sacred volume availed itself of the earliest instrumentality of abbreviated marks for its purposes. It is penned in languages most determinate and known. The former part lives in one which can never cease while the "tribes of the wandering foot and weary breast" are found in all the lands of the earth ; the second breathes through another which has always been felt to be the music of expression and the philosophy of thought. But as the inspiration of Scripture is not only in its meaning, but as far in its phraseology (for we hold a strictly verbal and organic illapse) as to constitute it an infallible medium of such meaning, so it was plainly intended that it should be translated into all the dialects of human speech. Whatever may be the deterioration of the process, it does not *necessarily* invalidate any thing of its authority, and impair any thing of its influence. The originals are very favorable to it by their union of copiousness with precision. Our Lord and his disciples sanctioned the principle by quoting from an uninspired version. And thus no embarrassment clogs the destined universality of " the lively oracles ;" though most solemn is the trust, and most jealous should be the care, of those who render them into the various languages of the earth. We can say of every such copy, and every such translation—executed with fidelity—" This is the word of God." And we

can, moreover, declare this confidence in strictest harmony with the *design* of that word, which, though given in particular tongues, merely made the first selection that it might be transferred from them into all. And it is a blessed spectacle which in our age we behold. This " word runneth very swiftly." But recently no barriers existed—not mountains, not seas—so formidable as the difficulties of language. They arrested ideas which might have spread through the community of mind, and checked feelings which could light up a universe. The harp of Zion could not rule its chords, and pour its melodies, in a strange land; the tones of taste and harmony, the magic sounds of Greece, would, beyond a certain boundary, be unintelligible, and he who spoke them would "be a barbarian." Through the dark night of persecution and superstition a scholarly penmanship traced the versions of many, and of the most important, idioms, until every polygraphic dream was surpassed by the powers of that wonder-working mechanism which gives to this result an indefinite multiplication and an inevitable perpetuity. And may we not imagine the joy of those sacred writers whose testimonies have been so long shut up in a speech unknown to the majority of our race—now that those testimonies are repeated in a hundred vernaculars of the earth! Moses is preached in every city! There is no speech nor language where the strain of David is not heard! With other tongues and other lips Isaiah speaks to the people! Paul, while there are so many kinds of voices in the world, impresses his signification upon all! And John hears, articulate and vocal, a great multitude of all tongues, surrounding the heavenly throne! How long was this delayed. But now of what usefulness are they conscious? What a course of successes may they predict! Nations, of which they had never heard, repeat their names! New worlds hang over their compositions!

The wells of their inspiration still rise and overflow! The awful instruments of their original announcement yet vibrate and ring! Their heaven refines and augments. With newer radiance each diadem burns, with fuller exultation each harp responds. Higher waves each palm, louder swells each song, while they continue to declare God's "glory among the heathen, his wonders among all people." But it was always designed that this revelation should be *preached* as well as *read.* In all ages, as to its objects, we may demand, " Have they not heard ? " Noah was the preacher of righteousness to the old world. The ministers of the Old Testament "read in the book of the law of God distinctly, and *gave* the *sense,* and *caused them* to *understand* the reading." Most confessedly is this a Christian ordinance. " How shall they believe in him of whom they have not heard ? And how shall they hear without a preacher ?" The sympathy of human manner attempers the dreadness of divine message; and the *standard* is within the reach of all—" faith cometh by hearing, and hearing by the word of God." The means of conviction and impression are thus uniformly written and parole.

2. It may be proper to justify the *aptitude* of the vehicle which God has prescribed for these moral purposes.

Whatever is mind and whatever is matter, that the intercourse may be maintained between them something most singular in its contrivance is demanded. It must be of the one substance or the other. Organs of sensation are therefore given us, and these mysteriously link us with the external world. Material as are the grossest and least susceptible parts, they are, in a way we know not, avenues to the soul ; bearing impressions to it which it corrects or allows, simplifies or compounds. It is not the eye which sees—the perception being a mental act—but without it there could be no vision. Now He who " knoweth our frame," who " formed the eye and planted

the ear," explains his mind and will in forms adapted to our sensible nature. Though he has immediate access to the soul, yet the soul only becomes intelligent and accountable by its commerce with that which is without; and, therefore, it is the "entrance" of his word into it which gives it "light and understanding." Our two principal mediums of impression are, sight and hearing. These swell the fund of our ideas far more richly and nobly than the other senses. They are in most frequent and influential operation, they partake most of the intellect. And, therefore, we are commanded to "search the *Scriptures;*" therefore the Apostles testified of these things and wrote these things; therefore they sought no higher appeal than "so it is written;" therefore they always "reasoned out" of the inspired volume as far as it was completed, and being inspired themselves, they were empowered to add "word or epistle." And still they "*preached* Christ crucified," they carried the "sound into all the earth," they "lifted up their voice and were not afraid." And these are the means perpetuated among ourselves. "The word is nigh" us; "whoso hath ears to hear let him hear." Now as it is obvious that a human being always blind and deaf could have no religious capability, because no mental existence—so we must admire this adoption of a simple method in impressing upon external sense spiritual conception. But it is only a temporary tribute to *sense;* faith and piety henceforth occupy the interior, "the inward man is renewed day by day," there is the "life of God," there is the heir of heaven walking "in the light." What is inferior in "this corruption and this mortal," "this vile body," and "this body of death," is made auxiliary to the highest ends of knowledge and purity. It refines what is corporeally gross into the index and instrument of all that is most transparent in thought and elevated in emotion; it displaces the associations of time by the visions of

eternity.   If revelation be blamed for its manner of addressing us, we have only to answer that it no further complies with the conditions of our lower nature than to make itself intelligible, and that, being once understood, it causes the spirit of man to expatiate amid scenes of more native excellence and congenial splendor.

3. The *tendency* of these means is sufficiently apparent. The "law which is perfect" is adapted to "convert the soul." The word which is engrafted is "able to save" it. The "word" which is truth, is calculated to sanctify it. And but that the circumstances which require these moral renovations present the barriers to its success, the Gospel might be left to win its own course and its own victory. It is so fit, so searching, so holy, that any state in the least susceptible must have yielded to it. Why does not the human mind at once embrace it? The reply is, that such is man's perverseness and enmity against religious truth that no foreign appeal, no objective reasoning, can overcome it. The power to change the heart must be exercised from within—that "exceeding greatness of power" which can penetrate it and then open it to the train of all holy reflections and motives. It does not resemble the bolt which rives the rock, but rather that invisibly forming and germinating influence which unfolds the rose-bud, developing its beauty and exhaling its fragrance—meeting, however, every external auspice in the vernal gale, the morning dew, the noontide heat. And these views lead to an important *distinction*—the depravity of *human nature* constitutes the occasion of divine influence, and not evangelical truth. It is not man's want of reason, but its perversion, which obscures revelation from him; it is his disrelish and dislike of its constituent principles. But while this influence communicates another disposition to the soul, (all that is wanted for its conversion,) it leaves the Gospel in its own independence. It strengthens none of its claims, it

heightens none of its attractions. It lays it under no obligations of revision or improvement. Man is the sole debtor, as he is the exclusive subject. The spirit of truth reveals it, but it is incapable of any change but to that altered view and feeling which depends upon a particular state of mind. The difference is of perception and regard, in which it is passive. Never let us speak as though it required any thing. Never let us represent it but as " the work of God which is perfect." Never let us disparage it by any comparisons which would describe it feeble and unworthy, but for a superadded might. It has no " weakness and unprofitableness ; " no imbecility and defect. And another *distinction* is consequent upon this ; man labors under no disqualification of *power*, (unless used scholastically,) but is restrained by a *rebellious will.* He *can* believe, he *can* repent ; he does both daily, when the testimony of faith and the cause of regret are of the slightest kind. His understanding is capable of giving credit, his heart of entertaining contrition. But he is morally disaffected ; his inclination is averse. This cannot excuse him ; this cannot vary his obligation. The authority of the Gospel is, all the time, the same. Otherwise a criminal might claim an acquittal upon the ground of disapproving the law he had broken, and of not feeling a wish to obey it ! Whatever a creature was at any time bound to do, morally considered, he must be irreversibly. The damned have not survived their duty to love their God ! Such distinctions are of the very argument which establishes the sufficiency of those means which Christianity presents, that sufficiency not being in the least degree affected by the necessity, only relative, of divine influence to remove our indisposition on the one hand, or by the existence of that indisposition on the other.

Still the voice urges, concerning Moses and the prophets—we subjoin, Christ and the apostles—"Let them

hear them!" And the appeal, founded on the completeness of apparatus, the fullness of discovery, the force of principle involved in Christianity, may not be unseasonably illustrated.

There is proof to satisfy every judgment.

Falsehood is not a gratuitous device. The fixed correspondence between words and things belongs to the earliest evolution of the mind, and cannot be evaded but for some countervailing intent. In indifferent and impartial circumstances veracity may be expected; it is the most easy and natural course. We ask, then, if the first disciples of the Gospel did *not believe* that *miracles* had occurred, what could induce them to invent the story? What did they gain? Men are swayed by the cupidity of wealth, by the fame of enterprise, by the love of ease. But these motives could have no place in minds which saw before them certain poverty, contempt, and death. Did posthumous honor allure them? The denier of a future state can never know this sentiment, and the believer in one would be unable to connect its hope with imposture. But again we ask, if they *did* believe such miracles, on what ground can their testimony be disputed? How arose it that men of far distant places, and as distant ages, (for the question of revelation is identical,) agreed together in so strange an impression, contrary to whatever was known or anticipated? Whence was the concord of parties held together by no common tie? By what charm did man, whose "days are few," make common cause with the stranger of another century, enter into his feelings, and interchange with him his own? But *prophecy*, which is intellectual miracle, yields evidence not less decisive. As it has been granted by the skeptic that nothing, however incredible, is to be rejected if the alternative be more incredible still, so the coincidences between the guess—if prophecy be only it —and the fulfillment of the guess, imply a chain of diffi-

culties overcome, and of improbabilities elicited, more than equal to the fact for which they are substituted, and without its confessedly competent agency. Look into the constitution of Christianity. What an unearthliness of character! What a sensitiveness of morality! What a divinity of piety! Call it a forgery, and either the weakest of men struck out the brilliant fable, or the most wicked wrought this creation of peerless excellence and virtue. Look upon the influence of Christianity. What has it not done? It has sown the seeds of civilization and refinement; banished vices upon which philosophy dilated without hesitation, and beauty gazed without a blush; forms the individual and the nation on a model of which the ancient sage was never wont to dream; and surrounds itself with a mild luster of loveliness, convincing as the insufferable blaze of its prodigies. It is a system of *persuasion.* "Let every man be fully persuaded in his own mind." Its teachers can say, "We persuade men," and its disciples, "We thus judge." There is nothing occult or coercive in it; the man must be determined to blind himself who disbelieves, to destroy himself who withstands, it!

There is attraction to awaken every interest.

Principles may convince by their naked truth, and yet leave the heart untouched. Abstractions may occupy some recess of the understanding, and never excite our warmer and more active emotions. But the Gospel is an expostulation with *self-love.* It calls on *shame, gratitude,* and *pity.* It lays hold of our *hope* and *fear.* With what a captivating grace does it visit us! It is the good news of salvation! Infinite compassion transfuses itself through all its discoveries and entreaties! "Why will ye die?" "Come unto me all ye that labor and are heavy laden, and I will give you rest." How solemn is its pathos, how pathetic is its solemnity! It is the weeping rebuke of mercy warning us into its arms!

He, and only he, can tell what music is in these truths and consolations on whose ear the sentence of the broken law has grated and its curse has rung. The harmonies of the universe have no strain like this, " I am pacified toward thee ! "

There is an appeal to every class of character.

When the philosopher tells me how my mental system —that which lies within my consciousness—is affected and governed—in what order its phenomena succeed, in what manner they influence, each other—I acknowledge the profundity of his examination into the laws and states of the human mind. When a physician not only determines my disease, upon a survey of its more obvious symptoms, but informs me of its every secret stage, each pain and languor known only to myself, I honor his acquaintance with all the particularities of morbid action. And yet in these instances there was a general ground of knowledge, a common subject of inquiry. The *mind* and the *disease*, investigated in one, might be inferred in all. But in *character* there is a more specific individuality. Its modifications are endless as they are unaccountable. And still Christianity, with the minutest observation and with an insulating power, makes the sinner tremble as though each warning was pointed at him, and rejoice as though each solace had been prepared for his relief. The self-conclusion is inevitable as that which the guilty monarch drew when there " came forth fingers of a man's hand," and he was convinced that they, of all his thousand guests, wrote his doom. And the convicted sinner equally realizes the personal reference of every invitation and promise ; and while he comes to Jesus it is to *him* it is said, "*Him* that cometh unto me I will in no wise cast out ;" and while he flies to refresh his thirst, it is to *him* the assurance is repeated, " I will give unto *him* that is athirst of the fountain of the water of life freely."

There is a provision for every extent of guilt.

The infinity of merit in the atonement of the cross does not seem to meet the full demand of the sinner's case. It is true that there is, that there must be, such infinity, but many current statements favor the idea of an *undirected* and *inapplicable* store. We hesitate not to go further: no statement would embody our convictions which did not set forth the atonement as universal in its character as it is infinite in its virtue—which did not assert that it was legislatively designed for all, and made the basis for the moral treatment of all. The fact of an excess, when that is but a necessary effect of circumstances, proves nothing, accomplishes nothing, consoles nothing : give it a meaning, a use, a direct intention, and there is an intelligible idea, an available blessing. And this is our rational consistency in calling on men to believe and embrace the testimony of the Gospel —not that there is a sufficiency only, but a warrant of that sufficiency—not that there is bread enough and to spare, but that it is placed on a " table of show-bread " —and that the Gospel makes such a constitution its express purpose and its unambiguous avowal. Why should we restrict and sophisticate its mighty generalities ? Can language have wider scope than it employs ? And therefore it is that the Gospel should be preached with the authority and power of a perfect confidence. We, " having believed, should also preach." We can never go beyond the word of the Lord in its *anointed character*, any more than in its *admitted efficacy.* There is not among the debtors of justice, the captives of sin, the prisoners of condemnation, an obligation which it is not *sincere in proposing* to cancel, a chain which it is not *commissioned* to burst, a sentence which it is not *ordained* to absolve.

It comprises the means of our regeneration.

Pardon only leaves us in a state of exemption from

punishment; it does not properly, nor necessarily, bestow a taste for purity and a disposition of obedience. A renovation of nature is as indispensable to the sinner as a reversal of condition. But the holy volume does not accomplish this effect, nor does the preaching of its contents; neither is it accomplished without their intervention and application. And therefore a " newness of spirit," though doubtless depending on an extrinsic cause, may be considered a *blessing* as well as a *truth* of the Gospel. For it not only enjoins that we " must be born again "--it not only expounds the manner and the agency by which the change is wrought—it is the appointed and exclusive contrivance. Foreign circumstances may induce men to think, to relent, to realize to themselves the truth; but nothing, save that truth, can sanctify. Where is the fanatic to be found who would maintain that the Holy Spirit illuminated the mind in evangelical principles, which never before, nor subsequently, had access to revelation? No matter how the truth has been injected into the mind—whether by education, by general report and impression, or by more direct methods—it is by this expedient that the agent of regeneration alone does, can alone, produce it. He has no other means; though He " searcheth all things, yea, the deep things of God." He is as morally unable to sanctify the heart without the Gospel, as He, who is " of purer eyes than to behold evil," is to pardon sin without the atonement. Such fact we learn from numerous and intelligible passages of Scripture. " The sword of the Spirit is the word of God." " In Christ Jesus I have begotten you through the Gospel." " Being born again, not of corruptible seed, but of incorruptible, by the word of God which liveth and abideth forever." Well, therefore, may we kiss the word as the rod with which the Comforter only smites to heal, " a rod out of the stem of Jesse." Well, therefore, may we venerate

the truth with a holy awe, even " tremble at " it, as the instrument which an Almighty hand has often wielded ; which bears the characters of its sacred appropriation; and which seems to retain a vibration of that power, and a glow of that splendor, which have enforced or accompanied its blessed use.

It supplies the motives for our conduct.

Itself the model of excellence, it illustrates its reasonableness and urges its pursuit. But it is not a preceptive morality, one of self-government and benevolence, to which it confines itself. It invites a higher class of duties. It calls for a constancy of profession unto beggary and death. A very crucifixion to the world, in all its present conveniences and sympathies, does it place among its foremost and paramount demands. Here is an inversion of nature. Here is a revolt of every ordinary idea and sensibility. And yet this is the heroic virtue which it has formed. In this virtue there is no blind enthusiasm, but its motives admit of the most discriminating inspection. Instead of claiming too much from man, man has become dignified in yielding himself up to the claim. Instead of receiving a sullen obedience, all has breathed alacrity and joy. They who, "for conscience' sake," were plundered of their earthly all, " took joyfully the spoiling " of their goods; and they who were summoned to death in its most cruel forms, counted not their lives dear unto themselves. There must have been high inducement to reconcile our nature to these evils. And Christianity is a system perfect in its motives. While it never quits our side by the hearth of domestic quiet and in the walk of peaceful avocation, always directing our ignorance and upholding our weakness, by soft whispers and gentle impulses counseling and guiding us, it forewarns of other scenes, and stands ready to arouse us with more stirring incitements; bids us follow it to the high place, and engage, on its behalf, in the joined battle; and when the trial seems too fiery, and the shock too overwhelming, it makes the duty sweet and the performance easy as to listen to the melody of the untraversed grove and gaze on the sunset of the calmest day.

It administers relief to our affliction.

Grief is a simple thing, and asks for commiseration and confidence. The manner of the application is often important as the solace itself. Kind must be the accent, the look, the touch. Now, the Gospel is "the *tender mercy* of our God." It exhibits him as "the God of consolation," as the "God that comforteth those that are cast down." It seeks out the abode and bosom of wretchedness. Tears are the attractions which it acknowledges, sighs are the calls which it obeys. It is the continued expression of the pity which, when commanding the empire of death to restore the brother to the disconsolate sisters of Bethany, itself could weep; which looked down from the cross of Calvary, and amid the unutterable horrors and portents of that scene, distinguished a mother's form, and soothed a mother's bereavement. O this is the religion of the forlorn and oppressed, the poor and needy! It opens its heart of infinite yearnings to them. It bends to hear each tale of woe. Its chosen station is close to the pallet of poverty and the bed of death. In the house of mourning it consecrates its home. It causes no tear but that of repentance, and that is sweeter far than the worldling's fullest, brightest tear of joy. Every other tear it loves and cares to dry, nor foregoes its soothing and healing course until it has carried the mourner whither no grief can follow him, and where "God shall wipe all tears from" his eyes. How lovely is the religion which can bid the rod of affliction to blossom, and make a smile play around the grimmest features of death!

And though, in arguing for the sufficiency of these

means, we distinguish between that which is moral, and that which is efficacious, yet we are justified in maintaining that *an influence* is connected with their dispensation The Holy Spirit is given to all " them that ask Him." Such influence cannot be uniform and essential; but it will surely vindicate its *sovereignty*, in the eyes of them to whom this quality is obnoxious, that the sinner never was refused who sought the boon. The want of a disposition toward it is a barrier the most strict and stumbling ; but " God tempteth no man," and disposition or will is the very subject of accountability. " The residue of the Spirit" is a portion of the fullness which dwells in Christ, and sinners are as welcome to a participation in his fullness as to an interest in his blood. Such influence could never be *necessary* to a righteous government and moral scheme ; and still its *promise* insures to Christianity a success, and to every suppliant an answer.

These are the means which God has founded, and which retain their perennial character. By them He saves them who believe. Other means we know not than the Bible unfolded to the eye and proclaimed to the ear. Circumstances of imperative authority, external to this book, enforce them. Institutes and appointments raise attention and habituate regularity. The Sabbath, the Church, the Baptismal rite, the Christian feast, are placed in the same connection. All have a tendency to convince and impress. Thus we are dealt with. Our rational apprehensions are addressed, our warmer affections are excited. These means survive all changes, and may be assimilated to the deeper springs of nature, the freshness of which cannot be impaired, nor their fullness exhausted ; or to the ordinances of heaven—fixed, pacific, unwearying, magnificent—and, like them, only to perish with the firmament itself.

But men indulge other sentiments. They would

fondly convince themselves that their unbelief is excusable because these means are not necessarily and inevitably resistless. They require a mechanical violence,
a physical force, to satisfy them. They must be put
into circumstances which shall leave them no liberty of
decision. By one of those unsound, though common,
maxims which are repeated until they are allowed, they
would confound an impression of sense and a result of
belief. "Seeing is believing," is the foolish saw which
comes to their assistance. Now there are not two acts
more contrary. The one depends upon an organ, and
the other upon a conclusion formed according to a
testimony. Should it be said that we believe the information of our senses, it is only a figurative form of
expression, unless in the lips of the man who, knowing
how certain speculatists have denied even the validity
of this information, measures, by these cautious words,
the steps by which he has become assured concerning
it. He who has extricated himself from the phantom
philosophy will only understand the language with
any distinctness, or employ it with any right. Now
we argue, that "if one went unto them from the dead,"
they would not "repent;" that if the moral instrumentality failed, the supernatural demonstration would not
succeed.

II. Any supplementary methods of conviction
and impression, founded upon miraculous agency,
would be inapposite and ineffective.

The *kind* of interposition which men might seek would
probably be very different; each would have his favorite
scheme and prevailing taste. Their sign would be
"either in the depth, or in the height above." Whatever
it was, it could remove no difficulty, as it satisfied but
one party. The allusion of the text is to the apparitions
of the dead. The grave is supposed to yield its prisoner;
the departed spirit, acquainted with "the eternal blazon,"

is conceived to reanimate and inform the lifeless body; again the familiar eye opens and the oft-heard tongue speaks; the once welcomed visitant of kindred and friendship is now clothed with all the authority and interest of a herald from the unseen world, and of an interpreter who can disclose its mysteries. No miracle could be more decisive, and then, as oral communication and dread discovery were associated with it, none could be more instructive. Nothing could exceed it in solemnity, power, and impression. It would not only be material but rational, not only a change wrought on brute substance but on conscious spirit—the recall of a soul from the gate of death, and from the region of immortality. It would be of little additional interest in what manner the scene was prepared—whether as a mysterious traveler the spirit joined itself to us, or whether as a radiant vision it burst upon us. Such a manifestation must comprise every advantage of miracle; and we shall principally avail ourselves of it, in the prosecution of the argument, though our remarks will concern themselves with the general question.

1. There is nothing which we feel to be so terrific as the thought of a spiritual presence, and a contact with the spiritual being. This may be variously accounted for; but, respecting the truth of the observation, there can exist no doubt. When the angel has stooped to our earth on some important mission, men have apprehended that they should surely die. When the specter has glared upon them, and, with sepulchral voice, has addressed them, their blood has curdled, their nerve has shrunk, their heart has turned to ice. It is not for us now to inquire whether these appearances have been real; this has been the effect. We neither beg nor rebut the question, at this step of remark, relative to another and immaterial world; but this is the popular impression. The most enlightened and dispassionate have known a

shudder and a trepidation. The horror of a Dion is far more natural than the phlegm of a Brutus. We sympathize with the disciples who, when Jesus walked on the sea, " were troubled, saying, It is a spirit ; and cried out for fear ; " who, when he suddenly presented himself among them after his resurrection, " were terrified and affrighted, and supposed that they had seen a spirit." Most terrific is the description which Eliphaz records of the midnight monitor who glided into his chamber and broke upon his solitude ; the shadowy outline, the abrupt narrative, but creates a deeper suspense, a more harrowing, thrilling sensation ! " Now a thing was secretly brought to me, and mine ear received a little thereof. In thoughts from the visions of the night, when deep sleep falleth on men, fear came upon me, and trembling, which made all my bones to shake. Then a spirit passed before my face ; the hair of my flesh stood up : it stood still, but I could not discern the form thereof ; an image was before mine eyes, there was silence, and I heard a voice." This is the sublimity of fear ; and it is only sublime by its fidelity to nature and fact. But is this a disposition and mood of the mind favorable to cautious deliberation and sober purpose ? Is the stupefaction and dismay, consequent on such a visitation congenial to inquiry and peace ? Would it not leave " thoughts beyond the reaches of our souls ? " Might it not endanger the empire of reason, and distract the temperament of fancy ? Religion is a " judgment of what is right ; " its requirement is a " reasonable service ; " its influence is not " the spirit of fear, but of a sound mind." Than consternation—the effect of *every thing supernatural*— nothing is more ill adapted to " the reason of the hope that is in us," unless it be utter indifference itself.

2. As all our ideas are related to our perceptions, language is necessarily built upon sensible analogies. The organs being the only mediums of present knowledge,

symbols and comparisons are the only methods of present illustration. Were any other language to be addressed to us, conveying to us any other thoughts, it would neither reach our sense nor coalesce with our intellect. Conceptions formed by incorporeal beings, and signified by ethereal representations, must be perfectly unintelligible to our compound nature, holding its only commerce with an external world. There was one (2 Cor. xii, 1, 4) who, for fourteen years, had revolved what occurred to him, and impressed itself on him, during a rapture in the third heaven. The traces were too serious and deep for any lapse of time, or change of circumstances, to impair. The visions of the Almighty had flushed forth upon his spirit; existences and modes of existence had risen before him such as imagination never attempted to realize and describe. Bodiless, impalpable essences gleamed across his view, which no known discourse of man could portray. He was girded in by a scenery which earthly elements and colors were not formed to paint. They were spectacles of which our world contained no type, and voices which could propagate no impulse on our atmosphere. What information does the descended Paul convey? What of the nature of that region, which of its glorious marvels, does he explain? And yet these mysteries were only not to be interpreted because they were incapable of interpretation—it was not lawful, only because it was impossible, to utter them. There is nothing common between the senses of embodied, and the ideas of disembodied, men. All reciprocation is precluded by their opposite conditions. Should, therefore, the minister of warning leave the spiritual world and alight on this, he could not make use of our impressions to superinduce his own. Let him, say the objectors, " testify unto them" who now live in this probationary scene. But they must be reminded that the testimony would be deficient, that whatever was removed

from the associations of our knowledge could only be pictured through them, and that whatever was more *explicit* than figure and allusion, would, to the same degree, be only more obscure and incomprehensible. The direct disclosure of spiritualism and eternity by one sent from the dead to the living, would be like confounding their language, that they might "not understand one another's speech."

3. Since it is not to be supposed that the wish of *every* one should be gratified in the time and manner of these resurrections from the dead—since none are sufficiently extravagant to suppose that any power would leave the question with each, "Whom shall I bring up unto thee?" —there must be some point of limitation. At that point commences the business of testimony. He who has seen the dead burst their cerements could not long conceal the secret. Unlike private opinion, the impression of this occurrence must have its way. It, during every moment of silence, would be a "fire shut up in the bones." And concealment would be as unjust as difficult. The miracle being "to testify," they who were signalized by its exhibition ought to make it known to others. And what would be the probable reception of the tale? A general suspicion would be immediately entertained of the narrator's solidity of mind. There would be suggestions of phantasma and excited fancy. Reference would be made to optical disease and spectral illusion. And the result of all might be, that the recital would not only be scouted, but that the man himself would, from the reasoning of some and the ridicule of others, abandon his own convictions, by having learned to discredit his own sensations.

4. The excitement of miracle is generally lessened by the nearer approach to its crisis and scene. The remark is borne out by somewhat analogous circumstances. Let us hear, from afar, of the pestilence—its dark march, its

desolating fury—its gradual encroachment—and the panic shoots through a community. Let the evil arrive —more calamitously and sweepingly than apprehended —recklessness takes the place of alarm, and levity of seriousness. The reverse we should deem more natural; but it is contradicted by notorious facts. And let us not suppose that miracles produced all the curiosity and stir which their character would justify. It is true that the Evangelists do not commonly state the influence of their Master's mighty deeds on the popular mind. Enough is, however, told to satisfy us that they were most convincing and resplendent; and that they who were their subjects or spectators disclosed them, though often charged to conceal them, and did " the more blaze them abroad." Here was publication. But did they raise the inquiry, or attract the notice, of the great and the learned? Did those, upon the very spot, trouble themselves to give them a passing survey? Would not such wonders have repaid a glancing eye, or slackened step, while the Pharisee hastened on? This momentary notice was not deigned. And we may cite the instance of Paul himself. All the plausibilities are, that his education in Jerusalem was conducted at the time of our Saviour's ministry. Many must have been the facilities for seeing Him who at last entered that city with triumph, and did his latest wonders in the Temple. It appears inconceivable that the sanguine youth, that the cultivated pupil, would omit an opportunity of marking His person, hearing one discourse, and beholding one achievement. It may be inferred that he never so much as saw him! To say nothing of the silence which he surely must have broken, if there were a single remembrance of Him whom he had persecuted, he speaks in this manner: "How shall we escape, if we neglect so great salvation; which at the first began to be spoken by the Lord, and was confirmed unto us by them that

heard him?" His exclusion is evidently from what was personal and not official; he having, by his miraculous conversion and rapture, been warranted to say, "And last of all, He was seen of me also, as one born out of due time." And if such a man was too prejudiced or too indifferent to seek a view of the Messiah's form, or to catch a tone of his voice, we may argue how many would follow the same course, and how uninfluential is miracle when it cannot excite even the attention necessary to examine it.

This is our first class of remarks, showing that these mighty works are little calculated to convert, from the horror of those who contemplate them disqualifying them to judge; from the impossibility of a perfect disclosure to our senses of realities with which the senses have no affinity; from the skepticism of mankind, which might not only withstand the evidence, but even corrupt the witness; and from the egregious insensibility which the closest vicinage to miracle, and the fullest opportunity of canvassing it, do not generally disturb. Another class of observation now presses upon us, relating to the positive incongruity of this instrument; the former demonstrated its inadequacy, this will establish its inadmissibility.

1. Unless miracle be sparingly used it loses its effect. The power which has wrought one may produce any number; but the same act, though repeated most monotonously, may be altered in its character. That which was miracle may now cease to be it. For the idea of this attestation is, that it departs and differs from the ordinary constitution of things. If the sun and moon stand still, if the laws of death be overcome, we observe these events because contrary to all tendency and arrangement as notified to us. Still if these events might be expected, if they followed in a regular course, though precisely identical in process and form, they

would altogether vary in import and evidence. Let a chain of miracles be drawn through every age, and around every individual, and the term is a solecism. The circumstance of frequency is the vitiating principle. But they who imagine that persuasion would follow a resurrection from the dead, necessitate a constant recurrence of these acts ; in a word, their demand for miracle destroys the very character, which can never attach to the grandest displays of Divine power, when interwoven into a strict order and uniform series.

2. The nature of the revelation, which we call the Gospel, is frequently set forth in Scripture ; it is " the record which God hath given of his Son ;" it is the " testimony of God " and " of Christ ;" it is a " witness to all nations ;" it is a " faithful saying ;" it is " the faithful word." The veracity of him who testifies is the common ground of belief in a testimony ; while the most satisfactory evidences of its truth may be found in the testimony itself. The operation of mind is necessarily one of assent and confidence ; until these be exercised, the subject is not brought into any connection with us, or into any capacity of influencing us. Christianity conveys to us the word of salvation, and it requires our belief of it. It comes in the shape of testimony, and credit is to be attached to it. " We walk by faith, not by sight." Its purpose is to divert us from material notices, and to bind us to the simple and cordial " belief of the truth." There must be a value in this purpose ; faith must be more fitting and useful than sensible impression. It must be more accordant with the Gospel, and more beneficial to ourselves, thus to arrive at the conclusion that it is true, and thus to acquire the way by which we may become interested in it. But miracle would trench upon the province and faculty of testimony ; would introduce sense to the disparagement of faith ; would throw back the dispensation from its

maturity; would unsettle the best known and most divinely pledged character which the "word of the truth of the Gospel" has ever received, as well as the strongest foundations on which human conviction has ever rested. "He that hath received his testimony [that of Christ] hath set to his seal that God is true." Grant but the prayer for miracle, and the Gospel is no longer a testimony, nor faith a grace!

3. Miracle belongs to an early and imperfect stage of the Christian revelation. It is a part of its first apparatus—of its scaffolding and machinery. Most necessary was it when the cause it asserted was new, to indicate it as a divine religion, and to urge it as a divine enforcement. But we now possess that state of consummated truth and blessing to which all this magnificence of the supernatural—this awful sway over inveterate disease and extinguished sense, elemental strife and demon rage—were but tributes of homage and means of confirmation. The canon of Scripture being complete, and whatever was preliminary being now adjusted, we may deem ourselves to occupy a most favorable position. We have the perfect volume with the perfect proof. Even in regard to the signs and wonders which surrounded Christianity in its infancy, as guardians and attendants, we may consider ourselves as most enviably circumstanced. We can behold them, from our present eminence, in their unity of rank and spirit. We can trace their analogy to the system which is now seen in all its tenderness and love. We can review them aloof from that bitter temper which disappointed ambition and exasperated prejudice foment. Nothing national, nothing ancestral, opposes our profession of their reality and grandeur. Their succession, their decisiveness as attestations, their beauty as emblems, strike us as they could not contemporary eyes. We may, therefore, congratulate ourselves that those evidences, which are most external, are really

more interesting *now* than at the period of their exhibition. Do we not see how they affected the primitive disciples ? Do we not learn their general acknowledgment from thé general conversion of mankind ? Do we not ascertain how they were appealed to by those who never took an uncertain ground ? We, so to speak, survey the scene from that central point at which the fall of light and the angle of vision are most happily adapted to excite our wonder and correct our apprehension. But now to call for miracle is to desire a return to the nonage and weakness of Christianity—is to forget or deny that superiority which is allotted to us on whom " the ends of the dispensation have come "—is to descend from the calm, in which we can explore the miracle of testimony, into the contentions which have often embroiled the testimony of miracle.

But if preternatural indications be *ineffective* as moral means, and if they can additionally be proved *illegitimate* in the present instance, a third class of reasonings will expose the causes of their *unsuitableness* to produce any true conversion, any saving result.

1. Conviction, when it reaches a certain point, is incapable of any *conscious* increase in its strength and practical influence. The most variously elaborated, the most frequently multiplied, demonstrations, would not very perceptibly fortify our belief if that were founded on one perfectly conclusive. We might be astonished and delighted; but our minds were assured, and our opinions formed, when we mastered the first. Millions, upon the present evidence of Christianity, have attained to a persuasion which left to them no doubt and exception—which suffered them not a hesitating moment and feeling between its maintenance and violent death—which blended itself with all that was intuitive and conscious in their minds. What could have made the confessor bolder, or the martyr more brave ? What could

have raised their faith, or strengthened their constancy? That evidence is before us, it deserves the most complete admission, and warrants the most decided assent. We need not wonder that miracle, therefore, fails to produce the boasted effect, and that the addition of any other would be abortive, since all are competent to adjudge the existing amount of evidence; the believer knowing that the highest pitch of his conviction cannot exceed it, and the unbeliever exemplifying that, if it does not satisfy him, no variation or increase of it could, though the letters were sunbeams and the sounds were thunders.

2. It is complained by the skeptic that the process of inquiry is circuitous—that the course of examination is slow—that writings are to be verified, witnesses to be tried, and motives to be sifted. He suggests a more ready method—let the debate be ended by an appeal to miracle. Be, then, such miracle performed. Being sensible, it could only be inspected by a definite number of persons; occurring at a given time as well as place, many contemporaries, and all posterity, must be unacquainted with its merits. The skeptic might now aver his full acquiescence in Christianity; he would confirm *his* judgment by that unanimous impression which had been made on *all* who witnessed the miracle along with himself. He and they report it, and expect to be believed. He and they consider that all dispute has ceased. But these parties only stand in the circumstances of the first Christians! They cannot employ more undoubting affirmations—they cannot be subjected to more rigid ordeals—they cannot furnish better proofs of veracity and tests of sincerity. Yet *they* reject the allegations of the first Christians, and hope that they themselves shall be believed! To say nothing of this inconsistency in their conduct, this improbability in their expectation —what would have been gained by the concession? The very men who disavowed Christianity, on account

of its peculiar evidence, upon the repetition of the same evidence at their own request, call upon all to embrace it. Thus the original system of examination and ground of belief—the butt of objection—is to be renewed. Age after age is to have its miracle, the testimony to that miracle, and the adherents to that testimony. Again and again the business of evidence is to be begun afresh; and that evidence, too, which if ever faulty and defective, must continue as faulty and defective through every step of its transmission. But this might not only be the cause of inefficiency in the miracle—the proposed arrangement would include another disadvantage. Might it not be deemed a reflection upon the *primitive* evidence, if it was, after this order, renovated? Would not the secondary series be equally disparaged by the third? Would not the succession be attenuated until the conviction of the most remote descendants would be, that a religion which was compelled to submit to these reiterated attestations, and still left men as incredulous and impatient of these attestations as before, *never did* possess a valid authenticity, and never ought to have challenged a reasonable faith.

3. There is a distinction between acts which are voluntary and involuntary. Every act, to be *moral,* or the subject of accountability, must be willingly and self-determinately performed. If my arm is seized by an external power and compelled to commit that from which my mind revolts, it is not within my responsibility. I am the passive, unconsenting instrument. Now, in the impressions made upon our senses, we are almost in the same predicament. Choice is denied us. We may close our eyes and stop our ears, but numberless sights and sounds are borne to these organs over which we have no control. A miracle might be executed before us. We could not fail to observe it. But this would be necessary and not optional, and therefore the observation

would partake of no moral quality.   What, that is commendable—what, that supposes disposition and motive—what, that refers to law and recompense, could such act contain?   It is not questioned that the *examination* of miracle may spring from a holy and a praiseworthy temper of mind.   But it is of the single process, through which the *senses* pass, that we now speak.   And if it be not a moral sentiment, we need not wonder that men are not "persuaded" by it; we need not wonder that it sets in motion no train of pious reflections and devout sensibilities.   It has only, so far, been a perforce admission; a nerve has been impinged, a sense has been excited, but an unreasoning and irreligious creature might have undergone the same obtrusion, and not have, more certainly than the man himself, resisted the proper review and the just inference.

4. When miracle has been displayed, there can be no doubt of its intention.   It is to call human attention to some great principle, some important truth.   It is the unison of almighty power with infinite love.   It certifies and urges revelation.   We might conclude, therefore, that men would never mark the one without following out the other.   And if this were so, miracle might have, in its consequences, a persuasive power.   But the ideas of the *reality* belonging to a supernatural occurrence, and of the *truth* involved in a particular religion which it has transpired to confirm, are not uniformly, not frequently, associated in the mind of the spectator.   Curiosity may gaze with a perfect vacancy of speculation.   We have now only to do with the fact as one of history.   Thousands were fed by our Lord through the most palpable operations of miraculous skill and might: thousands witnessed his cures of disease, and his exorcism of demons: yet how seldom did the conviction occur to them that, if these things were true, so also must be the doctrine he taught!

Herod " hoped to have seen some miracle done by him ; " but it is abundantly clear, that had his wish been gratified, he did not surmise that it would pledge him to the allowance of any particular religious system. The Pharisees even accused him of casting out devils by the prince of devils !* And if any proof be wanted to demonstrate how dissevered these convictions of a miracle and a mission may be, let us advert to the portents which solemnized the sacrifice of the cross. It is a terrific scene ! The noon of day is dark as the noon of night ! The silence of death is disturbed ! The vail of the temple is torn from the top to the bottom ! The solid globe trembles ! The massive rock splits ! Once the sun stood still on Gibeon; why is it stayed in its course, covered with sackcloth, turned into blood, over Calvary ? Graves have, at distant intervals, yawned and resigned their prisoners, why do so many now simultaneously rend, and why do so many of their sleeping captives, without a signal, rise ? The sanctities of the temple have, ere this, been profaned, but why is its tapestry now, without a visible agency, torn asunder ? Earth has known strange tremors, the land has been heaved into billows as the sea, but why does it now suffer these convulsions, and struggle with these throes ? Rocks, when God's " fury is poured out like fire," have been thrown down by him, but why do they now burst and shiver ? The multitude, the connection, the conjuncture

* How little competent the pagan world was to decipher the meaning and connection of those omens, which they esteemed real, may be gathered from the classical historians. Thus, Tacitus, in his Annals, (and we overlook not the sarcasm,) says: " Prodigia quoque crebra et irrita intercessere . . . quæ adeò sinè curâ deûm eveniebant, ut multos post annos Nero imperium et scelera continuaverit." In his History, relating the prodigies which foreboded the overthrow of Jerusalem, he marks the little and narrow impression they excited: " Quæ panci in metum trahebant."

of these phenomena, supplied an assemblage of awful demonstrations; they struck a panic, they produced a change of feeling and conduct. They, who had wagged their heads, now smote upon their breasts. It was "a compunctious visiting of nature," and nothing more. And only a few, and those from whom the confession might have been least expected, cried out, "Truly, this was the Son of God."

5. Supposing that there is no evasion of the lesson and doctrine inculcated by a miracle, it by no means follows that the mind receives them with cordiality and affection. The reasonable association may have forced itself upon it, that both are equally, and consecutively, true. But as the impression of miracle was violent, so the belief of that which it seals may be constrained. The heart may rebel against it. It may seem "as a strange thing." It may be endured as an object of terror and aversion. It may not be disputed, and yet not be loved. Men may regard it as Ahab did Micaiah—knowing he was a prophet, yet outraging him for prophesying only evil. They may be as unable to resist, as to cherish, the light; and like Satan, described by our bard, glance but at the sun, "to tell it how he hates its beams." The Gospel is a scheme of particular instructions. These may be mechanically enforced, or morally entertained. They may be assented to as moving in the train of a miracle; there may be a general apprehension of their meaning; and nothing short of enmity may scowl upon them. The bond, which shackles them to the mind, is no tie of its own; the supernatural evidence is the iron chain which, while it leaves it no liberty, softens no dislike. But when the understanding and the affections coincide with these propositions of truth—when every doctrine becomes endeared and every lesson attractive—when esteem is the effect of appreciation, and "faith worketh by love," then the entire soul is gained,

and every thought is captivated "to the obedience of Christ." The one process breaks, the other melts, the adamantine heart. The former compels, the latter wins, our conviction. In the first instance, it is the billow chafing the strand, lashing the shore; in the second, it is the ripple of the lake, when dimpled into beauty and when pulsing with music, spreading itself from the center in graceful circles, and kissing the flowery margin which rather protects than restrains it.

6. The inefficiency of miracle may be explained by an examination of the mind on which it is supposed to operate. Every mind has its tastes, its associations, and its habitudes. Its present nature or disposition is that of the deepest depravity. Men sin not accidentally and artificially. " Yea, they have chosen their own ways, and their soul delighteth in their abominations." In any other circumstances they would follow a course as sinful. The evil has its roots in the heart, and let it beat on earth or in hell, it is "desperately wicked." It is set upon it. The only method for its renovation is, that other tastes, associations, and habitudes be introduced. There must be established counteracting tempers and antagonist principles. But miracle is a " sign to them that believe not," and falls *without* them. It cannot, therefore, alter the prevailing bias. By the terror it inspires, by the check it imposes, it may suspend, but cannot destroy, it. The love of sin will be sure to restore its practice, when the powerful restraint, the diverting cause, is removed. Men will go on in their trespasses; nor would any external circumstance, however startling and tremendous, radically change, or effectually deter, them. A superficial application cannot reach to a disease whose cancerous fibers strike into the innermost core of the heart.

7. We may conceive, as revelation is a system of pure favor and mercy, of a difference in the extent of it

evidence. To those who desire a larger sum, we may suggest there might be less. And time was, when its present amplitude was much circumscribed. Yet, even then, men were required to embrace it. It was most reasonable for them to receive it as credible as important. What we may denominate the present excess, is therefore the effect of gratuitous favor. It is more than is demanded by the strictest exigencies of the case. Perhaps those who anticipated our period, asked the precise addition for their satisfaction which we now enjoy. It is the differential amount. And does not this prove, and should not this establish, that the argument of truth has always sufficed to convince, that the exhibition of truth has always been competent to impress, and that miracles, more or less numerous—the fact of a divine interposition and sanction being once settled—would leave mankind without any perceptible or conscious difference in their moral state and religious tendency?

8. However men may lay the burden of their unbelief on the scarcity and defectiveness of proof, we cannot doubt that there is wanting, on *their part*, what no mere proof can supply. They are not debarred by the fastidiousness or vigor of the reasoning faculty, by the peculiar turn of intellect, by the cautious habit of research, by being inured to habits of a severe logic and of a rigid demonstration. It is *impression* of which they stand in need. They have never duly weighed the subject. They have never assumed, for a moment, its results. They have never put, even on a supposition, its consequences, should they be confirmed. Their conduct is imprinted with egregious trifling. Seriousness they disclaim and despise. Other susceptibilities, before they commence their study of the evidence, must be awakened. It is not the ray that is wanted to dart on their reason, it is the lightning to strike and pierce their conscience. And men but hypocritically or self-deceivedly assert their

minology, more consequential reasoning. To this we reply, that Scripture was written on certain principles. The *first* was to exercise the mind—in comparing the whole, in developing the spirit, in drawing the inference: its meaning is clear, but it is not presented in rudiments, propositions, and axioms. It is to be sought, to be digested, to be systematized. However technicalities are avoided, there is a "proposition of faith." The *second* is to be a perpetual *test* to our state of disposition. To the pure, to the meek, to the upright, to the docile, to the humble, it shows its truth. These "see it," "taste it," and have "all riches of the full assurance of understanding." No dimness pervades divine revelation; the "light that is in us is darkness:" no vail is upon it; it is "upon our heart." And so long as "the natural man receiveth not the things of the Spirit of God," no argument could prove them to his judgment, no language could simplify them to his apprehension, no recommendation could endear them to his heart.

And let us remember that often as this excuse has been alleged, this plea adopted, it was never heard by Heaven but to be disowned and refused. And that surrounded by all the information, and possessed of all the warning, which shall ever be imparted to us, it becomes us now to decide. In vain we wait for another economy of things. In vain we ask for a more auspicious era. "There shall be no sign given." "The dispensation of the fullness of times." has evolved the last truth, and counsel, and hope. And now eternity unfolds its motive to urge our decision. There is a disclosure of heaven and hell. *The term for prayer is short.* This is a duty at least as important as that of intelligent conviction. Yet has it no scope in the place of torment. It can only ascend to Abraham's bosom to be rejected. It may expostulate, but it is beaten back upon the suppliant wretch. "Seek ye the Lord while

he may be found, call ye upon him while he is near." "Whosoever shall call on the name of the Lord shall be saved." *There is no term to retribution.* "The great gulf is fixed." Some may speak of the disciplinary flame. They may point their unhappy proselytes to the pit, as only a longer and rougher path to heaven. They may describe the misery of the lost as curative and salutary. But how have they learned to solve the difficulty which he, who "was called the friend of God," confessed? or contrived to throw the crossway over the abyss, impassable to spirits which might attempt the flight to soothe the lost, or escape to the blest?

O, it is plainly, incontrovertibly true, that we all sin, and all disbelieve, against declarations more pointed, against facts more stupendous, than any miracles. It is certain that nothing preternatural could conquer the apathy and the malignity which these cannot subdue. "We have a more sure word" of testimony than the gorgeous vision of "the holy mount." What could arouse, what impress, what soften us, if we can hear that "God was in Christ, reconciling the world unto himself," without rapt attention and bleeding emotion; if we can gaze on "Jesus, who delivered us from the wrath to come," without a weeping eye and a breaking heart? These are the higher wonders which men resist; the spectacles of merciful power, of unalterable love, which they withstand. He, who was "in the bosom of the Father," has tabernacled on an earth which was "made by him and for him," and was "God manifest in the flesh." The nature He assumed was the awful device and instrument for a sacrifice, which received all the merits, and developed all the purposes, of the Indwelling Divinity. He went down into the state of death: though the "Living Being, he was dead:" He rose from the grave, and bore our nature and our cause with him, not only as the subject of his

advocacy and government, but as an essential of his person, and the crown of his glory. It were easy, after evading and opposing these truths, to deride the most dazzling sign, and mock the most solemn voice, of the Almighty; to run "upon him, even upon the thick bosses of his bucklers." *Now* this conduct may find some apologist, and shelter itself in some pretext! *Now* it may be thought an honorable candor if some doubter shall exclaim, "Almost thou persuadest me to be a Christian!" *Now* it may seem no insolence to assert, that the religion which four thousand years were required to reveal only failed to convince; that the sentiments with which it was greeted only•fell short of a conviction that it was true; and that the creature to whom it was addressed did all but embrace it! But *then,* when all hearts are exposed—but *then,* when all men are arraigned—unbelief shall stand recorded and accursed, as the blasphemy of rebellion, as the extravagance of infatuation, as the madness of folly! No palliative will then occur, no sophism then flatter! "They shall proceed no further!"

Your faith, your obedience, are at this moment demanded upon substantive grounds, upon all-interesting reasons: you have the complement of evidence, and the accumulation of impression: justice dictates nothing superadded, and mercy asks no more! Therefore, "Say not in thine heart, Who shall ascend into heaven? (that is, to bring Christ down from above,) or, who shall descend into the deep? (that is, to bring up Christ again from the dead.) But what saith it? The word is nigh thee, even in thy mouth, and in thy heart; that is, the word of faith, which we preach; that if thou shalt confess with thy mouth the Lord Jesus, and shalt believe in thine heart that God hath raised him from the dead, thou shalt be saved."

V.

INCARNATE DEITY.

Let this mind be in you, which was also in Christ Jesus: who, being in the Form of God, thought it not robbery to be Equal with God. But made Himself of no reputation, and took upon Him the form of a servant, and was made in the likeness of men: and being found in fashion as a Man, He humbled himself, and became obedient unto death, even the death of the Cross.—Philippians ii, 5, 8.

We sometimes form ideals of moral beauty, archetypes of more than we have ever realized, images of wondrous and unattainable excellence. Such thoughts steal over our minds as the most exquisite and fair of all our intellectual creations, and unfold their endless variety with a kind of visioned enchantment. Like shoots of light they come and go: as dreams they gather and melt away. Few would be without these glowing visitations who have once enjoyed them; and few have enjoyed them without being improved. They form a world of their own, peopled with touching and majestic conceptions, breathing with intense and sublime aspirations. To this, we can retreat from the dull and gross repetitions of daily occurrence, we may escape from scenes which embitter and torment. These pictures of the mind not only preserve its sensibilities in their most delicate bloom, but rise upon us either as recollections of some former state, now most unaccountably obscured; or as the premonitions of another, prepared for us when

we pass from this earth, and refine from the meaner elements which at present encumber our spirits.

But there is one instance in which all such shadowings of fancy fall short of the original. I speak not now of the poet's inferiority to the task. I speak not now of the painter's incapacity for the theme. I speak not now of the abortive attempt of genius and art. It relates not to the spell of numbers, or the delineation of forms. Let the character of Him whom the text describes be contemplated. To whom shall we "liken," or shall it be "equal?" The noblest thoughts may be raised, the boldest imaginations may be exercised, and yet how most distantly they approach its idea, how most feebly they answer its reality? An undefined remembrance of its outline never strikes us in the manner with which we are occasionally affected, when, seeing an object for the first time, we cannot overcome the impression that we have been acquainted with it before. But with what resemblances and sympathies is this character to be identified? May it not challenge a perfect uniformity and originality? Where is the mind in which the pattern of it could be revolved and cast? To what prototype does it correspond, and according to which it is fashioned? It is an excellence which originates its own idea, a greatness which creates its own standard, a peculiarity of claims and attributes which circles forever in itself.

This character, as we peruse its record of severe simplicity and unconscious praise, must be regarded in the following manner—it was embodied in a living being, or it is but a lovely fiction; it did or it did not exist. If it did appear as a personal history, it could not belong to an *enthusiast,* since he can have no part in such holy prudence, profound discrimination, and unswerving consistency. And it can as little coalesce with the *impostor,* because his course must be most abhorrent from this

erect independence, this noble purpose, this disinterested meekness, this transparent simplicity, this indefatigable benignity. His religion is thus demonstrably established. But if this character be unreal—without foundation in truth, never possessing sphere for activity—there sprung from the mountains of Galilee and the banks of Gennesaret a marvel of imagination more sweet and more heroic than the magic of Greek and Roman poetry ever summoned into being, or molded into shape.

Though, if it were in our power, it would be most desirable to consider "the mind which was in Christ Jesus" as a *whole,* our faculties necessitate us to detach it into parts: as a sphere of light it overpowers and confounds us, we therefore must dissever and decompose its rays. And it will greatly depend upon the particular inquiry and argument, what may be the point in this assemblage of transcendent qualities to which we advert. Such is its compass, that there is nothing which it cannot illustrate.

The scope of this apostolic enforcement defines a portion of this character. Humility in condescension, disinterestedness in benevolence, are the properties selected. "Lowliness of mind," generous "looking to the things of others," are urged from their illustration in the temper and conduct of the Saviour. He is portrayed as a perfect specimen of these virtues. We are adjured to copy his example, and emulate his course.

It is no objection to the moral reasonableness of the imitation enjoined in the sacred writings that it often consults and pursues that which is infinite. There is before us, beyond the present opportunity, an eternal career. But for that infinite, the mind would reach a limitation, and then happiness must terminate with progression. We are therefore commanded to be "perfect as our Father in heaven is perfect:" to be holy "as He

who hath called" us is holy: to " be followers of God as dear children." Nothing, therefore, could be more rash and ill founded than to allege that the example pressed upon us in this connection must respect a simply finite or human being, because, otherwise, conformity to it would be hopelessly impracticable. It stands in the same rank of fitness and authority with those inspired directions and statements which describe, confessedly, the Supreme as claiming the imitation of his creatures, or stamping his resemblance upon them.

And assuredly, upon the most general survey of the case now cited to us, we shall conclude that Jesus Christ, who sets such a pattern, was more than man; that he existed in another condition previously to the adoption of our own; that the change to which he lowered himself was intended to denote an act and mark a principle of condescension; and that this condescension, to deserve the name, must be voluntary and spontaneous. But the condescension of a creature in not rivaling his Maker, of a responsible creature in becoming a servant, of a mortal creature in submitting to death, is not a very intelligible proposition, nor furnishes a subject very worthy of panegyric. At the first view, to say the least, the representation does not seem the most clear, nor the occasion of pressing it the most happily chosen. Some instance rather more abstinent from daring impiety may be conceived, a deeper degree of self-renunciation might be imagined. In the universal range of human conduct, among the generations of men, among the ornaments and lights of virtue—a superior portraiture of modesty, of diffidence, of shrinking sensitive withdrawment from notoriety and ostentation, could perhaps be selected. We are not immediately impressed with the sobriety and simplicity of style employed in recommending a person whose conduct had been only negative in its purest pretensions, and in all other respects had yielded

to the necessary laws of his being. There does, on the supposition that a man is anointed as an unparalleled model of forbearance in not presuming to be the Deity, and in acquiescing to be man, seem an effort, elaborate, if not extravagant, in thus emblazoning him. It is somewhat remote from a self-evident truth, why such a man on these grounds should take precedence of all those spirits who have walked humbly with their God. A few strokes commonly supply the biography of Scripture—nothing can be more chaste and inartificial than its ordinary method—but this, if justifiable at all, would seem of another class—the detail crowded, and the color overcharged. Let us remember that this description is affirmed of Him concerning whom it is written, " In his humiliation his judgment was taken away ;" who himself said, " I am meek and lowly in heart."

But there were circumstances which required the eulogists of the Saviour, if only man, to be henceforth most rigidly exact in stating his claims. It cannot be forgotten under what charges he was impeached and crucified. He was accused of no less a crime than *blasphemy.* None ventured to adduce it, in the sense of irreverence to the divine name, or disobedience to the divine law. His deep seriousness, his habitual devotion, were too plainly indicated by his temper and conversation to be doubted. He obeyed the temple-trumpet which sounded the hour of prayer. Each festival saw him among the pilgrim tribes. He spake of the Father with a hallowed awe. The night spent in devotion could not conceal its influence from the day. But his countrymen did suppose that his language intimated a near approach to the Infinite Nature; they understood him to assert an equality with it. It was common for him to declare himself the *proper,* the only begotten, Son of God. His mode of describing certain conjoint acts and sentiments between his Father and himself,

certainly strengthened the impression. "*We* will come unto him and make *our* abode with him." "That they may be one in *us*." The supposition that he arrogated to himself divine honors instigated his nation to adduce this heavy charge. His conduct, during the trial, did nothing most assuredly to dispel it. He asserted the truth of the allegation, upon the oath which was administered to him. The law was very clear: "He that blasphemeth the name of Jehovah shall surely be put to death." Lev. xxiv, 16. Nothing could outreach his blasphemy *if* he, merely born of woman, presumed to share the divine essence and throne; if he, "being man, made himself God." And this seemed equally implied in that title which he avowed—the King of the Jews. The Highest was emphatically their king. But to Pilate and Caiaphas he alike asserted and maintained that the claim was his. The ascription was conceded to him in scorn; he received, in this character, the mockery of homage; and beneath the unfurled sentence which proclaimed it, he was put to death. There were those who saw danger in this unqualified label of the cross. They would have marked a condition in it, but what "was written was written." If the Son of God did intend nothing that was divine, he had been grossly misconceived. We say nothing now whether his own language had been sufficiently limited. But according to this hypothesis of exclusive humanity, it became his Apostles to be most scrupulous when they "preached Jesus Christ their Lord." An immense evil had arisen from mistake, and mistake founded upon a peculiar style of language. It was time to correct it, and to substitute, for the occasion of it, a stricter course of annotation. The mischief must be repaired. But if our text be an earnest of this revised phraseology, this subdued manner; if this be the way in which the Apostles labored to break down the prejudices of men, as to the received, though mis-

taken, claims of their Master; if this was the expedient by which they depressed him from an imaginary rank, and contracted his honors within an inferior space; if so they lessened his prerogative, and if thus they abridged his dignity—then to disabuse mankind is hopeless, and " the last error is worse than the first."

Our embarrassment—if the description in the text be intended to signify that Jesus Christ was nothing more than human, and was furnished specifically to rectify the contrary opinion—is increased by recollecting the character and intention of the apostolic epistles. They were addressed to Churches, or believers. They served the purpose of reminding them, of reassuring them, of confirming them : they offer advice in difficulty, they point the particular application of principle. But they presuppose the profession of the Christian faith. They declare no new doctrine; only urging those to whom they are addressed to build up themselves on their most holy faith. And if the language, which we now consider, be but a reference to admitted opinion, and a stimulus to cherished piety, then what must have been the conceptions with which it readily cohered, and the affections with which it naturally mingled! What must have been the scheme of faith to which it answered, and the train of feeling into which it could flow! It is but a passing allusion; yet it announces that they who understood and justified it—whose minds could give it their assent, and whose hearts could vibrate their response—were not peculiarly straitened in their sentiments of the Saviour's person, nor exceedingly suspicious of the fervor with which they regarded his mission.

It is, therefore, observable that this allusive style is very cursory, as well as sudden, in the Epistles. There is no pause, no faltering—as though the idea would not be caught, or could be disputed. It is always suggested

without effort, and enforced without reserve; it is an approved and welcome thing. A modern writer* has truly remarked of these sacred penmen in their letters, "If they say any thing concerning the person of Christ it is in an incidental way, and not as if they were introducing any strange and astonishing discovery." The remark proceeds from an avowed opponent of all opinions and sympathies which can exalt and endear the Lord Jesus; but it is critically and religiously just. And we accept and apply it. The language of the text was not a "strange and astonishing discovery." It is "introduced" in an "incidental way." But then how irresistible is the inference, that the views were most elevated which this allusion did not shock, and that the hearts were prepared for every divine sensibility, in which it could strike a perfect chord!

These observations relate to the general structure, the superficial features of this passage: it is time that we should more closely inspect it.

I. WE ARE DIRECTED TO A STATE IN WHICH THE LORD JESUS SUBSISTED, ANTECEDENTLY TO PARTICULAR ACTS WHICH HE PERFORMED, AND WHICH RENDERS THOSE ACTS SO INTERESTING AND EXTRAORDINARY.

Whenever we think and speak of Deity, we feel our incapability of forming abstract ideas, and employing befitting expressions. And to discussions of the Saviour's divine nature this is often objected. But it equally applies to that which belongs to the first principle of all religion—the being of a God. Still if in that self-existing power and purity—if in that mysterious essence, of which these are but manifestations and attributes—there be nothing that we can fully comprehend or duly explain, are we therefore to forego all reverent inquiry, to suspend all moral exercise, because we cannot "find Him out unto perfection?" The divinity of Jesus Christ

* Belsham: Calm Inquiry.

does involve a most ineffable secret, a diversity of persons in the Godhead. We cannot look at the one fact without observing the necessary proof of the other. But such diversity could not, by any previous reasoning or induction, be shown improbable or contradictory, unless each being of finite nature was the standard and mirror of that which is infinite; and unless infinite being was a subject that could be included within human investigations, and shadowed by material analogies. It is vain to set one difficulty against another; but if that be adduced which implies a personal distinction, we contend that it is as explicable as the eternity and underived existence of that nature in which it inheres. It is most foreign to our taste to offer simile and illustration; but we deny the evidence of that simple unity in all finite things which has been affirmed, or that such notions of relation and quantity are inexorably to be transferred to Him whcse name is "I am that I am." With the information of Scripture on "the deep things of God" we resolve to satisfy ourselves; believing that it is not only sufficient for us, but that it is all which God could intelligibly reveal.

It is assumed that Jesus Christ was "in the form of God;" this is the *first* part of the proposition.

The phrase certainly denotes nothing of corporeal subsistence or dimensions. Accidents of this kind cannot attach to him who "is a Spirit."

It supposes nothing that is necessary to perfect and infinite nature, for it is capable of being accepted and laid aside. It cannot be divine *claim*, for all that we can understand by the term is inalienable and indefeasible. He "giveth not his glory to another." He "changeth not." Nor can it be divine *power*. He may cease to exercise it, but not to disallow it. "He fainteth not," nor is it a property optional and variable. And still less can it be divine *personality*. The language is

quite warranted by the inspired notice, "He is the brightness of" the Father's "glory, and the express image of his *person*." * Does not this assert not only the person of the Father, but also—as he is "the express image"—the person of the Son? Does not this assert, by the twofold implication of the term, the distinction to be of a personal character between the Father and the Son? But that cannot be intended here. For from it there could be no descent. And we should be loath, even did not the argument lead us another way, to enter into any dissertation, or attempt at dissertation, on the *modes* of the Infinite existence. There is "no manner of similitude" intimated in Scripture, and let us not invent one.

God has, however, appeared through certain mediums, and by certain manifestations, to his creatures. It has been in a manner most descriptive. He has bowed the heavens and come down. He has made his angels spirits, and his ministers a flame of fire. He has rode upon a cherub, and flown on the wings of the wind. The clouds have been his chariot, and the garniture of the sky has burnished his throne. His voice has been very powerful, and full of majesty. He has lifted himself out of his holy place. He has shown the lighting down of his arm. Men have been afraid of his tokens. The earth has melted. Thus, deity was beheld of old with a pomp of symbols, and with a grandeur—to adopt the language of poetic criticism—of machines. He was encircled with the Shechinah, attended by his hosts, and making proclamation of his titles. But sometimes the glory was more attempered, "the manner of the God" was vailed, and "there was the hiding of his power." Such was his style of appearance, indicative, characteristic, incommunicable. "It is as the appearance of the likeness of the glory of the Lord." And this outward display we consider to be "the form of God." The proper accom-

* Heb, i. 3. χαρακτηρ της ὑποστασεως αυτõυ.

paniments of the divine presence and manifestation are the only ideas we can associate with the term in this connection. Nothing model in his being and subsistence does he reveal, or can we understand. But as there must be proofs of his particular appearance—for " he is not far from every one of us "—these proofs may justly be designated his *form*, or peculiar manner of exhibiting himself.

But it is impossible to proceed any further without the inquiry, whether He, who is the Father; did ever thus appear? whether his office in the scheme of redemption did not preclude it ? The forerunner of Christ thus bare witness of him : " No man hath seen God at any time ; the only begotten Son, which is in the bosom of the Father, he hath declared him." And, accordingly, the Saviour adds a similar testimony : " Ye have neither heard his voice at any time, nor seen his shape." Though we strive not to know the original distinctiveness of the Son in the Godhead, yet as " the word who was God," there seems an essential fitness for revealing the divine mind, while, by official consecration, he was *sent* and " *anointed* to preach glad tidings."

The facts are these. There did oftentimes appear on earth, to the senses or the thoughts of men, one who could claim each divine prerogative and honor. An example may illustrate, at the same time, the plainest manner and the highest declaration of this awful visitant. We are expressly informed* that " Jehovah appeared unto Abraham in the plains of Mamre." Three men approach his tent. Two, afterward called angels, hasten to Sodom ; but Abraham " stood yet before Jehovah," who is described as promising the birth of Isaac, and receiving the earnest intercessions of the Patriarch on behalf of the cities so quickly " condemned with an overthrow." And the mysterious narrative is closed by the notice,

* Gen. xviii : passim.

" Jehovah went his way, as soon as he left communing with Abraham." This example might be easily enlarged; but its authority is decisive. More generally this being is denominated the *angel* of the Lord; though he appropriates the " great and dreadful name " of Jehovah, speaks in his own right, and suffers the presentation of the strictest worship. He is Jehovah, and yet *sent* of him —of Him, personally considered, who " dwelleth in the light which no man can approach unto, whom no man hath seen, nor can see." But " He and the Father are one." And the angel-relation of Jesus Christ is quite accordant with the Scripture account of him: " The Lord whom ye seek shall suddenly come to his temple, even the *messenger* of the covenant."

The conclusion is, in our opinion, inevitable: The Second Person of the Trinity, in anticipation of his incarnate sojourn upon earth, did frequently, through the interval of four thousand years, alight upon our globe, converse with our race, and renew the pledge of our salvation.

Who walked in Eden when the day of our offending began to decline? It was the Lord God whose voice the fugitives heard, and whose *form* they trembled to behold.

Who spake to Noah, and enjoined him to " prepare an ark to the saving of his house ? " The Lord gave the commandment, and " the Lord shut him in."

Who was he that, expressing the fervor of Jacob to detain him, and receive his blessing, wrestled with him until the dawn? The triumphant Israel saw " God face to face " at Peniel, as " he found him in Bethel, even the Lord God of hosts."—Hosea xii, 4, 5.

Who called unto Moses from the bush wrapped in the unconsuming flame? The angel of the Lord; but he explains himself by the most awful formula: " I am the God of thy father." And again, commissioning his serv-

ant to demand of Pharaoh the deliverance of his captive brethren, he adds, "Thus shalt thou say, 'I AM hath sent me unto you.'"

Who "came from Sinai and rose up from Seir?" Who "came with ten thousands of saints?" From whose "right hand went the fiery law?" "The *angel* spake to Moses in the Mount Sinai, and with the fathers." Acts vii, 38.

Who was "the angel sent before" that people? He was the Lord who looked out of the pillar, who dwelt in the cloud, who could extend or refuse the pardon of iniquity, who required the profoundest homage when he passed through the camp: "Neither let us tempt *Christ*, as some of them also tempted, and were slain of serpents." 1 Cor. x, 9.

Who was the Personage described in the vision of the Hebrew bards? They saw Him "traveling in the greatness of his strength, mighty to save." They heard "the name by which he should be called, Jehovah our righteousness." They beheld "the Son of man coming with the clouds of heaven," and obtaining "an everlasting dominion which shall not pass away."

Whether these appearances were more mystical, legislative, transient, permanent, visionary—One Being may be recognized in all. And when we remember that to him was confided the Jewish Church, that he was the source of its inspiration, we can understand how true is his pathetic appeal, "How *often* would I have gathered thy children!" since of old he "sent his prophets, rising early, and sending them." And in recalling the dread description he had given of his name in Midian, we can perceive how just is his language during "the days of his flesh:" "If ye believe not that *I am*, ye shall die in your sins. Even the same that I said unto you from *the beginning.*"

Nor is there any kind of manifestation implied in

"this form," but of which our Redeemer has availed himself. We may select the more prominent and signal circumstances which say, with infallible distinctness, "Behold your God."

Splendor is the emblem of Deity. "He covereth himself "with light as with a garment." "Our God is a consuming fire." "He is light, and in him is no darkness at all." "A fire devours before him." "There was under his feet as it were a paved work of a sapphire stone, and as it were the body of heaven in his clearness." So from Sinai did the people hear "the voice" of the Son "out of the midst of the fire." So when the Lord sat upon the "throne high and lifted up," such was the glory that "the house was filled with smoke." So when "the likeness of the firmament was as the color of the terrible crystal," "upon the likeness of the throne" He stood, "as the appearance of a man above upon it."

Title is announced whenever the Deity appears. He "passes by and proclaims himself." "Lift up your heads, O ye gates, and the King of glory shall come in. Who is the King of glory? The Lord of hosts, he is the King of glory." "He is the Living God." "He is the Holy One." And Christ is "the Lord of glory," the "Living Being, (Rev. i, 18,) and "Prince of Life :" He is the "Adonai and Jehovah :" He is "the thrice holy Lord of hosts," (John xii, 41 :) He is "Jehovah's Fellow :" nor is there any name and description inalienably divine, but is accorded to him without limit, reserve, and extenuation.

Agency is ascribed to the Deity when he descends to his creatures. He is universally and invariably working in all Nature and by all Providence : He "worketh all in all." He is acknowledged the Creator, Governor, Conservator, Judge. And Christ is enabled to say, "My Father worketh hitherto, and I work." "By him

were all things created that are in heaven and that are in earth, visible or invisible, whether they be thrones, or dominions, or principalities, or powers." "He is head over all things." "By Him all things consist." "All judgment is committed " to Him. "For what things soever the Father doeth, these also doeth the Son likewise."

Retinue forms an appendage to the revelation of Deity. Thousand thousands minister to him, and ten thousand times ten thousand stand before him. And the seraphim wait the Saviour's bidding, and swell his train which filleth the temple. And of Him was it foretold, and in Him was it verified, "The chariots of God are twenty thousand, even thousands of angels. Thou hast ascended on high, thou hast led captivity captive, thou hast received gifts for men." "He that descended is the same also that ascended far above all heavens, that he might fill all things."*

Worship is challenged by the Deity, and "Him only shalt thou serve." "The Lord is a jealous God." And yet did the writings of the Old Testament describe the Messiah as deserving and requiring equal honors. They predicted that all people should serve him, that all nations should bow down before him, that daily should he be praised. He, therefore, appropriated all divine rights, and received all divine glories, while upon earth —though it was no part of his mission to reveal his claim, and was a part of his humiliation to shade it. Nor can language be more authoritative than this: "That all men should honor the Son even as they honor the Father."

And during his stay on earth, he gave many a proof that the "form of God" was in his power and at his control; and his awful appearances posterior to his

* Psalm lxviii, 17, etc., compared with Ephesians iv, 8, etc.

resurrection, showed that what for a time he had deposed, he now permanently resumed.

In miracle he often "manifested forth his glory." Making bodily cure the seal of forgiveness, he did that which can be done by "God only;" and producing a change in the elements of nature, he constrained spectators to come and worship, saying, "Of a truth thou art the Son of God."

By his transfiguration, a majesty, so to speak, escaped him which he had studiously concealed; celestial legates waited upon him; the ancient blaze of the Holiest burned around him; his form became radiant and converted into the glory; and though the vision quickly passed, the impression was not so suddenly effaced from his person; for, descending from the mount, where the disciples had been "eye-witnesses of his majesty," straightway "all the people, when they beheld him, were greatly amazed, and running to him, saluted him."

At his ascension he bent to his purpose every material law, soared by a viewless energy through the regions of mid-air, was seen bearing away "with the clouds of heaven," entered "the everlasting doors," and became reinvested "with the glory which he had with the Father's own self before the world was."

To Stephen he stood disclosed "standing on the right hand of God:" the brightness of the scene kindled dled the martyr's fading eye, and cheered the martyr's pierced heart; and the saint broke away from his murderers, and sprung "to be with Christ" that he "might behold his glory."

Paul was struck to the earth by his glory outshining the meridian sun, and penetrated by his all-subduing voice bursting forth from that "heavenly vision."

And to John "one like unto the Son of man" appeared, and yet so dread and resplendent that the identity could scarcely be determined by him who had "leaned"

his head on " the bosom " now " girt with a golden girdle ;" who had beheld crowned with thorns the head and the hairs which were now " white like wool, as white as snow;" who had watched beneath the cross those eyes dim, and fix, and close, which were now " as a flame of fire ;" who had heard the nail driven through the feet which were now " like unto fine brass, as if they burned in a furnace;" who had received the dying commands of that voice which was now " as the sound of many waters ;" who had seen the right hand scoffingly filled with the reed, whose palm now held " seven stars ;" who had observed that mouth impiously struck, from which now gleamed " a two-edged sword ;" who had gazed on the countenance furrowed by care, swollen with grief, bathed in blood, which was now " as the sun shineth in his strength."

Heaven witnesses that He is " in the form of God:" He is " in the midst of the throne," he is " the light of the city." He is often the theme of distinctive praise by the angelic and redeemed throng; and the Lamb, with all his sacrificial associations, is added to the otherwise undistinguished Godhead—his memory is woven into every robe, and his name is chanted in every song.

And Judgment shall unfold his " form of God." " He cometh with clouds, and every eye shall see him." The universe shall " flow down at his presence." Heaven, earth, and hell, shall pour forth their multitudes at his tribunal. The moon shall be blood, the sun sackcloth, before the magnificence of that great and terrible day. And then all doubt shall vanish, reproach shall be taken away, " The Son of man shall come *in his own glory.*"

The argument, therefore, presses us, would this state and glory of Jehovah be lent to the creature? Could attributes and claims, by the which only can the Infinite Supremacy be acknowledged, be transferred to that which is limited, dependent, accountable, and mortal?

Must not such an arrangement, provided it were *possible*, induce a confusion most mischievous as well as bewildering? All our notion of *inert* matter is from its qualities; of *being*, from its qualities too. It is not the mention of the divine name which gives the idea of the Divinity: it is power, intelligence, truth, justice, purity, benignity, which are necessary to constitute it. The infinite possession, or, to use phraseology better adapted to our limitation, the highest *conceivable* elevation of these perfections, must belong to a being, and that Being we call God. Nor can any thing prevent us from *deifying* such a Being, because all our tests of thought, all our powers of conception, must pursue this reasoning, and must terminate in this result. The absurdity of the contrary course would be, that words must forsake their import, properties their relation—there could be no First Cause, no Ultimate Perfection, in the universe. God would be known by no discrimination of ideas, and his creatures could not be discriminated from him. Infinitude, omnipotence, self-existence, might be found apart from the Supreme Nature, and would furnish no guides to us in endeavoring to ascertain what that Nature was, in whom it subsisted, and how it stood related to ourselves. If Jesus Christ, " being in the form of God," at the same time is not God, then no predicates in language, no facts in induction, no accessories in idea, can establish the conclusion that there is such a being as God; or, if able to establish it in any given moment, to leave it on an ultimate and irrevocable tenure.

Nor is it unimportant to observe the *supposed independence* which the participle conveys: "*Being* in the form of God." It is spoken of no time, it is rested on no contingency. It is implied to be of an absolute nature. He may do other things, he may assume other characters, but he begins, if there be beginning to him, with *this;* and it is this which gives its infinite contrast

to his "dimness and vexation." It is this alone which can stamp a condescension on his form as a servant, and his fashion as a man. These latter changes belong to a *date*, and evolve from an *arrangement;* and thus differ from that superior condition *notwithstanding* which they were undertaken. And our minds must go back to the period before which he "became poor," when he was "rich;" before he was "made flesh," when his "glory" was that "of the only Begotten of the Father;" surrounded with the honor which measured his subsequent shame, and exalted on the height which discovered the depth of his subsequent humiliation. He sat in his own state, he wore his own glory, insphered in light, encircled by the angel-host, reposing on his conscious claim, enthroned in his own eternal power and Godhead.

II. THERE IS A SERIES OF ACTS TO WHICH WE MUST ATTEND, DERIVING THEIR SIGNIFICANCE AND PECULIARITY FROM THIS ANTECEDENT CONDITION OF JESUS CHRIST.

Though we have not satisfied ourselves that the amendment proposed on the passage is the more correct, or that it is any way more than barely tolerable, yet we would offer no objection to it. Let the reading be, "He thought it not a prey," something in his range and possession, but not to be retained. He did not, it must be meant, covet to be notoriously and obviously divine. And a certain pleasure seems felt by the projectors of the criticism, whose business is to blaspheme him, in associating with his character, though in negatives, the ravenous instinct of the beast and the successful plunder of the marauder—the quarry and the booty! But that we can concede this without danger, we should justify the common version. We should understand it as an assertion of strict coequality with every supreme claim and attribute. We should esteem it a consequent upon the form of glorious majesty which he had always possessed.

We should have repelled the merest supposition of rapine in this pretension. How could it be "robbery," for infinite knowledge to challenge its omniscience, infinite power to declare its omnipotence, and infinite purity to proclaim itself "incomparably glorious in holiness?" How could this be to wrong the "Majesty on high?" How could he thus desecrate the throne of God? It is "the throne of God and of the Lamb!" Therefore, said he: "All things that the Father hath are mine!"

But in an important sense the Saviour, for the purposes of his love, did not grasp at the honors and displays of the divine nature—willing to forego them, dismissing his train, and disguising his majesty. And we, therefore, in this descending succession of his acts "for us men, and for our salvation," remark,

1. *That he did not seek to retain an appearance of divine glory and coequality.*

But we, before this proposition is examined, must ask how it can consist with the fact of simple humanity.

For it shows what *might have been done.* The power of assuming, and the opportunity of rivaling, the Eternal was in his hand. It was no virtue to forbear what could not be realized. Like a "prey," it was already within the reach of Him who did not regard it with the avidity it might have excited, and who would not seize it. The acquisition which was easy, he declined. He suspended his claims, and abandoned the facilities he possessed, of making himself like God. But how is it to be conceived that this awful power could be lodged in a creature, or subjected to a creature's control? Balaam could not go beyond the commandment of the Lord; nor is he honored because he did not curse the host. When the Apostle speaks of his power and that of Barnabas to "forbear working," (1 Cor. ix, 6,) it refers to the labors of their hands, which often "ministered to their necessities;" and not to a discretionary custody of the miraculous

gift. This was never yielded up to human liberty, as are mind and body: it could never be turned by human caprice from the legitimate purpose of its donation. Nor is there supposition more monstrous, than that a creature can possibly wield against his Maker certain *supernatural* influences, freely given, and which, at any moment, might be withdrawn. The fables of mythology would become credible in comparison with this; and we might rather believe that Prometheus stole the fire of heaven, Phaëton obtained the guidance of the sun, and the Titans stormed the battlements of the sky, than that man ever was put into the situation, or endowed with the capacity, to compete with the Supreme.

Besides, applying this to Jesus of Nazareth, on the scheme of his mere humanity, it supposes what never did exist. When was he in "the form of God?" when was there pretext for appearing "equal with God?" At what point did he *begin* to sink? What is the *grace* of his condescension? Is this "form" the *moral likeness* of God? But religion must have taught him to aspire to it as his good and dignity; and there could be no virtue, to found an example to others, in disclaiming this pure ambition. Is it the *varied attestation* of his nativity? This was not withheld, but shone in the firmament, not only to lead the Magi to the stable, but to marshal the spirits of heaven for the celebration of the scene. It cannot be forgotten, too, that the impugners of his divinity treat the record of the star, the celestial choir, the oriental embassage, as a corrupt interpolation and perfect fable. Is it *miraculous agency?* Whoever can exert it may be said, in a sense, to have "the form of God." But then he divested himself of it, and did not challenge the implied equality. It must have been before his public ministry. There must be a time when he did, and a time when he did not, perform his mighty works. The time when he did, must *precede*

that in which he did not. If we look for "the form of God," we must look for it assuredly ere he laid it aside. Then it was in his earlier life. However, for thirty years, he wrought no miracle! These signs and wonders were reserved for his fuller office and later existence. It would therefore follow, that he desisted to emulate the powers of the Deity at the precise time of commencing their most signal display and self-directing majesty! But still it may be said that this presumption was obviated by his deference to his Father's authority, by his ingenuous acknowledgment that his power was but derived. This is not all the truth: for that deference and acknowledgment we will quickly account. There are deeds of power and mercy in his history which he most unexceptionably appropriates: many divine claims he advances, many divine honors he receives. After his resurrection, miracles are done *in his name*, and his followers *call upon it*.

And sufficient reasons may be offered to explain the conduct of any reasonable creature in refusing to make it a thing of overweening pride, of "vaulting ambition," to "be equal with God." These reasons are so palpable, and the consequences of infringing them are so frightful, that here can be no province for "any virtue," and no ground for "any praise." For the *attempt must be most impotent.* Angel might vie with angel, man with man, though their ranks were most extreme. It would be "the potsherds striving with each other." Between the highest seraph and the meanest reptile there are more points of assimilation than difference. But only madness, or that temerity of wickedness which exceeds it, could harbor the idea of supplanting Infinity by becoming infinite itself. "Hast thou an arm like God, and canst thou thunder with a voice like him?" The folly would be ridiculous, if the impiety were not more loathsome, which could snatch at the peerless glories of Him

who is "higher than the highest." "What is man?" "A worm," "a leaf driven to and fro," "crushed before the moth," "dust and ashes," "clay," "less than nothing," "lighter than vanity." "What is the Almighty?" All nations before him "are as nothing;" "the heaven of heavens cannot contain" him; he "layeth the beams of his chambers in the waters;" he "hath his way in the whirlwind and in the storm, and the clouds are the dust of his feet!" he "humbleth himself to behold the things that are in heaven;" "the nations move out of their holes like worms of the earth, afraid of the Lord our God." And not only were this mimicry of the Supreme beyond expression pitiful and abortive—as an *abuse of a solemn delegation* it would be most treacherous. Extraordinary endowments are supposed: these are committed to the creature for a particular end. It is a trust and stewardship. He is under a particular command, and doth his master "thank that servant because he did the things that were commanded him?" He receives a particular deposit, and "if ye have not been faithful in that which is another man's, who shall give you that which is your own?" Nor can it be a very honorable mention of the Lord Jesus, that, not being superior to man by nature, he did not attempt to engraft upon himself that which is divine; and that, being commissioned with large authorities, he absolutely restrained himself from employing them against that God and Benefactor from which they, in common with his very being, were received. But *every approach to a similar crime* is marked in Scripture with a singular reprobation. Lucifer said, "I will ascend above the heights of the clouds; I will be like the Most High." The prince of Tyrus is represented as declaring, "I am a god, I sit in the seat of God." There is no bolder blasphemy imputed to the antichristian superstition, than that its man of sin should oppose and exalt him-

self "above all that is called God, or that is worshiped; so that he as God sitteth in the temple of God, showing himself that he is God." A fear of judgment might well deter a creature from encountering the guilt of this vain and impious aggression. In these cited instances a most tremendous doom is threatened. And therefore when the pious have been placed in any circumstances which might leave their conduct at all equivocal in this respect, they have obtested against the honor which could have "robbed God." "Stand up," exclaimed Peter to the prostrate Cornelius, "I myself also am a man." "Why do ye these things?" cried the Apostles Barnabas and Paul: "we also are men of like passions with you." A "worshiping of angels" is not only forbidden, but when "the disciple whom Jesus loved" mistook the object of adoration, his celestial guide rebuked him: "See thou do it not." An implication that such a power was their own as could accomplish the miracle was the sin of Moses and Aaron at Meribah: "Must we fetch you water out of this rock?" And Herod was "eaten of worms," when elated with the flattery, "It is the voice of a god, and not of a man," because "he gave not God the glory."

These remarks must tend to convince us that there is a particularity in the person and history of Jesus Christ which renders his refusal to assume the divine form, and to insist on co-ordinate rank with the divine nature, an immense sacrifice, an infinite condescension. In no other view can it be worthy of esteem as the simplest moderation. The contrary supposition is absurd. The "lowliness of mind" which arrogates not to "set itself as the heart of God," banters alike with language and reason. Such disavowal is shocking to the piety which is "clothed with humility."

And yet upon earth he did not tenaciously retain, or openly reveal, his honor. "My Father," he said, "is

greater than I." Important information, circumspect admission, truly, if only the created being! Most emphatic and significant concession, if spoken concerning a voluntary and temporary abandonment of his proper sphere, and abatement of his external glory! There was an obvious propriety in the general suppression of the fact. It was to be gradually learned from a comparison of his claims and evidences with the inspired writings. It had especially to depend upon his resurrection from the dead, in which he was "declared according to the spirit of holiness," or his manifested divinity, "to be the Son of God with power." It seemed expedient, on general grounds, that it should be only partially and mysteriously intimated, subjected to a final proof. And therefore it was not made a prominent doctrine, or invariable lesson, of his mission; though to the inquiring disciple or the adjuring foe, no answer could be more distinct and unequivocal.

But there is one reason which the text alleges as the ground of this conduct: " He made himself of no reputation." We descend another step in the scale of his self-abasement.

2. *He divested himself, actually, of his appropriate and descriptive ensigns of divine nature and government.*

The original word is, "emptied himself." Of supreme claim and essence he could not be dispossessed; the reference must be to the "form of God." That he threw aside; discrowned his head, resigned his scepter, forsook his throne. He might have encompassed his person with legions of angels; a circlet-glory might have played about his brow; he might have come forth to our race with all his coruscating splendors. As the Messiah, he might have stooped to earth with all the indications of "a terrible majesty." He might have " stood upon the Mount of Olives," while it " cleaved in the midst thereof." He might have emerged from the holy of holies, burst

from between the cherubim, enshrined himself in the cloud, thundered out of the oracle, and reclined on the propitiatory seat. But his was a purpose of humiliation. This was a necessary means to effectuate his end. He must not bear witness of himself. He must not appear the God. The pretension and array of deity he must forego and suspend. There is, consequently, a reserve when he speaks of his person, whence he came, who he was, whither he went. He checks expression of reverential import applied to him, but often in the manner of a claim that is intentionally waived. It is a constructive and pregnant declension. Why, it is asked, did he not, if a divine being, surround himself with a corresponding state? Why should the power which girds the mountains and rules the sea not be displayed? Why should not the heraldry of his high praises be asserted? Why was not man apprised of *his* grandeur who now " came to his own? " Why did he not discover " the port of that eternal majesty that weighed the world's foundations? " Why, again it is asked, did the Son of God not announce himself? Why, " at the entry of the city," why, " from the housetop," did he not flash forth the evidence of his true rank and nature? Why did he not, as of old, employ the unambiguous asseveration, " I am the Lord? " Now it is strange that such questions should be asked; because all must admit that a revelation more naturally precedent, necessarily more simple, was withheld. It is allowed, by all the disputing parties, that he was the Christ. His claims to that character are admitted. The miracles which he wrought to confirm those claims, are admitted too. Yet nothing can be more certain than that he " charged his disciples that they should tell no man that he was Jesus the Christ." Of the scene on Tabor he " charged them to tell no man until the Son of man were risen from the dead." To the blind, whose sight he restored, he said, " See that no man know

it." He laid the same injunction of silence upon the cure of the daughter of Jairus. The cleansed leper and the tongue-loosed dumb were equally restrained. He imposed this interdict over even infernal spirits, that they "should not make him known." (Mark iii, 11, 12.) Can there be any difficulty in reconciling the reserve of a *divine* manifestation, when his *official* mission is intentionally kept back? May we not infer that stronger reasons delayed the dreaded revelation than those which suspended the more simple one? It will be asserted that there was no meaning in the terms from which we deduce his own declarations of deity, unless the disciples accepted that meaning. But fact and analogy will furnish a refutation. *Fact*—for it is often recorded that "they understood not the saying, and it was hid from them, that they perceived it not;" and that "they understood not these things at the first, but when Jesus was glorified, then remembered they that these things were written of him, and that they had done these things unto him." *Analogy*—for a type frequently has not a use in the present, but only in a future, time, by furnishing evidence of a divine foreknowledge, and illustrating a distant system of truth in a manner which only the divine establishment and direction of all things could command. "Now I tell you before it come, that when it is come to pass, ye may believe that I am." Perhaps the very familiarity of his followers with the Saviour will be pleaded against their most remote impression of his superior nature. But let it be observed that for such impression, quite independent of the fact, we do not contend; that the possession of miraculous powers, which is undenied, would be scarcely less felt a constraint upon mutual confidence and intimacy; and that an undefinable awe did occasionally steal over their minds, in some measure agreeable to the tremendous truth of his incarnation, "What manner of man is this?" "Of a truth thou

art the Son of God." "They were amazed." "They were afraid and wondered." And when he had risen from the grave, surmise and misshapen thought were compacted into a firm conviction, and the most incredulous of all *believed* and *answered,* "My Lord and my God!" Our answer, therefore, to the question, why he did not throw open at once the robe of concealment, and succinctly proclaim his rights, is this: It was a part of his humiliation not "to strive and cry, or to lift up his voice in the streets, until he had sent forth judgment unto victory." And to have urged his just prerogatives, to have stood up to his original claims, to have given to earth their proper proof, and to have extorted from it their perfect acknowledgment, would have been to retain that of which he "emptied himself," and must have frustrated his condescending purpose to "make himself of no reputation."

3. *He entered upon a course of responsible subordination.*

That voluntary temper which gives its influence to all these successive acts, discovers itself very obviously in the language of this idea: "He *took* upon him the form of a servant;" he laid hold of it, he caught at it, as the original may be expressed. And this deference plainly referred to a particular commission. I speak not my own words. "This is the Father's will which sent me." "I came down from heaven, not to do mine own will." "The Son can do nothing of himself, but what he seeth the Father do." "I am come in my Father's name." "My doctrine is not mine." It is most extravagant to affirm that any creature can *assume* the condition of accountability; and it is a gross misconception of the passage to treat this "form" of service as having relation to the insignia of slavery among men. We read not of any event in his history that can answer to a menial and servile lot. Poor he was, and received of others'

substance; but he was only the *servant of the Father.* Therefore was he foretold after this manner: "Behold my servant whom I uphold." "Behold, my servant shall deal prudently." "Behold, I will bring forth my servant, the Branch." And thus his own statements entirely accord with these predictions. What he teaches he has "learned of" his Father. He does not "speak of" himself. He seeks not his "own glory." Embassador from God, surety for man, there is committed to him a double trust. He must "lay his hand upon both." The wrongs of the divine government, the liabilities of the human race, he must alike redress and sustain. He was "made under the law." "The law" was "in his heart." In the constitution of mercy, which he represented by his person and sealed by his blood, he incurred this awful responsibility. He must pay to the law a perfect obedience, and exhaust its curse by enduring it. He must "fulfill all righteousness." No wonder, then, that we hear from his lips frequent allusion to a superior will. No wonder that he takes the posture of submission and subordination.

However we may be astonished at this fact of condescension, we cannot be that his language and manner comport with it. With all the meekness of conscious equality and voluntary obligation he seeks power from heaven; presents his praise, "Father, I thank thee!" urges his supplication, "Father, I pray for them!" expresses his resignation, "Father, not my will, but thine, be done!" With this spirit of *duty* he drinks the cup and bears the cross. The general language of Scripture responds to these views. Mediatorial suffering secures mediatorial reward. But subordination is still supposed. The Father hath given him "glory." The "name which is above every name," and which demands that "every knee should bow and every tongue confess," is tributary to the "glory of God *the Father.*" The Son must give

up the kingdom to God, *even the Father*."* Until the mediatory economy close, this style of phraseology, this representation of fact, must be expected. "Christ is God's." "The Head of Christ is God." Why should we think it equivocal, or feel it perplexing? What can better subserve the purpose and state the case? "*He took upon him the form of a servant*," and description must be true to such an occurrence, and all arrangement must be in harmony with it! And let us remember that he is the *servant*, though the exalted and rewarded one, until "the mystery of God be finished." "It is manifest that He is excepted who did put all things under him."

4. *He united himself to human nature by a perfect incarnation.*

It is a striking peculiarity of language, almost invariably employed by our Lord Jesus, in which he entitles himself the "Son of man." He repeatedly rejects the ordinary mode of address, and announces his own resolves and acts as those of that person: "The Son of man is come." "The Son of man must suffer many things." "That ye may know that the Son of man hath power to forgive sin." "Whom do men say that I, the Son of man, am?" We know that nothing is more common than for God thus to speak to man: "Thou, O son of man." But it is unprecedented for man thus to designate himself. We can enter into the solemn pathos of the dirge-like strain: "Man, that is born of woman, is of few days and full of trouble." But it would be a vain pleonasm to repeat this circumstance in every self-description. We are aware that it refers, in all probability, to a prophetic test; (Dan. vii, 13;) nevertheless it is founded upon a strict participation of human nature. That par-

* These salvos and limitations are sufficiently intelligible; "the Father," bearing rectoral power in the covenant, and representing the Deity, is thus *personally* contradistinguished from the Godhead.

ticipation was complete. He assumed the structure and the spirit of man. None of the radicals and constituents of manhood were wanting. "Forasmuch as the children are partakers of flesh and blood, he also himself likewise took part of the same." It does not very clearly appear why all this minute and specific information should be furnished respecting one of our race. It was not required by the possibility of the contrary supposition. It is needlessly alleged because there can be nothing in dispute. And yet we are repeatedly told that he " was made of a woman," that he " has come in the flesh," that he " was manifest in the flesh." And this humanity, or " flesh," is defined as the barrier to certain acts and sufferings, of which a superior nature is incapable. " Christ was put to death *in the flesh.*" " Of the fathers, as *concerning the flesh,* Christ came." He " was made of the seed of David *according to the flesh,* and declared the Son of God with power, *according to the spirit* of holiness, by the resurrection from the dead." Nothing more is demanded of us now, tempting as these passages are to criticism, than to note that, while the Saviour was unexceptionably human, he was so by no human necessity, and in opposition to a nature transcendent—unembodied and undying! There is something strange that he should be man at all! It lies within no creative law that he should come forth " in the likeness of sinful flesh." It is not birth, such as angels, and such as worms, obey. And therefore, as if by incidental but most forcible description, he is said by our text to have been "*found* in fashion as a man." Never was there equal discovery! It riveted the gaze of heaven, earth, and hell! It was the association of weakness with omnipotence, of contraction with infinity, of death with self-existence.

There is a device resorted to by those who would " cast him down from his excellency," which is quite impertinent to the argument at issue. Every verse of

Scripture, that implies his limited and assumed nature, is collected with much industry, and then, with equal parade, is urged in disproof of his Deity! Is it, then, that we believe less sincerely the fact of his manhood than themselves? Do they more resolutely than ourselves affirm that he ate, drank, slumbered, mourned, sighed, wept—felt the pulse of life and the pain of death? Can it be less necessary to our scheme to elicit the marks of dependence and limitation in " the man Christ Jesus?" Are there things which he does not know? Are there things which he cannot do? How else could he be man? These restrictions are as indispensable to constitute him human, as limbs and lineaments can be. They as truly indicate the soul, as these parts can characterize the body. There must be as proper growth in the mental faculty as there was in the material form. Let us shrink from no such statements. Let us allow that he was " very man." The mystery of condescension and love is here. We may adore him at the manger when the " holy child," and beneath the cross when the expiring sufferer. We may follow him in all the deep places of his humiliation. As he was " seen of angels," so let him be recognized by us. Awe, intensely overwhelming, will repress a vain curiosity, and heighten a solemn gratitude. We shall not evade any difficulty, but be prepared for the profession of all. Where he " despised the shame," we shall yield to none. And should testimony be subjoined to testimony in confirmation that he was " bone of our bone, and flesh of our flesh "—should every abasing ingredient in the present condition of our species, apart from sinful taint, be made to attach to him—should every imperfection and infirmity, belonging essentially to all created nature, be adduced to circumscribe him; we accept the pledge, we hail the proof, that he " was made in the likeness of men, and was found in fashion as a man!"

5. *He stooped to the most extreme depression of state.*

"Found" thus in another sphere and nature—the subject of an unparalleled transformation—he was not content with the point to which he had bowed himself down. He united himself to our nature in some of its most distressing and degraded forms. Far as he had sunk, he still "humbled himself." Palaces and thrones might have offered a little alleviation. They would have been earthly pinnacles by which to escape from a further descent into penury, trouble, and woe. But he is born of one who can only present the lowliest offering of the law, and whose travail of her illustrious man-child finds its hour in the stable. The supposed father is the carpenter, and he is known as the carpenter's son. He is "subject to his parents." "He is despised and rejected of men." He "has not where to lay his head." He is called the Galilean and the Nazarene of Galilee. He is denounced as concerting with Beelzebub, and as possessed of a devil. It was his to say, "I am a worm, and no man:" "Reproach hath broken my heart:" "They hate me without a cause." No contumely was spared. He was "spitefully entreated." "We hid our faces from him." "His visage was so marred more than any man's, and his form than the sons of men." And yet each indignity did he welcome, each outrage did he invite. They entered into his plan of condescension. They were a part of that "mixture" of which his cup was full. It is true, that in this spectacle of one so great and so despised, there is an awful mystery. That He should be " taken from prison and from judgment "—that he should be buffeted and blindfolded, that he should be scourged, that he should be mocked and set at naught—that they should " smite the Judge of Israel with a rod upon the cheek," (Micah v, 1,) that they should " shoot out the lip" at him, that they should loam and spit upon him, put the reed in his hand, and

twine the thorn around his head—such things involve a difficulty which we could not have explained. The God did not resent them with " rebukes and flames of fire ;" the Man, when " he was reviled, reviled not again ; when he suffered, threatened not." But the explanation has been afforded, the motive has been unfolded—and He who bore all this scorn—the victim of perfidy, and the prey of malice—has traced it to his own choice, and put it within his own adoption: " I gave my back to the smiters, and my cheeks to them that plucked off the hair: I hid not my face from shame and spitting !" Is this extreme depression inconceivable ! Do we ask how it came to pass that he was ingulfed in this abyss of woe and debasement ? " He humbled himself ! "

6. *He reduced himself to the necessity of death.*

It may perhaps be controverted whether the Saviour's body had, being unassociated with sin, any tendency to ailment, decay, and death. Our premises are barely sufficient for a decision. But it seems to have been his purpose not to take the form of an Adam, newly-fashioned by the Almighty Hand, but all the passive qualities and liabilities of Adam's most suffering offspring. That form, in its very organization, was adapted to receive all agonizing impressions. The assumption of a frail, dying body might be practicable, even if it was wholly unpolluted. Be the decision what it may, the submission to death was the same. For if not naturally obliged, then we see his independence of constraint; and if naturally obliged, this very independence took it up voluntarily with all its habitudes and conditions. Though it " behooved " him " to suffer," and though he must be " put to death," these obligations simply respected his own determinate plan. Men speak of death as " the debt of nature," and most incorrectly, since it is the due and wages of sin. And as it can only occur justly in this connection, and according to this award, He who " did

no sin," need not have gone " the way of all flesh," nor have bent to that which is " the visitation of all men." But these observations presuppose a superior nature, which has warranted the assumption of the inferior one, and which still imparted a voluntary merit to all its acts and compliances. For " what man is he that liveth, and shall not see death ? Shall he deliver his soul from the hand of the grave ? " We are not habituated to speak of that man as the humblest of his race, as meekly taking on him a yoke, as patiently allowing in himself a sacrifice, who at any time expires. We should not quite understand how it was that he consented to die. It would appear a very gratuitous epitaph to his memory that he " became obedient unto death." There is no great room for this freedom, and consequently for this virtue. " There is no man that hath power over the spirit to retain the spirit; neither hath he power in the day of death." Resignation to an evil is a proper temper, but a very improper boast. It is a grace of quiet, and not of public, fame. It cherishes, in secret, its smile and tear. Its unmurmuring voice, its serene aspect, its gentle heart, are not formed for ostentation. Never did it learn to glory of bearing that which it could not prevent. Never did it think itself something when it is nothing. But our Lord made choice of that, which to all others of human form is a necessity. He called to him all the snares, and pains, and terrors of death. He bade the monster strike him with its sting, but not until it had been compelled to crouch waitingly at his feet. He commanded the grave to open, and make a passage for his march. He had " power to lay down " his life, and " power to take it again." He delayed not, and hurried not, to die. He told each pang, and deliber-ated each gasp. And at his prefixed moment, and by his perfect authority, resigned his life, gave up the ghost. There, then, he bowed himself in conformity to

that dying nature which he had espoused for the salvation of a dying race. And are we required to tell how it was that He could suffer the stroke of death? How even that nature which was so mysteriously bound to the divine, could be the subject of passion and dissolution? How we can believe in the possibility, and set forth the necessity, of such a decease? How that ill could befall Him whom we profess as Immanuel, God with us? Our reply is instantaneous, "He became obedient unto death?"

7. *He yielded to death in a peculiar form.*

Crucifixion was a punishment the most acute, lingering, and odious. It fell to the lot of few. The sword, the stake, the ax, the hemlock, were the more frequent methods of dispatching the victims of justice. It was a ban and execration, the fate of the felon and the slave. It suspended the writhing wretch between heaven and earth, as unpitied by either, as renounced by both.

True, every reader of the prophecies must have expected a suffering Messiah. His "heel" was to be "bruised." He was to be "cut off." Bu the was predicted as a sacrifice, as a martyr, as a conqueror, in his death. There is a redeeming glory in these associations. There is a pomp in oblation. There is a force of moral dignity in the constancy of persecuted virtue. There is a blaze of renown cast over the dying conqueror—Fame blows its trumpet, and Victory prepares its wreath. But this was to be a sacrifice, a martyrdom, a conquest, by a cross, the abhorred engine of torture and shame. It is this which destroys the fascination of the imagery, dispels the charm of the poetry, and obtrudes itself upon us, stern, hideous, and revolting. For this consummation the Saviour contrived a preliminary language. He conjured all to take up his cross, to bear his cross; and they understood him to signify the lengths they

must go, and the dangers they must incur, for him. But thus a new cast of expression was molded, it mixed most naturally with the very facts of his religion, and it was extensively spoken whenever Christians told of mortifying the passions of the flesh, or surmounting the seductions of the world. The " likeness of his death " was ever present to them, the emblem of their every blessing, and the ensign of their every boast.

Yet the probabilities opposed such a means of death. It was not a Jewish punishment. Charged with the crime of blasphemy, a specific doom was adjudged to that crime—the guilty party was to be stoned. The malice of the priests and populace, however, blinded them to the discretion which might have, for a period, upheld their national integrity. They denied the possession of a power which the governor acknowledged. They forever put away from them the hope of a Christ, if this prisoner was not he : " We have no king but Cesar ;" " It is not lawful for us to put any man to death." Fatal self-renouncement! " The scepter " has departed from Judah, and the " lawgiver from between his feet ! " And of this surrender, the crucifixion of Jesus is the result : " That the saying of Jesus might be fulfilled, which he spake, signifying what death he should die." John xviii, 31, 32. It was, notwithstanding, sufficiently similar to an execution in the Mosaic code, to draw upon him a malediction as well as an ignominy : and the outcast, as extended on a cross, was also the accursed, as hanged on a tree.

The inference is, therefore, irrepressible—the end of these continually deepening acts of humiliation must be worthy of them. They were not performed for their own sake. They have nothing in common with superfluous expense or needless suffering. That end was our salvation by his atoning death. Not a degree in all this descending scale could be spared, not an intervening

step in the series might be remitted. There was no resting-place between his throne and his cross. The corn of wheat must "fall into the ground and die," if it would bring forth good fruit. The Son of man must be lifted up from the earth, to draw all men unto him. He is not "dead in vain." He sought not his crucifixion but "to put away sin," to "abolish death," to "destroy the works of the devil," to "bring us to God." Therefore he deigned so much, stooped so far, and sunk so low; therefore he groveled in "the dust of death," put on the ghastly attire of "his burial," and laid down his emaciated and scarred body in the tomb. What a suspense must holy spirits have felt as He was still seen to bend in his flight, as he still passed from higher to inferior measurements of abasement, as he still invented newer forms of reproach and agony, as he still plunged from deep to deep, and only ceased to sink when arrested by the cross and received by the grave!

Now two principles, already anticipated, must have governed these successive deeds. They were self-originated, strictly independent, purely voluntary; but this can be affirmed of no created relations. They were likewise in contrast with an antecedent state of being, rendering all these depressions of manhood and death new and strange. Nor do we evade the conclusion that he was as truly God as he was truly man; that he was equal with the Father in the Eternal Essence, while by taking on him our nature he was not ashamed to call us brethren.

And it is a dark feature of the system which explodes this great and all-important tenet of Christianity, that it reasons against the fact thus represented and indoctrinated, from the sources of an infinite condescension. There had been no room for the existence, no color for the sophism, of this blasphemy, had not He whom it denies vailed his glory and inverted his sphere. If the

" form of God" had been retained—if the hosts of heaven had been permitted to declare him—if the enshrinements of divinity had continued to signalize him—if he had not laid aside the phenomena of his proper state—all had bowed the knee, all had confessed his supremacy ! Had he " come to destroy men's lives," none of his enemies would have disallowed his rank. It belonged to human impiety, and still serves to distinguish it, that men should be found to take advantage of a forgone honor to discredit it, of a suspended claim to dispute its existence, of a voluntary prostration to deride the idea of any higher original. The manger is cited against his eternal beginning, and the cross against his power of an endless life. They would shackle him with his own bands of love. They would extinguish the glory by the vail which hid its splendor. Henceforth, as he sought not to appear equal with God, they will refuse his resumption of the prerogative. Henceforth they will resolve the form of the servant, and the fashion of the man, into the obligations of moral and physical necessity. Henceforth they will only endure in him the absence of the reputation which he mercifully shrouded. O guilty treason, which so attacks majesty by means of its condescension ! O foul ingratitude, which turns to contempt, and requites with scorn, the power which redeemed us, because of the mercy which refused no pang, no shame, required for the ransom !

The EXAMPLE which is founded upon the conduct of Christ, and which it is the design of the text to enforce on our imitation, seems to certify the conclusion that the Saviour is properly Divine. Humility and disinterestedness are portrayed in him that we may copy them. Our humility is the correct estimate of ourselves; it is the dictate, not of a voluntary depreciation, but a strict self-knowledge. Our disinterestedness is our sympathy with fellow-suffering; is related to a fixed standard of duty,

and a certain measure of reward, and therefore stands on opposite grounds to what is discretionary. But this high model is described as unnecessarily humble, and gratuitously benevolent. He comes freely from heaven to earth. He exchanges the form of God for the form of man. What lineaments, what lessons, what realities of the virtues, commemorated and commended, are here! This *is* lowliness of mind! This *is* looking on the things of others! But think of this Exemplar as never living but by human birth, as never subsisting but in human condition; think of him as the man, the mortal, the accountable agent; and then in what is seen his self-abasement? what can entitle him to be the pattern of all meek and retiring disposition? To make his boast that he did not emulate to be like God, is scarcely less audacious than to attempt it. To consider that there is any forbearance in this, is as foolish in its upstart vanity as it is hateful in its contumacious implication. Had the Saviour, being only man, resolved to hold divine equality as his spoil, not to be a servant, not to wear the human guise, not to be obedient to death, then had his history been an extravagance of presumption, his character had been a beacon of pride, "an execration, and an astonishment, and a curse!" He must have been classed with the fanatics or hypocrites who have affected divine names, and decreed to themselves divine honors! And had he, being no more than man, but forborne to do this, declined such rivalry, and assumed the position in created nature which he could not exceed, where would be the pre-eminence of the virtue, the justice of the applause? Forbearance to rebel is not fealty. He becomes not of necessity the saint, who is not the blasphemer; nor need he be humble who arrogates not the divine resemblance, and usurps not the divine throne. These are not the moral alternatives of the case. There may be other intervals in the scale. And when a virtue is affected on the plea of abstinence

from a vice, not only is ignorance expressed, but that vice is actually indicated. If, under the supposed circumstances, this was our Lord's humility, it would be pride; if this his piety, it would be profaneness. The withdrawment of such a purpose, the imposition of a stress upon such a refusal, the boast of such withdrawment, the mention of such refusal, would be a bravado of mockery and defiance toward the Most High, unknown to the pride by which the angels fell. Nor should we think of our nature's fall with any surprise, or with much disgust; since our attempt to "become as gods" was, in all comparison, so immeasurably inferior in its character of impiety and its outrage of expression. The defensive conduct we are compelled to pursue gives rise to this distressing peculiarity of the controversy. It is a bitter pain to speak of Him in this manner, to press the consequences of a false criticism and an irrational theology until they trench, though only most hypothetically, upon his dignity and truth.

Dear Christians, ye have "learned Christ." You have banished all doubts of his perfect claim to be equal with God. You discover, in all that at first may seem to oppose the conviction, only the facts of his incarnate humiliation and condescending grace. You cannot taunt him with these, nor employ them to impugn the prerogatives which they temporarily obscured. You cannot oppose such voluntary concealment and subjection to the divinity of him "whose right it is." You know that there is no real argument, any more than generous temper, in denying his celestial dignity from his earthly abasement, since the reality and virtue of his depression must constantly refer to his pristine ascendency. You rejoice, however this unholy strife assails the character and glory of the Saviour here, that you are approaching a world in which there can arise no darkening prejudice, no chilling doubt, but all is "quietness and assurance

forever." There you shall "see him as he is." There you, with all the powers of heaven, shall adore him! And while you fall down before him that multitude shall be filled with one sentiment, that service shall be devoted to one purport—all shall be wrapt in one vision, all shall be vocal with one strain; nor blasphemy mar a harmony or wound an ear!

It only remains that we revolve two lessons impressed upon us by these meditations.

1. *How admirable is the expedient of the Redeemer's incarnation.*

Man, when unfallen, being by the law of all created nature still dependent, required an object for love and a ground for rest. The Deity, simply considered in reference to him as worthy of complacency and favor, filled all his thoughts and attracted all his affections.

Man cannot be less dependent now that he is fallen. He is not only physically upheld, as is every holy being; but, morally destitute, spiritually helpless, he must owe the recovery of his happiness to a form of divine benevolence not necessary to the most perfect *lawgiver*, not applicable to a creature unless he has become a *transgressor*—that is mercy.

God was the source of perfect satisfaction, a portion, an all, to man when made upright, and pronounced very good; to man, the sinner, the fugitive, he was a source of terror and dismay. And from that hour in which his progenitor hid himself and was afraid, the Creator has not been in his thoughts, or has entered to distract them.

Where, then, should the conceptions and attachments of the human mind fix themselves? What might they embrace? They could not the Supreme, they must not the creature; they shrunk from the one, they distrusted the other; the first was a forbidden worship, the second a palpable idolatry.

Infinite wisdom and pity resolved the tremendous difficulty. Christ, in whom "dwelleth all the fullness of the Godhead bodily," "found in fashion as a man," clothed with a bodily form--the organ of the human spirit as well as the shrine of the indwelling divinity—Christ is the Mediate Object. "The Lord God dwells among us." The more intense and awful splendors are allayed and softened by this intervention. On a divine arm, which bears up the pillars of the universe, we hang our hope; into a human bosom, which itself has heaved with grief, we pour out our hearts with all their confidence and all their sympathy. Our awe chastens our esteem, and our esteem attempers our awe. This is the contact in which Deity and man may meet, the mysterious tie of underived and created being, the convergence of that which can array "the terrors of God" and that which is "touched with the feeling of our infirmities." This "Mediator is not of one," "he maketh peace in his high places," he "came and preached peace to you which were afar off." He has brought heaven to earth, he has raised earth to heaven. He took hold on our nature, nor relaxed his grasp until he had placed it, as proper to his very person, "in the midst of the throne." His heart, which was wrung with sorrow and pierced with violence —which yearned with filial love—which throbbed with friendly commiseration, sensitive to every impulse of pity, responsive to every importunity of woe—has not grown cold nor become estranged from those for whom it broke and bled; but expands as the index of infinite love and the channel of eternal good! "O the depth!" we may well exclaim; but it not only swallows our thoughts, it wells up the fullness of our joys!

Inane are the objections which our sciolists and witlings urge. Incomprehensible, it is alleged by them to be. Who ever doubted it? Is it not involved in the fact? "Without controversy, great is the mystery of

godliness: God was manifest in the flesh." As unparalleled, it is still demurred to; and singularly we are asked to find some likeness to it above or beneath. It is of itself incapable of support from any analogy and illustration. But if a fact, is not this inevitable? "The Lord hath created a new thing in the earth!" May these have another mind given them! May these cavils yield before the evidence of this stupendous wonder, the perception of its fitness, and the experience of its power!

2. *What a sublime example does the conduct of the Saviour afford!*

This being the basis of his unique and incomparable person, we behold in him dispositions the most varied, and yet the most consistent. Whatever independence can sway with the upright, or humility with the meek; what holiness with the pure, what forbearance with the lowly; what unwearied employment with the active, what sweet repose with the contemplative; what interest the generous mind can take in philanthropy, what on the contrary, the severer mind can in rigor and self-denial; what reverence greatness can raise in the noble, and esteem kindness can awaken in the tender; what incitement is in knowledge to fix the thoughtful, and in exertion to stimulate the ardent; what can enkindle zeal, and what inspire devotion; what can strike the saintly sage with veneration, and what win from the outcast penitent the smile of confidence and peace; what counsels the human soul in its true interests, and what composes the writhing limb and fevered pulse of the human frame; what exists but to heal the cup of life, and to soothe the sting of death; O, if such a combination of qualities be unlooked for on earth, be unhoped for in man, these are but some of the slighter touches, the fainter lineaments, of that character which "is full of grace and truth;" the dim reflections of that person in

whom all the awful and all the amiable are united; who, while angels bent at his feet, caught babes to his bosom, and pressed them to his heart; who, while demons fled affrighted from his rebuke, suffered to drop upon him the tears of the contrite and the mourner; who, amid his march of miracles, oft stood still to weep; who turned aside from his sterner and more heroic acts, to cherish friendly intercourse and domestic benignity; who, "lowly in mind," bore his own cross; who, looking not on his own things but the things of others, delayed to close his sufferings until he had secured his mother from destitution, promised the dying malefactor a place in his kingdom, and besought the forgiveness of his murderers! Thus pleasing "not himself," when he might have been most self-engrossed! Thus pouring "out his soul" of matchless love and pity "unto death," though in a moment he might have undeceived the mockeries of the multitude! Himself he will not save—though he might have left the world to perdition! He will not come down from the cross—though he might have left it for the throne! Such was his example, and we must follow his steps! Such was his temper, and "let the same mind be in you which was also in Christ Jesus." "Now if any man have not the spirit of Christ, he is none of his."

VI.

THE ATONEMENT.

BEHOLD THE LAMB OF GOD, WHICH TAKETH AWAY THE SIN OF THE WORLD.—John i, 29.

IT has been not unfrequently objected to the peculiar doctrines of Christianity, that they alone can be inferred from the later portions and epistolary compositions of the New Testament; that the Lord Jesus never seems to have intended them, and that it appears his disciples and general auditors never understood him to inculcate them. On this supposition we may account for much of their conduct who neither entertain nor profess any predilection for the evangelical verities. The narratives which are commonly styled *Gospels* are specially favored by them, and are conceived to supply a warrant for their skepticism and dislike. They argue that as these report the assertions of Messiah, the doctrine which fell from his lips in the very form of its utterance, the fidelity of the record must be less affected, and the accuracy of the expression less distorted, than when committed to other vehicles, and forced through other channels. But since error is always inconsistent, the apologists for one part of revelation at the expense of the other do not invariably attribute infallibility and pay deference to the Evangelists themselves. A way of escape is made practicable even from their decisions. The question of inspiration can offer to such parties no difficulty; it is held in a manner, if allowed at all, that renders it capricious as individual impression, and frail as human remembrance.

It may be incidentally remarked, that the sacred writers are manifestly unconscious of any disparity, and are far removed from any jealousy, whatever the province occupied by them. They contentedly take their place, and fill their department; honoring in each other " the self-same Spirit," and conceding the authority which they challenge for themselves. Thus Peter, whose opportunities of weighing the facts chronicled by the biographers of the Saviour were equaled by few and excelled by none, places all the epistles of Paul among " the other Scriptures." 2 Peter iii, 26.

Nothing would be more vain than to disguise the fact that the epistles do embrace more ample and explicit information touching the doctrines of the evangelical system; their definitions being more precise, and their arguments more extended. This was due to the advanced stage of the Christian dispensation in which they were written, and was to be expected from the descent of the Spirit, " who could not be given until Jesus was glorified." These larger accessions of knowledge, these brighter discoveries and accumulated proofs, far from dishonoring him, were announced and foretold by him : " What I do thou knowest not now; but thou shalt know hereafter." " I have yet many things to say unto you, but ye cannot bear them now." " When He, the Spirit of truth, is come, he will guide you into all truth." * For we should not forget that the doctrines are but expositions of the facts which occurred in the history of Christ. They are not theories, or simple principles, but the natural and intended construction put on circumstances which occurred in certain places

* There seems no propriety in the practice of the Roman and English Churches when their members sit without a thanksgiving to hear the Epistle, but rise to the Gospel with the sound of doxology— as though the latter were the fuller " mind of Christ " than the former—a position the reverse of truth.

and at certain times, together with reasonings well supported by them, and strictly deducible from them. Then could the doctrines be taught when the facts had not transpired? But while the Son of man lived on our earth, the cardinal facts of his mediation were unaccomplished. It remained for him to die and rise again. He, after his resurrection, interpreted these events to his disciples, who were to "teach all nations." Their instructions are those interpretations. We enjoy the benefit of his latest disclosures, when, "beginning at Moses and all the prophets, he expounded in all the Scriptures the things concerning himself." His historians received the same illumination, it is true; but then they adhered to the simple task of adducing what they had either seen or understood "from the very first:" his other inspired servants extracted the lessons and pursued the conclusions.

The very limited and even gross apprehensions of the disciples may furnish an additional reason for the partial concealment, or rather gradual development, of the Christian mysteries. The secular ambition which too often governed them is apparent in many of their questions to our Lord, and also in their replies to those which he suggested. They deprecated his death, and yet esteemed themselves able to "drink of his cup." And when that death was inflicted, and he was laid in the tomb, bitterly they spoke of their ruined expectations and blasted hopes. It never could have been possible to convince them that such catastrophe was necessary; its consummation induced them to inquire and compelled them to think, while the Risen Sufferer then witnessed to them, that thus it was written of him, and that so it behooved him to suffer.

Besides, it is the uniform plan of prophecy to intimate the future enigmatically and progressively. Forming a part in the scheme of universal government, these

characteristics of obscurity and partiality are requisite to sustain the authority of fixed law, and the freedom of human agency. But all the declarations made by our Lord partook of a prophetic nature. They should not, therefore, be so explicit as to enable the kindness of his followers, or the malignity of his enemies, to attempt, however ineffectually, any obstruction to his plans. He must move onward in his course undisturbed by their counterplots; they must proceed in their's unprompted by his prescience and unhampered by his will.

We do not, however, suppose that it would be difficult to demonstrate that whatever essentially belongs to the Christian system is included in the evangiles. They leave not unproved the divinity of Him who could say, " He that cometh from above is above all; he that cometh from heaven is above all." They leave not unasserted the atonement of Him who could say, "The Son of man came not to be ministered unto but to minister, and to give his life a ransom for many." They leave not explained the dominion of Him who could say, "My kingdom is not of this world." They leave not unpledged the influence of Him who could say, " I will pray the Father, and he shall give you another Comforter, that he may abide with you forever." These august truths are shrouded with no affected secresy. The books which record the corresponding facts, and not seldom announce the appropriate doctrines, are treatises " of all that Jesus began both to do and teach, until the day in which he was taken up." And as if no needless concealment should perplex them, see the pointed hand and hear the uplifted voice of him " that cried in the wilderness,"—who, giving utterance to every divine counsel, and fulfillment to every scriptural pledge, proclaims—while heaven and earth ring with echoes, " Behold the Lamb of God, which taketh away the sin of the world." A clearer insight into " the mystery of

godliness," a stronger attestation to "the truth as it is in Jesus," could not be supplied. It was not only to raise the vail, it was to uncover the ark.

The lamb has been accounted an image of innocence and gentleness. It has scarcely any means of defense, scarce any instincts of resentment; but is one of the most lovely emblems of each kindlier disposition that nature's numerous tribes afford.

But it is placed before us in Scripture as the animal peculiarly devoted to sacrifice. It was the common victim of the altar. Two were immolated every day for a "continual burnt-offering." To these another pair was added weekly for "the burnt-offering of the Sabbath." Seven more were required at each new moon. Sixteen were offered on the day of Pentecost, and fourteen when that of the Trumpets returned. This latter number was also due to the feast of Tabernacles during all the respective days it lasted, while other seven were added on the eight. Through the Passover seven lambs were presented as often as the same number of days occurred, with one more on that which immediately followed the first.

To the other sacrificial animals the Saviour is not directly compared, but this assimilation is frequent. The correspondences are frequently marked. "He is brought as a lamb to the slaughter." "Ye know that ye were redeemed with the precious blood of Christ, as of a lamb without blemish and without spot." Heaven is filled with the commemorative imagery. It gives prominence to every associated idea. It hangs high all the memorials of piacular infliction, suffering, and death. It breathes the incense of an oblation. It becomes the holy of holies to receive the votive gift. Christ entered it not without blood. Though sacred to peace and life, it is a scene impressed with vengeance and moral woe: resounding with accents of gladness, the "blood of

sprinkling speaketh" the stress and harmony of all. "The Lamb" is "on Mount Sion." He is the song, the light, the bridegroom, the temple; in the stream of his side the celestial robe acquires its purity, and the redeemed multitude never fail to rehearse that he "was slain." Surely these are not accidental mementoes, when the prevailing figure so little agrees with the various other descriptions.

Being designated the "Lamb of God," we learn that, in conformity with the terms of his humiliation, he was "chosen of God;" was sanctified, sealed, and sent by the Father; was set apart in human nature and mediatory office for the purpose of a sacrificial death. When revealed in his pre-existent honors, and when we connect with them the fact that "he was verily foreordained" as a lamb "before the foundation of the world," they seem the decorations which enwreath the victim, the presages of the fatal blow. The wood was heaped into its pile, the fire was fanned into its fury, the knife lay glittering with its keenest edge, and God provided the Lamb for the burnt-offering.

It can only concern us now to observe that the way in which a "lamb taketh away sin" is not very intelligible if the idea of sacrifice be exploded. In the emblematic qualities of the animal we find nothing to suggest the notion of removing guilt; and had a conception of muscular strength been sought, it would have been better conveyed by "a lion" coming up "from the swelling of Jordan." Between the circumstances of the Saviour's appointment and death and those of the Paschal Lamb, there may be traced a most striking resemblance. It is, however, to be doubted whether the allusion exists in the present connection. It is the general idea of sacrifice. Could the allusion be established, it would only confirm the particular end proposed in the death of the cross. It has, indeed, been insinuated that it was not

an expiatory rite, but a national solemnity and domestic service. It is surely forgotten, then, that the ministrations of the *temple* sustained, expounded, and consecrated these. And nothing can be more determinate than the language of the inspired volume in its extreme portions, when it either speaks of the shadow or the substance: "Thou mayest not *sacrifice* the passover within any of thy gates, which the Lord thy God giveth thee." "Christ our passover is *sacrificed* for us."

Little short of quibbling would it be to assign any restricted sense to "the world," as the term arises in the text. Though it must sometimes indicate the material frame, the Jewish State, the Roman Commonwealth, the sinful majority and embodied evil of mankind, yet nothing, save the prejudice of system and the recklessness of party, could ever define it here but as intending the *Human Race.* Respecting the particular application of this death, and the distinguishing grace which causes it, we have no present inquiry; nor have we to discuss the position that, dying in certain relative characters, such as spouse, shepherd, and surety, he determinately secured the salvation of a "peculiar people;" nor have we to argue that a security of efficiency was necessary to justify the means he expended upon his design, and to constitute his reward. In a substantive sense "the Lamb of God taketh away the sin of the world," that is, the species.

It is purposed, in the ensuing discourse, to treat of that which may be considered not so much a sentiment and part of the Gospel as its very self. For the sacrifice of Christ is the fact which alone gives validity, and the supposition which alone imparts consistency, to its entire system.

I. It will be necessary to offer some general explanations.

According as we notice the aspects of the Saviour's

death, we may occasionally vary our language. Has it a special reference to divine justice? It is a *satisfaction.* Does it contemplate injury and indignity offered by us to the character and government of Him " who ruleth among men ? " It is an *atonement.* Does it denote the consequences of that event toward ourselves ? It is an *expiation.* Should any object to words which are alleged to be without scriptural warrant, we reply that the phraseology of inspiration is significant, and that we best honor when we investigate it. It may be cited in the most literal manner to excuse thought, protect artifice, and supersede confession. The holy book is to be understood, and other language than its own must be the method of stating and avowing its meaning. But this is only a negative justification of our nomenclature; we can urge another more decisive. These terms are not unknown in the " lively oracles," " the Scriptures which" testified " of Christ" belonging to the former dispensation. They are there used of the *types ;* we maintain that this is sufficient sanction when we affix them to the antitype with a still ampler force and stricter application. Nor is it equitable for them who quarrel with our use of what we deem correlative and tantamount expression to persist in the practice themselves. What is their authority for the familiar employment of Deity, Providence, Christianity? Why mete to us a standard by which they cannot themselves abide? The word *atonement* may be *secular* in its use; as when offense and injury are repaired by certain amends, or are overlooked upon particular considerations. We have but to dismember it, and it presents the idea of unity, or being *at one*, to the very eye. Moses interposed to bring his brethren to peace; our version has it, " he would have set them at one again." (Acts vii, 26.) But as a *sacred* term, it implies the satisfaction made to justice, and substituted for the offender, in the form of a sacrifice. The guilt, or expo-

sure to punishment, is confessed ; the blow of that punishment is diverted from its proper course, and falls upon a third and representative party. As a religious ceremony the *offering* is well understood, and in all circumstances which connect it with the deprecation of penalty and the effusion of blood, is, of its own nature, generally allowed to be vicarious and expiatory. It cannot be a fitting expression of thanksgiving; it wars with all the melting calm of devotion; but sternly it reminds the transgressor of his desert, while it depicts at the same time the principle on which that award is arrested. An atonement is thus convertible with sacrifice; and both necessarily involve a compensative principle and a retributive act, strangely and mercifully turned aside from them on whom they should have fixed, and yet on another duly exacted and rigorously enforced.

We believe the death of Christ is such a transaction—that it is a sacrificial endurance in his person of our moral liabilities—that it is an infliction on him of what we had incurred—that it is the only honorable consideration on which divine justice can remit the culprit's sentence and receive the culprit's contrition—that it is a redress and a means of reconciliation—that it leaves our Maker with as strict consistency to pardon as he had ever known of necessity to punish—that it is, in fact, a contrivance to convince man of his deepest guilt by bestowing upon him his fullest salvation, and to impress the universe with the sublime sentiment that infinite purity hates sin as much as infinite mercy loves the sinner. Henceforth the ruler of heaven and earth can " declare his righteousness in the remission of sin," can " be just and acquit him who believeth in Jesus."

It must be noticed, and with most emphatic distinctness, that there is no reluctance in the Divine Being to receive the sinner, and to restore favor to him. Nothing that is good can he oppose; and this great amount of

happiness must be an object of his most perfect complacency. Evil of every kind is abhorrent to him, and is what he would not should exist, and what he bends all things to destroy. This is the reason and mode of his placability, his readiness to forgive, his delight in mercy. To make all his creatures blessed was his original design, is his constant work : and whatever mars and thwarts it antagonizes his will, known and moral, than which none other can be attributed to him. So far from the intervention of an atonement betraying such reluctance, it proves that there was a *disposition and a determination of mind* which, perceiving all the possible difficulties in its exercise, was prepared to surmount them all.

And by the atonement of the cross there is produced no *revolution of the divine character.* God is of one mind, his " counsel shall stand," he " changeth not." Essential excellence and necessary perfection, as well as absolute power and original authority, combine in him, and express themselves in his government. His nature is full of congenial activities, and his government of corresponding purposes. His immutability does not consist in a suspension of that which is " his work," nor in any limitation imposed upon his ever-developing counsels. And therefore, when the Saviour " offered up himself," though the divine character took a new aspect and entered a new relation, still there was the same hostility to sin, the same fidelity to law, the same impartiality of justice, the same beauty of holiness, as must invariably have united in the Deity whatever was his plan, and must have distinguished all his conduct toward intelligent and accountable beings. No course of time, no change of circumstance, could make these less or more.

It becomes us, consequently, to be very cautious how we speak of the *divine dispositions.* Many of the figures which indicate these must be interpreted with a

subdued sense. The passions ascribed to God shadow out properties incapable, from their changeless perfection, of excited intensity. The unfailing resolve, the calm majesty, of essential rectitude is his. The splendor of his glory never trembles with a varying light, nor shoots forth a wavering effulgence. When his " fury," his " hot displeasure," his " wrath unto the uttermost," are threatened or wreaked; when his vengeance seems impatient of delay and glowing for ebullition; when he is " pacified; " when his " repentings are kindled within him;" when he "retaineth not " his anger; when he inquires how he shall " give up;" when he waits to " be gracious;" when " his anger is turned away;" we must correct our first and crude impressions by those great illustrative principles which declare him to be " a Spirit," who " changeth not," " cannot be hindered," and " reproves " every notion that he is " such a one " as ourselves. The death of Christ is the only medium of mercy to the fallen race of man; but it appeased no divine emotion, neither could it augment the divine benevolence. It was the *effect*, and not the *cause*, of that benevolence; marking its existence, and not inducing its consent. The Deity *was* propitious; the atonement is the voucher of the fact; and upon its consummation neither his *reluctance* was removed, for it is his spontaneous act; nor was his *character* transformed, for it is his native delight; nor was his *passion* placated, for it is his manner of commending " his love " and showing his mercy. And the compatibility of this arrangement may be made plain. Should it be asked why God expended so much to realize his own will, and equally his pleasure, we reply: His moral perfections, with the respect due to them as the standards of all happiness in the universe—his moral rules, with the necessity of enforcing all their original exactitude to make them not only "just " but " good "—these are the grounds of

his conduct. He cannot deny himself. His will is but the activity of his nature, and that activity can only move in the line of eternal right. If he will pardon and renew the sinner, that is a good; but there would be an infinitely counter-active evil if that good were attained by any connivance at his sin, for the good of the creature would be the price of the faithlessness, injustice, and demoralization of the Creator! The atonement is God's resolve to be consistently merciful! Two Scripture passages may illustrate his method of procedure: passages we select for the purpose of *illustration*, without imposing on them any such meaning. " It is strange that God who can do all things " (this is the objection) " should not forgive it at once. Why should he allow a difficulty and a restriction? Why not act the Potentate? Why not burst through all by his omnipotence?" The objection blinks all moral principle. What upright man, of influence and wealth, *can* do all things whose consequences that influence and wealth would indemnify? *Can* he falsify and degrade himself? Does he not demonstrate his abhorrence of these alternatives best when he pronounces that he " cannot do them, and is incapable of them?" He can add nothing more. Who that is principled can contradict and oppose himself? So far as human predicament may exhibit divine obligation, the instance is complete. The law was *meant* and cannot be revoked; its menace was *intended* and cannot be reversed; and whatever is carried on beneath them must be serious, inflexible, and resistless. The *first* illustration from the inspired records is taken from the history of Job. God was willing and determined to pardon Eliphaz, Bildad, and Zophar. But it could only be in a certain way. They were to take a particular sacrifice, and to " go to his servant Job." They were to be indebted to a particular mediation. " My servant Job shall pray for

you : for him will I accept : lest I deal with you after your folly. And the Lord turned the captivity of Job when he had prayed for his friends." Here are institutes of expiation and intercession appointed by the Deity with whom they are to avail! But it is necessary that the creature who is saved should welcome and approve that salvation. He cannot be made happy in spite of himself. There must be concurring judgment and responsive will. The atonement is therefore required to be offered in a way most powerfully impressive to him. He must learn from it how guilty is he, how to it he is obliged, with an emphasis nothing beside could reveal. He must be as religiously as legally affected by it. It must as truly transform his disposition as alter his relation. And the second illustration we adapt from the language of Paul to Philemon : " But without thy mind would I do nothing ; that thy benefit should not be as it were of necessity, but willingly." Let the sinner behold and consider what a series of awful preparatives, of rigorous terms, of dread inflictions, was enforced, or otherwise there could be no redemption ; and he cannot but abhor that which was the occasion of the demand, nor fail to admire and to adore the love which met the demand, rose to its amount, and complied with its magnitude. And in this manner both the parties are, so to speak, morally and personally pledged : The Deity operates with " the counsel of his will," and man is " made willing," " persuaded," " drawn," and " brought nigh." A pardon, simple and abstract, had left God dishonored and belied ; man, penitent and rebellious— forever! But now is He better vindicated than he could be by the consequences of direct punishment ; and man, in the solemn lesson taught him, receives " the benefit " not of " necessity, but willingly."

- The moral defection of our nature had introduced a frightful innovation. This could not be overlooked.

Nothing must betray indifference to it. We were fore-warned that it should be resented. This issue alone could be arrested by some moral counterpoise. It could not be foregone, unless three ends were previously secured. *First*, the purity of the divine character must be cleared. Sin is an attack upon it, is its denial and insult, and any forbearance on its part to repel and avenge the wrong would be its own abandonment and compromise. Impunity would seem a connivance and misprision. If it resists not, it allows, its dishonor. The demonstration must be prompt and signal that evil cannot dwell with it, that a shadow of suspicion cannot settle upon its infinite perfection. *Secondly*, the recti-tude of moral government must be asserted. The law is either just or not, and the directing power is either true or not to itself and to us. Any relaxation would argue that it had been unduly strict, any suspension that it was recklessly vacillating, any infringement that it was frivolously inconsistent. The whole must be maintained, or it originally required too much, and dealt in unmeaning threats. Not a jot or tittle can pass away. And, *thirdly*, the well-being of all creatures capable of religion must be established. That of course finds its archetype in the divine character, and its ex-pression in the moral law. In proportion, therefore, as that character was debased, and that law was violated, the very source of intelligent and holy pleasure would be tainted. Man, instead of rising by an immortal progression to the resemblance and blessedness of the Deity, would behold in that Being a nature of caprice, and in his conduct an implied approval of evil. In that deterioration would be our decadence and ruin. Let any light view of sin be encouraged—let any screen be thrown over the offender—let any thing be done which tampers with the standard which is " ordained to life "— and the interests of the only good of God, and angels,

and man, are shattered and wrecked forever. These are the issues which, before a step can be taken toward our recovery, must be firmly and as notoriously insured. All, then, proves that there *was* a necessity to punish: the character, the law, the created system, of the Lord our God left him no alternative. If he refused, he must set a contradiction in that character, cause a repeal of that law, and drag down that system from all the happiness for which it was contrived, and all the honor of which it was susceptible. Failing in truth, he must have failed in every attribute of moral excellence, and so have wrested irrecoverably from us every sense of obligation, every hope of reward, every impulse of improvement.

The atonement is the punishment of sin—a condemnation of it, a sacrifice for it. It "puts," "takes," it "away." It "makes an end of it." It is an assertion of its "exceeding sinfulness," and a spectacle of the "fiery indignation" which has overtaken it. And around the altar of awful sacrifice, to which the victim was bound, and upon which the at once avenging and approving flame fell and kindled, we may read the inscription: "All His ways are judgment: a God of truth and without iniquity, just and right is he."

But henceforth the necessity to punish the actual culprits was withdrawn. It remained in no shape, and could place itself on no ground. The bolt had sped and spent. The justice is in the retribution, the mercy in the diversion of it from ourselves. Consistency gave choice of no other medium, and benevolence could not exceed that act. The "readiness to forgive," ascribed to the Holy One, is now exhibited, not by a gratuitous manifestation, but as counteracting every difficulty and lavishing every price. "There is now no condemnation to them who are in Christ Jesus." "Who shall lay any thing to the charge of God's elect? God that justifieth?

Who is he that condemneth? Christ that died? yea, rather, that is risen again: who is even at the right hand of God: who also maketh intercession for us?" No obstacle exists to the spontaneous overflow of infinite love. Whosoever will may drink "of the fountain of the water of life freely." This placability not only originates itself, but opens its own channel. It is *unconstrained*, for it directs its own means. It is *uncompelled*, for it constitutes its own necessity. It is *unbought*, for it defrays its own cost. The atonement stands to this placability in the precise relation of an act to its motive, and an effect to its cause. God is not propitious because Christ has become a sacrifice, but Christ has become a sacrifice because God is propitious.

This work of sacrifice must be invariably connected with that holy government which the Divine Being administers among men. It is an essential part of it. And we must surely perceive the advantage which arises from the circumstance of legislative appointment and sanction. It becomes its own reparation and decree. Not only does it receive its general and silent countenance—it springs from itself. Whatever there is of force in law, of wisdom in order, of majesty in authority, it acquires. The "throne of glory" must not be "disgraced." Jer. xiv, 21. The atonement disabuses and rectifies every mistaken suspicion and imputation which had ever passed over its sanctities. It "is upholden by mercy," as well as "established by righteousness." The arrangement is therefore placed upon these fixed and certain principles; and "it became Him, *for whom are all things, and by whom are all things*, in bringing many sons unto glory, to make the Captain of their salvation perfect through sufferings."

These views of the atonement once settled in the mind, we can infer many important conclusions. Its *character* stands out with a legal aspect. Therefore

the method of "justification" is by a "righteousness," which means that we are accepted on the ground of a moral equivalent: the state to which we are introduced is a "redemption" that is coupled with the condition of "a ransom." Every statement is of a forensic complexion. The whole work is a legislative and judicial one. The "sentence" comes forth from His presence, whose eyes behold the things that are equal." And does it not "assure our hearts," when justice becomes our advocate, and law our plea? The true ground on which this sacrifice finds its *necessity* is thus satisfactorily explained. To avoid the notion of a vindictive proceeding, a class of writers have made it their business to describe the fact as an expedient rather than a requirement. They conjecture that it is more related to wisdom than to the inflexible rules of justice. But *we* cannot understand how Infinite Wisdom should pursue any but the wisest plan, nor how that plan can be the wisest which is not the most true to equity and obligation. It is still necessary, to help our frailty and aid our discrimination, that we have recourse to that view of the divine character which distributes it into particular qualities or attributes. And then most clearly does it seem that such a sacrifice, in the disseverment of its flesh, in the libation of its blood, in the extinction of its life, was a requital of sin, a forfeit to justice, a compliance with an irreversible demand. It was not possible that this cup should pass from our Lord. Alternative would impeach the righteousness of this severe infliction. If it were chosen from among many—a something undebarred and unessential, a happy suggestion, a convenient device—it would be indefensible because gratuitous, unjust because not inevitable. Let us remember that "God is judge," that he will "in no wise clear the guilty," that he "will repay;" let us put into this remembrance the facts of the present case; and the stern-

ness of the principle which enforced the Saviour's death will appear but its impartiality, and both cannot fail to illustrate the mercy which as deliberately respected the standard of the claim as it tenderly undertook its discharge. The exaction of this suffering and death is of a moral order, and whatever transpired beneath it bears a similar impress. The *fitness* of such an expiation arises from this circumstance. "Mercy and truth meet together: righteousness and peace kiss each other." It is the perfect alliance between the divine government and the penitent sinner. Its aspect has not a frown, its sword no edge, for him. It only plants its terrors around him for his defense. Holiness shows the pattern, justice becomes the surety, truth swears the oath, of our salvation. It is thus said that "God is our salvation;" that he is "for us;" that he is "on our side;" that he "taketh part with us." How amazing the moral transposition, that He, who so lately exclaimed "I am against you," should protect us by that very shield on whose bosses we had rushed, and make the law we had broken the instrument of rescuing us from all the consequences of our transgression. It is therefore *available*. Not only is there need of a competent efficacy to remove the penalties of guilt, there must be representation of that efficacy to meet its fears. The affrighted sinner shudders at all the ideas of justice and the relations of law. He renounces all hopes from having kept, or from being able to keep, it. "The commandment" comes! Sin revives and he dies! But it is so ordered that he shall see the law "magnified and made honorable" in the pardon tendered to him. He shall behold the ministers of wrath in the train of love. He shall hear the very trumpet of Sinai, like the silver one of a feast, only "waxing louder and louder" with glad tidings of mercy and peace. His prepossessions of alarm are anticipated and allayed, while their occasion is constituted the title

of his happiness and the safeguard of his defense. Sweet thought to the trembling offender, that " God is *faithful and just* to forgive us our sins, and to cleanse us from all unrighteousness !" All questions concerning its *extent* must terminate when we take this view of the atonement. Be it remembered that it is a provision for vindicating the divine government, and exercising the divine mercy. That which is therefore *divine* is its only scale: what is divine must be infinite. Many inquiries may arise as to the nature, cause, and direction of its application; but its universal aspect and sufficiency are placed beyond dispute. It is that which would, all other circumstances being equal, enable the righteous Lord of our race to have mercy upon all men, and is a warrant for all men to seek that mercy. It is as much the enact ment of his government as the law itself; and still more than the law reflects and illustrates his infinitely holy character. We therefore put from us all supposition of arithmetical proportion and admeasured value between its worth and its experience; for its utilities consist in other relations than those which are human, and its design to benefit earth is subordinate to that which is only proper to God, and by which only he can bene- fit any portion of the universe—the glorification of him- self! It is with this reference of the atonement to the divine dominion that the Scripture says, "All things are of God, who hath reconciled us to himself by Jesus Christ."

We are fully aware that our business has, as yet, been simply that of *explanation :* and just reasoning compels that a subject be duly propounded ere we enter on its defense; but we now hasten to the *Confirmation of the Doctrine*, which will form

The Second Part of the Discourse.

1. The analogical argument is not to be overlooked, since it carries with it the double advantage of disprov-

ing the atonement to be contrary to other facts and laws well recognized among men, and of requiring this dispensation of the divine government to correspond with others. If all mediate instrumentality, all vicarious suffering, be unknown, be denounced; if it be an idea foreign to all our minds, and abhorrent to all our observations; we might, with some semblance of reason, demur to the first statement of such a doctrine. For in reasoning upon analogy, we adduce and collate all that we know and experience; this is but an investigation of things as ordered or suffered by the righteous disposals of Almighty authority; and when we gather our illustrations from other parts of that government to uphold and explain the sacrifice of the cross, we must remember that those other parts were made to reflect that sacrifice, and not that such sacrifice was accommodated to them. Analogy respects a system of operations, a constitution of things, which we contend must coincide with an *event* to which they all are tributary, and for the sake of which they alone have any existence.

Now it is most obvious that while we believe the Deity acts and speaks by the mediation of Jesus Christ, and employs his intervening agency, a world of contrivances on the same principle unfolds itself. Every benefit we enjoy is derived through some indirect channel. Being, sustenance, education, we receive from parents, benefactors, and teachers. The advantages of society are thus circuitously transmitted through all its countless links. So in the lower kingdoms of nature there is established a uniformity of what we call effects, arising out of what we term specific causes. Further and further we may trace the succession, in agents more remote and secondary, in means more subordinate and inconsequential. God gives and arranges all by this employment of power; and vehicles of power in constant dependence upon his control, and in unerring subserviency to his

purpose. If this should appear to us a characteristic and law of his general conduct, it is an argumentative presumption, and a natural expectation, that he will not, in such most glorious instance, vary his order and depart from his consistency.

The death of Christ differs, however, from all those prepossessions which have raised themselves upon a review of what is simply an interposition of ministries and means. It is much more; it involves the principle of *one suffering for another.* But this notion, abstracted from our particular subject, does not seem to shock the opinion and general sense of mankind. The annals of patriotism glow with bright names of self-sacrificing renown. Present good has been surrendered by a generous disinterestedness for the welfare of posterity. These models we admire, these heroic deeds we applaud. And when we look more minutely into the framework of every human community, we cannot fail to notice that almost all its good is purchased by necessary or voluntary inconvenience and pain. The parent denies himself repose and many a comfort for the better equipment of the child in the race of life; the child has often to repay the care which watched his infancy, by debarring himself of recreation which labor requires and competency might command. The artisan, to secure our dwellings and to clothe our persons, submits to occupations which shorten his days upon the earth. What are the original curses which still affect our nature? What is the cost of every life? What is the doom of its struggling support? And there are occasions when we should be accounted unnatural, did we not endanger health and existence for others. What parent would not extend the living shield of his bosom to protect his child? What Christian would refuse to die rather than forswear his profession? And, consequently, it revolts nothing that we are habituated to see, nothing which we are

instructed to approve, when a representation is made to us that the greatest possible happiness is apportioned by an infliction of suffering, and a self-devotement of philanthropy.

The fact that innocence often incurs the consequences of guilt is apparent, and proves that the actual case in question is by no means unknown to the present constitution of things. It is sufficient answer to the charge of any peculiar principle, that every observer is equally required to explain a similar one in surveying the history of communities and the progress of events. It is no more the embarrassment of revealed, than of natural, religion.

There is another class of parallelisms which is more distinct and substantive. We discover them in the field of Holy Scripture. Is the representative principle avowed in it? This is an important inquiry, because it must determine whether revelation, which is so conformable with the external arrangement, be also consistent with itself? Is it uniformly sustained by that volume, or abruptly introduced to serve a special purpose? In some instances we learn, that without mediatory suffering, an honor is put upon mediatory excellence. For the sake of the righteous, the wicked have been spared. Ten just men would have reprieved Sodom. "The Lord blessed" the Egyptian's house "for Joseph's sake." How often does "David's sake" turn away wrath from Judah. God gave to Paul all them who sailed with him. For the elect's sake the days of trouble are shortened. The earth cannot be hurt, neither the sea, nor the trees, until the servants of God are sealed in their foreheads. But there is a more determinate application of the principle. Facts are presented in which there occurs the inverted relation of guilt and impunity, innocence and suffering. The child of David dies for his father's sin. The crimes of Manasseh are avenged, long after he was buried in

the garden of Uzza. "I gave Egypt for thy ransom," said Jehovah to his ancient people, "Ethiopia and Seba for thee." He declares that he will visit "the iniquity of the fathers upon the children," and upon the children's children, "unto the third and to the fourth generation." It is not his ordinary tenor of conduct, but an exception to it, when he decrees, "The son shall not bear the iniquity of the father, neither shall the father bear the iniquity of the son." It is therefore a general principle of revelation, whose tone vibrates through the whole.

It is no part of our present duty to vindicate such course of procedure, and such avowal of purpose; the simple motive for adducing them is, to show that the principle does not innovate on any known law, or war with any sacred oracle.

2. Another argument may be added to this preparatory suggestion. It is merely mooted as negative. But the hypothesis is, that God does please to pardon. Now against a substitutionary principle, to which every analogy answers, and to which no authority is opposed, it is objected that it is superfluous, inasmuch as there are plainer and precedent means equally efficacious. Why, it is asked, fix upon a remedy foreign and doubtful, when every man possesses in himself the means of atonement and moral reparation? Why seek, in a punitive and vicarious act, that which is always at hand and in our power? Repentance is the alleged resource. It is affirmed that it is deprecatory and propitiating; that the present altered state of mind debars the very justice which would resent its former guilt and pravity. But it does not appear that there is any thing in the divine government to favor these positions. The consequences of an action prevail long after the action has been performed, and equally long after it has been made the subject of a bitter regret. Compunction and remorse have wrung scalding tears from the eye, have pierced the heart

with bleeding wounds. We "possess the iniquities of our youth." The arrears of former wickedness pursue us. Here is the sign of continued punishment, though there is the proof of sincere penitence. So far, therefore, every primary notice falsifies the conclusion. Nor does it seem reasonable that sorrow for offense should be accepted as a compensation for it. Between man and man, individually considered, this may sometimes be allowed; but when the laws and institutions of society are affected, it is never permitted. And our sins have their most serious evil in their invasion of an universal order and fitness, in their attack upon infinite purity and authority; so that, however they may injure our neighbor and ruin ourselves, we may warrantably exclaim, " Against thee, thee only, have we sinned!" And if repentance produce future amendment, that amendment only falls into the duty of that future; it can only supply the season as it arises, and meet the obligation as it falls. There is nothing retrospective in it, and cannot make it less true that we have hitherto done wrong. Where is the availableness to expurgate that wrong? What power is there to reverse its fruits? Still, if any doctrine be more explicitly the dictate of natural religion than another, it is that on all crime ensues a punishment. Whatever we sow, we also reap. It may not be an immediate issue, but at last it comes in its own appropriate form. There is a God who judgeth in the earth, if we only follow the silent operations of his undeclared will. But if repentance were the appeasement, then these strong links of succession must be broken, the ordinary pains of demerit must be remitted, and the vial of wrath cease to pour itself out upon them who mourned the past. The retributive character of the divine ordinations is *not* changed, and the entail is still on them whose dispositions and lives have been so greatly reformed. There is every disproof, in short, of the effi-

cacy ascribed to repentance and subsequent obedience, not only in Scripture, but in the province which reason loves to claim as its own, and to subject to its investigation. And it is unnecessary, therefore, for us to show that such repentance is inadequate to the extent and malignity of the crimes which it professes to deplore, and becomes their serious aggravation when it assumes the power to expiate them. He who receives the atonement weeps not to wash away his sins, but because they are washed away he weeps!

3. The use of similitudes is a very common and salutary practice in the work of instruction. It arouses attention, impresses memory, facilitates apprehension, and builds up in the mind a system of ready and pertinent illustrations. They constitute the source of all language, the basis of all writing; and what was suited to the infant history of our species, is still as adapted to the tender and unformed faculties of our infant nature. The fables and hieroglyphics of our childhood have not lost their power to entertain and discipline our maturer judgments and riper years.

And it was in this manner that God addressed the fathers of our race. He took them by the hand, and led them from step to step of knowledge. He made one thing tell of another. He put a sign, and taught a conception; he appealed to the sense, that he might reach the intellect. Upon such a principle the *ceremonial law* was constructed. It was a repository of types and representations. It drew the outline, and cast the shadow, of " good things to come." It " was a schoolmaster to bring us to Christ." Sacrifice was its characteristic institute. The altar was continually heaped with victims, and flowed with streams of blood. Sin was confessed over the offering, and the sinner found in it an atonement for his trespass. The whole was certainly prelusory, and it was " not possible that the blood of

bulls and of goats should take away sin." It is an idea which strikes in with no prepossession of man, and which finds nothing akin to it in his feelings. Tradition can account for its all but universal influence, but only a divine mandate for its original practice. There will be no hesitation with the Christian, that this expense of treasure and beastial life had a special reference to the death of the cross. That death is denominated a sacrifice. We believe that it was absolutely one, that it was such exclusively; that according to the strictest value of words, and the most rigid exaction of sentiments, it was a sacrifice of atonement. The alternative appears to us to be, that all the apparatus of magnificent forms, all the machinery of elaborate details, were unmeaning show and prodigal ostentation. But we are not ignorant that it is maintained that the death of Christ is only so styled allusively, that it is in accommodation to these ancient models.

The inquiry, then, between those who hold the atonement and those who renounce it, is, whether do the types determine the character of the Saviour's death, or does that death determine the character of the types? Is there the idea of sacrifice in the types because that death was truly sacrificial, or was that death regarded sacrificial in compliance with those types?

Now we ask why sacrifice should have been established at all, if it was incorrect to apply its meaning to that which it was established to introduce! Why should the perplexing error be injected into the human mind? Why should the stumbling-block be needlessly thrown in our path? Why was a figure sanctioned which all of the reality must disown and contradict? Why was the idea, perpetuated in every variety of manner, and under every pledge of solemnity, to be thrown away, to be denied, to be repudiated, at the very first moment it could be of use and application? Were the sacrifices of

four thousand years required to prove that the death of our Saviour was not a sacrifice ?

But there is another answer : the type must agree with the antitype, or the intended thing. It was established to forestall and indicate it. It might not be " the very image," but it is a close resemblance. It would defeat every intention were it otherwise, or were it less so than its own inferior nature compelled. Whatever in it is faint and dim, the *original* must define and illumine. That which " cometh after is preferred before." The homage is from the sign to the signification. Yet, in defiance of this simple rule, is the Saviour's death divested of a sacrificial import, is allowed the figurative name only in deference to particular ceremonies, is adjudged to have expiatory virtue only as a poetic trope ! The Jewish altar bows not down to the cross, the cross stoops to the Jewish altar ! The shadow depends not on the substance for its size and form, but the substance attributes its size and form to the shadow !

4. The *peculiar character* of the sufferings endured by our Lord supplies another argument in favor of their vicarious intention.

Two facts must be assumed ; indeed, into any controversy touching them it would be a shock to all piety, and a debasement of all reason, to enter. We deign not to dispute with the blasphemers or maniacs who could contest them. They lie at the basis of the whole argument. The *first* is the sinlessness in fact, and the impeccability in nature, of Him who is the " Most Holy," and " separate from sinners." The *second* is, the inalienable complacency of the Father in the Son, throughout the progress of his entire series of mediatorial acts and humiliations when " stricken, smitten of God, and afflicted." There was no taint of human corruption, no sentiment of divine displeasure ; his person

was the brightest perfection in the universe, and his work an expression of the richest benevolence which was ever diffused amid its realms.

These sufferings were of the most extraordinary severity and pressure. He was the " man of sorrows." They were on the body, on the mind, on every relationship and every stage of life. Strange is the hour when he rejoices in spirit; but it is a common thing for him to weep. In how many forms, from how many directions, with how many aggravations, did his sore travail oppress him ! He sank in deep waters; they went over his head, they came in unto his soul.

These sufferings were voluntary, or the results of voluntary engagements. He " gave himself for us." " He steadfastly set his face " to the scene on which he laid down his life of himself. And this is an uncommon circumstance, since our time is in the " hand " of God, with him are all our ways, and it is for him " to kill and make alive." To seek death is to undervalue the gift of life, and may be as suicidal an act as if we were to break open its sanctuary. But certainly such a self-disposing power is a most singular right, and perfectly at variance with the conditions of created being.

These sufferings were required by the most inevitable necessity. In harmony, however mysterious, with his freest agency and fullest choice, there was a moral and decreptive obligation which he obeyed. And when we remember Christ Jesus, his obedience to this twofold obligation is readily explained—the one is but the assent of his nature, the other is but the announcement of his will. Such necessity is his love of right, and his superiority to any violation of it. Therefore it is written that he ought " to suffer," that he must " be slain," that he was " delivered by the determinate counsel and foreknowledge of God," that the perpetrators of his crucifixion only did whatsoever the hand and the counsel

of God " determined before to be done." But this is a stress which it is by no means common to lay upon any human calamities ; nor can we conceive a case in which the cup of trial could not possibly be allowed to pass from us.

These sufferings were attributed to an immediately divine infliction. No adversity springs " out of the dust." But while there is no evil but the Lord hath done it, and the " Most High ruleth " among the children of men, there is a directness of purpose and conduct on his part in the history of the Saviour's humiliations unknown to any other. He " doth not willingly afflict nor grieve the children of men,"—" it *pleased the Lord* to bruise him, he hath put him to grief, he hath made his soul an offering for sin." Unless in proportion to the injustice of punishment is the divine pleasure in executing it, and according to the innocence of the subject is the divine delight over his extremest pains, we must necessarily conclude that there is a speciality in the present facts which alone can make them righteously defensible.

These sufferings were accompanied by the deepest depression of feeling. To his bodily sufferings perhaps some mortal agonies may be compared. In these he has been approached by men. One exception must be made —those bodily sufferings which were excited by mental griefs, which no bosom ever harbored save his own. This was his bloody agony in the garden, this was his unexpectedly-hastened death upon the cross. And it is beneath these conflicts of infernal assault, these depths of dread reflection, these visitations of divine infliction, that we mark a sinking, a recoil, a deprecating tone, a very despair. Such was his cry of parting life when his head bowed as much in dejection as in death. Bearing in memory who he was, and his own exemption from all that can barb an upbraiding mind, and lend scorpions

to an accusing conscience, we may justly inquire, why conscious rectitude and goodness did not preserve his brow from furrow, his voice from complaint, his heart from desolation. And still may we persist to ask, why martyrs should exhibit their high resolve, their glorious magnanimity, their dint of energy, and their rapture of meekness, when he would, though but for a moment, evade the necessity of the dire woes then beginning to gather around him, and the final stroke so presently to fall. Where was their collected serenity, when he was " sore amazed ? " Where was their triumphing courage, when he " was exceeding sorrowful, even unto death ? " The temper of endurance sufficiently decides that the sufferings were unequaled in their *character* and *design*, as well as in their poignancy and magnitude.

These sufferings indicate traces of a penal and judicial impress. Affliction may be kind by being corrective, but a fearful style of language is employed to denote acts of retributive wrath. The cup! " In the hand of the Lord there is a cup, and the wine is red; it is full of mixture ; and he poureth out of the same : but the dregs thereof, all the wicked of the earth shall wring them out and drink them." And never does Scripture ascribe to it one healing ingredient—it is " the cup of trembling," " the cup of fury," overflowing with " the wine of astonishment." The sword! Jehovah will " whet his sword ;" it " cannot be quiet," it is " filled with blood," it will " plead with all flesh." It is the instrument of devouring slaughter, and the symbol of inexorable law. And yet these are the tokens of that conduct which is pursued toward the Holy Jesus. " The cup which my Father hath given me, shall I not drink it ? " " Awake, O sword, against my Shepherd, and against the man that is my Fellow, saith the Lord of Hosts." But if there be any thing punitive in these sufferings, it can have no purport of personal demerit ; they must be in

some manner wielded against sin, which has only an accidental and temporary charge upon Him who now is made responsible for it. And if "forsaken"—if in such abandonment all the unmitigated consequences of sin be concentrated—if there be all its wormwood and all its curse—that "beauty of the Lord," that "light of his countenance," could only be eclipsed because the Immaculate Sufferer was brought into an unnatural relation, and beheld in a transposed sphere.

These sufferings, therefore, could not terminate on Him who bore them. When we sum up the preceding remarks, and connect them with those final causes which all divine acts must exhibit, we can reach no other conclusion than that a retribution so extreme, so voluntarily encountered, so indispensable, so immediately dealt by Heaven, borne with such dejection and consternation, flaming with such brands of penal wrath, could only be relative and impersonal; regarding some extrinsic due and represented interest. For if that retribution be exacted upon him strictly considered in himself, it is *unjust.* It would fail, therefore, in every end of moral government, neither encouraging virtue nor deterring vice. It must confound right and wrong, besides annulling all the sanctions which depend upon their different consequences. It could only destroy each incentive to excellence, and embolden guilt still further to presume. But as these alternatives are glaringly absurd and morally impossible, it is a position which establishes and balances itself, that all the sufferings of Christ are substitutionary in their cause, benevolent in their motive, and sacrificial in their effect. As it is the part of sound philosophy to gather up all facts independently of any particular system—and equally so, after the induction, to receive the one principle which can explain and harmonize them all —so we bring into a scheme all the circumstances of Him who "was wounded for our transgressions," and

having shown the inconsistency of every other solution, adopt the most worthy and satisfactory principle of expiation.

5. In an argument which respects a pure discovery of revelation, it would not be decent to omit all reference to those authorities and proofs which Scripture contains. It is much to find the general idea and assumption of the inspired volume; but we may be assured that we shall often discover the same in explicit sentences and naked declarations. These fill its range and determine its scope. Selection is the difficulty.

"For He hath made him to be sin for us, who knew no sin; that we might be made the righteousness of God in him." Can contrast be more marked, appointment more plain, and process more determinate?

"Scarcely for a righteous man will one die; yet peradventure for a good man some would even dare to die. But God commendeth his love toward us, in that, while we were yet sinners, Christ died for us." Is it possible so to overlook the construction of the passage as not to allow that Christ is here intended to die for us, as we might die instead of a righteous and philanthropic man?

"Christ hath redeemed us from the curse of the law, being made a curse for us." This is surely the strongest mode of stating his assumption of our penal liabilities.

"Christ hath once suffered for sins, the just for the unjust, that he might bring us to God." Can a vicarious idea be more distinctly announced?

Then we may reason upon the concurrent testimonies to the efficacy of the Saviour's *blood*—a sacrificial term—a term propounded always in connection with sin, or the covenant which remembers it no more—and always to be explained by that great axiom, "Without

shedding of blood is no remission." "This is my blood which is shed for many for the remission of sins." It can purge the conscience from dead works. It cleanseth from all sin. He is a propitiation through faith in his blood. "We have redemption in his blood." He has sanctified the people with his own blood. He has " washed us from our sins in his own blood." Is this a fortuitous description? Or is it a metaphor common to writers of the most different order of mind and style of composition?

The nicest attention to the use of the preposition selected by the sacred penmen, where they would inform us that Christ died *for* our sins, and gave himself *for* us, will satisfy the biblical student that substitution can only be intended. It need only be added that the case governed by that preposition—being dependent as a question of choice upon the particular shade of meaning in the writer's mind, the one sense requiring one and the other another—ascertains the most definite employment of it.*

* The force and perspicuity of the Greek prepositions are proverbial. The Apostles could not generally pretend to erudite scholarship; but the gift of tongues, and the afflatus by which they spoke and wrote, would certainly secure the most appropriate expressions. Paul was doubtless acquainted with some of the Attic models. Now, one of these parts of speech seems commonly selected by the New Testament. Προ, δια, περι, αμφι, and even occasionally προς, would have conveyed the idea of being for the benefit, or on the account, of the parties concerning whom they are affirmed. Αντι would be the next in conveying the impression of "instead," "in room," of another. But it seldom rises higher than *succession, sequence,* of the corresponding kind and natural order. Υπερ is the preposition most commonly used in this connection. Its primitive meaning is that of elevation, which is preserved in the notion of what we believe its scriptural intention. The representing party is raised above, over—he surmounts and overcomes the natural order of punishing the represented. The English reader may perceive this distinction in the following text: " Christ hath once suffered for (περι, about, because of) sins; the just for (υπερ,

And in conformity to this view of the Saviour's crucifixion is the common method of stating it. It is not casually, incidently, but systematically and advisedly, described as an offering, a sacrifice, a ransom, a propitiation, a redemption, a reconciliation, a making peace, a saving from wrath, a taking away of sin. This does not appear the most simple manner to narrate a mortal's death, or to illustrate a martyr's victory. And to this may be added his invested characters—he is a Saviour, a Mediator, a Deliverer, a Priest, a Surety, a Minister of the true tabernacle which the Lord pitched and not man. Nothing can be more intelligible than that such expositions should be given of his work, such descriptions of his character, if an atoning victim; nothing more incredible, if his purpose were only didactic.

6. There is an *implication* in Scripture equal to these *avowals*. And it is strange that any should so far tamper with its spirit as to speak of the Saviour's death with a disposition to degrade it. If any theme be secured by its own nature from ribald taunt and profanation, it is that awful fact. Will it be believed that it has been a current maxim with some, that it has no importance but as necessary to his resurrection, and that it is only useful as preliminary to it? That another and a loftier conception of it belongs to the sacred volume and the Christian economy, we need not pause to prove. Every thing vindicates its rank of infinite worth and glory.

This is to be observed when the first preachers of the Gospel announce themselves. They are " dead with Christ," they are " crucified with" him. Their language, because each sentiment, is determined by it. They seem entranced into a sublime abstraction and ecstacy, knowing nothing among men save Jesus Christ, even the

in the place of) the unjust." This is the invariable terminology of the New Testament. I, John ii, 2, introducing a *particular* view of the atonement, and omitting mention ·of the conscious agents, is no exception.

Crucified One. They would, under the most solemn forbiddance, only glory in the cross. This was their favorite contemplation; it gave fixedness to their thought, and fervor to their feeling; it formed the secret of every charm they employed, and the spell of every influence they commanded; it was their early visitation and their last.

Nor can we fail to notice that these first preachers of Christianity never refer to the death of the cross as *one* of the expedients by which the evangelical blessings are secured. It is not blended with miracle, teaching, or precept. It is set forth the exclusive means of salvation. He "his own self bare our sins in his own *body on the tree*." He "*gave his life* a ransom for many." And this is so remarkable, that his present mediatorial existence, his " power of an endless life " of priesthood, is contrasted with his death, and his death of blood. "Much more, then, being now justified by *his blood*, we shall be saved from wrath through him. For if, when we were enemies, we were reconciled to God by the *death* of his Son, much more, being reconciled, we shall be saved by his *life*." We are, indeed, informed by pseudo-christians that he is our Saviour by correcting our errors and by encouraging our virtues; it is enough that the Saviour himself, and the inspired interpreters of his mission, make our salvation depend upon one fact, and that is the *incarnate crucifixion*, " the body of his flesh by death," a sacrifice " offered once for all ; " to which the resurrection, without adding any thing to render it complete, stands simply related as a seal of its truth and a proclamation of its efficacy!

The importance attached by the first Christians to this *death* is seen in a sensitive delicacy whenever its singularity is likely to be confounded, or its virtue to be lost. " Was Paul crucified for you ? " was his own indignant remonstrance. Not for a moment could he

brook, not that the mistake should be entertained, but that there should be any feeling of partisanship toward him which, by possibility, unbelievers might so interpret. And in the same manner there is nothing which they so much deprecated, nothing at which they so deeply shuddered, as any compromise of the atonement on the cross. "Then," said they, unable to conceive of an equal catastrophe, "then Christ is dead in vain!"

The kingdom of the Lord Jesus, administered by him on earth, sanctifies and protects the memory of his death. His Church retains, in contradistinction to its general spiritualism of service, the symbols of his broken body and outpoured blood. This was the one point of which he required the remembrance; this is *our* distinctive badge and profession. "As often as ye eat this bread, and drink this cup, ye do *show the Lord's death* till he come." Therefore, from the night in which he was betrayed, have these tokens confirmed the faith, and nourished the piety, of them who love to confess their crucified Master; and these tokens shall continue to illustrate and cheer the faithful until the night when he shall come with his "sign in the clouds of heaven." "One generation shall praise" and declare this mighty act to "another." But can we escape the conclusion that the *death* which receives such signal honor, and such ever-during commemoration, contains in itself elements of wonder and interest which well authorize this homage?

And should it be thought that this *particular* of the Saviour's history is only suited for man in his present condition, and only held back from obsoleteness upon earth, we may ascertain whether the heaven of life, purity, and immortality bear its impression, and admit its memorial. Though we could never learn, from ourselves, "what passes there," a disclosure has been made to us. And he who should be suddenly rapt by a trans-

lation from the foot of the cross into the midst of " the things above," would not be conscious of a different thought or a successive feeling. All would be illuminated with a stronger splendor, and all be regarded with an intenser sensibility, but this would be the only change. The " heavenly things themselves " have been "purified " by this sacrifice. Hark to the celestial song, " Worthy is the Lamb that was slain." Admire those robes of white! "the souls of them that were slain for the word of God" are among the throng who wear them; but they owe no brilliance to the death, they derive no glory from the triumph of martyrdom; they are " made white in the blood of the Lamb." But will allusion be borne to the endurance and shame of the cross in a direct ascription to him who is the life? "Thou wast slain, and hast redeemed us to God by thy blood!" Or will not every memento of that death be henceforth studiously avoided, each association repelled, each scar effaced? Lo! stands the Lamb as he has been slain! Heaven is no place for flight from the recollections of Calvary! It is filled with the apparatus and monuments of atonement! Its atmosphere is brightened by it, redolent of it, vocal with it! There is its most sacred recess and depository! There is its shrine! Not one thought in the crowd of eternal ideas—not one note in the compass of eternal anthems—not one moment in the round of eternal ages—can there be but refers to " Christ crucified," and but evidently sets him forth before the eyes of the redeemed, " crucified among " them. With all its " many mansions," but one sympathy pervades the circuit of heaven; nor shall he find a place in one of them who " hath counted the blood of the covenant " a *common thing!*

So far, then, we have proceeded; and must maintain that when we examine Scripture—its records of primitive Christianity—its visions of eternal bliss—an injudi-

cious prominence, an unmeaning peculiarity, is attached to the sufferings of Christ; the stress laid upon them is most unwarranted, the regard challenged to them is redundant—save that they be strictly sacrificial!

7. The argument requires a further expansion. For it may be doubted by some whether we *do* increase the value of this *death* by clothing it with an expiatory character. They may conceive this is a corruption of its simple dignity. It therefore remains for us, in this scriptural argument, to press those views of it which are scripturally avouched, and to show that these can only answer to the idea of a great sacrificial transaction.

It will hardly be denied that if man be in that fallen state, in that predicament of guilt and depravity, which render his eternal punishment just—if he has wholly strayed and is utterly lost—that something more than instruction is necessary to restore him; that new and external relations must be established in his favor. Without begging the question, this must be the best interposition for us, the most efficacious remedy. But we cannot think it doubtful that the Scripture does state such facts. "They are all gone out of the way, they are together become unprofitable; there is none that doeth good, no, not one." "The heart is deceitful above all things, and desperately wicked." "Our righteousnesses are as filthy rags." "If our heart condemn us, God is greater than our heart, and knoweth all things." Something done for them will, in the apprehension of the most ordinary reason, be a thousand times better than a communication of knowledge or an exemplification of conduct. Nor, unless that be *done* which removes certain disqualifying circumstances, can the sinner make an approach to moral recovery or spiritual bliss.

The Gospel is *glad tidings.* It tells of pardon, life, and peace. Let us conceive a case. A criminal is in the hands of the executioner. Before his swimming eye

there stretches a curious, it may be a pitying, crowd. Perfect stillness reigns over the living mass, while the hideous preparations of death proceed. There is a mur-mur on its outer verge! A messenger proclaiming his errand lest he should come too late, forces, finds, a way through its densest center! Good news! resounds from every voice. The scaffold is attained! The half-dead wretch revives! How fires that but now glazed eye! How acute becomes that lately insensate ear! And now the rapturous information, at the first report of which the stroke was stayed, is more precisely unfolded! What! if after all, it were but a copy of the law that criminal had transgressed, and of the sentence he had incurred? Could there be a more fiendlike sport with anguish? Was mockery necessary to make that cup of ignominy and violence overflow? And yet, if the Christian redemption merely justifies its glad tidings by a recapitulation of our duty and an enforcement of our accountability, it raises a hope only to disappoint it; and opens our eye to the prospect of life only to em-bitter the agony of its close in death. It is a pretension of mercy, but a thing of despair! Let, however, some-thing be conveyed to us in the shape of a pardon—let it be proved that the pardon is based upon a moral satis-faction—that the satisfaction has been provided by mercy in consistent regard to justice—that a deliverance has been wrought out for us—and we hail it as " glad tidings of great joy." It is passing " from death unto life."

But it is a doctrine of inspiration that the death of Christ has not only an influence future to its occurrence, but that which is retrocessive. Faith in Him who " was to come "—the believing recognition in type and vision of his " day "—the persuasion of the " promises " " when afar off," was " counted for righteousness." The Gospel was preached unto Abraham. So true is this, that the

inspired writer is content to say, "Unto us was the Gospel preached *as well as* unto them." Heb. iv, 2. They "first," that is, they *before*, "trusted in Christ." But if you interpret the religion of the Gospel into a mere instrument of enlightening the human mind, of weaning it from idolatry, of inciting it to morality, how can it have this reflex power so expressly ascribed to it? How could it retrieve the errors and check the mistakes of former generations? Whatever its subsequent course, it could not throw back a ray of intelligence upon those large portions of our race which were long since swept among the dead. Here is the problem; this view only perplexes it. But if the death of Christ be sacrificial—if the Gospel be founded upon it—then may an *anticipated deed*, certain as though it was already transacted, be accepted in the sinner's room, and be attributed to him for his benefit—a constant provision and groundwork of acceptance, and always a competent object of belief. Being infallibly sure, it may be equally available for all old, and for all future, time. Its delay was but "the forbearance of God," and need not interrupt the "remission of sins that are past." By means of his death as the mediator of the new testament, there is the redemption of the transgressions that were under the first testament. Heb. ix, 15. Destroy this *character* of his death, and you render its prior efficacy impossible: admit it, and the Lamb is "slain from the foundation of the world." And in this sense only can we understand those expressions which relate to the infinite munificence of divine love in the *gift* of Jesus Christ—to the infinite rigor of divine justice in not *sparing him*—to the infinite delight of divine complacency in the "sweet-smelling savor" of his offering and sacrifice. And it speaks much for the superiority of this view over every other that opposes it, that, when the atonement is denied, the dignity of the Saviour is also rejected; proving

that in common apprehension the one is the higher work which incarnate deity must undertake, and that the other is a lower one which a human prophet can accomplish. Any conception of that death, in comparison with the idea of atonement, is like bringing for gold, brass; for silver, iron; for brass, wood; and for iron, stones! It is a certain exchange of ever-sinking depreciations!

There is a remaining branch of discussion which pertains to the *principle* on which the atonement was offered: the principle of substitution.

III. LET US ENDEAVOR TO DEFEND THE STRICT RIGHT AND PERFECT EQUITY OF THAT ARRANGEMENT WHICH DEVOLVES OUR PERSONAL LIABILITIES UPON JESUS CHRIST AS OUR SACRIFICIAL REPRESENTATIVE.

In ordinary contracts between man and man an independent party may become, by his own consent, responsible for the obligations and pledges of another. None can think it unjust if Judah be voluntarily detained in the room of his younger brother; or that Paul should make himself accountable for the debt and wrong of Onesimus.

In moral connections it is admitted to be much more difficult of application. But this seeming difficulty chiefly arises from a false supposition. It is imagined that the sinful act of the man is imputed to the Saviour, which is impossible—nothing can constitute it any other's act. Our depraved conduct, whatever is the *evil* of sin, can never belong to any history but our own, or attach to any being but ourselves. It is unphilosophical, it is irrational, that any separation can take place between what we have done and our doing of it. It is the most necessary of truths that the past cannot be obliterated or reversed. It is not in the power of omnipotence to make any fact unreal, any truth false. What has been, has been; what is, is. But there may

be a *quality* of sin, such a quality as has respect to an *external relation*, abstracted from it. The process of mind is as simple as to detach color from form. That quality in the present instance is guilt, or liability to punishment. If there were no law the same deed might be performed; it might possess all its inherent folly and unfitness; but it would not be a guilty, or in other words, a *punishable* deed. The punishment depends upon the law, the law upon the lawgiver, and the lawgiver upon infinite reason and purity. "The Lord is our lawgiver." Substitution therefore leaves "the things done in the body" just where they were, and only could be; but it undertakes that the obnoxiousness to consequences, so far as those consequences are not of sin's own nature but of the government under which it is committed, shall be displaced and shifted.

Another improper view has often embarrassed the subject. It is argued—or, perhaps, more truly, felt; that divine justice is an attribute of unrelenting sternness, of absolute vindictiveness, against the offender. It has nothing, we maintain on the contrary, that regards a personal aim. It hates no creature nor seeks his ruin. It concerns not itself with the person but the crime. If the obligation to suffer be separated from him, there is no further exposure. Its office is to protect right, and thus to insure happiness, and only to punish for the sake of enforcing this state of moral well-being. It is not implacable resentment, it is the care which embraces all the interests of the universe. Let the law be upholden, and any scheme which does this is consonant to its nature and may obtain its sanction. Moral righteousness is the love of all things.

The objection to the principle is considerably heightened by the impediments which obstruct it in the relations of human life. It is allowed that no civil

commonwealth could admit the transfer of capital punishment, though some cases may be conceived in which even this would invest a government with more apparent impartiality and terrible disinterestedness. Yet it is frankly acknowledged to be, in our circumstances, neither a feasible nor practicable commutation. But why? not, that if all the parties were capable of acting for themselves, it would be abstractly unjust, but because neither the laws of God nor man suppose a man's life to be his own. And then society would suffer were the worthy blotted from the living, and the wicked spared in their room. But it must always be remembered that these are groundless scruples against the interposition of Christ, for it was not " possible that he should be 'holden " of death. He arose from the grave with greater power to benefit them for whom he died. There was no subtraction of life and influence from the great moral system. We go not to his grave to weep there, as though he saw corruption ; he " dieth no more, death hath no more dominion over him." We are not weighed down by a possible suspicion that our salvation has been the cause of lessening his influence or abating his joy. Through us he has not been lost to others. His reward is founded upon his death. " Wherefore God hath given him a name above every name." We look on him whom we " have pierced, and mourn," " but we see Jesus crowned with glory and honor." Our gain is not his injury. We live not but by his life. We eat not " the sacrifices of the dead :" we " drink " not " the wine of the condemned ! " " He was raised again for our justification ! "

Substitution is not *unjust*, if the penalty of the law be inflicted ; nor *pernicious*, but the very reverse, if a stronger mark of its sincerity, and a more powerful expression of its even-handed justice be given by the moral system which superintends it—taking a more signal

retribution on the sin, by wreaking it on one infinitely superior to the sinner!

Christ thus represents us, and enters into that fixed, inevitable obligation to punishment which we had incurred by our revolt. In doing this he in no way mixes himself with our sinfulness, but proves himself most averse from it, is the object of infinite complacency in his work of expiating it, and stands at the most abhorrent extreme from it while enduring its appalling curses! Still as this is not the common and natural order of punishment—as it necessitates an arrangement somewhat extra-judicial—as many difficulties beset it which can only be obviated by a most singular combination of favorable circumstances—it may not be uninteresting to inquire into the power which exists to allow it—into the occasion which may be supposed to justify it—the rules which direct its permission—and the checks which limit its operation.

At what time, how far, under what conditions, is, then, substitution admissible? *

1. There must be a moral equivalent.

It is only a question of principle, and not of physical comparison. For in the very supposition of the case, the transferred punishment cannot be the *same*. The case is that of an innocent party suffering for the guilty.

---

* The writer was a good deal surprised to perceive in the posthumous sermons of the Rev. Robert Hall, a train of remarks so very similar to those of his own pages. He preached the substance of this Discourse at the Lecture in Heckmondwike, 1825. He was then solicited, by several of his brethren, to let it go to press. Perhaps it would not have now appeared, but that it might seem that he then declined from the consciousness of plagiarism. There is sufficient disparity in the topics, though the amount of numerals is the same, to show that his argumentation is independent: who could, indeed, hope to compare, in thought or style, with that most illustrious Author!

But the innocent, in such an act of noble benevolence, cannot feel regret, shame, remorse, or fear. Every thing approves him, he approves himself. And the present nature of such a case is *expiatory.* Now, no man can expiate his own offense. Punishment, personally borne, is not expiation. The character does not cease to be implicated when the penalty is spent. The sentence of death may be inflicted, it is the last retribution of earthly governments; but the crime remains what it was, and all its consequences endure long after the execution. And in sacrificial expiation there is a *victim.* Necessarily it must be different from them who have confessed their sins over it. Were it one of them, it could not be a proxy for them. And by parity and greater force of reasoning, it must follow that our Lord Jesus Christ was perfectly unsusceptible of conscious demerit, of painful repentance; could not be the object of displacency with heaven, nor feel a sense of having injured any being of earth. All that punishment of sin which is but its evolved consequence—which springs out of its very properties—he could never know. The bitter and keen mortification which is engendered of itself could never weigh upon his spirit. To all this scath and blast he was " the green tree," inconsumable; like that of Midian amid the lambent play of the enwrapping flame. How, then, can he supply an indemnity which, by every requirement and necessity, must be so dissimilar to the debt, and to the manner in which, otherwise, the debtor must suffer? How can he exhaust the punishment adjudged against us, and yet fail in so many of its characteristic severities? It is the consideration of His *person* which explains it all! What a *capacity* for suffering, what an *importance* of suffering, what a *validity* to suffering, does that person command! The effect cannot be less than infinite! And if the subjects of David could say, " But now thou art worth ten

thousand of us ;" what are our mortal interests when counterpoised by Him before whom " all nations are counted less than nothing and vanity?" Conceive him in his incarnate nature depressed, buffeted, agonized, crucified ; and *one* may represent *all*, and the *momentary* anguish of such a one may cancel the consequences of *eternity !* O there is a grandeur in his humiliation ! He puts the restraint upon his own energies, and the vail upon his own glories ! Still he is the Omnipotent and the Self-Existent. " Crucified through weakness "— " there is the hiding of his power !" (Habak. iii, 4.) Bowing his head in death—" he is the Living Being who was dead !" (Rev. i, 18.) Does not every advantage redound to the cause of justice and the enforcement of law when creatures, insignificant but for their guilt and their powers of bearing its consequences, are liberated in right of the intervening merit of voluntary suffering endured by Him whose single pang was greater than the endless gnawing of the worm which never dies though millions of millions were its prey, and who conferred on that suffering a value and a majesty which originate a claim which infinite righteousness is bound to answer and honored to fulfill. Moral government acquires every thing by the substitutionary transposition of " God manifest in the flesh " for " man whose breath is in his nostrils." (It is not only an equivalent, it is a priceless excess.) " The Lord is well pleased for his righteousness' sake :" he hath magnified " the law " and " made it honorable."

2. There must be a strict coincidence established between the representative and those for whom he mediates.

A repugnant class of qualities and circumstances would destroy that equilibrium which is virtually implied and morally obligatory. If there be necessity for condescension, it is to the same abject, or necessity for suffering

it is in the same passive, nature, which has offended. A general resemblance is not to be absolved. *Locality* prefers an urgent claim. Another region would confound the justice of the case, remove it to other associations, and entangle it in other questions. It belongs to this scene, its laws, its precedents, its usages. It has to do with "this building." Transport the action to distant worlds, and it conceals its meaning, and loses its effect. Earth was the theater of our revolt, and must be of our reconciliation. *Nature* is another requirement of this substitution. "He that sanctifieth and they who are sanctified" must be "all of one." A being of different qualities and susceptibilities might so resist the punishment devolved upon him that the punishment would become void and edgeless. This is conceivable in different ways. The essence might be too ethereal for a capacity of bodily pain. The temperament might be too dull and gross for the consciousness of intellectual and moral griefs. By a nature higher or lower than the one in question the infliction might be rendered only nominal and apparent—exquisite refinement on the one hand, and brute stupidity on the other, presenting so many points of repulsion and means of evasion. Man was the sinner, and man must be the victim. And though some modification of the *penalty* is absolutely necessary, still the suffering must retain much of *kind* and *identity*. Were it to be altered beyond the inevitable difference of the case, it would be taken out of that system which adapts appropriate punishments to particular offences. This is the bond of fitness as well as of denouncement. The connection is established and must be enforced. An adherence to this order and distinctiveness of sanctions conduces to deter the transgressor and support the commonwealth. Sin was committed, and sin must, with a strict correspondence to its specific sentence and tendency, be avenged. And when Jesus

undertook for us—when he put himself into our obligations—these coincidences were exactly observed. In no
remote sphere did he thus benevolently interpose. He
trod our planet as its native and inhabitant. He was
subjected to all its laws and influences. He subsisted
on its products, he moved among its scenes, he was
affected by its vicissitudes, respired its air, and obeyed
its attraction. He "came into the world to save sinners."
With no nature unlike our own did he invest himself.
Birth and mortality belonged to it; the nerve foliated
through his sensorium; the blood was propelled through
his frame; his tear was humor; his groan was breath;
his heart was flesh. His bosom heaved with emotion;
his countenance reflected the inner mind; he spoke by
the curious apparatus which gives articulation to sound;
his pores adjusted his animal heat, and at last discharged
his sweat of blood. He was taught; he learned letter
by letter; his mind was seen in all the different functions
of thinking, remembering, deciding, abstracting, suggesting; his feelings were those of love, gratitude, friendship, fear, anger. "Behold the man!" "In all things
it behooved him to be made like unto his brethren."
And all that characterized our *punishment*, apart from
the moral reflection and self-upbraidings of the sinner,
he came in the flesh to suffer. Death was the forfeit, so
far as it could touch the sensitive life and dislodge the
immortal spirit: his body became thus exanimate and
impassive, his soul departed from it. The separation involved in natural death was effected in himself. He
was "made a little lower than the angels *for the suffering of death.*" But there is a more fearful property in
death than the "wages of sin." There is a spiritual, a
"second death." As the former is the disseverment of
the soul from its body, so this is the disseverment of the
soul from its God. It is the dreadful rupture of all
merciful relations, and all congenial dispositions. Be-

ginning even now, this state is described as an alienation "from the life of God." "Your iniquities have separated between you and your God." "He that made them will not have mercy on them; and He that formed them will show them no favor." And this is the judgment passed upon them: "Depart!" "Everlasting destruction from the presence of the Lord!" And do the sorrows of Calvary fold within them any portion or counterpart of this terrible doom? Could it be that the Sufferer of the cross felt one darkening, one shade of this dreadful frown, fall upon his sinless spirit? "When "he tasted death for every man," was this gall and wormwood mingled in the cup? No remission was made in his favor. Every modification of the retribution but made it more extreme. And this, the tendency of all sin, the punishment included in it as well as decreed against it, was let loose upon him. Deity withdrew, hid its light, abandoned its victim! "My God, my God, why hast thou forsaken me?" That cry turned pale the sun! That cry proclaimed that sin is "evil and bitter," as it "forsakes God," and as the sinner is forsaken by him! That cry attested the reality of the imputation which laid our guilt on Christ, and the impartiality of that justice which avenged it on him! Had all the fires of divine wrath been uncovered and pointed against us—had the carcasses of our race been heaped on the ashes of our earth—that pyre would not have so distinctly signalized the certain and the appropriate punishment of the "abominable thing" which God hates.

3. There must be an explicit approval on the part of the government whose wrongs the substitute proposes to redress.

It may be assumed that such an arrangement cannot be forced upon a government, for it would be competent for any to demand the person of the delinquent. How-

ever just it may be to remit the claim, the claim is undeniable. Nor should the consent be reluctantly given, lest it betray a sense of hesitating and painful concession. It must be a voluntary and a cheerful act. And in applying these observations to the "kingdom which ruleth over all," we cannot but contemplate serious difficulties in the way of its agreement. There was no *precedent*, for however punishment had distributed itself upon the unoffending, they had individual demerit upon which it fell with perfect justice. And then that punishment never reached into eternity, but was only that which is temporary. No "soul" ever really was in another "soul's stead." There was no *tendency*. The natural order, the reasonable course is, that all crime shall be visited on the perpetrator; that he shall be held chargeable in his own capacity of endurance for all denounced against that crime; that he who is worthy of death should suffer it; that he should "be delivered to the judge," and that the judge should deliver him "to the officer," and he be "cast into prison." No other idea could occur to the mind; guilt being a personal quality, must be resented by a personal infliction. There was no *provision*. Each literal interpretation of the law decided that the "soul which sinneth, *it* shall die." Though a power is reserved of making the misconduct and punishment of one diffuse itself through a nation and a posterity, his personal relations are not merged in their's, but all alike retain an undivided responsibility. It was not possible that a code which showed what God required of man should contain an enactment authorizing, at any time, a confusion of all distinctions, and an exchange of all obligations. In the absence of precedent, tendency, and provision, it must rest with Infinite Authority to grant or withhold the permission. But if there be this permission, it must be notably declared: to be effective in its lessons as well as warrantable in its

results, all must understand it to be indisputable, and feel it to be unconstrained. And is the expiation of the Saviour's death a measure doubtfully recognized and tardily admitted by the King of men? "The Lord hath laid on him the iniquity of us all!" He has furnished the substitute! He has anointed and designated him to his mission! He has set him forth! He "gave" him! He "sent" him! He "upholds" him! He "glorifies" him! It is not his sanction to another's act, it is not his compliance with another's suggestion; it is his own spontaneous, unaided determination! We ask not whether his government approves the transaction, for we only learn the transaction from the manifesto of his government!

4. The act of the substitute should most clearly consist with his own right of conduct and freedom of choice.

It is not for any creature to desert his sphere. We have all a station and a duty, and we can never more than fill the one and satisfy the other. Each instant, each step, has its peculiar accountability. There can be no moral act unless it be unconstrained, the result of personal and self-prompted decision.

Now it might be conceived that, in some ordinary circumstances, man might supply the place of man, by greater leisure and superfluous resources, without any departure from his rank or abandonment of the obligations which cement him in society. It has been already stated that in the extreme case the delegation is inadmissible, because such society has the charge of every member's life, and must encourage, and as far as possible perpetuate, every loyal and virtuous subject's influence. But when we speak of the relations which exist between God and his creatures, the case puts on another complexion. *Man has fallen.* Who, then, of *creatures* shall, according to our argumentative supposition, represent him? Sinner cannot die for sinner, each perishes for

himself. He dies in "his own sin." Shall an angel take on him our obnoxiousness to punishment? Who, in the meantime, shall assume *his* place and execute *his* trust? What can release *him* from those high behests which called him into being, and still urge him in his activities? How could he acquire the independence to pass from orbit to orbit, or to interchange duty with duty? He only, then, can pay the debt who owes none; only can He become our surety who knows neither superior nor responsibility. And should one be found to make this dread engagement, the proofs of his freest volition must be unequivocal. Indeed, the act would declare the perfect heart and ready mind, for of an irresponsible being the motive must be uncontrolled. But there is an importance in the declarations of this entire acquiescence. And the history of our Divine Lord echoes with consent. "Then said I, Lo, I come: I delight to do thy will, O my God." Amid the scene of the transfiguration—the radiant cloud, the celestial embassage, the awful conversion of incarnate divinity into divine incarnation—they "spake of the decease" to be accomplished "at Jerusalem." The sight of the temple reminds him of his death, and the precious ointment of his burial. Every event is pervaded with this significance and association. He reads it every-where, and always hails it. He is "straitened" till it is accomplished. He enters Gethsemane to deliver up himself a captive, and passes to Calvary to die the death of a felon; the Lamb of God, unlike the victim which is blinded by its garlands, hastens with fixed eye and conscious pursuit to the altar whose trench is to drink his blood, whose fire is to consume his spirit, unfaltering and unshrinking to the last step by which he reaches its ascent, and the last moment in which he is bound to its horns; and there, as he is laid, he invokes the weapon to pierce his heart, and bids the flame, at once approving and avenging, fall!

5. The true ends of the legislative system, under which the substitutionary act occurs, must be answered.

Though it might sometimes be difficult to determine what object many a government proposes, save to pamper an imperial dotard and his parasitical court, every notion of law and sway is most oppositely distant. To uphold the dignity of power beyond the reach of intimidation; to establish justice where suspicion dares not gaze at it; to foster counsels and institutions of peace and amelioration; to neither bear the sword nor spread the shield in vain; to knit into the same bond prerogative and freedom, and to place the glory of the rule in · the happiness of the people—these are the great elements of duty and benefit in a proper administration. *Punishment is not an end,* it is only an alternative in the defeat of some legitimate purpose required by statesmanly wisdom and public good. It must be anticipated, threatened, and provided for; but it always supposes an injury which it cannot repair. It rather aims to deter than to compensate. It involves an injury as well as resents one. It abridges, as it may be, liberty and life. Though its neglect would be *more* pernicious, it can only exercise itself in certain disadvantages. If it can be avoided, without an appearance of betraying the honor of law and compromising the majesty of justice, the good secured is at least in the ratio of the evil prevented.

God has revealed to us a great moral system. His own glory is the end, which is promoted by communicating the largest share of holy felicity among his intelligent creatures. He must be just, for this is merely to allege that he must be consistent with his character and true to his law. Were he less just, to the same point would be the depression of every created interest. However difficult the lesson, the Christian learns it, and "gives thanks at the remembrance of his holiness!" Thus taught, he would not be saved if there was the

faintest risk that his salvation could cost divine dishonor. But if it can be achieved in perfect harmony with all that our Sovereign is, and all he has promulgated, we are warranted to say that it is not only competent but pleasant for him to work out such deliverance for us. He will have us know that in exercising loving-kindness, judgment, and righteousness he delights. When these can become conjoint acts there is a greater "delight," if we may be permitted so to speak, than they inspire in their separate qualities. Now if infinite justice be seen more resplendently awful in the death of our substitute than in our own; if a sum of happiness, the purest, and therefore the noblest, be secured to a "great number, which no man can number," all of whom must have been otherwise undone for ever—if no end of the legislative system beneath whose broad survey the twofold benefit is attained can be thwarted—each is made more manifest and left more secure. Nor do we decide with any partiality when we affirm that there is more of the God displayed in the sanction of justice to mercy, than in the consent of mercy to justice. It was never so much at the creature's peril to sin; it was never so fully afforded to the creature to be happy! And the song which pours forth the ecstasy of the saved shall through eternity repeat the strain: "Just and true are thy ways, thou King of saints!"

6. Some advantage should be gained, in allowing an act of substitution, above any connected with the more common proceeding.

It at once impresses us as a strange and irregular circumstance. It is not the natural step. It is a measure which asks much explanation. The order is inverted, the machinery is stopped. We may, therefore, reasonably seek for some expediency to counterbalance the very general idea founded upon the very general rule, that the person of the delinquent must bear the consequences of his crime.

Let us now conceive the results of guilt avenged upon man. Sooner or later all are " cast into hell ! " This catastrophe nothing could have precluded—it was the requirement of justice—it was the reward of sin. But no *punishment* is *reparation.* The wrong is done, the insult is offered, and nothing can destroy their substantial character. Sin would have been punished in our perdition, but the injury would have remained. Those eternal horrors would only have reflected the law eternally disobeyed, and signalized the lawgiver eternally dishonored ! Justice would foresee no term, and therefore no satisfaction. It would be a sacrifice whose " smoke " would ascend up " for ever and ever ; " never consumed, never accepted, " salted with fire," and " the fire not quenched." And then " the vengeance of eternal fire " would respect finite beings, and their sufferings could only, through all their progression, be finite. The multitude and the duration could never swell to an infinitude. There are features, too, of the divine character which must have continued, in a considerable degree, hidden from us. That justice is goodness we know ; the lost, in this conviction will feel the keenest aggravation of their doom. But *mercy* has in these consequences no scope, in fact, no *revelation.* The *fullest* exhibition of the infinite perfections cannot, therefore, be in the condemnation of the human race. All this would follow from letting things take their course, leaving law and equity to their simplest operations. This course has been interrupted, these operations stayed. Another arrangement has been introduced. It must plead certain advantages over the ordinary case. Now every point will be gained if it rectifies all the disadvantages. And in the substitutionary act there is *reparation* done to the government of God. It has been more honorably maintained than foully violated. The transgressor is made most penitent, and becomes " a new creature." He is

put into a train, and blessed with a principle, of endless obedience. But this is independent of any meritorious consideration on his part. The whole of that is in the Substitute! He has obeyed the law! He has vindicated the Lawgiver! More could not be done. It is *infinite* obedience and *infinite* vindication! That is accomplished which eternity would have been required to do, and which, therefore, never could be done. And now, too, mercy is disclosed, in combination with all the attributes of eternal excellence elicited into the brightest light, and impelled into the noblest action; no principle is left without its attestation, and no menace is denied its infliction; an amount of good is aggrandized whose measures are boundless and eternal; and Jehovah is beheld more inflexibly just, and more transparently holy, than any other system of conduct could have enabled him to appear, while he can " rest in love " and "delight in mercy! "

7. Such an arrangement should be incapable of any construction but as an act of favor and clemency.

It may be imagined that a government might find itself embarrassed by the circumstances of *number* and *extremity.* Its law is clear, its penalty is undebated; but to punish so many, and to such an extent, may seem impossible. It might then, so the imagined case may proceed, be induced to accept a principle of substitution. The motive would be divulged in the fact. Here was something not foreseen: the government is open, then, to the charge of ignorance. Here was something not to be firmly met: it is, then, capable of relenting. Here was something which could not be carried into effect: its executive, then, is weak and feeble. Here was something which shrunk from going too far; which deemed itself incapable of retrieving the consequences: it gives signs of imbecility and fear. It might cheerfully, therefore, accept or originate this method as less difficult and perilous; apprehensive that to deal the blow according to

the general regulations would overreach its strength and endanger its stability. It is to be easily inferred that no government can, with any regard to its consistency and dignity, suffer this interposition, unless all occasion is removed, all pretext is obviated, for speaking lightly of it, and behaving contemptuously toward it, among its subjects or surrounding states.

Now it is an interesting inquiry, Can this provision of a mediator, on the part of the divine dominion, be tortured into a readier expedient than individual retribution? was it introduced to save any hazard or to cover any indecision? does it present a trace of being an adoption in some unexpected crisis? O how little would it have been of loss to the territories of Him who "built all things," had our globe been blasted, had our species perished! How soon might he have supplied the void by another dwelling, and repeopled it by another race! How easily might he have dashed both to "pieces like a potter's vessel!" Thus far, as to power, there arose no dilemma. But when his "own Son" was the mark and sufferer—when he must expend on his sinless spirit the unalterable blow of condensed wrath against concentrated evil, then not to spare him, then to deliver him up, presented an excuse, if it could arise, for a pause and a mitigation. Then, if ever, was the temptation for justice to soften, for truth to unbend, for authority to relax! Such a case never having occurred, never to occur again, might it not form an exception? might not the universe, rapt into silent awe and trembling with vast excitement, as it gazed on the "Lamb" bound to the altar, have learned the lesson of impartial equity in this spectacle of stern preparation, though the sword, "bathed in heaven," had at that moment severed the cord and loosed the victim? It must not be—"His life" was "taken from the earth," and his substitution has clearly demonstrated, that, as this was

the most awful extreme divine government could ever encounter, so there is none for which it is not sufficient, and is not prepared ! And the sinner, while he accepts this reconciliation in the remembrance that God suggested the expedient and empowered the act, perceives how any course must have been less arduous and expensive than this; gathers new proof that justice will punish guilt wherever that guilt is charged; ascertains, as with an added sense, that this alternative was not a choice of difficulties, but a difficulty in comparison with which every other was a convenience; adores the immutability and grandeur of a law which, even in that conjuncture, could not abate a claim or check an infliction, and sinks beneath the idea of that mercy which received such a confirmation in selecting such a medium !

8. It should be unfailingly, necessarily, productive of its destined purpose and influence.

Experiments in government are dangerous things. Principles may be so well understood, and may so distinctly point to some new measures, that in working them out and molding them there is nothing rash, there can be nothing alarming—it is a logical conclusion. But when there are no lights, no guides, it is madness to embark on the deceitful element of speculation. A substitutionary arrangement might be suggested. It might approve itself to justice. On all sides it might be sanctioned. Each party might freely consent. It might even hold out a rational promise of efficiency. But it is a grave venture. Should it fail of success, the door is closed on all future attempt. The unnatural order of things, attracting a singular notice, would, from the event, be pronounced unjustifiable. The warrant, the equipment, the failure, would bring down general scorn. It would be accounted an innovation calculated to embroil every principle, and necessitating its own overthrow.

But how infinitely ruinous had been the abortive termination of that mediatorial scheme which pressed on our Lord for its accomplishment? While we shudder at the idea of this defeat, we know that it is a supposition only to be momentarily indulged that it may be indignantly resisted. If he had begun and had not been able to finish; if he had bowed beneath the weight; if he had come short of his purpose and our hope—salvation had been manifestly impossible. If his arm could not bring it, every other must wither in despair. But when the Father appointed him, he said, " Behold my servant, whom I uphold. He shall not fail nor be discouraged" until he " bring forth judgment unto victory." When he came forth he said, I know that I shall not be ashamed. His righteousness is " the righteousness of God." No suspense was upon his mind pertaining to the result. His resurrection from the dead, his effusion of the Spirit, his second advent, the happiness of his followers in his presence, his condemnation of the wicked, were themes on which he constantly dwelt. The glory with which he was to be glorified, " the joy set before him," he often predestined. His intercession and kingdom prove that he ran not uncertainly, that he was invincible! He thoroughly pleaded our cause. He " finished the work " given him to do.

But there is another way in which failure might attend a mediatory scheme. Let us suppose that it was embraced with a view to a great moral influence. Let us suppose that it was designed to excite fading allegiance; to recall a revolted race to the sense and practice of their duty; to impress the gazing nations with the wisdom and force of a new method of securing to the government which employed it the love and obedience of its subjects. Were it, after all, to produce the contrary effect, exciting them to jeer its authority and pre-

sume upon its forbearance, making it a laughing-stock to surrounding empires, egregious would be the confusion of its mistake, and irreparable the mischief of its experiment. And if the redemption of the Gospel weakened any obligation, lowered any duty, gave rise to any insinuation of fickleness, or afforded opportunity for any facility of resistance, fatally would it exceed its intention and contradict its aim. But it is a " kingdom of heaven," a celestial rule, on earth. It bestows life on the sinner, it inflicts death on his sin. Its " grace" inspires " reverence and godly fear." Our heart fears and is enlarged. We " fear the Lord and his goodness." Forgiveness is with God that he may be feared. Sin becomes " exceeding sinful :" obedience is the quickening element in which they delight, with native instinct, who are " alive from the dead :" authority assumes its most awful form, and purity its most piercing luster! Nor is this only the *fitting* influence : the Holy Spirit is given to *secure* it. And in all who lay hold on this covenant, who welcome this substitution, a sentiment of loyalty, of gratitude, of devotion, of sympathetic affinity, is implanted ; and becoming " obedient to the faith," they are " servants to righteousness unto holiness." They know and feel that they " have a master in heaven ;" they as " children are joyful in their King ;" they confess that " the works of his hands are verity and judgment: all his commandments are sure."

9. Such a regimen, as we now suppose, requires the most solemn publicity in its origin, its acceptance, and its accomplishment.

If there were carelessness of manner, it would appear indifferent ;—if haste, it would seem an undigested afterthought ;—if secresy, it would be suspected as a thing of shame. The deed must not be muffled, nor the stage be darkened : all must be placed before the keenest inspec-

tion, and be explained with the most unreserved ingenuousness. Breaking in upon the regulated practice and natural order, there must be every method taken to avow the fact and expose the reason. Should it be hurried or vailed, perfunctorily or clandestinely precipitated, a jealousy would be entertained of its correct principle, and a distrust of its honorable execution. It should be attended with the most solemn judicial forms, and be announced through the organ of the most reverend authorities. How inapplicable would any of these accusations be if they were directed against the interposition of our Redeemer! " Not without an oath " was he " made priest," and therefore a " surety." The inauguration was solemnized on a lofty stage, and through a prolonged season! How slow was the procession, and how public the spectacle! How elaborate was the rite! The arrangement was announced on the very day of our fall. Four thousand years repeated the pledge, and by symbolic action or living picture rehearsed the event in which it was fulfilled. Prophecy blew the trumpet before it, and " the shaking of all nations " sounded its prelude. Earth now heaved with expectation, then stood still in suspense. It came not unexpected, and found not man unprepared. It awaited " the fullness of times." " This was not done in a corner."

10. A substitutionary concert could not be suffered, but at distant intervals and on rare occasions.

It is necessary that the distinctions of conduct should be preserved, and its consequences be traced, if we would retain any vivid sense of virtue. But a frequent interchange of parties would tend to confound all such discriminations. If it be permitted to take place, it must be reserved for some signal conjuncture, in which it can neither be pleaded for impunity nor drawn into precedent. As an exception, it may emphatically vindicate its singularity and yet confirm the necessity of the

ordinary course from which it solitarily deviates: it could not become a frequent, not to say an ordinary, allotment without disturbing every relation and frustrating every law.

The vicarious offering of Christ is decisive of the question, as it can at all occur under the divine government. It need never more be proposed, it can never more be admitted. It is shut up forever. Nothing similar can it be quoted to sanction. With no other story can it coalesce. It stands like a pyramid in the desert, abrupt and incomparable. Expressions are multiplied to enforce the singleness of the act. " Christ was *once* offered to bear the sins of many." " Not that he should offer himself *often ;* for then must he often have suffered since the foundation of the world." " It is once for all ! "

Refine upon the most specious objections, conjure up the most hypothetical difficulties, cast them into any form, multiply them by any figure, conceive any circumstances, combine those circumstances in any manner, and the fact that Jesus represented our persons and expiated our sins upon the cross is only opposed by fallacy and anomaly, and rises with a majestic independence in its own truth, purity, and originality !

And this is our " ministry of reconciliation ! " He who in every age of the Church has exclaimed, " Behold me, behold me," (Isaiah lxv, 1,) has commissioned us to " cry aloud and spare not,"—" Behold the Lamb of God which taketh away the sin of the world." This is the evangelic proclamation ! It is an answer to man's most solemn inquiries, it is a supply for the soul's most urgent wants. Sweeter notice never fell on human ear, nor a lovelier spectacle ever rose on human eye. Alas, how many are there who have never given to him one fixed thought, or felt toward him one definite emotion ! We call them now to act a rational part, even should their

reason prove itself perverse in his rejection! No conduct is so insane as to spend life in indifference concerning such an object as to "*neglect* so great salvation!" We advance in our claim: He deserves not only your *attention* but your *admiration.* One believing perception will open to you an archetype of beauty, a standard of excellence, which romance never depicted, and poetry never dreamed. Like the noontide sun, it will fill your whole sphere of vision; and, as when you close the eyelid from that blaze, all mental images seem still teeming with its glow—so this will pursue the mind and tinge the feeling in the most forgetful mood, and amid the dullest sensibility. "Looking unto Jesus" is the exercise of every grace, the triumph of every principle, the perfection of every joy. Nor is our message told. "Behold the Lamb of God,"—it is for your life! As Noah, hasten to this ark!—As Lot, flee to this refuge! —As the serpent-bitten Israelite, gaze on this remedy!— As the dying thief, turn to this cross and this crucified One!—the sinner's throne of grace!—the sinner's object of confidence! "So we preach," nor envy we any other theme! Content, happy, most honored, are we to stand around the altar of Calvary; to invite along the avenues which lead to it, the outcast and undone; and to point them to the one sacrifice for sin. We are the merest attendants without a badge of priesthood—standing not to "offer," but to announce that the offering is consummated! We would be any thing or nothing;—but "a voice crying," or the echo of a voice—a line to this center, a mirror of this scene, a wand directing human eyes toward this spectacle! So be directed our living energy, so spent our dying gasp! Amen.

VII.

CHRISTIAN DOCTRINE OF DIVINE GRACE.

————◆————

AND IF BY GRACE, THEN IS IT NO MORE OF WORKS: OTHERWISE GRACE IS NO MORE GRACE. BUT IF IT BE OF WORKS, THEN IS IT NO MORE GRACE; OTHERWISE WORK IS NO MORE WORK.—Romans xi, 6.

THERE is not a more necessary and consolatory truth than this—reason allows it, revelation affirms it—"The work of the Lord is *perfect.*" Whatever he does, sustains its consistency and answers its end. Neither is there redundance nor defect. The question of degrees, the scale of dimensions, cannot alter the fact: whether the emmet or the leviathan, whether the atom or the world, each bears a stamp of entireness and self-sufficience. The most cautious inspection, the most fertile imagination, can discover no want, can suggest no improvement. You can relieve no difficulty, you can facilitate no process, you can heighten no result. The system of the individual is as faultless as that of the species, the economy of the particle as that of the universe. The grain imbedded on the shore, the star set among the constellations of the sky, in their differing ranks of constituted nature, exhibit the same matchless adjustment, fitness, and application.

Every "gift" that "cometh down" from God must be as "good and perfect." It is a boon of pure benignity. He openeth his hand. He "giveth liberally, and upbraideth not." "The gifts and calling of God" can-

not be revoked. His blessings are diffusely scattered, and lavishly bestowed. Through their boundless variety it is impossible to mistake their boundless munificence. "He loadeth us with benefits," but all are true to their character, and worthy of himself.

Counsel, in the sense of suggestion, co-operation, when understood as denoting aid, are words which can never express any acts of the creature toward this Infinite Being. He determines and operates alone. His plan is eternal as his mind, and his single arm puts aside all vaunted assistance when it bares itself to achieve it. This is his absoluteness and his supremacy. Hence those sublime demands which spare neither our ignorance nor imbecility. "With whom took he counsel, and who instructed him, and taught him in the path of judgment, and taught him knowledge, and showed unto him the way of understanding?" "Where wast thou when I laid the foundations of the earth? Who hath laid the measures thereof, if thou knowest? or who hath stretched the line upon it? Who laid the corner-store thereof?"

If, unaided, Jehovah hung the globe upon its center, and impressed its course; if all he does present manifestations of glorious independence; as little will he accept the advice, or seek the help, of his creatures in those purposes and deeds for whose consummation earth was only reared to be the scene, and providence is only impelled to form the machinery. Creation is all divine, providence is all divine, and grace must be all divine! We contend for its unmixed essence, its unconstrained exercise, its unrivaled triumph. It must be separated from all impurities, disengaged from all corruptions, and demonstrated to be the spring of divine goodness, to the exclusion of every other motive; and the basis of human hope, to the exclusion of every other support. This "pure religion" must be "undefiled."

The language of the text occurs in the conduct of an argument on the sovereignty of choice and distribution, which belongs to the prerogative of God, and which is involved of necessity in the operations of his grace. Critics have not been agreed on the genuineness of its latter section, many esteeming it the gloss of some scholiast, and adjudging the amount of authority in its favor to be defective. It is in itself, whatever may be the decision, clearly just and natural, being the converse of that sentence respecting which there can be no dispute. The sentiment of the part and of the whole is strictly one, and easily intelligible. The argument, of course, is relative. Though the terms are put questionably, not a doubt is implied of the certainty of *that* touching which they are used. *That something* is the doctrine which avers Christianity to be a system of *free favor* toward the guilty and miserable children of men; giving all its care to their need, without any admission of their claims, or balancing of their demerits. The inducement is entirely on the part of God; man from the beginning is merely regarded as unworthy and incapable of recovering himself. His destitution of title and recommendation wants no other proof than the circumstance that he is the *object of grace.*

I. THIS ARGUMENTATIVE ASSUMPTION OR PRESUPPOSITION MUST BE CONSIDERED BY US.

The present dispensation is only the enlargement and perfection of many: these have been progressively evolved; and all have coincided in their general nature and purport. They have been, indeed, but less or greater disclosures of the same plan, and have therefore been projected on the same principle. The "weakness and unprofitableness" of any were only comparative with that which succeeded, and were suited to the period which the one later and superior would have overborne. Grace is the characteristic which has traversed and as-

similated the long-extended series. But the evangelic constitution is its most distinct and professed exhibition. The *word* becomes a specific, as well as prominent, *term* in its language: the *conception* is indispensable for its right *interpretation*. Hence the Gospel is called, "the Gospel of the grace of God." The title in which it arrays the Father is, "the God of all grace." The testimony which it bears to the Son is put in the shape of the well-understood appeal, "Ye know the grace of our Lord Jesus Christ." The Spirit is the "Spirit of grace." This grace is uniformly stated as the cause of the electing purpose—the reason of our personal justification—the germ of that renovating process which brings back the moral disposition of the sinner to a standard of holiness and a center of good—the potent motive to all piety, as it is the prolific source of all favor. There is no other construction to be placed on the scheme or the operation of the Gospel but what those brief, definite, and most expressive statements of inspired authority so plainly and so repeatedly teach: "God, who is rich in mercy, for his great love wherewith he loved us;" "according to his mercy he saves us;" "according to his abundant mercy;" "according to his own purpose and grace, which was given us in Christ Jesus before the world began." These intimations are as full as language, are as emphatic as repetition, can make them; but who does not feel that there is a struggle for utterance which a finite medium resists, and an eagerness to convey a meaning which a finite intellect, with all its aids and efforts, never can receive?

We may be certain that Christianity is intended for a revelation of the divine glory. Did Jehovah forego his *claim* to be glorified in all things, did he forbear to *seek* to be glorified in all things, which all must admit to be the *highest possible* end, then he must act in a manner *less* than infinitely wise, *less* than infinitely pure, *less*

than infinitely authoritative, *less* than infinitely good. That which must be the end of all his plans and works, can only be more obvious and explicit in proportion to their value and magnitude. The impress of the design must enlarge and brighten with the grandeur of the achievement. The more important the measure, the more apparent ought to be the resolve to derive honor from it to the divine character and government. Such explanation, being all but self-evident, will scarcely be contested.

But upon this explanation an additional one must be laid. It may be the divine will to illustrate a particular form of his character, or what we intend by a single perfection. This is felt by us when little engaged in painful disquisition. The mountain tells us most naturally of the power which upraised and figured its lofty head; the valley, of the goodness which clothes it with verdure and fruitfulness; the firmament, of the skill which suspended in those heights its splendid handiwork; the ocean, of the riches of creative fullness, which supplies its deep sunk abysses, and makes it the element of multitudinous life. In this manner there may be a more special revelation of a divine attribute, the *occasion* more prominently illustrating one than another. Perhaps none would demur to this further explanation.

It may seem perilous, if not presumptuous, to institute comparison between the varied aspects of the divine character, as unfolded in the Christian system, because the tenor of that system appears to be to secure the perfect development of all. Redemption is the master purpose of divine wisdom, the fairest copy of divine purity, the crowning deed of divine power, the dreadest infliction of divine justice, the most costly boon of divine love. Whatever the light in which it is last surveyed, whatever the purpose for which it is last investigated, that light is always surpassing, that purpose transcendent.

As it revolves, each compartment of the complex wonder is pronounced to be its capital excellence and distinctive glory. We now cannot doubt that it was intended to magnify wisdom, and we exclaim, "He hath abounded toward us in all wisdom and prudence." And then we do not question that it was intended to enforce justice, "to declare his righteousness for the remission of sins, to declare, we say, at this time, his righteousness." Once more, we decide it must have been to signalize his power; and instead of seeking a sign, we adore that which eclipses a thousand signs, "Christ the power of God." Again, the faithfulness is so vividly portrayed, that its fulfillment must have been the impulse of all, and we sing, "He hath visited his people" to "perform the mercy promised to our fathers." This prejudice and infirmity of mind is not a vice inherent in it, but rather a proof of the limitation of its faculties. The "angels" who "desire to look" into these things, are not described as acquiring them at a glance, or indeed capable of pursuing them without an effort. And if their piercing eyes cannot penetrate and compass them all at once, a very inferior portion of this magnificence will fill our whole vision, absorb our whole thought, and overwhelm our whole heart. Still every point cannot be most prominent, and every changing opinion cannot be alike conformed to truth. Nor are we left to ourselves to resolve the question. We might naturally make our longest pause, and breathe our fullest ecstacy, upon the mercy, as the predominant feature, and the excelling indication: "For thy goodness' sake, O Lord!" But what saith the Scriptures. "That even so grace might reign through righteousness unto eternal life, through Jesus Christ our Lord." "To the praise of the glory of his grace." "That in the ages to come he might show the exceeding riches of his grace, in his kindness toward us, through Christ Jesus." Such is the

deeply engraven, the strongly emblazoned, superscription of our religion.

The design of the Gospel once fixed, we possess the best key to its nature, and the truest index to its constitution. That must have its basis in grace which is intended to display and aggrandize grace. Among the different versions and representations of the Gospel we should be careful to select that which gives to this principle all its descriptive marks and appropriate honors. Let us leave the altar in its native simplicity, knowing that to lift up our tool upon it is to profane it. Let us leave the diadem in its ample outline, without confounding it by any settings of our own.

In endeavoring to disabuse the idea of grace, we must concern ourselves with much that is gross in ignorance, impious in temerity, and wily in sophistry. We must be painfully affected with the coarse effrontery and the perverse ingenuity of those who cannot bend to the ascertained condition of human nature, or to the gratuitous promptitude of divine interposition.

The more ignorant and audacious contention, that human actions can literally challenge and deserve approval and favorable recompense—that they can, though the agents are utterly depraved, be the subjects of merit—when thus boldly declared and contumaciously urged, is generally discarded. Against this more stupid avowal and wanton bravado of error and self-righteousness we are not often cited to appear. The hostility is more subtle, more evasive; the wolf wears the sheep's clothing; Satan is transformed into an angel of light; it is not the analysis of the substance, but the detection of the enemy! But they who oppose the doctrine of the atonement, have been incited to allege an incompatibility between it and the grace for which we plead. With considerable adroitness, they present themselves as champions of the free favor which contemplates sin-

ful man, at the same moment in which they despise the great expedient by which it only can be justly revealed and consistently sustained.

Hateful hypocrisy! Whence this unwonted part, this sudden zeal? Where is the braggart morality of the philosopher and worldling now? How is it that the boast of merit and the urgency of claim no longer swell on high? Strange proselytism and marvelous transformation! They are guided only in their blasphemy of their Saviour's name, and their rapine on the Saviour's Gospel, by the fear that grace, in such a connection, will not be worthily free or adequately spontaneous! How have they been misunderstood! They could not concur with us, because we were not unequivocal as themselves in spreading the honors of infinite grace! They would go further, but we stop short in its full exhibition and fearless averment! They would apply a principle to all its extent, which we gainsay and cramp! True it is, that neither the sound nor signification was until now so rife and lavish! But then the emergency that may be served, the success that may be won! Hitherto they kept their mouth with a bridle. The fire was shut up in their bones. The power of repression at length yielded. The holy indignation made a way for its lightning. Who would not make the grace of God a watchword, even if the idea be despised in the heart, if by its prepossessing character and vulgar association a deeper thrust be aimed at Christ's pre-eminence, and a darker slur be cast on the peculiarities of Christ's Gospel! The opposition, by these means, is so consistent and so characteristic! Their jealousy of grace is sensitive to that degree that they cannot endure the cross as an adjunct, or Him who hung upon it as its dispenser! Conjectural criticism, materializing skepticism, flippant invective—the arrogant monopoly of reason, the supercilious contempt of the catholic faith, the treatment of

the blood of the covenant as a common thing, and the paring down of our religion to a meager nullity—all originate in profound homage and meek submission to the pure and uncompounded grace of God!

It is thus the sophism is enunciated: Redemption supposes the infliction of the penalty, though it be shifted from the individual delinquent to his substitute; this is to attribute it to barter and compensation, and not to mercy; to describe it as actually purchased, and not freely bestowed. "For," say our opponents, "that which you call mercy is not free—your surety has paid the ransom, has canceled the claim. Our archetype of mercy contradicts such notions. It asks no victim, it exacts no term. Therefore the doctrine of grace is our peculiar tenet, for we supplicate as a pure favor what you may sue out as a strict right."

"Our soul is exceedingly filled with" this "contempt." The answer to this shallow parade of reasoning is as easy as undeserved. No lion need come out of Lebanon to tread down the thistle. The following observations may not be inapposite or useless:

The atonement is the effect of divine grace and placability.

Its oblation produced no change in the divine mind. Jehovah is not merciful because Christ has died, but Christ has died because Jehovah was merciful.* The Father sent the Son. It pleased the Lord to bruise him. God is never said to be " reconciled in Christ;" but as in " Christ, reconciling the world to himself."

Christianity, whatever may be its compensative prin-

---

* The reader must excuse the recurrence of this thought, simple, essential, as it is, so much does common language overlook or distort it. Even the intercession of Christ is nothing but the perpetual remembrance of the mediatorial process by which God had mercy, and his perpetual consistency with it. He "has respect unto his covenant." "He causes his ear to hear."

ciple, is entirely independent of man in its contrivance and provision.

"The grace which bringeth salvation" is in no sense impaired by any arrangements which had a reference to ourselves. Antecedent questions of justice and satisfaction could not injure the display of that love which was equally in the Father and the Son; which was equally evinced in inflicting and enduring death. It wears but one expression toward us, who, instead of making overtures of peace, still need a creative and a resurgent power to induce us to fall in with them; who, instead of selecting the Mediator, now only call him the Lord by the Holy Ghost; who, instead of approving and welcoming the remedy, were scandalized, until another mind was given, by its refusal to us of the smallest share in its honors.

The death of the cross is only a means to the most benevolent end.

We must reason inversely to all general modes of argument if we can imagine that the grace, which is spread throughout the plan, is weakened or depreciated by the existence of certain moral difficulties in the way of its accomplishment. The benefaction is not commonly reduced in its value by its cost, nor a deliverance by its peril. There must be a maintenance of right, there must be a resentment of sin; but these preliminaries shall all consist with the pardon of those to whom the violation of that right, and the commission of that sin, have been traced. Is the grace of God the greater, or the less, when encountering no difficulty, or when encountering it to overcome it? Is the grace of God more brightly, or more faintly, glorious when associated with moral principles, or when disregarding them? It is easy to speak of grace, disjoined from the atonement, as unconstrained; but that which recognizes an atonement is perfectly, absolutely, so, for it effectuates its

purpose by the atonement; and, if constrained, is only held to what is right by the immaculateness of its nature, in the same manner in which God cannot err or lie. Who is affected at the thought of divine benevolence when nothing urges and when nothing opposes it? Who is not affected when the strait and struggle of human fondness are borrowed to inculcate the infinite effort of that love which surrendered the ineffably endeared "Beloved," who was in its bosom; when we are left amid the pantings of wonder, the musings of gratitude, with such an intensive, transcendental description as this, "He spared not his own Son, but delivered him up for us all."

So the Bard represents the Messiah addressing the eternal Father:

> "Man shall find grace;
> And shall grace not find means, that finds her way,
> The speediest of thy winged messengers,
> To visit all thy creatures, and to all
> Comes unprevented, unimplored, unsought?
> Happy for man, so coming; he her aid
> Can never seek, once dead in sins and lost;
> Atonement for himself or offering meet,
> Indebted and undone, hath none to bring."

The Gospel, while it upholds the claims of the divine law, has an exclusive bearing upon us as sinners.

Let the awful negotiations between the Father, who is in the Son, and of the Son, who is in the Father—who are one—be whatever they were—the sinner has no righteousness or claim. There may be a moral necessity that he shall be saved, but that necessity is perfectly foreign to any thing in himself. God is faithful and just to forgive us our sins, but it is only through the countenance of mercy he can smile upon our lost condition. We can only be seen, and treated with, upon that level. We can only hope that through the grace

of our Lord Jesus, we shall be saved. We can suppose a case in which the loss of a soul should be an injustice to the Saviour's desert, and a robbery of his reward; but that injustice and robbery could not pass through him, and retain the same character toward the soul that was lost. That soul would have justice done to it; its salvation being a question not of justice but of grace.

No blessing of the Gospel is, in any legitimate sense, the subject of purchase.

Such phraseology is, at least, without the sanction of Scripture, if it be not in contradiction to it. Christians are "the purchased possession;" they are "bought with a price." But the "sure mercies" of the covenant are thus unfitly represented. God was ready to forgive and sanctify, but there was an impediment. This was none other than the inconsistency into which these acts of favor would hurry him, if unattended by a fulfillment of his holy law. The atonement is the removal of that impediment in the prevention of that inconsistency: "the fullness of the blessing of the Gospel of Christ," henceforward, had merely to flow without check or restriction.*

We, therefore, affirm that these conceptions of divine grace are best calculated, and are exclusively adapted, to place it in a true light and on an honorable foundation. We combine all the perfections of the Godhead: we allow for all the moral difficulties of the case: we proceed on admitted and established principles, rather than assumed and arbitrary: we make much stress of the counteracting circumstances which others think did not

* It is strange how this vendible language was introduced. The Noncomformist Fathers abound in it. The compositions of Watts employ it very commonly. No preacher, in modern times, used it more than the late pre-eminent Robert Hall. Notwithstanding these high examples, the Author cannot but deem it unwarranted by the letter, and inexpressive of the sense, of Scripture: incorrect in itself, and lending countenance to Socinian objections against our system.

exist, and of that travail of mercy which others describe as most easy and self-indulgent : we appeal not to the vagueness of conjecture, but to substantial proofs and monumental facts !

It is plain that a connection between the grace of God and the work of Christ, was never suspected by the earliest teachers of the Gospel to be irreconcilable. They bound them together as cause and effect, as design and execution. They contemplated them while they advanced from the germination of the seed to the maturity of the fruit. " Being justified freely by his grace, through the redemption that is in Christ Jesus." " By the righteousness of one the free gift came upon all men, unto justification of life."

The Gospel being then considered and admitted by us to be a system of grace, the text opposes certain terms to each other which are essentially extreme and incoherent. We must, then, attempt to prove,

II. That the grace which is so pre-eminent cannot be confounded with any inferior or incongruous principle.

We often have to reason on the fixed use of terms. Hence the virtue of definition. This is necessary to all perspicuity and fairness of argument. Endless are the controversies, and as ignoble, when differing amounts of signification are attached to the same pass-word. You know that some terms have exactly the same meaning. These are familiar to your ears as synonyms. Other terms are called inconvertible. They cannot be substituted or interchanged. They are not only, after research, discordant, but on their surface declare a diametrical, a transverse alienation. Such are these conflicting phrases. They are incompatible as any two elements that cannot meet without an overpowering, a neutralization, of one or the other : repellant as any two orbs which, having dashed

together, could never lose the shock, but must still fly asunder.

Grace is free favor: it can be related to no right, and contained in no law. It is extra-judicial; whenever bestowed, it depends upon the mere will of him who exercises it, or, upon what is the same thing, his voluntary pledge and agreement. If this latter be withdrawn, there may be a forfeiture of integrity and fidelity; but it is only so far unjust to those deprived of it, that a claim arose out of it; but no injustice accrues to them, considered in their original circumstances. A simple test of grace is presented by the following inquiries; ought it to be exercised? can it be righteously withheld? If we affirm the one, if we deny the other —it may be obligation, debt, reason—it cannot be grace, for this principle never owes itself to its object; and in not showing it, the person still is just. If there is any necessity for it, save that of demerit and its misery, it "is no more grace."

Work is individual action or conduct. It comprehends whatever is done in the body—speech and deed, sentiment and feeling. It embraces the whole range of our moral agency. It implies those particular qualities which provoke praise or condemnation. This course of accountable behavior is properly

Personal. We all feel possessed of a something which we cannot transfer. We are the same, notwithstanding changes of time and character, with our former selves. Whatever we have taken part in still attaches to us. We reap what we have sown. We cannot escape the consciousness that we are what we are. It is a solemn thought that our doings, however distant in point of season, and various in point of complexion, are but an accumulation of our responsible being—the identifying proofs, the mysterious links, of our personal character and history!

Work must be voluntary to be accountable. If I am compelled to do what I disapprove, the hand is mine, but that hand is only a mechanical instrument of another's will: the act is not mine, for the inward soul resisted it. It may be, however, that men shall deny their freedom on unreasonable grounds. They may allege the force of their appetites and their affections: but what are these, except so many biases of the will? Motive is not only consistent with liberty, but there could be no liberty without motive. That cannot be an involuntary action when we act from ourselves, independently of external coercion.

Work, therefore, goes to form the general character of the moral agent. That which a creature is known by, his prevailing conduct, from which we infer what it would be under any circumstance, and what it will be at any period—conduct, which, while it is more tangible, lays open much of the understanding and the heart—this we denominate character. We all perceive what it intends, however difficult may be its philosophical explication. It depends upon habit, and habit weaves itself out of conduct. A succession of works forms a habit, a variety of habits mold a character. Such has merit or demerit; we attach weight, respect, esteem to it, or frivolity, contempt, reprobation. Human character, as "God searches and knows" it, is far more, it is the naked attitude of "the hidden man of the heart:" the form of innermost thought, the peculiarity of innermost disposition.

But if this be the just delineation of *work*, it cannot be employed indiscriminately with *grace*. No mixture could be more heterogeneous. They denote things which have nothing common between them.

Grace is opposed to *work* as it is extrinsic of the person. It reaches us from another source. It implies an external relation. It is the favor of an independent

Being upon us, his once revolted creatures. Personal qualities it may inspire; but its origin is supernal and divine.

Grace is opposed to *work*, as it is independent of the volition. Man had no desire to be saved in this manner; and since the day that our first parent hid himself and was afraid, "there is none that seeketh after God." Each heart has yet to be turned, or else "ye will not come unto" Christ "that ye may have life." And even if man felt the wish, that could not command the grace, which is sovereignly free. It is the "kindness of God our Saviour," "who doeth as it pleaseth him." Grace directs our will, which it finds all stubbornness and pride against its influence. "God worketh within us to will and to do of his own good pleasure." "So then it is not of him that willeth, nor of him that runneth, but of God that showeth mercy."

Grace is opposed to *work*, as it most jealously and tenaciously challenges that merit and honor which virtuous and sinless obedience claims, and the divine code awards. "To him that worketh is the reward not reckoned of grace, but of debt." "The man who doeth these things shall live by them." "If Abraham were justified by works, he hath whereof to glory." But the sinner, "saved by grace," disclaims all such "confidence of boasting." Though most active, though "always abounding in the work of the Lord," he is described in the sacred writings as "one that worketh not, but believeth on him who justifieth the ungodly." This "work of faith and labor of love" are of another essence. And grace *will* gather the revenues of its honor, and the tributes of its praise. There must be no possible mistake. Each crown of spiritual excellence and of celestial glory must be cast at its feet. "The Lord alone shall be exalted." "He that glorieth, let him glory in the Lord." That the claims of grace may not pass into

momentary dispute, how does inspired truth throw man back on his nothingness in snatching him from his ruin! One example may suffice: "*For by grace are ye saved through faith.*" Then there is something for self-gratulation! "*And that not of yourselves, it is the gift of God.*" Then that faith is not inert, and works will follow! But these have no part in the matter of justification: "*Not of works, lest any man should boast.*" Then works are wrought by us, and so may we plead something self-determining and characteristic! But the last pretense is doomed to fall. "For we are His workmanship, created in Christ Jesus unto good works." So perishes the pile of human frowardness and vanity; but by its side rises the sanctuary, whose pattern is in the Eternal Mind, whose altar retains the fragrance of a sacrifice offered once for all, whose foundation was hewn from the Rock of Ages, and whose "headstone was brought forth with shoutings, crying Grace, grace unto it!"

Here then are unalterable, eternal distinctions. Some numbers can never quadrate, some lines never converge, some substances never mingle; and these terms can never be transposed, these alternatives can never be reconciled. Sooner call cold and heat the same, darkness and light the same, death and being the same, than imagine that grace and work can be compromised, or can replace each other. This would be a chaos beyond the poet's dream.

We shall find occasion, notwithstanding their discrepancy and collision, to regret the various attempts made to consubstantiate them; and must proceed to remark,

III. THAT THESE ARE OFTEN VIOLENTLY TORTURED INTO AN UNNATURAL ALLIANCE AND INTERMIXTURE AMONG THE SYSTEMS WHICH PROFESS TO EMBODY THE EVANGELICAL DISPENSATION.

Confessions and symbols of doctrinal faith may pass

under different names, and may be abetted by different parties. The practiced and vigilant eye detects the fraud. The combatants cannot take their aim from the clouds of dust which their onset has raised. Extremes, it is proverbial, sometimes meet: but though this is sufficiently unmeaning, unless it apply to what is simply nominal and not real, still all error, however combined, however varied, however particularized, retains a certain uniformity.

Grace has been "turned into lasciviousness"—been represented as existing without any holy evidence. Men have "continued in sin that grace may abound." But it is plain that *work* not signifying obedience inspired by grace, but some claim against it, men will not build up *grace* with *work*, but rather cement *work* with *grace.* This is therefore the coalition, or, if the word may be tolerated, the jumble, against which we protest.

That system cannot reconcile itself to the idea of grace which proceeds upon the *merits* of human conduct. We do not say that innocence deserves, in the strictest acceptation of the word, the divine favor, but it is a fit subject of reward: for as it must respect a law, it must be dealt with according to that law. But the innocence of a rational creature (and its application to one irrational, savors more of poetry than theology, and of absurdity than both) is the effect of inducement. All law, however seemingly harsh the proposition, is an appeal to self-love. It is better, or it is worse, as the subject obeys or infringes it—a law implying sanctions. Such innocence may claim, if not on the right of proportionate merit, yet on the ground of express stipulation, a particular measure of benefit. As God is not "unrighteous in taking vengeance," so he is not "unrighteous to forget" what he has promised to remunerate. All moral conduct is of itself rewardable. Still we remember the different circumstances of our race at

present. They are circumstances of absolute defection and ruin. The resistance of Christianity to all merit is, that such merit is impossible; that its existence is fictitious; that its supposition is monstrous; that its boast is an act of most unreasonable hardihood and impious contumacy. It militates, not against the doctrine of merit, without which there could not be a moral government, but against the guilty phantasy that man can secure and retrieve himself in virtue of it. It is an arrest, not upon the principle, but upon his application of it. It does not uproot this tree of life, without which innocence would be robbed of paradise, and paradise would be emptied of innocence, but only interposes lest he should put forth his hand that is already polluted by another stealth, and whose pollution this additional outrage would but confirm. We, therefore, often hear of the efficacy of repentance; and, if in so many words the title of virtue is not alleged, the illegality of punishment is loudly denounced. How many who profess to look for salvation to mercy, raise an outcry " like an armed man," against their perdition being agreeable to *justice!* They forget that merit is a relation of justice; that no creature can ever be treated but according to justice; that there is an unalterable rule of admeasurement; that sin has desert, and shall have the wages; while a lapsed being can only be recovered to a perception and habit of excellence by unmerited goodness, so that all this excellence must be void of claim, constituting but a part of that gratuitous recovery.

Any system which rests human acceptance on a foreknowledge of some attractive qualities of character, cannot reconcile itself to the true notion of grace. It would be difficult to find where this view gains any advantage over the simple, undisguised consultation of the creature's claim. It would be as difficult to point out how any supposed embarrassment of these questions can be re-

lieved by such a view. God sees the end from the beginning; there can, therefore, be no real distinction between the anticipation of certain virtues and his retrospective concession to them. The cause is the same, beheld from different directions; and we but throw farther back that perplexity which, referred to whatever date, is equally irresoluble. But even allowing such anticipation, fallacious as it is, when intended to explain what it only displaces, another question arises. Whence originates this foreseen confidence, godly sorrow, and holy love? Foreknowledge is not potential; it is as independent of what it regards, as what it regards is of it. "Who can bring a clean thing out of an unclean?" "Do men gather grapes of thorns, or figs of thistles?" Why any creature falls, why any fallen creature does the vilest abominations, are inquiries which are hampered with no dilemma; a creature left to himself, by his law of being—having no claim to be kept, for this sustentation is favor, not justice—will go away with " a perpetual backsliding;" and there is nothing "earthly, sensual, and devilish," but of which he is capable. No superadded force is wanted to depress him. But how with his "heart," which is "desperately wicked," does he "believe unto righteousness?" Who has smitten the rock, and melted it into streams of grief? Who has turned the "wilderness" into "the fruitful field?" If, therefore, it is an anticipation of the sinner's self-cherished excellence, it is evidently not of grace but work, whatever be the question of time; and if it be an anticipation of what God will do in us and for us, his own "good word," which he "will begin and will perform," then it is not of work but grace, though regulated by a digested purpose, and not an existing fact,—by what is to be, and not what is.

Any system which reckons on the self-determining power of the human will, cannot be reconciled to the

legitimate purport of *grace.* Whatever a man prefers, he wills; or whatever he wills, he prefers; he inclines, he chooses. Here lies the strongest proof of his depravity, that he loves it; and here is the great argument for his moral liberty, that he voluntarily thinks, speaks, and does his sinful pleasure. Is he excusable in breaking the law, because he does not desire to obey it? Or does he, by the prevalence of such desire, cease to be free? "Yea, they have chosen their own ways, and their soul delighteth in their abominations." It will be readily granted that all good in the creature originates with the Divine Being. That influence which produces this good, whether light, impulse, grace, or any other term, shall describe it, is either general or partial. All do not benefit from it, but some do. The former fact we could explain, did we believe it common, which we think negatived by Scripture, and did we believe that God would bestow any thing unavailing. But how is it that some do benefit from it? We shall be told that they, unlike the rest, improve it. Then they are only indebted to grace as are all mankind. They are not more so than any of the lost. They make themselves to differ. Yet the question returns: How is it that their will, which is but the bias of their tainted nature, elects the part of good? How is it that it takes grace by the hand, and aids its operation? Should it, in answer, be said, that unless this influence be common, man is unjustly governed, it would follow that a government must provide for the principle, as well as the claim, of allegiance in all its subjects, and that, becoming a business of government, it must leave the station of a favor to take that of a right. But it is a poor consummation of an energy which is more stupendous than that which creates out of nothing, and quickens whom it will, that it would have converted the creature, if the creature might have been induced to permit it! Such self-determining power,

a power to rise above all the known tastes of the soul, would involve, in this connection, something more determined, more resistless, than the " exceeding greatness " of Jehovah's power, " according to the working of his mighty power ! "

Any system which accounts the Gospel as a provision of simple opportunity and facility to man to save himself, cannot be reconciled to a due consideration of grace. This has been called, in somewhat uncouth phrase, a salvable state. It proceeds on many errors, and engenders more. It commonly takes for granted that the divine law is let down in its requirements and sanctions, as though God had miscalculated and overreached his prerogative in these announcements and safeguards of his will. It generally goes to confirm the sentiment, that a certain line of demeanor will have a pacifying and propitiating effect upon the mind of the Lawgiver, who has already deferred so greatly to his creatures, that he has exposed himself to a necessary implication of previous harshness in exaction and punishment. But where now stands the work of Christ? According to the same hypothesis, it has brought about this state of things: that is, instead of magnifying the law, and making it honorable, he has stamped an ambiguity on it, and virtually annulled it; he has died, that man might see that sin was not so evil, and that its consequences ought not to be so dreadful! And after this indignity done the " Holy One and the Just," assigning him the work of " destroying the law," what a mockery of his saving office does it leave him! Man, having been brought into a condition far freer from restraint, and far more exempt from retribution, than before, by the advent of his Saviour, now is able to do what would have been little and useless, until the milder code was introduced, but what is very laudable and satisfactory under the amended form of duty! Still, nature is weak, and pas-

sion strong; there may be a deficiency after all. If the tears of repentance cannot wipe out every stain, if the many virtues cannot countervail all the numerous imperfections, then (I tremble to give language to these deformities and horrors of blasphemy!) shall the " blood of the covenant" complete the almost perfect task! Is this grace or work? By this construction of Christianity, Jesus deigns nothing more than to put us into a capacity, and furnish with a chance, of saving ourselves! And by the view we must take of his design, never are we to invoke his righteousness and expiation but when, after our best and most strenuous self-justifying efforts, we feel that a little more may be required to give our case its last claim and perfect recommendation! Blessed Jesus! thus art thou put to " an open shame!" First thou art made " the minister of sin," in reducing a law which is " holy, just, and good ; " and then the friend of presumption, in crowning the labor of those who " go about to establish their own righteousness!" This is the estimate of thy stripes!—this is the glory of thy wounds! " A goodly price that thou art prized at ! "

Any system which vindicates the prerequisite to interest in the Gospel, as inclusive of all the virtues, is irreconcilable with a worthy interpretation of grace. It need not be insisted on that faith is this prerequisite; it is the condition (we retain the terminology of our soundest divines) to " the fellowship of the Gospel." The reason for this constitution is assigned in Scripture most unequivocally; it " is of faith, that it might be of grace." There must, therefore, be an aptitude in this instrument for this end. It must be transparently illustrative of this object. But is not the reason of its constitution often placed on other ground? Is it not often stated that faith seminally contains reliance, love, patience, zeal, and general obedience? Is it not warranted as the guaranty of the best and purest conse-

quences? Is not the stress laid upon its prospective effects? Strip the disguise from this, and faith is vindicated for " its works foreseen." " If it be of work, then is grace no more grace." But all who are in similar error will not feel this application of the argument. These are quite indignant at those simple views of faith which some, who attempt to think for themselves, entertain. Would you take away, they exclaim, all efficacy from faith, as though it could do nothing of itself? Would you resolve it into sheer mental exercise? Would you have us saved by the faith of devils? To this we answer, that no faith can have any more or less qualities in itself; that nothing is so dependent for its character on objective accidents; that it must be influenced solely by the veracity of the witness, and the nature of the testimony; that faith of its own nature has not a saving point beyond brotherly kindness and charity; that the faith of devils is an insupposable case, as there is no " word of the truth of glad tidings " addressed to them; that the process of intellect, by which they believe that there is no provision of mercy in their instance, and by which their rage and despair are awakened, assures us of the reverse; for this is a " faithful saying, that Christ Jesus came into the world to save sinners;" and we have " joy and peace in believing." Faith can neither justify nor purify; it is the Gospel which only can do the one or the other. It is from the Gospel faith derives all its influence to " justify without the works of the law," and to " purify the heart." Faith only recognizes God as sincere, and the Gospel as true and all-important; and this is its whole use in these great transactions. As men never believed in two ways, or by two mental states, so happy would it be if, when they spoke of our " precious faith," they thought more of the matter believed, and analyzed the manner less. It is very possible to contend for

faith, and to refine upon it, until it becomes a very righteousness, a more splendid and elaborate " work."

Any system which varies the universal freeness of the Gospel by moral differences in man, cannot be reconciled to adequate impressions of grace. Without distorting or forcing into one another the things which differ, Christianity surveys all men in their need of salvation and in their ruin without it. Their guilt of a thousand hues, their depravity of a thousand features, all exhibit them in this predicament of equal need and ruin. In its grandeur it seizes on these generalities, knowing that the debtor of fifty pence and the debtor of five hundred are leveled to one condition, and because they have "nothing to pay," it frankly forgives them both. But have we no idea, though we perhaps will not confess it to even ourselves, that some have inferior occasion, and more ready welcome, than others? Could we, with the same unfaltering tone, proffer these blessings for immediate acceptance and for immediate relief to the ornament and the outcast of society, to the cloistered sage and the condemned felon? Instead of addressing the inquiring sinner, " And now why tarriest thou?" do we not feel more disposed to subject him to trial, and to rack him by suspense? It is difficult to be practically consistent; and there are few, though they are most devoted to the Gospel for its grace, that have not hesitated, in particular circumstances, whether all should be told, whether a gradual and medicated preparation of its truth should not be substituted—whether a regimen almost irritating should not precede the soothing balm. But no one has discretionary power here. It is his duty to "testify the Gospel of the grace of God." And this view flings a burning rebuke upon those who pretend to honor grace by the rejection of all conditions. Yet among the " perverse things which they speak, to draw away disciples

after them," these are foremost in erecting conditions which the Gospel never contemplated, and its ministry never acknowledged. They tell us that we must bear no general message, that we should address only certain descriptions of character; that when we find a particular amount of convictions and emotions, there only can we be suffered to disclose the " plenteous redemption." Their idea of grace is, that it must find a congeniality in the sinner; but if magnet there must be, it is of little importance what be its precise attraction, it is only a question as to the kinds of work. We preach to the uncalled, to call them; to the unimpressed, to impress them; to the unconvinced, to convince them. Otherwise our commission would be partial and specific, not to " every creature," and to " all people," but determined by human character and discriminative qualification.

Any system which founds our duty upon a bestowment of grace, is irreconcilable with its very principle. Grace may or may not be exercised, may be withheld, may be withdrawn. But obligation depends upon law, upon expediency, and when it is moral, its grounds are immovable. Grace therefore can never be a reason of duty, nor can duty cease to bind us because of the non-intervention of grace. Yet why is it that many say that all men ought to believe? Their answer is, that all have grace. Why is it that many say that the duty is confined to some! Their explanation is, that only some have grace. Thus obligation is made to travel the same course, and to measure itself by the same extent, as that which is under no necessity to exist at all! God's authority is thus suspended upon his mercy, and we should become unaccountable had he forgotten to be gracious! And I beg you will remember two things which are equally true, but by no means contradictory: that gracious influence is necessary to salvation, but

not to moral rule—is necessary for a sinner in order to be saved, but cannot be to a moral agent in order to be governed.

You will not fail to observe with what jealousy the sacred writers denounce any encroachment upon the province of grace. As justification is its first expression and act, they set around it a guard of the most solemn cautions. Circumcision was the only rite that the Jewish converts wished to retain; they sought and struggled hard to mingle this with " the righteousness of God by faith." It seemed a harmless peculiarity. But it was a foreign infusion in that element which must be purely integral. It was opening the door to other intrusions. It was a declaration that something might, and must, be added to that on the simple ground of which we are accepted. And how does an Apostle regard it? As so irreconcilable with the profession and truth of Christianity, that he who was guilty of it " was a debtor to do the whole law,"—that Christ should profit all such as were circumcised nothing, that " Christ was become of no effect unto them," that they " had fallen from grace." And as sensitively as we feel the slightest particle in some delicate sense, or a jar through the frame when the quick of some nerve is most gently pressed, so should we watch against any thing, however minute and seemingly innocuous, that would detract from the purity, by blending itself with the essence, of grace! O how strange is it that men should labor to corrupt this divine principle, to throw strange fire on the altar which burns with the heaven-kindled flame! to adulterate the " feast of fat things!" They extract bitterness from the sweetest flowers in the " garden of the Lord," and distill poison from the leaves which " are for the healing of the nations." They recast the Gospel in their own mold, and mutilate its natural proportions according to their own model. They receive the heavenly to debase it into the

earthly. They now complain of the conditions of the Gospel as too free, and then of its precepts as too severe; here they allege its salvation to be too easy, and there too arduous; first, it leaves them nothing, and afterward too much, to do; their complaint that it represents them as utterly helpless, is followed by another, that it expects scarcely any thing short of superhuman excellence from them; and thus their wayward objections give a sort of reality to the parable of the children sitting in the market-place, and calling one to another, and saying, " We have piped unto you, and ye have not danced; we have mourned unto you, and ye have not lamented." A less theoretic view of this subject remains to be taken. And we proceed to observe,

IV. THAT THESE CLASHING AND REPUGNANT PRINCIPLES ARE EQUALLY EXTREME IN THEIR PRACTICAL EFFECTS.

How differently they explain Christianity!

If *work* predominate over *grace*, the Gospel is the republished law. This law is what it was, or it is not. If it is, then why call that the " Gospel of peace " which only tells of war? why speak of " the hope of the Gospel " when Sinai has not spent a thunder, or allayed a curse? Why rejoice in the republication of a law with greater clearness in those rules which we have violated, and greater terribleness in those penalties which we have incurred? Is this the " ministration of righteousness," in contrast to " the ministration of condemnation? " Is it thus that " the hand-writing of ordinances, which was against us, and which was contrary to us, was nailed to the cross? " But if the law, in its new form, be not what it was, then it is extenuated. It becomes what theologues have called remedial; and it is the consent of God, to accept less than he originally required,—he has lowered his demands on our obedience. But this is not only impossible in Him " with whom is no variableness," but

one or the other of these implications must be just—either that the original claim was exorbitant, or that its abandonment is derogatory. View, then, the state of the question. The Gospel, if the *unabated law*, is a message of despair. All the expectations formed of it were mockery, and all the statements, furnished by itself, are turgid exaggerations. The Gospel, if the *extenuated law*, does not raise " glory to God in the highest," but changes that glory into whatever is short-sighted, fickle, and inconsistent; nor need we exult, for in the prostration of that law sinks the standard of our good, falls the pattern of our dignity! The " perfect love," with which it dispenses, would have been the perfect happiness of which this act consequently despoils us. But let grace have the pre-eminence; let the tender mercy of our God visit us; what a change comes over the " great salvation ! " What light passes through it! What significance impresses itself on it! It is pardon to the guilty, it is renovation to the depraved, it is relief to the wretched, it is restoration to the undone! It undertakes the whole burden, and condescends as far as we have sunk! It never pauses until it has found out " our low estate," and never relaxes its effort until it has lifted us from it. What different things the gospel of *work* so defined, and the gospel of *grace* so illustrated!

How oppositely they affect the mission of Christ!

That coming " into the world," that coming " in the flesh," that coming unto the hour which consecrated him as a victim for sacrifice, is described as a strenuous labor, as a signal consummation. He " endured the cross," and " despised the shame," upon an urgent necessity. This cause must be worthy of such dread expense. He is always represented as unassisted. He " trod the winepress alone." He, his own self, " bore our sins, in his own body, on the tree." Such is the sense of the inspired page respecting it,—his interposition was greatly

conceived, and greatly done. And such is the sense, which, "if it be of grace," is fully supported. He "hath perfected for ever them that are sanctified." It is not a small, uncertain product of benefit which he realizes. He "is made unto us wisdom, righteousness, sanctification, and redemption." We "are complete in him." We honor *grace* in the degree to which we honor the mediation of Christ. "I do not *frustrate* the *grace* of God; for, if righteousness come by the law, then Christ is dead in vain." But "if it be of works," at once the Saviour's mediation is degraded. Though the means are the same, how dwindled is the issue! Though he bled and died, the prodigious cost is redeemed by no corresponding advantage! A subserviency to our convenience is all we concede to him! For what did he "pour out his soul unto death?" According to this unworthy calculation, to follow in the train of the sinner who strives to save himself, ready to lend his aid, should occasion require it! the armor bearer to the warrior who may not need him, but who is ennobled by his attendance, and secured by his service! The employment of "the true God and eternal life," in such salvation of such sinners, is inglorious beyond all comparison. It is to put the new piece of cloth to the old garment, while the tatters hide and shame it! It is to make up our all-but-sufficient sum, that we may purchase our own freedom! It is to unloose one hand of the fettered prisoner to enable him to boast that, with this solitary exception, he unshackled every other limb!

How inversely they influence the human mind!

Grace supposes a certain state of feeling in its recipient. "God resisteth the proud, and giveth grace to the humble." That humility is proper in the creature as derived and dependent; that it is proper in the creature as fallen from his Maker's likeness and favor, is beyond the reach of doubt. It is equally indubitable that God,

in all his dispensations, aims to repress every opposite disposition. "The proud He knoweth afar off." He will be acknowledged as the Giver of all good. Nothing does he more reprobate than even the inclination to say in the heart, "My power and the might of mine hand hath gotten me this wealth." Assumption of independence is the "cursed thing," the root of every evil, the stamp of every crime. This, particularly, applies to religion. There can be no offense equal to that of corrupting or rejecting a religion which only humbles by declaring the truth of our own condition, and by proffering a salvation adapted to the helplessness and demerit of that condition. The God of this religion can suffer no one to "glory in his presence." "Boasting is excluded," necessarily and intentionally. Now, whether of these two principles is the better fitted to inspire that humility of dependence which every relation of the creature, and much more every adjunct of the sinner, dictate? There is all the difference of claim and suppliance: "God, I thank thee that I am not as other men are!" "God be merciful to me a sinner!" The Gospel repeats, "By *grace* ye are saved;" it adds the reason, "Not of *works*, lest any man should boast." But the spirit of grace, in contradistinction to *work*, is not only the spirit of humility, but of obedience. We may conceive of an obedience beneath the scourge of fear, the constraint of interest, the impetus of ambition. These are either passions which are quickly exhausted, or which cannot survive frequent mortifications. The conduct they will urge is not framed for its own sake. They are the chains in which the convict works, or the unpalatable restraints of self-denial necessary to him "who striveth for the mastery." But we can conceive of an obedience prompted by gratitude for some great benefit; we can conceive of it being congenial to the taste, as well as responsive to the feeling, of the grateful party; we can conceive of

that twofold moral influence pressing upon the spirit so equally from without and within it, like the atmosphere upon the bodily frame, that all exists with spontaneousness, and all moves with facility. Whether will comprehensive or contracted views of divine mercy—whether will the Gospel, flowing from grace, or founded on work—whether will fear and self-seeking, or sympathy and gratitude—produce the larger share and purer kind of holiness and worth? The one will be ostentatious, clamorous, arrogant, intermittent, evasive; the other retiring, meek, lowly, continuous, indefatigable. The former will be "eye-service," the latter of "goodwill." "To whom little is forgiven, the same loveth little."

The incongruity is thus plainly declared in the effects which severally follow the admitted ideas of "grace" and "work." They cannot be transmuted in substance, or interchanged in operation. Their mutual adoption is therefore inconsistent, and no juxtaposition can give them affinity with each other. They are the rock and sand; they are the gold and clay; they are the day and night. "If by grace, then it is no more of works: otherwise grace is no more grace. But if it be of works, then it is no more grace: otherwise work is no more work."

There is a tone of remonstrance in these words, which speaks to all who place their hope elsewhere than on the simple mercy of God in the provision of a Saviour. There are those who would dissociate these ideas. Of God we know nothing but in Christ; and of his mercy nothing but in the cross of Christ. There only justice and clemency meet; there only can the pardoning Creator and the penitent creature approach each other; there only may we in one focal view behold that "God is light," and that "God is love;" that the "righteous Lord loveth righteousness," and that "he delighteth in

mercy." These are the fairest images that ever entered the human mind; the most stirring of conceptions, the most touching of sensibilities. These are the sentiments we most fondly cherish, and most earnestly recommend. We would " make all men see what is the fellowship" of this " mystery!" And can you be so " vain in your imagination," can your "foolish heart be so darkened," that you refuse the living " waters," for no other reason than that they are given " without money and without price?" If bidden to " do some great thing," would you not have done it? What is your attempt? If you seek to be justified by the law, avow it, and be consistent. The law will justify perfect obedience, but only that. It has no clause of grace. Offending " in one point, you are guilty of all." " Cursed is every one that continueth not in all things which are written in the book of the law to do them." You may appeal to the judgment-seat; but see that your case be irrefragable in the argument of your sinlessness, or never commit yourself to the headlong extremity. Ah! what strange infatuation prejudices you against the wisdom of this gracious expedient, and blinds you to its necessity? Is it too groveling to accept what God so generously bestows? Will you make your own terms, in contravention of his? Can you only object that he as freely as abundantly pardons? Must you be saved in a manner that shall blot from the act all importance, and leave you without any obligation? Then banish yourselves from the companionship of broken and contrite hearts. Then find a heaven of your own, in which you may pour the full melody of a self-applauding song, and dazzle with the radiant majesty of a self-adjusted crown. " Talk no more so exceeding proudly; let not arrogancy come out of your mouth: for the Lord is a God of knowledge, and by him actions are weighed!"

But let us " cut off occasion from those who seek occa-

sion," though we err by a tautology of statements. The *work* to which *grace* is opposed, is some presumed ground of merit; something that wars against the ready, thankful, and earnest compliance of the sinner with the tendered salvation of the Gospel. We do not "sin, that grace may abound," but we honor grace, in teaching us that "denying ungodliness and worldly lust, we should live righteously, soberly, and godly." Condemnation cannot coexist with obedience; condemnation is reversed, that obedience may be promoted. Our heart is turned, at the moment that our conscience is "purged from dead works to serve the living God." We work no longer for the life of safety, but from the life of principle. We know that we cannot be justified by our works, but we know that without works faith is dead. We rejoice that we are redeemed who "were under the law," but do not consider ourselves "without law to God, but under the law to Christ." We believe that God imputes "righteousness without works;" and that the "purpose" is not of works, "but of him that calleth;" but as cordially do we believe that "this is a faithful saying," and to be affirmed constantly, "that they who have believed must be careful to maintain good works." They are depicted as "zealous" of them, ready to do them, fruitful in them, and when they die, "they rest from their labors, and their works do follow them." These are their necessary uses, and their splendid honors. Be it yours, dear Christians, to emulate them: that while your sentiments give to this blessed grace its purest definition, and your feelings accord to it its warmest praise, your lives may present its most illustrative specimen, most accurate comment, and most beautiful delineation! Amen.

VIII.

THE SON OF GOD ANTICIPATING HIS REWARD.

From henceforth Expecting till his Enemies be made his Footstool.—Hebrews x, 13.

Whatever may be the description of that knowledge which an omniscient being must possess regarding future events, or whatever is the manner in which future events must shape and unfold themselves to an infinite mind, they can simply be considered as future still. Futurity supposes a relation to present time, and only by admitting that relation can we properly conceive the idea which it intends. From analogy we might therefore infer, as well as from the necessity of the case demonstrate, that this distinction will enter into the judgments of the Uncreated Intelligence, " the only wise God." Though " there is no searching of his understanding," he " is a Spirit," he is " the Father of spirits ;" and consequently some resemblance must obtain between his knowledge and our own. Such events are not, indeed, contingent because future, futurity being equally susceptible of certain arrangement with the immediate instant. To the Eternal they will stand revealed absolute as his nature, fixed as his decree. To him there can be nothing problematical, nothing casual; he must foreknow all things, and can only know what is already sure. What has constituted that inevitably sure would form another question, and belongs to another class of inquiries ; but a prescience of future contingencies, of

what perhaps may or may not be, is a contradiction in terms. It is vain to say that this perception is merely of their doubtful nature, that they are known as uncertain—for this confesses an ignorance of the issues, and boasts an information than which no thinking creature can have less. What we contend for is, that the perfection of divine knowledge does, by no means, subvert or overlook the succession of passing and remote events. For this succession is a fact. Instead of things being of one date, they gradually transpire. A child cannot fail to discriminate the order in which one circumstance follows another. Then if nothing of this fact of sequence presents itself to the mind of God, there is a something actually existing which he cannot recognize, and which all finite apprehension cannot but observe! His eye detects not what every other necessarily seizes! It is not by these verbal perversities, these false reasonings, that we "glorify God as God." The thought of his consciousness must always agree with reality, and the light which inspheres him must be invariably reflected from truth. It is nothing short of absurd to state " that the *future* is *present* " with him. Things are positive and rigid: and though the judgment day be clearly foreseen and truly determined—though he has appointed the very aspect of its scenery and the very moment of its consummation—yet it is future to the Judge as it is to ourselves. This being a substantive fact, cannot be more or less true, or vary its truth by any law of relation to higher or inferior natures. Our estimate and impression of that future period will most seriously differ from the glance with which Deity meets, and the survey with which he comprehends it. To us, who are " of yesterday," the distance may seem vast; fancy and computation may sink beneath the attempt to expect it; while in the judgment of Him who " inhabiteth eternity," the postponement may contract to a span and dwindle

to a point—" a thousand years are as one day !" And this mode of statement He himself warrants. He distinguishes between his intentions and his acts : " declaring the end from the beginning, and from the ancient times the things that are not yet done, saying, My counsel shall stand and I will do all my pleasure." Nor can it be any derogation from him thus to separate the " things which differ." For what is futurity ? What is it but that arrangement which He has laid down for the ordinary evolution of his own purposes, for the proper succession of events.

These remarks are capable of an application to our present design. When " the Son of God," " the Lord from heaven," interposed to become the " mediator between God and man," he contemplated certain results arising out of that mediation, and sought, in those results, his recompense of reward. The subjection of all things to himself was the specific end of whatever he taught, performed, and suffered in this strangely-kind capacity ; and no indemnity inferior to this could he accept for infinite privations and woes. He demands the accomplishment of this plan, which really is only constituted to give greater effect and wider scope to his benevolence. The triumph he awaits is a triumph of mercy. The victory he will achieve is the overcoming of evil by good. The spectacle he will exhibit is a world subdued by love. In crushing all adverse principle, all counter-working malice, he is but true to this purpose of benignity, and but cares to establish the well-being of the universe. There is not a world and community of intelligent beings unthreatened and unendangered while any hostile force is left without duly-meted punishment and invincible restraint. To insure this determination, the oath of Jehovah has gone forth. Because " he could swear by no greater," he has " sworn by himself." It rests upon " the immutable

things in which it is impossible for God to lie." But it is yet future, it is still reversionary. There is "a set time," and "an expected end."—"now we see not yet all things put under" Him, who has acquired their right and shall receive their possession! He is "heir of all things," and is "expecting till his enemies be made his footstool." This, then, robs him of no glory, and divests him of no claim as "God over all;" for exactly similar representations are employed in cases which leave no doubt with any that the Supreme Divinity is to be understood. Ah, if a hundredth part of the express condescensions avowed by the Divinity had been announced by Jesus Christ—in hearkening to hear—in looking down from heaven to behold—in leading man, to prove him and to know what was in his heart—in "repenting," in "turning"—how would the enemies of his coequality have numbered and displayed them to deny the perfection of his knowledge, and the consistency of his will! Every explanation is welcome to reconcile the humble language, the deepest accommodation, of the Father: the faintest approach to such gracious mien, the rarest imitation of such voluntary meekness, is always to be quoted against the divine majesty and prerogative of the Son! The alternative in the former instance is to maintain the condescension of Supreme Power, in the latter to deny Supreme Power from the condescension. "The way of the Lord" *is* "equal: but as for them, their way is not equal." They make the invidious distinction, turning every statement, which in the one argument they admit most congruous with all that is divine, into a compulsory process, a determinate law, limited to the creature, demonstrative of the man. Little would their utmost objection, indeed, establish; since His person consists of human circumscription and infinite essence!

Let us "seek the things which are above, where

Christ sitteth at the right hand of God." Him "the heaven" has received "until the times of restitution of all things." On him every eye of celestials is turned, to him their every harp is struck. Pierce through every sphere of light, every throng of spirits. Above those sons of the morning, those creatures of beauty and of bliss, how do his glories pre-eminently shine! He is "in the midst of the throne!" He is the center of all attraction, sympathy, and joy! "The Lamb is the light thereof." But who can explore his bosom and search his heart? Who can divine the thoughts which engage, and pursue the visions which wrap, him? His countenance, his attitude, his station, his office, all bespeak a calm but deep emotion; a hope which beats high but unperturbingly. Some lofty project occupies him, some glorious conception transports him, and we can now pronounce its actual purport. We not only catch, as in a mirror, the expressions of the "visage which was more marred than any man's," and from which hereafter "the earth and the heaven shall flee away;" but we feel the very throb of the heart which the spear transfixed, while it pulsates with "the expectation" of the ascendency which the cause it cherished in life, and clung to in death, and lays hold of forever, is preparing to establish and destined to command. We see not only the array of "the glory and honor" with which Jesus is crowned—we have access to the secrets of his breast!

Let us consider this expectation,

In the peculiarity of its scope.

Evil of every kind has forced its entrance into this world. How subtle is its form, how malignant is its influence, how wide-spread is its diffusion! It has drawn to itself that of other natures and spheres. The enemy came in like a flood. But here is its deepest hold and intrenchment: here, too, is the theater of its most notorious publicity and most restless activity. It is more

than doubtful whether, in any dwelling-place of the universe, there can be found so many different elements of evil, or such multiform combinations of them. Everywhere the leprosy has eat in itself, has fretted the pillars which bear up the earth, and struck through it until it has become like the tainted habitation of old. *We* are "altogether an unclean thing." Having brought the abomination into our house, we have become "a cursed thing" like it. It stamps us with its own image. It transforms us into its own nature. It implicates us in its own doom. There is, consequently, an idea of hostility in every scriptural representation of sin. It is the hostility of rebellion against God, it is the hostility of fraud, murder, and perdition against man. It does the law and character of the Deity a moral injury; the interests of human welfare it contravenes and betrays. But this hostility requires, on the part of all loyal creatures, an opposing feeling, a disgust of its perfidy and a horror of its cruelty. For as good is the only will of the Creator, if we be "followers of that which is good," we must be on his side. Since it has no standard but his infinite excellence, love to him implies reprobation of whatever is adverse. That excellence is holy beauty, of which benignity is only a part. The emotion which corresponds to it is holy esteem and complacency, and therefore a contrast necessitates a disrelish and an execration. Hence the righteous One is represented to be the hater and avenger of evil, because of his fidelity to perfect good in universal purity; and all his creatures who are followers of him "as dear children," participate in the same disposition, and arm for the same war. *He* is only inimical to that which is essentially pernicious, and *they* seek alone the overthrow and extirpation of a destructive principle, which can only exist and operate to the harm of all being and the wreck of all happiness. Malevolence cannot mingle with such a cause, nor enter

on such a pursuit. " Judgment shall return unto right-eousness: and all the upright in heart shall follow it."

The submission of all accountable creatures to God is not only reasonable, but indispensable to their well-being. Then only can they " walk at liberty." A revolt supposes a blinding and seductive influence which is incompatible with the freest, or which is the same, the most congenial and native, exercise of the soul. The balance of the mental and moral powers is deranged. Justice takes its prisoners too. So that in fitness and in law the very good of the creature is abused. Voluntary subjection is his dignity and his happiness. And therefore, when every statute of divine government, and every plan of divine benevolence, insist upon this subjection, it is really but requiring the party who yields to bless himself. Instead of exacting, in this requirement, a harsh and capricious measure, without it God could make no creature happy: it is the indispensable condition of whatever good he can bestow or we can receive.

Now our text pledges that the enemies of Christ shall " be made his footstool." The preceding remarks will explain the beneficence of this hostile purpose, so far as it supposes the ultimate happiness which it is necessary to produce and secure. But we do not disguise that it involves the eternal misery of certain beings who have so identified themselves with the evil which is the sole object of vengeance, that they must bear all its disgrace, and suffer all its demerit.

At once, then, we are ready to declare that the inspired account of divine benevolence is far from supposing the final happiness of all. To rescue one fallen angel it has never interposed: though it redeems from among men " a great number which no man can number," it leaves others to the due reward of their deeds.

We only cite two popular objections. Why, in the first place, it is asked, has not God mercy upon all?

But surely an earlier reply is demanded to the question, Why has he mercy upon any? A universal amnesty is not to be forced upon him who need not ever exercise mercy, though he must always execute justice; and the probability is, that were none " set forth for an example," the ends of moral government would be compromised, and the enormities of sin be forgotten. And a second inquiry is, Why should not these enemies be annihilated, if they cannot be forgiven, rather than be perpetuated in penal existence? Destruction is no law of this created system, no menace of this moral probation; and He who made beings for immortality will not, on account of any change in their character and relation, undo his work and deny himself. It is his will that they live; and this tendency of an endless life is impressed upon them. The question is not, what he could accomplish, for a being independent of his power and pleasure there cannot be. It was an unalterable purpose; and this is the reason of their immortality, as it is of their existing at all. To recall that immortality would confess the law to be too severe, and its consequences to have been unforeseen. It would impeach its principles and its sanctions. It would be to snatch the culprit from its grasp. Besides, we should thus recognize a collision of divine perfections. We distinguish between those more natural and more moral. Power is of the first, justice of the second, class. Let the blow fall which shall extinguish some being. Notwithstanding the reasoning of certain metaphysicians, we hold the effect possible. But would it not be a hideous supposition that justice was defeated by power? that force clashed with right? that arbitrariness prevailed over law? Taking the Bible with us, we advisedly denounce the vain conceit of universal happiness, and the strange suggestion of spiritual annihilation. From the same authority, we learn that there are enemies who shall be " made his footstool "—a phrase which.

cannot denote any thing salutary and propitious to those who are thus prostrated and abased. They are placed beyond the limit of remedy and hope. "He that made them will not have mercy on them; and he that formed them will show them no favor."

It is somewhat difficult to class the enemies of Christ. The characters of their hostility are recklessness and desperation. However unworthy and despicable, we cannot make light of their aggressions. Their course is most mischievous, though their subversion is sure. They may, perhaps, be enumerated in the two following divisions.

There are particular beings who are his foes. Creatures of his power, endued and sustained by him, are found leagued against him. They "will not have" him "to reign over" them. Their intellect, with all its faculties and passions, strives against his authority and his cause. Fiends and wicked men are alike guilty. We are not disposed to think of Satan less than of a most formidable adversary. He "had the power of death," having introduced it. The power of the kingdoms of the world, and the glory of them, was, in a very credible and substantive sense, delivered to him and to whomsoever he would give it. It is not his boast, but an infallible description furnished of him, that he is the "prince" and "god of this world." He has fortified it as his own monarchy, and converted it into his own temple. He is represented as "a strong man armed, who keepeth his palace," and his goods are in peace. His is a gloomy but a royal state. His is an iron throne and a serpent crown. His is a train of willing vassals and victims. His dominions lie in undisturbed quiet. Neither is his title questioned nor his yoke felt to gall. Insurrection there is not among his captive slaves, nor complaint. The "treasures of darkness" he keenly watches and resolutely guards. And when we remember that the

"angels excel in strength," that this apostate was probably shorn of none in his fall—when we further consider the consummate artifice of such close inspection into human nature, and of such accumulated experience of it—when we still add the intensity of hatred which burns amid his stupendous powers and gives them their fatal direction—it were folly for us to attribute to him little importance, or to think of him with light concern. In him we behold what *sin* is, and what is its desert; the lofty proportions and vast capabilities of his nature are informed and dilated by it, and its sentence is branded on his thunder-scarred brow. It is the fearful consequence of joining in his rebellion, of making this "agreement with hell," that human beings become "enemies to God by wicked works;" that they are dealt with as confederates; and that if finally incorrigible and implacable, if at length they do not "recover themselves out of the snare," they must "depart into the everlasting fire prepared for the devil and his angels." It is only meet that this common revolt be counteracted with the same spirit of determined opposition as that in which it is waged; that when creatures rebel and vex his Holy Spirit, he should be "turned to be their enemy," and to fight "against them." The divine character, the universal interest, each idea of government, each ground of law, demand the suppression of this treason, and overthrow of those who have conspired together in it.

To these beings, the Scripture subjoins certain hostile principles, which under the vail of allegorical allusion, and by the aid of bold personification, are denominated foes. Sin, as a criminal, is "condemned in the flesh." The world, as an adversary, is "overcome." Superstition is antichrist, that wicked one, the man of sin. Idolatry is a dragon, having a power, a seat, and "great authority." Persecution is a "woman drunken with the blood of the saints." War sits on the "red horse, and there is

given unto him "a great sword." Religious imposture is "the false prophet." Death is the "last enemy;" the grave is taunted with its "victory;" Hades is defied with "its gates," "follows with death," and is cast along with it "into the lake of fire." All these evils will find a subversion. They are among "the enemies" who shall become his "footstool." Signal displeasure shall be manifested against them. As opposed to whatever was comely and beautiful, just and kind, they shall be denounced and destroyed. But it is plain that all their hostility drew its dint from living intelligence, from accountable nature,—and the punishment must therefore fall on that which is sentient and susceptible. To beings shall their odiousness be exposed, and on beings their resentment must be visited. The subjection of these inimical forces is the grand design of the Saviour's advent into our earth. "For this purpose was the Son of God manifested, that he might destroy the works of the devil." He hath "put away sin." He "gave himself for our sins, that he might deliver us from this present evil world." The various forms of depravity which exist in the passions of men, and which have even corrupted the character, while they pleaded the sanction, of his religion, he will, at his second appearing, "consume with the spirit of his mouth, and destroy with the brightness of his coming." He will "swallow up death in victory."

The tendencies of Christianity co-operate with this design. They are precisely adapted to "put enmity" between the seed of the serpent and of the woman. They set us in the strictest resistance to all evil as an usurpation. We know that the Gospel conjures us to be "reconciled unto God;" that it is a system of allegiance and love; that it is the appointed means of excluding from our earth, and eradicating from our nature, all that is detrimental and untoward. It does not

palliate the evil, but resolves to dry its source and kill its root. The "Author and Finisher of our faith" is therefore described in the gradual process and ultimate triumph of his truth as separating all alloy and disengaging all worthlessness—"sitting as a refiner," having "his fan in his hand" that he may "thoroughly purge his floor." And when he reduces his enemies to the condition of his "footstool," it will be the righteous vindication, dread as is the act, of his benevolence, which all these hostile natures existed to thwart, and all these hostile principles operated to embarrass.

Now these perverse abettors, and monstrous forms, of guilty variance with the Saviour, he awaits on his throne to see entirely subjugated. These enemies must be overthrown. Their purposes shall be baffled; their energies shall be subdued. In vain shall they writhe beneath the feet then planted upon them! They shall bite the earth and lick the dust! From their promised greatness, from their towering ambition, they shall be hurled to the ground, and become the footstool of Him who was "despised and rejected" of them! This figure supposes

Defeat. Long since was the basis of his victory laid, its title established. He, upon the cross, made "an end of sin," and destroyed death. Then was "the judgment of this world," then was "the prince of this world cast out." He encountered their united shock and prevailed. No future struggle can resemble the past. He has won, and only has to apply, the victory. "The Lamb shall overcome." He who conquered when "crucified in weakness," can be disconcerted by no force, and impeded by no difficulty. Even now his most inveterate enemies gasp beneath their death-wound. But the vengeance is yet to be wreaked. The triumph is yet to be displayed. At present the spoil is not sufficiently gathered, nor the host refreshed. Still these enemies find no hope in the future. They have not even the desperate hazard before

them of another combat. Their destiny is cast. Their struggles, however oft repeated, and however long extended, are in chains. They cannot meet again their awful Antagonist; no more can they recoil before him. He has "bound the strong man." The deed is done. The weapons of their war have perished. Soon shall "the army of the aliens" be brought forth. Our Jesus has imprisoned them in their refuge. And as the Israelitish chief dragged the kings from the cave of Makkedah, and summoned his warriors to "put their feet upon the necks of these kings,"—so, having "bruised" our enemies under our feet, the "Captain of our salvation" shall "tread them in his anger and trample them in his fury," while he calls upon an applauding universe to confess his fame and sing his victory! "There are the workers of iniquity fallen; they are cast down, and shall not be able to rise!"

Nor does the image which implies *defeat*, less import *Degradation.* Evil is highly flattered and powerfully supported in the present state of things. It throws an intrepidity and daring around it. Much exists to encourage it. "Hand" joins "in hand." It enthrones itself upon "high places." "The multitude" does it. It finds countenance in the communities, institutions, and laws of men. It calls every association of a proud honor to its aid. There is every effort, every contrivance, to evade the sense of shame. But then a new, though the just, feeling shall seize upon the enemies of the common good. Reproach shall cover them. Inly shall they shrink. Low shall they crouch. Their deformity will be unvailed. Their purpose shall be detected. All eyes must shun, all hearts detest them. Nothing can survive to cheer their spirits, to rally their resources, or to redeem their excesses. And now awaking "to everlasting contempt" —the very "footstool" of Him whom they were too

haughty to acknowledge, and too stubborn to serve—they suffer the doom threatened by the Eternal Sire against the enemies of the Son: "I will beat down his foes before his face, and plague them that hate him." "All that are incensed against him shall be ashamed."

And this similitude denotes also

Subserviency. Now does the Saviour "rule in the midst" of his enemies. He can "put in their hearts" to fulfill his will. He allows not of their independence, whatever may be their boast. Their "wrath" praises him. They "are made for the day of evil." He knows their abode, and their going out, and their coming in, and their rage against him. They have their use in his plan: they are the slaves, and not even the mercenaries, who hew wood and draw water for the erection and service of his temple. And in that day of anticipated triumph, they who took "counsel together to break his bands asunder," shall be shown, through all their unwitting course, to have ministered to him: and then shall become instrumental to his state. They shall be thrust into a very "footstool" for him. From them, not only harmless but accessary to his royal dignity, he shall exact a final service. They shall swell his pomp and express his grandeur! While they gnash beneath him, not only shall their overthrow teach their powerlessness to mate with his strength, but prove that their hostility to his perfect benevolence gave the darkest hue to their guilt, and constituted the most exasperating provocation of their punishment! Thus "the Lord will take vengeance on his adversaries, and he reserveth wrath for his enemies." He will wound their head; he will clothe them with shame; he will see his desire upon them. And though this requires a terrible retribution, it is necessary that mischief and misery may cease, and that "destructions may come to a perpetual

end." And when He "treads down" them who stumbled and fell, it is no tyrannic sway, no cruel parade: it is Benevolence sitting in its state. it is sceptered Mercy and enthroned Love!

Having pursued the scope of the expectation which is cherished by the Saviour, let us consider it

In the period of its commencement.

It takes its rise with a certain date, it follows in a particular order. "From henceforth,"—that is, upon some scene being past, some epoch having expired.

A scene how strange! It commenced with a manger, and ended with a cross. It was constituted of misery, and consummated by death. It was an eclipse of infinite majesty. It was the travail of eternal Might. He stooped from heaven to the "lowest parts of the earth." He sunk from the regions of immortality into the grave. Constantly that scene evolved with new ignominy and enlarged woe. But it is fled, never to be repeated!

An epoch how tremendous! It was the crisis for which all time was born, and upon which all history was balanced. The interval it included measured such moments and years as never rolled before or since. To this fullness of times all had culminated, and by it all are impressed. With the suspense of that crisis the universe vibrated. But it is numbered, never to be recalled!

Still the original term may yield a more extended meaning: that which is left, or what remains, the rest is, that He should expect "till his enemies be made his footstool." Hitherto something preliminary and necessary had always intervened. The expectation depended on some condition, and looked through some medium. It is now unbroken and unmixed. It is a free and commanding vision. Nothing confuses and embitters it. It rises serenely, it advances steadily, it opens

unallayed; no more to be secured, but simply meditated and uninterruptedly enjoyed. What, then, was the restriction- until now? What was that requirement which stood up before his mind, and darkened this glorious prospect?

He must endure the most inconceivable sufferings.

From eternity they had risen on his view. When he rejoiced, by benevolent anticipation, in the "habitable part of the earth," he contemplated it as a stage for their endurance. Gethsemane was there as well as Eden; the river which watered the garden in which the first Adam was placed did not ravish him more with its sweet music than Kedron then murmured mournfully on the ear of the second Adam, as if ready to drink his tears; and the original tree which was "made to grow out of the ground," contained the germ of the cross. He beheld, when bidding the deluge to subside, the hill Calvary, more prominent to his eye than the peak of Ararat, emerging from its bosom. He foresaw, when he rained fire upon Sodom, "the great city, which is spiritually called by that name, where he was crucified." His death was perpetually imaged in bleeding mysteries, and announced by prophetic oracles. Had he been able or disposed to forget it, the reiteration of its signs was too frequent, and the assertion of its horrors too distinct. "The harp, with a solemn sound," was struck by many an inspired bard to strains still more intense and articulate, as the time drew nigh when he should tabernacle with us. During that sojourn, these omens thickened upon him in ever-accumulating succession. There was neither respite nor pause. Each association of external objects took this character; all his thoughts and his allusions declared this presentiment. He computed time by this index. "My hour is not yet come!" "The hour is at hand!" "The hour is come!" "Save me from this hour!" When was the minute, where was

the point, in which the presages of his agony and crucifixion did not lour before him? The path of the Victim, the procession of the Sacrifice, reached back to his "goings forth which were from of old, from everlasting." —"It is finished!" He shall not suffer another pang, nor the thought of another. He "dieth no more." No intimation, no suggestion, of woe can pass his mind. No complaint, no deprecation of pain, can escape his tongue. He has thrown all that which was once the gloomy and bitter future into the past. It lies in the "dark backward and abysm of time." Before him stretches the unclouded scene of peace and joy. He expatiates in it without check or possible dejection. There grows not in it a thorn, there rests not on it a shadow. He looks out from his throne, and, conscious that his sufferings have entirely and eternally ceased, merely awaits "till his enemies be made his footstool."

Ere this expectation could be unreservedly indulged, *He must lay the basis of his mediatorial offices.*

Being sent to save mankind, rejoicing in the purpose, he had to surmount certain moral exigences. These respected divine claim and human incapacity. Without sacrifice God could not allow, without sanctification man would not accept, "the Gospel of salvation." For both these ends, it cannot be too often repeated, provision must be made. There must be a counterbalancing desert to man's demerit, and a counteracting influence to man's indisposition. Christ has undertaken for us. He must, therefore, substitute an equivalent righteousness, and exercise an efficient energy. We must be pardoned for "Christ's sake," we must be renewed by the "Spirit of Christ." The whole is a special work which he was to accomplish, and from it arises a special title, which he applies. "He is able to save to the uttermost:" but this ability is as much a right, as a competency, to exe-

cute the deed. He has "obeyed the law," he has borne our sin and curse. We are saved, not in deference to his pre-eminent virtue and exalted dignity, as children have "found grace" because of their parents, but we are saved in regard to a series of positive acts performed, a succession of positive sufferings endured, for the express design of saving us. Upon these the mediatorial relations and characters of our Lord depend. Only by this course does he become a prophet, priest, and king. And this work which the Father gave him to do had hitherto obstructed the spectacle of this final subjugation. While it remained, it filled the sphere of thought and attention. "It is finished!" His oblation can never require another grain of incense to enrich its "sweet-smelling savor," nor can his endless intercession find another plea besides his obedience "to the death of the cross." And it is now for him, without this pre-engagement distracting and intercepting the view, to cherish the future, amid which stands no difficulty and arises no labor—a scene of sweet refreshment and calm repose. He aspired to these offices that he might control all things by the power, and for the triumph, of his love. His blood was our ransom from the demands of justice, and his power is employed to "save us from our enemies, and from the hand of all that hate us." And having so fulfilled "all righteousness," the diadem is set upon his head, and heaven is his throne, that this prospective reward may stand forth to him with a definite outline and living truth. He need deserve no more to win it; and whatever of particular commission was necessary to obtain his title he has executed. His eyes, "like unto a flame of fire," gaze upon the vision of his final glory, dispreading in its amplest folds, and irradiated with its strongest splendors. "For He that is entered into his rest, he also hath ceased from his own works, as God did from his."

Previously to the unrestrained enjoyment of this catastrophe to the universal plan, the Son of God

Must overcome his spiritual adversaries.

Fallen angels had taken us captive. Our circumstances, in the first instance of probation, and in all others of depravity, gave a facility to their malign purpose. But we do not think that Scripture ever affixes to this power obtained over us any idea of right. It is a violence, a rapine, but not a lawfully founded rule. And therefore, to the best of our judgment, the Scripture does not express our deliverance under any notion of equitable redemption. It is not to be indemnified, but overthrown. Satan set up his "power of darkness," but "greater is He that is" for "us, than he that is in the world." It was power which should assail, and not price which might remunerate. "A stronger than he" must overcome him, and take from him "all his armor wherein he trusted," and divide his spoils. But it is a necessary inquiry, how created strength can, for a moment, hold combat with omnipotence? We traverse not now the realms of poetry, but of far more magnificent truth. Let it be remembered, according to some of our earlier statements, that it was not in the mind of the "great God our Saviour" to annihilate the existence, or suspend the agency, of any accountable creatures; and therefore they opposed him not with their derived power, but their spontaneous malice. They were "left at large to their own dark designs."* But it contradicts all reason, that this strife should have partaken of a physical character; that mountains torn from their roots, and linked thunderbolts, should have been the weapons. Such an encounter "makes arms ridiculous, useless the forgery of brazen shield and spear."† "He that sitteth in the heavens" would "laugh, the Lord" would "have them in derision." It is not, then, a trial, a shock, of

* Milton.   † Ibid.

strength whose issue must be easy and immediate: it is a struggle in connection with particular moral means, and certain moral principles. Did this tyranny arise out of our sins? In their counteraction the tyranny is quelled. Did wicked maxims and practices uphold the tyranny? Its falsehood yields to truth, its treason to fealty, its mischief to good. Did this tyranny enslave the human race? It crumbles before that salvation which "makes us free indeed." Did this tyranny erect on earth a rival influence? It is broken to pieces by the kingdom which the Redeemer raises in the human heart, the kingdom which destroys all hostility and has no end. Did this tyranny indirectly, though consequentially, form a part of the penalty which guilt incurs? It is dissolved wherever that penalty receives a remission. Did this tyranny consolidate itself in the "ignorance and blindness" of our nature? It is stricken to its center by every exposure of its machinations and delusions. Now all this is the history of the event. Jesus must have the *official qualification* of the mediator in order to wrest his people from this infernal seizure. Thus only did he equip himself and become "mighty in battle." Justice, until then, could not suffer the liberation. But when he died to expiate sin, to establish righteousness, to secure a glorious liberty, to "receive for himself a kingdom," to repeal "all condemnation," to "wound the head out of the house of the wicked, by discovering the foundation unto the neck," he effectually closed with his enemies, met them in the plain, and secured their irretrievable discomfiture. Thus he substantiated his supremacy, and disarrayed the traitor host. And their fall is so much the more abject, as it was not wrought by simple power, by an appeal to force, but by confirming great and important principles, which are irreconcilable with every rebellious attempt, and subversive of every rebellious system.

We have in the evangelic record an account of the Messiah's death; but nothing seems more remote from every circumstance of victory. No such enemies as these appear, nor is there a demonstration of their attack. Hasten to the scene. There is an engine of torture! And is this to be the standard of the war? There is a place of execution! And is this fit theater for the enterprise? There is a cry of despair! And is this the voice of one who shouteth for mastery, and who findeth a spoil? As if in mockery of that weakness and woe, we are informed by an inspired commentator that He blotted " out the handwriting of ordinances that was against us, which was contrary to us, and took it out of the way, nailing it to his cross: and having spoiled principalities and powers, he made a show of them, openly triumphing over them in it." Was ever history and description more at variance? " He nailed the handwriting to his cross!" The superscription of his offense is there, and the hammer has driven nails through his hands and feet to suspend him on it. " He spoiled!" Instead of stripping others, the soldiers part his raiment among them, and upon his vesture cast lots. " Principalities and powers!" All rank and authority are leagued against him, and have succeeded in destroying him. " Made a show of them openly!" He is transfixed, naked, insulted, pierced, a spectacle to heaven and earth. " Triumphing over them!" His murderers gloat over him as *their* victim, while they deridingly shake their heads, and barbarously sit " down to watch him there." " In it!" The cross is no vantage-point from which to deal the blow that shall scatter the enemy as chaff. Yet this is the infallible construction upon the death of Calvary, and therefore " the mount " must have been " full of horses and chariots of fire." To Him, who there " set up his ensign," stood revealed the presence and the agency of spirits that desired this death, and had com-

plotted with man to secure it. For "Satan entered into the heart of Judas," and the crucifixion was the master-piece of his stratagem, and the burst of his rage. He deemed that it must be a downfall to the cause of Him who had come to "bruise" his head. And O, what furious joy he felt when the traitor kissed Him: when the multitude demanded His death: when the governor outraged every sense of justice in His condemnation: when He was hurried away to the place of skulls: when He was uplifted on the tree: when the spear was thrust into His heart: when He bowed his head: when He was laid in the grave. The blow in which was collected the vengeance, and in which fell the aim, of four thousand years, at that moment struck him down! "How art thou fallen, O Lucifer!" Dread was then thy distrac-tion! Ghastly then was thy despair! Caught in thine own toils! Crushed by the recoil of thine own engines! Then learnedst thou what is hell! Thy chain had never lacerated until it received this rivet; thy fire had never consumed until it was reddened by this blast! Then thy captivity was taken captive! Then thy counsel was turned into foolishness! Then thou didst betray thy-self! Then thou wast cast down! The conflict was real in proportion as it was moral! Human sense could not apprehend it. There was no blazonry of arms. There was no "shouting at noontide." But in a field impalpable to our eye, and with a din impalpable to our ear, the adversaries confronted and strove. And a con-cussion of powers must then, by other beings, have been as distinctly felt as when this earth, in mysterious sym-pathy, rocked with surprise and quaked with fear; an array must have been observed by them, more dazzling than had the stars in their courses fought against each other; or had the rout fallen, like lightning, from heaven. "It is finished." Our champion overcame. Nothing was wanted to secure the conquest. He looked around

the battle scene, but all was complete. Henceforth he resigns himself to "the vision which is for an appointed time," and "though it tarry," waits for it. He will contend no more. No other enemy can arise. Victory has sheathed his sword for ever. And it only remains that he dictate his terms, that he apply his successes, that he distribute of his spoils, that he dispose of his captives, that he recline beneath his palms!

What then *now* intervenes requires no such suffering, labor, and conflict. Not that we make light of those mediatorial functions which he still executes, nor that we can imagine his state of reward supposes any notions of inactivity. He lives for the most important ends. He intercedes. He reigns. We are "saved by his life." He is "our life." "Because he lives," we shall live also. He "abideth a priest continually." His "throne is forever and ever." In both these offices he "is consecrated for ever more." But then he only pleads and presents the merit of his blood, and only sways and enforces the "all power," given to him "in heaven and in earth." No idea of difficulty, no circumstance of trial, remains. "We have such a High Priest, who is set on the right hand of the throne of the Majesty in the heavens." He "is Lord of all." Whatever are his enemies, he "despises their image." And though we must conceive of his constant agency, it is marked with the utmost possible facility, it is "the working whereby he is able even to subdue all things unto himself." All moves on in an unbroken train. The progression sweeps majestically forward, embodying the scenes of prophecy, and ushering in the ages of peace. He hastens "it in his time." He rests from pain, from toil, from strife; not with indolent repose, but refreshing activity. "His rest is glorious." He "fainteth not, neither is weary,"

This expectation must be considered
In the Temper of its Indulgence.

During the life of our Lord on earth, a desire of the reward which depended on his death is very perceptible. As it was promised to him, because his soul was "made an offering for sin," that "the pleasure of the Lord" should "prosper in his hand," so he ever and anon anticipates this glorious sequel to his labor and woe. It cannot be too constantly remembered, too vividly impressed, that the result is one of the divinest charity; that it is the largest possible amount of the purest possible happiness for the greatest possible number of moral beings. Therefore each incident, though apparently slight, offers occasion of triumph and warrant of hope. When the inhabitants of Sychar came forth to examine the truth of the report which had been conveyed to them of the stranger sitting on Jacob's well, He said to his disciples, "Lift up your eyes, and look on the fields; for they are white already to harvest." Having observed the "great faith of the Centurion," he exclaimed, as though this was the specimen and earnest of a believing world, "I say unto you, that many shall come from the east and west, and shall sit down in the kingdom of heaven." Certain Greeks would see him, and when their curiosity was testified to him, he was elated with a holy transport: "The hour is come, that the Son of man should be glorified." When Mary poured the spikenard over his head, he declared with an emphatic assurance of the future, "Verily I say unto you, wheresoever this Gospel shall be preached in the whole world, there shall also this, that this woman hath done, be told for a memorial of her." These scenes, these triumphs, attracted his loving heart, and constituted that "joy set before him" on account of which he "endured the cross and despised the shame." And now he has "for ever sat down on the right hand of God, from henceforth *expecting* till his enemies be made his footstool."

It is a somewhat unusual term, and in this connection

inspires high and animating thoughts, involves strong and solemn pledges, which embolden and " assure our hearts." Nor is it possible to conceive of this expectation without supposing a concentration of mind upon the destined result. All things in their appointed dates and stages are exposed to his knowledge. The plan of the universal future is spread out under his eye. " Hell is naked before him, and destruction hath no covering." What changes of dynasty, what revolutions of empire, what causes of vicissitude, are laid bare to his glance ! No moment, no event, can he overlook. The number of our hairs he cannot mistake, nor the fall of the sparrow can he neglect. He is " the first and the last." But this final object engrosses him. All his thoughts linger here. It absorbs his dearest will. He pierces whatever is intermediate to rest his attention upon its scene, and to expatiate amidst its glory. Occurrences derive all their value and interest to his eye from their relation to the issue which he now undivertedly regards, and according as they are accessory to " his glorious appearing," when he shall triumph over all the powers of darkness and the occasions of woe.

Circumstances might sometimes tempt us to distrust the earnestness of this expectation. Obstacles are suffered, delays are brooked, which we determine could be prevented, or, if they must arise, could be instantaneously repressed. This is but the re-appearance of our common error—the supposition that power, in the sense of force, should control moral agency and expedite moral government. His rule is directed, in consistency with the probation of man, to stem the torrent, to draw it off into other channels, to render its proudest waves demonstrative of the strength, and subservient to the speed, of the ark which rides over them. But never can his anticipation grow indifferent and languid. The most fervent ardor of the saint, the collective zeal of the Church, is

coldness itself when compared with the strength of his desire. Never has it wavered, never can it decline. He is as resolved upon it as when he descended to earth and arose to heaven, that he might appropriate the right and adjust the attainment.

And this expectation is formed in a manner most worthy of the mind which cherishes it. It is a perfect prescience. Hope lends the reality no exaggeration, fancy decks it in no fiction, but it arises before the Saviour in the very shape of truth and fact. It shines upon him, though from afar, with a steady light and perfect delineation. We cannot "steadfastly look to the end." The vista dimly twinkles before our eye through means vast and complicated. "We know in part, and we prophesy in part." We confound and often lose the glimmering. He predestines and seizes it. The vision approaches or retires at his bidding. His comprehensive survey embraces only that which it contains. It is not now brighter and then more faint; it owes nothing to a varying gleam; it stands out distinctly beneath the sun of his own noon, and to the all-searching scrutiny of that foreknowledge with which there is nothing dark and precarious!

The serenity which distinguishes this expectation blends most beautifully with its dignity. The passions of man cannot adequately represent the emotions of His bosom. Nothing is more disquieting to our feelings than hope deferred. We are ruffled with the excitement of any prospective gratification. Agitation marks the excess of our joy, and our feeble power of entertaining it. But He who "has sat down, expecting till his enemies be made his footstool," dwells in the purest calm. He diffuses around him an infinite repose. No anxiety sits upon his brow. No doubt depresses his heart. The light which informs him of the future is soft as it is piercing. He has nothing to learn, nothing

to resolve. In the settlement of his plan and the certainty of his reward he lives assured, he exults meekly. His "very rapture is tranquillity." * Many events perpetually occur which seem untoward and perplexing. They spread consternation upon earth. "The kingdoms are moved." "Men's hearts fail them with fear." The pious are "filled with the cup of astonishment." "Truth has fallen in the street." "The spirit of heaviness" has palsied the energies and anticipations of the Church. But these things have never reached his atmosphere, nor disturbed his peace. They have thrown no obscurity over his prospect, and have struck no chill through his breast. He has beheld the temple arise, "growing" like a stately tree with all the certainty and quiet of a vegetation ; and the troubled times in which it was built have not grieved his eye, nor have the ax and the hammer, employed in its erection, wounded his ear. His eternal conception presses forward to its realization without effort and misgiving; and his unvarying expectation, itself an element of calm, leans placidly, and rests untremblingly, upon the ultimate consummation. The scenery of prophecy thickens in interest and rapidity as it hastens to its close; and in passing characters and events a reality is given to its awful action. We cannot but perceive that there is a shaking of the "heavens and the earth." All things seem to feel the eve of a solemn crisis. Signals are streaming, alarms are ringing, on every wind ! The oldest relations are cut asunder, the most massive foundations are dissolved. A restlessness of innovation, and an impatience of restraint, hold contest with a pertinacity of power and a dotage of prescription. Billow chafes with billow. The maddest theories are propagated, the wisest expedients are spurned. Anarchy is demanded, liberty is denied. Kings, as

* Young.

if they saw the mystic fingers which write their doom, start from their thrones: the tumult of the people, like the noise of the sea, declares that the mounds of authority are giving way before it. The storm will have its drift! The earthquake will force its vent! The flood will rend open its channel! But the Divine Expectant observes and disposes all. His glorious seat vibrates not to the shock, his tranquil mind is not embarrassed by the turmoil. The seals may be broken, the trumpets be sounded, the vials be discharged; there may be " lightnings, and voices, and thunders;" yet He stands with undiscomposed mien, and with majestic serenity—the Lamb upon Mount Zion, " meek and gentle," giving " rest " to all the " weary " who come unto him, and existing in " quietness and assurance forever."

The confidence of His mind is the secret of that sweetly calm decision which distinguishes this Expectation. Time was when despondency saddened it. Not only did his approaching sufferings dismay him, but he deplored the absence of success. His language took the cast of complaint. "Who hath believed our report? " " I have labored in vain, I have spent my strength for naught and in vain." But, since he " ascended on high," whatever events have transpired, they could not thwart his design or deject his spirit. Nothing has hung in suspense. Nothing has been the cause of vexation. When every eye has been strained to observe " the thing coming on the earth," when there have been " great searchings of heart," his tone never faltered, his courage never misgave. Still he has said, I know that I shall not be ashamed. He sees the goal. The shadow of his hand falls upon the spoil. He has " the substance of things hoped for " in his infinite knowledge and decretive will. " He shall send forth judgment unto victory. He shall not fail nor be discouraged till he have set judgment in

the earth, and the isles shall wait for his law." He beholds from above, with a sureness and exactitude which no mortal ideas and instances of certainty can convey, the ready obedience of some, the involuntary surrender of others, the eternal subjection of all. The conversion of his "enemies into his footstool" is the sign that they who have overcome, are sitting on his "throne," even as He overcame and is seated with his Father on his throne.

This expectation draws with it an infinite complacency. He who "hateth nothing that he hath made,"* seeks the greatest measure of good. He, in this special act of punishment, pursues the plan which shall secure good the most enlarged and pure. He is swayed by no jealousy of authority, by no eagerness of revenge. Our wishes often give rise to our hopes, our hopes to our expectations. That order of feelings, which we denominate personal, has a blinding influence, and we are sometimes aware of their contrariety to our duty, as well as the general interest. But in "Jesus Christ the righteous," whatever is kindly and beneficent is wise, and holy, and equitable; an eternal reason directs it; an infinite excellence impresses it; an almighty power enforces it; it is His prosecution of created happiness by the only legitimate means, and according to the only admissible principles. Well, then, may He rejoice that his enemies shall become his footstool. So long as they have any license of power, they have a capacity of mischief. Confusion and misery are their delight. To defeat the end of all moral being is their settled purpose. They wield but instruments of destruction. They revel in ruin. They exult in every species of falsehood, misrule, and wrong. And when he is rapt into this vision, he cannot fail to "desire it with desire." Then shall he tread out the last train of dis-

* Ash-Wednesday Collect of the English Church.

order, stifle the last atom of evil, extinguish the last coal of strife, disable the last weapon of cruelty, and purge the universe of those hostile elements which have so long jarred and shattered it. Then He redeems the pledge of his nativity, then he has fulfilled the purport of his mission, then he has realized the fruit of his death, and the songs of angels rise to celebrate the consummation of the plan whose earliest dawn they hailed; and no fuller strain do they need for the close than they swelled over the commencement, " Glory to God in the highest, and on earth peace, good-will toward men!"

The *influence* of this expectation must be powerful. It cannot be cherished without attracting to it the sympathies of the intelligent and moral creation. It draws every thing after it. The universe rolls in its direction. It gives the law and bias to whatever exists. As all things were created by Jesus Christ, so were they *for him*. He has constituted the vast machine, he still impels each spring and controls each movement, while the grand result is educed from that real, though unapparent, unity which combines all its parts, and harmonizes all its operations. And it is a solemn thought, that a dread anxiety pervades all the evil and the good. Demons "know their time is short," and would not be " tormented before the time!" They turn their malignant eye to Him who is "henceforth expecting till his enemies be made his footstool;" they shrink before his brow of might and confidence; they read, in awful characters imprinted on it, their certain perdition; and all their hopes wither in the conviction that his assurance, thus expressed and vindicated, cannot be disappointed. The " souls under the altar " become importunate, their blood utters its voice to mingle with their prayer, and they exclaim, " How long, O Lord, holy and true!" Expostulation ascends from earth, and " the elect cry

day and night" unto God. Even this vehement longing descends still lower, and "the earnest expectation of the creature waiteth for the manifestation of the sons of God." The very frame of nature is seized with this emotion, and "the whole creation groaneth and travaileth in pain together until now." The "vanity," which yet debases the creature, shall be speedily removed and his use be vindicated; the teeming birth of the material system shall make it forget its pain; "the floods" shall "clap their hands," and "the hills be joyful together before the Lord, for he cometh to judge the earth."

And thus, dear Christians, if we ourselves conceive this expectation, if we yield up our hearts to it, with what a kindred of all that is holy and lovely are we united, with what a general impulse are we urged forward, what a cloud of witnesses is present to our eye, what a unison of voices bursts upon our ear! Into what a fellowship have we entered! What a sympathy do we share! We lean upon the bosom of Jesus until our heart catches the glow, and returns the throb, of his!

It remains for us to contemplate this expectation In the Certainty of its Realization.

He is not described by the text as active to seize it. In many points of view his part is fulfilled. His task is accomplished. Other agency is now chiefly to be employed. Whatever devolves upon him must be consistent with a state of reward and rest. And the language denotes that there is a train of arrangements, a system of causes, which will infallibly terminate in this result. He therefore awaits it now as sure, and soon as real. "For so the Lord said unto me, I will take my rest, and I will consider in my dwelling place like a clear heat upon herbs, and like a cloud of dew in the heat of harvest;" his repose and meditation are like the purest sunshine and the softest vapor.

Argumentation is vain when the certainties are so absolute; but the following reasons may be assigned:

Explicit engagement. The manner in which the Son obeyed the will of the Father—the proof that he was always "about it," that it was "his meat to do it"—must reflect the necessary converse, that whatever the Father promised, shall be completely ratified and deserved. These pledges illustrate the "purpose purposed in Christ." It involves official subserviency and personal condescension; it insures official recompense and personal exaltation. As by office, and as in person, he was made lower than his Co-equal in the Godhead, so now that office challenges a distinctive homage, and so that person emits a peculiar glory, with this reference, "The Lord said unto my Lord, Sit thou at my right hand, until I make thine enemies thy footstool." Jesus the Lord cited this passage in the days of his flesh, and with it confounded the enemies of his divinity. "If, then, David called *him Lord,* how is *he* his *Son?*" He did not explain, but they felt the rebuke; and ere the Scripture was closed he "sent and testified in the Churches, I am the *Root* and *Offspring* of David!" This declaration of truth must therefore be fulfilled. And what can be more beautiful than the confidence which the Saviour always evinces when surrounded by the circumstances of his deepest depression: "I have set the Lord always before me:" "Thou wilt not suffer thine Holy One to see corruption:" "I knew that thou hearest me alway:" "This voice came not because of me, but for your sakes."

Mediatorial government necessitates this final act.

"He is the head over all things." "At the name of Jesus every knee" shall "bow, of things in heaven, and things in earth, and things under the earth." "In all things" he must "have the pre-eminence." He must deliver its subjects, sustain its principles, and confirm its

ends. But all is subject to misinterpretation, and exposed to confusion, if its enemies are left to their way unpunished, and their onsets are borne unrepelled. As that government or kingdom is to be " delivered up to God even the Father," it must be resigned in its perfect state. It must be cleared of every imputation, and lifted above every charge. This, therefore, cannot be while the powers of evil are " going about seeking whom they may devour." Having gone forth to war, he cannot return without making his enemies captive. He re-appears with no empty pageant, he advances with no barren triumph; he drags at his chariot-wheel the dire and ruthless adversaries of holiness and peace. "He puts down all rule, and all authority and power." And when he has at last reduced them to " his footstool " then will he lay aside the badges of his specific royalty, will dissolve the particular modification of universal government over which he now presides, will merge all distinctions into an economy which shall eternally exist without recurrence of evil or appearance of foe—though his Person will forever be the object of unreserved worship, and the medium of divine manifestation.

Conscious right secures this realization. Men may mistake their claims, but the Saviour perfectly weighs his own. He deserves not an enemy. His is " a right scepter." He knows that the subjugation of every enemy is just. Even he indignantly regards them. His " fury, it upholds him." He " will heap mischiefs upon them," and spend his " arrows upon them." He " will not pity, nor spare, nor have mercy, but destroy them." His patience, his meekness, his commiseration, can no longer endure that the benevolent purpose of his heart should be resisted; and he "pours out his indignation" upon the enemies who have refused to be comprehended in it themselves, and have sought to oppose its extension to others. " The Son " is " angry ! " It is " the wrath of the

Lamb!" What a necessity must there consequently arise for this retribution; and how unblenching the resolve must be to "ease" him of his "adversaries," and "avenge" him of his "enemies," which can be formed in such a gracious heart, and be mused with such a calm complacency.

Nothing, then, can convict us of unreasonableness when we indulge this expectation. Does omniscience forecast, and infallibility certify, it? What, then, if scorn be our lot? What if, when we surrender ourselves to this hope, we be regarded as visionary? Nothing but that which invalidates its certainty and impeaches its propriety can deny our right, and annul our duty, to share in it. If for us it is idle, and for us it is vindictive, then need not Jesus await, then should not Jesus foster, it. We only catch the glow of his bosom, we only follow the direction of his eye. Nor can we fail to perceive that in this emulation, whatever would be otherwise extravagant is redeemed. We know that our "Redeemer liveth, and that he shall stand at the latter day on the earth." "Behold, he cometh with clouds, and every eye shall see him." The infatuation is with them who boast that they can descry a different result. Their "expectation shall perish." He "frustrateth the tokens" of these "liars," and maketh these "diviners mad." "Their everlasting confusion shall never be forgotten." But how rational will seem their part, how appropriate their temper, who "against hope believed in hope," who "waited for the Son of God from heaven," who "looked for, and hasted unto, the coming of the day of God!" They have a warrant which nothing can weaken, and a confidence which nothing can shake. "They that wait for him shall not be ashamed." And they bind this hope to them without acrimony or malevolence. They desire the era of peace. They would keep the festival of love. Rancor fills not their breast.

Resentment envenoms not their tongue. The very overthrow they seek is but the necessary sacrifice for the triumph of happiness and the ascendency of good. And the Avenger will let these enemies "fall by their own counsels;" he will "cast them out in the multitude of their transgressions;" for they have rebelled against him.

It must therefore follow, that we should imitate the Saviour in the manner of contemplating this future victory. He expects it. With the impression of his wounds still inhering in his flesh, he "with patience waits for it." Little have we done to promote it, little do our spirits conform to it, yet we are displeased with the delay. We would give each event a straighter impulse, we would desire for time a swifter wing. It is an affected feeling, and oft a sorry plea. Our task is prescribed. On us the honor is devolved of taking a part toward the accomplishment of the expectation. As soon might the clay remonstrate with the independence of the potter, as soon the "ax boast itself against him that heweth therewith," as we complain of our allotted labor and deferred hope. The "worm Jacob," blind as feeble, must not arraign the Father's power over the times and seasons, nor count "the Lord slack concerning his promise." "The zeal of the Lord of hosts will perform this." Actively let us serve, meekly let us wait; ready to strive, resigned to suffer; and "go our way till the end be; for we shall rest and stand in our lot at the end of the days."

It is important, too, that we expect the same issue which, at this moment, the ascended Son of God anticipates. Let us take heed that we suspend it on no favorite hypothesis. Let us not flush the horizon with the colors of our vain imagination. Let us not seek a *sectarian* triumph. Let us be prepared to exult in it, whatever it may be, knowing that wherever it contradicts us,

it only opposes so much ignorance, prejudice, and sin: it can reverse no real interest, it can crush no worthy hope. The altar of victory shall be dedicated to truth and righteousness; and bigotry and partisanship, instead of being priest or god, shall bleed as one of its earliest offerings.

Ah, the happiness of yielding ourselves to our Sovereign Redeemer! "He has bought us with a price." No longer are we Satan's slaves, but the "Lord's freemen." No longer do we fight against God, but "the haters of the Lord" have "submitted themselves unto him." What a fellowship have we entered! Being "joined to the Lord" we are "one spirit!" His plan, his cause, his expectation, are our own. "We are laborers together with" him. We are committed to his success, and are warmed with his benevolence. We "flow together to the goodness of the Lord." We follow an infinite movement, an almighty sway. We are made "willing in the day of" his "power." And are any of you disposed to resist? Are you hardened to disobey? Cast, cast yourselves at his feet; cast yourselves where otherwise you must lie; embrace those feet while you bow before them, that you be not trodden beneath them; wash them with your tears that they may not at last spurn you, and make you their footstool! He shall not want the allegiance which proves the beneficence, nor the overthrow which vindicates the supremacy of his rule! "Through the greatness of thy power shall thine enemies submit themselves unto thee!"

If you "will walk contrary" to him, He will "walk contrary unto you!"

IX.

THE HEAVENLY COUNTRY.

———•———

BUT NOW THEY DESIRE A BETTER COUNTRY, THAT IS, A HEAVENLY: WHEREFORE GOD IS NOT ASHAMED TO BE CALLED THEIR GOD. FOR HE HATH PREPARED FOR THEM A CITY.—Hebrews xi, 16.

THE emigrant who, in any degree, feels the native tie, and cherishes the patriot throb—who, to any extent, loves the birthplace of his friends, and the burying-place of his fathers—cannot uproot himself from his proper soil without painful efforts and bitter struggles. You need not ascribe to him any excess of sentiment, any poetry of character, aught of romance, an approach to refinement: allow him his proportion of our common nature, and the pang of the separation which tears him from his country's attachments, and banishes him from his country's scenes, will well nigh divide his heart. Wild and haggard may be the region where first he drew his breath; a region of iron boundary, cheerless frost, and immitigable sterility. But what skies can reflect so much beauty? What landscapes can picture such sweet content? All, however bleak and desolate, has an attraction for his taste. The loud tempest is his refreshment, the hoarse torrent his music, the dark forest his shade, the ocean-breaker his sport. Forced to leave it, that land becomes more than ever endeared. He hurries forth from it, and fears to look on it again while he heaves his farewell sigh, and

to pause, and all but make him desire to recede. The absence of all that can familiarize is a check to his ardor. He knows, and has tried, this scene; he must now migrate to a country strange, and in which he is inexperienced. He must forget the change of day and night, summer and winter: he must abandon animal instinct and social institution: he must lay aside the store of bodily and mental labor: he must close his eye on that smiling group which shared his morning embrace, and his evening blessing. "It is certain," that of all that he has acquired, and of all that may cling to him " he can carry nothing out." And then, too, the only avenue to this land for which he departs is through the appalling transformation of death. It is so " appointed," nor is there chariot to help us in its evasion. If we " are alive and remain " to hear the trumpet which shall wake around us all the dead, " the last trump " shall signalize a " change " on us, not less humbling and severe. It is only natural to fear death, and Christian faith does not destroy that nature, but introduces considerations stronger and more absorbing than its fear. Death is, in itself, a fatal loss, and vast must be the indemnity to make it gain. Death itself is a terrible evil, and immense must be the counteraction to turn it into good. Nor is this all. Who people that unseen country? Not creatures of flesh and blood, not the earthly forms of our interest and love, but a spectral race. Spirits there have their element and home. And have we not shrunk at the recital, however supposititious, of their visitation to earth? Have we not shuddered, when even in the paroxysm of grief we have besought the remembrance and apostrophized the manes of departed friends, lest we should be answered by their spirit-voice, and folded in their shadowy bosom? And it is often a thought of intense anxiety to the saint, that, a spirit himself, his converse shall soon be confined to

spirits. And it is not an Enoch and an Elijah who, by their human array, can quench the ghastly apprehension: it is the glorified humanity of Jesus, the " last Adam," who "is made a quickening spirit."

What, then, can relieve the deep solicitudes of him who stands on the verge of life, and puts forth his foot for this mysterious journey! What can cause him to feel each footfall along that path, safe and pleasant? What can give him assured peace, as he steps across the confines of that solemn land, and as at that moment he becomes a spiritual citizen of a spiritual world?

It is delightful for us to know that the comparisons we have hitherto employed, and which we think perfectly just in our use of them, if man had no stricter information than his reason supplies, are greatly mitigated and really destroyed by the present condition of the Christian pilgrim drawing near to heaven! For heaven is not to him a state of view and emotion wholly new, though he has not explored its scene. Let the traveler, however remote his stray, find something congenial to his own latitude and country, and the sense of alienation is redeemed. Should he unexpectedly discover the daisy of his native fields, or catch the wood-note that had caroled from his native groves—should he hear his mother-tongue—should he enjoy the right and protection of some institution at which his youthful heart had learned to bound—though the earth's diameter struck through between his sojourn and his own dear land, even that sojourn would only be less to him than home. And the Christian has now much akin to heaven. His heart is there. Eternal life abides in him. Now he possesses the principles which heaven but matures, and cherishes the affections which it but expands. Hence the connection between the present and the future. Here must be the heir, if yonder be his inheritance. Here must be the laborer, if yonder be his rest. Here must be

the candidate, if yonder be his reward. As he now adds excellence to excellence—as he is not "barren nor unfruitful"—"so shall an entrance be ministered unto him abundantly into the everlasting kingdom of our Lord and Saviour Jesus Christ." Thus he comes "to the city of the living God, the heavenly Jerusalem, and to the spirits of just men made perfect," though still himself in the body, and subject to all the requirements of this mortal life. It is the same song which he sings in the "house of his pilgrimage" and in his "Father's house:" a fainter, and sometimes a broken strain while toiling on the road, swelling to its most ecstatic compass when he reaches the threshold of endless security and joy. O! fair, and bright, and inconceivable as is the celestial, it shall overpower no true principle, it shall reverse no just feeling: nor can it burst strangely upon them who have rejoiced "with joy unspeakable and full of glory." And again does the comparison fail. Have we supposed a home and then an exile? and the anguish of abandoning the one and going into the other? These parallels must be transposed. This is the Christian's exile—there is his home! He is born from above. He is of God. Whatever his present lot, whatever his share of this world's good, his "portion is not in this life," he has "in heaven a better and more enduring substance." Welcome to him shall be the mission of that angel who comes to take him hence. It will be the captive's return! Then will the exile hasten to be loosed! He shall be seen going up to his fatherland. He leaves strangers for kindred. He forsakes bondage for liberty, poverty for wealth, pain for pleasure, combat for triumph, turmoil for rest, sin for holiness, death for immortality. Nor can he know one gloomy disappointment. No casualty has injured, no death has invaded, the scene. Breathless has often been the suspense, agonizing the conviction, of the traveler when

he has sought a parent's or a brother's house. The last request of the expiring patriot is, that he may be laid in his country's mold. Nor is there a faster bond than that which unites the freeborn to the place of his fathers' sepulchers. But the Christian "wayfaring man" need indulge no such foreboding. He may repair from his captivity to his country, and no urn shall fix his mournful gaze, and no grave sadly invite him to go and weep there. Infirmity is only an idea necessary in remembering what was, and death is a recollection but incidental to "the former things which are passed away."

And we are now carried back to a distant date of time. The interesting record, contained in the text, of patriarchal simplicity and intentness, exhibits the concordance of true religion under every dispensation. And shame may well scorch our cheek, and cast down our spirit, if we, with our clearer illuminations and nobler privileges, should still hold to a world which, without reluctance, they resigned; nor pant for a "better country," because a "heavenly" one, after which they so greatly and constantly pursued, now that it does not arise, as it did to them, enveloped in haze, and shrouded in figure, but spreads itself out with a definiteness of outline, and basks glowingly beneath splendors which those "new heavens" alone can shed on that "new earth," in both of which "dwelleth righteousness."

I. WE PROPOSE TO EXAMINE THE ARGUMENT OF THE TEXT, SO FAR AS IT JUSTIFIES THAT SPIRITUAL AND HEAVENLY PERCEPTION WHICH THESE PERSONS EXHIBITED.

"But now they desire"—that is, it is plainly indicated by their entire conduct—"a better country, that is, a heavenly." The eldest born of the Church—the fathers of that holy line which yet extends, and shall always be succeeded by a holy progeny until the perfection of its number and glory—were in a particular state, and under

a " carnal dispensation," which might have been expected to induce, if not suffered to excuse, a secularity of mind. But instead of yielding themselves to what was low and groveling in hope, whenever they received a mixed promise they separated what was spiritual from what was temporary; and far from terminating their desires upon the earthly, always rose to the standard of the heavenly. They were not disposed to overlook the settlement of their posterity, and to neglect the fortunes of the nation which should descend from them; but they knew " the things which differ," and esteemed " the glory of the terrestrial " to be one, and " the glory of the celestial" to be "another." They were thankful for that land which their seed should occupy; but it was not Siloam's stream, nor Ephron's palm which filled their hearts with their " chief joy; " another river made them glad, and another tree gave them its " fruit for meat," and " its " leaf for medicine." Abraham was called from Chaldea to be the father and prototype of the faithful in every age. No event is more singular and comprehensive. The most important transactions proceed from it. "From thence is the Shepherd, the Stone of Israel." His two immediate successors participate in his honor, and the triune Jehovah pledges himself to this saintly triad. This is His name forever; and his memorial unto all generations. There may be a mystery of the Persons in the oath—the faithful Creator, the Man-victim, the Spirit of supplication. Not, however, to press this idea, let us remark the conduct of this great ancestor. He " obeyed." He believed that the distant country which he was commanded to visit should be for " his inheritance." Unheard of by him, even to its very name, " he went out, not knowing whither he went." Having reached it, "he sojourned in the land of promise as in a strange country." He dwelt "in tents"—more durable habitations being denied him—" with Isaac and Jacob, the heirs of

the same promise." Though God had sworn by himself, though the symbols of his majesty had moved between the disparted members of the sacrifice, yet only is the reversion of Canaan granted to his "friend." And the stranger learns that centuries must elapse before his descendants shall take possession of it. Did he repine? Did he, upon a more delayed fulfillment than had been surmised, "stagger through unbelief?" A better construction occurred to his mind. The land had been promised to him. But literally it could only belong to the people who shall spring from him. Was it in no sense *his?* Was there no *personal* blessing, when, for his protection and that of his patriarchal children, though "few in number, yea, very few, and strangers in it, God reproved kings for their sakes, saying, Touch not mine anointed, and do my prophets no harm?" He, in common with them, felt no disappointment. The less was distantly future; the greater was near and real. The noble and fertile territory which they should never till and rule, and in which their ashes should only claim a tomb, led them at once to a richer interpretation of the promise. As they looked forth upon it from point to point, from mountain to mountain, as it smiled in its beauty and swelled in its grandeur—as the breeze bore its treasured sweets, and harped its wild symphonies— this was the suggestion of their minds, that a land whose every breath was fragrance, and every wellspring music, was never intended to bound their views and sate their cravings, but was furnished to be the type of spiritual existence. "He looked for a city which hath foundations, whose builder and maker is God." And they "plainly declared that they sought a country"—surely not that which they had quitted— surely not that which their children could not enjoy for ages—then it was not terrene; and if a "better" it must be "heavenly."

How false and debasing, we may cursorily observe, is the theory which restricts the knowledge, and even religion, of the ancient saints to a providential government, rather than allowing it a reference to invisible sanctions. Such a government did obtain, but it respected its own evidence; while the piety of its subjects entirely depended upon a belief of eternal rewards. Without this, the piety which regarded arrangements simply confined to this life, though they were most immediately divine, would be nothing more than a balance of practical convenience, an adjustment of earthly good. With what force and satisfaction of conviction does this inspired comment on patriarchal history make its appeal to us! and with what absolute authority does it exonerate the heaven-commissioned claimants on that promised land from the cupidity of spoil, and the ambition of conquest! *

It tends also, when we dwell upon these annals of ancient spiritual-mindedness, to vindicate the clearness as well as depth of piety, which were proportioned to the revelation then known. Certainly these founders of Israel were hardly, if at all, eclipsed by any of their descendants. They saw the visions of the Almighty. With infrequent exceptions, a retrograde seems to have taken place after they had gathered up their feet. And though a single star may have risen here and there of brighter ray in that hemisphere, such a resplendent constellation was never equaled amid all its hosts. Happy would it have been for the Jewish Church if the "kindness" of its "youth," and "the love" of its "espousals,"

* In these animadversions the great features of Warburton's hypothesis are noticed. The author would desire all to read the "Divine Legation," as he knows not a writer in greater favor with himself, nor one from whose *episodes* he has derived more instruction. Dean Graves, on the Pentateuch, should be consulted at the same time for a corrective.

had been perpetuated through the progress of its age, and by the constancy of its fidelity.

But it was upon no constructive reasoning of their own that they superinduced their hope. Faith must have a testimony, and expectation a ground. The warrant is thus stated: "God is not ashamed to be called their God." He had entered into covenant with them. He attested that relation with particular seals, and founded it upon particular promises. And our inquiry must be into the connection between such a compact, and the reasonableness of their hope, that there was a "better country;" in other words, to justify from the tenor of the one, the fitness of the other.

Now so great a stipulation, so solemn a pledge, as Jehovah swore to these patriarchs, could only be interpreted into a spiritual boon. A grant of soil, a promise of posterity, would not have required nor admitted this majesty of formula, and seriousness of protestation. He only becomes our God in a manner worthy of his moral grandeur, and our religious capability. And we have the exposition of its meaning from the lips of Jesus Christ himself. "Have ye not read," said he to his captious assailants, "that which was spoken unto you by God, I am the God of Abraham, the God of Isaac, and the God of Jacob? God is not the God of the dead, but of the living." Be it remembered that this was spoken originally "touching the resurrection of the dead." But intermediately there was a subsisting life. God can stand in no relation of covenant to the dead, for the spirit's self always lives, and its life is the earnest of the body's renovation. This, then, is the argument: He was their God: he would remain their God when their dust mingled with the clods of the country which they should never possess: but he is God of the living only: therefore they should live as long as it continued true that he was their God: their conscious

spirits must consequently wing their flight to a separate state, where spirits find their home: and if the spirit was made happy in the inheritance of "a heavenly country," the corresponding frame could not be forgotten by Him who had bound himself to the safety and good of the whole man.

And well they reasoned from the letter to the spirit of the covenant: justly they concluded that He who engaged himself, on the very honor of his perfections, and on the very security of his resources, to be their God, had reserved better things for them. The Lord was the portion of their souls; therefore did they trust in him. Their eye grew indifferent to the "glory of all lands;" for they were rapt in contemplations of a celestial scene over which their covenant God, having invited and entitled them to it by the most explicit ratifications, would array all his "beauty," and diffuse all his "goodness."

Nor let us deem that covenant dissolved. We claim it still, while it unfolds far clearer signs and ampler promises—"He is our God," and "we are his people." It rests upon an undying priesthood and suretyship. It has characterized all dispensations, and shall survive all. However they may be "shaken," this is of "the things which cannot be shaken," but must remain. And therefore is there often seen in the statements of the New Testament, and the predictions of the Old, almost an appearance of anxiety that the covenant with the patriarchs should be remembered by us in its original terms. We are called on to pass under its bond, and to renew it for ourselves. "We are blessed with faithful Abraham." "We, as Isaac was, are the children of promise." We call ourselves "by the name of Jacob," and surname ourselves "by the name of Israel." "He hath commanded his covenant for ever!"

II. It is now proper that we should attend to THAT PARTICULAR OBJECT OF DESIRE WHICH THESE PATRI-

ARCHS BELIEVED TO EXIST IN CONSEQUENCE OF SUCH
DIVINE RELATIONSHIP.

Abraham had been apprized that his descendants
should be in servitude and oppression during four hundred years. He was only a stranger in the land, and
never had a greater possession in it than that of a burying-place. Even this he acquired not under the guaranty of promise, but according to the valuation of its
owner, and by purchase in "the current money of the
merchant." His son and grandson knew this, and therefore entertained no hope of calling the land in which
they sojourned, at any period of their lives, their own.
They desired it not: but "a better country."

But a "better country" than this, earth did not contain. It was "a delightsome," and "a pleasant land;"
"a goodly heritage of the hosts of nations." It was
variegated and intersected with all the elements of sublimity and beauty, with whatever was bold and gentle.
It was prolific without a miracle, and the subject of a
periodical one. It was a wealthy place. Aromatic herbs
covered its hills, and the fairest flowers decked its glens.
The rose was in Sharon, and the lily in the valleys. The
voice of the turtle was heard in the land. There roamed
the vine, and there clustered the date, and there hung
the pomegranate. The cedar towered on the mountains,
and the myrtle skirted their sides. No human hand
could raise the clusters of Eshcol. The south wind passing over the gardens, caused the spices thereof to flow
out. The seasons revolved in their variety, but with a
blended sweetness. There was the upland breeze, in
which the fir could wave its arms, and the softer air in
which the olive unfolded its blossoms. The sun smote
not by day, nor the moon by night. The birds sang
among the branches. The dew lay thick on Hermon.
There was balm in Gilead. The lign-aloe drooped from
the river bank. Kedron and Jordan poured forth their

streams. The rain also filled the pools. Lakes glistened in the landscape, and cooled the drought. Beautiful, for situation, was Mount Sion. The cattle browsed on a thousand hills. The excellency of Carmel, and the glory of Lebanon, set their pinnacles against the deep azure of Canaan's sky. The year was crowned with goodness. The Lord God cared for that land, and his eyes were always upon it. At the stated periods fell the early and the latter rain. The pastures were clothed with flocks. The plowman overtook the reaper, and the treader of grapes him that sowed seed. The barns were filled with plenty, and the presses burst out with new wine. The little hills rejoiced on every side. Precious fruits were brought forth by the sun, and precious things were put forth by the moon. The earliest pass, the valley of Achor, was a door of hope. The vineyards distilled the pure blood of the grape. The fountain of Jacob was upon a land of corn and wine. The inhabitants were filled with the finest of the wheat. It flowed with milk and honey. Its heavens dropped fatness. It was surrounded with munitions of rock. The deep, couching beneath, spread its sure defense. The land might be called Beulah. The distant glimpse of its prospect refreshed the dying eye of Moses; and of all thine earthly territory, it is emphatically thy land, O Immanuel!

When, therefore, the comparison is employed respecting this country, we may be sure that its superiority is not one of earthly climate—a more salubrious atmosphere, a more exuberant soil—for a better country than Palestine the horizon did not gird, the sky did not pavilion; the comparison must be justified by adducing qualities which belong to no sublunary scene, and no earthly condition. And it is " better" as it is,

    1. *The antitype of that land.*

You can easily understand that an emblem should be

inferior to the reality.   It would be unfitting were the first to exceed the second.   Such a transposition would be unnatural.   The herald does not equal the personage of his announcement.   The index cannot compare with the object of its direction.   And in like manner there may be a type of the celestial world.   A country of confined space may intimate its extent; a stability of definite duration may figure its permanency.   This is all that material symbols can denote of pure spiritualism; this is all that human conceptions can comprehend of eternal existence.   We cannot have " the very image of the things; " we must be content with the truest representations of which either they admit, or which our mediums can receive.   And that the country which the patriarchs visited, just tarrying to pitch a tent or buy a tomb, was such an earnest of heaven, is demonstrative from the text.   If they " desired a better," there were some points of parity, and some suggestions of relation, between it and that.   When, leaning upon the top of their staff, they took their survey and made their resignation of the one, it was because the one stood in the order of picture and pledge to the other.   It was therefore only reasonable that, when they learned that this land, " the joy of the whole earth," was the specimen and surety of another, it must be a " better,"—else why this furniture of illustration for that which had no transcending claim?   These wandering saints were reminded and reassured of a glorious reversion by the fruitfulness and beauty of the realms through which they passed; but they wished not to linger there for the moment which detained them from an entrance into that fairer and more resplendent scene, of which it was the imperfect sign and inconsiderable installment.   With no indiferent eye did they look forth on that enchanting prospect —with no spurning footstep did they disdain that votive ground—with no listless ear did they drink in " the

melodies of woods, and winds, and waters." * But these were only the ministrations of external sense to their piercing faith, and " served unto the example and shadow of heavenly things." And if this was the antitype toward which the pilgrim hastened, and for which the patriarch sighed, it must be " better " than the terrestrial land, since it was

2. *The spiritual perfection of its sensible immunities.*

It will be perceived that nothing can be more foreign from our design than to disparage the country which God promised to the fathers. It would be treason to the rhetoric, as well as strength, of the argument. That country can scarcely be delineated with too fascinating and imposing hues. It had the spontaneousness and verdure of a paradise. But it was " of the earth, earthy." Its mercies and privileges belonged to the present state; but if " better " can be found, it must be by the conversion of what is external into blessings which are native to the soul, and enduring as eternity.

Did that country descend by *inheritance?* " They got not the land in possession by their own sword, neither did their own arm save them; " but the Lord's right hand, and his arm, and the light of his countenance, because he had a favor unto them. Constantly is it called their " own land." Constantly are they said to " inherit the land." They were regarded as its destined proprietors. " The inhabitants of Canaan " melted away; " sorrow " took hold of the " inhabitants of Palestina; " and God brought his people in and planted " them in the mountain " of his inheritance. So the righteous shall " inherit the kingdom prepared for them from the foundation of the world." In Christ " also we have obtained an inheritance." And it is " incorruptible, undefiled, and fadeth not away."

Was that country given by *promise?* The engage-

* Coleridge.

ment into which Jehovah entered with the fathers he never forgot. He heard the cry of his people " out of the iron furnace; " he knew their " walking through this great wilderness: " " he remembered his holy promise, and Abraham his servant; and brought forth his people with joy, and his chosen with gladness." So " this is the promise that He hath promised us, even eternal life." It is " the promise of eternal inheritance; " and they who obtain it, realizing all in one, " inherit the promises."

That country was the abode of *satisfaction.* Its name was associated with plenty. The inhabitants ate that which was good, and delighted in fatness. It was " not as the land of Egypt," where they " sowed the seed," and by the process of irrigation watered it with their " foot, as a garden of herbs; " but it was " a land of hills and vallies," and drank " water of the rain of heaven." The manna, " the rock that followed them," and the other miraculous supplies, were now superseded. And yet, in the idea of physical abundance, there is somewhat cloying. Appetite is soon sated and palled. We disgust what we desired; we loathe what we loved. And it is only in religion we can discover the secret of happiness rising with its means, and the possibility of enjoyment through all its additions. And it is only in heaven that this faculty can fully expand. There, is constant longing; there, exhaustless supply; and there, unabating zest. Impressive is the beauty with which this thought is imaged: " They shall hunger no more, neither thirst any more"—they shall not experience one painful sense of want and craving—" For the Lamb, who is in the midst of the throne, shall feed them, and shall lead them unto living fountains of waters"—the wish, so to speak, never having time to become the uneasy dearth, being swallowed up, at each moment, in the infinite plenitude.

That country was the asylum of *life.* Genial air and

high cultivation procured many sources of health. There were plants of kindliest virtues. But rather do we now allude to the promise of longevity. "That thy days may be long in the land which the Lord thy God giveth thee," sanctions "the first commandment with promise." "Length of days" is a reward frequently proposed to encourage the ancient piety and zeal. These are denominated "the days of heaven" upon the earth. How many were the harms from which they were now protected while sitting under their vine and their fig-tree! How innocently jocund was youth, and how serenly meek was age, "old men and old women" dwelling in "the streets of Jerusalem, and every man with his staff in his hand for very age; and the streets of the city full of boys and girls playing in the streets thereof!" And if "the carcasses of them who believed not fell in the wilderness," and "with long life" they were blessed who entered into the promised land, yet this was not an invariable bestowment nor necessary good. Often was it interrupted, and a "Jesse went for an old man in the days of Saul." It is in heaven that we shall "reign in life." The immortality of the wicked is never called "eternal life:" for it wants the honors, the joys, the ends of life; and though they live, it is as they now are, "they are dead while they live." But the righteous "go into life eternal." And there is no stronger expression that the Saviour can use; and though he speaks of present recompense to his self-denying follower as in the measure of a "hundred fold," with compressed simplicity and dignity he but promises, "and in the world to come, eternal life."

That country was the seat of *rest*. No more did the tribes wander in the desert; no more were they harassed by march after march, still leaving the destined goal; no more were they smitten before their enemies, but "Jerusalem was a quiet habitation," and "Israel

dwelt safely." "As a beast goeth down into the valley," invited after its labor by the cooling shade, "the Spirit of the Lord caused him to rest." And a "promise is left us of entering into rest." There are moments when we should welcome, perchance, a retreat of any kind from mortal bitterness, and even pointing to the grave might say, "There the weary are at rest!" And this is true, if we carry not a thought, if we wing not a hope, beyond its margin. The grave—how still, how tranquil! Its inmates suffer no adversity, foment no strife, harbor no fear. They "know not any thing." "Their thoughts perish." The rich and the poor meet together, the proud and the mean are laid beside each other, captives are as bold as conquerors, slaves are as attended as kings, neither is there advance nor repulse, disdain nor recrimination, the equality of mankind here adduces its proof, and the spirit of leveling here gluts its rage; without a distinction, an annoyance, a passion, they are all at rest. There is the one house appointed for all living; the bed on which all await their sure, their last, and it may be, their only repose. Thither we may escape from the din and bustle of the world; its follies will not pursue us, its excitements will not agitate us, its votaries will not disturb us. There only can we be secured from the inroad of its cares, and be withdrawn from the jar of its discords. Thither we may escape from the passions which consume all earthly peace, the gnawing of envy, the canker of avarice, the sting of remorse, the tumult of vengeance, the fang of despair. The fever which parched our blood shall chill, the fierce throbbings of desire shall subside, and the uproar of contending lusts shall settle and hush into the quiet of our kindred earth. Thither we may escape from each skyey influence, the summer's drought and winter's cold will fall alike unheeded on our dwelling, spring will not mock by its budding, nor autumn sadden us by its decay.

Thither we may escape from the keen inflictions of poverty; we shall all of us have the apparel, tenement, pillow, and service we can want. Thither we may escape from the painful days and wearisome nights appointed to us: our eyes will not be held waking, nor will our sleep depart from us. Thither we may escape from the broken heart which bereavement has smitten; a parent or a child may be let down into the grave where we molder, and yet shall we not weep. Thither we may escape from slander and detraction; their rumor will not taint our peace nor reach our abode. Thither we may escape from insensibility, unkindness, and ingratitude; there can be no colder hearts than those which then perish in our bosoms, to beat and warm no more. It is a moody thing to say, "There is rest!" Can this be all? It is a common lot. To all our race the grave throws open such dreary refuge. Thousands hide themselves in this sanctuary, loaded with most direful guilt, pursued with most execrated memory. And is there no rest to which the spirit of the Christian springs? Is there no quiet reserved for it but the undreaming sleep of the guilty dead? Is this the end of his faith—the cessation of remembrance, the extinction of consciousness, the destruction of thought? Is this the consummation of his hope—reduced to the clay and the clod? Shall not his spirit, when his flesh rests in its bed, walk in its uprightness? Shall he not, when he falls asleep in Jesus, awake in his image? Shall not he who died in the Lord be present with the Lord? O, beyond that dull, that common, that debasing stupor, "there remaineth a rest for the people of God." We will not point to the grave, and welcome, as our rest, the defense from trouble, and release from care, which it affords; we will look to the heavens for the peace of our sabbath, for the security of our refuge, for the endearment of our home! Nor let us imagine, when "we rest

from our labors," that our minds shall become inert: or that we shall cease to be creatures of duty. Obedience must always be the happiest, and only happy, condition of man. But many of our present obligations spring out of our sinful state: we "war with the flesh," we "watch lest we enter into temptation," we "resist the devil"—that he may flee from us. These exercises must be painful. But as in the heavenly country the Lord will give us rest from our enemies round about, there will be no danger demanding vigilance, nor evil taking repulse.

And it is a "better country" than that which these patriarchs now traversed, for it

3. *Completes and perpetuates all the religious advantages and recommendations which they anticipated us forming the true dignity of that land.*

"The excellency of Jacob" did not depend upon simply physical blessings. Its "trees were full of sap;" honey dropped from its rocks; it was overspread with "grass for the cattle, and herb for the service of man;" it was "enriched with the river of God, which is full of water;" "the outgoings" of its "morning and evening" rejoiced; "all the chief spices" perfumed its air, and "a plentiful rain" confirmed this "inheritance when it was weary." Beautiful was Tirzah, and comely was Jerusalem. But "glory dwelt in the land." It was the one which "God had chosen for himself." He, when "he divided to the nations their inheritance," set the bounds of the people "according to the number of the children of Israel." A "glorious high throne" was its sanctuary. What nation was so great, who had God so nigh unto them? What nation was there so great, that had statutes and judgments so righteous? It was the high place of sacrifice to the whole earth. It was the holy precinct in which dwelt the symbols of the divine glory, and in which were solemnized the ministrations of the

divine service. And its characteristic glories were those of purity and worship.

There was a distinctive holiness. The very soil claimed this appropriation ; and when its inhabitants denied this to it, then were " they scattered among the heathen, that the land might enjoy her sabbaths." The people were incorporated into a church, which is repeatedly called " the congregation ;" and our Saviour acknowledged it as a " fold." Paul, too, recognized its members as sons and heirs " under tutors and governors, until the time appointed of the Father." Periods were enumerated to them by a calendar of sacred feasts. When first they entered that country, it was under most solemn impressions. " Israel was holiness unto the Lord, and the first-fruits of his increase." The " dwelling-place " which Jehovah had " desired " for his rest was a " habitation of justice and mountain of holiness." Inspiration expressly calls Canaan " the holy land," (Zech. ii, 12 ;) and it deserved the title better when Immanuel "came unto his own," " came unto his " temple. And, though poetry may have idolized, and chivalry have profaned, the localities of " those holy fields over whose acres walked those blessed feet, which eighteen hundred years ago were nailed, for our advantage, on the bitter cross,"*—still who could tread it as common ground, and sternly dispel the visions which hover around it ? And yet how much of the sanctity which impressed itself on that land is extrinsic and accidental—of the nature of association, and dependent on sentiment? How stiff-necked was the people ! The prophets prophesied falsely ! The offering of the Lord was abhorred ! The ways of Zion mourned ! They spake all manner of blasphemy against the Son of man ! They crucified the Lord of glory ! But the holiness of that country which the patriarchs sought

* Shakspeare.

was not imaginary and mutable: it is sincere, perfect, and abiding. It can never exhibit the spot of deformity, or the wrinkle of decay. The happy people who inhabit it stand "without fault before the throne of God." They can no more come into condemnation, nor be ensnared by sin. Exemption from every kind of evil is their reward. Nothing can enter it "which defileth." The purity is resplendent as the sea of glass, and exhaustless as the river of life. The mind cannot suffer the momentary contamination of vain thought. The heart cannot waver with momentary influence of an irregular desire. Each breath is praise, each feeling love, each act obedience. Nothing shall suggest doubt of others, or demand jealousy over ourselves. The "people are all righteous." That is the holy land!

And the country which formed the patrimony of Israel was devoted to *distinctive worship.* It was occupied by "a kingdom of priests." It was consecrated to "ordinances of divine service." Its gates were praise. It was "a house of prayer for all people." Cloud followed cloud of incense, oblation reeked after oblation of blood. They knew what they worshiped. In His temple did every one speak of His glory. To enable them to take possession of it as the site of that fane in which He should be "glorious in holiness, fearful in praises," the sun stood still on Gibeon, and the moon in the valley of Aijalon. Still often incense was an abomination; vain was the oblation; it was "iniquity, even the solemn meeting;" "their fear" was "taught by precept of men." Where are the true celebrants of *such* worship? of worship without pause and satiety? It is remarkable that while heaven is described by the similitudes of the ancient Jerusalem, it is noted by the apocalyptical seer that "he saw no temple therein, for the Lord God Almighty and the Lamb were the temple of it." It was only fitting that when praise is incessant and eternal,

He who is its object and medium should become its sanctuary too, so that he "inhabits" as well as receives it! "They rest not day and night!" "His servants shall serve him!"

And as Canaan was but the type, the sensible model and imperfect specimen, of all the blessings which are included in "the better country," so is it affirmed, what indeed might be assumed, that it is "*heavenly.*" The original word not inaptly expresses the force of our own. The first is derived from an etymon signifying to excite;* the other from one which expresses height and elevation.† The lofty moves our admiration. And it is frequently used to denote another order of things from any we have known—a state of purer existence and nobler joy. It tells us of that which we cannot learn but on the testimony of Him who is "the Lord from heaven." Our hope is "laid up in heaven." Our inheritance is "reserved in heaven." In heaven is our "better substance." "The house not made with hands" is "eternal in the heavens." We admit that we cannot unfold its import or seize its strength. It is a term which, however positive in itself, rather expresses our ignorance than overcomes it. All we know is what the contrast teaches—"As is the heavenly, such are they also who are heavenly: and as we *have* borne the image of the earthy, we *shall* also bear the image of the heavenly."

And it furnishes a pleasing illustration of the argument couched in the text, that the patriarchs are particularly revealed to us as having entered into heaven, and as holding in it a most distinguished place. If they "gave commandment concerning" their "bones," it was that they might express their confidence in the reality of the more glorious region which the place of their sepulchers adumbrated. The "Israelite indeed" thought of "Abra-

* Ὁρω.   † Heaſian, to heave, to raise.

ham's bosom:" and our Lord assured his hearers that Abraham, Isaac, and Jacob were in the kingdom of God. Thus are they defended on the highest authority; and it is manifested that their hope was no idle dream, but that "the steps of their faith" conducted them surely to the reality of the "better country, that is, a heavenly."

It may be permitted to us to mark "the blessed hope" which we thus obtain of sharing with them that possession, since "without us they could not be made perfect." What a contrast has every departing saint experienced who has gone forth by death from this inferior, to that transcendent, state. They have only been "absent from the body to be present with the Lord." However "wrought for the self-same thing," however meetened "for this inheritance," however foreordained "unto glory," yet the transition from the extreme of weakness and suffering, from the overwhelming abasement and rending struggle of the mortal strife, into the sudden brightness and perfect rapture of the Vision, and this too in "a moment, in the twinkling of an eye;" such a transition it is impossible to describe, for the single step appropriates heaven, and the single moment commences eternity! Gaze on the expiring, the glorified Christian! At one moment seized by death; the next, free from its grasp forever! At one moment filled with the deep consciousness of various depravity; the next, standing unreprovable and unblameable in the sight of God! At one moment racked by pain and wasted by disease; the next, knitted into the vigor of an eternally-renewing youth! At one moment what all must pity; the next, what all must envy! At one moment surrounded with tears and sighs; the next, with smiles and acclamations! At one moment lamented by mortals; the next greeted by angels! At one moment gasping in agony and convulsion; the next, pouring forth the melody of a ceaseless song! At one moment the nerveless emaciated hand just raised by

attendants; the next, waving a palm of victory, and striking a harp of gold! At one moment the parched lip gently touched with moisture; the next, drinking "the rivers of divine pleasures!" At one moment the darkened chamber accommodated to the shutting sense, and concealing the ignominious form of death; the next, the subject of such precaution shining out like a sun in the kingdom of his Father!

Surely, if the children of the captivity forgot not their own land, what sensibilities should our present expatriation, and our future return, awaken! "By the river of Babylon," there they "sat down," yea, they wept, when they "remembered Zion." They "hanged their harps upon the willows in the midst thereof." Their right hand had not "forgotten its skill" to rule the chords, nor had their voices lost the power of inspired song; but rather should it be forgotten, and their hand fall lifeless by their side—rather should their tongue cleave to the roof of their mouth than they forget Jerusalem—than they cease to prefer Jerusalem above their most valued delight. They could not "sing the Lord's song in a strange land." They felt the cruelty of the exaction which "required mirth" from them in their mournful desolation. And "when the Lord turned again the captivity of Zion," they "were like them who dreamed." Then was their mouth filled with laughter, and their tongue with singing. The desert became a "highway" for their trackless but certain course: patriotic instinct led them, and the wayfaring men, though fools, could "not err therein:" age resigned its infirmities, weak hands were strengthened, and feeble knees confirmed: original incapacity was overcome, "the eyes of the blind" were "opened," and the "ears of the deaf" were unstopped, and the "tongue of the dumb" sang: external nature, in its grimmest forms, became propitious, "the solitary place" was "glad for them, the desert"

blossomed abundantly, the " parched ground" became a pool, and " the thirsty land springs of water:" the ferocity of serpents and beasts was subdued, " dragons" left " their habitation," " no lion nor any ravenous beast" crossed their march: whatever were their perils, " the ransomed of the Lord" returned and came " to Zion with songs and everlasting joy upon their heads:" and amid those scenes of holy memory and historic exultation, they obtained "joy and gladness, and sorrow and sighing" fled away!* And should we not evince that this world is uncongenial to us, that it is a region through which we only pass, that we are " strangers and sojourners," that we have put on the gear of pilgrims, that we are hastening homeward, that we have already in sight our native land? "The world will love its own" —have we secured its hate? If we "are not of the world," is the demarkation apparent? Should not the moan of the exile mingle with our song? Should not our strain swell more rapturously as we approach the heavenly strand? Earth is but our road, life but our travel, and eternity but our destination! And still as we advance let the lessening objects of sense be more lightly esteemed by us; and as the heavenly country opens on our view, let us speed forward, let us rejoice thankfully—let its music warble from our tongue, and its glory flash from our brow!

III. Let us remark that plan of ultimate habitation which these patriarchs were to discover and enjoy in the country of their fond desire and earnest research.

We cannot but shudder at infinite immensity. We may be told of a boundless country, and though " a heavenly," only be confounded and dismayed. Our feebleness, which has its " foundation in the dust," needs a more minute and local settlement. The emigrant is dis-

* Isaiah xxxv, chap. passim.

heartened by the vastitude of the country which he enters, uncertain whither to proceed, and where to stop. And after the same manner, a fixed habitation is required by the departed spirit, seeking rest and refuge in eternity. In the thought of that eternity, all its powers, its very self, are lost. It desires, as it strives to conceive of the length and breadth of even the heavenly country, a particular allocation. And when it is separated from the present sphere, an all-directing voice shall speak to it, "Come up hither;" nor shall it wilder a forsaken and homeless thing, but "enter through the gate into the city." Such a residence has every spirit found, "knowing God, or rather, known of him." "He has prepared a city," and the Saviour has endeared it still more by impressing on it characters still more tender: "In my Father's house are many mansions: if it were not so, I would have told you. I go to prepare a place for you." The man who would refine away the materialism of the celestial world has yet to learn the nature of the human mind, must retract all belief in the properties of that Incarnate Person the peculiarity of which consists in its relation to space, distracts the attention with what is inconceivable by being indefinite, and leaves to himself and others an abstraction cold as the moon-beam, and as fickle too.

There *is* a city, "the heavenly Jerusalem!" "God has devised means that his banished ones be not expelled from him." Long since the first pilgrimage commenced. Tribe after tribe has gone forth from the house of bondage. Column has pressed upon column through the wilderness. Millions have still before them the struggle of the outset; millions are toiling onward among the briars and thorns of the way; millions have accomplished the journey, and are singing in the height of Zion. "They go from strength to strength; every one of them in Zion appeareth before God." And when we

examine the reasons why such a figure is employed, why this is called a *city*, two very obvious remarks suggest themselves.

1. Heaven is a *community*. For the civic is a corporate state of society, in which equal rights are enjoyed and equal obligations are imposed. It presumes the strictest agreement and fellowship. The cities of Israel were still more social than ordinary ones can be. They were allotted to kindreds and families. Each citizen could point to his mural inheritance, and dwelt among his own people.

Even now the Christian is one with his brethren that are in the world; he is one with " the whole family in heaven and earth : " he is no more a stranger and foreigner, but a fellow-citizen " with the saints, and of the household of God." And his name is in " the book of life," and his citizenship is in heaven, and he has " the earnest of his inheritance." " The Church of the first-born " wait for their younger brethren, until all shall be " made perfect in one ! "

Excellence of the highest order just shows itself among us to disappear. It is as though the bloom of paradise were on it, and contact with earth would defile it. Whither does it find its way ? What collects the beautiful exhalation? How much holy influence is withdrawn ! How many precious examples set in our horizon ! The sun goes down while it is yet noon ! The jewels are only exhibited while the hand is making them up to set them in the crown which fadeth not away ! Treasure after treasure is detached, pillar upon pillar falls ! " The godly man ceaseth, the faithful fail from among the children of men." And often the preparations seem too elaborate for the race, the munitions of war too mighty for the victory. What education has been received, and scarcely has a lesson been inculcated in return ! What presage has been signalized to perish unredeemed ! But not a fragment has been lost. All is stored up in heaven.

Worth and goodness feel its attraction, and tend to it as their center. They "reach forth unto those things which are before," and "seek those things which are above." They there can find a congenial atmosphere, and acquire a native growth. Deeply are we impoverished by the loss; but death is their gain, and the acquisition of a region which they were designed to adorn, and fitted to enrich. True greatness and virtue are transplanted from our waste into that soil. The fruits of holiness are deposited in that garner. From the first saint who passed thither, until him who shall be the last, that city has kept a "feast of ingathering." Hourly, momentarily, have its inhabitants multiplied. One after another has been joined to them. The pious have found the still more devout, the zealous the still more fervent. They who sowed, and those who reaped, rejoice together. Its gates are not shut at all by day, and there is no night there. From the four winds are accessions constantly rendering it more wealthy and blessed. Can it be a little thing to "walk with the nations of the saved?" Can it be,—to commune with "faithful Abraham," to see "the end of the Lord" in Job, to listen to "the sweet singer of Israel," to hail the "mother of our Lord" and learn from her what she "pondered in her heart," to sympathize with the emotions of "the disciple whom Jesus loved, and to "fall on Paul's neck," not weeping that we "shall see his face no more," but rejoicing that he has now "received us forever?" A thousand avenues open from earth into heaven, "thither the tribes go up" for whom God has prepared this city, and soon that assemblage shall be complete. Then what was taken away shall be restored; and the high, sweet qualities which escaped from this unpropitious clime shall obtain the favor they deserve, and take the station to which they are entitled. Ah, that is "the holy city, New Jerusalem," and the residence of the holy!

And not only is it the ultimate abode and metropolis of all the faithful, the " Zion " which collects and embraces all her " precious sons," but there they exist in the most entire agreement of love. Consentaneous is every thought and temper. With an endless modification of character, and as endless a diversity of reward, no possible interruption can arise to their harmony. The concord is absolute. The bond of perfectness excludes the most distant encroachment, or most subtle insinuation, of envy, suspicion, and distrust. Not only is hate unknown, but every seed is destroyed from which it could spring. The misconstructions of motive, the dissensions of · opinion, the alienations of habit, which sever the righteous here, will be replaced by generous confidence, unerring sentiment, and inseparable union. There no forbearance can be exercised, nor forgiveness exchanged. No wall of partition will divide, no contrariety of disposition repel. Fellowships of mind and sympathy will exist, now foretasted by few, and comprehended by none. There thought will flow into thought, and feeling blend with feeling. The " city is compact together." Peace is " within its walls, and prosperity within its palaces."

2. Heaven is an enduring place. With a city we connect what is massive in foundation and structure. The emporium of government, and the mart of trade, it arises in strength. It seeks to fortify itself against time as well as hostility. Architecture boasts its solid grandeur, and power entrenches itself in its sure defense. The village may be rapidly overthrown or deserted, but the towered state and might of the city look down scornfully upon the threatened attack, nor heed the stream of ages more than the river which skirts its walls, and reflects its pinnacles. Yet where are those things of a vaunted eternity ? Where are the cities of Nimrod, Cecrops, Nebuchadnezzar, and even Augustus ?

Vanished like a mountain-mist, past like a watch in the night. But our city is not built on the sands of earth, the waves of time—it is deep-based in the rock of eternity! " Here have we no continuing city, but we seek one to come." As if to express its durability, we are informed that it has " twelve foundations." The crash of worlds would spend itself without marring a trace of its beauty, or shaking a stone of its building.

Sometimes, indeed, the cities of the earth have survived their living populations. They have stood uninhabited like Thebes, or been scathed as Pompeii into a city of the dead. But it is the ordinary law that " the mourners " should " go about the streets." It is not only from the " gate " of a Nain that " a dead man is carried out." However the piles of earth defy the shock and waste of ages, man " is of few days." His own works deride his little span of life. But the city which God has prepared, is as imperishable in its inhabitants as its materials. Its pearl, its jasper, its pure gold, are only immortal to frame the abode of immortals. No cry of death is in any of its dwellings. No funeral darkens along any of its ways. No sepulcher of the holiest relics gleams among the everlasting hills. Violence is not heard in the land. There is no more death. It is destroyed and obliterated. Its last ensign has disappeared. Its very name has perished. It is " swallowed up in victory."

And high is our dignity, and triumphant should be our joy, if " grace hath been showed from the Lord our God, to give us a nail in his holy place, that our God may lighten our eyes, and give us a little reviving in our bondage." Yonder is our city-home! We carry our muniments in our bosom. In its archives our names are enrolled. We are citizens " of no mean city." As its battlements rest against the sky, what hands

wave from them, what anthems float over them, to quicken our activity, and greet our approach! "We have a strong city: salvation will God appoint for walls and bulwarks!" Certain is our present claim: but it awaits the grandest avowal. And He who is "our forerunner" will ratify the investiture, and write upon us "the name of the city" of our God. Inaugurated on the set thrones of that royal, presenting the censers "filled with odors" of that templar, city—surveying, on the one hand, its wealth, its magnificence, its robes and crowns, its every inhabitant a king—encircled by the holy memorials, on the other, the crystal laver, the golden altar, the ark of the testament, the Lamb of the sacrifice, each worshiper a priest, . . . ah! how may we look down upon the proudest honors and richest treasures of the noblest city which ever oppressed earth with its foundations, or emulated heaven with its summits!

And can we be satisfied with any other portion? Were the kingdoms of the earth, and the glory of them, now shown and proffered to you, must you not "desire a better country?" It is well that we "learn to be content;" a necessary lesson and an arduous attainment. But this world contains not an element of satisfaction. Our soul finds within all its breadth, no peace nor rest. It knoweth us not. We are but journeying through it. Thankful for a path, whether rugged or smooth, we still pursue our way. We would be benefactors as we press forward, and our invitation is to all, "Come with us and we will do" you "good; for the Lord hath spoken good concerning Israel." Could we but make them feel the urgency and grandeur of our enterprise! Could we but induce them to abandon this place devoted to vanity and doom! Shine out, O city of our God! Attract their eyes, captivate their hearts, who now "mind earthly things!"

For you, dear Christians, it only remains that you keep your fixed resolve, and hasten toward the land which God has promised, and the city which he has prepared. Barter not your pilgrim's staff for a monarch's scepter! Put not off your sandals, though potentates would stoop to anoint your feet! Be yourselves, and their wealth will be no bribe, and their power no temptation. Spurn their dalliances! Brave their frowns! Your diadems will blaze forth when kings are bound "with chains and nobles with fetters of iron!"

Strangers here, a stranger conflict will soon demand your faith and patience. The last step of pilgrimage is the most severe. It is still left for you to die. The summons of this mortality resounds, and falls on many a timid ear, chill and startling as that of old, "Go over Jordan." Cold and dark is the wave we must pass. Whether we cross it at the most shallow ford or the most eddying depth, whether at its narrowest or broadest reach, it yet is to be past. But lo! the heavenly country and holy city rise before you! Close they rise upon the other margin! They mirror themselves on the stream! Sometimes, as it is ruffled, the reflected image is broken, but as frequently restores itself; and assures us that the imperfect view should be ascribed to the agitation of the medium, while Reality exists in its unwavering majesty, and even overhangs the waters which waft us thither! Amen.

X.

DEISM NO REFUGE FROM JUDGMENT.

For then how shall God judge the world.—Romans iii, 6.

The abruptness of this inquiry sufficiently proves that the fact, which is the subject of it, is established beyond dispute. It is adduced as an essential and primary truth. Other points might require adjustment and defense; but this is too plain an axiom, too sure an event, to admit of argumentation. It is made a standard of appeal; and in all such cases the appeal must be allowed, on every side, to be valid and unexceptionable. The inspired writer, therefore, intended that there was nothing more obvious than the appointment, more general than the admission, more indispensable than the necessity, of the Final Judgment.

Had occasion existed for discussion, had there been need of reasoning, Paul would have exhibited his capacity to undertake either, or his masterdom of both. Whatever he most cursorily touches, he arrays in light. He seems to dismiss each topic exhausted, until he renews it. He loves the sublimely terrible. If there be one chord more awfully sonorous than another, it is that he strikes. On the introduction, for instance, of this particular theme, he is wont to rise into his loftiest majesty of sentiment and expression. Sometimes, in a tone of clear dispassionate statement, he affirms it to be "a righteous thing with God to recompense tribulation,"

Standing at the bar of Felix, he " reasoned of" it, poured out in its vindication all the strength and opulence of his mind; and though his well-directed proofs are not recorded, they made the royal culprit " tremble." It was an intellectual sway ennobled with a moral triumph. Summoned to account for his opinions before the high court of Areopagus—encircled by the lights and ornaments of Grecian jurisprudence, eloquence, and logic—raised as in mid air, while temple and statue gleamed beautifully around him—he proceeded by a cautious, and apparently incidental, train of remarks, into a powerful series of reasonings; reminds that judicature of another tribunal; by a rapid transition passes from that pending investigation to a more solemn scrutiny; and cites these functionaries, the very impersonations of an awful justice, before a Dreader Judge. Was ever human mind so susceptible of its impression, and capable of its description? His spirit seemed clothed with its pomp, and resonant of its trumpet. He only failed when the thought and language of creatures must necessarily fail. Could mortal power have embraced the realities of that august transaction, his was the imagination to give them a terrific vividness, his was the energy to set them forth with a faithful certitude. But a single turn of interrogation better serves his purpose now. It carries conviction, and compels assent. Tolerating no reply, brooking no suspense—the truth, the justice, of the demand instantaneously, intuitively, flashes upon us! " How, then, shall God judge the world?" is, in other words, to say, that it is a universal impression, an undeniable truth, an inevitable conclusion, that God will, and even must, judge the world!

It is the common device of infidelity to rest the truth of such judgment upon the question of a particular revelation. It attacks the Gospel: now this Gospel presumes the fact at issue: and the attack is supposed, if success-

ful in the first case, to be invincibly so in the last. It is not doubted by these adversaries but that both must fall together. Let but Christianity be disproved, and they hesitate not to affirm that the whole theory of a judgment is subverted. They covert, they hope to make a deadly, thrust. But they sophisticate the matter. They take for granted that this doctrine is a distinctive feature of the Christian system. They hope to find this assumption convenient, and the argument based upon it availing. But assumption cannot be more false, nor argument more bootless. The religion of the Saviour presupposes the judgment, but does not constitute its ground: it explains its nature, but does not give it existence. It imparts to the sinner hope and solace, amid his conjecture of its horror, and his foreboding of its doom. But reject it, repeal it! Still man is not released from duty, nor exempted from retribution. These are elements of a moral condition, which are primordial to all specific dispensation of divine government. These may be discerned among the original characteristics which attach themselves to our nature itself. Rule, surely, precedes mercy —and penalty, forgiveness. The mercy and the forgiveness cannot be the reason of the rule, or the cause of the penalty. If criminals be arraigned, if an amnesty be declared to all who will accept it, how absurd would it be to ascribe to the amnesty the previous arraignment! That, manifestly, is something antecedent and independent: and though clemency had not interposed, still would the law have remained the same, and would still require for its support an administrative and executory power.

So that we are willing to meet the skeptic on his own ground. You need not be a Christian, to be a probationer for " eternal judgment." You do not, on the refusal of any claims purporting to be those of a divine revelation, cease to be accountable, or throw aside the

candidateship for reward and punishment. This arises out of an earlier relation, it is a predicament of moral being. You cannot, however you deal with any revealed pretension, make the last day a pendent to it: you cannot, in any shipwreck of faith, engulf this consequent of the simplest admission of a first Cause: prostrate, as you may, the pillar of inspired truth, and establish the cheat of the inspired pages, you cannot rend down the judgment which shall be set, nor blot out the books which shall be opened. If you destroy all that intervenes between you and that last great day, that day must break. Had our God not come at any time, had he never interrupted the silence of the ages, he will then "come, and not keep silence." This is due to the constitution of things. Whatever else may be controverted and escaped, this is alike infallible and inevitable!

We must attempt, therefore, to place it on grounds unconditional of our "professed subjection to the Gospel of Christ."

I. THE MOST CORRECT IDEAS WE CAN ENTERTAIN OF THE DEITY REQUIRE THAT THERE SHOULD BE A JUDGMENT.

Holy Scripture does not take to itself the honor of discovering that there is a God. It distinctly allows that the evidence of this fact is in the works of his hands. It would not be in the power of any book to furnish it. The first notion, that there is a maker, must be suggested by the things he has made. The rational creature who infers not "the invisible things of God" from the operations of his power, intelligence, and benignity, is "without excuse." These "may be clearly seen." But it may be asked, Is it only "the fool who hath said in his heart, There is no God?" Were not the ancient sages also ignorant? We must answer this to the shame of their base artifice: "When," or although,

"they knew God, they glorified him not as God, neither were thankful." The information which their perceptions could derive from the vast fabric of earth and sky had once sufficed to convince them. That which might "be known of God" was "manifest in them," for God had "showed it unto them." The knowledge was lost when they willfully blinded others, and in some degree became the dupes of their own duplicity. But this was a moral retribution—fitting punishment following voluntary guilt—they "changed the truth of God into a lie . . . they did not like to retain God in their knowledge." Whatever was the corrupting influence of their systems, each individual gazed forth on the same wondrous premises, and might have wrought out for himself the same necessary conclusion.

Strength and skill are the two most early impressions induced by a survey of creation. The greatness of the act is unquestionable. The subservience of that act to all the wants and habitudes of living beings is demonstrative. Such a combination of properties supposes an active benevolence, directing all to purposes of happiness and utility. But the impression of justice is not spontaneously obtained. The course is not so much of observation as reflection. We proceed with a more circumspect examination. We are compelled to admix different ideas, to compare remote phenomena, and having reasoned, to pronounce our deliberations. Still there are reasonings by no means abstruse, founded upon what we see around us and feel within us, which cannot fail to conduct to the assurance that there is "a God who judgeth in the earth."

We cannot regard mankind with any closeness of investigation without finding that sentiments of duty, and principles of conscience, actuate them. Hoodwinked as their apprehensions, debased as their standards, of religion may be, still they have universally exhibited a

religious bias and capacity. "Their thoughts" have accused or excused "one another." They knew "the judgment of God." They "are a law unto themselves." None should be more ready to embrace such statements than the impugners of revelation; and none, when such statements are found convenient, do lay greater weight upon them. For it is from the sufficiency of reason and the moral sense they hope to invalidate the authority, by showing the superfluousness, of any but natural religion. Enough, they tell us, is already taught; the lessons are plain to every eye, and the dictates to every ear! They ask no volume but that of nature, and wish no interpreter but that of man! Creation is their temple, and they worship at the altar of no "unknown God!" Such are our common data—but how are they to be pursued? We differently account for them; but as to their character and existence we have no dispute. Have all nations a fear of disobeying a higher power? Have they a dread of punishment? Resort they to means of expiation? Then this is the collective suffrage of the species. It proclaims that where there is guilt there is justice; that the sinner awaits the execution of a sentence; that there is a universal assent to the doctrine of a judgment —our only present question, since the time, order, and manner cannot affect its equity or reality!

As we can trace a general uniformity in the divine procedure, an analogy between the various acts of the Great Agent of all, so we find that however interrupted, the original plan is speedily restored. The deviation is partial and transient, and the disturbed machinery reverts to its more precise and regular movements. An infinite care is extended toward the physical world. The cloud-rack disparts, and the bright, calm heaven glows above us; the chafed ocean rocks itself to rest. If, therefore, this love of order, and perseverance of arrangement, govern the realms of matter, an equal vigi-

lance will pervade the dominion of mind. But mind is susceptible of certain disorder, and it may present to the allseeing Eye a scene of frenzy and misrule. Should no cognizance be taken of this violation inflicted on the more precious harmonies of spiritual existence? Mechanical power is competent in the one case, for it is unconscious matter on which it operates; but moral nature is the subject of ascertained law and proper disposition—it must not be therefore coerced but regulated. It may persist in this wrong, its will may lead it forward in a succession of guilty conduct, and now what is left even to the Supreme but to punish? What other check but punishment can be supposed? He who controls the objects of sense, cannot be insufficient or indifferent to control, agreeably to its own laws, that mysterious essence which constitutes all the value and all the character of man, whom He has set over the works of his hands! The question is, whether the God who upholds each atom, and enforces each law, of the universe, will suffer the human spirit all its waywardness of folly and crime without restriction—that is, with indulgence and impunity?

We are conscious, whatever may be our present state of vitiation, (a state we do not ask our opponents to allow, but a belief in which we feel perfectly to comport with the ensuing averment,) we are conscious of being differently affected by different kinds of conduct. It will be impossible to portray certain excellence or vice without exciting in the spectator esteem or disgust. The most debased will not be wholly unimpressed. Something of an original taste survives in all, and it is scarcely capable of an entire perversion. Reason, in every distinctive acceptation, must have perished if *it* be extinguished. Unbending integrity, melting charity, meek simplicity, high-souled independence, the rescue of innocence, the resistance of oppression, these awe or charm,

raise our admiration or inspire our love. It is a law almost irrepressible. Bodily distortion and deformity do not more certainly move within us unpleasant feelings, than moral incongruities jar and pain. How is it that these forms of virtue and vice produce such concurrent effects? How may we explain it, that men have at all times united in these sentiments? What poet could ever make vile and cruel passion agreeable; and what painter could ever win, for the figure of infamy, our complacent emotion? The triumph of these masters might be proudly successful—their spell might soften, their composition might relieve—but the themes themselves could only displease. Say, that this is an essential law of mind—say, that it is dictated by a fixed constitution of things—say, that it is an acknowledgment of a proportion and scale as true in morals as a standard of what is straight and crooked is in physics—what is such law, such constitution, such proportion and scale? It must be the divine will—its sympathy or aversion—impressing itself on each mind, and reflecting itself from the general system. You shrink from evil, you are attracted by good, because your Creator has so constituted you to be impressed. But then we cannot evade the inference, that He must mark his displeasure, that He must be consistent with these declarations of his purpose; and that, since He loves good and hates evil infinitely more than we can do, He must call them to account who thwart and disobey these primary perceptions. He cannot impel us in one way, and proceed himself in the contrary!

All the preceding statements presume a rectitude in the Deity. Is his government stretched over mind! Has he made virtue beautiful? Then he respects no man's person, then he elicits the qualities of conduct, he "looketh upon the heart," by him "actions are weighed." He must entertain an essential disposition to execute

righteousness in approving or condemning; and will make it plain to others, to all rational beings, that he is not only invariable in this purpose, but that this purpose is suggested by an equal invariableness of nature.

And surely our adversaries will not refuse us the right to ascribe to the Supreme all known and conceivable excellence. Whence, but from this " eternal Power and Godhead," can the capacity to discriminate excellence be derived? Whence, but from this source, can excellence itself have emanated? But we see it only in distinct, and often broken portions; and not in its perfection of symmetry and fullness. And as virtuous greatness cannot consist without justice, so we must cause this attribute to inhere in every thought and representation of the Deity, the denial of which to a creature leaves him confessedly the bane and disgrace of his kind. And the proof, that if God be infinite in *any* attribute he must be in *all*, is irrefragable; he is therefore just in a degree and to an extent worthy of him who "governs the nations upon the earth."

Indeed, his justice is necessary to his less disputed perfections. Is he wise? then the plan of his wisdom must not be frustrated. Is he powerful? then the temerity which trifles with it, and the hardihood which scoffs at it, must be overthrown. Is he good? then his beneficence must not be turned aside from the objects to which it is directed, nor be converted into a weapon against himself. Justice is but the perseverance of his wisdom, the determination of his power, and the victory of his love. It is the only security of his purpose, protection of his character, and guardianship of his creation.

But more will be granted by the intelligent Deist. He will clothe the God whom he confesses with certain relations. That God is a father: and the poet of nature sang a truth, " We are his offspring." Requires that

family no discipline? Shall no difference be made between the obedient and the disobedient children? That God is a governor: for it is presupposed by the argument that such a law is now, and always has been, extant, as to make a dogmatic revelation unnecessary. Has that law no sanctions? is there no honor, no self-respect, which obliges the lawgiver to enforce them?

The great rudiments of justice are widely and deeply engraven on the present system; and the very exceptions to the universal rule, the very delays of the universal administration, only render the doctrine more credible, the fact more urgent, that there shall be a judgment, in which man will receive "according to the things done in the body." Invest the First of Beings with one moral quality—the boast of this species of skepticism—and not only cannot this event be disproved, but all our reasonings on that one quality render it plausible, and leave it imperative!

II. The dignity of human intellect and capacity enforces it.

Man is endowed with a capability of knowing different things, of distinguishing their properties, and of choosing between their claims. He obeys no impact like the material body, nor follows the instinct of the simple animal: he prefers, he refuses, he outstrips his fellow, he improves on himself. Who can limit his power? What can stop his progress? The elements are his tributaries. He can change their forms, and invent new uses for them. He yokes the winds, and lightning stays for his experiment. And he may be, as yet, only in the infancy of his energies, and but at the threshold of discoveries which no fancy can paint. What realms may open for his invasion, and yield to his sovereignty!

But why was he made? To eat, and drink, and

sleep? To care only for himself? To build houses, and ply his different arts? While the majority evince so feeble an activity of intellect, were they created to aggrandize by contrast, what the few master-spirits have done, and what the mind they represent can always achieve? We cannot but notice the vanity of his common pursuits and their disparity to his character. None can exceed our estimate of his faculties; but the fact is as certain as it is mournful, that they are strangely degraded. And when we look upon "the vain show" in which he acts his part, and "the pride of life," with its gewgaw pageantry and tinsel pomp—when from palaces we descend to the menial drudge, his hapless lot and bitter privation—we demand, is this the nature of which we vaunt? is this the creature whose brow looks up to heaven, and whose spirit mingles with divinity? What does man better than the thousand tribes which fill the air, roam the earth, and cleave the flood? The hue of Paradise may vein the clod; there may lie hidden in the spirit the imperfect sinew, and callow down, of wings which could dispread themselves for an immortal flight. The inquiry relates to what is; and all must admit that human nature is the subject of a lamentable perversion.

And that this idea of perversion may be duly considered, we should remember that we can apply it to none other creature within this visible economy. When we think of the sun, we never suppose that it had a nobler use; the stars keep their orbits and travel their rounds; spring raises nature from the grave of the year; and the ordinances of heaven are established. Still "all is very good;" and if "subject to vanity," it is the folly to which it ministers, and not any taint upon itself. It may be "made to serve with" our iniquities, but itself basks in the smile continually which erst glanced on it. Man only has abused his nature, and

corrupted his way. He is the solitary failure! His powers give magnitude to his guilt and his perniciousness. He has fallen, and dragged down the pillars of earth in his fall.

Of all terrestrial creatures he is the only religious one. The scenes around him, and the feelings within him, allow him no alternative. The Deist confirms this impression, and speaks of a natural religion, suitable for man and common to him. And if man be the only religious creature, he is the only creature who can understand religion. You may, by hope and fear, arouse the brute; you may teach it to interpret your looks and tones; but a producing cause, a code of fitness, a spirituality of retribution, surpass any capacity it has to understand. But why was man thus enabled to appreciate ideas of moral accountability? Is it not a distinction of his being? Must it not denote the will of his Maker? Hence arises the necessity of a judgment. For how great a waste of intellect and moral feeling is included in sin! What a depravation of heart is supposed in voluntary irreligion! What is their guilt who throw off an allegiance which they only can approve! For what have they to answer! And can He, whose purpose these endowments express, suffer all this perversion without inquisition and rebuke? Can He behold himself mocked in his plan, and robbed of his glory, without one frown of his disapprobation? Can skepticism impute to its God a leniency, or rather a supineness, like this? The doctrine of final causes would, under such argument, be an empty theory: design there could be none; law must be repealed; government might break its scepter; for man, constituted religious, susceptible of its influence, and intelligent of its nature, jeers its supposition, spurns its authority, withholds its service; while his God, who required it, and should have received its homage, cares not to notice the neglect, nor to resent the indignity!

III. The partially developed character, and the mixed nature, of the present system, intimate that there shall be a judgment.

It would be difficult for any reasoning creature to conclude that the present was a final state. There is so much of life passed in infancy and demanded for education—the period of the longest is so brief, and that of each so uncertain—toil consumes so large a part, while refreshment from toil one scarcely less—such buddings of genius are prematurely blighted, and mind often retains such freedom and triumph amid the dissolution of the body—that every thing seems to intimate another scene of existence, in which the highest aims and employments of the soul, in its earthly abode, may be resumed. Were this world all—were all our mortal life—how melancholy would be the wreck of its abortive enterprises. Sensuality and gain would best agree with its littleness; and where men attempted better things, we should be summoned to deplore the distorted growth of intellect, the outspread wing of the soul beating against the bars of its cage. And if a reasoning creature would infer that only an incipient character belonged to the present state, the inference would still more readily recur to him who exercised moral reflection. How confused are those arrangements which should distinctively belong to virtue and vice! Does not crime frequently succeed? Is not excellence depressed? Though enough exists to satisfy us that there is a plan and rule of justice, is there not equal proof that this plan and rule are never perfectly enforced? If they were fully carried out, would not the effect be so great that society would generally invert itself? The " prosperity of the wicked " has awakened the most masculine minds to wonder, and the most holy hearts to mourn.

The view which best and alone relieves this strange position of human affairs, is that which impresses a pro-

bationary character on the present state. Our Maker will now "prove what is in" our heart. It is a necessary condition of such a discipline, that wickedness shall be left to itself. Therefore it stalks so giantly, and uprears its towering front. Misery is entailed by its course, and its success is founded upon suffering. Though "the evil bow before the good, and the wicked at the gates of the righteous," they seek their extermination. The meekness, the forbearance, the rectitude of the pious are thus established; there is a constant scrutiny of their pretensions, an ordeal of their excellences. This mixed state must continue, unless there be a constant interposition to repair and adjust it; but then there could be no liberty, no opportunity given for the collision of rival principles, and the reaction of opposite characters. It arises out of moral agency, and is inseparable from moral probation. The consequence is, that "many are purified and tried; but that the wicked do wickedly." There are "the tears of the oppressed, and on the side of their oppressors there is power."

If such a condition of things be found under the dominion of the Just One, whose "eyes behold the things which are equal," it cannot be the *whole* of that system which he administers : if its partial character be intended for the regimen of a probation, then it must point forward to some period and mode of *decision*. But this is the very *judgment* which we affirm, necessary to resolve all temporary perplexities, and to balance all former derangements.

Nor let it be objected to, that the delay is long: it would be as reasonable to complain of the succession of mankind. All are to be treated alike; and the system must endure with the species. It proves not that "the Lord hath forsaken the earth." It warrants not the wicked to "contemn God, or to say in his heart, Thou wilt not require it." "Sentence" may be promulgated

"against an evil work," though it is not "executed speedily." There can be no need of any addition to the acts and resources of His government. There is no implication and ground of suspicion that any thing dubious waits to be explained, any thing feeble to be enforced, any thing vague to be defined. The patience of this government may rather augur its efficiency. It is too majestic to be provoked, too strong to be tempted from its fixed arrangements. Its forbearance reveals its dignity. God ceases not to reign when he refuses to strike. If the objection ever was powerful, it is hourly diminishing. We who are Christians, tell our antagonists that the end is at hand. Judgment lingereth not. The retribution, which has an eternity in which to expand, wants not to precipitate its measures. It will be sufficiently early. None will complain that it was too tardy then. Let not foolish men try to urge it on. Would ye taunt it into haste? Such a God as the opponent allows can suffer this delay without derogation: nor let him turn from us when we declare from the Bible that *our* God "knoweth how to reserve the unjust unto the day of judgment to be punished."

These are facts which the Deist observes—how can he escape, admitting as he does the existence of a Deity, the pressure of the conclusion that he must judge his creatures?

IV. The tendencies of conduct in the present state will greatly increase the probability of a judgment.

Particular consequences are perceived by all to attend particular acts. We are happy or miserable according to the nature of those acts. Exultation in crime is nearly impossible. It is true that men may exult in some success which crime has accomplished, but there are few who would not avoid the crime itself. Theft was necessary to the acquisition, murder to the revenge; but the

means are perhaps subjects of complacency to none. Shame, misgiving, and remorse fill the guilty heart. Something more than the fear of punishment torments— it is the hideous aspect of the deed. "Look on it again, they dare not." Justice, on the other hand, integrity, temperance, kindness, impart to the mind a cheerfulness, a peace, a glow of satisfaction, which no guilty excesses bring. It is the consciousness of being right. But it is more, it is the influence of that consciousness on an order of natural sensibilities as adapted to receive pleasure from it as the eye from light, and the ear from music. It is not the loud plaudit which bids us rejoice: it is the internal welling up of a native spring.*

And we may commonly discern that there is connection between sin and suffering besides that of the self-upbraiding mind. Fraud overreaches, violence recoils on, itself. One false step induces a second, and the entire life stumbles from it. This is the principle of distributive justice—we receive according to our works. The most distant results are held by the attachment of some most unconsidered and early act. "Justice commends the ingredients of our poisoned chalice to our own lips." In the abandonment of an evil course, we cannot promise ourselves a reversal of its former consequences.

* This sentiment is well illustrated by Socrates, in his dialogue with Hippias: "Αγραφους δε τινας οισθα, εφη, νομους; Τους γ᾽ εν παση, εφη, χωρα κατα ταυτα νομιζομενους. Εχοις αν ουν ειπεν, εφη, ὁτι οι ανθρωποι αυτους εθεντο; Και πως αν, εφή, ὁιχε ουτε συνελθειν απαντες δυνεθειεν, ουτε ομοφωνοι εισι; Τινας ουν, εφη, νομιζεις, τεθεικεναι τους νομους τουτους; Εγω μεν, εφη, θεους οιμαι τους νομους τουτους τοις ανθρωποις θειναι." "Knowest thou not that there are certain laws which are unwritten?" He answered, "You allude to those which are every-where in force." "But you do not maintain that all men agreed to constitute them?" "Surely not, for mankind could not meet on one spot, or communicate by one language." "How then were these universal laws founded?" "I cannot but conclude that this was the work of the gods."—XENOPHON, MEMORABILIA. Chap. 4.

The retribution is often explicable from the nature of things, which is only another mode of saying, from the counsel of the divine will operating in so sure a way that it may be constantly anticipated, and made a ground of confident persuasion. But there is also much to show, if not a more direct agency on the part of God, a more immediate interference. Who can shake from him the belief that He has so acted and may so act?

We require not to be reminded that this argument may, at first sight, appear conflicting with our purpose. If even now " virtue is its own reward, and sin educes its own punishment—if this system of moral tendencies be now operative—how can another adjudication be made to seem necessary? You have proved too much." Our answer is of two kinds. The *first* respects the possibility of these consequences being defeated, and these tendencies warped, by particular circumstances. The audacious sinner becomes, by as *certain a law* of sin as that which binds up misery with it, *infatuated* and *hardened.* His " judgment is fled to brutish beasts." The very mercy which makes it a " bitter thing" is survived. He is " past feeling." He ceases to know the proper anguish of shame and remorse as he increases the number and the enormity of his offenses. And has he his desert? The self-inflicted punishment has long since failed. In its suspension is there no voice which announces that the earlier pain attendant upon sin was the preintimation of a deeper and more poignant despair, when it can no longer blind the mind and sear the conscience? that it was the first stirring of " the worm which never dies," afterward chilled into torpor by the sinner's self-neglect and scorn of all remonstrance from without and within, but to warm itself into activity and fury, where nothing can loosen its hold or soothe its bite? And the systems of superstition which abound in our world give not a chance to those punishments which depend upon the

reproof of the mind. Licentiousness raises no blush of shame, for it enters into the orgies of some worship; the mother feels a satisfaction in infanticide, because, whatever the pang, a superior power is supposed to ordain the sacrifice; and the child applies the brand to the funeral pile, on which his living mother lies, with all the strength of filial piety. Other sentiments fill the heart, and turn aside the current of its best emotions. But there is a *second* vindication of our argument. The traces of justice, or of that which deals with every thing and relation as it is, are not invariably apparent because narrowed and impeded by sin. And that probationary character, which we have endeavored to prove belongs to the present state, could not be sustained if justice were uniform and instantaneous in its exercise. For virtue would then at once claim its reward, without any necessity for the faith which now relies upon a promise of the future, or for the patience which now meekly awaits it. And then, too, the transgressor would be struck down by the curse, without a power to accumulate his guilt, or a hope of repenting it. There is a sufficiency of evidence to prove that God is manifestly just, and to protect the inference that he must be so when the manifestation is withheld; and both cases combine to show that it is a reasonable expectation, and an absolute dilemma, that he shall "judge the world in righteousness."

And since man is now capable of forming these sentiments, and cherishing these feelings, can they be simply related to the passing life? Do they abruptly expire at death? Is their possessor treated with no distinction above the brute? Are they the decorations and riches of a vessel to be shivered by a blow?

V. The visitations of calamity, public and personal, contribute much illustrative evidence to the fact.

Phenomena have, indubitably, occurred more than

difficult to reconcile with the innocence of man, or the indifference of his Creator toward his demerits. We contend not for their judicial character in any invidious sense, and assure the infidel that our Bible pointedly condemns any such interpretation. If a man be born blind, it reminds us that there is no proof that he has particularly and enormously " sinned, nor his parents ; " * if a tower fall on a company of persons, or a tyrant ruthlessly massacre those who are engaged in the very act of religious worship, it warns us not to suspect that they " were sinners above all men," but to keep in mind the certainty, if impenitent, of a more tremendous perdition.† We invite not the infidel to give credit to those prodigies of horror which we, upon the assertion of our Bible, believe. He may deny—whatever profane history shall allege, however awe-struck nature shall corroborate— that Sodom and Gomorrah were destroyed with signal vengeance, and tread the strand of Asphaltites, as of the fairest lake which mountains embosom and lilies skirt. He may deny that Euphrates and Tigris wash ruins of any fearful import and prophetic ban ; and listen unimpressed to their murmuring streams. He may deny that any supernatural power has plucked the Edomite from his rock, and bid the denationalized Hebrew wander over the earth. He may deny that ever one surge of wrath swept around our globe, and calmly survey its convulsed stratification, confusedly heaped and capriciously dislocated, as he would the veins of some columned marble. He may dissociate from every catastrophe, all moral liability and all penal pursuance. But still there have been vast and manifold natural evils. The storm, the flood, the volcano entombing cities, the earthquake swallowing alive the flying multitude, the pestilence withering nations in its blast, are forms of confessed evil, whatever be their relative cause. But they are

* John ix, 3.   † Luke xiii, 1, etc.

strictly *just.* They leave no impeachment on the divine government. Yet how are they just? If they who have suffered were thus dealt with, what millions have escaped? Is there not a presumption here that these calamities are but specimens and omens of a universal judgment, of the *quick* and *dead?* It may be easy for philosophers in their halls of science and museums of research to speak of these visitations as following a physical order, and resolvable into a material law. Phlegmatically, they may tell that thus atmospheres are ventilated; and that fires, pent up in central forges, thus scatter their ashes and blow their flames. But the human mind will feel that there is a notice taken by them of sin, and will deprecate of heaven their occurrence. We are wholly at the sport of the elemental war, and our spirits are troubled that something more is meant than nature's momentary start and disturbance in the adjustment of itself. And the *partiality* of these effects cannot be pleaded in reproof of our argument. Whatever might be the equipoise between those who are implicated and exempted—though "two men should be in one bed, and the one be taken and the other not;" though "two women should be grinding together, and the one be taken and the other left;" though "two men should be in the field, and the one be taken and the other left;" yet this equal division proves an unequal treatment. And, therefore, we conclude that there is a prospective arrangement which shall explain the reason of what now seems severe, and shall attach a universality to what is circumscribed—thus establishing that all His scattered and partial inflictions have shadowed out a general rule and pledged a final arbitration!

VI. THE CLAIMS OF UNIVERSAL CONSENT ARE ON THE SIDE OF A JUDGMENT.

We popularly speak of conscience, and many a flattering title has been given to it. Yet it is to be feared

that the general opinion is fallacious. For when we call it monitor, the vicegerent of heaven, the inward oracle, the starry ray—is there not an impression that it must be right to follow its authoritative guidance? But what can be more contradictory than the consciences of mankind? It cannot be a distinct power of the soul, or a state in which all souls may be expected to discover themselves—it is nothing but the conception a man takes of religious duty, the judgment of his mind on what involves the relations which unite him to his Maker. Still while it is the simplest mental act, it closes with an original capacity and law of our being. We were made accountable creatures. It does not glance over us as do many indifferent opinions—it falls in with the primal bias of our nature. Conscience, then, is man's judgment about his religious obligations, he being designed and impelled to form one. And does not this, however taught, by whatever creed it may be regulated, solemnly assure us of such an issue? Does it not, with its steadiest index, denote it? Does it not, with its deepest knell, forewarn it? Why does it make cowards of us all, but that it converts us all into candidates who shall be summoned to this dread tribunal? He is but a sophist who, though he does not reason against the common opinion of material things which the progress of science often corrects, derides the deeper sympathies and moral impressions of mankind.

Traverse the earth—enter the gorgeous cities of idolatry, or accept the hospitality of its wandering tribes—go where will-worship is most fantastic and superstition most gross—and you will find in man " a fearful looking for of judgment." The mythology of their Nemesis may vary—their Elysium and Tartarus may be differently depicted—the metempsychosis may be the passage of bliss and woe—still the fact is only confirmed by the diversity of the forms in which it is

presented.   If this be an *innate law of susceptibility*, then it must have been impressed by the Creator.   But was it a false expectation of which man was made the dupe ?   Or could his Creator thus sport with his happiness ? *   If it be not innate, then it is a universal *tradition*.   Still, whence did it originate ?   What was its source ?   Is it to be traced to an original pair, or any other presumed stems of the human family ?   It is, then, what the earliest progenitors believed.   But there must have been an inducement and a ground.   Their conviction may sustain that of their posterity, but what sustained their own?   The cause may be displaced again and again ; the fulcrum may be shifted, the difficulty may be removed ; but it is only grown more serious and formidable by the prevarication.   For surely if man at his creation (and we hold no debate with the asserters of an eternal succession of creatures !) believed that God would judge the world, it was one of the most simple and early lessons which His finger ever traced on the table of the human heart.   That which was always believed by the species, though an Epicurism of the few has labored to resist, must have its basis in what is settled and immutable.†

* Nature, whose dictates to no other kind
  Are given in vain, but what they ask they find.—POPE.

† Bayle, in his Dictionary, (Rotterdam, 1867,) has the following remarks, which are not the less weighty because he was not favorable to Christianity : " Toutes les religions du monde, tant la vraye que les fausses, roulent sur ce grand pivot, qu'il y a un juge invisible qui punit, et qui recompense aprés cette vie les actions de l'homme, tant exterieures qu'interieures.   C'est de lā que l'on supose que decoule la principale utilitè de la religion ; c'est le principal motif qui eût animé ceux qui l'auroient inventeé.   Il est assez évident qu'en cette vie les bonnes actions ne conduisent pas au bien temporal, et que les mauvaises sont le moyen le plus ordinaire et le plus sur de faire fortune : afin donc d'empêcher l'homme de se plonger dans le crime, et de le porter a la vertu, il auroit été necessaire de 'lui proposer des peines, et des re-

The *probable* is the only kind of evidence we have hitherto employed. *We* are not to be blamed for this, because if the term be understood in the acceptation of the schools, " probable " is the only kind of which any moral subjects admit, not even excluding those which are historical; and if only taken in the vulgar sense, we have resorted to it in compliance with the necessity of our argument, and the predicament of our opponent, leaving our own " more sure word of prophecy."

But it must be felt that the greater part of what has been already advanced implies the doctrine of a *future state.* Though we have not formally propounded it, almost all has necessitated the inference. For the *judgment* which we seek to argue as true and certain, does not in any proper shape occur on the stage of this world, or during the term of this life. It has to do with the departed spirit; its review and sentence are reserved for an invisible region, and its influence forms the character of an immortal duration. It is for others to contend that an existence bounded by death is a complete existence; that the awful enigmas which surround the thinking being await no ultimate solution; that the stewardship of so many trusts as are committed to man, will not be required; and that Jehovah has ordained no era at which he will vindicate his government, and roll the clouds and darkness which have shrouded it eternally away. Our belief of a judgment forbids the thought that this is the only scene and life, and debars the fell hazard of annihilation !

And an examination of the deistical writers cannot fail to convince us that few, in any tangible sense, embrace the immortality of the soul. Herbert is an exception; but his natural theology is but a stolen likeness of

compenses après cette vie. C'est la ruse que les esprits forts attribuënt à ceux qu'ils pretendent avoir été les premiers Autours da la religion."—Page 1087.

Christianity. Others have been more consistent, and forbear to put such extravagant assumptions into their premises. Shaftesbury and Bolingbroke constantly intimate, that at most the doctrine is unsettled, that it is indifferent; and that any reference to future rewards and punishments is incompatible with a love of virtue. The French Encyclopedists, if they belong not to a class of deeper infidelity, openly explode it. Scarcely any of the present day will allow for a moment the immateriality of the mind; and therefore it cannot be expected that they should believe that it survives the stroke of death. The resurrection of the body it were foolish for them to anticipate but on the voucher of a divine revelation. The nearest approach that the majority make who believe at all in a future state, is that of a chemical reproduction without consciousness; while the small portion who retain the doctrine of an escape, a preservation of the intelligent principle at the deposition of the body, stand like wrecked mariners on some slippery rock, with the ocean constantly rising upon them. It is unquestionable that they, who repel with equal decision the charge of Atheism and the profession of Revelation, (and whom therefore we allot to the middle community of them who avow a First Cause, and affect to decipher from constituted nature His righteous will)--it is fully proved that they, with very rare exceptions, believe not in the immortality of the soul, nor in any future state of retribution.

So far we speak to facts; but we do not wonder that such immortality should be denied by the free-thinker. It consists not gracefully with infidelity. It is too vast a consummation for its system. The point rises not from its pyramid, the pyramid is built upon its point. The Deist seems to watch his opportunity to shake off the unwieldly incumbrance. He cannot find use nor solace in it. But we would remind him that a judgment

is not invalidated should Christianity be disproved, so the immortality of the human soul is not falsified on the same alternative. And yet how many shelter themselves in this sophism from the fear of immortality! How many think that they shall not live forever, if it can be shown that a revealed religion is unfounded! Impotent folly! like the hope of the hunted ostrich, burying its eyes in the sand, that not seeing its danger, its pursuers may not behold their prey!

It is only just that this inconsistency should be put in its true light. Christianity affirms our future existence as its postulate. It is not the revelation of the fact, but a description of its nature, and a provision for its beatification. And it is for him who impugns "the word of life," still to bear the burden of his own immortality as he can! The only difference between him and his fellow-travelers toward eternity is, that he has thrown away the torch and the staff, which the others acknowledge to enlighten and help them!

The argument must rest with the infidel: he must prove that man is *not* immortal: for this is the obligation on any one who sets himself in defiance of general consent.

Now whatever is may still be: a body impelled into motion continues in motion: and the presumption is, that man, who at present exists, will always exist, unless the strongest reasons can be opposed. Is such a contrivance likely to perish? And if he continue to exist, should not his being, as it advances, become more grave? extricated from its littleness of pursuit, and disciplined of its frivolity in taste? Is not his immortality the pledge of a more solemn state of things? Can the *grub* of time be the *butterfly* of eternity?

Death will, however, be urged as the palpable extinction of the being. But no man will assert that then a single atom of the body is destroyed. The organic

structure is altered; fiber and fluid are decomposed; the whole enters into new combinations, but not a particle is lost. Why may not the same be true of the soul? It was held by the body—the body has been affected by mechanical causes which could not reach the soul—the soul has become disengaged. Many changes took place in that body through life, and yet the soul was the same. And to the last, amid the wreck of its corporeal vehicle, how often does it triumph! I speak not of the hero, the martyr, the patriot who kisses the block, the chief who chants the death song, but of one whose springs of life are all shivered, and all his vigors spent. There a lambent fire plays, which no chill and damp of death can extinguish. There a might puts forth itself, victorious in that grasp beneath which all things wither. And have we not witnessed the holy spectacle? The mind rising in majesty, while all its barriers were falling from around it! the gem flashing with new brightness, while its setting was destroyed! It is then greatest when it might be expected to yield; then freest when it might be expected to waver; then boldest when it might be expected to shrink! "Death is thus a spontaneous act, a more ardent prayer of the mind."* Are not then the probabilities strongly in favor of the soul's independence and indestructibleness? And should a desire be felt to confuse the properties of matter and spirit, of which the human being in his present state is compounded, we shall again remit the disputant to the common sense of mankind. All allow them to be as different things as differing and inconvertible properties can prove them. And whatever physiological hardihood has dared, we wait with perfect composure for it to prove—that man is a mere machine; that intellect is the result of organization and a modification of matter most subtilized and attenuated; that thought is an effect of refined substance

* De Staël.

27

and arrangement, even though it will allow that no more of grossness enters into its nature than into the effluvium of a rose, and the tone of a vibration. And if soul and body be such foreign essences, how can it be supposed that they are subject in themselves to the same accidents or perish by the same fates?

And on the supposition that there is no immortality for man, let the skeptic attempt to vindicate the character of his God. It cannot be denied that it is the fervid aspiration of our nature that the cessation of being is regarded by us as the greatest possible infliction, and that each yearning of our bosom disposes us to " give all that we have for our life." Something of this feeling, we admit, may have been benevolently given, though death were the last scene of all, as a precautionary instinct, that we might prize and guard so important a deposit. But this is a nobler tending of our being. It cannot bear that its garner of affections and its treasure of purest delights shall, in a moment, be crushed. It cannot endure that its high studies and wonderful acquirements shall be instantaneously blotted into night. It cannot brook the sudden transition from the intellectual soar, into the sleepless clod. And yet the Theist must conceive that the Deity has raised these hopes to crush them, and taught men to ascend a mount whence they might descry the boundless prospect, that they might die on that mount. And thus represented cruel to man, he is described as equally unjust to himself. His creatures, made capable of understanding him, are perplexed with his conduct, but confide in its destined explanation. They have seen only " a part of him." They have heard but a passage of an infinite history, and beheld but a scene of the eternal drama. They " wait the great teacher, Death, and God adore !" But while their spirits are rapt in anxiety, they perish in the suspense ! ready to burst into the

song of wonder, love, and praise, their lips are sealed in endless silence!

Let, then, the unbeliever consider his case. He is hastening to judgment! He will soon enter eternity! His rejection of Christianity does not, to the slightest degree, alter these laws of his being. For him there is no pause, no choice. He is borne resistlessly forward. However his spirit may recoil, his step cannot. Each moment, each pulse, testifies his progress. He is always accountable, and shall live always. Let him now look into his futurity. Is he not aghast at the bleak, dreary prospect? Little knows he of his Judge. He is just; but may he not be capriciously so, since his operations, as far as we have seen them, are not uniform? May he not be relentless in his justice, since innocence, when connected with any guilty party, has been frequently destroyed in the same blast of wrath? If merciful, may he not withhold it, for often the cry of misery has been ungranted? He is invested with no fixed character, and acts upon no assigned rule. Intimations and conjectures are the only elements out of which he can gather to himself any manner of similitude. Such a God is the creature's work: he is vanity, and cannot save! And is it a light thing to meet a God at uncertainty? Is it a light thing to stand before a God only hitherto recognized from the most contradictory appearances? Is it a light thing to find the possible terror without the possible relief? And what is the immortality which such a person may expect? Has he any proof that a future life may not be far more painful than this? Has he any proof that the pains from which death here releases us, may not there perpetuate themselves without release? Has he a presentiment how that duration is to be occupied? Does he trace a way-mark along that mysterious road? The Atheist has no appeal but to mechanical chance: the Deist none but to moral fickleness. What, with their views,

may not await them! If there be no God, as the former says, then the fortuitous power which happily composed his form below, may in some far-off world leave him as miserable as lurking poisons and gnawing griefs can make him; the chance which caused this life to be agreeable, may render his immortality horrible—may drive it where tempest only resounds and darkness dwells—may exile it from all sympathy and intercourse to an impenetrable solitude—may abandon it to a despair so unutterably deep, that it cannot hope that a God exists to finish its miseries! And if there be such a God, as the second affirms, then there may be the severity of justice, perchance the mildness of forbearance. But a darker cloud may cross the prospect than that of a dread uncertainty. He has not disproved revelation to the confutation of millions: perhaps never unfailingly convinced himself. Should Christianity be true; should it contain the precise information our understandings require, and the exact remedy our transgressions need; should it be all that was wanted to unvail the character and purpose of nature's God; then what must be the remorse of the spirit that passed through its light without irradiation, and walked beneath its pity without blessing! And be it as he thinks: ah, what has infidelity, such as his, to fill immortality! With his views of human nature and divine government, how shall it not linger and fatigue? What transport has his religion ever awakened, what song has it ever attuned, to swell through the compass of each successive period? It knows nothing of gratitude for eternal deliverance, nothing of tender humility, nothing of awe at the mysteries of one ceaseless agency to save the sinner, nothing of sweet penitence. It has no assurance of a congeniality between the condition of the immortal and his abode. It has no pledge that the welcome of his first greeting, beyond this present state, may not degenerate into cold neglect. It has no security that new

creations may not divert the attention he now enjoys, while he may be cast away as the refuse of a system which has completed its ends. O bitter immortality, in which no object relieves, no remembrance harmonizes, no promise assures! O cold uncertain lengthening out of a being which is vanity and vexation of spirit! In vain ye call to the mountains and rocks, Fall on us! Ye seek death and cannot find it; and desire to die, and death flees from you! Rev. ix, 6.

And it may be added, that—be it a reduction to absurdity, or an argumentative appeal to shame—nothing intervenes between a belief of revelation and a denial of the Deity. The concession of such a being is inconsistent without a moral character; and his moral character is inconsistent without an assent to Christianity. The Theist has no retreat, no stand; all that he knows of God requires a future, all that he divines of the future blasphemes a God. Painful as is the plea, we must urge it; and we cannot but decide that the Atheist is the more consistent of the two.

After this delay, tedious and even circumlocutory but for the sake of the argument, it is our unspeakable satisfaction to introduce "the glad tidings" of Christianity. And here we may, before we disclose all its blessed intelligence, publish an argument implied in it against the disputer of its claims. Twelve men promulgated it, and even they were not secularly qualified to recommend it. Let Christianity be a fable! Then is it but a human device. But it attests that all men believed in some judgment; receiving, assuming this, if it were not so, it would be a mockery on human nature. It could have no success had it not met such dread foreboding; it could never have undeceived the world of this universal impression. Yet these impressions did, or did not preexist. If they did, then man is all this, agreeably to our argument, independently of any belief in revelation;

if not, then must revelation, from the first promise until now, have spread these unnatural impressions among the human race. Either horn of the dilemma is fatal to infidelity.

Christianity would appear founded upon an anticipation of our circumstanees as accountable and immortal creatures. And there are those who thus reduce and stint it. They have no more sublime conception of it than that it explains our obligations, and certifies our prospects. They think it is only the light of reason made to burn more brightly, and but the voice of nature speaking with unprecedented distinctness. With them the Gospel is but the re-enacted law. But is it good news to inform the sinner of a code he has violated, and of an immortality, rather than endure which it were better that he had not been born? Far other are its proclamations! they declare the pardon of our guilt, the purification of our nature, and the conversion, by these means, of an undone eternity into an eternal good. On Mount Zion is deliverance, and there is holiness.

And let him who will confess that he is something more than a being religious and imperishable—that he is a sinner—think of the importance which belongs to the inquiry, "How can man be just with God?" The Christian doctrine calms the shudder of the culprit, and assures him of pardon and acceptance.

Justification is a term of Scripture, and Scripture must decide its own use of the term. It cannot be, according to its conventional import, a vindication of rectitude, an assertion of innocence, for it places "the whole world guilty before God." It cannot declare that which is not true, nor constitute that which is not real; and therefore it cannot declare nor constitute the sinner otherwise than he is. But it may treat man as righteous without any contradiction, or in other words, it may reverse his doom. It does not "impute his trespasses unto him." It does

not exact their punishment. Now this manner of dealing with the sinner is called "the righteousness of God." It is a singular phrase, because righteousness is more naturally connected with the enforcement of a sentence upon guilt. But it has thus enounced its glorious peculiarity. It treats us as righteous on the ground of a righteousness. Then it must be another's. And this righteousness must be produced in obeying the precept, and enduring the penalty, of the law. Can this, however, be a moral consideration, on the weight of which millions of millions may be justified? This depends upon a relative matter. Who has "brought in" this "everlasting righteousness?" "Jesus Christ the Righteous." His infinite dignity of person has stamped an equal character on his work. And therefore its "righteousness" is contrasted with "condemnation." (2 Cor. iii, 9.) O wonderful provision! Mercy employs a righteousness as the medium of its exercise; but then that righteousness she herself has yielded!

And as there is but one ground on which a holy God can meet and receive the sinner—a righteousness—it must be that of his Messiah or our own. Nor can these be confounded and admixed. Wholly must the business proceed on the one or the other. We must be justified by works, or without them. They must be reckoned to us, or abjured. The law demands our love to God with all our heart, and love to our neighbor equal to that we possess for ourselves. It denounces punishment against all disobedience. We may be assured that it cannot be relaxed in its conditions or sanctions. In vain you think that it is not in earnest, or that it contains in itself a remedy. It is law! It is the law of God! Has he required too much? Will he annul his statute? Can he change? Abide by your choice. If you demand a right, no right shall you be refused. Let justice be your claim, and never can this be denied to the creature who pleads

it. But you must keep to the rigid, unblenching ideas of right and claim. You must mean by them what God intends. You stand forth and answer for yourself! You sue acceptance! You challenge your personal title to it! Have you a spotless obedience to adduce? Perhaps now you resort to evasion. You substitute sincerity. You oppose good works to them which are evil. You deprecate the strictest severity. You admit an imperfection, and seek a mitigation. But thus you recall your appeal. Now you vary your process. Boldly you push your way to the judgment-seat. Nothing has been done, but according to your own urgency. You undertook your defense. Blame us not if we carry you further than your imagined restriction. The deed is all your own. The defiance you have sounded, the arena you have selected, the scrutiny you have braved! You have appealed unto justice; unto justice you shall go! Ah, again consider, be of another mind, " humble yourselves under the mighty hand of God." He will meet, can only meet, you at the Cross! " He hath made Him to be sin for us who knew no sin, that we might be made the righteousness of God in Him." When He shall " call to the heavens from above, and to the earth, that he may judge his people"—when all " these things shall be dissolved "—when shall roll along the heavens the dread echoes of " the last trump"—say, whither then will you fly? on what then will you lean? Will you rush on the sword of justice, or into the embrace of mercy? Will high-crested pride then disdain this righteousness of God by faith, " the garment of salvation," that there may flutter around its own deformity but shameful tatters and filthy rags? Jehovah will lack no attestation of his uprightness; he will be " justified " when he speaketh, and " be clear" when he judgeth; " the heavens shall declare his righteousness, for God is judge himself." He would have " declared even at that time his righteous-

ness in the remission of sins," but the vain-glorious sinner has " provoked him to jealousy," dared him to rigor, and plucked the bolt from his hand!

But Christianity, addressing us as creatures of accountability and immortality, proposes another and an equal benefit; and while justification blends itself with judgment as a forensic inquest, sanctification is not less important and essential to indicate and conduct the process of a moral discrimination. He will then gather his saints unto him. His elect will he bring from the four winds of heaven. His servants are sealed. If a man love God, the same is known of him. The Lord knoweth them that are his.

Suppose that a man is pardoned, nay, more, is accepted; that the sentence of a violated law is withdrawn, and the thunder of the angry Deity sleeps; suppose that every legal restraint and barrier to his intercourse with an infinitely holy God is removed, and that the light of that God's revealed countenance is thrown with mildest luster around him; still, with a contrariety of temper, and repugnance of character, in what a tremendous difficulty is he involved! And what is that? Not of guilt, we argue that to be canceled; not of punishment, we presume that to be reversed. Yet is there a mountain he cannot level, a great gulf he cannot pass. It is his unrectified nature, it is his unconquered self! Though God should not repel him, though heaven should not exclude him, he carries in his own bosom the foul disqualification for all good, for all use, for all happiness! Did he attempt to approach the altar before the throne and burn incense, the leprosy would rise up in his forehead; nor would it require the attendants of the temple to thrust him from its courts, for, like the smitten monarch, he "himself would hasten also to go out." Though he might still be welcome to abide under his Father's roof, with the restlessness of the prodigal he would soon once more

exile himself. How could he bear to meet that eye in whose pure beam he read his shame? How could he dwell upon those features in which he saw no reflected image of his own disposition? How could he clasp those feet on which he had never let fall a tear of penitence? How could he listen to that voice whose accents would only jar on his untuned soul? If the disqualification of the human mind for the divine service and vision were but only a partial obliquity, it might retrieve itself; if it were only an interspersion of the good with a little evil, the evil might be subdued by the good; if it were only the warm passion of youth, age and discipline might eventually control it. But it is an estrangement, an apostasy of the heart. It is utter ungodliness. Marvel not that we say unto you, " Ye must be born again." Thus is imprinted a mark of holy distinctiveness, of a separation for a holy use, which the angels shall recognize and respect when the final discrimination shall be made between the righteous and the wicked, the wheat in their sheaves, and the tares in their bundles!

What then are we? " We must give account." We must live forever. This is the ordination, whether a revealed religion accost us or not: whether or not Christianity be a revealed religion. " God will bring us into judgment." But if ever such revealed religion could adapt itself to our necessities, what is comparable with Christianity? It is one anticipation of our wants, an entire answer to our forebodings. It is regulated upon the principle of our condition. It prepares us for the trumpet which otherwise would sound, and for the tribunal which, in the most different circumstances, would be equally erected. It meets us in the way by which we approach this dread consummation with its blessings. For that assize it provides a plea—for that discrimination a character. It goes with us to

the bar, and accompanies us through immortality. Like the Saviour, what it hath "seen and heard," that it "testifieth;" like the Saviour, it hath gone "to prepare" for us. Beneath its influence the tribunal becomes a sanctuary, and immortality no longer dispreads away a cheerless blank or possible disgust of being, but a prospect lovely as it is interminable—the scene of a right activity and of a conscious progression. Infidelity pulls down every refuge, repels each remedy, and only interposes for the sinner to stand between him and any help. It leaves him with "the works of the law written in his heart," under all his self-conviction—and with "the wounded spirit" unsoothed, which "none can bear"—but no peace does it suggest, no hope can it impart. It serves but to exasperate the accusation of conscience, and to barb the sting of remorse. It deepens the suspense of life, and haunts the bed of death. It flings us on our destinies as unfeelingly as hopelessly!* But Christianity is the religion which we want. It makes light of nothing. It does not teach us to lesson our estimate of judgment and immortality in order more indifferently to meet them. It throws all its energy and pomp into their description. It excites us to the measure of our faculty to muse, and to the fullness of our capacity to feel. Of "that great and terrible day of the Lord," it utters warnings only inferior to the reality. It has no office of reducing and allaying the scenery. It makes all that can belong to that catastrophe most serious. It has heightened all. It has enlarged our responsibility, and consequently our account. The grandeur of Him who "cometh in clouds," owes itself to this system of mediatorial grace.

* How justly might we exclaim with the poet, though not with his impious sarcasm, when we describe infidelity,

"Tantum religio potuit suadere malorum!"

Lucretius, De Rerum Natura. Lib. I.

Much of "the terrors of the Lord" arises from the very love "which passeth knowledge." It is not a small thing to pass from evangelical overture and hope to the irrevocable sentence. The religion of the Cross superadds to whatever is most rigorous and most august in those transactions. It gives a more piercing clangor to the trumpet; and burnishes, with a fiercer magnificence, the judgment-seat. And yet is there a peace which it bestows so soft and sure, that even now, with these portendings within us, "our hearts condemn us not;" and there is a process, which it conducts, so distinctive that we may say, "Now are we the sons of God." Let it come as "travail on a woman," as "a thief in the night," as "the lightning which shineth from the east unto the west," "we, through the Spirit, look for the hope of acquittal by faith." "Wherefore we labor, that whether present or absent, we may be accepted of Him. For we must all appear before the judgment-seat of Christ." The "testimony of Jesus" teaches us how to "love his appearing." Leaving it in all its majesty, it clothes it with whatever is attractive. "All judgment is committed unto the Son." He wears our nature, and returns with "the sign of the Son of man!" The pierced one, He comes again "unto salvation!" The thunder-blast is but "the voice" of your "Beloved!" The rich garniture of heaven, as it unfolds "the great white throne," marks but the lofty midway which invites you "to meet the Lord in the air!" And from the final conflagration you shall rise, like the angel that appeared to Manoah, as from an altar-flame, to the heaven whither he returned, wafted on the very fire of the sacrifice, and amid the very breath of the incense! Amen.

XI.

JESUS CHRIST CREATOR AND LORD OF THE UNIVERSE.

For by Him were all things Created, that are in Heaven, and that are in Earth, visible and invisible, whether they be thrones, or dominions, or principalities, or powers: all things were Created by Him, and for Him.—Colossians i, 16.

It is a solemnly bold adventure of mind to revert to the period, deep hid among "the years of the right hand of the Most High," when this world we inhabit—so prominent in interest, so vast in dimension, so ancient in date, according to the manner in which such creatures must be affected by all comparisons of feeling, size, and duration—yet such an atom to the revolving systems, such a spark to the central luminaries of the universe—did not exist. Inconceivable by us is the gulf of its void, the midnight of its extinction. Frightful solitude! Its darkness had never been irradiated, its depth never sounded, its waste never explored. Unbroken had been that long interval of silence, unrelieved that large field of space. For we know that there could not but have been a moment in which our earth was not; when the question was between nothingness and creation; when not a particle of matter and beam of light appeared to denote that it should soon bend into convexity and burst into splendor. "Before the mountains were brought forth, or ever he had formed the earth and the world, even from everlasting" there was a God. "The An-

cient of Days" arose! At his command accumulated the elements of things—rude, huge, shapeless—into the mass which he now prepared for the materials of our habitation. But how unlike that pile, the abode which it was destined to build! No life filled its caverns, no vegetation mantled its surfaces, no beauty relieved its horrors, no order compacted its parts. "The earth was without form, and darkness was upon the face of the deep." What a confusion of substances! What a rush of waters! What a deformity of aspects! What a whirlwind of opposing causes and contending powers sweeping over it, strewing desolation, bellowing rage! What could still that uproar? subdue that anarchy? attune that jar? Again He arose, "even He that abideth of old." He declared "the end from the beginning, and from ancient times the things that are not yet done, saying, My counsel shall stand, and I will do all my pleasure." Long lay the type of creation in his searchless bosom. From eternity it had there been revolved. It now emanates in the perfection of beauty. It now beams out with the self-furnished evidences of wisdom and of love. Chaos hears and obeys! The work is begun and swiftly hastens to its consummation. The waters fall back to appointed channels; the solid masses are fixed to sustain and bind a framework of a thousand orders and kinds; the distorted twinklings of light are embodied and find "their tabernacle in the sun;" the rugged shapes swell into lovely forms, and melt away into enchanting landscapes; the repulsive differences of attraction, instead of agitating the globe to its center, gird and balance it; the latent seeds of each fair flower and luscious fruit break out along the river which flowed in Eden to water the garden; and the wild war of discords hushes into the soft sunrise, and fragrant breath, and holy calm of a Sabbath dawn, in which God rested from his work and "was refreshed," (Exod. xxxi, 17,) in

which man, "made upright," stretched forth his hands to his Father-creator, with songs of praise comely for one so upright, and with the effectual fervent prayer of one so righteous; in which higher intelligences took a holy sympathy, and performed a benevolent part—while, hanging with wondering delight over the teeming scene, the sons of God pressed into view and shouted for joy!

On one question there can be no dispute. This world must have had an origin, that origin must have consisted with a cause, that cause must have been intelligent, that intelligence must have been ultimate, that ultimate power must have been supreme, that supremacy must have been divine, or what we call and know by the awful name of God. But we are unwilling to trust further to reason when we can command the ground of revelation. Our convictions are not so much the deductions of argument as the results of faith. And when scorn has spit its spleen—when infidelity has mooted its cavil—when we have listened to each grave disquisition on spontaneous outbirth and self-generative life—when we have even attended to the last absurdity and closing pretext of eternal matter—this is our reply: "Through faith we understand that the worlds were framed by the word of God." "But this they willingly are ignorant of."*

* As the whole of the ensuing discourse attempts nothing but the exposition of a doctrine which never could have been known but by revelation, it may be well to let the reader understand how that revelation is regarded by some who boast their title to the Christian name: "With the Rationalist it is reason alone that decides in matters of faith, and in the adoption of religious doctrine. The Scriptures are to him nothing more than any other human book. He allows their authority only when they coincide with his own convictions; and that, not as the determining grounds of those convictions, for these he regards as true on their own grounds of reason, but simply as an illustration that others also, wise men of former times, have thought and believed in the same manner. The Rationalist considers the assumption of a direct supernatural revelation as inadmissible and groundless.

But why was this orb, stored as it is with inexhaustible resources, peopled as it is with swift successions of inhabitants—why was it reared? Was it just to circle its mazy path? Was it only to deck immensity with another gem? Was it simply to intersect the infinite vault above, around, beneath us, with another beacon and way-mark? Were all the mighty springs of this complex machine wound up, all its wheels set in motion, that the experiment might be concluded, All is vanity? or that the complaint might be justified, Wherefore hast thou made all men in vain? No! it is appropriated to a noble service, to a magnificent use. Sooner shall it wander from its course and start from its sphere, than this purpose shall be frustrated and reversed. And who is the Claimant to the world's creation and the world's design? Christians! He "whose worthy name ye bear;" He in whose "cross ye glory;" He "whom the nations abhorred;" He whom "we esteemed not,"—He is "the Almighty!" "He is Lord of all." His voice woke up universal existence, and his hand bound it to his purpose. He uttered its fiat! He imposed its law! As the stage of transactions at once most dread and benevolent; of interests the most sublime and precious; He hung our earth upon nothing! And when first this new and unknown Star arose, it pointed not, like that of Bethlehem, the course of mercy to some other world over which it bent and shone, but flashed from the brow of the firmament as her chosen care, her palace-home, and spread a dayspring of salvation over the realms of heaven, and the hosts of God.

He sees in the Scriptures nothing more than a human book, in which noble and wise men of former times have laid up, entirely in the ordinary manner, the results of their reflection and investigation upon the truths of religion"!!!—Letters on Rationalism, by Dr. Rohn, General Superintendent and First Court Preacher, Weimar. This is Neology, the fondling of Socinianism, and the more consistent of the two.

The text, clearly and strongly as words can serve, propounds these facts of Christ's *work* and *property*—it asserts him to be the *efficient* and *final* cause of the entire creation. Such are the truths affirmed, and such are the themes we propose for meditation.

I. Those ideas which we attach to him who is our Creator are due to the Lord Jesus Christ, he having produced the universal system of being.

This is represented as no partial operation of his power—as employing itself in no contracted spot—or as only developing itself in this earth, with the sky which pavilions it, and the satellite which attends it, its oceans and continents, its lakes and isles. It wanders not alone; but a sweet fellowship of sister-spheres is bound together, cheering each other from afar, and from one telling it to all of a mutual law and indissoluble bond. Within the limits of this smaller economy burns the sun, so that in the act of creation, from which our abode arose, we necessarily include all the planetary apparatus, knowing that then the center was fixed, and that each globe was launched in its circlings around it. The mundane and sublunary form only a little fragment of the work, an inferior department of the great transaction. And what are the few worlds which sweep with us about the same source of life and light? Massive, ponderous, in themselves; some of them immensely larger than our own, running wider revolutions, and drawing after them brighter trains. But even this one solar family, recognizing and claiming members in the outskirts of space— it is as nothing to what the eye can command, nothing to the visible! What constellations are thrown over the firmament in all the profusion of beauty and magnificence! And when the unaided sense has roamed to its utmost ken, and gazed to its utmost strength, it may call the instruments of science to its assistance; and it shall look out on ampler territories, and take hold of larger

notices. Now we leave our nook. We speak in no terms of exaggeration when we describe what we see as bods, and floors, and clouds of stars. As we pierce the awful altitudes we ascend to new wonders. Apertures constantly open, and we are just suffered a glimpse into them. Heaven spreads above heaven, new arrangements stand revealed, and celestial bodies, in shapes hitherto undeveloped, flame as at the portal of the eternal throne, to guard its access and proclaim its terribleness. Yet even there are proofs that discovery has not closed its researches; still avenue verges from avenue, and height rises into height. And after all, this is but the outer court of "His high and holy place." But how much more of the universe is invisible! Matter may subsist in forms of which we have no conception; nor can wo doubt that it may extend indefinitely. And a thousand essences may inhere in the constitution of things that the qualities by which we discriminate matter cannot denote, and the senses by which we determine it cannot examine. Spirit through all its rank, the instinct of the worm, the wisdom of the angel, must be comprehended. It includes the hierarchy of " thrones, dominions, principalities," and " powers; " and not only " the elect angels," but " the angels that sinned." The summary of these operations is, " all things that are in heaven and that are in earth."

It is not an unnatural inference that a divine interposition was necessary to produce this effect. What wisdom may be traced in the contrivance of all things! their arrangement in system, their subserviency to utility—the appropriateness of the part, the perfection of the whole. How little do we know of our own frame, and yet what a workmanship is it, as far as we comprehend it, of wonderful designs and adaptations! How much more are we perplexed when we apply our scrutiny to the mind, its connection with the body, its independence of such connection, its power to invent and

combine, its susceptibility of emotion, its challenge of immortality! Who can conceive the intelligence which measured all this subordination of agency, and adjusted all this correspondence of result? Power is an attribute as essential as wisdom to the consummation of this plan. Understanding this in no lofty sense, attaching to it only an executory idea, there are no known, no conceivable modifications of created force and strength which could originate the meanest atom. Mechanism may obviate risk, save time, and economize labor; but it cannot add a particle to the mass of the universe: it may most strangely transform substances, but it cannot call one into existence. In the accommodation of this dwelling and its furniture to our capacities and wants, we read a goodness equal to the wisdom and power which creation demonstrates; nor is it unworthy evidence of a divine act. For in this we see the end for which wisdom has suggested, and power has constructed, the phenomena of human nature, together with all the scenery and convenience of its abode. Nor can we fail to remark that authority of the highest order is demanded for the right of this stupendous work. It lies not within any prerogative of which we can conceive—less than divine—to break the pause of eternity, to cover space with being, and to place creatures not only beneath a constant protection, but a moral rule. It belongs only to Him whom none can interrogate, " What doest thou? " To " reason's ear " one testimony is borne; and all things proclaim that " the hand which made us is divine."

After all, revelation is the only authoritative standard of appeal. The different theories which have been advanced of an energetic principle, and pregnant cause, and mysterious incubation, are unsubstantial as the shadows which brooded over the dark abyss ere the fabric of nature was deposited in it, while the sayings and explanations of Scripture are firm and unyielding as the

" world " which, in comparison with its " generations," " abideth for ever."

In pursuing the argument, we admit that the work of creation does not necessarily prove, apart from the averments of inspiration, the absolute deity of him who accomplishes it. There are beings transcendently superior to man, and yet they are but creatures. One of those who " excel in strength " may surpass all our notions of limitation and control; he may be " clothed with a cloud," he may have " a rainbow upon his head," his face may be " as the sun," he may " set his right foot upon the sea, and his left foot on the earth." It would be presumptuous to say that a power to create could not be delegated to them, unless we possess an infallible contradiction. Besides, creation, whatever be its breadth, and depth, and height, is but a finite effect. We talk of infinite space ; and as its supposed boundary must be in space or not, it is easy to see that the boundary may be removed, must retreat, for ever. This is, however, rather metaphysical subtlety than solid truth; but our question is not with space, whatever it be, but with a particular occupation of it. We say that that occupation of it, being but a finite result, does not indispensably prove an infinite agent. Our concession is, therefore, twofold: that we cannot, by any original reasoning, adjudge what trust and task God may assign to a creature ; and, that a determinate work cannot argue an omnipotent cause.

" What saith the Scripture ? " We open it to ascertain the precise value, and the legitimate scope, of the creative act; and the character of Him who exclusively and necessarily performs it. The following series of observations will elicit the bearing of the sacred volume on this question.

1. *The creative act is uniformly ascribed to the Deity.*

" God that made the world and all things therein, seeing that he is Lord of heaven and earth, dwelleth not

in temples made with hands. He giveth to all life, and breath, and all things. In Him we live, and move, and have our being." "In the beginning God created the heaven and the earth." "God rested on the seventh day from all his works." "Now he that built all things is God." No language can be more precise, no suffrage more concurrent. And this coincides with those features of decisive energy which indicate Him who is "excellent in working." He "calleth those things which be not as though they were." And he educed them by direct command, "so that things which are seen were not made of things which do appear."

2. *This act is the ground on which the highest claims and honors are required for the Divine Nature.*

A primary duty which we owe to God is the acknowledgment of his being and government by worship. Nothing can be more reasonable and binding. And yet it is rested upon the announcement that he is Creator. "Let all the earth fear the Lord, let all the inhabitants of the world stand in awe of him: for he spake and it was done; he commanded and it stood fast." "Know ye that the Lord he is God; it is he that hath made us, and not we ourselves; enter into his gates with thanksgiving, and into his courts with praise: be thankful unto him, and bless his name." "Thou, even thou, art Lord alone; thou hast made heaven, the heaven of heavens, with all their hosts; the earth, and all things that are therein, the seas, and all that is therein, and thou preservest them all; and the host of heaven worshipeth thee." Nehemiah ix, 6. "Fear God, and give glory to him; and worship him that made heaven, and earth, and the sea, and the fountains of waters." This is the sanction of the Sabbath. He who "in six days made heaven and earth" is entitled to our homage, whoever he be: and a former proposition has established that the creator is God. The faithfulness of

his declarations to his creatures lies at the basis of his moral government over them; since, could a momentary doubt arise in respect to his voracity, they would lightly esteem his law, with all its safeguards of reward and punishment. But it is upon the creating deed that he suspends the certainty of what he promises and threatens, thus urging our faith, because as he is the creator, it is impossible for the creator to deceive. "Thus saith God the Lord, he that created the heavens, and stretched them out, he that spread forth the earth; and that which cometh out of it; he that giveth breath unto the people upon it, and spirit to them that walk therein." "For thus saith the Lord that created the heavens; God himself that formed the earth and made it, he hath established it; he created it not in vain, he formed it to be inhabited; I am the Lord, and there is none else. I have not spoken in secret, in a dark place of the earth: I said not unto the seed of Jacob, Seek ye me in vain: I the Lord speak righteousness, I declare things that are right." "And the angel sware by Him that liveth for ever and ever, who created heaven, and the things that therein are, and the earth, and the things that therein are, and the sea, and things which are therein, that there should be time no longer." It follows, then, that whoever is our maker, may demand our most unqualified credence, and that no credence can support itself on so warrantable a hold. He who formed us from the dust, and "speaketh to us from heaven," is one and the same. It is observable, that when the Supreme arrays himself in his peculiar majesty, when the saints sing most rapturously of his glory, the achievement of creation is mutually alleged. It is felt that an indubitable pre-eminence must belong to him who could signalize it. "To whom then will ye liken me, or shall I be equal? saith the Holy One. Lift up your eyes on high, and behold who hath created these things. Hast thou not

known, hast thou not heard that the everlasting God, the Lord, the Creator of the ends of the earth, fainteth not, neither is weary." "For, lo, he that formeth the mountains and createth the wind, and declareth unto man what is his thought, the Lord, the God of hosts, is his name." "When I consider thy heavens, the work of thy fingers, the moon and the stars, which thou hast ordained; what is man that thou art mindful of him? and the son of man that thou visitest him." None, then, can be higher than the Creator; and He who is "higher than the highest," alleges not a nobler boast. The manner in which the grandeur of this operation is adduced, to give terror to divine menace, and richness to divine consolation, bespeaks it to be a divine act itself. "Woe unto him that striveth with his Maker." "The great God, that formed all things, rewardeth transgressors." "He that made them shall have no mercy on them, and he who formed them shall show them no favor." . . . . "Thy Maker is thy husband." "But now, saith the Lord that created thee, O Jacob, and he that formed thee, O Israel, Fear not." "The portion of Jacob is not like them, for he is the former of all things." "I, even I, am he that comforteth you: who art thou, that thou shouldest be afraid of a man that shall die, and forgettest the Lord thy maker, that hath stretched forth the heavens, and hath laid the foundations of the earth?" "I will not contend forever, neither will I be always wroth: for the spirit should fail before me, and the souls which I have made." It is therefore obvious that the greatest distributive happiness or misery must be awaited from the hand which fashioned the universe.

3. *The creative act is invariably recorded and enforced for the glory of the Being from whom it proceeded.*

It is a monument of praise to none other but himself. It stands for a witness to his skill and might. Whenever it is described, it is for the purpose of his aggran-

dizement. No intervening object is admitted, no superior is supposed. He who has devised and completed this work shall receive its attestation and bear its glory. And therefore we find that Jehovah is constantly adorned for this "operation of his hands." "Bless the Lord, all his works, in all places of his dominions." It is resolved into his will: "For thou hast created all things, and for thy pleasure they are and were created." Not only does it prove his absolute pleasure, but his skillful arrangement: "The heavens declare the glory of God, and the firmament showeth his handywork. Day unto day uttereth speech, and night unto night showeth knowledge." Thus his wide dominion is proclaimed: "The earth is the Lord's, and the fullness thereof; the world and they that dwell therein: for he hath founded it upon the seas, and established it upon the floods." The source, conservation, and tendency of these works is identical: "For of him, and through him, and to him, are all things: to whom be glory forever." And, indeed, we should be unable to sustain one pious reflection, if creation did not express, and stand to honor, its original. But now, in not severing the act from the agent, we can exclaim, "O Lord, how great are thy works, in wisdom hast thou made them all!" "For thou, Lord, hast made me glad through thy work. I will triumph in the works of thy hands." "The works of the Lord are great, sought out of all them that have pleasure therein." "All thy works shall praise thee, O Lord; and thy saints shall bless thee!" We refer from the building to the architect: we "rise from nature up to nature's God."

4. *The creative act is the basis of natural religion.*

Effect supposes cause; and that primary system of morals which "nature teaches," and which reason allows, is but an inference from the one to the other. Can the world have been constituted by a fortuitous concourse

and dance of atoms? Can it have always been? We are shut up to one conclusion, that it is a work, that it is a contrivance, and that the producing power still presides over it. The simple inquiry then is, What does this Power require of us? what are our obligations to our Creator, and those other creatures especially which belong to the same kind? Natural religion but asks, Who hath spangled that firmament? who hath made this world? It then acknowledges Him as the ascertained object of worship and umpire of right. Now this bright volume of heaven, and this fair spectacle of earth, are unfolded with an adaptation and a design to teach us the being and character of their Author. "Hath it not been told you from the beginning? have ye not understood from the foundation of the earth?" "The invisible things of him from the creation of the world are clearly seen, being understood by the things which are made, even his eternal power and Godhead." Men saw an economy of things which could not be accidental; and that which might be known of God was manifest in them, for God had showed it unto them. Had they given it the thought which their trifling cares engross, or had they liked to retain this knowledge, they would have spurned any equivocation. Their soul would have followed hard after God, and their inquiries would have ended in adoration of his greatness, and in obedience to his will. "God hath made of one blood all nations of men for to dwell on all the face of the earth. That they should seek the Lord, if haply they might feel after him and find him. Forasmuch then as we are the offspring of God, we ought not to think that the Godhead is like unto gold, or silver, or stone, graven by art and man's device." "Are there any among the vanities of the Gentiles that can cause rain? or can the heavens give showers? Art thou not he, O Lord God? therefore will we wait upon thee, for thou hast made all these

things." This is the resolve of impartial investigation ; but there is an end to natural religion, there remains but irreconcilable confusion, if the Creator be not the ultimate source, the supreme essence, of all. The only dictate of our circumstances, as rational moral creatures, is, that we obey Him who·has constituted us such creatures. Nor is there another right in God to govern us, but that he made us ; nor reason for us to obey him, but that we were made by him. Our dependence and obligation must rest on the same ground.* " Where is God my maker ? " " This is the whole of man."

5. *The creative act is the general argument employed in the reprobation of idolatry.*

In showing the folly of worshiping our own inventions, God has often resorted to the severest irony. He has derided the image of human fabrication, because the craftsman has of the same tree made the idol, burned part in the fire, baked bread on it, and roasted flesh by it. (Isa. xliv, 15, etc.) But a more refined polytheism supposed an inferior race of agents ; a class of œons,

* What our great Poet puts into the mouth of Sin, "the snaky sorceress," when she addressed Satan, is the exact inference of nature :

> " Thou art my father, thou my author, thou
> My being gavest me ; whom should I obey
> But thee, whom follow ? "

And still truer to the argument are " the orisons " in which he makes our progenitors adore :

> " These are thy glorious works, Parent of good,
> Almighty ! Thine this universal frame
> Thus wondrous fair : Thyself how wondrous then !
> Unspeakable, who sitt'st above these heavens
> To us invisible, or dimly seen
> In these thy lowest works ; yet these declare
> Thy goodness beyond thought, and power divine."
>
> PARADISE LOST, Books II and V.

who were the formers of particular works and presidents of particular departments. These were interposed between man and God. These are swept away by a stroke. "I am the first and the last. Is there a God besides me? yea, there is no God, I know not any." The error was in placing those who by "nature are no gods" in the rank of creators, and yielding corresponding homage to them. An exception was frequently made on behalf of a first cause, but it quickly lost any practical influence. They "worshiped and served the creature more than the Creator, who is blessed forever." In this spirit the Apostles subverted every system which encroached on the exclusive prerogative and distinction of the Deity. "We preach unto you that ye should turn from these vanities unto the living God, which made heaven, and earth, and the sea, and all things therein:" and "left not himself without witness." And with the same spirit the Prophets foretold the downfall of those fictitious powers, since they had not the slightest claim to the original ground of all worship, the constitution of the universe; "the gods that have not made the heavens and the earth, even they shall perish from the earth, and from under these heavens."

6. *The creative act is adduced as the sanction and emphasis of those specific blessings which we discover and derive from the evangelic revelation.*

Whatever are the truths we recognize in the scenery around us, those which His written word discloses are of another character. It is the Gospel of salvation. God magnifies his word above all his name. But while he subordinates all things to this purpose, it is only because he is creator that he is competent to act. The right to interpose for the rescue of the rebel-creature is in the being to whom the creature owes existence, and therefore fealty. Who but he can treat and regulate his own handiwork? Who can deliver out of his hand? Scrip-

ture therefore urges this idea: "He that is our God is the God of salvation." Our redemption is not only his sufferance, but his doing. He whose temple of nature we profaned, rears the altar for the expiation of the sacrilege. Read we of reconciliation? "All things are of God, who hath reconciled us to himself by Jesus Christ." Are the mediation and atonement exhibited? "It became him, for whom are all things, and by whom are all things, in bringing many sons unto glory, to make the Captain of their salvation perfect through sufferings." Is spiritual illumination described? "God, who commanded the light to shine out of darkness, hath shined in our hearts, to give the light of the knowledge of the glory of God, in the face of Jesus Christ." Is divine protection recommended? "Wherefore, let them that suffer according to the will of God commit the keeping of their souls to him in well-doing, as unto a faithful Creator." Is the "heavenly calling" narrated? "It pleased God, who separated me from my mother's womb, and called me by his grace, to reveal his Son in me." Then if this coincidence be just; if he who created, also redeems; our redemption must be indisputable as creative right, and efficient as creative energy; but, for an instant, allow that creation may be the work of an agent inferior to God, and this redemption, henceforth attributable to an inferior agent, is despoiled of its worth, and shorn of its grandeur.

7. *The creative act is alleged to have been unassisted and undivided.*

"Where wast thou when I laid the foundations of the earth?" "Who hath measured the waters in the hollow of his hand, and meted out heaven with the span? Who hath directed the Spirit of the Lord, or being his counselor hath taught him?" "I am the Lord that maketh all things; that stretcheth forth the heavens alone; that spreadeth abroad the earth by myself." "O give thanks

unto the Lord, who alone doeth great wonders; to him that by wisdom made the heavens; to him that made great lights; for his mercy endureth forever." He " alone spreadeth out the heavens," he " maketh Arcturus, Orion, and Pleiades, and the chambers of the south." " Other gods," and " strange gods," he covers with scorn and blasts with vengeance. He sought not aid of his strongest, he consulted not with his wisest, creatures; " behold, he put no trust in his servants; and his angels he charged with folly."

Such are the revealed descriptions of the creative act; it is a work appropriated to the Deity; it is discriminated as a work most distinctive, and signalized as one most transcendent. And it is now scarcely necessary to repeat, that this work terminates in the fountain of all power and life. If the greatest Being, the cause of every other being, is not the Creator, then have we never heard of him, nor been brought into contact with him. Then have our conceptions been absorbed in some intermediate object. Then has no clew been furnished to us that we may find out " the true God, the living God, the everlasting King." The scale which we have climbed has not carried us further than the throne of some exalted creature. Far off, in hopeless distance, the God of gods may dwell, but there is no access to his presence-chamber. This mighty fabric is not his work; forms no ground for his claim to worship, veracity, pre-eminence, and power to " kill and to save; " does not witness to the glory of his skill and dominion; teaches no lesson of his character and will; justifies the idolatry of the secondary being who planned and accomplished it; lends no authority to the message of salvation; and yet excludes any possible demand on the part of another, because it was a single-handed and unaided deed of might and fame.*

* The classical reader may be reminded of Evander's embarrassment, in Virgil: " Quis Deus, incertum est." Æneid 8.

But without limit, reserve, or qualification, this creative act is ascribed to Jesus Christ: is attributed to him with all the clearness which language can convey, and all the force which reiteration can express. Two instances only do we select. "In the beginning was the Word, and the Word was with God, and the Word was God. All things were made by him. In him was life. He was in the world, and the world was made by him, and the world knew him not. And the Word was made flesh, and dwelt among us." John i, 1, etc. The identity of this Word with the Lord Jesus Christ admits of no rational dispute. Whatever a spurious criticism has hardly asserted, the phraseology most positively declares his formative interposition. And no tribute can be more decisive and abundant than the language which the Psalmist addresses to Jehovah: "Of old hast thou laid the foundations of the earth: and the heavens are the work of thy hands. They shall perish, but thou shalt endure: they shall be changed: but thou art the same, and thy years shall have no end." But the writer of the Epistle to the Hebrews hesitates not to make an application of that sublime apostrophe to the Son of God. Psalm cii, 25, 27; Heb. i, 10–12.

It will be, after all, the suggestion of some, that this is but a delegation. We repeat that we will not go into any abstract question of what organs and ministers of his purpose the Deity may select and prepare. We renew our concession that a work of great power does not prove an almighty agent, and a determinate result does not demonstrate an infinite cause. Not that this can avail any argument, for the work must be always inferior to him who effectuates it. But the argument of revelation abides! And then, if Jesus Christ be not a Divine Person, and only accomplished the creation in the capacity of an instrument, contradiction presses upon contradiction. A creature's act is said to be divine! on

that service he rests his claim to divine honors! the universe expands to manifest his divine perfections! all the oracles of nature resound with his divine behests! idolatry changes its character, and he deserves to be surrounded with divine praises! evangelic mercy emanates from him, and is consequently clothed with divine credentials! he shares the burden of the omnific decree, and destroys the independence of divine avowals! The proofs of omniscience, of irresistible energy, of paramount authority, are devolved on the act of creation; if it bear not out the proofs, then we can never know that such attributes exist; and if it does bear them out, then do they converge in Christ. But such convergence in him must be of right or of permission; the former supposition declares that he is their Infinite Possessor; the latter, that he is deified by an actual communication of perfections, a creature made underived, a mortal constituted self-existent, a being of frailty and want invested with omnipotence! The Saviour constantly puts his claims upon this—that he did what no other man had done, and that he did the works of the Father.

The impossibility of delegation is not more glaring than that of comprehending a created agent under the general language of our text, and of other portions of the inspired record. "By him were all things created." "Without him was not any thing made that was made." The terms are universal and unqualified. There is not an effect he did not produce; not a being whom he did not originate. Then if a creature, he comes within his own creation! He summons himself into existence! But as this is absurd, the latitude of the ascription excludes him from every order of creatures, however exalted, and leaves him in the full and awful absoluteness of the God!

As it is inconceivable that Christianity can encourage that plurality of gods which it has ever been the folly of men to suppose and their bane to adopt, so a consistent

view must be presented by it in all its disclosures con-cerning the Deity.   The Trine Subsistencies in the Divine Essence furnish that view.   And it is in accordance with the great plan of redemption that the principal agency in creation was undertaken by the Lord Jesus. As the Godhead is one and ineffably consentaneous, while we predicate this work of the Son we cannot surmise the inactivity of the Father and the Spirit.   "The Father worketh hitherto."   "The Spirit of God moved upon the face of the waters."   The reign of Christ, his present peculiar province, does not imply that God as God ceases to reign.   Nor is this an uncommon necessity of interpretation.   Our Lord says, "The Father judgeth no man, but hath committed all judgment unto the Son;" but all will admit that an invariable forbearance cannot be meant, and that we must not insist on a rigid exclusion.

All, then, that has ever been appropriated to the Creator—all that inspired historians have narrated and inspired instructors have taught, and inspired bards have sung, is "the glory due" to the Saviour of mankind. "By his Spirit he hath garnished the heavens."   "He fashioneth their hearts."   Can we, after this, be betrayed into an excessive tone?   Can we sing praises too lofty?   Does not nature first teach us that the Supreme is our Maker? and does not revelation then inform us that Jesus is that Supreme?

It is only equitable to remind you that Scripture has been cited to lessen and subdue these representations: particular passages which are alleged to imply subordination and instrumentality.   "But to us there is but one God, the Father, of whom are all things, and we in him; and one Lord Jesus Christ, by whom are all things, and we by him."   "God, who created all things by Jesus Christ."   "By whom also God made the worlds."   The critical answer is, that the preposition by no means ne-

cessitates the idea of subservient action, for it is applied in cases which admit of no controverted application.* And often it intends the efficient cause.† The theological refutation is, that God is often said to do things by God, or, as we think, one Person by another Person of the Deity, where the second cannot be instrumental in any sense of inferiority to the first. "Jehovah rained down upon Sodom fire and brimstone from Jehovah out of heaven." "I will have mercy upon the house of Judah, and will save them by the Lord their God." Hosea i, 7. Admit the personal distinctions, and how simple is all! Deny them, and how every thing remains inexplicable!

Let, then, the scriptural argument be reviewed—let these difficulties, if they still be felt to continue such, be arrayed against it—and what will justice demand for the verdict? Invert your position, take the difficulties for your faith, and the faith for your difficulties—let that which you now cannot but believe for its resistless weight, be sacrificed in behalf of the few scruples which you cannot satisfy—have you gained a more argument-ative advantage, or a more rational quietude? Is it not rather the seat of the scorner, than the stronghold of a triumphant assurance?

But even they who know the "mystery of God, and of the Father, and of Christ," (Col. ii, 2,) who see in the adorable distinction of Divine Persons the principle which permeates and explains the whole scheme of sal-vation, may not, at once, perceive the reason of that instrumentality which these few quotations of our oppo-nents do, in some sense, most assuredly attach to Christ in the creation of the world. Be it, then, remembered that long ere the created system arose, the purpose of Grace was established in the Divine mind, and was the

* Ὅτι ἐξ αὐτοῦ καὶ Δι' αὐτοῦ καὶ εἰς αὐτὸν τα πάντα. Rom. xi, 36.
† Πιστὸς ὁ Θεός, Δι οὐ ἐκλήθητε κ. τ. λ. 1 Cor. i, 9.

subject of a Divine arrangement. Jesus was the appointed Mediator, the Legate of the Father, the Anointed of the Spirit: " the Lord God and his Spirit " covenanted to " send him," (Isa. xlviii, 16.) Creation is, therefore, a mediatorial act and dispensation; and it was an honor conferred on Christ, who was " set up of old, from everlasting," to retrieve it when it should sink into sin. Still mediation is officially subordinate; and therefore creation may be considered as much in obedience to the will of the Father, who is invested with official supremacy and headship in the covenant, as redemption is often declared to be according to His will. And the specific right in the creation, which is the reward of "his obedience unto the death of the cross," is thus made consistent with his relative subordination— it was an honorable distinction to create, it was a dreadful part to redeem, and the possession of all things is now founded upon the double right, that He gave them their existence, and paid for them their ransom.

The context has, however, been urged as incompatible with these claims of the Saviour. He is declared to be " the image of the invisible God, the firstborn of every creature." The language is expressive of inheritance, the peculiar dignity of Him who is ruler of the family. It alludes to his resurrection. It is desired, by the adversaries of his divinity, to include him, from this expression, among the creatures. But this will poorly help their wretched cause. The text is illative. It will then be their outrage upon reasoning, which they fain would foist upon Scripture—He is a creature, " for by Him were all things created, that are in heaven, and that are in earth, visible and invisible, whether they be thrones, or dominions, or principalities, or powers: all things were created by Him and for Him. And He is before all things, and by Him all things consist!" Is this the way they take to establish their exclusive

rationalism? Or is it their method of evincing the high veneration felt by them toward the inspired volume?"*

We are at a loss to know how moral demonstration can be more compact and overwhelming than that which may be built up from Scripture in favor of the truth, that Christ is the Creator of the universe, and that, consequently, he is the Eternal God. If the Bible is to be compared with the responses of the Delphic Oracle, or with the leaves of the Cumæan Sybil, then all its statements may be vague and undeterminate, and we may exercise our ingenuity upon them; but if it be unerring as Israel's pillar, and infallible as Urim and Thummim's sacred lot, then let us never deviate from its course, nor prevaricate with its decision. Blessed Saviour! It is no hard pass to which we come, no painful conclusion to which we are reduced, when on the brow which bent toward us

---

* It is proposed by them, indeed, to resolve this system, which Christ has created, into "thin air." They would treat it as a figurative description of the Church on earth and in heaven. Christ was the first member of it, and founded it! With wondrous versatility they can turn spiritual into material, and material into spiritual, things. Literal or allegorical wait alike on their wand. Macknight is at a loss to know what is meant by "a new modeling of the angelic hierarchy," which he says is the version which some give of the text. I cannot help him out, unless the idea be taken from a batch of peerages, and a list of promotions, on some national festivity. But were he living now, he might save himself all trouble, for angels are generally voted by this school among popular errors and vulgar superstitions. Belsham draws a comparison between Jesus Christ and Napoleon Buonaparte, to illustrate the text. And having shown that the Emperor of France was "the creator of all new distinctions, high and low, whether thrones or dominions," etc., adds, "the language which is true of Buonaparte in a civil sense is applicable to Jesus Christ in a moral view; but it no more implies pre-existence, or proper creative power, in one case than in the other." What a religion must that be which needs such argument, and encourages such impiety!—LETTERS TO CARPENTER.

we read thine infinite majesty—in the eye which melted over our woe we discern thine infinite knowledge—and when we behold thine arm, which brought salvation, "lighting down" among us, as much energized with infinite power as laden with the blessings of infinite love! "Lo, this is our God; we have waited for him, and he will save us!"

But if the Lord Jesus be the Maker of all things, he must have a right of the most unqualified property in them: if by him were "all things created that are in heaven and in earth," heaven is his throne, and the earth is his footstool—"He is head over all things!" And this the text establishes. "All things were made for him."

II. HAVING ATTRIBUTED ALL THOSE CONCEPTIONS TO THE SON OF GOD WHICH ENTER INTO THE MOST ABSO-LUTE SENSE OF HIS CREATIVE WORK, WE STILL FURTHER MAINTAIN THAT THIS WORK MOST UNDIVERTEDLY CON-TEMPLATED HIS MEDIATORIAL POSSESSIONS AND GLORIES.

There are two species of foreknowledge ascribed to God in the sacred volume which are the most wonderful forms of even foreknowledge. He is acquainted with acts, however future, having their motive in the freest agency of man. We choose our own way: no coercion forces our will, no restraint shackles our liberty. But He ascertains what shall be that way, the object of that will, and the fruit of that liberty. "I am sure that the King of Egypt will not let you go." "I knew," he said to his people, "that thou wouldst deal very treacherously, and wast called a transgressor from the womb." The murderous usurpation of Hazael was thus anticipated; Jesus "knew from the beginning who should betray him;" and though "the hands" were not the less "wicked" which perpetrated his crucifixion, yet he "was delivered by the determinate counsel and foreknowledge of God," and "those things which God before

had showed by the mouth of all his prophets, that Christ should suffer, he so fulfilled." "Thou understandest my thoughts afar off." But Jehovah can realize what would be the issue of circumstances if totally different from what they are. "O that Israel had walked in my ways! I should soon have subdued their enemies the haters of the Lord should have submitted themselves unto him." "Woe unto thee, Chorazin! woe unto thee, Bethsaida! for if the mighty works had been done in Tyre and Sidon which have been done in you, they had a great while ago repented, sitting in sackcloth and ashes." "And thou, Capernaum! which art exalted unto heaven, shalt be brought down to hell! for if the mighty works which have been done in thee had been done in Sodom, it would have remained until this day." "Such knowledge is too wonderful" for us. "O the depth of the riches both of the wisdom and knowledge of God!" Here is a twofold glory—prescience of what is determinable by the most unrestricted volition, and of what is contingent upon the most opposite results !

These principles are now to be applied : these forms of divine knowledge must now be traced in their operation.

We are assured that the universe was reared by the Son of God for his own sake, his purpose and interest. It exists by his will, and for his use. We are, moreover, assured that this is not a supplementary and amended design upon a previous derangement. It is not an appendage, something original having miscarried and failed. Often in our disappointments, when some speculation is defeated and some plan foiled, we avail ourselves of a second suggestion to redeem the mortifying discomfiture of the first. We would repair the discredit. We would save the wreck. We turn ourselves to that which is next in utility and importance. We cannot endure that all our

sanguine measures, all our collected materials, should be reduced to confusion and converted to waste. The world having apostatized, being abandoned, has Jesus our Lord, in that crisis, consented to bend it to his cause? Thrown aside, as a thwarted and alienated thing, did he then first determine to take it up into his counsels and agencies? Did he only then stamp on it the characters of his property, and impress on it the conditions of his employment? No: it is his workmanship, his instrument: it was launched from his hand, it rolls in his service! Here is the reason of its primeval construction and of its perpetuated course. This is the only solution of its varied phenomena, the only moral of its mysterious scenery, the only scope of its massive architecture. This is the cause which arrests the conflagration of the elements, and which detains the signal prepared to announce "that time shall be no longer." But for this, the sun would cease to cheer us in our days and seasons; earth would dispread one blasted waste of thorns and briars; and every spot would disclose the bed of the dying or the bier of the dead. This is the upholding principle, the conservative element, the retrieving counter-check against the dreadful penalty, and the equally dreadful tendency, which would hurry it to despair and sink it in ruin!

But it is impossible for even the dullest apprehension to overlook the difficulty which lies in these statements: for if this world was raised for the exhibition of Christianity, for the development of its truths, and the distribution of its blessings, it renders certain (a more correct term than inevitable) the introduction of sin. In some sense it *does;* but not by originating it; not by necessitating it; not with any complacency of adaptation; not with any manner of connivance; not with any construction that it is a congenial agent, or disguised good. But if such be the prologue of the awful drama, there is no

more objection to it as a comprehensive anticipation of the whole forward to its final catastrophe, than can be raised against the prediction of its several parts. Many prophecies declare that such wicked men shall arise, and such wicked acts shall be performed : it must be certain, then, such shall be the event, but the event does not depend upon the prophecies. Besides, there is a class of futuritions which we may denominate negative certainties. That a creature must be imperfect, and limited, and dependent, simply requires the proof that he *is* a creature. That no creature can be otherwise formed, only wants the proof of the self-evident fact, that no creature can be independent of Him who formed him. That such a creature is justly dealt with in being left to the necessary laws of his nature, merely asks the proof which arises from the inverse proposition that then it must be unjust to form any creature at all. That no moral sustentation is due to the creature, but seeks the proof that favor or grace is no term of justice, and can never be needed to set it with an honorable aspect before the intelligent universe. And on these grounds the defection of man was certain, as most justly treated, as most freely left, as most infallibly foreseen! For as little can these negative certainties be questioned as the noblest demonstration of mathematical truth, which is, after all, evolved from a point, a thing of no quantity, and really a nothing.*

It will be objected that there is no variety of evil which God could not prevent. This is one of those

---

* I believe that greatest master of divinity, that more than Augustine of our age, the late Rev. Dr. Edward Williams, of Rotherham, has somewhere in his writings a similar figure. I remember not where it is to be found. It will be a happy bait to that man who will be content to seek it, though he should find it in the last sentence his mortal hand ever impressed! When he is read and understood, the deterioration of the modern ministry (and some assert it) will be an unsupported charge.

views of omnipotence which we hold to be most unfounded. If it be intended that almightiness need not have made rational creatures, what is the value of the gratuitous remark? If it be meant that such power can interfere to change the necessary tendency, or can be employed to alter the laws, of moral agents, we deny that it ever existed in the Divine Being or ever can. To say that power could have excluded sin from the creation, is a most illogical and inapposite statement; for it either denotes that it might have forbidden the existence of accountable nature, or that, such accountable nature existing, it might have imposed violent restraint upon it. And therefore we feel ourselves justified in avowing—harsh as the denial may sound, opposing all the rules of thinking as many may deem it—that the moral constitution of intelligent creatures being once presumed, God could not, in their simply equitable regimen, and according to their unquestionably moral probation, prevent the entrance of sin!

Let us, then, consider the operation of that Infinite Intelligence concerning which we have spoken. He, "in whom are hid all the treasures of wisdom and knowledge," discriminated what the most perfect freedom would accomplish, and what the most inverted condition of man's first nature would insure. These we propound as facts. Moral rectitude and moral accountability are our stays. Whatever the apparent collision, both are equally attested and equally credible. And foreseeing these results, was the Divine Being to abandon his creation, to leave upon it "the line of confusion and the stones of emptiness?" Was it unworthy of his government, which undertakes our world as its trust and care, to mark each crisis, overrule each perversion, and provide for each exigency? Should it be subject to surprise, and unprepared for dilemma? Ought it not to be ready to turn to its own advantage and vindication the

malice of its foes?   Can an entire dereliction of the race to destruction be the only method in which it can disabuse itself of all connivance at human rebellion?   Nor is our ignorance solitary here.   Many consequences are certain, though we know not the reason or the medium by which they are educed.   Moral certainties, the most general ground of confidence, are not easily explained : the deductions of science it would be more than arduous, in frequent instances, to connect with their elementary axioms; while the relations of cause and effect, which at first may appear so simple, still confound the keenest speculations, and excite the most conflicting opinions. After the same manner, though in an infinitely higher degree, we must forget our littleness and exceed our province when we attempt to define the awful intervals between what divine omniscience clearly foreknew, and divine purity must abhor, and divine government does permit.

And though the hypothesis which conceives the bower of Adam to be prepared as the abode of innocence, and which asserts the race that he federally represented to possess in him the liberty of pursuing faultless immortal excellences, is doubtless just and incontestably true; yet we are warranted to rest on a purpose anterior to formation, and more stable than the caprice, of man. We know that man had the choice and power of good and evil; we know that his freedom was not, to the most imaginable point, interrupted and infringed; we know that there is not a sophism more perverse and guilty than that which the ancient transgressors employed : " We are delivered to do these abominations ; " we know that sin is what, we are most fully authorized to say, God would not to exist and continue; we know that nothing but its foresight, its hatred, and its determined counteraction, can be admitted into his councils or allied to his plans; but we are also constrained to

acknowledge (sweet necessity that is laid upon us!) that Christ created the world for himself, resolving to restore what would be alienated, and to establish what would be disputed; thus becoming its owner, and constituting it a primary contrivance, an original vehicle, for that great exercise of mercy which is denominated "the Gospel of the grace of God." For if made by Christ in his distinctive character, it must be for the distinctive transaction which that character supposes, having as little reference to a state of innocence as it has to an award of vengeance. He "came not to destroy men's lives:" he "came not to condemn the world, but that the world through him might be saved." He therefore projected its scale and drew its map; fixed the axis on which it should turn, and the orbit within which it should travel. Hence we read of "the eternal purpose purposed in Christ Jesus our Lord;" of the "hope of eternal life which God, that cannot lie, promised before the world began;" of "the hidden wisdom, which God ordained before the world unto our glory;" of "the precious blood of Christ, who verily was foreordained before the foundation of the world." Did not these designs require a development? and was not such development the plan after which this fabric was hewn, the pattern according to which this temple was constructed?

Fact, indeed, seems more opposed to the conclusion that "all things were made for Christ," than even theoretic difficulty. The world, upon a most cursory recollection of history, upon a most superficial glance over the present, stands forth in absolute contradiction. Its race is in revolt, and "abased unto hell;" and itself is abused to crime, and made subject to vanity. The phraseology of Scripture habituates and obliges us to speak of it as a world whose course is sinful, whose repulsion is to all goodness, and whose "friendship is enmity with God." It even compels us to stamp a stronger com-

plexion on our remarks; for this world has a prince and a god of its own! It has formally thrown off its proper allegiance, and apostatized from its proper devotion; it has openly avowed its preference of that accursed spirit who enthralls and defiles it, and has elaborately converted itself into the usurper's hold and the idol's house!

So fearful have been the crimes acted upon the stage of our world—such have been its convulsions and plunges of iniquity—that we are told, though then its days were young, "It repented God that he had made man on the earth, and it grieved him at his heart." Yet this only expresses his view of our nature's evil failure, and his sense of the odiousness which marks its defection from rectitude and obedience; and strong as is the language, it derogates nothing from his infinite complacency in recovering that very nature, nothing from his delight in that mercy he has exercised toward it, nothing from "the good pleasure of his goodness" in that great system of redemption which has swallowed up every purpose, and superinduced itself upon every law, of the creation—its noblest bulwark and its concentrated glory!

It may be tauntingly said, that scarcely a sign exists of this appropriation of all things to Christ, that "all things continue as they were from the beginning of the creation." We may select an illustration, by no means inapt, from one portion of the earth; and thus we shall reason from the particular to the general. Canaan was destined, when each circumstance was most unpropitious, to be the goodly heritage and holy land devoted to the ministrations of the divine worship, and consecrated by the symbols of the divine presence. It was given by promise unto Abraham. His descendants were to form the Israelitish Church. It was from that moment their's. Its localities were described, together with their use, ages before that Church had passed its frontier. Even

Zion was noted in the sublime song of Moses, though he was never to enter the promised territory, and though forty years transpired ere he caught its distant prospect: " Thou shalt bring them in, and plant them in the mountain of thine inheritance, in the place, O Lord, which thou hast made for thee to dwell in, in the sanctuary, O Lord, which thy hands have established." Exod. xv, 7. How was it, then, that they were so long excluded from possession? The iniquity of the Amorites was not yet full. But Judah was saved, and Israel dwelt safely, after the long term of centuries which had been originally forewarned. And then we behold them occupying that fair country—its citizens rather than its conquerors. Yet still that " mountain " was impregnable against them. Hundreds of years rolled on, and it was still a fortress of their idolatrous enemies. And it was in a far subsequent period, that from the steep of that long-allotted hill, " on the sides of the north," arose the temple where Jehovah had of old determined to record his name and find his rest. Was this a later consideration? Or was the applicability of Palestine for the nation, and Zion for the temple, accidental? Was it then discovered that the area of the country was of the adequate admeasurement; and that the mountains round about Jerusalem did furnish a platform, a buttress-ledge, most eligible for that awful pile? We can answer these questions in inspired strain: " When the Most High divided to the nations their inheritance, when he separated the sons of Adam, he set the bounds of the people according to the number of the children of Israel." For this constitution of things regarded the religious benefit of mankind. " Thus saith the Lord God, This is Jerusalem: I have set it in the midst of the nations and countries that are round about her." Ezek. v, 5. And Paul reasons upon the same purport of the facts: "He hath determined the times appointed, and the bounds of their

habitations, that they should seek the Lord," their opportunities favoring, and their vicinities assisting, so important an end. Nor is it more improbable that earth shall yield itself to the sovereignty of Immanuel, and that he shall be Lord over its whole extent, than that the land of the Amorite should be filled with a people who "were holiness unto the Lord," and that the citadel of Jebus should be displaced for the temple to which kings brought presents, and in which a nation adored!

And we are supported in this view of earth's first design and final destiny by the manner in which the "thoughts of peace and not of evil" were breathed to our original parents. We had rebelled, and the day of our transgression declined apace. How do we shudder when we think of its hurrying moments and falling shades! How do we tremble with the fugitives, and seek out their retreats! The Lord God descends! His voice is heard while he walks in the garden! Surely "the indignation is accomplished!" Surely the blow shall now be struck! O, wondrous reversal of the sentence! He "will have mercy." "He will abundantly pardon." He is "come to seek and to save that which is lost." That evening shall not close in despair. That sun shall not go down on wrath. "The cool of the day" brings with it a token of pity, placid as its calm, soft as its twilight, gentle as its dew, soothing as its lull, beautiful as its western sky, fair as its vesper star! All was then ready to be divulged. All was then adjusted for immediate operation. In that earliest promise all the rudiments of human salvation were comprehended. Every economy, every fact, in the history of redemption, has only been its enlarged construction and progressive fulfillment. And we know that there was a heaven for the penitent child of man even then provided, and that a "door was opened in it" for his entrance, since "the kingdom was prepared from the foundation of the world." Matt. xxv, 34.

And when we observe the absence of all surprise from the divine announcement, together with the unde-layed disclosure of a plan which at once began to extend its cheering influence, and took a grasp of all earthly time and interest, we cannot withstand the proof that redemption is the key to creation, and that "all things were made by Christ and for him."

There is a species of proof very delicate in itself, but yet capable of forming a strong addition to the evidence that our earth was created to receive the mysterious manifestation of the eternal Son. We all admit the adaptation of the external system to human wants and circumstances. We must all admit that—notwithstand-ing the moral defection of our race, and the consequent change in the external system—much of this adaptation is preserved. Nor is that change, so far as we can trace it, of the extreme character which might have been augured from the magnitude of the defection. If we may be allowed the remark, we should say that the very conditions of innocence were framed with a reference to a facility of transition from a former to the present state of things. Why was man " taken out of the ground ? " Why was not his material texture woven of finer and more ethereal elements ? Can we evade the conclusion of the expected and certain issue ? Can we doubt that the creature who would die was constructed of mate-rials so gloriously transformed that the workmanship triumphed over their inferiority, yet of materials which were fitted by their own nature to corrupt, to resolve into their first atoms, and readily to sink into all the humiliations of death ? Thus did He, who made the world, place our unfallen nature in perfect happiness ; but still, knowing its self-determined course, prepared a natural order of punishment which should only, in the least degree, disturb the general system ; and raised a fabric upon a plan so true to his foreknowledge, that it

could be left to settle—though modified, not deranged, by the most fearful vicissitude !

The subserviency of his works to his purposes requires a more distinct illustration; and we may trace in them

I. THE SCENES OF HIS MEDIATION.

While many theories have been broached on the reasons of the Deity in selecting for the stupendous scheme of mercy a world so diminutive, a race so insignificant, —it is sufficient for us to state that we know not that any others are involved in the guilt to require it. We are quite willing to speak of our nature as most depraved, but we must contest every imputation that it is mean. Nothing intelligent, accountable, immortal, is or can be of little importance. Against mind and eternity the comparative smallness of our planet, and the absolute feebleness of our corporeal structure, cannot be seriously weighed. The argument of dimensions is gross and blind. And this earth does take a rank of precedence, even overlooking its moral interest; for it would seem that from its original elements the sun was lighted up, that it commenced the train in which other worlds were fabricated, that it will implicate some in its destruction, and " draw a part of the stars of heaven " after it. But the safer exposition of the divine conduct is this: that we being chiefly, if not exclusively, the objects, our globe was most suitable for the transaction; that if there were other purposes, it still contained facilities and offered occasions which perhaps none other possessed; that any system of mercy not immediately proposed, not expressly adapted to our condition, must fall short of it; that whatever expedient was capable of removing our guilt and " countervailing our damage," may easily reach upward and spread widely, may embrace the most remote varieties, may release the most intricate combinations, of circumstances in which other creatures can be placed, may bear on all orders of intelligence and all classes of

being, may vibrate to the extremities of the universe. And we know that this economy of grace, though it descends not low enough to rescue fiends, rises sufficiently high to unite and establish angels. And, therefore, whether it have ulterior intentions or not, the mediation of Christ has adopted this earth as its principal scene and center.

It was the stage of his advent. He "came into the world." He "came in the flesh." "He dwelt among us." His conception, birth, life, death, entombment, were "of this building." He was "the second Adam, the Lord from heaven." He who said, "Let us make man," was "made of a woman." And that track of earth in which he drew his first breath and heaved his last, hallowed by his agony and crucifixion, is therefore denominated "Immanuel's land." Thither he "descended"—"came down from heaven." In his human nature it was an actual change of place and relation. That He should walk our earth! be subject to the skyey influences! be tossed by the raging waves! toil along the dusty roads! suffer thirst and hunger! have a place where he abode, (John i, 39,) only less a wonder than that he should not have where to lay his head! O favored orb! What footsteps once impressed, what eyes once surveyed, thee! Whom didst thou bear, though transfixed on a cross, and buried in a grave!

It is the site of his Church. Here is the rock whence it is hewn, and the hole of the pit whence it is digged. Here too is the foundation laid, the precious corner-stone. It is gathered out of all nations, and from the four winds. Other beginning it cannot have, though its perfection is in those first-born members who are written in heaven. It must have its birth and nourishment in the present state. From guilt and depravity it is called, redeemed and sanctified. And well is it for the earth that it contains this "peculiar people." They are the

dew, the salt, the light, the "everlasting foundation," the "substance," of it. Judgment is arrested for their sake : " I cannot do any thing till thou be come thither." " Hurt not the earth, till we have sealed the servants of God in their foreheads." And the language of Scripture clearly expresses the subordination of all things to their benefit : "And I have put my words in thy mouth, and I have covered thee in the shadow of nine hand, that I may plant the heavens, and lay the foundations of the earth ; and say unto Zion, Thou art my people." Isaiah li, 16.   Nor shall their dignities be long deferred; but " the kingdom, and dominion, and the greatness of the kingdom under the whole heaven, shall be given to the people of the saints of the Most High." Daniel vii, 27.

It is the sphere of his influence.   Of the Spirit it is said, "The world seeth him not."   He is the "Spirit of Christ," and carries on the most singular operations. And within the circuit of our earth, though millions remain unconscious, he pours a spiritual light into the understanding and infuses a divine light into the heart. As there is a perpetual virtue emitted through the kingdoms of nature, molding new forms and repairing old decays—putting forth energy and beauty ;—so a virtue, equally inscrutable, moves in the minds and consciences of men, creative as well as restorative, by which all the visions of moral loveliness are passing into reality—hidden seeds are swelling to fruits of holiness, and rising to trees of righteousness, plastic powers begin to unfold the fair scenery of the new heavens and the new earth !

It is the receptacle of his most complacent operations. It is evident that creation must stand in the order of means to an end.   It is evident that the end can be the only equivalent for the labor and expense of the means. It is evident that this end is human redemption.   This is the treasure which enriches the field, the diadem which

gives splendor to the palace, and the shrine which constitutes the holiness of the sanctuary. In comparison with all other purposes, this is pre-eminent above them all, as the temple is to the gold, and the altar to the gift. It is "the pleasure of the Lord." The principalities and powers learn from the Church the manifold wisdom of God. This was the "joy set before" the Saviour. This "satisfies" him for "the travail of his soul." O! not when he nerves the warrior's arm, not when he kinkles the statesman's ardor, not when he directs the philosopher's research, does he rejoice in his noblest workmanship, does he smile upon his dearest success; but when he exhibits his grace in the renovation of minds, the conversion of hearts, the salvation of souls—then he bodies out his fullness of purpose—rests in his love—and overlooking all meaner things, disdaining all inferior spoils, leaves this vast result for "a name, an everlasting sign, that shall not be cut off."

It is the arena of his most glorious victories. Heaven once rung with the shout of conflict, and Satan, with his host, was hurled down to hell. It must have been a momentary strife which demanded but one crushing repulse of power. "Neither was their place found any more in heaven." But circumstances render the terrestrial war of another character and duration. And from the moment, when "enmity was set" between the woman's Seed and the Tempter in Eden, down to the crisis of the final decision at Armageddon, the battle has never failed, nor can the combatants be parted. And He who has "girded his sword upon his thigh," has followed one career of triumph. Success has he made sure, and added to success. At intervals he has cheered his soldiers, "As I have overcome." He has been seen by them at the different stages of the contest, "Conquering and to conquer." And long as earth shall endure, the pedestal shall expand upon which his monu-

ment is built, and new trophies shall be brought in to be hung around it!

It was only likely that when we were informed of the use to which the Lord Jesus devoted his universe, that the particular notice should be of our earth. But when we recollect the transactions of infinite importance which have occurred upon it, the improbability of similar events in any other, the manner in which they engaged the everlasting mind, their celebration in heaven and through eternity, we need not wonder that it is a focal point of interest and instruction to all beings and worlds. Nor will it be reasonably objected that our planet is comparatively small, and therefore cannot be thus sublimely distinguished. What has that to do with the selection? Is it not the method of divine conduct to exalt them of "low degree?"   Is not such an experiment of awful principles independent of the platform? And as the natal city of the Saviour was "the least among the cities of Judah," and yet the new luminary, the "consenting planet" of heaven, gleamed a vertical ray on its littlenesss, its trembling turret, and mouldering wall;—so, were our habitation reduced a thousandfold from its present dimensions, still would it be great and illustrious in the lessons it has taught, in the measures it has matured, and in the triumphs it has unfolded!

And not only is earth the principal scene of the Saviour's mediation, heaven likewise sustains its part. " Amid the glory which He had with the Father before the world began," he expatiated in the prospect of the world which should be formed, and " rejoiced in the habitable parts of the earth." "For our sakes he returned on high," but he "entered not without blood," but with it "purified the heavenly things themselves." " He maketh peace in high places." " He ever liveth to make intercession for us."   Redemption is the concen-

trating attraction to every order of the celestial inhabit-ants, and forms their " new song ! "

Nor is there a spot of space but which he could com-mand, if a vantage ground for his purpose. Is it heaven? He is there! Is it the invisible world? He is there! Is it the uttermost part of the sea? He is there! Is it the outer verge of space! It is not out-lawed from his authority, nor rent from his control. Every-where he could fix the awful machinery to move the moral universe, and all the stars of the firmament would follow his Sun-banner, and fight in their courses for him.

All things were " made for Christ," as they are

II. THE TRIBUTARIES TO HIS PRAISE.

This is not doubtful of " things in heaven," of the heavenly orders. " Thrones " fall down before him, " dominions " obey, " principalities " discrown them-selves in his presence, " Powers " yield. " All the angels of God worship him." " All are made subject unto him."

And it is worthy of notice, that when in the humblest condition of humanity, when he " made himself of no reputation," when " many were astonished " at his marred image and form, there was always a contrast, a redeem-ing might, which vindicated his superior nature and uni-versal rule. He is born, and the choirs of heaven salute the swaddled child. He is presented in the temple, and beneath a supernatural influence the aged saints confess him, and then depart to die. He is tempted, and angels minister to him. He is baptized, and the Holy Ghost, in the bodily shape of a dove, rests upon his head. He hungers, and feeds thousands at his will. He thirsts, and turns water into wine. He slumbers, and awakes to still the tempest. He weeps, and calls the corrupting dead from the grave. He is in agony, and a voice thunders from heaven that as he had been glorified, he

shall be glorified again.   He is taken captive, and more than twelve legions of ministering spirits hover round him, impatient to rescue him.   He is put to death, and throws open Paradise.   He is laid in the tomb, and an earthquake rolls away the stone to release him who could not be holden of death, and whose flesh could not see corruption.

And " all things " have owned, and served, and glorified him!   Especially may we notice the devotement of the visible system to him, in all its properties, agents, and operations.   Among these we may enumerate

Natural symbols.   We think there is nothing extravagant in the sentiment, that the most striking signs of the external world were contrived on purpose to represent and recommend him, and were intended to construct a language adapted to this principle, and not arbitrarily wrested and constrained.   And whither can we turn but bright syllables are imprinted of a Saviour's worth ? and full-toned voices reach us, which enounce his glory ? Sun, and star, and tree, and rock, and river, are the ready mediums of comparison, and are consecrated as the universal speech, whose, " sound is gone out into all the earth, and its words unto the end of the world." " O Lord, our Lord, how excellent is thy name in all the earth !"   " They shall fear thee as long as the sun and moon endure, throughout all generations."   The objects of physical nature were not alone thus appropriated as his shadows.   He has called forth

Personal representatives.   They who had an individual existence, and pursued an accountable history, were often taken out of their own station, lifted above their own sphere, and transformed into living types of his office and character.   Even Adam, the least probable likeness of a deliverer and redeemer, does not pass into his grave without having been exhibited for a " sign,"

and was presented to his posterity, not only as their destroyer, but as "the figure of Him that was to come." Nor do we properly conceive of this representation when we place it upon a coincidence; the resemblance was determined for the type, not the type determined upon the resemblance, as Melchisedec was "made like unto the Son of God." And still there are those who walk our earth as his remembrancers and imitators—who are his retrospective types—they are "the glory of Christ," "because as he is, so are they in this world." But nature inert, and even immaterial, yielded to his

Miraculous authority. The material world was his servant and ready instrument. A new luminary took its place in heaven, and was the auspice of his birth. The winds and sea obeyed him. The deaf heard his most soothing whisper; the blind gazed after him who had given them sight; the dumb, with the ecstacy of their new faculty, spake his goodness and sang his praise; the loathsome crust of leprosy fell, and the ghastly array of death unloosed, before him; and having thus made matter and its laws passive to him, he not only gathered an eclipse around his cross, and soared buoyant on "the wings of the wind" to heaven, but he healed distempered minds, commanded demons and they fled, recalled spirits and they returned! And we learn that there ascends to him

Incessant homage. We want a finer sense, and then we might perceive that there was a service, and a service of praise extorted from his enemies. "For the Scripture saith unto Pharaoh, Even for this same purpose have I raised thee up, that I might show my power in thee, and that my name might be declared throughout all the earth." "Surely the wrath of man shall praise thee." He "surnames" a Cyrus, though that prince "had not known him." The Assyrian, though "he meant not so, neither did his heart think so," was "the

rod of his anger." He hath "created the waster to destroy." God puts in the heart of the ten kings "to fulfill his will, and to agree, and give their kingdom unto the beast, until the words of God shall be fulfilled." And the effect of these combined agencies is stated to be most harmonious; and one who stood in a more favorable position than ourselves, "heard every creature which is in heaven, and on earth, and under the earth, saying: Blessing, and honor, and glory, and power, be unto Him that sitteth upon the throne, and unto the Lamb for ever and ever."

But "all things" are "for Christ," since they are

III. THE ACCESSORIES TO HIS PURPOSE.

The great events of science and art are left to the general operation of the human mind, though we do not exclude the continued direction of Deity. But man, as merely an intellectual being, is not chiefly the object of his care. His interpositions take place in our moral history, and for our religious good. And we may observe the subserviency of human inventions to these superior purposes. Why were they not earlier? The discovery of the compass? The revolution of the earth? The expedient of printing? The moral sense of man was not roused, the utility of these instruments of knowledge could not therefore be secured, and "the fullness of times" was necessarily delayed. We deny not that this delay is wrapped up in deep mystery. Yet the advocates of the natural sufficiency of reason in all affairs of religion, gain nothing by advantageous comparison. Have they outstripped revelation in the race? Did they sooner read their volume of earth and sky? But there is one view of this delay which we think generally neglected, though important. The loss of the first revelation of divine things is always pointed out by Scripture to have been willful and most guilty. "The times of this ignorance God winked at;" not by indifference, not

by connivance—not in forbearing to punish, not in refusing to amend—but in positive retribution; punishing by his most effectual manner of abandoning, "giving up," "letting alone," and "casting off;" "suffering all nations to walk in their own ways." The delay was, therefore, at least in part, judicial. And as we know that "Christ is God over all," he superintended all those preliminaries, and allowed all those postponements, which might be necessary to give men a clear idea of the Gospel, a just impression of its evidence, and so favorably to usher it in before men, that it might be raised beyond the most captious suspicion. And in these statements we must not forget that "the Gospel was preached" ere the garden of innocence was closed upon us, and was efficacious to "every one who believed" during the four thousand years which preceded its more economical establishment.

This world is therefore not "a wandering star," abandoned in wrath, discarded from use, rushing to destruction, but is still held for a design, and turned to an account the most glorious. Its Maker has not renounced nor disowned his property. It may be a rebel, but he is still its Sovereign: it may be a recusant, but he is still its Lord. And through the ancient story of our race, we can mark satisfactory proofs of his continued control and activity—apparent episodes of the great drama, but really preserving its unity, and hastening its catastrophe! Where shall we go in quest of illustration?

Enter the harvest-field of Bethlehem. There is a gleaner following the reapers, who is a subject of interest, not only to all that know her affliction, but to all that can anticipate her posterity. "Her hap to light" was the guidance of Providence and verification of prophecy: "how the matter fell" was weighed in an eternal balance. And hence sprung a name which was "famous in Israel," and the line is perpetuated "whose

are the fathers, and of whom Christ came." The Moabitess who left her land to put her "trust" under the wings of the Lord God of Israel, is honored as the ancestral mother of the Redeemer; and not only could boast of a David as her descendant, but David's Lord.

Enter the palace of Shushan. A vail is lifted up, and we behold a new class of agencies employed to introduce the Christian dispensation. There is an orphan maid: she is next seen with the royal crown of Persia upon her head; her foster-parent being privileged, in consequence, to sit in the king's gate, detects a conspiracy against the life of the king; a proud courtier is offended at the disrespect shown him by this kinsman of the queen; he seeks in his anger the destruction of the Church; having well plotted it, he becomes intoxicated by the favors heaped upon him; he consents to a means of revenge, pitiful in its malignity; and then a restless fever in the veins of the monarch leads to his bitter discomfiture in the triumph of his rival, and in his obligation to pronounce it; he is hurried on to his fate; the covenanted race, which he would exterminate, are rescued and avenged; while even the heathen acknowledge that "he has fallen before the seed of the Jews," and all must allow that the bereft and captive daughter of that people "came to the kingdom for such a time as this."

But it is unnecessary to trace the manifold ways in which all things have been administered to promote the cause of Christ. And now that "the government is upon his shoulder," now that he is officially advanced to the magistrature of the universe—the activities of intellect, the discoveries of enterprise, the accumulations of wealth, the vicissitudes of empire, the revolutions of time, the assaults of infidelity, the machinations of hell, shall fall into his plan, and be made occasions of his glory. All things must be "gathered together in Christ." All his enemies shall be made his "footstool." And he

shall at last exclaim, in assertion of his complete subjection of every adverse power to his sway, "It is done: I am Alpha and Omega, the beginning and the end, the first and the last."

And here He will erect his final monarchy. We disclaim any aggrandisement but that which is spiritual. And as "he was the Desire of all nations," as "the powers of heaven were shaken" for his manifestation, so all things shall contribute to introduce him. "He shall reign whose right it is." "He shall take to himself his great power, and reign." He shall have "dominion from sea to sea." "Yea, all kings shall fall down before him, all nations shall serve him." And when every government shall but reflect divine justice, and every subject shall but obey true religion—then, when the Gospel is written in every law, and is seated in every breast—when Christianity is the only standard of jurisdiction and the only measure of allegiance—then, when the temper of Jesus shall be the spirit, and the testimony of Jesus shall be the letter, of every code—when authority is without pride, fealty without distrust, and love without dissimulation—then, when holy truth has spread its leaven through the entire mass, as well as each separate element of civilized life and social being—then voices shall be heard in heaven, saying, "Now is come the kingdom of our God, and the power of his Christ." "The kingdoms of this world are become the kingdoms of our Lord, and of his Christ." The heathen are his inheritance, and the uttermost parts of the earth are his possession. And that we might not despair, he left not our world ere he had proclaimed, "All power is given unto me in heaven and in earth."

And, did we not fear too large an extension of the discourse, we might argue the CONNECTION between the Saviour's creation and the proprietorship of all things: justice to the subject forbids its total neglect.

A more important inquiry cannot arise: Is our Maker also our Saviour? Does He, whose command filled Nothing with matter, and gave beauty to the Formless mass, bear our nature, and "plead our cause?" Does He, who spread abroad the heavens as a curtain, and as a tent to dwell in, build the refuge of our hope? It is a joyous hour when we can conclude, "He that is our God is the God of salvation."

And at once we are impressed with the difficulty of our salvation. Constituting the design of this created system, it must be a more worthy deed than creation itself. Yet can we imagine no power greater than is necessary to create, and Scripture does not encourage and warrant us to do so. Then that energy which is the highest in our conception, and which, according to inspired authority, is ultimate, is demanded to recover us from the effects of sin. What must be that "abominable thing!" How appalling must be the ruin which it has entailed upon us! If that "very word of grace" which saves us were not "strong as that which built the skies;" * if that "arm" did not bring "salvation," on which universal nature hangs its weight; our case were hopeless, our doom inevitable, our species lost! The crisis came; and "where sin abounded, grace did much more abound!" A moral creation sprung up in its own loveliness; man stood once more erect "after the image of Him who created him;" our fallen nature beamed forth again as "His workmanship in Christ Jesus;" and that Power which peopled immensity with being, and illuminated it with a thousand suns, still operates with its fullest energies in the production of spiritual light, vitality, and beauty.

And not less distinctly are we taught, by this connection, the efficiency of the "great salvation." The heart has its tremors and misgivings, and will sometimes

* Watts.

inquire whether there be put forth all that strength to save which was required to create us? whether there be all that earnestness and determination of purpose which the prodigious monuments of constituted nature attest? But what should be the heart's relief when we discover that our salvation is the cause of all that the universe contains of vast, and fair, and radiant; that it impresses the law of every atom, and the motion of every world; that the Creator stamps his seal upon it, and enforces it equally with his most tremendous mandates; that he bids the spirit go in peace, undisturbed as the sublime emanations which constantly spread from him through his works; that He prescribes the holy liberty of the regenerate, who sustains the moon when she walks in brightness with her sisterhood of stars; that He ordains the life of the soul who is the author of existence so multifarious and boundless, that the difficulty is to show what is not living entity and structure; that "the Gospel is the power of God unto salvation." This is "a propriety none can feel," "but who can smiling say, My Saviour made them all!"* O ye who tremble because He is omnipotently great, because he doeth wonders, because yon heavens with their hosts are his, because he can kill both body and soul, because he can blast with a breath and wither with a frown—never did his might unfold itself as in this operation of mercy; and though the fact of "Christ crucified" may appear to vail and frustrate "the exceeding greatness of this power," it is its noblest medium, its grandest proof, its brightest spectacle. "It is the Power of God."

A fitness is apparent in this arrangement. Our earth, being dishonored, the measures to avenge or purify it must be with him who had made it. The cause is his. No interposition could be suggested to him, much less

* Cowper.

forced upon him. He alone can act. But if he so determine, we cannot fail to admire the moral propriety of his agency. He had "dedicated this house," and he now will see whether the dedication has been respected. No other power could have the right to cast it down, or to renew its original intention. He has resolved to rescue our world. Hence arises the meetness of deriving the reparation from him who is aggrieved, and the pardon from him with whom it was to punish. Surely the Creator knows the value of his works and the nature of his laws; what can retrieve the wrong done to the one, and expiate the insult offered to the other; and if he be "well pleased," whence can arise demur? "It is God that justifieth." "If God be for us, who can be against us?" He is therefore described as claiming his people: "I will say to the north, Give up: and to the south, Keep not back: bring my sons from far, and my daughters from the ends of the earth: even every one that is called by my name: for I have created him for my glory, I have formed him; yea, I have made him." And inanimate nature is represented as rejoicing with sympathy in the redemption of man: and as invoked by Him to expressions of a jubilant gladness: "Sing, O ye heavens; for the Lord hath done it: shout, ye lower parts of the earth: break forth into singing, ye mountains, O forest, every tree therein, for the Lord hath redeemed Jacob, and glorified himself in Israel." "Drop down, ye heavens, from above, and let the skies pour down righteousness: let the earth open, and let them bring forth salvation, and let righteousness spring up together: I the Lord have created it."

And thus a parallelism and analogy is constituted between the material and moral systems; and signs are borrowed from the one to denote the other. "He who sitteth on the throne saith, Behold, I make all things new." A sun of righteousness bursts out to dispel

spiritual darkness; the troubled sea, which cast up mire and dirt, is hushed and cleansed; earth yields her increase; instead of the thorn there comes up a fir-tree, and instead of the briar the myrtle-tree; man is a new creature in Christ Jesus; the law of the Spirit of life stirs a sweetly freshening balm; the new heavens and the new earth are so resplendent that the former cannot "be remembered nor come into mind." Nor is this all: the world of nature ministers to the world of grace, and to it at once owes its existence and its respite from the final doom.

And it is worthy of notice that in those strongest passages where the Deity challenges any rival, where he assures us that "he is the Lord, and that there is no God beside him," where he calls upon his creatures to "know from the rising of the sun, and from the west, that there is none beside him," the Lord Jesus is certainly intended.* "I have sworn by myself, That unto me every knee shall bow, every tongue swear." So that his supreme divinity and personal distinction are at the same time unequivocally averred.

And most rightful is his possession of all things. "His hand hath laid the foundation of the earth, and his right hand hath spanned the heavens: when he called unto them, they stood up together." "They were made for him." He built our earth to be an ark of safety, and a sanctuary of mercy. He spread over it the covering of his atonement, and will sway it with the scepter of his grace. "The people shall fall under him." "Every thought shall be brought into captivity to his obedience." And the world, which he created and which he saved, shall confess his title, and bring forth its diadem of many crowns to place upon the head of Him who is "the Efficient Cause of the creation of God!" When, therefore, we are engaged in promoting

* Isaiah xlv, 6, compared with Rom. xiv, 10, 11; Phil. ii, 10, 11.